lonely planet

Trans-Siberian Railway

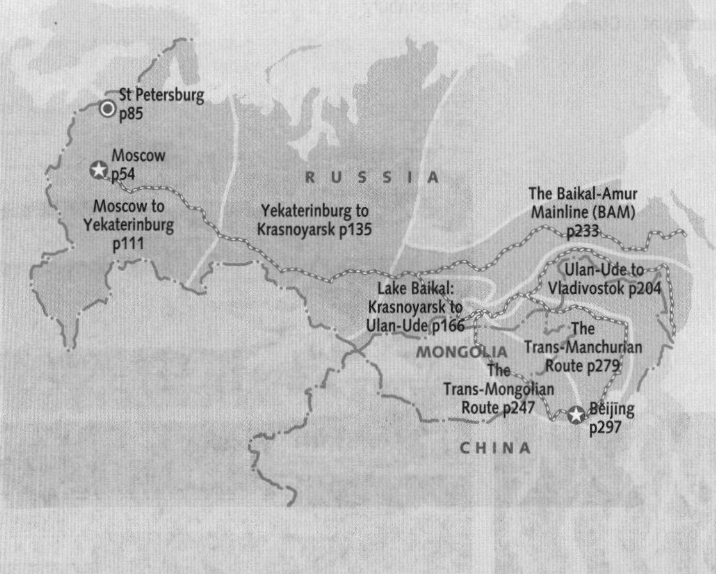

Simon Richmond,
Mark Baker, Stuart Butler, Trent Holden, Adam Karlin, Michael Kohn,
Ali Lemer, Tatyana Leonov, Tom Masters, Thomas O'Malley,
Leonid Ragozin, Adam Skolnik, Regis St Louis, Mara Vorhees

PLAN YOUR TRIP

ON THE ROAD

06PHOTO/GETTY IMAGES ©

LENA SIB/SHUTTERSTOCK ©

DRIED OMUL FISH, LAKE BAIKAL P184

Contents

FORBIDDEN CITY, BEIJING
P301

Welcome to the Trans-Siberian Railway

Snow-dusted or sun-kissed steppe and taiga, the Gobi Desert and the Great Wall – the Trans-Siberian routes unite landscapes and experiences into the journey of a lifetime.

Jewel in the Crown of the Tsars

No other rail journey can compare to the Trans-Siberian Railway, once hailed as 'the fairest jewel in the crown of the Tsars'. Today the name is shorthand for a web of tracks, fanning out from Moscow and European Russia across seven time zones to the Pacific edge of Asia. Survivor of revolution, wars, natural calamities and extreme weather, this historic iron way provides access to both contemporary metropolises and timeless villages, as well as beautiful landscapes.

Choice of Routes

Trans-Siberian journeys are packed with wow moments. We defy you not to get a kick out of marching across the cobbles of Moscow's Red Square, wandering around Běijīng's Forbidden City or taking in the glorious panorama of Vladivostok's Golden Horn Bay. The more adventurous will certainly want to explore -and possibly plunge into – icy Lake Baikal, or ride with nomads across Mongolia's magnificent steppes. There's also the Baikal-Amur Mainline (Baikalo-Amurskaya Magistral; BAM) passing through remote and stunning parts of Siberia.

Cultural Contrast

While aboard the train, embrace the chance to interact with your fellow passengers and learn a little about their respective cultures as you share with them something of your own. You'll discover, if you haven't already, that Russians in particular are among the kindest people you could meet, ever ready to share their provisions and engage in conversation. So whether you're on the Trans-Siberian Railway simply for the sake of the journey or for the access it provides to Russia, China and Mongolia, prepare yourself for a magnificently rewarding experience of changing landscapes and cultures, people, and of life on the rails.

Slow, Rewarding Travel

The opportunities to alight and explore what was once one of the world's most forbidding and feared destinations are now only limited by your time, budget and imagination. With an average speed of 60km/h Trans-Siberian services are not for travellers in a hurry. There's probably never been a better, more comfortable time to travel, with improved train facilities, online ticketing and a proliferation of affordable Western-style hostels and other accommodation along the way.

Why I Love the Trans-Siberian Railway

By Simon Richmond, Writer

Etched on my memory is the research trip I made for the first edition of the *Trans-Siberian Railway* guidebook: I was arrested on a platform and separated from my luggage (including computer, notes and nearly all my money), which continued on the train into Siberia. The day was saved by a wonderful collection of Russians who pulled together to reunite me with all my belongings. Awesome engineering feat it may be, but it's the chance to make friends and connect with Russians and other nationalities on the Trans-Siberian Railway that really makes the journey so special.

For more about our writers, see p416

Above: Trans-Siberian train near Lake Baikal (186)

Trans-Siberian Railway

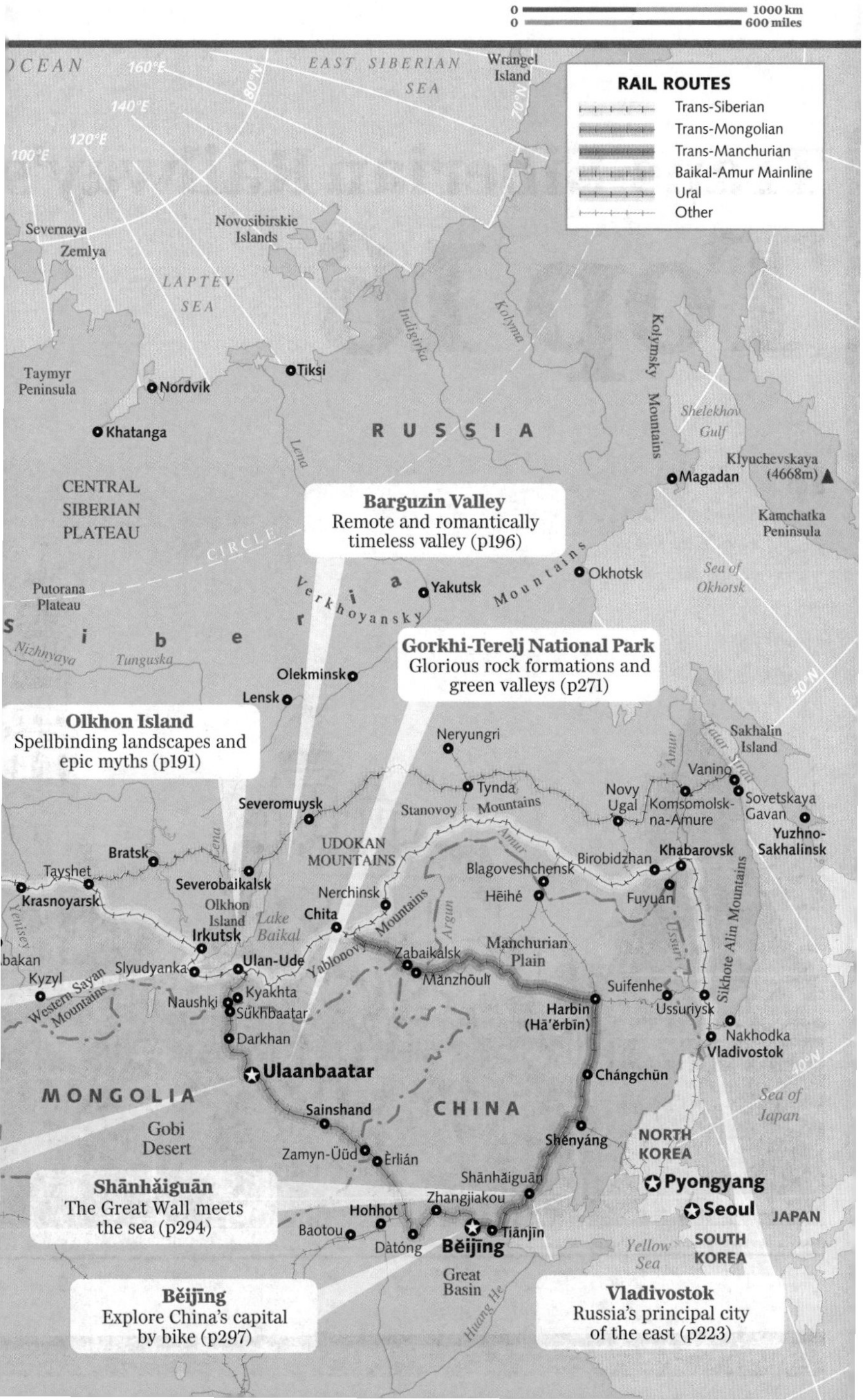

0 1000 km
0 600 miles
RAIL ROUTES
Trans-Siberian
Trans-Mongolian
Trans-Manchurian
Baikal-Amur Mainline
Ural
Other
OCEAN
EAST SIBERIAN SEA
Wrangel Island
160°E
140°E
120°E
100°E
80°N
70°N
Severnaya Zemlya
Novosibirskie Islands
LAPTEV SEA
Indigirka
Kolyma
Kolymsky Mountains
Taymyr Peninsula
Nordvik
Tiksi
Khatanga
RUSSIA
Lena
Shelekhov Gulf
Klyuchevskaya (4668m)
Magadan
Kamchatka Peninsula
CENTRAL SIBERIAN PLATEAU
Barguzin Valley
Remote and romantically timeless valley (p196)
CIRCLE
Putorana Plateau
Verkhoyansky Mountains
Yakutsk
Okhotsk
Sea of Okhotsk
Siberia
Nizhnyaya Tunguska
Gorkhi-Terelj National Park
Glorious rock formations and green valleys (p271)
Olekminsk
Lensk
50°N
Olkhon Island
Spellbinding landscapes and epic myths (p191)
Neryungri
Sakhalin Island
Amur
Tatar Strait
Vanino
Tynda
Novy Ugal
Komsomolsk-na-Amure
Sovetskaya Gavan
Severomuysk
Stanovoy Mountains
Yuzhno-Sakhalinsk
UDOKAN MOUNTAINS
Amur
Birobidzhan
Khabarovsk
Bratsk
Blagoveshchensk
Tayshet
Severobaikalsk
Krasnoyarsk
Nerchinsk
Hēihé
Fuyuan
Yenisey
Olkhon Island
Lake Baikal
Chita
Argun
Ussuri
Sikhote Alin Mountains
Irkutsk
Yablonovy Mountains
Manchurian Plain
Abakan
Zabaikalsk
Ulan-Ude
Slyudyanka
Mănzhōulǐ
Kyzyl
Western Sayan Mountains
Kyakhta
Suifenhe
Naushki
Harbin (Hā'ěrbīn)
Ussuriysk
Sükhbaatar
Nakhodka
Darkhan
Vladivostok
Ulaanbaatar
Chángchūn
40°N
MONGOLIA
CHINA
Sea of Japan
Sainshand
Gobi Desert
Shěnyáng
NORTH KOREA
Zamyn-Üüd
Èrlián
Shānhǎiguān
The Great Wall meets the sea (p294)
Shānhǎiguān
Pyongyang
Zhangjiakou
Hohhot
Seoul
JAPAN
Baotou
Dàtóng
Běijīng
Tiānjīn
Yellow Sea
SOUTH KOREA
Great Basin
Huang He
Běijīng
Explore China's capital by bike (p297)
Vladivostok
Russia's principal city of the east (p223)

Trans-Siberian Railway's Top 16

1

Moscow's Kremlin & Red Square

1 This ancient fortress (p62) is the founding site of Moscow and the ultimate symbol of political power in Russia. Within its ancient walls you can admire the artistry of Russia's greatest icon painters, gawk at the treasure trove that fuelled a revolution, shed a tear for Russia's great and tragic rulers, and climb the tower for an amazing panorama. Flanking the northeastern wall of the Kremlin, Red Square is dominated by bold towers and the colourful domes of St Basil's Cathedral.

Life Aboard the Train

2 Imagine it as an overland cruise. The great pleasures of Trans-Siberian travel (p44) are the on-board rituals of eating, sleeping and simply gazing through the windows at the unfurling landscape. The height of luxury are trains such as the *Golden Eagle*. Better, though, are regular RZD trains, where you'll meet ordinary Russian travellers, who have a real knack for making the compartments a home away from home. Amble along to the restaurant car and pal up with the *provodnitsa,* the female train attendant who cherishes her carriage as her own little fiefdom.

SERGEY FOMENKO/SHUTTERSTOCK ©

2

VOSTOK/GETTY IMAGES ©

CHRISTIAN KOBER/GETTY IMAGES ©

Běijīng by Bike

3 In order to get under the skin of Běijīng, hire a bike and cycle like mad through the city. Navigate twists and turns, thread through alleys, down boulevards and around landscaped parks, and the city will reveal itself as a fascinating mosaic of charming old *hútòng* (narrow alleyway) neighbourhoods and 21st-century architectural wonders. Biking Běijīng puts you at ground level with the locals, and there is a tangible sense of camaraderie as you pull up to an intersection and push off together as if in a massive bike rally.

Russia's Sacred Sea

4 The exiled Old Believer Avvakum found it to be a bountiful paradise where all was larger than life: mountains and rocky gates that rose into the heavens, and pure waters brimming with fish. Lake Baikal (p186), the world's largest freshwater lake, still has the power to amaze whether you glimpse its sapphire waters from the train as it skirts the southern shore or disembark to get an even closer look. For those who like to hike, also consider tramping part of the splendid Great Baikal Trail.

Mongolian Landscapes

5 Mongolia is a beautiful country. Get into a Russian 4WD or van and your Mongolian travel mates will be crooning about the blue waters of Lake Khövsgöl, the singing sand dunes of the Gobi Desert (above) and the glaciated peaks of the Altai Mountains. Closer to Ulaanbaatar, it's easy to make day or overnight trips to Gorkhi-Terelj National Park (p271) amid the glorious rock formations and green valleys. For an experience that combines natural landscapes and wildlife viewing, visit Khustain National Park, where wild *takhi* horses roam across the pristine grasslands of central Mongolia.

St Petersburg's Hermitage

6 Standing proudly at the end of Nevsky pr, Russia's most famous palace houses its most famous museum, the Hermitage (p89). Little can prepare most visitors for the scale and quality of the exhibits, including a staggering number of works by Rembrandt, Rubens, Picasso and Matisse. In addition to paintings, there are superb antiquities, sculpture and jewellery on display, and if that's not enough, you can also wander through the private apartments of the Romanovs, for whom the Winter Palace was home until 1917.

Great Wall of China

7 Just as there are two sides to every coin, there are two opinions about the Great Wall. For the Chinese, the Wall represents a marvellous architectural achievement, accomplished with enormous human effort and advanced technical designs. For Mongolians, it represents nomadic strength, power and determination, for only the fiercest of warriors could force another people to construct such a colossal defensive work. For Trans-Siberian travellers, the Wall is a majestic ending (or starting) point to the long cross-continental journey.

6

7

8

9

Vladivostok

8 Capital of Russia's Far East and a major port, Vladivostok (meaning 'lord of the east') has been on a roll after being remade for an economic summit in 2012. Asia's rising star has a new branch of the Mariinsky Theatre and the Hermitage. Take in beautiful Golden Horn Bay from one of the city's myriad viewpoints, or join the frenzy of activity with a ferry cruise. Check out the impressive suspension bridge spanning the bay. Suddenly those San Francisco comparisons don't seem quite so preposterous.

The Arts of Moscow

9 Moscow's performing and visual arts scenes are a major drawcard. Classical ballet, music and theatre have traditionally been at the heart of Russian culture. Today, exciting and creative artists are experimenting with new forms of theatre, painting, music, sculpture and dance. If you have your heart set on classical opera or ballet at the Bolshoi Theatre (p80), or icons at the State Tretyakov Gallery, you won't be disappointed. But try to catch the experimental cultural scene, too. A ballerina dancing in front of the Bolshoi Theatre (p80)

Barguzin Valley

10 The remote and romantically timeless Barguzin Valley (p196) is said to have been the birthplace of Chinggis (Genghis) Khaan's mother. It is one of the Baikal region's most attractive places and, despite the trickle of visitors finding their way into the region these days, remains one of the least visited spots around Lake Baikal. Snow-dusted peaks and curious rock formations gaze down upon a landscape dotted with salt lakes and fairytale wooden villages, where horse carts and sleighs are more numerous than cars.

Historical Tobolsk

11 Formerly the capital of Siberia, Tobolsk (p149) is today renowned across Russia for its magnificent kremlin. Crowds are rare, though, and if you come on a weekday you are likely to have the grounds almost to yourself. The kremlin is perched high above the old town, a part of Tobolsk where you lose track of time as you explore the endless wooden buildings and dramatic churches. Tobolsk is off the main Trans-Siberian route, but its charms are well worth the detour. St Sofia Cathedral, Kremlin, Tobolsk (p150)

Naadam in Ulaanbaatar

12 You don't have to travel far to find Mongolian culture; it's right in Ulaanbaatar. During Naadam (p263) proud examples of national pastimes, such as archery, wrestling, horse racing and *shagai* (anklebone shooting) are played out before enthusiastic crowds in traditional dress. National foods *huushuur* (mutton pasties) and *airag* (fermented mare's milk) are consumed in great quantities. Naadam is also a great time to catch traditional performances including the other-worldly *khoomi* (throat-singing). Archers on horseback during Naadam

Novosibirsk

13 Once viewed as an intimidating monolith, Novosibirsk (p153) has blossomed into one of Russia's most hip and hospitable metropolises. Siberia's unofficial capital boasts a delightful range of accommodation, an up-and-coming restaurant and bar scene, and friendly locals. It's a perfect stop-off for rail-weary souls looking to unwind with a big night out on the town, and also offers worthy museums, Siberian wooden architecture and a lively music and arts scene. Main train station, Novosibirsk

KOSTIN SS/SHUTTERSTOCK ©

KATVIC/SHUTTERSTOCK ©

Tradition in Siberia

14 Siberia's villages and small towns may be gradually sinking back into the enormous landscape, but Siberians (Sibiryaki) survive and see themselves as the purer essence of Russia – the way Russians elsewhere used to be. Tradition expresses itself in hospitality and acceptance of strangers (and their odd ways). You'll see traditional Siberian *izby* (wooden houses) everywhere: beside the railway, along rivers and lake shores, hiding deep in the forests or on proud display in Irkutsk or the university town of Tomsk (p159). Wooden lace window, Tomsk (p159)

Suzdal's Idyll

15 Ding-dong ring the bells of a few dozen churches as you ride your bike through the streets of Suzdal (p119), lined with wooden cottages and lush gardens. This is Russia as it would have been, if not for the devastating 20th century – unpretentious, pious and very laid back. Some of the best religious architecture is scattered around, but you can just as well spend all day lying in the grass and watching the river before repairing to a *banya* (bathhouse) for the sweet torture of heat, cold and birch twigs.

Olkhon Island

16 Sacred to the shamanist western Buryats, enchanted Olkhon (p191) sits halfway up Lake Baikal's western shore. It's obvious why the gods and other beings from the Mongol *Geser* epic chose to dwell on this eerily moving island, though today it's more likely to be a bunch of backpackers you meet emerging from a cave. The island's landscapes are spellbinding, Baikal's waters lap balmiest on its western shore and if you're after some Siberia-inspired meditation, there's no better spot.

Need to Know

For more information, see Survival Guide (p369)

Currency

China: yuán (¥); Mongolia: *tögrög* (T); Russia: rouble (R)

Language

Mandarin (China); Mongolian, Kazakh (Mongolia); Russian (Russia)

Visas

Required for most nationalities for Russia and China and for some in Mongolia. Apply three months ahead.

Money

ATMs are plentiful in Russia and in big cities and towns in China. Widely available in Mongolia's regional capitals.

Mobile Phones

Prepaid SIM cards are available in Russia, China and Mongolia for unlocked phones.

Time

Russia has 11 time zones. Moscow time (three hours ahead of GMT/UTC) is used at Russian stations. Ulaanbaatar and Běijīng are five hours ahead of Moscow.

When to Go

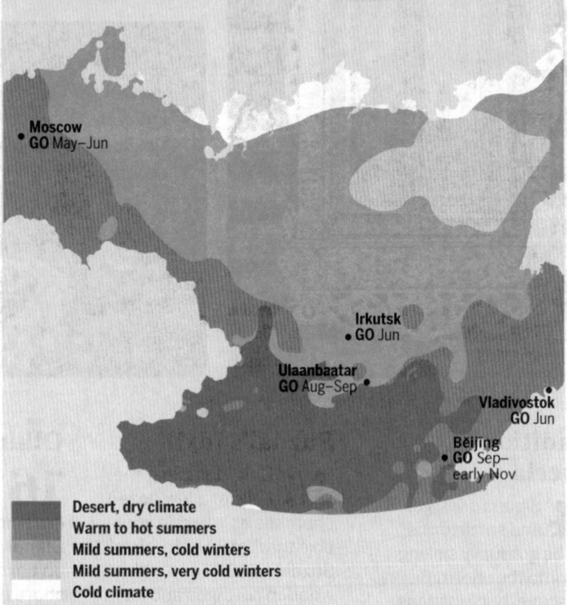

High Season (Jun–Aug)

- China: peak June to August; hot, but rainstorms offer respite.
- Mongolia: peak June to August; rain late July to August; book everything early around Naadam.
- Russia: peak June to early September.

Shoulder (May & Sep–Oct)

- China: April and May plus September and October; most pleasant weather.
- Mongolia: May and September some ger (yurt) camps closed, fewer tourists, weather changeable.
- Russia: beautiful but can get chilly.

Low Season (Nov–Apr)

- China: December to February; cold and dry. Fewer tourists (except around Chinese New Year).
- Mongolia: some ger camps and smaller guesthouses closed.
- Russia: plan indoor pursuits or winter sports; take saunas.

Useful Websites

Lonely Planet (www.lonelyplanet.com/trans-siberian-railway) Destination information, hotel bookings, traveller forum and more.

Ctrip (http://english.ctrip.com) Hotel-booking and air-ticketing website for China.

Mongolia (www.mongolia.travel) Government travel site.

Way to Russia (http://waytorussia.net) Comprehensive online travel guide.

Important Numbers

Russia international access code	☎8, wait, then ☎10
China police	☎110
Mongolia police	☎102
Russia police	☎02

Opening Hours

Banks 9am–noon and 2–5pm Monday to Friday

Restaurants 10.30am–11pm

Shops 10am–10pm

Daily Costs

Budget: Less than US$50

➡ Dorm bed: Russia ₽700–800; Mongolia US$7–15; China ¥40–60

➡ Cafe or street-stall meals: Russia ₽200–500; Mongolia US$4–7; China ¥40

Midrange: US$50–200

➡ Double room in a hotel: Russia ₽2000–3000; Mongolia US$75–150; China ¥200–600

➡ Restaurant meal: Russia ₽500–1000; Mongolia US$8–14; China ¥80–100

Top End: More than US$200

➡ Double room in a hotel: Russia more than ₽3000; Mongolia more than US$150; China more than ¥600

➡ Restaurant meal: Russia more than ₽1000; Mongolia more than US$14; China more than ¥100

EXCHANGE RATES

For current exchange rates, see www.xe.com.

CURRENCY	VALUE	CHINA	MONGOLIA	RUSSIA
Australia	AU$1	¥5.3	T1974	₽46
Canada	C$1	¥5.4	T2012	₽47
Europe	€1	¥7.9	T2964	₽70
Japan	¥100	¥5.9	T2217	₽52
New Zealand	NZ$1	¥4.8	T1802	₽42
UK	UK£1	¥8.9	T3350	₽79
US	US$1	¥6.6	T2475	₽58

Arriving in Russia, China & Mongolia

Sheremetyevo, Domodedovo and Vnukovo airports (Moscow) Aeroexpress (https://aeroexpress.ru/en) trains connect to the city centre from all three airports (from ₽420, half-hourly 5.30am to 12.30am, 35 minutes).Taxis (₽2000 to ₽2500) take at least an hour; this varies wildly with traffic.

Běijīng Capital International Airport The subway Airport Express runs every 10 minutes (6.30am to 11pm; ¥25). It is 30 minutes to the city centre. Taxis cost between ¥90 and ¥120 (30 to 60 minutes to the city centre).

Chinggis Khaan Airport (Ulaanbaatar) Organise bus pick-ups through hotels (US$15 to US$20). Official taxis charge a fixed price of around T20,000.

Getting Around

For most, if not all, of your Trans-Siberian journey you're going to be getting around on the train, but sometimes you might need or want to take an internal journey. Check train times and make bookings with the trip planning section of Russian Railways' website (http://pass.rzd.ru).

Train This will be your main way of getting around, with many overnight services between far-flung cities.

Air To speed up sections of the route. Only book airlines with solid safety records.

Bus For getting to places not covered by the train. Sometimes faster than local *elektrichka* train services.

Car/Taxi Sometimes the only way to get to really remote destinations.

For much more on **getting around**, see p383

First Time

For more information, see Survival Guide (p369)

Checklist

➡ Make sure your passport is valid for at least six months beyond the expiry date of your visa

➡ Arrange your visa

➡ Check airline baggage restrictions

➡ Check travel advisory websites

➡ Tell banks and credit-card providers your travel dates

➡ Organise travel insurance

What to Pack

➡ Good walking shoes – Trans-Siberian cities are best explored on foot

➡ Phrasebooks, minidictionary or translation apps

➡ Earplugs and eye mask for napping on trains, noisy hotels and during long White Nights

➡ Sense of humour and a bucketful of patience

Top Tips for Your Trip

➡ Consider using a specialist travel agency to arrange visas, make key transport bookings and hire guides.

➡ Treat yourself to a stay at a business or luxury hotel over the weekend when many often drop their rates substantially to cover the shortfall in business customers. Big discounts can also be had on hotel rack rates for online bookings.

➡ Rail tickets can be booked online or at stations 60 days in advance. There are sometimes discounts for advance bookings made online.

➡ Fixed-price business lunches, common in Russian cities, are a great deal and an ideal way to sample the cuisine at fancier restaurants.

What to Wear

Informal dress is generally fine. However, Russians do make an effort when they go to the theatre or a posh restaurant – you should do likewise if you want to fit in. If you're planning on exploring on foot, a comfortable pair of waterproof walking shoes will come in handy, as will an umbrella or rain jacket.

In winter, bundle up with several layers before going out and bring a long, windproof coat to stay nicely warm. Hats and coats are always removed on entering a museum or restaurant and left in the cloakroom.

Dress codes are more casual in China and Mongolia.

Language

In Russia, China and Mongolia, English speakers are more common in the big cities than smaller towns and the countryside. Learning Cyrillic and a few key phrases will help you enormously with decoding street signs, menus and timetables – this is also the case for Mongolia where Cyrillic is used, too.

Money

- If prices are listed in US dollars or euros, you will still be presented with a final bill in roubles in Russia.
- ATMs linked to international networks can be accessed across Russia, China and Mongolia. Credit cards are commonly accepted in the big cities but don't expect to be able to use them in more off-the-beaten-track spots and rural areas.
- Inform your bank and/or credit-card provider of the dates you'll be travelling in Russia, China and Mongolia to avoid your card getting blocked.

For more information, see p377.

Bargaining

Prices are fixed in shops, but at souvenir markets, such as Izmailovo in Moscow, polite haggling over prices is a good idea.

Tipping

When to tip In Russia, customary in restaurants, cafes and bars, optional elsewhere. Less common in China and Mongolia.

Restaurants Leave small change or about 10%, if the service warrants it.

Guides Around 10% of their daily rate; a small gift will also be appreciated.

Taxis No need to tip as the fare is agreed either before you get in or is metered.

Hotels Only in the most luxurious do you need to tip bellhops, and only if service is good.

Etiquette

Russians are sticklers for formality and can be superstitious; Chinese and Mongolians are a little more relaxed. Follow these tips to avoid faux pas.

Visiting homes In Russia, shaking hands across the threshold is considered unlucky; wait until you're fully inside. Always bring a gift. In all three countries, remove your shoes and coat on entering a house.

Religion Dress accordingly and conservatively when visiting churches, mosques and Buddhist and Taoist temples in all three countries.

Eating and drinking In China help fill your neighbour's plate or bowl at the dinner table. Vodka toasts are common at shared meals in Russia and Mongolia – it's rude to refuse and traditional (and good sense) to eat a little something after each shot.

Eating

Gourmands should park their expectations before embarking on an extended Trans-Siberian journey: luxury train trips apart, these services don't offer high-end dining and, although dining cars have improved over the years, few travellers would cite train food as being a highlight. That said, alighting at stops along the Trans-Sib and its international routes is a brilliant opportunity to dig into regional Russian, Mongolian and Chinese cuisines. At stations and on train platforms you can also pick up excellent fresh foods and produce to fuel on-board picnics.

Sleeping

For much of your Trans-Siberian journey your bed will be on the train, but at either end of your trip and most likely at points along it you'll be looking for more traditional accommodation. For major cities it's a good idea to book a night or two in advance. Elsewhere you can usually just turn up and find a room.

Hotels From Soviet-era unreconstructed edifices to luxurious and contemporary.

Hostels, B&Bs and homestays Plenty of hostels along the Trans-Siberian routes; not so many B&B or homestays, but worth trying for a true Russian hospitality experience.

Ger camps A Mongolian accommodation option.

If You Like...

Good Food & Drink

Cafe Pushkin Splurge on a *haute-russe* feast amid faux 18th-century opulence at this Moscow restaurant. (p76)

Omul This fish is sold smoked to passengers at Slyudyanka station and elsewhere around Lake Baikal. (p184)

Pozy (Buryat dumplings) Filled with a blend of pork and beef; best enjoyed in the authentic setting of a ger. (p183)

Hikes & Walks

Great Baikal Trail Volunteer to help build a path around the world's largest freshwater lake – or hike the parts that have been completed. (p188)

Frolikha Adventure Coastline Trail A relatively demanding 100km route along Lake Baikal's northeast coast – worth every mosquito bite and blister. (p240)

Great Wall of China Walk over the mighty ramparts of the Great Wall to get a sense of its long history and significance. (p321)

Gorkhi-Terelj National Park This popular park, 55km northeast of Ulaanbaatar, is great for hiking as well as other outdoor adventures. (p271)

Iconic Architecture

St Basil's Cathedral The most internationally recognised and architecturally exquisite building in Russia. (p61)

Forbidden City China's standout imperial residence, home to two dynasties of emperors and their concubines. (p300)

Gandan Khiid Ulaanbaatar's most famous Buddhist monastery is notable for its three-storey Migjid Janraisig Süm. (p257)

Tobolsk A magnificent kremlin looks down upon the city's picturesque old town. (p149)

Severobaikalsk railway station Symbolic of the brave new world in concrete the BAM was meant to represent. (p239)

Majestic Landscapes

Gobi Desert Where camels slurp water from wells and lone horsemen gallop alongside the train. (p273)

Northern Mongolia Gers (yurts) dot the landscape and rushing streams meander into the distance. (p249)

Suzdal A time capsule of rural Russian life with wooden cottages and golden cupolas. (p119)

Multicultural Encounters

Tatar Kazan For total Tatar immersion, travel the route to Siberia via Kazan, Tatarstan's capital, where you'll find a thriving Muslim culture. (p123)

Nomad hospitality On Mongolia's vast plains hospitality is a time-honoured tradition. Expect to receive endless bowls of tea, snacks and vodka shots.

Carriage connections On the train the Chinese are usually thrilled to chat with foreigners. On Russian trains the art of conversation reaches its highest forms. (p47)

Ivolginsky Datsan The epicentre of the Russian Buddhist world is contained within an ever-expanding compound of temples, prayer wheels and monks' quarters. (p203)

River Trips & Rafting

Tuul River Paddle a canoe down the Tuul River, outside Ulaanbaatar on fun day or overnight trips with Nomadic Journeys. (p259)

St Petersburg Relax aboard one of the Anglo Tourismo boats that cruises around St Petersburg's rivers and canals. (p99)

Top: Cafe Pushkin (p76), Moscow.

Bottom: Gandan Khiid (p257), Ulaanbaatar

Moscow Avoid traffic jams and feel the breeze on your face while you get a new perspective on Moscow's most famous sights with Radisson River Cruises. (p71)

Komsomolsk-na-Amure Choose between mellow multiday floats and one-day white-water whirlwinds in the wilds surrounding this key BAM hub. (p244)

Views from the Train

Bratsk Dam One of the most spectacular moments on the BAM route comes when the train trundles across the towering Bratsk Dam. (p238)

Slyudyanka No stretch of the Trans-Siberian Railway is more photogenic than the section between Slyudyanka and Posolskaya along Lake Baikal's shoreline. (p192)

Approaching Běijīng Less than one hour outside the city (p297) the train rolls through some 60-odd tunnels, each time emerging with stunning views.

Ulaanbaatar Whichever direction you arrive from, the sprawl, congestion and chaos of Ulaanbaatar (p253) make for an engrossing sight.

Month by Month

TOP EVENTS

Harbin (Hā'ěrbīn) Ice & Snow Festival (China), December–February

Easter (Russia), March or April

Lunar New Year (China, Mongolia), January, February or early March

White Nights (Russia), June–July

Naadam (China, Mongolia), July

January

Much of Russia, northern China and Mongolia are in deep freeze during this and subsequent months. It's cold outside, but the train will be warm (or stifling hot).

Russian Orthodox Christmas (Rozhdestvo)

A religious fast from morning to nightfall on Christmas Eve (6 January), followed by a feast that includes roast duck and the porridge *kutya*. Special masses at midnight.

Lunar New Year (Spring Festival)

The Chinese New Year is family-focused, with dining and gift-giving of *hóngbāo* (red envelopes stuffed with money) and a week-long holiday. In Mongolia it's a good time to be invited to a family celebration.

March

Strong winds, sub-zero temperatures, snow and dust storms hit Mongolia. Temperatures are still low in northern China and Russia, but days are significantly longer.

Pancake Week (Maslenitsa)

Folk shows and games are staged to celebrate the end of winter, with lots of pancake eating before Lent in Russia.

April

Slush in Moscow and less savage temperatures in Siberia. Northern China remains cold, and in the Mongolia–China border regions April is like March. Gradually the weather improves.

Easter (Paskha)

Easter Sunday in Russia begins with midnight services. Afterwards, people eat *kulichy* (dome-shaped cakes) and *paskha* (cheesecake) and exchange painted wooden Easter eggs.

May

Everywhere the weather is warming up and the tourist season is getting under way. In Mongolia some ger (yurt) camps open. Snowfall may still occur, especially in the north. All of China is on holiday for the first four days – avoid.

Victory Day

On 9 May, this Russian public holiday celebrates the end of WWII, which Russians call the Great Patriotic War. Big military parades in Moscow and St Petersburg are well worth attending.

Great Wall Marathon

Experience the true meaning of pain while getting your Great Wall sightseeing done (http://great-wall-marathon.com).

June

Much of China is hot and getting hotter, southern Siberian cities can get sticky, and in Mongolia temperatures are climbing to the pleasant mid- to high 20s (Celsius).

White Nights

Russia's cultural capital, St Petersburg, hosts a huge party as days lengthen. Events run until late July.

Dragon Boat Festival

Find yourself the nearest large river and catch all the waterborne drama of dragon-boat racers in this celebration of one of China's most famous poets.

Moscow International Film Festival

Russia's premier film festival runs for 10 days in June/July and includes retrospective and documentary cinema programs as well as the usual awards. (p71)

July

The grasslands of Inner Mongolia turn green; in southern Siberia and elsewhere in Russia temperatures can soar. This is Běijīng's warmest month. Mongolia gets heat waves, hitting 40°C in the Gobi.

Kamwa Festival

The 'ethno-futuristic' Kamwa Festival, taking place in late July in Perm and Khokhlovka, brings together ancient ethno-Ugric traditions and modern culture. (p131)

Naadam Festival

Mongolia's premier summer sports festival erupts in July. The date is fixed in Ulaanbaatar (11 to 12 July) but changes from year to year in other cities and towns. In China, the same occurs in Inner Mongolia.

Red Bull Trans-Siberian Extreme

International athletes compete in the world's longest bike race, covering 9283km from Moscow to Vladivostok (www.redbull.com/int-en/events/red-bull-trans-siberian-extreme-2017).

August

Train prices in Russia can spike during this month as many people take holidays – book ahead if you want to travel on particular services along the Trans-Siberian route. Rain storms in Běijīng; less dusty in Mongolia.

Golden Naadam

This late-summer sports festival (usually held 21 August) takes place at Terelj, Mongolia.

Mongolia Bike Challenge

Mongolia draws serious mountain bikers for this rally. The route of the challenge (www.mongoliabikechallenge.com) varies each year, covering about 1500km through fine landscapes.

Roaring Hooves Festival

Often held at a remote location in the Gobi Desert, this international music festival (www.roaringhooves.com) can be staged anywhere in the country.

September

The fleetingly lovely *tiāngāo qìshuǎng* ('the sky is high and the air is fresh') autumnal season in Běijīng.

Gobi Marathon

Go for a 42km run (www.gobimarathon.org) in one of the world's most inhospitable deserts. Try not to die.

Mid-autumn Festival

Celebrated in China on the 15th day of the eighth lunar month and also called the Moon Festival. Locals devour cakes stuffed with bean paste, egg yolk, walnuts and more.

December

Short days and long nights keep many people inside for most of this month. If you're prepared it's the best time to see freshly snow-covered landscapes.

Harbin (Hā'ěrbīn) Ice & Snow Festival

In China, Hēilóngjiāng's capital Harbin is all aglow with rainbow lights refracted through fancifully carved ice statues. (p287)

Sylvester & New Year

Russians and Mongolians celebrate New Year's Eve enthusiastically, usually with lots of beer, vodka and fireworks.

Choosing Your Route

Contrary to popular belief, the Trans-Siberian Railway follows not a single route but several, from European Russian to the Russian Far East and inner Asia. There are a number of differences between each of the main lines and a variety of alternatives.

General Online Planning

The Man in Seat 61 (www.seat61.com/Trans-Siberian.htm) Most informative and current site for train travel in Russia, Mongolia and China (and other countries). Also has suggestions on getting to the railheads and on ferry services.

Lonely Planet (www.lonelyplanet.com) Use the Thorn Tree forum.

Railway Timetables

Russian Railways (http://pass.rzd.ru/main-pass/public/en)

Tutu.ru (www.tutu.ru; in Russian)

Yandex (http://rasp.yandex.ru; in Russian)

German National Railways (www.bahn.de) Has English page for seaching timetables.

China Train Guide (www.chinatrainguide.com)

China Highlights (www.chinahighlights.com)

Initial Decisions

Start by asking yourself the following questions:

Do I want to travel only in Russia? For many travellers, only the classic **Trans-Siberian** route between Moscow and Vladivostok will be of interest. But you can also use part of this route to connect with the **Baikal-Amur Mainline (BAM)** that starts from Tayshet and terminates in Sovetskaya Gavan, or to branch out to other destinations east of Moscow along Russian Railways' vast network.

Do I want to use the train to get to or from Běijīng? The two main options are the highly popular **Trans-Mongolian** linking Moscow and Běijīng via Ulaanbaatar in Mongolia, or the Moscow–Běijīng **Trans-Manchurian** service that goes only via Russia and China. Other alternatives involve crossing the Amur River by ferry at either Blagoveshchensk (110km off the main Trans-Sib route) or Khabarovsk and continuing by rail to Harbin (Hā'ěrbīn), which has good rail links with Běijīng. Trains from Harbin also run to Suífēnhé, from where you can make an onward connection to Vladivostok.

Do I want to extend my rail journey beyond the major termini? The most popular option here is to start or finish in **St Petersburg**. If you're really going for it, there's nothing stopping you train-hopping into Russia from the Atlantic coast of Portugal and then all the way beyond Běijīng to Vietnam – a journey of over 17,000km!

Trans-Siberian: From Moscow to Vladivostok

This classic route runs between Moscow and Vladivostok mostly following the historic path of Russia's first railway across the subcontinent. Trains roll for 9289km across steppe and through taiga on a journey that takes at least 143 hours (around six full days) from the capital to the Pacific.

Should you stay on the train for the full journey, the experience is like being on a long voyage through the Russian heartland: the scenery alternates between the sublime (along the shores of Lake Baikal) and the monotonous (seemingly endless taiga or the constant clatter of freight trains passing).

During peak travel season in the summer you'll likely find yourself in the company of fellow long-distance passengers (some of whom on the *Rossiya* will be foreign travellers) for several days, if not the whole journey. However, most Russians generally only travel shorter overnight sections of this route, so you'll have a chance to meet a wide range of people.

Trains & Prices

The *Rossiya* (train 1/2) is the prime-choice *firmeny* (higher quality or premium) train on the route, departing Moscow on odd days and, with exceptions, departing Vladivostok on even days (five days, 23½ hours). It's best used for nonstop travel or for long sections of the route such as Moscow–Irkutsk and Irkutsk–Vladivostok.

At the time of research the following prices were those for the Moscow–Vladivostok journey booked online through Russian Railways. Prices vary with season and extra comforts.

Platskart (open compartment with bunks) ₽15,261

Kupe (4-berth compartment) ₽29,864

SV (also called *lyuks;* 2-berth compartment) ₽81,101

Train 99/100 This Moscow–Vladivostok service goes via Yaroslavl every other day (six days, 16½ hours). *Platskart* is ₽10,917 and *kupe* ₽32,332.

Flagship Trains for Shorter Hops

Because tickets on the *Rossiya* are among the most expensive on the route, travellers who wish to break the journey along the way are better off using other trains to connect. Other *firmeny* services include:

001Г/002Й Moscow–Kazan (*Premium*) Has a luxury *myagkiye* carriage, compartments sleeping two with their own toilet and shower.

15/16 Moscow–Yekaterinburg Goes via Kazan.

29/30 Moscow–Kemorovo (*Kuzbass*) Leaves Moscow usually on odd days; useful for stations as far as Novosibirsk on the Trans-Sib line.

37/38 Moscow–Tomsk (*Tomich*) Leaves Moscow usually on even days, Tomsk on odd.

55/56 Moscow–Krasnoyarsk (*Yenisey*) Leaves Moscow usually on odd days, Krasnoyarsk on even.

Trans-Mongolian: From Moscow to Běijīng via Ulaanbaatar

This route is a popular one because it takes travellers on a coherent journey across three distinct cultures, landscapes and languages – even if not every traveller on the train is coherent after the 7826km between Moscow and Běijīng! You will need up to three visas.

The major train servicing this route is the weekly Chinese train K3/4 (also appearing on Russian timetables as 33/43), which takes 5½ days between Běijīng and Moscow, travelling via Dàtóng and Èrlián in China, Ulaanbaatar in Mongolia, and Ulan-Ude in Russia. A highlight of the journey is that it traverses part of the Gobi Desert in Mongolia. Many travel agencies offer stopover packages with a night or two in a Mongolian ger (the traditional collapsible yurt dwelling).

Between Ulan-Ude and Moscow the train follows the same route as the Trans-Siberian from Vladivostok, crossing European Russia via Nizhny Novgorod. It's the most comfortable of the regular trains and uses Chinese locomotives, carriages and staff.

At the time of research the fares on this route with train K3/4 were US$652 for hard sleeper booked with CTrip travelling westwards, and ₽31,031 (US$525) for *kupe* travelling eastwards booked online with Russian Railways.

Trans-Manchurian: From Moscow to Běijīng via Manchuria

The weekly Trans-Manchurian train 19/20 goes via Chita to Zabaikalsk, the border town on the Russian side where the bogies are changed before the train crosses to Mǎnzhōulǐ in China. The entire journey is 8988km and takes six days and two hours from Moscow to Běijīng, via Nizhny Novgorod in European Russia.

The two important things to remember about this route are that it uses Russian rolling stock and staff and it does not pass through Mongolia. (You will only need visas for Russia and China.) It can also be combined with a stopover in Harbin. Most of your fellow passengers will be Russians or Chinese doing shorter hops.

At the time of research, the eastbound prices for train 20 *(kupe)* were ₽34,587 (US$585). Westbound on train 19 (hard sleeper) it was US$720, booked via CTrip.

Baikal-Amur Mainline (BAM)

A Soviet-era project, the BAM – an alternative trans-Siberian route – is entirely within Russia, beginning in Tayshet, a rail junction east of Krasnoyarsk (and almost 4800km east of Moscow). It skirts the northern tip of Lake Baikal at Severobaikalsk and terminates 4287km east of Tayshet at Sovetskaya Gavan. Many travellers exit shortly before this at Vanino, however, as there's a ferry here to Sakhalin Island. Getting to and from the eastern railhead of the BAM can be inconvenient, and your best rail hub is Komsomolsk-na-Amure, 13½ hours before the terminus.

Unlike other routes, the BAM largely passes towns lacking historical character, as most were founded in order to build the line. This is grubby-window and taiga country. The BAM weaves through dramatic mountain landscapes rising to over 3000m, cuts a swath through seemingly endless taiga that fringes the track and plunges suddenly into the darkness of tunnels up to 15.3km long.

Severobaikalsk is the major stop for relaxing on Lake Baikal. Stops at Bratsk, Tynda and especially Komsomolsk-na-Amure are popular for short breaks from the poetic rattle of rail life.

Invariably, travelling on the BAM involves taking short hops, such as from Tayshet to Komsomolsk-na-Amure, and from Komsomolsk-na-Amure to Sovetskaya Gavan.

Alternative Routes & Transport

With notable exceptions, such as train 15/16 (which goes via Kazan) and train 99/100 (which goes via Yaroslavl), the major trains cross European Russia via Nizhny Novgorod. Unless you decide to make a detour via Petropavlovsk in Kazakhstan (Kazakh visa required), the route from the Ural Mountains into Central Siberia is simple: along the main line from Yekaterinburg through cities such as Tyumen, Omsk, Novosibirsk and Krasnoyarsk. After that, lines begin to fan out again.

ON A BUDGET?

Trans-Manchurian Budget Route

Moscow to Irkutsk (*platskart* €101, three days 14 hours); stopover in Irkutsk; Irkutsk to Zabaikalsk (*platskart* €44, 31 hours); Zabaikalsk to Mǎnzhōulǐ (bus €6); stopover in Mǎnzhōulǐ; Mǎnzhōulǐ to Běijīng via Harbin (hard sleeper €50, 22 to 32 hours). Total transport cost: approximately €201.

Trans-Mongolian Budget Route

Moscow to Ulan-Ude (*platskart* €106, three days 16½ hours); stopover in Ulan-Ude; Ulan-Ude to Ulaanbaatar (bus €22, 10 hours); stopover in Ulaanbaatar; Ulaanbaatar to Èrlián (hard sleeper €60, 12½ hours); Èrlián to Běijīng (sleeper bus €28, 10 hours). Total transport cost: approximately €216.

INTO NORTH KOREA

North Korea's Dear Leader Kim Jong-Il famously travelled into Russia and back on a 21-carriage armoured train. What is less known is that it is, in theory, possible for lesser mortals to make a similar train journey between Russia and the 'hermit kingdom'.

To be granted a visa to North Korea you must be signed up for an organised tour with a guide, so it's best to first contact agencies such as **Koryo** (https://koryo-group.com), **Juche Travel Services** (www.juchetravelservices.com) and **Regent Holidays** (www.regent-holidays.co.uk) for more information.

See www.seat61.com/NorthKorea.htm for details of the North Korean and Russian Railways services linking Moscow and Pyongyang, some of which may *not* be approved for tourists by the North Korean authorities. If you are determined to cross by rail from Russia to North Korea, tourists are permitted to use the trains that shuttle a few times a month between Hasan on the Russian side and Tumangan across the border – it will take time and money to organise. An alternative is to arrange a flight to Pyongyang from Vladivostok – these go at least once a week.

The established rail route into North Korea for tourists is the Běijīng–Pyongyang service (23½ hours, four per week). A Pyongyang–Dāndōng service (6½ hours, daily) is now also available. Dāndōng is around four hours train ride east of Shěnyáng, which is on the Trans-Manchurian route.

Budget & Border Alternatives

There are many ways to cut costs, but border hopping is a good one. Don't forget, however, that you will also need to stay overnight in some places, in which case add up to €50 per night for a midrange hotel.

Russia–Mongolia Border

The Russia–Mongolia border on the Trans-Mongolian route is at Naushki on the Russian side and Sükhbaatar on the Mongolian side. There's also a road border at Kyakhta-Altanbulag which is convenient for the Ulan-Ude–Ulaanbaatar bus.

Lake Baikal–Ulaanbaatar

Good options are trains (263/264; or 362 on Russian timetables) between Irkutsk and Ulaanbaatar (₽6591, 27 hours), and the once- to twice-weekly 5/6 (also on timetables as train 63) between Moscow and Ulaanbaatar, which stops in Irkutsk.

From Ulan-Ude (Russia) you have bus, train and flight options (p202).

Mongolia–China Border

The border (p274) between Mongolia and China crosses at Zamyn-Üüd (Mongolia) and Èrlián (China). This is often a sleepless leg, as most trains cross at night.

Russia–China Border

The border between Russia and China on the Trans-Manchurian is at Zabaikalsk (Russia) and Mǎnzhōulǐ (China). There are numerous train and bus options (p284). Other border crossings (p27) are in the Amur and Primorye regions of Russia.

Alternatives: Amur & Primorye Regions

Much of the northeastern border between China and Siberia is an oft-forgotten region along the Amur River. Here it's possible to roam Siberian forests and visit dwindling settlements of northern minorities, such as the Daur, Evenki, Hezhen and Oroqen.

Khabarovsk (Russia)–Fǔyuǎn (Fuyuan, China)

Switch countries on the ferries plying the river between Khabarovsk and Fǔyuǎn (90 minutes), which cost ₽4500 including tour and overnight lodging.

Blagoveshchensk (Russia)–Harbin (China)

Blagoveshchensk is off the Trans-Siberian main line. This approach involves crossing the Amur River by frequent boat to/from Hēihé (return ₽1650, 15 minutes), from where there's an evening train to Harbin. From Harbin there are good connections to Běijīng.

TOP STOPOVERS

The only practical way to break a journey is to buy separate tickets.

Moscow–Vladivostok

Nizhny Novgorod Situated on the Volga River, 'Nizhny' has some good museums and a lively food and culture scene. High-speed *Strizh* (seats from ₽1131) and *Lastochka* (seats from ₽765) trains run from Moscow; both take 3½ to four hours and complement conventional services. The nightly premium train 35/36 *Nizhegorodets* (*kupe* ₽2473, 7¼ hours) has luxury twin berths with shower and toilet (₽5352).

Yekaterinburg The unofficial capital of the Urals. Allow three days to explore nearby sights, or at least a week to explore a chunk of the region. The flagship 15/16 service (*kupe* ₽4813, 25½ hours, daily) travels from Moscow via Kazan.

Tyumen The first of the large Siberian cities after you leave Yekaterinburg has the advantage of being the springboard for an easy side trip off the main line to historic **Tobolsk**, with its magnificent kremlin overlooking the Irtysh River (allow a minimum of three days so you have at least one full day in Tobolsk). The premium service connecting Moscow with Tobolsk, via Tyumen, is the 59/60 *Tyumen* (*kupe* ₽6642, 38 hours).

Novosibirsk Russia's 'third city' and the unofficial capital of Siberia. Two to three days will give you a taste of the city. Add a couple of more days if you decide to branch off to nearby **Tomsk**. Anyone with a week or more up their sleeve for an extended side trip should consider bussing to the Altay Republic, as its Mongol-Turkic heritage offers an interesting cultural contrast on this route.

Krasnoyarsk An attractive city situated on the Yenisey River, it provides opportunities for extended side trips into **Tuva** – again, offering an ethnic contrast – or north to **Yeniseysk**.

Harbin (China)–Vladivostok (Russia)

Trains from Harbin run as far as Suífēnhé, from where you have to change trains to make an onward connection to Vladivostok. Much simpler is taking a direct flight from Harbin to Vladivostok or vice versa.

Vladivostok–Sovetskaya Gavan

A through carriage on the daily train 351 links the Trans-Siberian Railway with the BAM, travelling via Khabarovsk and Komsomolsk-na-Amure between Vladivostok and Sovetskaya Gavan (*kupe* ₽5801, 40 hours).

Amuro-Yakutskaya Mainline (AYaM)

At research time, this new line into Yakutia had been completed between Tynda on the BAM via Neryungri to just beyond Tommot. As passenger train services are yet to commence, most travellers continue to Yakutsk from Neryungri by minivan or jeep.

Railhead Extensions

If you have the time consider taking a train rather than a plane to the railheads. At the Moscow end, the choices lead to many cities of Western and Central Europe, whereas from Běijīng the options include Vietnam and Hong Kong. From Vladivostok you can also connect to South Korea and Japan by ferries.

St Petersburg

Russia's old imperial capital can be used as an alternative starting point. It's easy to connect from here to Moscow by either high-speed Sapsan day trains (from ₽1985) or slower overnight services (*platskart* from ₽996). However, there are also several services, some of which bypass Moscow, to whisk you straight towards the Urals and beyond, including:

Train 13/14 Starting/terminating in Novokuznetsk, this service stops at Perm, Yekaterinburg, Tyumen, Omsk and Novosibirsk on the main Trans-Sib route.

Train 39/40 With carriages originating from or bound for various destinations in Kazakhstan, including the capital Astana; also pauses in Perm and Yekaterinburg.

Train 59/60 The *Volga* premium service links Nizhny Novgorod with St Petersburg via Vladimir and Moscow.

Irkutsk and Lake Baikal Irkutsk is easily the most popular of the stopovers, and for one reason: Lake Baikal. If you arrive in Irkutsk during the day and immediately step into a *marshrutka* (collective taxi), you can be sipping a drink on the lapped shores of the world's largest freshwater lake in just over an hour. A three- to four-day stopover is the absolute minimum if you want to at least dip a toe into the Baikal region. Irkutsk is also the base for longer side trips to **Olkhon Island** or the **Tunka Valley**. The most popular pastime during a short Baikal stopover, though, is simply lotus eating (more accurately, smoked-fish eating) in **Listvyanka** or other accessible small towns on Lake Baikal.

Ulan-Ude Travellers have been known to stop here just to see with their own eyes the monumentally oversized head of Lenin's memorial. Buryat and Buddhist (with doses of shamanism) culture are also drawcards.

Khabarovsk Stop here for the flavour of a historic and lively Amur town. The premium train 5/6 *Okean* connects Khabarovsk with Vladivostok (*kupe* ₽2100, 11 hours) and half the price of a similar ticket on the *Rossiya*.

Moscow–Běijīng

In order to break a Moscow–Běijīng journey in, say, Irkutsk, it's best to take a Russian domestic train and then pick up the twice-weekly train 5/6 at Irkutsk for Ulaanbaatar, followed by the once- to twice-weekly K23/24 between Ulaanbaatar and Běijīng.

Ulaanbaatar Mongolia's capital is the main stopover on the Trans-Mongolian route.

Harbin A late 19th-century Russian enclave in Manchuria.

Train 71/72 The premium *Demidovsky Express* service connecting St Petersburg with Yekaterinburg has 1st-class carriages and also stops in Perm.

Train 145/146 Trains to/from Chelyabinsk run on odd days and go via Moscow, Vladimir, Nizhny Novgorod, Perm and Yekaterinburg.

European Russia

Helsinki–St Petersburg Four high-speed Allegro trains (2nd class from ₽2012, 3½ hours), plus *Lev Tolstoy*. Ferries and buses also do the route.

Helsinki–Moscow via St Petersburg daily train 31/32 (*Lev Tolstoy; kupe* from ₽6151, 14 hours).

Moscow–Tallinn *Kupe* from ₽5169, 15 hours, daily.

St Petersburg–Vilnius *Kupe* ₽9933, 13½ hours. As this train skirts through Belarus you will need a transit visa for that country.

Paris–Berlin–Moscow A weekly service connecting Paris and Moscow via Germany, Poland and Belarus (*kupe* from ₽20,683, 39 hours). You will need a Belarus transit visa.

Berlin–Moscow The new twice-weekly Strizh (Swift) service is a faster, more modern train connecting Berlin and Moscow with four classes of carriage (*kupe* from ₽11675, 22½ hours).

London–Moscow via Brussels, Berlin & Warsaw Take the Eurostar train to Brussels, then a high-speed train to Berlin and change to the train to Warsaw; from here you can connect to Moscow. Using the cheapest tickets this can be done for around €213 total one way.

Běijīng

Běijīng–Hanoi Four-berth rail sleepers, twice-weekly trains, departing Běijīng Thursday and Sunday, and Hanoi (Vietnam) Tuesday and Friday. The journey takes 40 hours. Soft-sleeper tickets from Běijīng cost ¥2063. London to Saigon by rail takes about two weeks (see https://www.seat61.com/Vietnam.htm).

Běijīng–Hong Kong Hard sleeper ¥601, 24 hours, every two days. A high-speed train also connects Běijīng with Shēnzhèn (¥936, 10½ hours, twice daily) from where you can take the metro on to Hong Kong, thus completing the journey in under half a day.

Vladivostok (By Sea)

Vladivostok–Donghae (South Korea) From US$205 one way, 20 hours; continues to Sakaiminato (Japan; from US$265 one way, 43 hours).

Itineraries

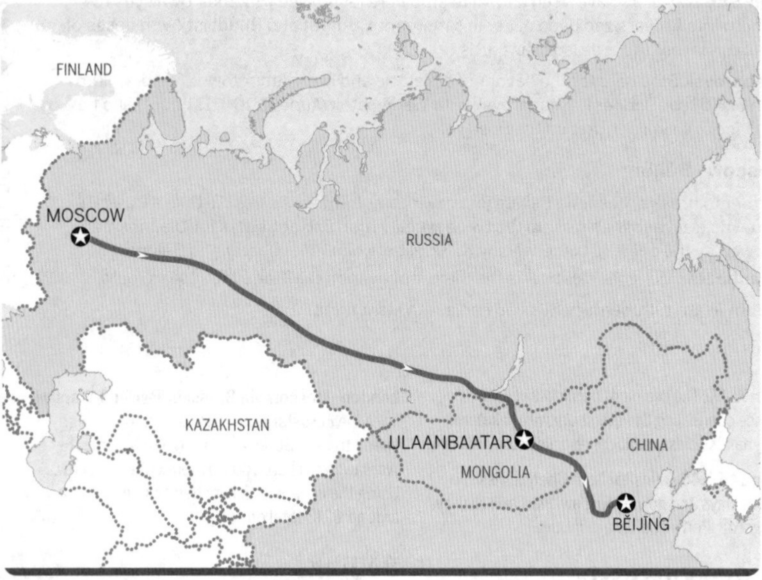

2 WEEKS The Trans-Mongolian Route

This highly popular journey is a chance to compare and contrast the cultures and landscapes of Russia, Mongolia and China. The train journey in itself takes almost six days, which allows several days in each of the three capital cities for exploration.

In **Moscow**, allow at least three days, during which time you should see Red Square and the Kremlin, and take in at least one large gallery. Also give yourself a couple of days at least to see the sights of **Ulaanbaatar**. At the other end of the line in **Běijīng**, the Forbidden City, the Great Wall, the Summer Palace and Tiān'ānmén Square will each take a day. Along the way, taiga, steppe and desert unfold in a mesmerising landscape panorama, with views of iconic Lake Baikal, the Gobi Desert and the Great Wall of China.

A nonstop itinerary is best suited to travellers who want to see Moscow and Běijīng, enjoy the changes of landscape and experience life on the train as it transitions from Europe to Asia. It can be covered in either direction, but if you wish to spend time in Moscow at the start of the journey, a transit visa will not suffice.

4 WEEKS The Trans-Siberian Route

Although this route can be done in either direction, we suggest going against the general flow from east to west. The route takes six days without stopovers on the *Rossiya,* the premium train 1/2, which means the absolute minimum required for this itinerary is one week. However, it is best done with stopovers over three to four weeks, and can easily be tailored to your own schedule.

Vladivostok, situated on a stunning natural harbour, merits several days to enjoy Russia's Pacific seaboard. It's also worth taking a break of a couple of days at **Khabarovsk**, a lively city on the banks of the Amur River that's an overnight hop from Vladivostok. Save another couple of days for **Ulan-Ude**, a fascinating city where Russian and Buryat cultures mingle, and from where you can venture into the steppes to visit Russia's principal Buddhist monastery, **Ivolginsky Datsan**. Just west of Ulan-Ude the railway hugs the southern shores of magnificent **Lake Baikal**. Allow at least five days to see the lake, visit the equally lovely **Olkhon Island** and spend time in **Irkutsk**, one of the Trans-Siberian's most important rail junctions.

Krasnoyarsk, on the Yenisey River, affords the opportunity for scenic cruises along one of Siberia's most pleasant waterways and can easily be visited on a two-day stopover to see the city itself and the nearby Stolby Nature Reserve. Also well worth a stop are the big city **Novosibirsk**, from where you can branch out to the charming Siberian town of **Tomsk**, and **Tyumen**, the access point for **Tobolsk** with its historic kremlin overlooking the Irtysh River.

Crossing the Ural Mountains into European Russia, schedule a stop in **Yekaterinburg**, a city stocked with interesting museums and sites connected to the murder of the last tsar and his family. Further west, **Nizhny Novgorod** has some good museums and restaurants plus a thrilling cable-car ride. Don't miss the tranquil Golden Ring towns of **Vladimir** and/or **Suzdal**, both packed with onion-domed churches, and a million miles away from the manic pace of modern **Moscow**. If you have time, finish up in the old imperial capital of **St Petersburg**.

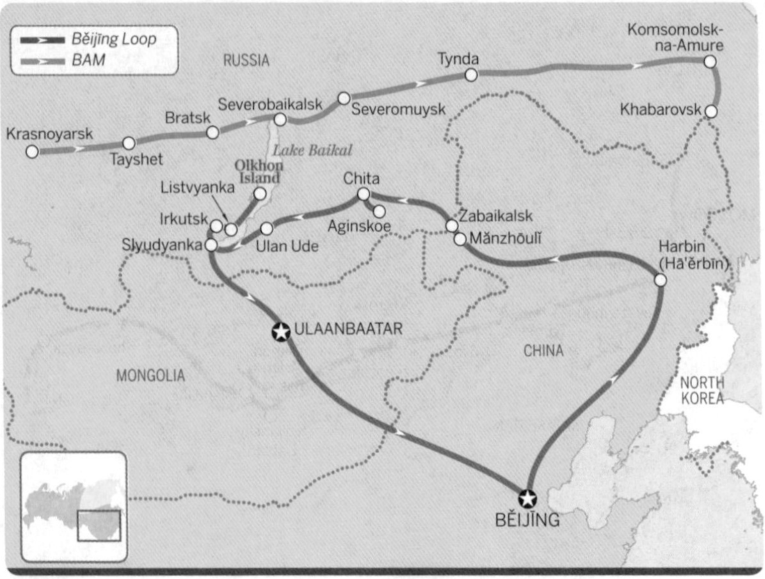

3 WEEKS Běijīng Loop

This circular itinerary starts and finishes in Běijīng and can be done in either direction. Allow time in China's capital to see some of the key sights.

An excellent overnight service connects Běijīng with **Harbin (Hā'ěrbīn)**. Russians came here at the end of the 19th century to build the railway, and handsome architectural evidence of their stay remains. The Chinese–Russian border lies an overnight train ride away at **Mǎnzhōulǐ**. If you're not on one of the weekly Trans-Manchurian services that continue across the border and through to Moscow, it's a process of hopping on a bus across to **Zabaikalsk** on the Russian side, where you can reconnect with trains through to **Chita**. Strike out to a couple of beautiful Buddhist monasteries at **Aginskoe**. Detour west from **Ulan-Ude** to Lake Baikal, where bases for exploring the lake include **Slyudyanka**, **Irkutsk**, **Listvyanka** and **Olkhon Island**.

Complete the loop by heading to **Ulaanbaatar**, which merits a couple days stopover. It's a two-night journey back to **Běijīng** through the Gobi Desert.

2 WEEKS BAM

The 3400km Baikal-Amur Mainline (BAM) travels through some of Siberia's most rugged landscapes and is a worthwhile trip for those seeking an alternative Trans-Sib adventure.

The line officially starts in the drab town of **Tayshet**, but the closest big city, **Krasnoyarsk**, has an airport. At **Bratsk** the train crosses a 1km-long dam. The town also has an excellent open-air ethnographic museum where you can see many traditional Siberian buildings. **Severobaikalsk**, on the northern tip of Lake Baikal, is the best base for exploring this relatively unvisited end of the lake.

En route to **Tynda** the line climbs over and burrows through mountains, the longest tunnel being 15.3km at **Severomuysk**. Home of the BAM construction company's headquarters, Tynda offers a BAM museum and a native Evenki village. Continue working your way east to **Komsomolsk-na-Amure**, the largest and most attractive city on the line and a great place to ponder the sacrifices and achievements made by hardy Soviet pioneers. Finish up your journey in **Khabarovsk**, which is on the main Trans-Sib line and has an airport.

Booking Tickets

Online train ticket booking has made securing your dream Trans-Siberian adventure only a few clicks away from reality. However, in some cases it may be necessary to buy tickets at local stations or use an agent to help you secure the seats you want.

Classes of Ticket

Once you've decided what route to follow (p24), you next need to consider how much comfort you'd like to travel in and when – both decisions will impact the price you'll pay for your tickets.

Russian *firmeny* (premium) trains have a higher standard of service and carriages but usually cost more. They provide a fast, useful connection, mostly between regional centres and Moscow or St Petersburg. There are various classes of compartments (p45).

Trans-Siberian & Trans-Manchurian

These routes use Russian rolling stock. When booking, you often have the choice of a mixed-sex or women-only *kupe*, although this is not always guaranteed.

SV (1st class or soft class) Two-berth compartments.

Kupe (2nd class) Four-berth. Berths 33 to 36 are alongside the toilet and can be noisy. The lower the number, the closer you are to the attendant. Note that there may be a discount offered on tickets for the top bunks.

Platskart (3rd class or hard class) Carriages sleep 54 passengers in compartments with partitions. Bunks also line the corridors. Not available on the Trans-Manchurian.

Classic Trains

Train 1/2 (westward/eastward) *Rossiya* runs between Moscow and Vladivostok.

Chinese train K3/4 (Trans-Mongolian) runs between Moscow and Běijīng via Ulaanbaatar.

Train 19/20 *Vostok* runs between Moscow and Běijīng via Manchuria.

Also useful is the 5/6 service connecting Moscow and Ulaanbaatar.

Advance Bookings

Agencies can facilitate earlier bookings in all countries.

China For C, D, G and Z express trains from 10 to 20 days before departure; for others it's five to 10 days.

Mongolia In Ulaanbaatar tickets to Moscow or Běijīng are available a day before departure.

Russia From 60 days ahead.

Online Timetables

CTrip (http://english.ctrip.com/trains) For Chinese trains.

Russian Railways (http://pass.rzd.ru) Check specific routes and times.

INDIVIDUAL OR GROUP?

The choice used to be 'individual or package', but these days tour agencies also create packages for individuals. These range from semi-individual arrangements where you are 'bundled' with several other travellers and a local guide might meet you briefly at a stop, and perhaps even drive you around town for an hour, to fully fledged group tours with a guide to take care of your needs. At the top end of the scale, packages on higher-comfort or luxury trains such as *Tsar's Gold* and *Golden Eagle* have their own itineraries and stops. These often include extras you can't otherwise get, such as tailor-made stopovers with a program for the whole group or a stretch of the spectacular Circumbaikal route. Prices are accordingly higher.

Trans-Mongolian K3 & K4

This service uses Chinese rolling stock.

Deluxe two-berth Showers shared by two compartments.

Hard class four-berth Similar to the Russian *kupe*.

Higher-Comfort & Luxury Trains

If your budget stretches to it, there are a few special train services with more luxurious carriages, offering compartments with their own toilets and showers, and fancy dining cars and bars. These services are typically used for package tours and while none are cheap, they do include day trips off the train, all meals and at least one night's hotel accommodation at either end of the train trip.

You are unlikely to meet many ordinary Russians, Chinese and Mongolians on these trains, apart from the staff; passengers tend to be well-heeled and older than the average train traveller.

Golden Eagle

The **Golden Eagle** (www.goldeneagleluxurytrains.com) is the most luxurious and expensive of Trans-Sib train services. It offers three classes of cabin (Silver, Gold and Imperial Suites), all with private shower rooms, as well as a bar-lounge carriage and restaurant carriage. Prices for a 15-day itinerary between Moscow and Vladivostok in Silver Class single/double occupancy compartments start at US$23,500/33,790.

Imperial Russia

Russian Railways run the **Imperial Russia** (http://rzdtour.com/en) service between Moscow and Běijīng via Ulaanbaatar. There are four classes of travel (VIP, Business, First Class Plus and First Class), with rates for a 15-day tour in a First Class single/double occupancy compartment costing €7225/10,700.

Tsar's Gold

The most affordable of the luxury trains is **Tsar's Gold**, a train that can be booked via a variety of Trans-Sib tour operators, including Mir Corporation (p38) and Regent Holidays (p38). It has six cabin categories: the Bolshoi Platinum and Bolshoi classes both have en suite bathrooms; the Nostalgic Comfort Class, Superior Plus, Superior and Classic cabins all share bathrooms. The tour itinerary also typically includes overnight stays in hotels in Irkutsk and Ulaanbaatar to break up the time spent on the train between Moscow and Běijīng. Rates for the 15-day itinerary for single/double occupancy start from US$12,095/17,390.

Where to Buy Tickets

While you obviously can buy tickets directly at local stations, this isn't always the most convenient or preferable thing to do – especially when you are trying to secure seats for specific dates.

If your itinerary is straightforward, you can use the website or app for **Russian Railways** (РЖД, RZD; ☎8-800 775 0000; www.rzd.ru) to secure your Trans-Siberian journey. A small discount for tickets purchased online may also be available.

Alternatively, there's the option of using local or international travel agents and booking offices. This will be more expensive (possibly up to 30% pricier than doing it yourself), as you are paying commission on top of the ticket prices; the plus side is that the agent, rather than you, spends time organising what may be complicated bookings. Some agents are also experts in stitching together a complete itinerary with hotels, guides etc.

Things to Note

➡ Have your passport and those of fellow travellers handy for all international and distance rail bookings – whether online or at the station.

➡ If you need to have your tickets on the train booked earlier than 60 days in advance, then you will have to use the services of a travel agency or tour company that can guarantee this for you.

➡ In order to book in advance on a westward route on the Trans-Mongolian (train K3) and the Trans-Manchurian (train 19), you will need to use China International Travel Service (CITS) or local or international tour and travel agents, and you usually need to board in Běijīng. Agencies in Harbin (Hā'ěrbīn) and Mǎnzhōulǐ can also arrange tickets on the Trans-Manchurian into Russia.

➡ From Ulaanbaatar, you can't be certain of an advance reservation on the Trans-Mongolian train 3 or train 4 as they won't know how many places are available.

➡ In Russia, avoid using the international trains for domestic routes: they are usually more expensive than nonpremium trains and tickets are difficult to come by outside Moscow.

➡ If you can't buy a ticket in advance because the train is full, it may still be possible to negotiate a berth with the attendants on the platform when the train arrives.

➡ Unless otherwise stated, the prices listed by Lonely Planet are usually for 2nd-class, four-berth compartments (*kupe*) and don't include meals.

PRICES & SERVICES

Price Comparison by Class – Trans-Siberian & Trans-Manchurian

ROUTE	SV	KUPE	PLATSKART
Moscow–Vladivostok (train 1/2)	₽81,101 (US$1373)	₽29,864 (US$505)	₽15,261 (US$258)

Price Comparison by Class – Trans-Mongolian K3 & K4

ROUTE	DELUXE (2-BERTH)	SOFT SLEEPER (4-BERTH)	HARD SLEEPER (4-BERTH)
Moscow–Ulaanbaatar (UB)–Běijīng (train K3/4)	₽55,502 (US$940)	n/a	₽31,031 (US$525)
Moscow–Běijīng (train 19/20)	₽53,984 (US$914)	n/a	₽34,587 (US$585)
Běijīng–Ulaanbaatar (train 23, Tue service only)	US$339	US$313	US$240

Prices are for September 2017.

Services

When you book, you will often see a range of prices. The higher ones are with services, usually meaning meals, often a newspaper and cleaner toilets. These are common symbols you will see online.

CLASS	SERVICES
platskart 3 P (3 П)	not air-conditioned
platskart 3 E (3 Э)	air-conditioned
kupe 2 K (2 К)	not air-conditioned, no services
kupe 2 L (2 Л)	air-conditioned, no services
kupe 2 U (2 У)	not air-conditioned, with services
kupe 2 E (2 Э)	air-conditioned, with services
spalny vagon (1st class) 1 L (1 Л)	air-conditioned, no services
spalny vagon (1st class) 1 B (1 Б)	business class, air-conditioned, with services
additional letters МЖ	male-only carriage

HOW TO BUY & READ YOUR TICKET

When buying a ticket in Russia, it's a good idea to arrive at the station or travel agency prepared. If you don't speak Russian, have someone who does write down the following information for you in Cyrillic:

- How many tickets you require.
- Your destination.
- What class of ticket.
- The preferred date of travel and time of day for departure.

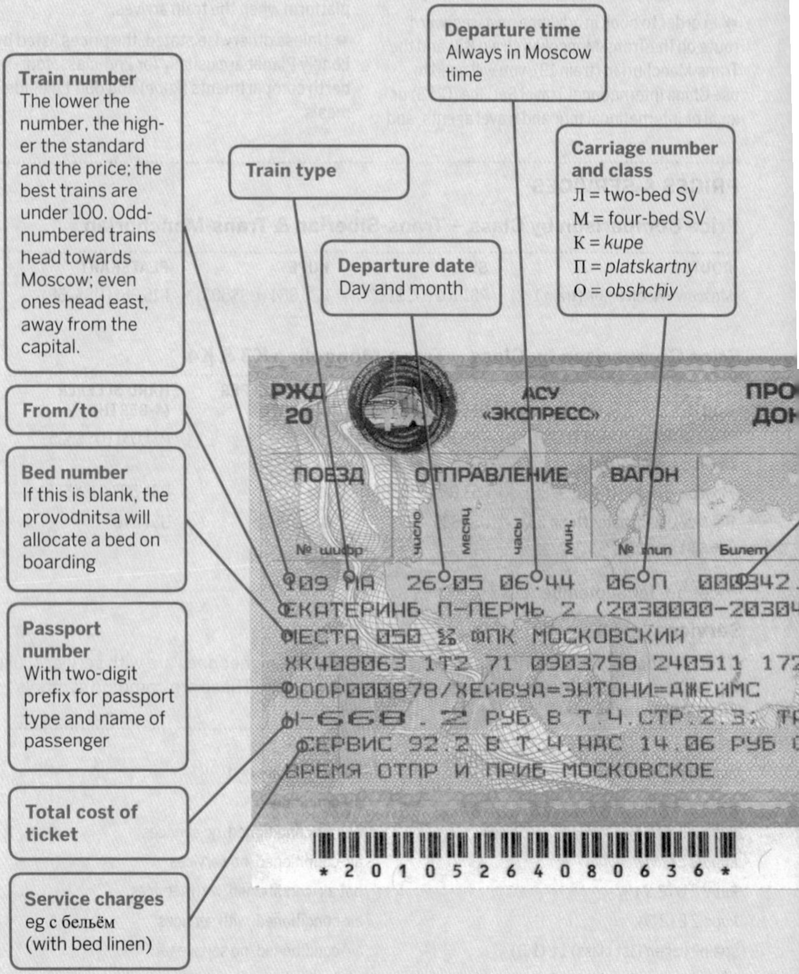

Also bring your passport; you'll be asked for it so that its number and your name can be printed on your ticket. The ticket and passport will be matched up by the provodnitsa (female carriage attendant) before you're allowed on the train – make sure the ticket-seller gets these details correct.

Tickets are printed by computer and come with a duplicate. Shortly after you've boarded the train the provodnitsa will come around and collect the tickets: sometimes they will take both copies and give you one back just before your final destination; often they will leave you with the copy. It will have been ripped slightly to show it's been used. Hang on to this ticket, especially if you're hopping on and off trains, since it provides evidence of how long you've been in a particular place and may prove useful if you're stopped by police.

Sometimes tickets are also sold with separate chits for insurance in the event of a fatal accident, or for bed linen and meals, but usually these prices appear on the ticket itself.

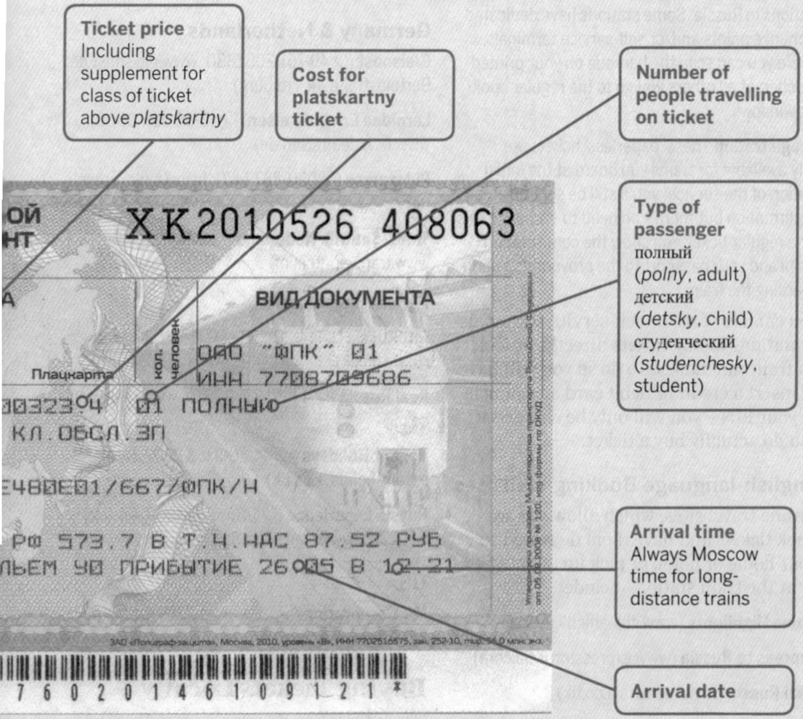

Buying Your Own Tickets Online

Online booking options for Russian trains are very good as you can use RZD's website (http://pass.rzd.ru) or app, or the websites of agents to buy an e-ticket. The Russian Railways site allows you to book and pay for Russian domestic train services using a credit or debit card (most foreign ones are accepted), up to 60 days prior to departure. You will need to set up a user profile in order to purchase the ticket. During the booking process, when asked to fill in 'document type' you should pick 'foreign document' and then enter your passport number.

Electronic Tickets

RZD has two types of electronic tickets:

e-tickets These are coupons detailing your 14-digit order and 14-digit e-ticket numbers. Print them out and exchange them for paper tickets at stations in Russia. Some stations have dedicated exchange points and/or self-service terminals, where you can scan the barcode on your printed voucher; at all others you go to the regular booking windows.

e-registration These 'paperless' tickets are only available for trains you board at the initial station of the service; you'll still be sent an email confirmation but there's no need to exchange this for a regular ticket. You show the confirmation email and your passport to the *provodnitsa* upon boarding the train.

You can also use the self-service terminals at stations to buy tickets directly, or look up train timetables. To do so you will have to insert a credit or debit card and punch in your PIN – you will only be charged if you do actually buy a ticket.

English-language Booking Websites

Online travel sites, which allow you to book tickets and have them delivered to your home or hotel, or pick up at an agency or at the train station, include:

China Highlights (www.chinahighlights.com)

Express to Russia (www.expresstorussia.com)

Real Russia (www.realrussia.co.uk)

Svezhy Veter (www.svezhyveter.ru)

Trains Russia (www.trainsrussia.com)

UFS (www.ufs-online.ru)

Visit Russia (www.visitrussia.com)

Tour & Ticket Agencies

While it will be more expensive, buying tickets from agents is often the most convenient option. Many local operators are also equipped to take bookings from abroad.

Australasia

Sundowners Overland (☎61-3-9672 5386, 1300 133 457; www.sundownersoverland.com)

China International Travel Service

CITS (www.cits.net) Usually the cheapest agency for booking a service from Běijīng. Unless you use one of the recommended agencies, it's pretty much the only way. The following are CITS overseas representatives:

Australia (www.travman.com.au)

France (http://fr.cits.net)

USA (www.citsusa.com)

Germany & Netherlands

Gleisnost (☎49-761-205 5130; www.gleisnost.de; Bertoldstraße 44, Freiburg)

Lernidee Erlebnisreisen (☎49-30-786 0000; www.lernidee-reisen.de)

Pulexpress (☎030-887 1470; http://pulexpress.de)

Trans-Sputnik Nederland (☎020-797 9800; www.trans-sputnik.nl)

UK

IntoRussia (☎44-20-7603 5045; https://intorussia.co.uk)

Real Russia (☎44-20-7100 7370; www.realrussia.co.uk)

Regent Holidays (☎44-20-3733 2907; www.regent-holidays.co.uk)

Russia Experience (☎1-8665 224308, 44-845 521 2910; www.trans-siberian.co.uk)

USA

Mir Corporation (☎1-206-624-7289, 1-800-424-7289; www.mircorp.com)

Buying Tickets Locally

The international trains, especially the Trans-Mongolian, are popular; if this is the train you want it's risky to wait and book locally. Generally it's easier getting tickets if you're going west rather than east, and summer is busier than winter.

Russia

Tickets can be bought online, at Russian Railways booking offices and many of the private railways' booking offices in Russia (ж/д касса). For a list of Russian Railways ticket offices, see the English-language page of their website (http://pass.rzd.ru) under 'passenger information' then 'services' then 'ticket offices'.

At all major stations there are ticket machines that can be used to buy tickets directly or to pick up tickets bought online, using your credit or debit card. If these are not available you will have to fall back on the staffed ticket windows – an unappetising prospect as the sellers rarely speak any other language than Russian and lines at these windows can be long and tend to move slowly. Before you do this, look around for a **service centre** (сервисный), where staff may speak some English and can help book your ticket for a small fee (around ₽250).

If all of the above fails, local travel agencies with English-speaking staff should be able to assist in securing tickets.

Mongolia

In Ulaanbaatar, you cannot buy tickets in advance for the Běijīng–Moscow or Moscow–Běijīng trains, because staff in Ulaanbaatar won't know how many people are already on the train. You can only buy a ticket for these trains the day before departure (although you could try asking two days in advance). If you have trouble booking a berth, ask your guesthouse manager or hotel reception desk for assistance.

China

It's cheaper to buy your ticket at the station, but tickets can be bought online at the following and collected from any train before travel (China DIY Travel is the cheapest):

China DIY Travel (www.china-diy-travel.com; 6 Chaoyang Park Nanlu; 朝阳公园南路6号; commission per ticket $10)

China Trip Advisor (www.chinatripadvisor.com)

CITS (www.cits.net)

Arranging Your Visas

You will almost certainly need a visa for Russia and China, and possibly one for Mongolia, too. Arranging these is generally straightforward but can be time consuming, bureaucratic and – depending on how quickly you need the visa – costly. Start the application process at least a month before your trip.

General Need to Know

- Visas are *not* issued at land borders.
- Visas are valid for entry within three months of issue, so don't apply for them too early.
- Visas are most easily obtained from your country of residence.

China

A visa is required for travellers from the vast majority of countries.

Mongolia

Citizens from a handful of countries need no visa for visits of up to 30 days; likewise US citizens don't need a visa for visits of up to 90 days (if they register with immigration within seven days). Other nationalities can apply for a 30-day tourist visa for which an invitation is sometimes required if you apply outside your country of residence.

Russia

Apply in your country of residence and you will first need an invitation. A tourist visa is valid for up to 30 days, nonextendable. Business visas allow more time – up to three years for US citizens.

Planning

Keep an eye on political events, as they can suddenly make visas more difficult to procure or renew.

Costs

Unless otherwise noted, the following fees are for single-entry tourist visas and don't take into account processing costs by agencies when used.

China

UK £151

USA US$200

Other nations US$110

Mongolia

Australia AU$230

UK £40

USA No need for visa for visits of up to 90 days

Russia

Australia Both tourist and work visas issued in 10/two working days are $135/270

Most EU countries Tourist/work visas issued in four to 10 working days cost €61/141; visas issued in one to three days cost €96/185

UK Tourist and work visas issued in five working days/next working day cost £108/187

USA Tourist or work visas issued in 10/three working days cost $123/213

Agencies

The following agencies can arrange visas for China, Mongolia and Russia and are especially useful for Russian visas.

Action-visas.com (www.action-visas.com)

CIBT (http://cibtvisas.co.uk)

Comet Consular Services (www.cometconsular.com)

IVDS (www.ivds.de)

Real Russia (http://realrussia.co.uk)

VisaCentral (http://visacentral.com)

VisaHQ.com (http://russia.visahq.com)

Invitations can also be arranged with:

Express to Russia (www.expresstorussia.com)

Way to Russia (www.waytorussia.net)

Embassy Websites

China (www.fmprc.gov.cn/mfa_eng/wjb_663304/zwjg_665342 or www.chinese-embassy.info)

Mongolia (www.mfa.gov.mn/?page_id=16975)

Russia (www.mid.ru/en/main_en)

Visas for China

Apart from visa-free visits to Hong Kong and Macau and useful 72-hour visa-free transit stays (for visitors from 51 nations) to Běijīng, Shànghǎi (144-hour visa-free transit), Guǎngzhōu, Xī'ān, Guìlín, Chéngdū, Chóngqìng, Dàlián and Shěnyáng, among others, you will need a visa to visit China. Citizens from Japan, Singapore, Brunei, San Marino, Mauritius, the Seychelles and the Bahamas do not require a visa to visit China so long as the visit is less than 15 days. There remain a few restricted areas in China that require an additional permit from the PSB. Permits are also required for travel to Tibet, a region that the authorities can suddenly bar foreigners from entering.

A standard, 30-day single-entry visa can be issued in four to five working days. In many countries, the visa service has been outsourced from the Chinese embassy to a compulsory Chinese Visa Application Service Centre (www.visaforchina.org), which levies an extra administration fee. In the case of the UK, a single-entry visa costs UK£85, but the standard administration charge levied by the centre is an additional UK£66 (three-day express UK£78, postal service UK£90). In some countries, such as the UK, France, the US and Canada, there is more than one service centre nationwide. Visa Application Service Centres are open Monday to Friday.

A standard 30-day visa is activated on the date you enter China, and must be used within three months of the date of issue. Travel visas of 60 days and 90 days are harder to get but possible just by applying. To stay longer, you can extend your visa in China.

Having a visa mailed to you will take up to three weeks. In the US and Canada, mailed visa applications have to go via a visa agent, at extra cost. In the US, many people use the **China Visa Service Center** (☎in the US 800 799 6560; www.mychinavisa.com), which takes 10 to 14 days.

From Mongolia & Russia

Getting a Chinese visa in Ulaanbaatar is possible, but takes between one and four working days (depending on what level of service you pay for) and involves queuing and paperwork. You must provide one passport photo, proof of departure from China (eg an air or train reservation), proof of a booked hotel stay of three nights and a bank statement. In practice, travellers often obtain all this from any travel agency in Ulaanbaatar and simply cancel afterwards.

In August and early September lines are long due to students queuing up for visas. At these times the line starts to form at 6am (or earlier). Before the embassy opens, the guard will give out a limited number of tickets. If you don't get a ticket, it's highly unlikely you'll get inside that day. For updated information, see http://mn.china-embassy.org.

In Russia, China has consulates in St Petersburg, Moscow and Khabarovsk. At the very least an invitation letter and/or hotel booking, travel itinerary and an onward flight are usually required.

Registration & Extensions

There's no individual registration requirement when you enter China. Remember that if you go to Hong Kong or Macau (which are visa-free for many nationalities) you'll need a new visa or a double-entry visa to return to the mainland.

The Foreign Affairs Branch of the local **Public Security Bureau** (PSB; 公安局; Gōng'ānjú) deals with visa extensions.

Visas for Mongolia

A 30-day tourist visa is easily obtained at any Mongolian embassy, consulate, consulate-general or honorary consulate.

If you are travelling to Mongolia from a country that has no Mongolian consulate, you can pick up a 30-day tourist visa on arrival at the airport in Ulaanbaatar. You'll need T108,000 (or US dollar equivalent) and two passport photos – you should also have a pre-approval letter from an organisation or company in Mongolia.

Citizens of the following countries can stay in Mongolia for up to 90 days without a visa: Belarus, Brazil, Kazakhstan, Kyrgyzstan, Macau, Serbia, Ukraine and the USA. If they stay less than 30 days, nothing needs to be done, other than having their passport stamped when they enter and leave the country. If they stay more than 30 days, they need to register.

Citizens of Canada, Germany, Israel, Japan, Laos, Malaysia, Russia, Thailand and Turkey can stay visa-free for up to 30 days; Philippines passport-holders can stay for 21 days without a visa and Hong Kong citizens can stay visa-free for up to 14 days.

A single-entry transit visa costs between US$30 and US$60, depending on where you apply for it. You will need to show your train or plane ticket and a visa for the next country (Russia or China). Transit visas (which cannot be extended) are valid for 72 hours from the date of entry, which will only allow you to get off the Trans-Mongolian train in Ulaanbaatar for a very short time before catching another train to Russia or China.

To check the current situation on visas see http://caravanistan.com/visa/mongolia.

From China & Russia

Always try to call ahead at Mongolian embassies as hours change frequently. Invitations are not usually required, but this can be arbitrary and change quickly; it's worth being prepared if you're short of time.

Registration & Extensions

If you stay less than 30 days, you don't need to register. All visitors who plan to stay more than 30 days *must* be registered within seven days of their arrival. Registration costs T1000.

Visitors can extend visas on a per-week basis up to four days before their expiry. A one-week extension is T27,000, then T3600 for each additional day. If you are late extending your visa then you will pay an additional fine of T200,000.

For extensions, registration and exit visas, go to the **Office of Immigration, Naturalisation & Foreign Citizens** (INFC; ☎19001882; Airport Rd; ⏲9am-1pm & 2-6pm Mon-Fri) in Ulaanbaatar.

Getting a visa extension outside the capital can be difficult and your passport may need to be sent back to Ulaanbaatar anyway.

Visas for Russia

Everyone entering Russia needs a visa and should apply before leaving home. The Russian Embassy in Běijīng (p375) has been known to issue visas and **Legend Tour** (☎11-315 158, 9919 3843; www.legendtour.ru; Seoul St, Chonon Burt Center Bldg, 3rd fl, What3words: isolated.emulating.fronted; ⏲9am-1pm & 2-6pm Mon-Fri) in Ulaanbaatar is often successful.

Tourist Visa

For most travellers a tourist visa (single or double entry and valid for a maximum of 30 days, nonextendable, from the date of entry) will be sufficient. Travel agents, Russian hotels and specialised visa agencies can provide the invitation.

Business Visa

If you plan to stay longer than a month, it's advisable to apply for a business visa. These can be issued for three, six or 12 months (or three years for US citizens), and are available as single-entry, double-entry or multiple-entry visas. They are valid for up to 90 days of travel within any 180-day period. You don't need to be on business to get one of these visas, but you must have a letter of invitation from a registered Russian company or organisation (arranged via specialist visa agencies).

Transit Visa

For transit by air, this visa is usually good for up to three days. For a nonstop Trans-Siberian Railway journey, it's valid for 10 days, giving westbound passengers a few days in Moscow; those heading east, however, are not allowed to linger in Moscow.

Private Visa

Valid for up to three months and can be issued for single or double entry. To get one you'll need an official invitation certificate from relatives or friends you'll be staying with (this is a big hassle for them to get; applying for a regular tourist or business visa is far simpler).

Application

If the agency is not handling the application as well, you need to lodge it yourself at the consulate. Costs vary depending on the type of visa applied for and how quickly you need it. Check the rules well in advance.

Russian embassies in many countries have contracted separate agencies to process the submission of visa applications and check everything is in order; these companies use online interfaces that direct the relevant information into the standard visa application form (available at https://visa.kdmid.ru/PetitionChoice.aspx). In the UK, the agency is **VFS.Global** (http://ru.vfsglobal.co.uk) with offices in London and Edinburgh; in the US **Invisa Logistic Services** (http://ils-usa.com) has offices in Washington, DC, New York, San Francisco, Houston and Seattle.

Immigration Form

Immigration forms are produced electronically by passport control at airports. Take good care of your half of the completed form as you'll need it for registration and could face problems while travelling – and certainly on leaving – without it.

Registration

Visas should be registered within seven days of arrival, excluding weekends and public holidays. The obligation to register is with the accommodating party – your hotel or hostel, or landlord, friend or family if you're staying in a private residence.

If you're staying at a hotel or hostel, the receptionist will register you for free or for a small fee (typically around €10). Once registered, you should receive a slip of paper confirming the dates you'll be staying at that particular accommodation. Keep this safe – that's the document that any police who stop you will request to see.

If staying in a homestay or rental apartment, you'll either need to make arrangements with the landlord or a friend to register you through the post office. See http://waytorussia.net/RussianVisa/Registration.html for how this can be done and for more details on the whole process.

Every time you move city or town and stay for more than seven days, it's necessary to go through the registration process again. There's no need to be overly paranoid about this, but the more thorough your registration record, the less chance there'll be of running into problems. Keep all transport tickets (especially if you spend nights sleeping on trains) to prove to any overzealous police officers exactly when you arrived in a new place.

It's tempting to be lax about registration, and we've met many travellers who were and didn't experience any problems. Note that you will not be asked to show registration slips when leaving from Russia's airports.

However, if you're travelling for a while in Russia and particularly if you're visiting off-the-beaten-track places, it's worth making sure you are registered at each destination, since it's not uncommon to encounter fine-hungry cops hoping to catch tourists too hurried or disorganised to be able to explain long gaps in their registration.

Extensions

Extensions are time-consuming and difficult; tourist visas can't be extended at all. Avoid the need for an extension by initially arranging a longer visa than you might need.

Life on the Rails

Whichever route you choose to travel along the Trans-Siberian Railway, you'll have to adjust to an extended period spent living on a train with all its associated quirks and rituals. Come prepared for that experience and your journey will be all the smoother and more enjoyable.

Internet Resources

Circumbaikal Railway (http://kbzd.transsib.ru)

CNVOL.com (www.cnvol.com) Covers train travel in China.

Man in Seat 61 (www.seat61.com) Mark Smith's definitive website.

Meeting of Frontiers (http://international.loc.gov/intldl/mtfhtml/mfhome.html) Online collection about Russians exploring America and vice versa. Under 'Digital Collections' you'll find an original Trans-Siberian guidebook dating from 1900 and rare books and photos, many relating to Siberian and Far East travel and exploration.

Russian Railways (http://eng.rzd.ru/vtour/index.html) A virtual tour inside the *Rossiya*.

Trans-Siberian Railway Encyclopaedia (https://trans-siberian-railway-encyclopedia.com) Download Robert Walker's all-encompassing book here.

Trans-Siberian Railway Web Encyclopaedia (www.transsib.ru) Not updated, but still a mine of useful background detail.

Arriving & Boarding

- Russian trains are super punctual, so allow enough time at the station for formalities and buying last-minute supplies before scheduled departures. Check the name of the station closely on your ticket and arrive at least 30 minutes before scheduled departure.
- Wait for the platform (платформа) and track (путь) to be displayed on the departure board.
- Keep your ticket and passport safe but accessible so you can show them for boarding.

A–Z on the Train

Bedding

Fresh sheets and pillowcases, blankets and a handtowel are provided. If the cost isn't included in your ticket (it often is) then you'll pay the *provodnitsa* a small charge for these.

Carriage Layout

Facilities in the carriage will depend on the class of travel, but generally the layout is as follows. On the left as you enter is one bathroom; alongside that is the attendant's compartment. Opposite this compartment is the all-important samovar with hot water for beverages, and directly opposite this, inset on the wall near the attendant's compartment, is (in theory) potable water.

Under no circumstances drink the water in the bathrooms; the best and safest water on the train comes from the samovar.

The rest of the carriage is made up of nine closed compartments (1st/SV and 2nd/*kupe* class) or 54 open beds (3rd/*platskart* class). At the other end of the carriage is a second toilet. The rubbish bin is inside a box opposite the second toilet.

Classes & Comforts

In theory, all but the cheapest carriages are air-conditioned in summer and heated in winter – that's why the windows are locked shut (though sometimes you'll be able to open them). In practice, air conditioning can break down or a compartment can be stiflingly overheated.

Some Russian 2nd-class compartments are entirely single-sex these days, although this is not available on all trains.

Deluxe 1st Class & Tourist Trains

Deluxe 1st class is available on train K3/4 (Trans-Mongolian). This entails roomy, two-berth compartments with showers shared between two compartments. Train K23/24 between Běijīng and Ulaanbaatar has a similar deluxe 1st class with showers.

A handful of scheduled trains, including the 001Г/002Й *Premium* Moscow–Kazan service and 53/54 (http://grandexpress.ru/en) linking Moscow and St Petersburg, have a luxury *myagkiye* carriage with compartments sleeping two with their own toilet and shower. Tourist trains such as the *Golden Eagle* have the option of even more luxurious compartments.

1st Class/SV

This class of compartment, called SV (short for *spalny vagon,* or sleeping wagon) or *lyux,* has only two berths, so there's more room and more privacy. They usually also have TVs on which it is possible to watch DVDs. The *provodnitsa* has DVDs for a small fee (there's nothing to stop you from bringing your own, although they'll need to work on a Russian DVD player, compatible with region 5).

2nd Class/Kupe

The compartments in a *kupeyny* carriage (2nd class, also called 'compartmentalised' and often shortened to *kupe*) are standard on long-distance trains. These carriages are divided into nine compartments, each with four reasonably comfortable berths, a fold-down table and enough room between bunks to stand and undress.

In every carriage there's one half-sized compartment with just two berths. This is usually occupied by the *provodnitsa,* or reserved for railway employees, but there is a slim chance that you may end up in it, particularly if you do a deal directly with a *provodnitsa* for a train ticket.

3rd Class/Platskart

You either love them or hate them, and it's worth experiencing these carriages at least once to decide for yourself. A reserved-place *platskartny* carriage, sometimes also called *zhyostky* ('hard class', or 3rd class) and usually abbreviated to *platskart,* is essentially a dorm carriage sleeping 54. The bunks are non-compartmentalised and arranged in blocks of four running down one side of the corridor and in two on the other, with the lower bunk on this side converting to a table and chairs during the day. They're ideal for one-night journeys. In summer the lack of compartment walls means they're not usually as stuffy as a *kupe* can be. Many travellers (women in particular) find *platskart* a better option than being cooped up with three (possibly drunken) Russian men. It's also a great way to meet ordinary Russians.

However, on multiday journeys some *platskart* carriages can begin to resemble a refugee camp, with clothing strung between bunks, a great swapping of bread, fish and jars of tea, and babies sitting on potties while their snot-nosed siblings tear up and down the corridor. Only the hardy would want to do Moscow to Vladivostok or similar nonstop journeys this way.

If you do travel *platskart,* it's worth requesting specific numbered seats when booking your ticket. The ones to avoid are 1 to 4 (next to the attendant and samovar, which means a lot of activity) and 33 to 36 (next to the toilet). Corridor bunks are numbered from 37 (the lower bunk near the toilet and smoking vestibule) to 54 (the upper bunk near the *provodnitsa*). Odd numbers are always lower bunks; even numbers are upper bunks. The bottom side berth bunks (ie the odd numbers) are shorter than the rest. Anyone over 180cm (6ft) tall will find the 'pedial overhang' uncomfortable, if not downright untenable.

Finally, it's worth experiencing *platskart* while you can, as as Russian Railways announced plans in 2013 to replace these carriages with more comfortable rolling stock in the near future – they are seen as an anachronism in contemporary Russia.

4th Class/Obshchiy

Also called 4th class, *obshchiy* (general) is unreserved. On long-distance trains the *obshchiy* carriage looks the same as a *platskart,* but when it's full, eight people are squeezed into each unenclosed compartment so there's no room to lie down. Suburban trains normally have only *obshchiy* class, which in this case means bench-type seating. On a few daytime-only intercity trains there are higher-grade *obshchiy* carriages with more comfortable, reserved chairs.

Clothing

Loose fitting, comfortable and layered is our advice. Russian train attire often consists of synthetic tracksuit pants, a T-shirt and pullover (or sweatshirt) and thongs (flip-flops) or sandals. In contrast to Russian big-city streetwear, this is not high fashion, but it's highly functional. Variations on this theme – such as loose-fitting jeans and using the tracksuit pants as pyjamas – are a good compromise between style and comfort. In winter, a warm jacket or overcoat and a warm hat and gloves, as well as face and lip cream against cold, should be kept close by for station stops.

Be aware of polite signals or requests by others that you should briefly leave the compartment so that the person can get changed – mostly, this happens just after departure and before arrival.

Electricity

In the age of manifold hand-held devices and digital cameras, power outlets can be a problem in some carriages, especially on older Russian trains. These have a couple of 110V outlets for razors, but often a 2nd-class carriage will have only one 220V socket, located halfway along the corridor. Ask politely, however, and you can often use a power outlet inside the attendant's carriage. Modern 1st-class and many newer 2nd-class carriages also have power outlets in the compartments.

Essential Items

- Pocketknife with corkscrew and openers, plastic or metal mug, plastic or metal cutlery (a metal camping set that fits together is useful)
- Lightweight torch (flashlight)
- Money belt, neck pouch or ankle stash
- Toilet paper, a small medical kit (the attendant also has one) and whatever hygiene articles you need; buy some from the attendant, or top up at platform kiosks
- Earplugs or a sleeping mask if white noise or bright light bother you
- Bottled water
- An electrical plug adaptor if required
- Comfortable clothing suitable for the season, and slip-on footwear

Food

Platform Food

Shopping for supplies on station platforms is part of the fun of the Trans-Siberian Railway (note, however, that in Mongolia and China you will find very little food available on platforms). It's a good idea to have plenty of small change on hand, but you'll rarely have to worry about being overcharged.

The choice of items can be excellent, with bread, fresh dairy products, ice cream, grilled chicken, boiled potatoes, home cooking such as *pelmeni* (dumplings) or *pirozhki* (savoury pies), buckets of forest berries and smoked fish all on offer. Through Siberia you'll always find sellers of fresh pine or cedar nuts. Check the use-by dates on packaged platform food.

Compartment Picnics

Instant noodles have made great inroads into Russia's rail system, but serious eating still tends to involve sliced chunks of cucumber and tomato in summer, more often than not cured sausage, perhaps fish, perhaps a cold dish someone prepared at home, all washed down with beer, tea or vodka. A cloth or newspaper is often spread carefully across the compartment table, then the food is unpacked lovingly and eaten with relish. After that – if it's lunch – everyone usually dozes off. If you buy plentifully on the platforms and have the right travel companions, compartment picnics will be a true highlight of your trip.

Strictly speaking, alcohol cannot be carried onto the train; it can only be bought from the restaurant car or the snack seller. In practice, Russians invariably bring their own.

Some train tickets include snacks or small meals that will be distributed by the *provodnitsa*.

Restaurant Cars & Buffets

The restaurant cars are changed at each country's border, so en route to Běijīng you will get Russian, Chinese and possibly Mongolian menus (although it's unlikely there will be a car attached between the Russian border and Ulaanbaatar).

In restaurant cars, a full meal with accompanying drink typically costs US$20 to US$30, paid in local currency. The cars are open from approximately 9am to 9pm local time, although their hours in Russia are highly unpredictable. With time-zone differences, knowing when to turn up is almost impossible to guess. Generally, Chinese restaurant cars have the best food. On Russian menus, the dishes with prices written alongside them are the ones available that day.

Some trains, especially on the Baikal-Amur Mainline (BAM), only have a buffet car with high tables, but these afford good panoramas of the landscape. In the restaurant car there's often a table of pot noodles, chocolate, alcohol, juice and the like.

As well as vendors who go through the carriages with snacks, *provodniki* offer their own drinks and nibbles. Prices are not as cheap as at the kiosks or station halts.

A restaurant or buffet car can be a good place to meet people, or get away from them, depending on the time of day or night and standard of food and service. On some low-grade Russian trains you'll find few signs of edible food or human life, however, except for a few bored staff and the telltale smell of something having been cooked there some time in the distant past. On other trains, the standard isn't too bad.

Interacting with Passengers

Politely greeting fellow travellers when you first enter the compartment, or greeting new arrivals, is a good icebreaker. Let things develop at a natural pace, though. Offering food, even as a token gesture, is de rigueur and remains the best way to cultivate a good travelling relationship.

Russians are masters of the art of conversation, so if you're travelling alone it will be easy to meet people. Chinese travellers are also curious and like talking to foreigners. Sometimes the trolley lady selling drinks and snacks will combine business with pleasure by sitting down for a rest and conversation. If you chat for a long time, it's usual to buy a drink or snack in return. Keep small change for this –

SHE WHO MUST BE OBEYED

On any long-distance Russian train journey you'll soon learn who's in charge: the *provodnitsa*. Though sometimes male (*provodnik*), carriage attendants are usually women.

Apart from checking your ticket before boarding the train, doling out linen, and shaking you awake in the middle of the night when your train arrives, the job of the *provodnitsa* is to keep her carriage spick and span (most are very diligent about this) and to make sure the samovar is always fired up with hot water. They will have cups, plates and cutlery to borrow, if you need them, and can provide drinks and snacks for a small price.

On long journeys, the *provodnitsa* works in a team of two; one will be working while the other is resting.

Initially, a *provodnitsa* can come across as quite fearsome. Very few will speak any language other than Russian. All look as smart as sergeant majors in their RZD uniforms – and just as ready to knock you into shape if you step out of line! However, if you're polite and respectful to your *provodnitsa*, and bestow on her plenty of friendly smiles, chances are high that she will do her best to make your journey a very pleasant one.

snack sellers can disappear into the taiga for several hundred kilometres in order to break the high notes. The more skilled deliver the best vodka and conversation on the train.

If you have difficulties with a fellow passenger (a loud DVD player is a possible issue), sort it out locally, but if that fails, the *provodnitsa* can swing into action.

Luggage

How much to bring will be a compromise between weight and comfort. The baggage allowance per adult on Chinese international trains is 35kg (20kg on domestic trains). On all Russian trains it's 36kg (50kg in 1st class).

Before boarding, stow things needed for the journey in your day pack; the rest can be locked in your baggage and stored either inside the base of the bottom bunk (you can lift up the bunk) or in the luggage space above the door.

Time Zones

The Trans-Siberian route between Moscow and Vladivostok crosses seven of Russia's 11 time zones. Moscow has its clocks permanently on winter time (GMT/UTC plus three hours), which means that when clocks go forward in spring in Europe and elsewhere, the relevant time differences decrease by one hour. Like Russia, neither China nor Mongolia observe daylight-savings time. The following table lists times at different locations when it's noon in Moscow:

WHERE	TIME	GMT/UTC
Běijīng	5pm (17.00)	+8hr
Ulaanbaatar	5pm (17.00)	+8hr
Yekaterinburg & Tyumen	2pm (14.00)	+5hr
Omsk & Novosibirsk	3pm (15.00)	+6hr
Krasnoyarsk	4pm (16.00)	+7hr
Irkutsk & Ulan-Ude	5pm (17.00)	+8hr
Vladivostok	7pm (19.00)	+10hr

Clocks and timetables on trains and at stations show Moscow time *(Moskovskoe vremya)*. Local time is known as *mestnoe vremya*.

The best way to cope with the time zones is to drink plenty of bottled water, avoid overdoing the alcohol and shift your meals and bedtime back or forward according to local time. Travellers who take strong medication will need to exercise caution and seek advice from their doctor before setting out.

Toilets & Showers

The toilets on all major trains are Western type. Unless the train has a closed-system biological toilet (some modern or refitted carriages have these), toilets will be locked before and after arrival at a station. In larger cities, this might include one hour before arrival and one hour after leaving the station, although 10 to 20 minutes on each side of town is more usual. The schedule is attached to the toilet door.

There are no showers in passenger carriages except in 1st class on a few top-quality trains, so a flannel is useful for washing at the basin. Most *firmeny* (premium) trains, however, have a shower cubicle in the service wagon, next to the restaurant car. There is a small fee (usually around ₽150) to use it; the *provodnitsa* can organise a visit to this carriage. Apart from soap and the usual toiletries, you should pack or buy sufficient toilet paper, although a good attendant will keep the toilets supplied and shipshape. Use the bathroom bin to dispose of sanitary objects. A clothes hook situated in the bathroom is useful for hanging up your day pack or toiletries bag while you go about your ablutions. A pair of rubber flip-flops (thongs) is also recommended to save standing on the floor in your bare feet.

Safety & Safekeeping

Russian and Asian trains are generally safe, but be security conscious, especially if you're travelling alone.

➡ Keep your valuables and documents with you at all times in a zipped or buttoned-up pocket. Don't flash large amounts of cash or your credit cards around.

➡ Money belts and ankle stashes are useful, but storing documents and valuables inside your pillowcase while you sleep is the safest stash.

➡ Ask someone you trust to keep an eye on any bag containing valuables while you are away.

➡ If you're alone in a compartment, ask the *provodnitsa* to lock it while you go to the

CROSSING THE BORDERS

The Trans-Mongolian Railway crosses the Russia–Mongolia border at Naushki-Sükhbaatar, which can take anything from six to 11 hours. Crossing the China–Mongolia border takes about five hours, and the bogies of the carriages are changed to the local gauge here.

The Trans-Manchurian Railway crosses the Russia–China border between Mǎnzhōulǐ (China) and Zabaikalsk (Russia), which takes about half a day. Again, the bogies must be changed. Remember: toilets are always locked at stops and during bogie changes.

restaurant car or get out at long station stops (never leave luggage completely unattended in an unlocked compartment).

➡ Lock your compartment door from the inside at night and use the additional metal security latch on the door.

➡ Generally, the more alcohol there is in play, the more safety is an issue. In the rare case that you are molested by a fellow passenger, inform the attendant. If you feel unsafe, a move or swap can be organised.

Smoking

Smoking is not allowed anywhere on the train or, officially, on station platforms (even though you may see fellow passengers taking a puff here). If you are caught smoking, you may be liable for a fine.

Wi-fi

On Sapsan trains between Moscow and St Petersburg and Moscow and Nizhny Novgorod, paid wi-fi access and 3G coverage is available. Russian Railways has plans to roll out on-board wi-fi for some other premium train services and routes.

Mobile-phone coverage is available all along the main Trans-Siberian lines and 3G is available in places, so if you have internet access on your phone, you may still be able to get online in the midst of Siberia (but no promises!).

Station Stops

Many of the stops along the Trans-Siberian and Asian routes are for two minutes. Halts of 10 to 20 minutes are common at larger towns or junctions, and sometimes extend up to six or seven hours at borders. From some platforms you have enough time to dash into the station, but let the *provodnitsa* know in advance and don't dilly-dally – trains won't wait for you!

➡ A timetable of station stops (in Cyrillic) hangs in the carriage, but these times are not set in stone. Check the schedule (or take a photo of it), but also double-check with the *provodnitsa* when you get off.

➡ All train clocks show Moscow time. It's useful to be bi-temporal, eg keeping your watch on Moscow time and a mobile device on local time.

➡ Take your ticket and passport with you. You might be asked to show them to police on the platform (rare) or to get back on (if you have unremarkable features).

➡ If you miss your train, inform station staff immediately. They will try to organise alternatives so you can catch up with your luggage. But don't count on it.

Journey at a Glance

Our coverage of the Trans-Siberian Railway includes the major cities in which you may start or finish your journey (Moscow, St Petersburg and Běijīng) and bite-sized chunks of the overall Trans-Siberian route, heading east from European Russia into Siberia and onwards to the Russian Far East and termination in Vladivostok. There are also descriptions of the Trans-Mongolian and Trans-Manchurian routes (both of which terminate in Běijīng) and the Baikal-Amur Mainline (BAM) from the points they diverge from the main Trans-Siberian railway. Each route has its own appeal but all are united by the experience of being on the train itself. Our details will help you plan where best you might want to make a stop along the way.

Moscow

History
Art
Performing Arts

Historical Landmarks

The Kremlin shows off the splendour of Muscovy's grand princes. St Basil's Cathedral recounts the defeat of the Tatars. And on Red Square, Lenin lies embalmed.

Glorious Galleries

The illustrious Tretyakov and Pushkin Galleries are only the beginning of the art in Moscow, where contemporary artists and their patrons are taking over former factories and warehouses to display their works.

Theatre & Dance

The city's classical performing arts are still among the best in the world. Nowadays, even the most traditional theatres are experimenting with innovative arrangements and cutting-edge choreographies.

p54

St Petersburg

Palaces
History
Art

Imperial Splendour

Grand imperial palaces line the embankments of the Neva River, its tributaries and canals. Restoration over the past two decades has been painstaking; the results are breathtaking.

Revolutionary Road

St Petersburg has revolution in its DNA: from Peter the Great's determination to forge a new Russia by opening the country to the rest of Europe, to Lenin's leadership of a coup in 1917, which led to the creation of the world's first communist state.

Staggering Collections

The Hermitage collection is unrivalled. The Russian Museum boasts its own unique collection of Russian painting from icons to the avant-garde.

p85

Moscow to Yekaterinburg

Scenery
Culture
Outdoors

Crossing the Urals

The Ural Mountains form a physical and metaphysical divide between Europe and Asia. The Volga River is a highlight; the scenery is most beautiful just east of Kungur.

Multicultural Mashup

Nizhny Novgorod offers an insight into Volga life as well as a wonderful kremlin. Perm has refashioned itself as a 'contemporary art capital', while the less-travelled Kazan and Yaroslavl routes offer insight into Islamic (Kazan) and Orthodox (Yaroslavl) cultures.

Getting Active

Perm is a fine base in the Urals for hiking, rafting or horse riding; Kungur has easy access to canoeing, cycling and cross-country skiing.

p111

Yekaterinburg to Krasnoyarsk

Scenery
City Life
Architecture

Into the Taiga

Vistas of dense taiga alternating with farmland unfurl gradually outside your window as you travel deeper into Siberia. On a winter journey, a blanket of snow makes the unchanging look romantic and beautiful.

Big City Lights

They don't call Novosibirsk the capital of Siberia for nothing – enjoy a slew of quirky museums and monuments, a relaxed big-city vibe and pulsating nightlife.

Wooden Lace

Tobolsk and Tomsk, both slight detours off the main Trans-Siberian route, are worth visiting for their attractive wooden buildings with intricately carved facades. Tobolsk also has a handsome, ancient kremlin.

p135

Lake Baikal: Krasnoyarsk to Ulan-Ude

Baikal Views
Outdoors
History

Siberian Pearl

Lake Baikal is the highlight, even viewed through the carriage window. Summer waters lap in shades of blue; winter white-outs melt the frozen lake into its alpine backdrop.

Make a Splash

A chilly plunge into Baikal is said to add seven years to your life! Not game? Then give winter dog sledding and ice fishing on Baikal a go.

Exiles & Indigenes

The peoples of the Baikal region have lent it a colourful and varied history, especially since the 17th-century Russian Cossacks collided with Mongol Buryats. Later came Tibetan Buddhists, aristocratic Decembrists and revolutionaries. Museums explain all.

p166

Ulan-Ude to Vladivostok

Urban Life
River Life
Religion

End of the Line

Even if Vladivostok wasn't the Trans-Sib terminus it would still be well worth visiting for its remarkable harbour, hilly location and great range of museums and cultural centres.

Riverside Promenades

The fortunes of Siberian cities are shaped by rivers, especially the Amur. Lively promenades along the banks are part of the appeal in Blagoveshchensk and Khabarovsk, one of the Far East's most happening cities.

Religious Life

Spin prayer wheels at the *datsan* (Buddhist temples) in Aginskoe and Tsugol, both reached from Chita. Learn about Stalin's plan to create a Jewish Zion at Birobidzhan.

p204

The Baikal-Amur Mainline (BAM)

Scenery
Outdoors
Architecture

Taiga & Tunnels

Stare into limitless taiga, strain to view the top of a mountain, then plunge into a long, dark tunnel. The BAM bucks and weaves, skirts 3000m-high peaks, rattles over mountain brooks and burrows into earthquake-prone mountainscape.

Base for Baikal

Severobaikalsk is a superb base from which to explore the surrounding wilds on foot, by bike, on the water or snow. The Great Baikal Trail can be accessed from town.

Soviet Architecture

The Soviet-futuristic BAM stations at Severobaikalsk and Tynda are worth a visit in their own right as are the heroic mosaics in Komsomolsk-na-Amure.

p233

The Trans-Mongolian Route

Scenery
Religion
Outdoors

Steppes & Desert

Taiga gives way to Mongolia's rolling hills, which ease into grassy steppes. Further south the train travels through the Gobi Desert, and once in China it's back to grasslands and spectacular mountain scenery.

Buddhist Art

Some stunning Buddhist monasteries can be visited in Mongolia, including Amarbayasgalant and Gandan. In China, the Yúngāng Caves, crammed with carved Buddhas, are not to be missed.

Saddle Up

Gorkhi-Terelj National Park is an excellent destination for horse riding, mountain biking or hiking. For wildlife viewing, try Khustain National Park.

p247

The Trans-Manchurian Route

Winter
History
Quirkiness

Ice & Snow

The Harbin (Hā'ěrbīn) Ice & Snow Festival runs from early December to late February and is the city's main claim to fame.

The Manchus

Make a stop in Shānhǎiguān, where the Great Wall meets the sea, or Chángchūn, home to the Manchu Imperial Palace. Harbin has its own unique history, filled with architectural treasures.

Quirky Sites

Mǎnzhōulǐ is a slightly oddball destination, with its hip-hop statues on the streets and gigantic *matryoshka* doll park. In Harbin you can kick back in Stalin Park, one of the last parks to retain the dictator's name, as well as visit an Orthodox church.

p279

Běijīng

Shopping
Architecture
Food

Markets

For a brand-new wardrobe on the cheap, bargain at the Sanlitun Yashou Clothing Market. For more traditional items, browse the ancient shops and stalls of Dashilar silk street or Pānjiāyuán Market.

Imperial Icons

The Great Wall, Forbidden City, Temple of Heaven and Summer Palace – to name just a few. But don't overlook the best of old Běijīng and relaxing bike rides through its winding alleys and tranquil parks.

Culinary Delights

Gastronomes will be salivating at the capital's amazing selection of Chinese cuisine. Peking duck is the city's signature dish, but head to Wangfujing to try out China's most exotic street snacks.

p297

On the Road

St Petersburg p85
Moscow p54
RUSSIA
Moscow to Yekaterinburg p111
Yekaterinburg to Krasnoyarsk p135
The Baikal-Amur Mainline (BAM) p233
Ulan-Ude to Vladivostok p204
Lake Baikal: Krasnoyarsk to Ulan-Ude p166
The Trans-Manchurian Route p279
MONGOLIA
The Trans-Mongolian Route p247
Beijing p297
CHINA

Moscow

Includes ➡

Best Places to Eat

- ➡ Delicatessen (p75)
- ➡ Cafe Pushkin (p76)
- ➡ Khachapuri (p76)
- ➡ Kitayskaya Gramota (p78)
- ➡ Lavka-Lavka (p75)

Best Places to Stay

- ➡ Hotel National (p72)
- ➡ Hotel de Paris (p72)
- ➡ Godzillas Hostel (p72)
- ➡ Loft Hostel 77 (p72)
- ➡ Bulgakov Mini-Hotel (p73)

Why Go?

Moscow (Москва) is the start or the end point for your train journey across Mother Russia. If you are travelling east to west, you will be relieved – after days (or weeks) of train travel – to reach the cultured, cosmopolitan capital, brimming with opportunities to immerse yourself in history; to indulge in world-class music and art; to feast on fabulous food; and to sample the nightlife in a city that never sleeps. If you are travelling west to east, you may be relieved to depart – to escape the overwhelming urbanity, the bumper-to-bumper traffic, the nonstop noise, the panic-inducing prices. Either way, Moscow is an exhilarating and confounding contrast to the rest of Russia.

Soak it up. Examine the art and move to the music; splurge on a ritzy restaurant; stay out till sunrise; get lost in the crowds. Once you board that train, you may not get to do it again.

When to Go

Moscow

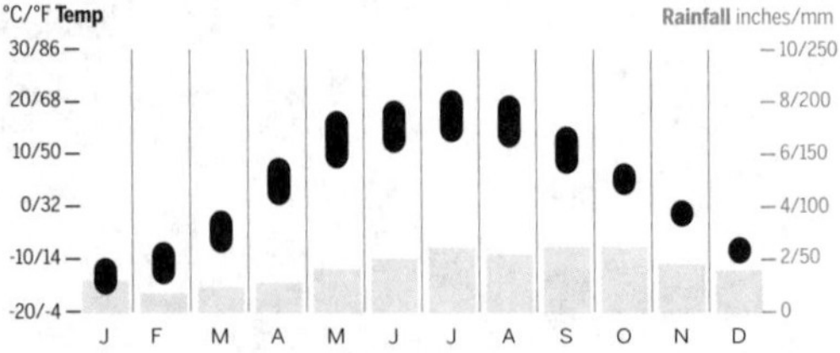

May & Jun Long daylight hours and mild temperatures entice locals to sit at summer terraces.

Sep The capital celebrates City Day, as the foliage turns the city splendid oranges, reds and yellows.

Dec The snow-covered city hosts its premier cultural event, the December Nights Festival.

Arriving by Air

If you arrive by air, you will fly into one of the city's four airports. The majority of international flights go in and out of Domodedovo and Sheremetyevo International Airports; the other two airports are Vnukovo and Zhukovsky. All airports except Zhukovsky are accessible by the convenient Aeroexpress train (p84) from the city centre.

If you wish to take a taxi from the airport, go to the taxi desk (or straight to the dispatcher) for an official airport taxi, which will charge between ₽2000 and ₽2500 to the centre. Note that driving times vary wildly depending on traffic.

Arriving by Rail

Rail riders will arrive at one of the central train stations. All trains from St Petersburg arrive at Leningrad Station, while Trans-Siberian trains from the east arrive at Yaroslav Station or Kazan Station. These three railway stations (p83) are clustered around Komsomolskaya pl, a bustling square just northeast of the centre. From here, you can hop on the metro (Komsomolskaya) for a quick, easy ride to your destination. Alternatively, most taxi companies offer a fixed rate of ₽400 to ₽600 for a train-station transfer.

Guided Tours

Moscow is a big, overwhelming city with a strange alphabet. Letting the locals show you around is a good way to get your bearings and learn something along the way.

Moscow Free Tour (Map p60; ☎495-222 3466; www.moscowfreetour.com; Nikolskaya ul 4/5; guided walk free, paid tours from €31) Offers a free walking tour, led by knowledgeable and extremely enthusiastic guides. Did we mention it's free?

Moscow 360 (☎8-985-447 8688; www.moscow360.org; tours per group from ₽2000) For unique and informative walking tours (all free!) as well as a bigger-picture tour by air-conditioned minivan (not free).

Moscow Mania (www.mosmania.com; 2hr walk from ₽3500) Fifty-plus specialised tours led by a passionate team of historians.

Moscow Bike Tours (☎8-916-970 1419; www.moscowbiketours.com; 2½hr tour US$40-60) Cover more ground and see more sights, while getting fresh air and a bit of exercise.

NEED TO KNOW

Most Moscow museums close on Monday, but the Kremlin and the Armoury close Thursday instead. Many museums close once a month for 'sanitary day', usually the last week of the month.

Fast Facts

- Telephone code: ☎495, ☎496, ☎498, ☎499
- Population: 12.5 million
- Time zone: GMT/USC +3 hours

New in Moscow

Park Zaryadye (p62) Moscow's newest park has four different microclimates (representing Russia's geographic zones) and four museums.

Vladimir I Statue (p63) You can't miss this massive memorial to the founder of the Russian state, just outside Alexander Garden.

Gulag History Museum (p65) A new location and nine times more exhibition space for this important institution.

Metro Upgrades Metro riders are now enjoying free wi-fi and English-language station announcements.

Resources

Moscow Times (www.themoscowtimes.com) Moscow's leading English-language newspaper.

Expat.ru (www.expat.ru) Run by and for English-speaking expats in Moscow.

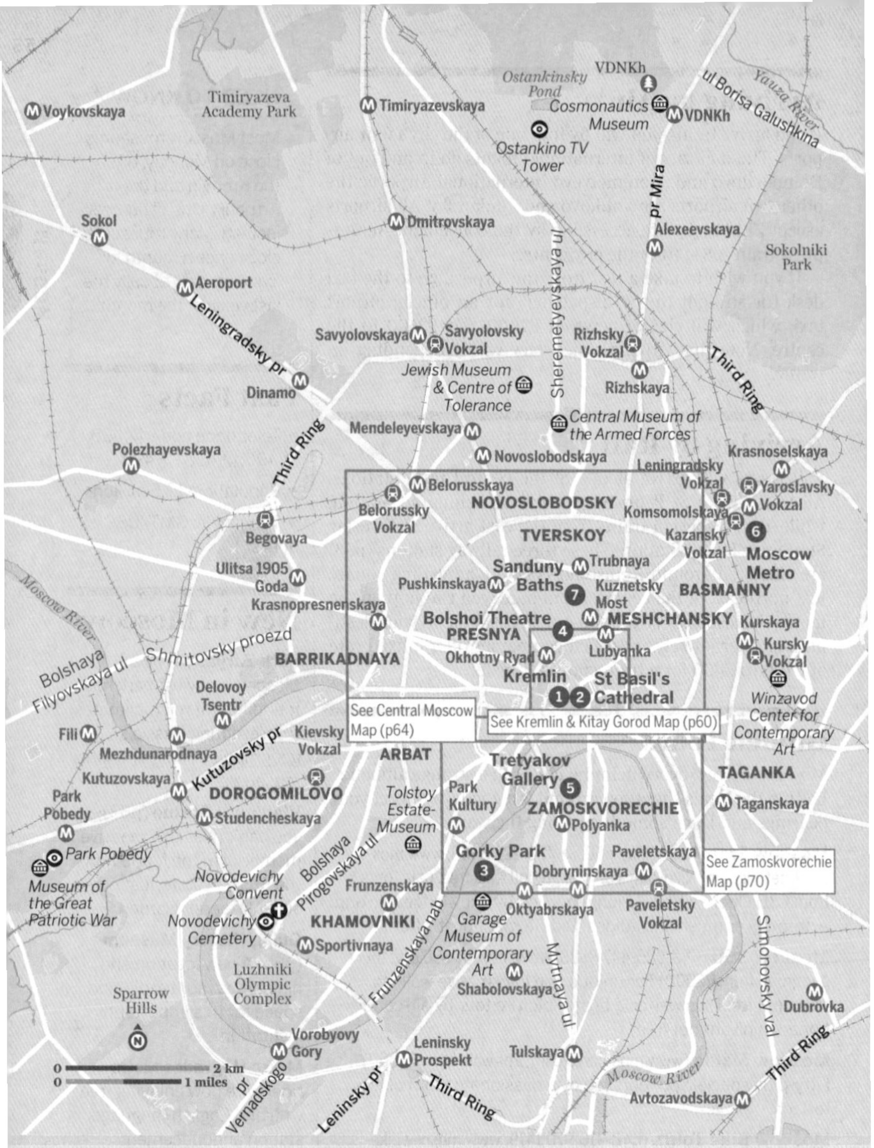

Moscow Highlights

1 Kremlin (p57) Explore 500 years of artistic mastery, political power and spiritual devotion.

2 St Basil's Cathedral (p61) Marvel at the multicoloured, multidomed spectacle on Red Square.

3 Gorky Park (p68) Be as active or as lazy as you wish in this wonderfully gentrified and iconic park.

4 Bolshoi Theatre (p80) See *Swan Lake* and other performances at this historic theatre.

5 Tretyakov Gallery (p68) Ogle the icons, peruse the Peredvizhniki and contemplate avant-garde art.

6 Moscow metro (p84) Go underground for cheap travel, a history lesson and art exhibit all in one.

7 Sanduny Baths (p69) Steam your cares away at this luxurious *banya*.

History

Moscow's recorded history dates to the mid-12th century, when Yury Dolgoruky constructed the first Kremlin on a strategic spot atop Borovitsky Hill. Moscow soon blossomed into an economic centre.

In the 13th century, the Mongols burned the city to the ground. The Golden Horde was interested in tribute, and Moscow was conveniently situated to monitor the river trade and road traffic. Moscow's Prince Ivan acted as tax collector, earning himself the moniker 'Kalita' (Moneybags), and Moscow developed into a regional capital.

Towards the end of the 15th century, the once diminutive duchy emerged as an expanding state under the reign of Grand Prince Ivan III (the Great). To celebrate his successes, he imported a team of Italian artisans for a complete renovation of the Kremlin. The city developed in concentric rings outward from this centre. Under Ivan IV (the Terrible), the then capital city earned the nickname of 'Gold-Domed Moscow' because of its multitude of monastery fortresses and magnificent churches.

In 1712 Peter the Great startled the country by announcing the relocation of the capital to St Petersburg. In the early 1800s, Moscow suffered further at the hands of Napoleon Bonaparte. But after the Napoleonic Wars, Moscow was feverishly rebuilt and industry prospered.

When the Bolsheviks gained control of Russia in 1917, the capital returned to Moscow. Stalin devised an urban plan for the city: historic cathedrals and monuments were demolished; in their place appeared the marble-bedecked metro and neo-Gothic skyscrapers. In the following decades, Moscow expanded at an exponential rate.

Moscow was the scene of the most dramatic events of the political transition of the early 1990s. Boris Yeltsin led crowds protesting the attempted coup in 1991, and two years later he ordered the army to blast the parliament into submission. Within the Moscow city government, the election of Mayor Yury Luzhkov in 1992 set the stage for the creation of a big-city boss: his interests range from the media to manufacturing. While the rest of Russia struggled to survive the collapse of communism, Moscow emerged as an enclave of affluence.

Early in the new millennium, Moscow was a target for terrorist attacks linked to the ongoing crisis in Chechnya. Over the next decade, suicide bombers in Moscow made strikes in metro stations, at rock concerts, on trains and aeroplanes, and in the international airport, leaving hundreds of people dead and injured and reminding Muscovites that there is no end in sight to the Chechen crisis.

In 2010, long-time mayor Luzhkov lost his job. The new boss Sergei Sobyanin promised a shift in focus – away from big business and huge construction projects towards improving the city for regular-guy residents. Almost a decade down the line, the results are visible. Moscow is gradually but noticeably becoming an easier, cleaner, more pleasant place to live.

Not all Muscovites are satisfied to sit back and accept politics as usual. In 2017, for the first time in years, a wave of anti-corruption protests took place in Moscow (and around the country). With the presidential election in 2018 – and Putin's certain participation – there are bound to be more. But most Muscovites are not in the mood for revolution.

Sights

Kremlin & Kitay Gorod

Both at the very heart of Moscow, Red Square and the Kremlin are the starting points for any visit to the capital. The surrounding streets of Kitay Gorod are crammed with churches and old architecture.

The apex of Russian political power and once the centre of the Orthodox Church, the **Kremlin** (Кремль; Map p60; ☎495-695 4146; www.kreml.ru; ₽500; ⏲10am-5pm Fri-Wed, ticket office 9.30am-4.30pm Fri-Wed; Ⓜ Aleksandrovsky Sad) is not only the kernel of Moscow, but of the whole country. From here, autocratic tsars, communist dictators and modern-day presidents have done their best – and worst – for Russia.

Covering Borovitsky Hill on the north bank of the Moscow River, the Kremlin is enclosed by high walls 2.25km long, with Red Square outside the east wall. The best views of the complex are from Sofiyskaya nab across the river.

Before entering the Kremlin, deposit bags (for free) at the left-luggage office, beneath the **Kutafya Tower** (Кутафья башня; Map p60) near the main ticket office in **Alexander Garden** (Александровский сад; Map p60; Ⓜ Aleksandrovsky Sad). The entrance ticket covers admission to all five church-museums and the Patriarch's Palace. It does not include the Armoury, the Diamond Fund

The Kremlin

A DAY AT THE KREMLIN

Only at the Kremlin can you see 800 years of Russian history and artistry in one day. Enter the ancient fortress through the Trinity Gate Tower and walk past the impressive Arsenal, ringed with cannons. Past the Patriarch's Palace, you'll find yourself surrounded by white-washed walls and golden domes. Your first stop is ❶ **Assumption Cathedral** with the solemn fresco over the doorway. As the most important church in prerevolutionary Russia, this 15th-century beauty was the burial site of the patriarchs. The ❷ **Ivan the Great Bell Tower** now contains a nifty multimedia exhibit on the architectural history of the Kremlin. The view from the top is worth the price of admission. The tower is flanked by the massive ❸ **Tsar Cannon & Bell**.

In the southeast corner, ❹ **Archangel Cathedral** has an elaborate interior, where three centuries of tsars and tsarinas are laid to rest. Your final stop on Sobornaya pl is ❺ **Annunciation Cathedral**, rich with frescoes and iconography.

Walk along the Great Kremlin Palace and enter the ❻ **Armoury** at the time designated on your ticket. After gawking at the goods, exit the Kremlin through Borovitsky Gate and stroll through the Alexander Garden to the ❼ **Tomb of the Unknown Soldier**.

TOP TIPS

➡ **Online Purchase** Full-price tickets to the Kremlin churches and the Armoury can be purchased in advance on the Kremlin website.

➡ **Lunch** There are no eating options. Plan to eat before you arrive or stash a snack.

Assumption Cathedral
Once your eyes adjust to the colourful frescoes, the gilded fixtures and the iconography, try to locate *Saviour with the Angry Eye*, a 14th-century icon that is one of the oldest in the Kremlin.

BOROVITSKY TOWER

Use the entrance at Borovitsky Tower if you intend to skip the churches and visit only the Armoury or Diamond Fund.

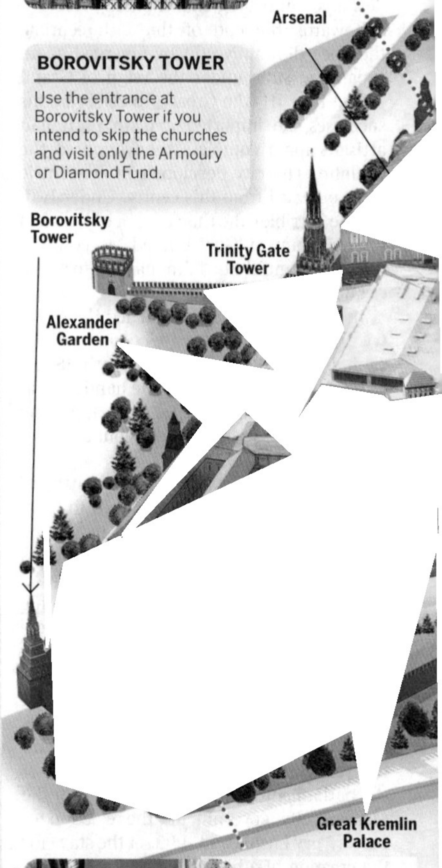

Armoury
Take advantage of the free audio guide to direct you to the most intriguing treasures of the Armoury, which is chock-full of precious metalworks and jewellery, armour and weapons, gowns and crowns, carriages and sledges.

Tomb of the Unknown Soldier

Visit the Tomb of the Unknown Soldier honouring the heroes of the Great Patriotic War. Come at the top of the hour to see the solemn synchronicity of the changing of the guard.

TOWER TICKETS

Sessions at the Ivan the Great Bell Tower take place six or seven times a day, mid-May through September. Purchase tickets at the Kremlin ticket office 45 minutes before the session.

Ivan the Great Bell Tower

Check out the artistic electronic renderings of the Kremlin's history, then climb 137 steps to the belfry's upper gallery, where you will be rewarded with super, sweeping vistas of Sobornaya pl and beyond.

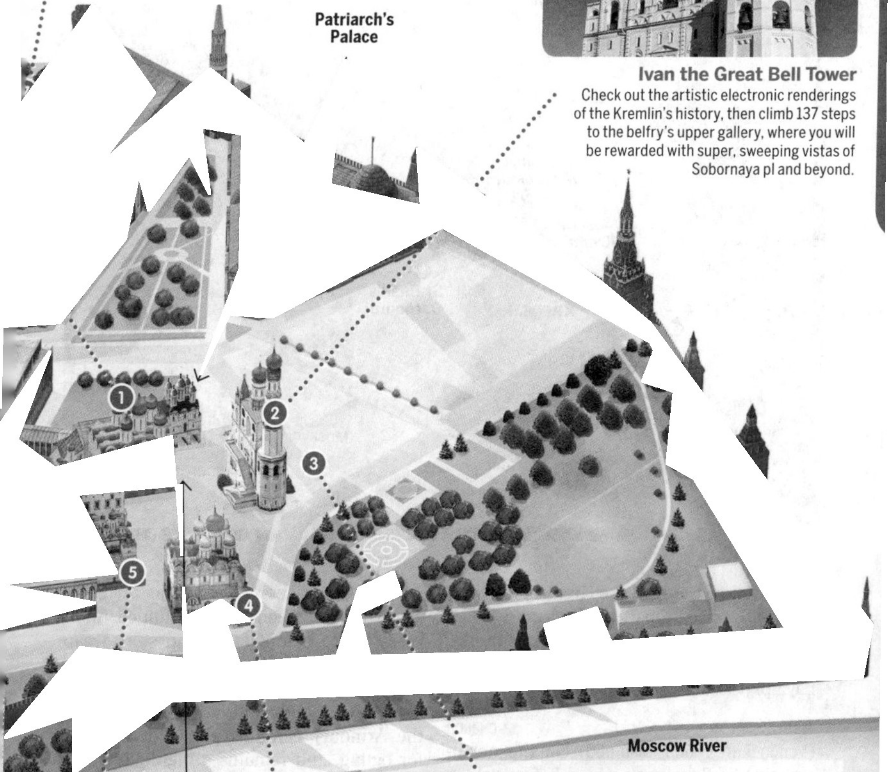

Tsar Cannon & Bell

Peer down the barrel of the monstrous Tsar Cannon and pose for a picture beside the oversized Tsar Bell, both of which are too big to serve their intended purpose.

Annunciation Cathedral

Admire the artistic mastery of Russia's greatest icon painters – Theophanes the Greek and Andrei Rublyov – who are responsible for many of the icons in the deesis and festival rows of the iconostasis.

Archangel Cathedral

See the final resting place of princes and emperors who ruled Russia for more than 300 years, including the visionary Ivan the Great, the tortured Ivan the Terrible and the tragic Tsarevitch Dmitry.

The Kremlin & Kitay Gorod

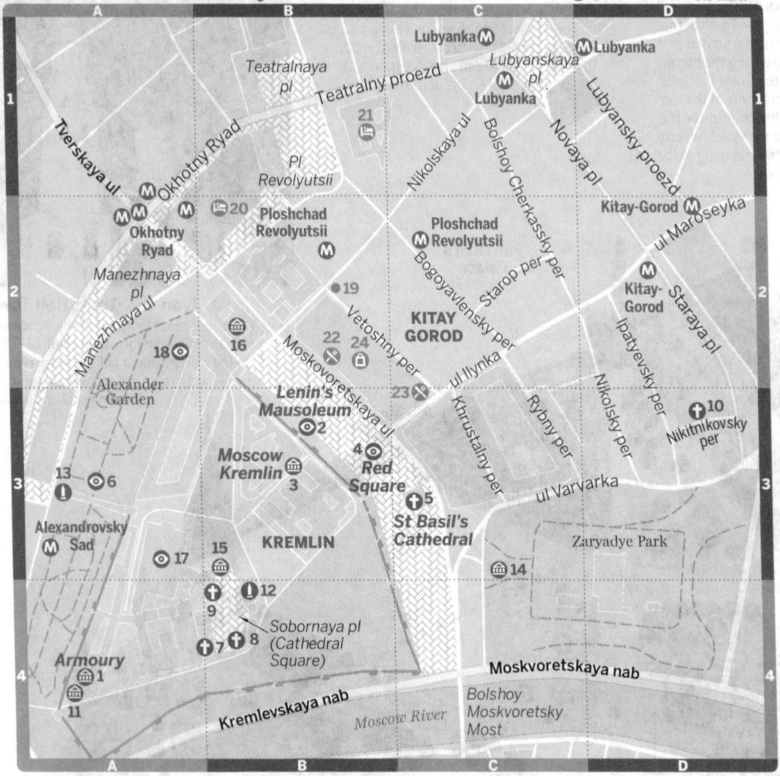

Exhibition or the Ivan the Great Bell Tower, which are priced separately.

Photography is not permitted inside the Armoury or any of the buildings on Sobornaya pl (Cathedral Sq).

Assumption Cathedral CHURCH

(Успенский собор; Map p60) On the northern side of Sobornaya pl, with five golden helmet domes and four semicircular gables facing the square, the Assumption Cathedral is the focal church of pre-revolutionary Russia and the burial place of most of the heads of the Russian Orthodox Church from the 1320s to 1700. A striking 1660s fresco of the Virgin Mary faces Sobornaya pl, above the door once used for royal processions. If you have limited time, come straight here. The visitors entrance is at the western end.

★ Armoury MUSEUM

(Оружейная палата; Map p60; adult/child ₽700/free; ⏲tours 10am, noon, 2.30pm & 4.30pm Fri-Wed; Ⓜ Aleksandrovsky Sad) The Armoury dates to 1511, when it was founded under Vasily III to manufacture and store weapons, imperial arms and regalia for the royal court. Later it also produced jewellery, icon frames and embroidery. To this day, the Armoury contains plenty of treasures for ogling, and remains a highlight of any visit to the Kremlin. If possible, buy your time-specific ticket to the Armoury when you buy your ticket to the Kremlin. A one-hour audio guide is available to point out some of the collection's highlights.

Ivan the Great Bell Tower TOWER

(Колокольня Ивана Великого; Map p60; ₽250; ⏲10am-5pm Apr-Oct) With its two golden domes rising above the eastern side of Sobornaya pl, the Ivan the Great Bell Tower is the Kremlin's tallest structure – a landmark visible from 30km away. Before the 20th century it was forbidden to build any higher in Moscow. Purchase a ticket to the architec-

Kremlin & Red Square

tural exhibit inside for a specifically timed admission to climb the 137 steps to the top for sweeping views.

Archangel Cathedral CHURCH

(Архангельский собор; Map p60) The Archangel Cathedral at the southeastern corner of Sobornaya pl was for centuries the coronation, wedding and burial church of tsars. It was built by Ivan Kalita in 1333 to commemorate the end of the great famine, and dedicated to Archangel Michael, guardian of the Moscow princes. It contains the tombs of almost all of Muscovy's rulers from the 14th to the 17th century.

Annunciation Cathedral CHURCH

(Благовещенский собор; Map p60) The Annunciation Cathedral, at the southwest corner of Sobornaya pl, contains impressive murals in the gallery and an archaeology exhibit in the basement. The central chapel contains the celebrated icons of master painters Theophanes the Greek and Andrei Rublyov.

Diamond Fund Exhibition MUSEUM

(Алмазный фонд России; Map p60; ☎495-629 2036; www.gokhran.ru; ₽500; ⊙10am-1pm & 2-5pm Fri-Wed) If the Armoury hasn't sated your lust for diamonds, there is more in the Diamond Fund Exhibition. The fund dates back to 1719, when Peter the Great established the Russian Crown treasury. These gemstones and jewellery were garnered by tsars and empresses, including the 190-carat diamond given to Catherine the Great by her lover Grigory Orlov. The Great Imperial Crown, encrusted with 4936 diamonds, was the coronation crown of Catherine the Great and successive rulers.

Security is super tight and you are not allowed to bring cameras, phones or bags of any sort.

Patriarch's Palace HISTORIC BUILDING

(Патриарший дворец; Map p60) Built for Patriarch Nikon mostly in the mid-17th century, the highlight of the Patriarch's Palace is perhaps the ceremonial **Cross Hall** (Крестовая палата), where the tsar's and ambassadorial feasts were held. From here you can access the five-domed **Church of the Twelve Apostles** (Церковь двенадцати апостолов), which has a gilded, wooden iconostasis and a collection of icons by leading 17th-century icon painters.

Red Square & Around

Immediately outside the Kremlin's northeastern wall is **Red Square** (Красная площадь; Map p60; Krasnaya pl; Ⓜ Ploshchad Revolyutsii), the 400m-by-150m area of cobblestones surrounded by a spectacular architectural panorama that never fails to send the heart aflutter, especially at night.

★ **St Basil's Cathedral** CHURCH

(Покровский собор, Храм Василия Блаженного; Map p60; adult/student ₽400/150; ⊙ticket office 11am-5pm Nov-Apr, to 6pm May-Oct; Ⓜ Ploshchad Revolyutsii) At the southern end of Red Square stands the icon of Russia: St Basil's Cathedral. This crazy confusion of colours, patterns and shapes is the culmination of a style that is unique to Russian architecture. In 1552 Ivan the Terrible captured the Tatar stronghold of Kazan on the Feast of Intercession. He commissioned this landmark church, officially the Intercession Cathedral, to commemorate the victory. Created from 1555 to 1561, this masterpiece would become the ultimate symbol of Russia.

★Lenin's Mausoleum MEMORIAL

(Мавзолей Ленина; Map p60; www.lenin.ru; Krasnaya pl; ⏲10am-1pm Tue-Thu, Sat & Sun; Ⓜ Ploshchad Revolyutsii) FREE Although Vladimir Ilych requested that he be buried beside his mum in St Petersburg, he still lies in state at the foot of the Kremlin wall, receiving visitors who come to pay their respects. Line up at the western corner of the square (near the entrance to Alexander Garden) to see the embalmed leader, who has been here since 1924. Note that photography is not allowed and stern guards ensure that all visitors remain respectful and silent.

State History Museum MUSEUM

(Государственный исторический музей; Map p60; www.shm.ru; Krasnaya pl 1; adult/student ₽350/100, audio guide ₽300; ⏲ticket office 10am-5pm Mon, Wed, Thu & Sun, to 9pm Fri & Sat; Ⓜ Okhotny Ryad) At the northern end of Red Square, the State History Museum has an enormous collection covering Russian history from the time of the Stone Age. The building, dating from the late 19th century, is itself an attraction – each room is in the style of a different period or region, some with highly decorated walls echoing old Russian churches.

Park Zaryadye Pavilion MUSEUM

(Павильон парка 'Зарядье'; Map p60; Moskvoretskaya ul) FREE This glass-dome pavilion was the first element of Park Zaryadye to open to the public. A creation of Sergei Kuznetsov, the pavilion was designed as an 'observation deck' for the ongoing work on the park. Construction was not actually visible from the pavilion; rather, the central chamber is wallpapered in QR codes – a surprisingly appealing look – that contain maps, designs, photographs and other information about the new park. At the entrance, visitors receive tablets which they can use to decode the electronic exhibits.

Church of the Trinity in Nikitniki CHURCH

(Церковь Троицы в Никитниках; Map p60; Ipatyevsky per; Ⓜ Kitay-Gorod) Hidden between big government blocks, this little gem of a church is an exquisite example of Russian baroque. Built in the 1630s, its onion domes

MOSCOW IN ...

Two Days

Spend a day seeing what makes Moscow famous: **St Basil's Cathedral** (p61), **Lenin's Mausoleum** (p62) and the **Kremlin** (p57; including the bling in the **Armoury**, p60). After lunch, stroll through Kitay Gorod discovering the countless 17th-century churches. Dine on trendy ul Petrovka, perhaps at **Lavka-Lavka** (p75), then take in a show at the world-famous **Bolshoi Theatre** (p80).

On your second day, admire the art and architecture at **Novodevichy Convent** (p67), then head next door to the eponymous cemetery. Make your way into the Arbat district for an afternoon of art appreciation at the **Pushkin Museum of Fine Arts** (p67) or at one of the smaller niche galleries. In the evening, stroll along the Arbat enjoying the atmosphere of old Moscow.

Four Days

On your third day, get an early start to beat the crowds to the **Tretyakov Gallery** (p69). Grab lunch at **Mizandari** (p77) at Red October, then stroll along Krymskaya nab, where you can frolic in fountains and explore the outdoor art gallery at **Art Muzeon** (p68). Then head across the street to **Gorky Park** (p68) for bicycle riding or boat paddling. Stay into the evening for drinking and dancing under the stars.

Reserve the morning on your last day for shopping at **Izmaylovsky Market** (p81), crammed with souvenir stalls. On your way back to the centre, make a stop at **Winzavod** (p69) to see the arty happenings in one of Moscow's former industrial spaces. Indulge in a farewell feast at **Cafe Pushkin** (p76).

and tiers of red-and-white spade gables rise from a square tower. Its interior is covered with 1650s gospel frescoes by Simon Ushakov and others. A carved doorway leads into St Nikita the Martyr's Chapel, above the vault of the Nikitnikov merchant family, who were among the patrons who financed the church's construction.

Vladimir I Statue MONUMENT
(Памятник Владимиру Великому; Map p70; Borovitskaya pl) In 2016 Vladimir Putin unveiled a new monument dedicated to his namesake Vladimir I, ruler of Kyivan Rus from 980 to 1015. At 17m high, the massive statue towers over the surrounding Borovitskaya pl. Vladimir is credited with uniting the fledgling Russian state and establishing the Orthodox Church.

DON'T MISS

TOMB OF THE UNKNOWN SOLDIER

This **tomb** (Могила неизвестного солдата; Map p60) contains the remains of one soldier who died in December 1941 at Km41 of Leningradskoe sh – the nearest the Nazis came to Moscow. This is a kind of national pilgrimage spot, where newlyweds bring flowers and have their pictures taken. The inscription reads: 'Your name is unknown, your deeds immortal.' Every hour on the hour, the guards perform a perfectly synchronised ceremony to change the guards on duty.

Tverskoy & Novoslobodsky

Although mostly a commercial district, Tverskoy is dotted with museums and boasts the excellent Hermitage Gardens – a much-needed escape from the city madness. Beyond the Garden Ring, several major attractions are found in the quieter Novoslobodsky district and around VDNKh metro (orange line).

★**Hermitage Gardens** PARK
(Сады Эрмитажа; Map p64; www.mosgorsad.ru; ul Karetny Ryad 3; 24hr; M Pushkinskaya) FREE All the things that have improved Moscow parks no end in recent years fill this small, charming garden to the brim. Today, it is possibly the most happening place in Moscow, where art, food and crafts festivals, and concerts, occur almost weekly, especially in summer. Apart from the welcoming lawns and benches, it boasts a large children's playground, a summer cinema and a cluster of food and crafts kiosks. Come here to unwind and mingle with the coolest Muscovites.

Museum of Soviet Arcade Machines MUSEUM
(Map p64; 495-628 4515; http://15kop.ru; ul Kuznetsky most 12; incl tour ₽450; 11am-9pm; M Kuznetsky Most) Growing up in 1980s USSR was a peculiar, but not necessarily entirely bleak experience. Here is an example – a collection containing dozens of mostly functional Soviet arcade machines. At the entrance, visitors get a paper bag full of 15-kopek Soviet coins, which fire up these recreational dinosaurs that would look at home in the oldest episodes of *Star Trek*.

Jewish Museum & Centre of Tolerance MUSEUM
(Еврейский музей и Центр толерантности; 495-645 0550; www.jewish-museum.ru; ul Obraztsova 11 str 1a; adult/student ₽400/200; noon-10pm Sun-Thu, 10am-3pm Fri; M Novoslobodskaya) Occupying a heritage garage, purpose-built to house a fleet of Leyland double-deckers that plied Moscow's streets in the 1920s, this vast museum, filled with cutting-edge multimedia technology, tackles the uneasy subject of relations between Jews and the Russian state over the centuries. The exhibition relates the stories of pogroms, Jewish revolutionaries, the Holocaust and Soviet anti-Semitism in a calm and balanced manner. The somewhat limited collection of material exhibits is compensated for by the abundance of interactive video displays.

Central Museum of the Armed Forces MUSEUM
(Центральный музей Вооружённых Сил; 495-681 6303; www.cmaf.ru; ul Sovetskoy Armii 2; adult/student ₽200/100; 10am-4.30pm Wed-Fri & Sun, to 6.30pm Sat; M Dostoyevskaya) Covering the history of the Soviet and Russian military since 1917, this massive museum occupies 24 halls plus open-air exhibits. Over 800,000 military items, including uniforms, medals and weapons, are on display. Among the highlights are remainders of the American U2 spy plane brought down in the Ural Mountains in 1960 and the victory flag raised over Berlin's Reichstag in 1945.

Central Moscow

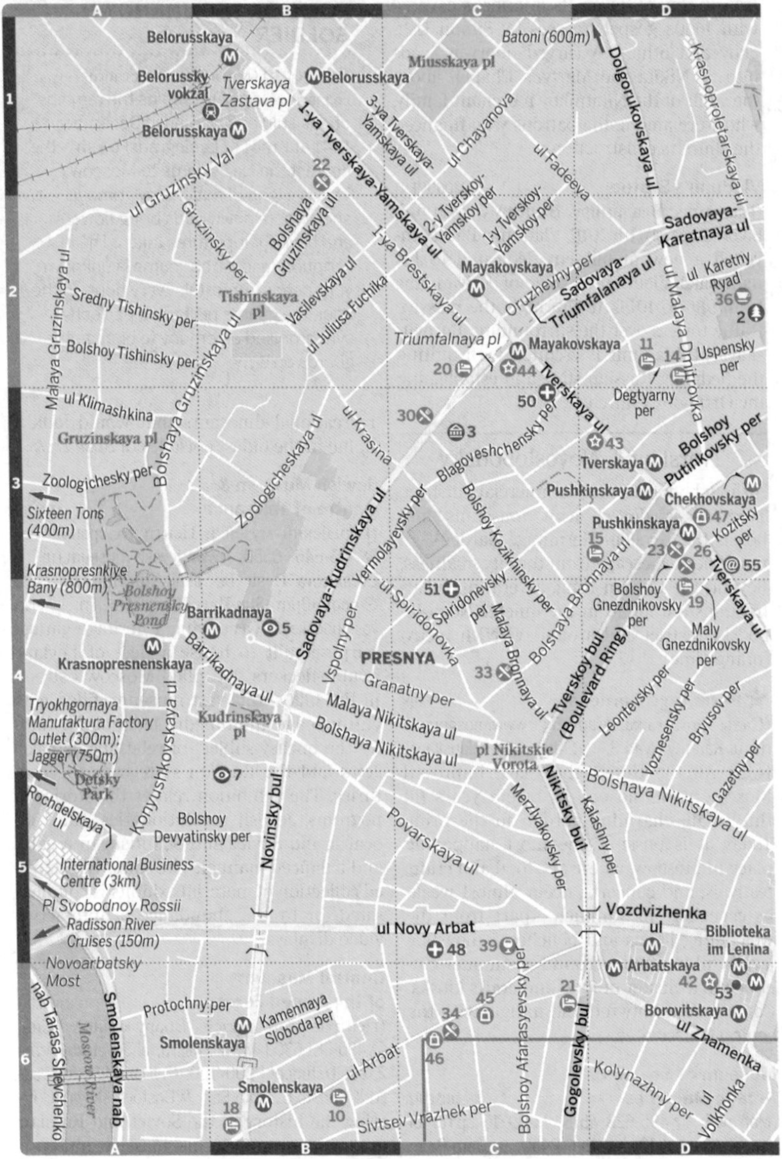

Ostankino TV Tower LANDMARK

(Останкинская башня; ☎8-800-100 5553; https://tvtower.ru; adult/child ₽1000/500; ⏲10am-10pm Mon-Thu, to 11pm Fri-Sun; Ⓜ VDNKh) When the Ostankino TV Tower was built in 1967, it was the tallest free-standing structure in the world (surpassing the Empire State Building). At 540m, it is now fourth on the list.

The 337m-high observation deck is open for visitors. A super-speedy lift whisks passengers up in less than 60 seconds. From

the top, there are 360-degree views and – horror! – a bit of glass floor.

Gulag History Museum MUSEUM

(Музей истории ГУЛАГа; Map p64; ☎495-621 7310; www.gmig.ru; 1-y Samotechny per 9 str 1; adult/student ₽300/150; ⏰11am-6pm Tue, Wed & Fri, noon-8pm Thu; Ⓜ Dostoyevskaya) Stalin's genocide is a subject many Russians prefer to forget rather than reflect on, but this modern multimedia space serves as both a learning centre and a memorial to

Central Moscow

Sights

1 Gulag History Museum E1
2 Hermitage Gardens D2
3 Mikhail Bulgakov Museum C3
4 Moscow Museum of Modern Art E3
5 Moscow Planetarium B4
6 Museum of Soviet Arcade Machines F4
7 Narkomfin B5

Activities, Courses & Tours

8 Sanduny Baths F3

Sleeping

9 Brick Design Hotel G3
10 Bulgakov Mini-Hotel B6
11 Chocolate Hostel D2
12 Fasol Hostel G4
13 Godzillas Hostel E2
14 Golden Apple D2
15 Hotel de Paris D3
16 Hotel National E5
17 Hotel Savoy F4
18 Jedi Hostel B6
19 Loft Hostel 77 .... D4
20 Peking Hotel C2
21 Russo Balt Hotel C6

Eating

22 AQ Kitchen B1
23 Cafe Pushkin D3
24 Delicatessen E2
25 Golodny-Zloy F3
Gran Cafe Dr Zhivago .... (see 16)
26 Khachapuri D3
27 Kitayskaya Gramota G3
28 Lavka-Lavka E3
29 Seven E3
30 Stolle C3
31 Technicum E4
32 Tsvetnoy Food Court F2
33 Twins C4
34 Varenichnaya No 1 .... C6
35 Voronezh E4

Drinking & Nightlife

36 32.05 .... D2
Balalaechnaya .... (see 45)
Noor / Electro .... (see 43)
37 Sisters Cafe H4
Time-Out Rooftop Bar .... (see 20)
38 Ukuleleshnaya H4
39 Zhiguli Beer Hall C5

Entertainment

40 Bolshoi Theatre E4
Bulgakov House & Theatre .... (see 3)
41 Nikulin Circus on Tsvetnoy Bulvar F2
42 Rhythm Blues Cafe D6
43 Stanislavsky Electrotheatre D3
44 Tchaikovsky Concert Hall C2

Shopping

45 Association of Artists of the Decorative Arts C6
46 Russian Embroidery & Lace C6
47 Yeliseev Grocery D3

Information

48 36.6 Arbat C5
49 36.6 Basmanny G4
50 36.6 Tverskaya C3
51 European Medical Centre C4
52 International Clinic MEDSI G1
53 Russian State Library D6
54 Ziferblat Pokrovka H4
55 Ziferblat Tverskaya D3

the millions who perished in concentration camps for 'enemies of the people'. The centrepiece display of objects handmade by prisoners is especially moving.

Moscow Museum of Modern Art MUSEUM

(Московский музей современного искусства; MMOMA; Map p64; www.mmoma.ru; ul Petrovka 25; adult/student ₽450/250, joint ticket for 3 venues ₽500/300; noon-8pm Tue, Wed & Fri-Sun, 1-9pm Thu; M Chekhovskaya) A pet project of the ubiquitous artist Zurab Tsereteli, this museum is housed in a classical 18th-century merchant's home, originally designed by Matvei Kazakov (architect of the Kremlin Senate). It is the perfect light-filled setting for an impressive collection of 20th-century paintings, sculptures and graphics, which include both Russian and foreign artists. The highlight is the collection of avant-garde art, with works by Chagall, Kandinsky and Malevich.

Presnya

Presnya is Moscow's largest administrative district, encompassing some of the capital's oldest neighbourhoods as well as its newest development at Moscow City. The area around Patriarch's Ponds has become one of the city's best areas for dining.

★ **Moscow Planetarium** PLANETARIUM

(Московский планетарий; Map p64; www.planetarium-moscow.ru; Sadovaya-Kudrinskaya ul 5; Large Star Hall ₽550-750, Small Star Hall ₽100-200; 10am-10pm Wed-Mon; M Barrikadnaya) The planetarium has become one of the biggest and brightest stars on the Moscow museum circuit, now incorporating all kinds of high-tech gadgetry, interactive exhibits and educational programs. The centrepiece is the Large Star Hall (the biggest in Europe!), with its 25m silver dome roof, a landmark that is visible from the Garden Ring. Narration for the shows is available in multiple languages.

★ **Mikhail Bulgakov Museum** MUSEUM
(Музей Михаила Булгакова; Map p64; www.bulgakovmuseum.ru; Bolshaya Sadovaya ul 10; adult/child ₽150/50; ⏲noon-7pm Tue, Wed & Fri-Sun, 2-9pm Thu; Ⓜ Mayakovskaya) Author of *The Master and Margarita* and *Heart of a Dog*, Mikhail Bulgakov was a Soviet-era novelist who was labelled a counter-revolutionary and censored throughout his life. His most celebrated novels were published posthumously, earning him a sort of cult following in the late Soviet period. Bulgakov lived with his wife, Tatyana Lappa, in a flat in this block, which now houses an **arts centre and theatre** (Булгаковский Дом и Театр; Map p64; www.dombulgakova.ru; 1st fl, Bolshaya Sadovaya ul 10; ⏲1-11pm, to 1am Fri & Sat) on the ground floor, and a small museum in their actual flat.

Narkomfin NOTABLE BUILDING
(Наркомфин; Map p64; Novinsky bul 25; Ⓜ Barrikadnaya) The model for Le Corbusier's Unité d'Habitation design principle, this architectural landmark was an early experiment in semicommunal living. Designed and built in the 1920s by Moisei Ginzburg and Ignatii Milinis, Narkomfin offered housing for members of the Commissariat of Finances. In line with constructivist ideals, communal space is maximised and individual space is minimised. Apartments have minute kitchens (or none at all) to encourage residents to eat in the communal dining room. Tours are available through **Moscow ArchiGeek** (Москва Глазами Инженера; ☎499-322 2325; www.archigeek.ru; tours from ₽1200).

Arbat & Khamovniki

These side-by-side districts are rich with culture. Moscow's most famous street, **ulitsa Arbat**, is something of an art market, complete with portrait painters and soapbox poets, while the nearby streets are lined with museums and galleries.

★ **Pushkin Museum of Fine Arts** MUSEUM
(Музей изобразительных искусств им Пушкина; Map p70; ☎495-697 9578; www.arts-museum.ru; ul Volkhonka 12; single/combined galleries ₽300/550; ⏲11am-7pm Tue, Wed & Fri-Sun, to 9pm Thu; Ⓜ Kropotkinskaya) This is Moscow's premier foreign-art museum, split over three branches and showing off a broad selection of European works, including masterpieces from ancient civilisations, the Italian Renaissance and the Dutch Golden Age. To see the incredible collection of Impressionist and post-Impressionist paintings, visit the **19th & 20th Century Art Gallery** (Map p70; www.arts-museum.ru; ul Volkhonka 14; adult/student ₽300/150; ⏲11am-7pm Tue-Sun, to 9pm Thu; Ⓜ Kropotkinskaya). The **Museum of Private Collections** (Музей личных коллекций; Map p70; www.artprivatecollections.ru; ul Volkhonka 10; entry prices vary; ⏲noon-8pm Wed-Sun, to 9pm Thu; Ⓜ Kropotkinskaya) shows off complete collections donated by private individuals.

★ **Cathedral of Christ the Saviour** CHURCH
(Храм Христа Спасителя; Map p70; www.xxc.ru; ul Volkhonka 15; ⏲1-5pm Mon, from 10am Tue-Sun; Ⓜ Kropotkinskaya) FREE This gargantuan cathedral was completed in 1997 – just in time to celebrate Moscow's 850th birthday. It is amazingly opulent, garishly grandiose and truly historic. The cathedral's sheer size and splendour guarantee its role as a love-it-or-hate-it landmark. Considering Stalin's plan for this site (a Palace of Soviets topped with a 100m statue of Lenin), Muscovites should at least be grateful they can admire the shiny domes of a church instead of the shiny dome of Ilyich's head.

★ **Novodevichy Convent** CONVENT
(Новодевичий монастырь; Novodevichy pr 1; adult/student ₽500/250, photos ₽300; ⏲grounds 8am-8pm, museums 9am-5pm Wed-Mon; Ⓜ Sportivnaya) The Novodevichy Convent was founded in 1524 to celebrate the taking of Smolensk from Lithuania, an important step in Moscow's conquest of the old Kyivan Rus lands. The oldest and most dominant building on the grounds is the white Smolensk Cathedral, with a sumptuous interior covered in 16th-century frescoes. Novodevichy is a functioning monastery. Women are advised to cover their heads and shoulders when entering the churches, while men should wear long pants.

Novodevichy Cemetery CEMETERY
(Новодевичье кладбище; Luzhnetsky pr 2; ⏲9am-5pm; Ⓜ Sportivnaya) FREE Adjacent to the Novodevichy Convent, the Novodevichy

WORTH A TRIP

PARK POBEDY

The Great Patriotic War – as WWII is known in Russia – was a momentous event that is still vivid in the hearts, minds and memories of many Russian citizens. Meaning 'Victory Park', magnificent **Park Pobedy** (Парк Победы; www.poklonnaya-gora.ru; Kutuzovsky pr; dawn-dusk; ; Park Pobedy) FREE is a huge memorial complex commemorating the sacrifice and celebrating the triumph of the war. Unveiled on the 50th anniversary of the victory, the park at Poklonnaya Hill includes endless fountains, monuments and museums, as well as a memorial church, synagogue and mosque.

The park's centrepiece is the **Museum of the Great Patriotic War** (Центральный музей Великой Отечественной Войны; www.poklonnayagora.ru; ul Bratiev Fonchenko 10; adult/child ₽300/200; 10am-6pm Tue-Sun Nov-Mar, to 8pm Apr-Oct; Park Pobedy) housing hundreds of exhibits, including dioramas of every major WWII battle the Russians fought in, as well as weapons, photographs, documents and other wartime memorabilia. The building also contains two impressive memorial rooms: the Hall of Glory honours the many heroes of the Soviet Union, while the moving Hall of Remembrance and Sorrow is hung with strings of glass-bead 'teardrops' in memory of the fallen.

Cemetery is one of Moscow's most prestigious resting places – a veritable who's who of Russian politics and culture. Here you will find the tombs of Bulgakov, Chekhov, Gogol, Mayakovsky, Prokofiev, Stanislavsky and Eisenstein, among many other Russian and Soviet cultural luminaries. The most recent notable addition to the cemetery is former President Boris Yeltsin, whose tomb is marked by an enormous Russian flag.

Zamoskvorechie

Meaning 'Beyond the Moscow River', this area offers two major collections of Russian art (the old and new Tretyakov galleries), a gentrified park belt along the Moscow River and the reconstructed Danilovsky Market (p77), a magnet for foodies from all over the city.

★Gorky Park — PARK

(Парк Горького; Map p70; 24hr; ; Oktyabrskaya) FREE Moscow's main city escape is not your conventional expanse of nature preserved deep inside an urban jungle. It is not a fun fair either, though it used to be one. Its official name says it all – Maxim Gorky's Central Park of Culture and Leisure. That's exactly what it provides: culture and leisure in all shapes and forms. Designed in the 1920s by avant-garde architect Konstantin Melnikov as a piece of communist utopia, these days it showcases the enlightened transformation Moscow has undergone in the recent past.

★Garage Museum of Contemporary Art — MUSEUM

(495-645 0520; www.garagemca.org; ul Krymsky val 9/32; adult/student ₽400/200; 11am-10pm; Oktyabrskaya) The brainchild of Moscow art fairy Darya Zhukova, Garage is one of the capital's hottest modern-art venues. In mid-2015 the museum moved to spectacular new digs in Gorky Park – a derelict Soviet-era building, renovated by the visionary Dutch architect Rem Koolhaas. It hosts exhibitions, lectures, films and interactive educational programs, featuring Russian and international artists. A good cafe and a bookstore are also on the premises.

★State Tretyakov Gallery Main Branch — GALLERY

(Государственная Третьяковская Галерея; Map p70; www.tretyakovgallery.ru; Lavrushinsky per 10; adult/child ₽500/200; 10am-6pm Tue, Wed & Sun, to 9pm Thu-Sat, last tickets 1hr before closing; Tretyakovskaya) The exotic boyar castle on a little lane in Zamoskvorechie contains the main branch of the State Tretyakov Gallery, housing the world's best collection of Russian icons and an outstanding collection of other pre-revolutionary Russian art. Show up early to beat the queues. The neighbouring **Engineer's Building** is reserved for special exhibits.

Art Muzeon & Krymskaya Naberezhnaya — PUBLIC ART

(Map p70; Park Kultury) FREE Moscow's answer to London's South Bank, Krymskaya Nab (Crimea Embankment) features wave-shaped street architecture with Scandinavian-style wooden elements, beautiful flowerbeds and a moody fountain, which ejects water randomly from many holes in the ground to the excitement of children and adults alike. It has merged with the Art Muzeon park and its motley collection of Soviet stone idols (Stalin, Sverdlov, a selection of Lenins and Brezhnevs) that were ripped from their pedestals in the post-1991 wave of anti-Soviet feeling.

New Tretyakov Gallery GALLERY
(Новая Третьяковская галерея; Map p70; www.tretyakovgallery.ru; ul Krymsky val 10; adult/child ₽500/200; ⌚10am-6pm Tue, Wed & Sun, to 9pm Thu-Sat, last tickets 1hr before closing; Ⓜ Park Kultury) Moscow's premier venue for 20th-century Russian art, this branch of the Tretyakov Gallery has much more than the typical socialist-realist images of muscle-bound men wielding scythes and busty women milking cows (although there's that, too). The exhibits showcase avant-garde artists such as Malevich, Kandinsky, Chagall, Goncharova and Popova, as well as nonconformist artists of the 1960s and 1970s who refused to accept the official style.

Red October ARTS CENTRE
(Завод Красный Октябрь; Map p70; Bersenevskaya nab; Ⓜ Kropotkinskaya) FREE This defiant island of Russian modernity and Europeanness is a vibrant arts centre filled with cool bars, restaurants and galleries. With an aptly revolutionary name, the former Red October chocolate factory looks straight into the Kremlin's eyes – a vivid reminder that Russia is not all about totalitarian control and persecution.

Meshchansky & Basmanny

These districts flank the little Yauza River in the eastern part of the city. The latter is largely comprised of old factories, now renovated to house innovative contemporary galleries, boutiques and clubs.

★**Winzavod Center for Contemporary Art** GALLERY
(Винзавод; www.winzavod.ru; 4-y Syromyatnichesky per 1; Ⓜ Chkalovskaya) FREE Formerly a wine-bottling factory, this facility was converted into exhibit and studio space for Moscow artists in 2007. The post-industrial complex is now home to several art and photo galleries, as well as a few funky gift shops and boutiques. Even if you're not in the market for the art world's next big thing, you can hang out at the cafe or catch a film or a lecture at one of the entertainment venues.

★**ArtPlay** GALLERY
(☎495-620 0882; www.artplay.ru; ul Nizhny Syromyatnichesky per 10; ⌚noon-8pm Tue-Sun; Ⓜ Chkalovskaya) FREE A 'design centre', ArtPlay occupies the buildings of the former Manometer factory and is home to firms specialising in urban planning and architectural design, as well as furniture showrooms and antique stores. Considering the architectural emphasis, there is perhaps less for the casual caller to see, although there are always diverse and dynamic rotating exhibits in the display spaces. Come here to feel the pulse of new Moscow.

Activities

★**Sanduny Baths** BATHHOUSE
(Map p64; ☎495-782 1808; www.sanduny.ru; ul Neglinnaya 14; ₽1800-2800; ⌚8am-10pm Wed-Mon, second male top class 10am-midnight Tue-Fri, 8am-10pm Sat & Sun; Ⓜ Kuznetsky Most) Sanduny is the oldest and most luxurious *banya* (hot bath) in the city. The Gothic Room is a work of art with its rich woodcarving, while the main shower room has an aristocratic Roman feel to it. There are several classes, as on trains; regulars say that second male top class is actually better than the premium class.

Krasnopresnkiye Bany BATHHOUSE
(Краснопресненские бани; ☎men's banya 495-255 5306, women's banya 495-253 8690; www.baninapresne.ru; Stolyarny per 7; ₽1400-1900; ⌚8am-11pm; Ⓜ Ulitsa 1905 Goda) Lacking an old-fashioned, decadent atmosphere, this modern, clean, efficient place nonetheless provides a first-rate *banya* (hot-bath) experience. The facility has a Russian steam room, a Finnish sauna, a plunge pool and massage services.

Capital Shipping Co BOATING
(CCK, Столичная Судоходная Компания; ☎495-225 6070; www.cck-ship.ru; adult/child 1hr cruise ₽900/700, 2-day pass ₽2400/2000) Originally, these ferries were simply a form of transportation, but visitors realised that riding the entire route was a great way to see the city, and CCK eventually developed fixed routes with higher prices. Nowadays, ferries ply the Moscow River from May to September; board at one of six docks for a cruise ranging from one to two hours.

Zamoskvorechie

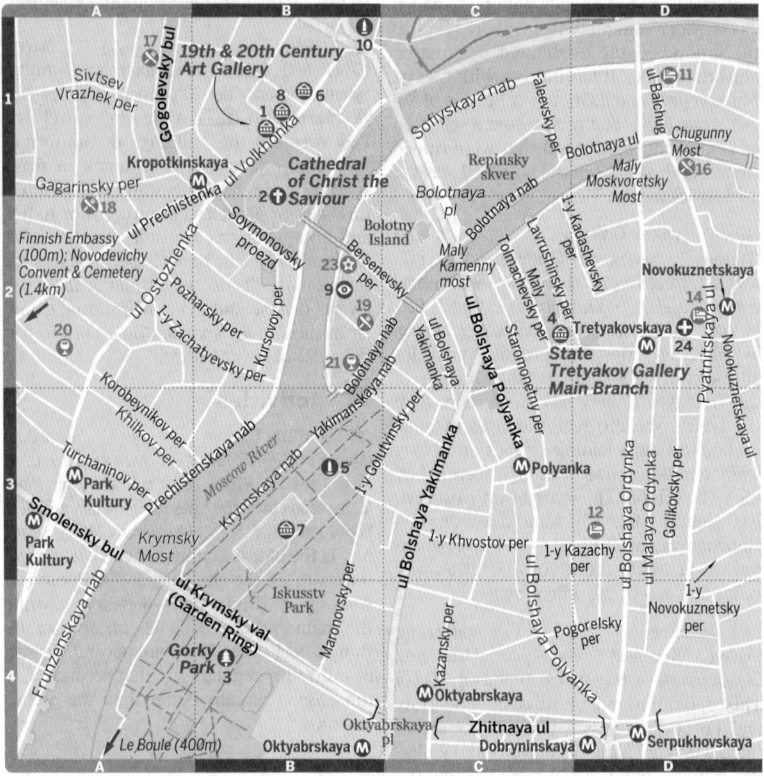

Zamoskvorechie

Top Sights
- 1 19th & 20th Century Art Gallery B1
- 2 Cathedral of Christ the Saviour B2
- 3 Gorky Park B4
- 4 State Tretyakov Gallery Main Branch C2

Sights
- 5 Art Muzeon & Krymskaya Naberezhnaya B3
- 6 Museum of Private Collections B1
- 7 New Tretyakov Gallery B3
- 8 Pushkin Museum of Fine Arts B1
- 9 Red October B2
- 10 Vladimir I Statue B1

Sleeping
- 11 Hotel Baltschug Kempinski D1
- 12 Na Kazachyem D3
- 13 Ozerkovskaya Hotel E3
- 14 Three Penguins D2
- 15 Troika E1

Eating
- 16 Björn D1
- 17 Chemodan A1
- 18 Elardzhi A2
- 19 Mizandari B2

Drinking & Nightlife
- Bar Strelka .... (see 23)
- 20 Dom 12 .... A2
- 21 Gipsy B2

Entertainment
- 22 Moscow International House of Music F3
- National Philharmonic of Russia .... (see 22)
- 23 Strelka Institute B2

Information
- 24 36.6 Zamoskvorechie D2

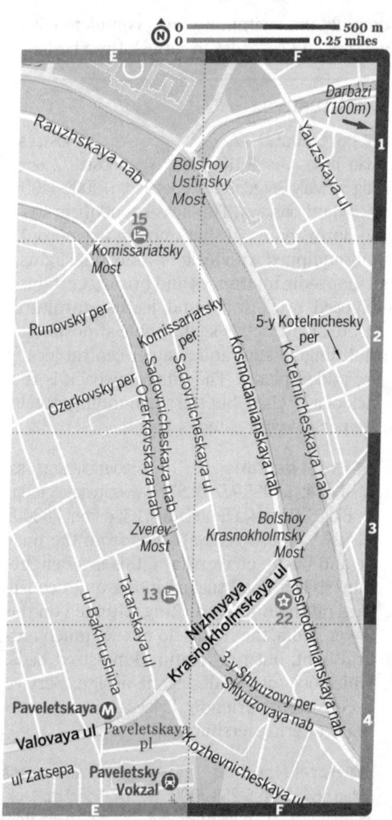

Radisson River Cruises BOATING
(www.radisson-cruise.ru; adult/child from ₽750/550; Ⓜ Kievskaya) The Radisson operates big river boats that cart 140 people up and down the Moscow River on a 2½-hour cruise, departing from the dock in front of the hotel and from the dock in Gorky Park (p68). In summer, there are five or six daily departures from each location (check the website for times).

Festivals & Events

Golden Mask Festival THEATRE
(www.goldenmask.ru; Mar-Apr) This festival involves two months of performances by Russia's premier drama, opera, dance and musical performers, culminating in a prestigious awards ceremony in April.

Moscow International Film Festival FILM
(www.moscowfilmfestival.ru; Jun/Jul) This 10-day event in June/July attracts filmmakers from the US and Europe, as well as the most promising Russian artists. Films are shown at theatres around the city.

City Day CULTURAL
(Sep) City Day, or *den goroda* in Russian, celebrates Moscow's birthday on the first weekend in September. The day kicks off with a festive parade, followed by live music on Red Square and plenty of food, fireworks and fun.

Moscow Biennale of Contemporary Art ART
(www.moscowbiennale.ru; Sep) This month-long festival, held in odd-numbered years in September (and sometimes in different months), has played a key role in establishing the capital as an international centre for contemporary art. Venues around the city exhibit works by artists from around the world.

December Nights Festival ART, MUSIC
(www.arts-museum.ru; Dec) This prestigious annual festival in December is hosted at the Pushkin Museum of Fine Arts (p67), with a month of performances by high-profile musicians and accompanying art exhibits.

Sleeping

Hotels have become more affordable for foreigners, due to the weak rouble, but Moscow is still not a cheap place to sleep. The city is flush with international luxury hotels, but more affordable hotels are harder to find. Fortunately, a slew of hostels have opened, and more midrange accommodation is now also appearing, usually in the form of 'mini-hotels'.

Kremlin & Kitay Gorod

★ **Hotel Metropol** HISTORIC HOTEL $$
(Map p60; 499-501 7800; www.metropol-moscow.ru; Teatralny proezd 1/4; r from ₽10,000; ; Ⓜ Teatralnaya) Nothing short of an art nouveau masterpiece, the 1907 Metropol brings an artistic, historic touch to every nook and cranny, from the spectacular exterior to the grand lobby and the individually decorated (but small) rooms. The breakfast buffet (₽2250) is quite an affair, with an extravagant feast served under the restaurant's gorgeous stained-glass ceiling.

Four Seasons Moscow HISTORIC HOTEL $$$
(Map p60; 499-277 7100; www.fourseasons.com; Okhotny ryad 2; r from ₽27,000; ;

M Okhotny Ryad) Long a fixture on the Moscow skyline, the infamous Hotel Moskva was demolished in 2003, but Four Seasons reconstructed the old exterior, complete with architectural quirks. The updated interior, of course, is contemporary and classy, with over 200 luxurious rooms and suites, as well as a fancy spa and a glass-roofed swimming pool.

Tverskoy & Novoslobodsky

Godzillas Hostel HOSTEL $
(Map p64; ☎ 495-699 4223; www.godzillashostel.com; Bolshoy Karetny per 6; dm ₽700-950, s/d ₽2200/2800; ❄ @ 📶; M Tsvetnoy Bulvar) Tried and true, Godzillas is Moscow's best-known hostel, with dozens of beds spread out over four floors. The rooms come in various sizes, but they are all spacious and light-filled and painted in different colours. To cater to the many guests, there are bathroom facilities on each floor, three kitchens and a big living room with satellite TV.

Chocolate Hostel HOSTEL $
(Map p64; ☎ 8-910-446 1778; www.chocohostel.com; Degtyarny per 15, apt 4; dm ₽600-700, tw/tr ₽2600/3300; @ 📶; M Pushkinskaya) Chocolate lovers rejoice – this charming hostel will soothe your craving. Bring your favourite brand from home for their collection. In return you'll get simple, friendly accommodation – colourfully painted rooms with metal furniture and old-style parquet floors. Bonus: bikes available for rent!

Golden Apple BOUTIQUE HOTEL $$
(Map p64; ☎ 495-980 7000; www.goldenapple.ru; ul Malaya Dmitrovka 11; d from ₽5100; ⊖ ❄ 📶; M Pushkinskaya) A classical edifice fronts the street, but the interior is sleek and sophisticated. The rooms are decorated in a minimalist, modern style – subdued whites and greys punctuated by contrasting coloured drapes and funky light fixtures. Comfort is paramount, with no skimping on luxuries such as heated bathroom floors and down-filled duvets.

Hotel Savoy BOUTIQUE HOTEL $$$
(Отель Савой; Map p64; ☎ 495-620 8500; www.savoy.ru; ul Rozhdestvenka 3; r from ₽13,000; ⊖ ❄ 📶 ≋; M Lubyanka) Built in 1912, the Savoy maintains an atmosphere of tsarist-era privilege for its guests, and is more intimate and affordable than other luxury hotels. All rooms are equipped with marble bathrooms and Italian fittings and furnishings. The state-of-the-art health club includes a glass-domed 20m swimming pool, complete with geysers and cascades to refresh tired bodies.

Presnya

★ **Loft Hostel 77** HOSTEL $
(Map p64; ☎ 499-110 4228; www.hostel-77.com; Bldg 3a, Maly Gnezdnikovsky per 9; dm ₽1000-1400; 📶; M Pushkinskaya) This sweet spot offers stylish dorm rooms (if that's not an oxymoron), fully equipped with lockers, individual lights, orthopaedic mattresses and privacy curtains. Exposed brick walls and leather furniture create an attractive shabby-chic atmosphere. Multilingual staff and a super-central locale are added pluses. The only drawback is the lack of a kitchen, but the surrounding streets are packed with eateries.

★ **Hotel de Paris** BOUTIQUE HOTEL $$
(Map p64; ☎ 495-777 0052; www.cityhotelgroup.ru; Bldg 3, Bolshaya Bronnaya ul 23; d from ₽6800; P ❄ 📶; M Pushkinskaya) Steps from the hustle and bustle of Tverskaya, this is a delightfully stylish hotel tucked into a quiet courtyard off the Boulevard Ring. Situated on the lower floors, the rooms do not get much natural light, but they feature king-sized beds, whirlpool tubs and elegant design. Service is consistently friendly. Prices drop on weekends, offering terrific value.

★ **Hotel National** HISTORIC HOTEL $$$
(Map p64; ☎ 495-258 7000; www.national.ru; Mokhovaya ul 15/1; d with/without Kremlin views from ₽14,600/9700; ❄ 📶; M Okhotny Ryad) Now operated by Starwood Resorts, this 1903 beauty occupies a prime location at the base of Tverskaya ul, across from Alexander Garden. As such, some rooms have magnificent views of the Kremlin (worth the extra roubles). Original artwork lines the walls and antique-style furnishings grace the premises. The rooms themselves are classically luxurious.

Arbat & Khamovniki

Jedi Hostel HOSTEL $
(Map p64; ☎ 929-681 0041; http://jedihostel.com; 4th fl, 2-y Smolensky per 1/4; dm/d from US$11/40; ❄ @ 📶; M Smolenskaya) This place exudes (and requires) good vibes, with its wacky and wonderful mural-painted walls and pillow-strewn 'lounge zone'. Dorm beds are actually little 'pods' with shades that ensure complete privacy. Lockers, kitchen and laundry facilities are available. Get the door code before you show up.

★**Bulgakov Mini-Hotel** HOTEL $$
(Map p64; ☎495-229 8018; www.bulgakovhotel.com; ul Arbat 49; s/d from ₽3600/4000; ⊖@☜; Ⓜ Smolenskaya) The classy rooms, graced with high ceilings and *Master and Margarita* inspired art, are as good as it gets in Moscow for this price, especially considering the primo location. The bathrooms are tiny but they are private. Enter the courtyard from Plotnikov per and use entrance No 2.

★**Hotel Grafskiy** BOUTIQUE HOTEL $$
(Отель Графский; ☎499-677 5727; www.grafskiyhotel.ru; Bldg 5, ul Lva Tolstogo 23; s ₽6000-8000, d ₽7700-9000; P❄☜; Ⓜ Park Kultury) Live next door to **Leo Tolstoy** (Музей-усадьба Толстого 'Хамовники'; www.tolstoymuseum.ru; ul Lva Tolstogo 21; adult/student ₽400/200; ⊙10am-6pm Tue, Wed & Fri-Sun, noon-8pm Thu; Ⓜ Park Kultury) at this new boutique hotel, in a building dating from 1866. Both service and style are simple but quite delightful. Some of the 38 rooms have exposed brick walls or loft-style ceilings. Outside the Garden Ring, this neighbourhood is still pretty lively, with a number of restaurants and bars in the immediate vicinity.

★**Russo Balt Hotel** BOUTIQUE HOTEL $$$
(Map p64; ☎495-645 3873; www.russo-balthotel.com; Gogolevsky bul 31; s ₽13,500-15,000, d ₽15,400-16,900; ❄@☜; Ⓜ Arbatskaya) With 15 rooms in an exquisite art deco building, the Russo Balt is as intimate and elegant as it gets in Moscow. Standard rooms are on the small side, but the whole place is beautifully decorated with period furnishings and original artwork, with the utmost attention to detail. Highly recommended.

Zamoskvorechie

Three Penguins HOSTEL $
(Три Пингвина; Map p70; ☎8-910-446 1778; www.3penguins.ru; Pyatnitskaya ul 20, str 2; dm/d ₽750/2600; ☜; Ⓜ Novokuznetskaya) This very small hostel is located in a converted flat with a comfy (we'd even say intimate) common area in the building best identified by Illarion cafe, just off Pyatnitskaya ul. Apart from the dorms, it features four doubles – two regular and two with bunk beds.

Troika HOTEL $$
(Map p70; ☎495-204 2226; www.hoteltroyka.ru; Sadovnicheskaya ul 5; r from ₽4000; ❄; Ⓜ Novokuznetskaya) This tourist hotel has a top-notch location across the bridge from Red Square, which makes it great value for money. All rooms are on the 1st floor of an 18th-century building with bare-brick walls and vaulted ceilings typical of that age.

Na Kazachyem HOTEL $$
(На Казачьем; Map p70; ☎495-745 2190; 1-y Kazachy per 4; s/d from ₽7600/8600; ⊖❄☜≋; Ⓜ Polyanka) Set in the historic heart of Zamoskvorechie, Na Kazachyem recreates the atmosphere of an 18th-century estate. The light-filled atrium, bedecked with a crystal chandelier, and 15 classically decorated rooms provide a perfect setting for old-fashioned Russian hospitality. Reduced rates on weekends.

Ozerkovskaya Hotel BOUTIQUE HOTEL $$
(Озерковская гостиница; Map p70; ☎495-783 5553; www.ozerkhotel.ru; Ozerkovskaya nab 50; s/d incl breakfast from ₽2900/3500; ⊖☜; Ⓜ Paveletskaya) This comfy, cosy hotel has only 27 rooms, including three that are tucked up under the mansard roof. The rooms are simply decorated, but parquet floors and comfortable queen-sized beds rank it above the standard post-Soviet fare. Add in attentive service and a central location (convenient for the Aeroexpress Train to Domodedovo Airport), and you've got an excellent-value accommodation option.

★**Hotel Baltschug Kempinski** HISTORIC HOTEL $$$
(Балчуг Кемпински; Map p70; ☎495-287 2000; www.kempinski-moscow.com; ul Balchug 1; r with/without view from ₽13,600/12,000; ⊖❄☜≋; Ⓜ Kitay-Gorod, Ploshchad Revolyutsii) If you want to wake up to views of the sun glinting off the Kremlin's golden domes, this luxurious property on the Moscow River is the place for you. It is a historic hotel, built in 1898, with 230 high-ceilinged rooms that are sophisticated and sumptuous in design.

SLEEPING PRICE RANGES

The following prices refer to a double room with a private bathroom. Breakfast is not included unless otherwise indicated.

$ less than ₽3000

$$ ₽3000–15,000

$$$ more than ₽15,000

SERVICED APARTMENTS

Some entrepreneurial Muscovites rent out apartments on a short-term basis. Flats are equipped with kitchens and laundry facilities, and they almost always offer wi-fi access. The rental agency usually makes arrangements for the flat to be cleaned every day or every few days. Often, a good-sized flat is available for the price of a hotel room, or less. It is an ideal solution for families or travellers in a small group.

Prices for apartments start at around ₽5000 per night. Expect to pay more for fully renovated, Western-style apartments. Although there are usually discounts for longer stays, they are not significant, so these services are not ideal for long-term renters.

Moscow Suites (495-233 6429; www.moscowsuites.ru; studios from US$100;) Slick apartments in central locations on Tverskaya or Novy Arbat. Airport pick-up and visa support are included in the price.

Intermark Hospitality (495-221 8922; www.intermarksa.ru; 1-/2-room apt from ₽5800/6800;) Catering mostly to business travellers, Intermark offers four-star accommodation in the city centre.

Enjoy Moscow (8-916-976 4807; www.enjoymoscow.com; apt from US$120;) Has a range of apartments in the Tverskoy district. Apartments vary in size and decor, but the company provides responsive, reliable service.

HOFA (8-911-766 5464; www.hofa.ru; s/d from €33/52, apt €44-67;) Authentic (and affordable) stays in a Russian family's apartment (with or without the family).

Moscow4rent.com (495-225 5405; www.moscow4rent.com; studios from US$83) Centrally located flats, with internet, satellite TV and unlimited international phone calls.

Meshchansky & Basmanny

Fasol Hostel HOSTEL $

(Map p64; 495-240 9409; http://fasol.co; Arkhangelsky per 11/16 str 3; dm from ₽900, d with shared bathroom ₽3100; M Chistye Prudy) The entrance to this hostel, hidden in the courtyards amid 19th-century apartment blocks, looks unassuming. However, with over 80 beds, this popular and professionally run place is a major-league player. Dorms, sleeping six to eight, are decorated with psychedelic wall paintings; bunk beds come with body-friendly mattresses, curtains and individual lights, allowing guests to enjoy full autonomy.

★ **Brick Design Hotel** BOUTIQUE HOTEL $$

(Map p64; 499-110 2470; www.brickhotel.ru; Myasnitskaya ul 24/7 str 3/4; s/d from ₽6200/7100; ; M Chistye Prudy) Not only is this boutique hotel cosy, thoughtfully designed and very centrally located, it also doubles as an art gallery, with original works by Russian 20th-century conceptualist artists adorning the walls. That's in addition to a very tasteful combination of modern and antique furniture. Visitors also rave about the breakfast, which comes fresh from farms near Moscow.

Eating

Foodies will be thrilled by Moscow's dining options, from old-fashioned *haute-russe* to contemporary 'author cuisine'. The ban on imported foodstuffs means that chefs are finding innovative ways to utilise local ingredients, rediscovering ancient cooking techniques and inventing new ones in the process.

Discounts of up to 25% are sometimes available for dining before 4pm. Alternatively, many places offer a fixed-price 'business lunch' during this time. This is a great time to sample some of the pricier restaurants around town.

Kremlin & Kitay Gorod

Stolovaya No 57 CAFETERIA $

(Столовая 57; Map p60; 495-620 3129; https://gumrussia.com/shops/stolovaya-57; 3rd fl, GUM, Krasnaya pl 3; mains ₽200-300; 10am-10pm; M Okhotny Ryad) Newly minted, this old-style cafeteria offers a nostalgic recreation of dining in post-Stalinist Russia. The food is good – and cheap for such a fancy store. Meat cutlets and cold salads come highly recommended. This is a great place to try 'herring in a fur coat' (herring, beetroots, carrots and potatoes).

Bosco Cafe ITALIAN $$$

(Map p60; 495-620 3182; https://gumrussia.com/cafe/bosco-cafe; GUM, Krasnaya pl 3; pasta ₽500-1000, mains ₽1200-2000; 10am-10pm; M Ploshchad Revolyutsii) Sip a cappuccino in view of the Kremlin. Munch on lunch while the crowds line up at Lenin's Mausoleum. Enjoy an afternoon aperitif while admiring St Basil's domes. Service is lacking and the menu is overpriced, but this cafe on the 1st floor of the GUM mall is the only place to sit right on Red Square and marvel at its magnificence.

Tverskoy & Novoslobodsky

Batoni GEORGIAN $

(499-653 6530; www.batoni-kafe.ru; Novoslobodskaya ul 18; mains ₽300-600; 11.30am-midnight; M Mendeleyevskaya) Among myriad Georgian places in Moscow, Batoni is about the loveliest and the most scrupulous at sourcing all the right ingredients for century-old recipes. *Pkhali* (walnut paste) snacks, *khachapuri* (Georgian cheese bread) and lamb shashlyk kebabs are all up to Mt Kazbek–high standards. For a proper taste of Georgia, order a bottle of Mukuzani or Kindzmarauli – the country's best reds.

Tsvetnoy Food Court INTERNATIONAL $

(Map p64; 495-737 7773; www.tsvetnoy.com; Tsvetnoy bul 15, str 1; tapas ₽100-400; noon-10pm; M Tsvetnoy Bulvar) The two upper floors of Tsvetnoy Central Market shopping mall are filled with refined delis and cafes, some of them outstandingly good. Little snacks hailing from Basque Country in Spain have generated a bit of a cult following for Tapas & Pintxos, on the 5th floor. The Dagestani dumpling shop on the 6th floor makes for equally exciting culinary travel.

★ **Lavka-Lavka** INTERNATIONAL $$

(Лавка-Лавка; Map p64; 8-903-115 5033; www.restoran.lavkalavka.com; ul Petrovka 21, str 2; mains ₽500-950; noon-midnight Tue-Thu & Sun, to 1am Fri & Sat; ; M Teatralnaya) Welcome to the Russian Portlandia – all the food here is organic and hails from little farms where you may rest assured all the lambs and chickens lived a very happy life before being served to you on a plate. Irony aside, this is a great place to sample local food cooked in a funky improvisational style.

★ **Delicatessen** INTERNATIONAL $$

(Деликатесы; Map p64; www.newdeli.ru; Sadovaya-Karetnaya ul 20; mains ₽500-800; noon-midnight Tue-Sun; ; M Tsvetnoy Bulvar) The affable and chatty owners of this place travel the world and experiment with the menu a lot, turning burgers, pizzas and pasta into artfully constructed objects of modern culinary art. The other source of joy is a cabinet filled with bottles of ripening fruity liquors, which may destroy your budget if consumed uncontrollably (a pointless warning, we know).

Golodny-Zloy FUSION $$

(Голодный-Злой; Map p64; 495-792 7105; http://perelmanpeople.com/restoran/golodnyy-zloy; Tsvetnoy bul 2; mains ₽500-700; noon-midnight Sun-Thu, to 2am Fri & Sat; ; M Trubnaya) Filling up with white collars from the business centre above it, this trendsetting establishment combines unlikely ingredients and cooking methods with unfailingly excellent results – just try its smoked-mussel soup or dorado cooked with sorrel. Visual art is also involved, with each dish designed to entertain the eye as much as to please the stomach.

Seven EUROPEAN $$

(Map p64; 495-205 0277; Dmitrovsky per 7; mains ₽500-900; 8am-11pm; M Teatralnaya) You'll find a pleasant mix of post-industrial and theatrical in this dimly lit space, where low-hanging chandeliers and comfortable chairs make for a long and enjoyable evening. The menu mirrors the city outside – inventively cosmopolitan with a sprinkle of Soviet nostalgia and a strong bias towards domestic meat and vegetable producers.

Technicum EUROPEAN $$

(Map p64; 495-230 0605; www.tehnikumbistro.ru; ul Bolshaya Dmitrovka 7/5, str 2; mains ₽480-650; 9am-midnight; M Teatralnaya) Casual, friendly and focused on taste, rather than trying to impress with shocking exoticism, Technicum is one of the places that shape the modern outlook of Moscow's culinary scene. The laconic menu contains a short list of fish and meat dishes (note the outstanding mutton with aubergine) as well as soups, including an exemplary borsch (beetroot soup) served with Borodinsky rye bread.

Voronezh INTERNATIONAL $$

(Воронеж; Map p64; www.voronej.com; ul Bolshaya Dmitrovka 12/1, str 1; mains ₽300-720; 9am-9pm; M Teatralnaya) Its darkened, scarlet-coloured interior makes this bistro look a bit like an oriental opium den, but it is in fact a carnivore temple, where patrons seem to fall into a deeply meditative state while

WORTH A TRIP

VDNKH

Palaces for workers! There is no better place to see this Soviet slogan put into practice than at **VDNKh** (Ⓜ VDNKh), which stands for Exhibition of Achievements of the National Economy. The place feels like a Stalinesque theme park, with two opulently decorated fountains and a series of palatial pavilions, each designed in its own unique style to represent all the Soviet republics and various industries, from geology to space exploration. A thorough reconstruction, under way at the time of writing, is expected to breathe new life into the area.

Approaching VDNKh from the metro, the soaring 100m titanium obelisk is a monument 'To the Conquerors of Space', built in 1964 to commemorate the launch of Sputnik. In its base is the **Cosmonautics Museum** (www.kosmo-museum.ru; ₽250; ⏲11am-7pm Tue, Wed & Fri-Sun, to 9pm Thu; Ⓜ VDNKh), featuring cool space paraphernalia such as the first Soviet rocket engine and the moon rover Lunokhod. An inspiring collection of space-themed propaganda posters evokes the era of the space race.

munching on their burgers and excellent pastrami sandwiches. One of the best places for lunch in the city centre.

Presnya

★ Stolle — CAFE $

(Штолле; Map p64; www.stolle.ru; Bldg 1, Bolshaya Sadovaya ul 3; mains ₽200-400; ⏲8am-11pm; ; Ⓜ Mayakovskaya) The entire menu at Stolle is excellent, but the *pirozhki* (savoury pies) are irresistible. A 'stolle' is a traditional Saxon Christmas cake: the selection of sweets and savouries sits on the counter, fresh from the oven. It may be difficult to decide (mushroom or meat, apricot or apple?), but you really can't go wrong.

★ Twins — RUSSIAN $$

(Map p64; ☎495-695 4510; www.twinsmoscow.ru; Malaya Bronnaya ul 13; mains ₽650-1750; ; Ⓜ Tverskaya) Swoon-worthy identical-twin chefs Sergei and Ivan Berezutskiy bring their contrasting tastes and creative talents to this delightful restaurant. The brothers take a thoroughly modern approach to Russian cooking, with ingredients procured from all corners of the country. Seating is on the pleasant terrace or in the classy, kitschy dining room.

★ Khachapuri — GEORGIAN $$

(Хачапури; Map p64; ☎8-985-764 3118; www.hacha.ru; Bolshoy Gnezdnikovsky per 10; khachapuri ₽220-420, mains ₽430-690; ; Ⓜ Pushkinskaya) Unassuming, affordable and appetising, this urban cafe exemplifies what people love about Georgian culture: the warm hospitality and the freshly baked *khachapuri* (cheese bread). Aside from eight types of delicious *khachapuri*, there's also an array of soups, shashlyk (kebabs), *khinkali* (dumplings) and other Georgian favourites.

★ AQ Kitchen — MEDITERRANEAN $$

(Map p64; ☎499-393 3224; http://aq.kitchen; Bolshaya Gruzinskaya ul 69; mains ₽700-1200; ⏲noon-midnight; ; Ⓜ Belorusskaya) AQ stands for Adrian Quetglas, the Argentinian chef who is the brains behind this creative endeavour. With huge windows and stressed-wood details, the shabby-chic interior is a perfect setting for the eclectic menu. Look for Moroccan chicken with couscous, grilled squid with romesco sauce and other unexpected delicacies.

Gran Cafe Dr Zhivago — RUSSIAN $$

(Гранд Кафе Dr Живаго; Map p64; ☎499-922 0100; www.drzhivago.ru; Mokhovaya ul 15/1; mains ₽540-1200; ⏲24hr; Ⓜ Okhotny Ryad) An excellent breakfast choice before visiting the Kremlin, this round-the-clock place mixes Soviet nostalgia with a great deal of mischievous irony in both design and food. The chef has upgraded the menu of a standard pioneer camp's canteen to near-haute-cuisine level, with masterfully cooked porridge, pancakes, *vareniki* (boiled dumplings, like ravioli) and cottage-cheese pies.

★ Cafe Pushkin — RUSSIAN $$$

(Кафе Пушкинъ; Map p64; ☎495-739 0033; www.cafe-pushkin.ru; Tverskoy bul 26a; business lunch ₽620-930, mains ₽1000-2500; ⏲24hr; ; Ⓜ Pushkinskaya) The tsarina of *haute-russe* dining, offering an exquisite blend of Russian and French cuisines. Service and food are done to perfection. The lovely 19th-century building has a different atmosphere on each floor, including a richly decorated library and a pleasant rooftop cafe.

Arbat & Khamovniki

★ Varenichnaya No 1 RUSSIAN $
(Map p64; www.varenichnaya.ru; ul Arbat 29; business lunch ₽290-340, mains ₽220-490; ⏲10am-midnight; ; M Arbatskaya) Retro Soviet is all the rage in Moscow, and this old-style restaurant does it right, with books lining the walls, old movies on the B&W TV, and Cold War–era prices. The menu features tasty, filling *vareniki* and *pelmeni* (Russian-style dumplings), with sweet and savoury fillings. Bonus: an excellent house-made pickled vegie plate to make you pucker.

Usachevsky Market MARKET $
(☎8-999-003 0030; www.usachevsky.ru; ul Usachyova 26; mains ₽200-600; ⏲9am-9pm; M Sportivnaya) An old market has been taken over by hipster foodies, who instantly filled the premises with little eateries serving Georgian, Uzbek, Italian, Israeli and you-name-it cuisine, as well as shops representing small-scale Russian food producers, such as Kostroma Cheese. It's a great place for lunch and shopping, if you happen to be nearby.

★ Elardzhi GEORGIAN $$
(Элarджи; Map p70; ☎495-627 7897; www.ginza.ru; Gagarinsky per 15a; mains ₽600-800; ⏲noon-midnight; ; M Kropotkinskaya) Moscow's Georgian restaurants are all very tasty, but this one is also tasteful. You'll be charmed from the moment you enter the courtyard, where live rabbits and lambs greet all comers. Sink into a sofa in the romantic dining room or on the light-filled porch; then feast on delicacies, such as the namesake dish, *elarji* (cornmeal with *suluguni* cheese).

★ Chemodan RUSSIAN $$$
(Чемодан; Map p70; ☎495-695 3819; www.chemodan-msk.ru; Gogolevsky bul 25; mains ₽900-1950; ; M Kropotkinskaya) A unique opportunity to sample Siberian cuisine (rare, that is, for those who don't frequent Siberia). The menu highlights game meat, regional seafood and wild fruits and berries (and pine cones). The dining room is decorated with old photos and antiques, creating a romantic atmosphere that any adventurer would be happy to return home to. Highly recommended.

Zamoskvorechie

★ Mizandari GEORGIAN $
(Map p70; ☎8-903-263 9990; www.mizandari.ru; Bolotnaya nab 5, str 1; mains ₽300-500; ⏲11am-11pm Sun-Thu, to midnight Fri & Sat; M Kropotkinskaya) Georgian restaurants in Moscow tend to be either expensive or tacky. This small family-run place is neither. Come with friends and order a selection of appetisers, such as *pkhali* and *lobio* (both made of walnut paste), *khachapuri* (Georgian cheese bread) and *kharcho* (rice with beef or lamb soup). Bless you if you can still accommodate a main course after all that!

★ Danilovsky Market MARKET $$
(www.danrinok.ru; Mytnaya ul 74; mains ₽400-600; ⏲8am-8pm; M Tulskaya) A showcase of the area's ongoing gentrification, this giant Soviet-era farmers market is now largely about deli food cooked and served in myriad little eateries, including such gems as a Dagestani dumpling shop and a Vietnamese pho-soup kitchen. The market itself looks very orderly, if a tiny bit artificial, with uniformed vendors and thoughtfully designed premises.

★ Björn SCANDINAVIAN $$$
(Map p70; ☎495-953 9059; http://bjorn.rest; Pyatnitskaya ul 3; mains ₽600-1200; M Novokuznetskaya) A neat cluster of fir trees on a busy street hides a Nordic gem that deserves a saga to glorify its many virtues. This is not an 'ethnic' restaurant, but a presentation of futuristic Scandinavian cuisine straight out of a science fiction movie. From salads to desserts, every dish looks deceptively simple, visually perfect and 23rd century.

Meshchansky & Basmanny

★ Dukhan Chito-Ra GEORGIAN $
(☎8-916-393 0030; www.chito-ra.ru; ul Kazakhova 10 str 2; mains ₽300-500; ⏲noon-11pm; M Kurskaya) It's a blessing when one of the most revered Georgian eateries in town is also one of the cheapest. The object of worship here is *khinkali* – large, meat-filled dumplings – but the traditional vegie starters are also great. The rather inevitable downside is that the place is constantly busy and there is often a queue to get in.

★ Darbazi GEORGIAN $$
(☎495-915 3632; www.darbazirest.ru; ul Nikoloyamskaya 16; mains ₽590-1500; ⏲noon-midnight; ; M Taganskaya) The vast majority of Georgian restaurants focus on the most popular, tried-and-true fare, such as shashlyk (meat kebabs) and *khinkali* (dumplings).

This classy place goes far beyond these, listing less well-known delicacies with almost encyclopaedic meticulousness. Our favourite is *chakapuli* (lamb cooked in white wine with tarragon) and *megreli kharcho* (duck in walnut sauce). Definitely go for one of the desserts, such as *pelamushi* (red grape mousse).

★**Kitayskaya Gramota** CHINESE $$
(Китайская грамота; Map p64; ☎495-625 4757; http://chinagramota.ru/; ul Sretenka 1; mains ₽400-1200; ⊙noon-midnight; Ⓜ Sretenskaya) Ignore the fact that the waiting staff are dressed as Mao's soldiers; this is the place to try outstanding Cantonese fare in an atmosphere echoing that of the Opium War's decadence. A true culinary magician, the Chinese chef turns any ingredient – from hog paw to octopus to simple milk – into a mouth-watering delicacy.

Drinking & Nightlife

Pedestrian streets such as ul Arbat and Kamergersky per are hot spots for strollers and drinkers. Red October (p69) in Zamoskvorechie is packed with diverse drinking establishments while Gorky Park (p68) has plenty of summer spots.

Tverskoy & Novoslobodsky

★**Noor / Electro** BAR
(Map p64; ☎8-903-136 7686; www.noorbar.com; ul Tverskaya 23/12; ⊙8pm-3am Mon-Wed, to 6am Thu-Sun; Ⓜ Pushkinskaya) There is little to say about this misleadingly unassuming bar, apart from the fact that everything in it is close to perfection. It has it all – prime location, convivial atmosphere, eclectic DJ music, friendly bartenders and superb drinks. Though declared 'the best' by various magazines on several occasions, it doesn't feel like they care.

32.05 CAFE
(Map p64; ☎8-905-703 3205; www.veranda3205.ru; ul Karetny Ryad 3; ⊙11am-3am; Ⓜ Pushkinskaya) The biggest drinking and eating establishment in Hermitage Gardens, this verandah positioned at the back of the park's main building looks a bit like a greenhouse. In summer, tables (and patrons) spill out into the park, making it one of the city's best places for outdoor drinking. With its long bar and joyful atmosphere, the place also heaves in winter.

Presnya

★**Time-Out Rooftop Bar** COCKTAIL BAR
(Map p64; http://hotelpeking.ru/timeout-rooftop-bar; 12th fl, Bolshaya Sadovaya ul 5; ⊙noon-2am Sun-Thu, to 6am Fri & Sat; Ⓜ Mayakovskaya) On the upper floors of the throwback **Peking Hotel** (Гостиница Пекин; Map p64; ☎495-650 0900; www.hotelpeking.ru; Bolshaya Sadovaya ul 5/1; r from ₽7600; ❄☜; Ⓜ Mayakovskaya), this trendy bar is nothing but 'now'. That includes the bartenders sporting plaid and their delicious concoctions, specially created for different times of the day. The decor is pretty impressive – particularly the spectacular city skyline view. A perfect place for sundowners (or sun-ups, if you last that long).

Jagger BAR
(www.jaggercity.ru; Bldg 30, Rochdelskaya ul 15; ⊙noon-midnight Mon-Wed, to 6am Thu-Sat, 2pm-midnight Sun; Ⓜ Ulitsa 1905 Goda) Tucked into the courtyard in the old **Tryokhgornaya** (Трёхгорная Мануфактура; www.trekhgorka.ru; ⊙9.30am-8.30pm Mon-Sat, 10am-6pm Sun; Ⓜ Barrikadnaya) manufacturing complex, Jagger is a super-hot bar with a super-cool vibe. Excellent cocktails, sharp clientele and laid-back atmosphere are characteristic of a new Moscow nightlife that is cosmopolitan and cultured, not over-the-top outrageous. Still, you have to know where to look for this place. And you have to look good.

Arbat & Khamovniki

Dom 12 WINE BAR
(Map p70; www.dom12cafe.ru; Mansurovsky per 12; ⊙noon-6am; Ⓜ Park Kultury) Eclectic and atmospheric, Dom 12 may be the perfect place to attend an event or chat with friends over a glass of wine. The cosy interior is enhanced by natural materials, comfy chairs and low lighting. Besides the excellent wine list, the place offers poetry nights, lectures, concerts and dancing. Delightful!

Balalaechnaya CRAFT BEER
(Балалаечная; Map p64; www.balaykabar.ru; ul Arbat 23; ⊙noon-midnight; Ⓜ Arbatskaya) There is nothing too complicated going on here, and that's the beauty of it. Lovely handcrafted *balalaikas* (traditional Russian stringed instruments) for sale on the wall, and tasty handcrafted beer on tap. Live acoustic music on 'Spiritual Thursdays'.

WORTH A TRIP

SERGIEV POSAD

Blue and golden cupolas offset by snow-white walls – this colour scheme lies at the heart of the Russian perception of divinity and the **Trinity Monastery of St Sergius** (Свято-Троицкая Сергиева Лавра; info 496-544 5334, tours 496-540 5721; www.stsl.ru; 5am-9pm) FREE is a textbook example. In Russia it doesn't get any holier than this monastery, for the place was founded in 1340 by the country's most revered saint. St Sergius of Radonezh was credited with providing mystic support to Prince Dmitry Donskoy in his improbable victory over the Tatars in the Battle of Kulikovo Pole (1380). Soon after his death at the age of 78, Sergius was named Russia's patron saint. Since the 14th century, pilgrims have been journeying to this place to pay homage to him.

Note that the monastery is an active religious centre with a visible population of monks in residence. Visitors should refrain from photographing the monks, female visitors should wear headscarves and men are required to remove hats before entering the churches.

Sights

Built in 1423, the squat, gold-domed **Trinity Cathedral** (Троицкий собор) is the heart of the monastery, as well as its oldest surviving building. The tomb of St Sergius stands in the church's southeastern corner, where a memorial service for him goes on all day, every day. The icon-festooned interior, lit by oil lamps, is largely the work of the great medieval painter Andrei Rublyov and his students.

The star-spangled **Cathedral of the Assumption** (Успенский собор) was modelled on the cathedral of the same name in the Moscow Kremlin. It was finished in 1585 with money left by Ivan the Terrible in a fit of remorse for killing his son. To the left of the main entrance is the rectangular **tomb of Boris Godunov**, the only tsar not buried in the Moscow Kremlin or St Petersburg's SS Peter & Paul Cathedral.

Nearby, the resplendent **Chapel-at-the-Well** (Накладезная часовня) was built over a spring that is said to have appeared during the Polish siege of 1608–10, in the Time of Troubles. The five-tier baroque **bell tower** (колокольня) – at 88.5m, the highest in Russia – took nearly 30 years to build (from 1741 to 1770), and once had 42 bells, the largest of which weighed 65 tonnes.

Getting There & Away

Take the express commuter train (₽160, one hour, six daily) from Moscow's Yaroslav Station. A handful of long-distance trains call at Sergiev Posad daily on the way to Yaroslavl (*platskart* ₽1200, three hours).

Zhiguli Beer Hall BREWERY
(Пивной зал Жигули; Map p64; www.zhiguli.su; ul Novy Arbat 11; beer ₽210-350; 10am-2am Sun-Thu, to 4am Fri & Sat; ; M Arbatskaya) It's hard to classify this old-style *stolovaya* (cafeteria) that happens to brew great beer. The place harks back to the Soviet years, when a popular *pivnaya* (beer joint with stand-up tables) with the same name was a Novy Arbat institution. The minimalist decor and cafeteria-style service recalls the heyday, although it's been updated with big-screen TVs and a separate table-service dining room.

Zamoskvorechie

★ **Bar Strelka** CAFE, CLUB
(Map p70; www.barstrelka.com; Bersenevskaya nab 14/5, bldg 5a; 9am-midnight Mon-Thu, to 3am Fri, noon-3am Sat, noon-midnight Sun; ; M Kropotkinskaya) Located just below the Patriarshy most, the bar-restaurant at the Strelka Institute (p81) is the ideal starting point for an evening in the Red October (p69) complex. The rooftop terrace has unbeatable Moscow River views, but the interior is equally cool in a shabby-chic sort of way. The bar menu is excellent and there is usually somebody tinkling the ivories.

★ **Gipsy** CLUB, CAFE
(Map p70; www.bargipsy.ru; Bolotnaya nab 3/4; 6pm-1am Sun-Thu, 2pm-6am Fri & Sat) Euphoria reigns in this postmodern nomad camp of a bar with its strategic rooftop position on Red October (p69). The decor is bright-coloured kitsch, which among other oddities means fake palm trees and toilet doors covered with artificial fur. The DJ and live-music repertoires are aptly eclectic.

Meshchansky & Basmanny

★Ukuleleshnaya BAR
(Укулелешная; Map p64; ☎495-642 5726; www.uku-uku.ru; ul Pokrovka 17 str 1; ⊙noon-midnight Sun-Thu, noon-4am Fri & Sat; Ⓜ Chistye Prudy) In its new location, this is now more of a bar than a musical instrument shop, although ukuleles still adorn the walls, prompting an occasional jam session. Craft beer prevails on the drinks list, but Ukuleleshnaya also serves experimental cocktails of its own invention. Live concerts happen regularly and resident Pomeranian spitz Berseny (cute dog) presides over the resulting madness.

★Sisters Cafe CAFE
(Map p64; ☎495-623 0932; www.cafesisters.com; ul Pokrovka 6; ⊙noon-11pm; 📶; Ⓜ Kitay-Gorod) This cosy and quiet cafe-cum-bar has a distinct feminine touch about it – as if Chekhov's sisters have finally made their way to Moscow and started a new life here. Cheapish smoothies, lemonades and teas are on offer, but the wine and cocktail lists are equally impressive.

☆ Entertainment

★Bolshoi Theatre BALLET, OPERA
(Большой театр; Map p64; ☎495-455 5555; www.bolshoi.ru; Teatralnaya pl 1; tickets ₽100-12,000; ⊙closed late Jul–mid-Sep; Ⓜ Teatralnaya) An evening at the Bolshoi is still one of Moscow's most romantic and entertaining options for a night on the town. The glittering six-tier auditorium has an electric atmosphere, evoking over 240 years of premier music and dance. Both the ballet and opera companies perform a range of Russian and foreign works here.

After the collapse of the Soviet Union, the Bolshoi was marred by politics, scandal and frequent turnover. Yet the show must go on – and it will. The Bolshoi has recently undergone a much-needed renovation; in 2011, the theatre reopened the doors of its main stage after several years of work, revealing expanded theatre space and glittering mouldings. The smaller New Stage (Novaya Stsena), remodelled in 2003, also hosts performances.

Stanislavsky Electrotheatre ARTS CENTRE
(Map p64; ☎495-699 7224; http://electrotheatre.ru; ul Tverskaya 23; Ⓜ Pushkinskaya) Renowned performance artist Boris Yukhananov has revived this old theatre as Moscow's hottest venue for experimental performance and visual art. Dance, music, cinema and theatre form a sparkling cocktail of genres and there is not a day without something new, strange and exciting going on.

Tchaikovsky Concert Hall CLASSICAL MUSIC
(Концертный зал имени Чайковского; Map p64; ☎495-232 0400; www.meloman.ru; Triumfalnaya pl 4/31; tickets ₽800-3000; ⊙concerts 7pm, closed Aug; Ⓜ Mayakovskaya) Home to the famous Moscow State Philharmonic (Moskovskaya Filharmonia), the capital's oldest symphony orchestra, Tchaikovsky Concert Hall was established in 1921. It's a huge auditorium, with seating for 1600 people. Expect to hear the Russian classics, such as Stravinsky, Rachmaninov and Shostakovich, as well as other European favourites. Look out for children's concerts, jazz ensembles and other special performances.

Moscow International House of Music CLASSICAL MUSIC
(Map p70; ☎495-730 1011; www.mmdm.ru; Kosmodemyanskaya nab 52/8; tickets ₽200-2000; Ⓜ Paveletskaya) This graceful, modern glass building has three halls, including Svetlanov Hall, which holds the largest organ in Russia. Needless to say, organ concerts held here are impressive. This is the usual venue for performances by the **National Philharmonic of Russia** (Национальный филармонический оркестр России; Map p70; ☎495-730 3778; www.nfor.ru), a privately financed, highly lauded, classical-music organisation. Founded in 1991, the symphony is directed and conducted by the esteemed Vladimir Spivakov.

Nikulin Circus on Tsvetnoy Bulvar CIRCUS
(Цирк Никулина на Цветном бульваре; Map p64; ☎495-625 8970; www.circusnikulin.ru; Tsvetnoy bul 13; tickets ₽400-2500; ⊙box office 11am-2pm & 3-7pm; Ⓜ Tsvetnoy Bulvar) Founded in 1880, this circus is now named after beloved actor and clown Yury Nikulin (1921–97), who performed at the studio here for many years. Nikulin's shows centre on a given theme, which serves to add some cohesion to the productions. There are lots of trapeze artists, tightrope walkers and performing animals.

Kremlin Ballet BALLET
(Кремлевский балет; Map p60; ☎495-620 7846; www.kremlinpalace.org; ⊙box office noon-8pm; Ⓜ Aleksandrovsky Sad) The Bolshoi Theatre doesn't have a monopoly on ballet in Moscow. Leading dancers also appear with

the Kremlin Ballet, which performs in the **State Kremlin Palace** (Государственный Кремлёвский дворец; Map p60; ☎495-620 7846; www.kremlinpalace.org/en). The Bolshoi is magical, but seeing a show inside the Kremlin is something special too. The repertoire is unapologetically classical. The box office is near the entrance to the Biblioteka im Lenina metro station.

Sixteen Tons LIVE MUSIC

(Шестнадцать тонн; ☎495-253 1550; www.16tons.ru; ul Presnensky val 6; cover ₽600-1200; ⏲11am-6am; 📶; Ⓜ Ulitsa 1905 Goda) Downstairs, the brassy English pub-restaurant has an excellent house-brewed bitter. Upstairs, the club gets some of the best Russian bands that play in Moscow and occasional first-rate or semi-obscure Western groups. Show times are subject to change so check the website for details.

Rhythm Blues Cafe LIVE MUSIC

(Блюз Кафе Ритм; Map p64; ☎499-697 6008; www.rhythm-blues-cafe.ru; Starovagankovsky per; cover ₽500-1000; ⏲shows from 7.30pm; Ⓜ Aleksandrovsky Sad) If your dog got run over by a pick-up truck, you might find some comfort at the Rhythm Blues Cafe, with down-and-out live music every night, plus cold beer and a whole menu of salty cured meats. Great fun and a friendly vibe, with people actually listening to the music. Book a table if you want to sit down.

Strelka Institute ARTS CENTRE

(Map p70; www.strelkainstitute.ru; Bersenevskaya nab 14/5; Ⓜ Kropotkinskaya, Polyanka) This institute is the focal point of the development at the Red October (p69) chocolate factory. Aside from the course offerings and the popular bar (p79), Strelka brings a healthy dose of contemporary culture to Moscow, hosting lectures, workshops, film screenings and concerts.

Shopping

GUM MALL

(ГУМ; Map p60; www.gum.ru; Krasnaya pl 3; ⏲10am-10pm; Ⓜ Ploshchad Revolyutsii) Behind its elaborate 240m-long facade on the north-eastern side of Red Square, GUM is a bustling shopping mall with hundreds of fancy stores and restaurants. With a skylight roof and three-level arcades, the spectacular interior was a revolutionary design when it was built in the 1890s, replacing the Upper Trading Rows that previously occupied the site.

WORTH A TRIP

IZMAYLOVSKY MARKET

Never mind the kitschy faux 'tsar's palace' it surrounds, **Izmaylovsky Market** (www.kremlin-izmailovo.com; Izmaylovskoye sh 73; ⏲10am-8pm; Ⓜ Partizanskaya) is the ultimate place to shop for *matryoshki* (nesting dolls), military uniforms, icons, Soviet badges and some real antiques. Huge and diverse, it is almost a theme park, including shops, cafes and a couple of not terribly exciting museums.

Serious antiquarians occupy the 2nd floor of the wooden trade row surrounding the palace, but for really good stuff you need to come here at an ungodly hour on Saturday morning and compete with pros from Moscow galleries. Keep in mind that Russia bans the export of any item older than 100 years. Feel free to negotiate, but don't expect vendors to come down more than 10%. This place is technically open every day, but many vendors come out only on weekends, when the selection is greater.

Yeliseev Grocery FOOD & DRINKS

(Елисеевский магазин; Map p64; Tverskaya ul 14; ⏲8am-9pm Mon-Sat, 10am-6pm Sun; Ⓜ Pushkinskaya) Peek in here for a glimpse of pre-revolutionary grandeur, as the store is set in the former mansion of the successful merchant Yeliseev. It now houses an upscale market selling caviar and other delicacies. It's a great place to shop for souvenirs for your foodie friends back home.

Flakon SHOPPING CENTRE

(www.flacon.ru; ul Bolshaya Novodmitrovskaya 36; Ⓜ Dmitrovskaya) Flakon is arguably the most visually attractive of all the redeveloped industrial areas around town, looking a bit like the far end of London's Portobello Rd, especially during the weekends. Once a glassware plant, it is now home to dozens of funky shops and other businesses. Shopping for designer clothes and unusual souvenirs is the main reason for coming here.

Russian Embroidery & Lace GIFTS & SOUVENIRS

(Русская вышивка и кружево; Map p64; ul Arbat 31; ⏲11am-8pm Mon-Sat, to 5pm Sun; Ⓜ Smolenskaya) Considering the lack of flashy signs and kitsch, it would be easy to miss this plain storefront on the Arbat. But inside there are treasures galore, from elegant tablecloths and napkins to delicate handmade sweaters and embroidered shirts.

Association of Artists of the Decorative Arts GIFTS & SOUVENIRS
(Ассоциация художников декоративно-прикладного искусства; AHDI; Map p64; www.ahdi.ru; ul Arbat 21; 11am-8pm; M Arbatskaya) Look for the ceramic number plate and the small sign indicating the entrance to this 'exposition hall', which is actually a cluster of small shops, each showcasing arts and crafts by local artists. In addition to paintings and pottery, the most intriguing items are the gorgeous knit sweaters, woolly coats and embroidered dresses – all handmade and unique.

Information

DANGERS & ANNOYANCES

Moscow is mostly a safe city.

- As in any big city, be on guard against pickpockets, especially around train stations and in crowded metro cars.
- Always be cautious about taking taxis late at night, especially near bars and clubs. Never get into a car that already has two or more people in it.
- Always carry a photocopy of your passport and visa. If stopped by a member of the police force, it is perfectly acceptable to show a photocopy.
- Your biggest threat in Moscow is xenophobic or overly friendly drunks.

EMERGENCY

Tourist Helpline 8-800-220 0001/2

Universal Emergency Number 112

INTERNET ACCESS

- Almost all hotels and hostels offer wi-fi, as do many bars, restaurants and cafes. It isn't always free, but it is ubiquitous. There is also free wi-fi on the metro and at hot spots around the city.
- To use the free wi-fi, you will be obliged to register your phone number to obtain a pass code. Some services only accept Russian telephone numbers, in which case you may have to ask a local to use their number.
- Most hostels and hotels offer internet access for guests who are not travelling with their own device. Internet cafes are a thing of the past.
- Also popular is shared work space, which offers a comfortable work space, functional wi-fi, and sometimes drinks and snacks, for a per-minute or per-hour fee.

Russian State Library (Map p64; ul Vozdvizhenka 3; 9am-9pm; M Biblioteka imeni Lenina)

Ziferblat Pokrovka (Циферблат; Map p64; www.ziferblat.net; ul Pokrovka 12c1; per min ₽3; 11am-midnight Sun-Thu, 11am-7pm Fri & Sat; M Chistye Prudy)

Ziferblat Tverskaya (Циферблат; Map p64; www.ziferblat.net; Tverskaya ul 12c1; 11am-midnight; M Pushkinskaya)

MEDICAL SERVICES

Hospitals

Moscow is well served by sparkling international-style clinics that charge handsomely for their generally excellent and professional service: expect to pay around US$100 for an initial consultation. Both the International Clinic MEDSI and the European Medical Centre accept health insurance from major international providers.

Botkin Hospital (495-945 0045; www.mosgorzdrav.ru; 2-y Botkinsky proezd 5; 24hr; M Begovaya) The best Russian facility. From Begovaya metro station, walk 1km northeast on Khoroshevskoe sh and Begovoy pr. Turn left on Begovaya ul and continue to 2-y Botkinsky proezd.

European Medical Centre (Map p64; 495-933 6655; www.emcmos.ru; Spirodonevsky per 5; 24hr; M Mayakovskaya) Includes medical and dental facilities, which are open around the clock for emergencies. The staff speak 10 languages.

International Clinic MEDSI (Map p64; 495-933 7700; https://medsi.ru; Grokholsky per 1; 24hr; M Prospekt Mira) Offers 24-hour emergency service, consultations and a full range of medical specialists, including paediatricians and dentists. There is also an on-site pharmacy with English-speaking staff.

Pharmacies

36.6 Arbat (Map p64; ul Novy Arbat 15; 9am-10pm; M Arbatskaya)

36.6 Basmanny (Map p64; ul Pokrovka 1/13; 9am-9pm; M Kitay-Gorod)

36.6 Tverskaya (Map p64; Tverskaya ul 25/9; 24hr; M Mayakovskaya)

36.6 Zamoskvorechie (Map p70; Klimentovsky per 12; 8am-10pm; M Tretyakovskaya)

MONEY

ATMs widely available. Credit cards accepted by most hotels and restaurants.

POST

Main Post Office (Map p64; Myasnitskaya ul 26; 24hr; M Chistye Prudy)

Getting There & Away

TRAIN

Yaroslav Station (Ярославский вокзал; http://yaroslavsky.dzvr.ru; Komsomolskaya pl; ; Komsomolskaya), the main station for Trans-Siberian trains, serves Yaroslavl, Arkhangelsk, Vorkuta, the Russian Far East, Mongolia, China and North Korea; some trains to/from Vladimir, Nizhny Novgorod, Kostroma, Vologda, Perm, the Ural Mountains and Siberia; and suburban trains to/from the northeast, including Sergiev Posad.

Kazan Station (Казанский вокзал; http://kazansky.dzvr.ru; Komsomolskaya pl; ; Komsomolskaya) serves trains to/from Kazan and points southeast, as well as some trains to/from Vladimir, Nizhny Novgorod, the Ural Mountains and Siberia.

Leningrad Station (Ленинградский вокзал; http://leningradsky.dzvr.ru; Komsomolskaya pl; ; Komsomolskaya) serves Tver, Novgorod, Pskov, St Petersburg, Vyborg, Murmansk, Estonia and Helsinki. Note that sometimes this station is referred to on timetables and tickets by its former name, Oktyabrsky (Октябрьский).

Belarus Station (Белорусский вокзал; http://belorussky.dzvr.ru; Tverskaya Zastava pl; ; Belorusskaya) serves trains to/from northern and central Europe, as well as suburban trains to/from the west, including Mozhaysk and Borodino. This is also where you'll catch the Aeroexpress Train (p84) to Sheremetyevo international airport.

Kiev Station (Киевский вокзал; www.kievsky-vokzal.ru; Kievskaya pl; ; Kievskaya) serves Kyiv and western Ukraine, as well as points further west, such as Moldova, Slovakia, Hungary, Austria, Prague, Romania, Bulgaria, Croatia, Serbia and Greece. This is also where you'll catch the Aeroexpress Train (p84) to Vnukovo international airport.

Pavelets Station (Павелецкий вокзал; http://paveletsky.dzvr.ru; Paveletskaya pl; Paveletskaya) serves points south, including the Volga region and Central Asia. This is also the departure/arrival point for the Aeroexpress Train (p84) to Domodedovo international airport.

Kursk Station (Курский вокзал; http://kursky.dzvr.ru; pl Kurskogo vokzala; Kurskaya) serves Oryol, Kursk, Krasnodar, Adler, the Caucasus, eastern Ukraine, Crimea, Georgia and Azerbaijan. It also has some trains to/from Rostov-on-Don, Vladimir, Nizhny Novgorod and Perm.

Rīga Station (Рижский вокзал; http://rizhsky.dzvr.ru; Rizhskaya pl; Rizhskaya) serves Latvia.

Most stations have a separate ticket hall for suburban trains, usually called the Prigorodny Zal and often tucked away beside or behind the station building. These trains are usually listed on separate timetables and may depart from a separate group of platforms.

AIR

Sheremetyevo (Шереметьево; 495-578 6565; www.svo.aero) international airport, 30km northwest of the city centre, is the largest airport in Moscow. The Aeroexpress Train (p84) makes the 35-minute trip between Sheremetyevo (located next to Terminal E) and Belorussky vokzal every half-hour from 5.30am to 12.30am.

Domodedovo (Домодедово; 495-933 6666; www.domodedovo.ru) international airport, located about 48km south of the city, is the city's largest and most efficient international airport. The Aeroexpress Train leaves Paveletsky vokzal every half-hour between 6am and midnight for the 45-minute trip to Domodedovo.

About 30km southwest of the city centre, **Vnukovo** (Внуково; 495-937 5555;

TRAINS TO/FROM ST PETERSBURG

All trains to St Petersburg depart from Leningrad Station. Coming from St Petersburg you'll board at Moscow Station (p108).

Overnight

There are about a dozen overnight trains travelling between Moscow and St Petersburg. Most depart between 10pm and 1am, arriving the following morning between 6am and 8am. On the more comfortable *firmenny* trains, such as the Red Arrow (Красная стрела) or Grand Express (Гранд Экспресс) a de-luxe sleeping carriage is between ₽12,800 and ₽16,400, 1st-class compartment (two-person cabin) around ₽16,300, while a 2nd-class *kupe* (four-person cabin) is ₽2800. Less fancy trains offer 3rd-class *platzkartny* (dorm-style sleeping carriages) for ₽1570 and even sitting-only carriages for ₽890.

Sapsan

These high-speed trains travel at 200km/h to connect the cities in around four hours. There are six to eight daily departures between around 5.30am and 7.30pm. Comfortable 2nd-class seats start at ₽1300, while super-spacious 1st-class seats run from ₽5000.

www.vnukovo.ru) international airport serves most flights to/from the Caucasus, Moldova and Kaliningrad, as well as domestic flights and a smattering of flights to Europe. The Aeroexpress Train makes the 35-minute run from Kievsky vokzal to Vnukovo airport every hour from 6am to 11pm.

Opened in 2016, Moscow's fourth international airport, **Zhukovsky** (Жуковский; ☎ 495-228 9600; http://zia.aero), is about 40km southeast of Moscow. The new airport mostly serves Central Asian destinations, and it is a hub for Ural Airlines.

BUS

Bus service may be useful for destinations that are not served by train. The **central bus station** (Центральный автовокзал, Щёлковский автовокзал; ☎ 499-748 8029; www.avtovokzaly.ru; Ⓜ Shchyolkovskaya), sometimes called Shchyolkovsky bus station, is located 8km east of the city centre.

Getting Around

TO/FROM THE AIRPORTS

The three main airports – not yet including Zhukovsky – are accessible by the convenient **Aeroexpress Train** (☎ 8-800-700 3377; www.aeroexpress.ru; one way ₽420; ⏲ 6am-midnight) from the city centre; reduced rates are available for online purchases. Alternatively, order an official airport taxi from the dispatcher's desk in the terminal (₽2000 to ₽2500 to the city centre). Save some cash by booking in advance to take advantage of fixed rates offered by most companies (usually from ₽1500 to ₽1800 to/from any airport). Driving times vary depending on the traffic.

BOAT

For new perspectives on Moscow's neighbourhoods, fine views of the Kremlin, or just good, old-fashioned transport, a boat ride on the Moscow River is one of the city's highlights. Capital Shipping Co (p69) offers a two-day pass, so you can get on and off wherever you wish.

METRO

Most visitors won't need anything but Moscow's super-efficient metro system, which allows you to get to pretty much anywhere in the city without complicated bus or tram routes. Connecting to the metro, an overground railway ring line (Moscow Central Ring) circles the city, which may be useful for some sights on the outskirts.

Moscow has a unified ticketing system. All tickets are essentially smart cards that you must tap on the reader at the turnstiles before entering a metro station or on the bus. Most convenient for short-term visitors is the red Ediny (Единый) ticket, which is good for all kinds of transport and available at metro stations. Depending on your time and logistics, you can choose between buying a ticket good for a single trip for ₽55, two trips for ₽110, 20 trips for ₽720, 40 trips for ₽1440 or 60 trips for ₽1700.

If you are staying in Moscow for more than a few days, it is recommended that you get a Troika (Тройка) top-up card, also available at metro stations. It works on all kinds of transport and gives a slightly cheaper rate than Ediny.

If your accommodation warrants taking a bus or tram to the nearest metro station, you may consider buying a 90 Minutes card (single trip ₽65), which includes one metro ride and an unlimited number of bus/tram/trolleybus rides.

Another ticket type is TAT, which is only good for trams, buses and trolleybuses, but it is of little use for most visitors.

The 150-plus stations are marked outside by large 'M' signs. Trains are generally reliable: you will rarely wait on a platform for more than three minutes. Nonetheless, they do get packed, especially during the city's rush hours.

Maps & Signage Stations have maps of the system at the entrance and signs on each platform showing the destinations. The maps are generally in Cyrillic and Latin script, although the signs are usually only in Cyrillic. The carriages also have maps inside that show the stops for that line in both Roman and Cyrillic letters.

Transfers Interchange stations are linked by underground passages, indicated by *perekhod* (underground walkway)signs, usually blue with a stick figure running up the stairs. Be aware that when two or more lines meet, the intersecting stations often (but not always) have different names.

TAXI

These days, most people use mobile phone apps, such as **Yandex.Taxi** (Яндекс.Такси; https://taxi.yandex.com), to order a cab. This solves the language barrier issue to an extent, given that you know the precise departure and destination address. If you have the app, try to make sure it's easy to park where you are, otherwise the driver will start calling you and asking questions in Russian.

You can also order an official taxi by phone or book it online, or get a Russian-speaker to do this for you. Normally, the dispatcher will ring you back within a few minutes to provide a description and licence number of the car. Most companies will send a car within 30 minutes of your call. Some reliable companies offer online scheduling.

Detskoe Taxi (Детское Такси; ☎ 495-765 1180; www.detskoetaxi.ru) 'Children's Taxi' has smoke-free cars and car seats for children.

Lingo Taxi (www.lingotaxi.com) Promises English-speaking drivers (and usually delivers).

New Yellow Taxi (Новое жёлтое такси; ☎ 495-940 8888; www.nyt.ru)

St Petersburg

Includes ➡

Best Places to Eat

- ➡ EM Restaurant (p103)
- ➡ Cococo (p102)
- ➡ Gräs x Madbaren (p101)
- ➡ Yat (p102)
- ➡ Duo Gastrobar (p103)

Best Places to Stay

- ➡ Soul Kitchen Hostel (p100)
- ➡ Baby Lemonade Hostel (p99)
- ➡ Alexander House (p100)
- ➡ Rachmaninov Antique Hotel (p99)
- ➡ Rossi Hotel (p100)

Why Go?

Beautiful, complex and imperious, with a hedonistic, creative temperament, St Petersburg (Санкт-Петербург) is the ultimate Russian diva. From its early days as an uninhabited swamp, the 300-year-old city has been nurtured by a succession of rulers, enduring practically everything that history and nature's harsh elements could throw at her. Constantly in need of repair but with a carefree party attitude, Petersburg still seduces all who gaze upon her grand facades, glittering spires and gilded domes.

Even if you don't plan to start or end your train journey in St Petersburg, it would be a shame not to visit the city. The long summer days of the White Nights season are particularly special – the fountains flow and parks and gardens burst into colour. The icy depths of winter have their own magic, and are the perfect time for warming body and soul in all those museums and palaces.

When to Go

St Petersburg

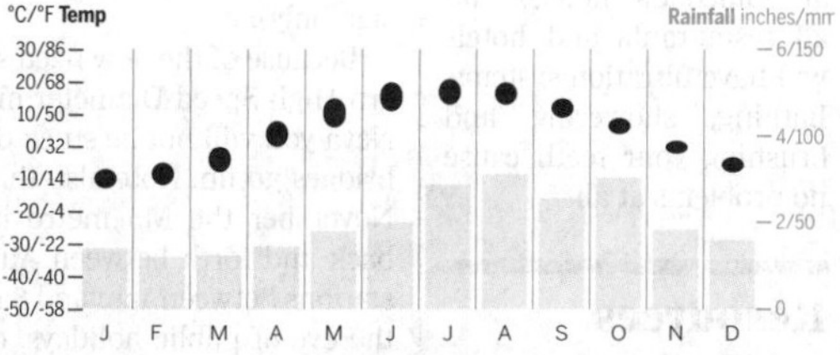

Mid-May–mid-Jul The White Nights, when the sun never sets, is the most popular time to visit.

May & Sep A great time to visit summery St Petersburg without the crowds of the peak months.

Nov–Jan Dark and blanketed in snow, winters in St Petersburg can be magical.

NEED TO KNOW

Take advantage of deals such as the Hermitage's two-day ticket, which allows you access to all its sites over 48 hours, or the Russian Museum's four-palace ticket that does likewise over three days.

Fast Facts

- Telephone code: 812
- Population: 5.28 million
- St Petersburg time: GMT+4

Don't Drink the Water

Tiny traces of *Giardia lamblia,* a nasty parasite that causes stomach cramps, nausea, bloated stomach, diarrhoea and frequent gas, have been found in St Petersburg's water. There's no preventative drug so it is worth taking precautions against contracting it.

To be absolutely safe, only drink water that has been boiled for 10 minutes or filtered through an antimicrobial water filter. It's safe to accept tea or coffee at someone's house, and all restaurants and hotels will have filtration systems. Bathing, showering and brushing your teeth cause no problems at all.

Resources

In Your Pocket St Petersburg (www.inyourpocket.com/russia/st-petersburg)

Visit Petersburg (www.visit-petersburg.ru)

Arriving in St Petersburg

Most people arrive at St Petersburg's Pulkovo International Airport (p108) from where an official taxi costs between ₽800 and ₽1000 to the city centre; if you book one via an app it's likely to be ₽700. Alternatively, take bus 39 (35 minutes) or 39A (20 minutes) to Moskovskaya metro station for ₽35, then take the metro from Moskovskaya (Line 2) all over the city for ₽45.

Arrivals from Helsinki by train come into the Finland Station (p108), while those coming by train from Moscow will arrive at the Moscow Station (p108); both terminals are connected to the city's metro. Cruise ships and ferries arrive at several docks scattered around the city.

HISTORIC RAILWAY STATIONS

St Petersburg's oldest and most elegant rail terminal is Vitebsk Station (p108), originally built in 1837 for the tsar's private train line to Tsarskoe Selo. The current building dates from 1904 and is partly graced with gorgeous Style Moderne interiors.

While you're at Moscow Station (p108) look up at the expansive ceiling mural in the main entrance hall. There's also a striking giant bust of Peter the Great in the hall leading to the platforms.

Finland Station (p108), rebuilt in the 1970s in rectilinear Soviet style, is where Lenin arrived in April 1917 after 17 years in exile abroad and gave his legendary speech atop an armoured car. Walk out onto the square that still bears Lenin's name and you'll see a statue of the man himself at the far end.

Bridges Up!

From mid-April until late November major bridges across the Neva rise overnight (usually between 1am and 5am) to allow ships to pass through the city. You can check the full, up-to-date timetable at www.razvodka-mostov.ru (in Russian only).

Because of the new fixed suspension bridges on the Western High Speed Diameter highway across the mouth of the Neva you will not be stuck either side of the river when the bridges go up. Note also that between May and the end of November the M5 metro line shuttles every 20 minutes back and forth between Admiralteyskaya and Sportivnaya stations between 1am and 3am on Saturday and Sunday and the eve of public holidays, creating an easy way to get between the islands and the Historic Heart.

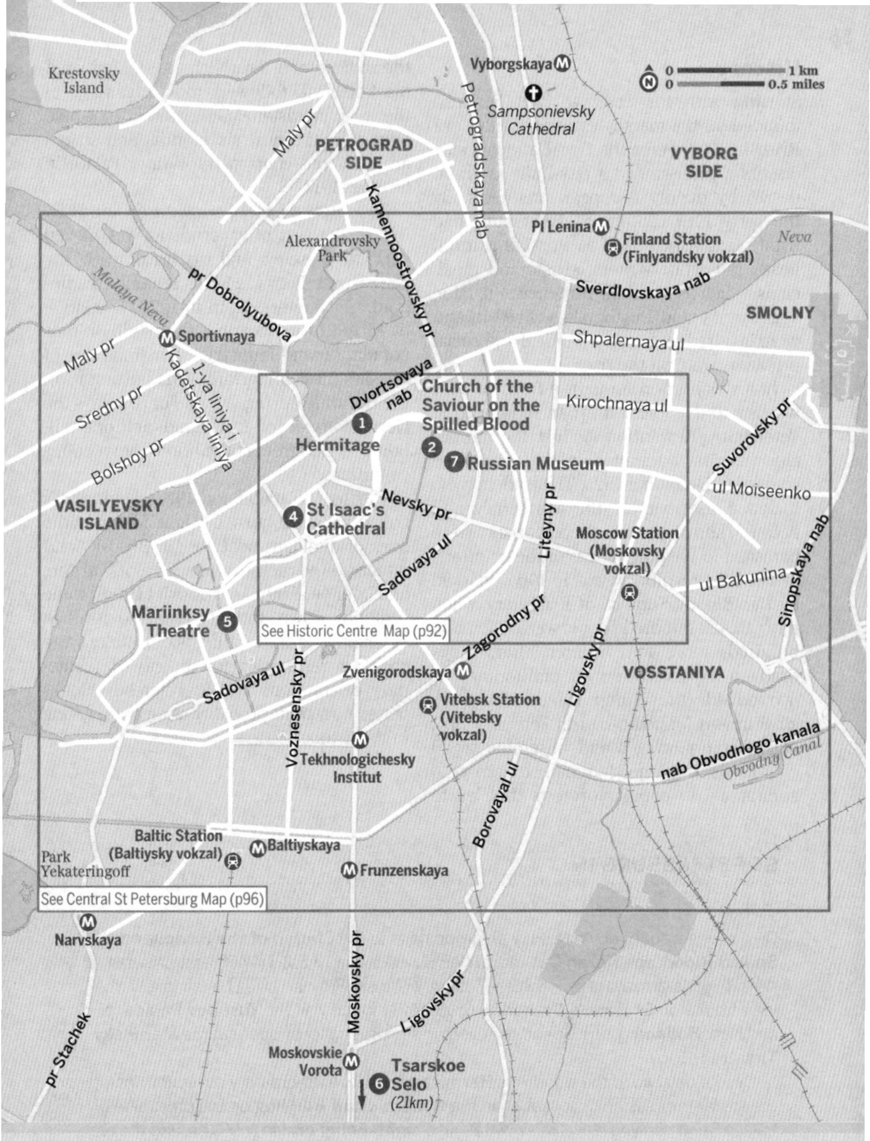

St Petersburg Highlights

❶ **Hermitage** (p89)
Spending a day (or more) in the one of the world's unrivalled art collections.

❷ **Church of the Saviour on the Spilled Blood** (p89)
Witnessing the amazing kaleidoscope of colours that is the city's most iconic church.

❸ **White Nights** Revelling with locals during the ethereal endless daylight of the summer.

❹ **St Isaac's Cathedral** (p93) Climbing the enormous dome for a bird's-eye view of the imperial city.

❺ **Mariinsky Theatre** (p106)
Watching a ballet or opera at this historic theatre.

❻ **Tsarskoe Selo** (107)
Heading out of town to see Catherine the Great's incredible summer palace.

❼ **Russian Museum** (p92)
Seeing the sublime collection of Russian art, from icons to the avant-garde.

History

Starting with the Peter & Paul Fortress, founded on the marshy estuary of the Neva River in 1703, Peter the Great and his successors commissioned a city built to grand design by mainly European architects. By the early 19th century St Petersburg had firmly established itself as Russia's cultural heart. But while writers, artists and musicians – such as Pushkin, Turgenev and, later, Tchaikovsky and Dostoevsky – lived in and were inspired by the city, political and social problems were on the rise.

Industrialisation brought a flood of poor workers and associated urban squalor to St Petersburg. Revolution against the monarchy was first attempted in the short-lived coup of 14 December 1825. The leaders (who included members of the aristocracy and became known as the Decembrists) were banished to the outer edges of the empire.

The next revolution was in 1905, sparked by the 'Bloody Sunday' of 9 January when more than a hundred people were killed and hundreds more were injured after troops fired on a peaceful crowd petitioning the tsar outside the Winter Palace. The tsar's government limped on, until February 1917, when food shortages and miserable social conditions in the newly renamed Petrograd culminated in popular protests that led to the abdication of Tsar Nicholas II. Lenin and his Bolshevik followers took advantage of the weak Provisional Government that held power for the next six months and staged an audacious coup in the Winter Palace in October 1917.

To protect the city during the ensuing Civil War, the seat of government was moved back to Moscow, and, to break with the tsarist past, Petrograd was renamed Leningrad after Lenin's death in 1924. The city – by virtue of its location, three-million-plus population and industry – remained one of Russia's most important, thus putting it on the frontline during WWII. For 872 days the Germans besieged Leningrad, and one million perished from starvation in horrendous conditions.

During the 1960s and 1970s Leningrad's bohemian spirit burned bright, fostering the likes of dissident poet Joseph Brodsky and underground rock groups such as Akvarium, and later on, Kino. As the Soviet Union came tumbling down, the city renamed itself St Petersburg in 1991. Millions of roubles were spent on restoration for the city's tercentenary celebrations and St Petersburg looks better now than probably at any other time in its history.

ST PETERSBURG IN ...

Two Days

On day one wander down Nevsky pr, dropping in to the **Church of the Saviour on the Spilled Blood**, and **Kazan Cathedral** (Казанский собор; ☎812-314 4663; http://kazansky-spb.ru; Kazanskaya pl 2; ⏲8.30am-7.30pm; Ⓜ Nevsky Prospekt) FREE. Also take in the view from atop **St Isaac's Cathedral** (p93). After lunch visit the **Yusupov Palace** (p95) and **New Holland** (p95). Spend the evening seeing a ballet or opera at the **Mariinsky Theatre** (p106).

Devote day two to the wondrous **Hermitage** and its extraordinary collection, including the stellar Impressionist collection in the **General Staff Building** on the other side of Palace Sq. When you leave, relax by taking a **sightseeing cruise** (p99) around the canals, followed by dinner at **Cococo** (p102), enjoying contemporary takes on traditional Russian cuisine.

Four Days

On day three start at the **Peter & Paul Fortress** (p95) to see where the city began. Wander across the bridge to Vasilevsky Island and see the **Strelka** (p95) and the fascinating **Kunstkamera** (p98). Later, catch a taxi or bus to the **Erarta Museum of Contemporary Art** (p95) at the other end of the island.

Travel out to Peterhof on day four to wander the lovely grounds and admire the fountains. On returning to the city, make a tour of the superb **Russian Museum** (p92). Top off the night with cocktails at one of St Petersburg's cosy bars such as **Apotheke Bar** (p105).

Sights

Historic Heart

★State Hermitage Museum MUSEUM

(Государственный Эрмитаж; Map p92; www.hermitagemuseum.org; Dvortsovaya pl 2; combined ticket ₽700; ⏲10.30am-6pm Tue, Thu, Sat & Sun, to 9pm Wed & Fri; Ⓜ Admiralteyskaya) The Hermitage fully lives up to its sterling reputation. You can be absorbed by its treasures for days and still come out wanting more. The enormous collection (over three million items, only a fraction of which are on display in 360 rooms) almost amounts to a comprehensive history of Western European art. Viewing it demands a little planning, so choose the areas you'd like to concentrate on before you arrive.

Catherine the Great, one of the greatest art collectors of all time, began the collection. Nicholas I also greatly enriched it and opened the galleries to the public for the first time in 1852.

It was the post-revolutionary period that saw the collection increase threefold, as many valuable private collections were seized by the state, including those of the Stroganovs, Sheremetyevs and Yusupovs. In 1948 it incorporated the renowned collections of post-Impressionist and Impressionist paintings of Moscow industrialists Sergei Shchukin and Ivan Morozov.

The museum consists of five linked buildings along riverside Dvortsovaya nab. From west to east they are:

➡ **Winter Palace**

This stunning mint-green, white and gold profusion of columns, windows and recesses, with its roof topped by rows of classical statues, was commissioned from Bartolomeo Rastrelli in 1754 by Empress Elizabeth. Catherine the Great and her successors had most of the interior remodelled in a classical style by 1837. It remained an imperial home until 1917, though the last two tsars spent more time in other palaces.

➡ **Small Hermitage**

This part of the museum evolved from a series of buildings constructed between Palace Sq and the Neva between 1764 and 1769, and was used by Catherine the Great as a retreat and to house the art collection started by Peter the Great, which she significantly expanded.

➡ **Great (Old) Hermitage**

Facing the Neva, this section of the museum (also known as the Large Hermitage) dates from the time of Catherine the Great. It mainly houses Italian Rennaissance art including works by Leonardo da Vinci, Raphael, Giorgione, Titian, Botticelli, Caravaggio and Tiepolo.

➡ **New Hermitage**

Facing Millionnaya ul, the New Hermitage was built for Nicholas II in 1852, to hold the growing art collection and as a museum for the public. Designed by German neoclassicist architect and painter von Klenze, the historically preserved rooms house the museum's collections of ancient art, European paintings, sculptures and decorative art.

➡ **Hermitage Theatre**

(Map p92; ☎812-408 1084; https://hermitagetheater.com; Dvortsovaya nab 32; online tickets from ₽8300; Ⓜ Admiralteyskaya) Designed by Giacomo Quarenghi, this intimate neoclassical auditorium was once the private theatre of the imperial family, and stands on the site of the original Winter Palace of Peter I.

★General Staff Building MUSEUM

(Здание Главного штаба; Map p92; www.hermitagemuseum.org; Dvortsovaya pl 6-8; ₽300, incl main Hermitage museum & other buildings ₽700; ⏲10.30am-6pm Tue, Thu, Sat & Sun, to 9pm Wed & Fri; Ⓜ Admiralteyskaya) The east wing of this magnificent building, wrapping around the south of Dvortsovaya pl and designed by Carlo Rossi in the 1820s, marries restored interiors with contemporary architecture to create a series of galleries displaying the Hermitage's amazing collection of Impressionist and post-Impressionist works. Contemporary art is here, too, often in temporary exhibitions by major artists.

Palace Square SQUARE

(Дворцовая площадь; Map p92; Dvortsovaya pl; Ⓜ Admiralteyskaya) This vast expanse is simply one of the most striking squares in the world, still redolent of imperial grandeur almost a century after the end of the Romanov dynasty. For the most amazing first impression, walk from Nevsky pr, up Bolshaya Morskaya ul and under the **triumphal arch** (Map p92).

★Church of the Saviour on the Spilled Blood CHURCH

(Храм Спаса на Крови; Map p92; ☎812-315 1636; http://eng.cathedral.ru/spasa_na_krovi; Konyushennaya pl; adult/student ₽250/150;

The Hermitage

A HALF-DAY TOUR

Successfully navigating the State Hermitage Museum, with its four vast interconnecting buildings and around 360 rooms, is an art form in itself. Our half-day tour of the highlights can be done in four hours, or easily extended to a full day.

Once past ticket control start by ascending the grand ❶ **Jordan Staircase** to Neva Enfilade and Great Enfilade for the impressive staterooms, including the former throne room St George's Hall and the 1812 War Gallery (Room 197), and the Romanovs' private apartments. Admire the newly restored ❷ **Great Church** then make your way back to the Neva side of the building via the Western Gallery (Room 262) to find the splendid ❸ **Pavilion Hall** with its view onto the Hanging Garden and the gilded Peacock Clock, always a crowd pleaser.

Make your way along the series of smaller galleries in the Large Hermitage hung with Italian Renaissance art, including masterpieces by ❹ **Da Vinci** and ❺ **Caravaggio**. The Loggia of Raphael (Room 227) is also impressive. Linger a while in the galleries containing Spanish art before taking in the Dutch collection, the highlight of which is the hoard of ❻ **Rembrandt** canvases in Room 254.

Descend the Council Staircase (Room 206), noting the giant malachite vase, to the ground floor where the fantastic Egyptian collection awaits in Room 100 as well as the galleries of Greek and Roman Antiquities. If you have extra time, it's well worth booking tours to see the special exhibition in the ❼ **Gold Rooms** of the Treasure Gallery.

TOP TIPS

- Reserve tickets online to skip the long lines.
- Bring a sandwich and a bottle of water with you: the cafe isn't great.
- Wear comfortable shoes.
- Bear in mind the only cloakroom is before ticket control, so you can't go back and pick up a sweater.

Jordan Staircase
Originally designed by Rastrelli, in the 18th century this incredible white marble construction was known as the Ambassadorial Staircase because it was the way into the palace for official receptions.

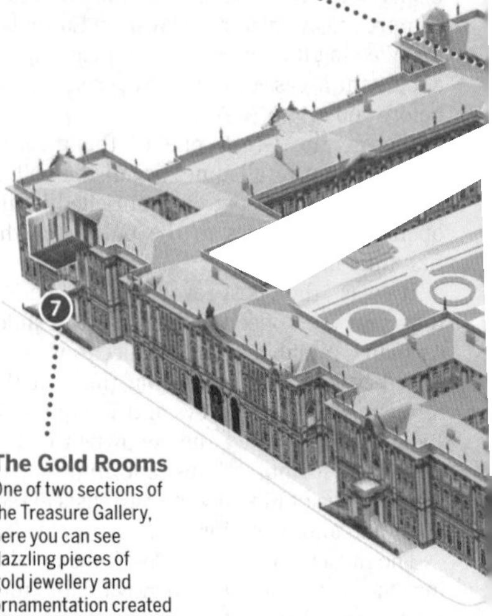

The Gold Rooms
One of two sections of the Treasure Gallery, here you can see dazzling pieces of gold jewellery and ornamentation created by Scythian, Greek and ancient Oriental craftsmen.

Great Church
This stunningly ornate church was the Romanovs' private place of worship and the venue for the marriage of the last tsar, Nicholas II, to Alexandra Feodorovna in 1895.

Rembrandt
A moving portrait of contrition and forgiveness, *Return of the Prodigal Son* (Room 254) depicts the biblical scene of a wayward son returning to his father.

SUPERSTOCK/GETTY IMAGES ©

Da Vinci
Along with the *Benois Madonna,* also here, *Madonna and Child (Madonna Litta;* Room 214) is one of just a handful of paintings known to be the work of Leonardo da Vinci.

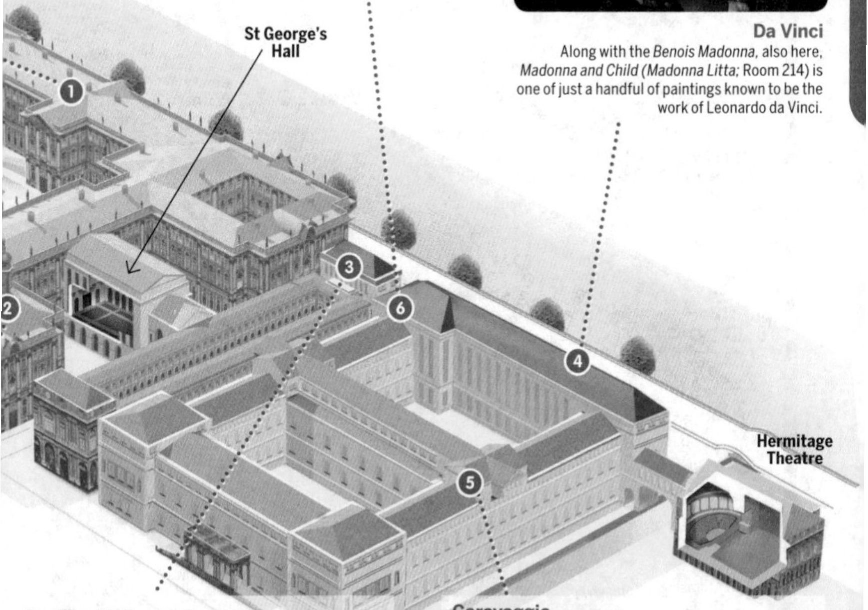

Pavilion Hall
Apart from the Peacock Clock, the Pavilion Hall also contains beautifully detailed mosaic tables made by Italian and Russian craftsmen in the mid-19th century.

Caravaggio
The Lute Player (Room 237) is the Hermitage's only Caravaggio, and a work that the master of light and shade described as the best piece he'd ever painted.

ANATOLY SAPRONENKOV/GETTY IMAGES ©

Historic Centre

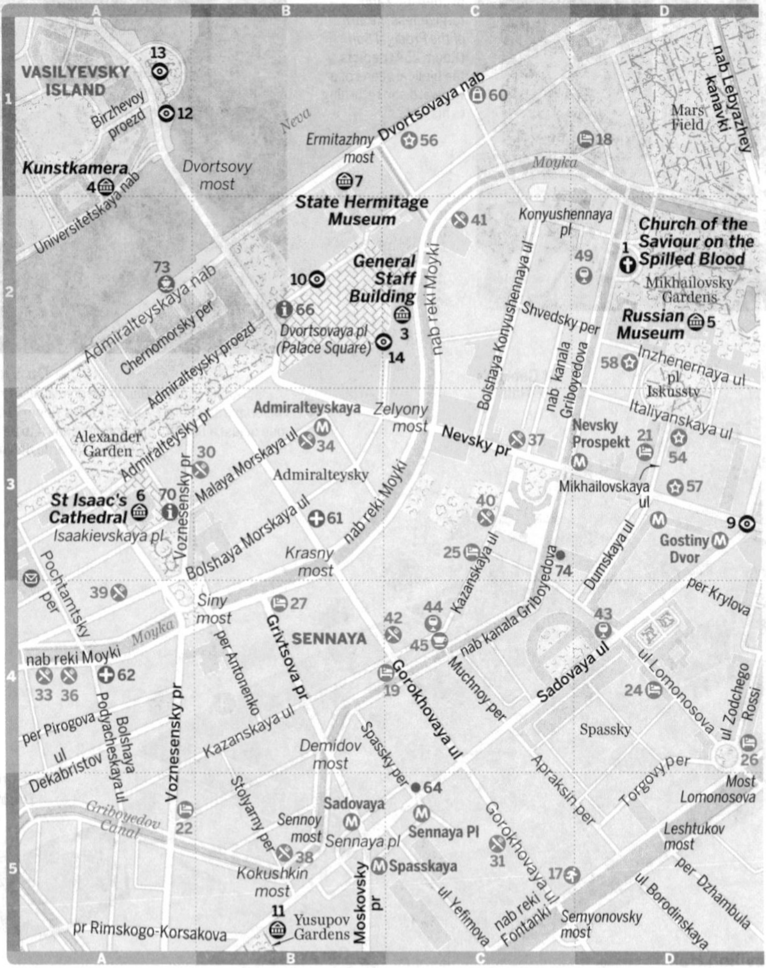

⏲10.30am-6pm Thu-Tue; Ⓜ Nevsky Prospekt) This five-domed dazzler is St Petersburg's most elaborate church with a classic Russian Orthodox exterior and an interior decorated with some 7000 sq metres of mosaics. Officially called the Church of the Resurrection of Christ, its far more striking colloquial name references the assassination attempt on Tsar Alexander II here in 1881.

★ **Russian Museum** MUSEUM

(Русский музей; Map p92; ☎812-595 4248; www.rusmuseum.ru; Inzhenernaya ul 4; adult/student ₽450/200; ⏲10am-8pm Mon, 10am-6pm Wed & Fri-Sun, 1-9pm Thu; Ⓜ Nevsky Prospekt) Focusing solely on Russian art, from ancient church icons to 20th-century paintings, the Russian Museum's collection is magnificent and can easily be viewed in half a day or less. The collection includes works by Karl Bryullov, Alexander Ivanov, Nicholas Ghe, Ilya Repin, Natalya Goncharova, Kazimir Malevich and Kuzma Petrov-Vodkin, among many others, and the masterpieces keep on coming as you tour the beautiful Carlo Rossi–designed Mikhailovsky Palace and its attached wings.

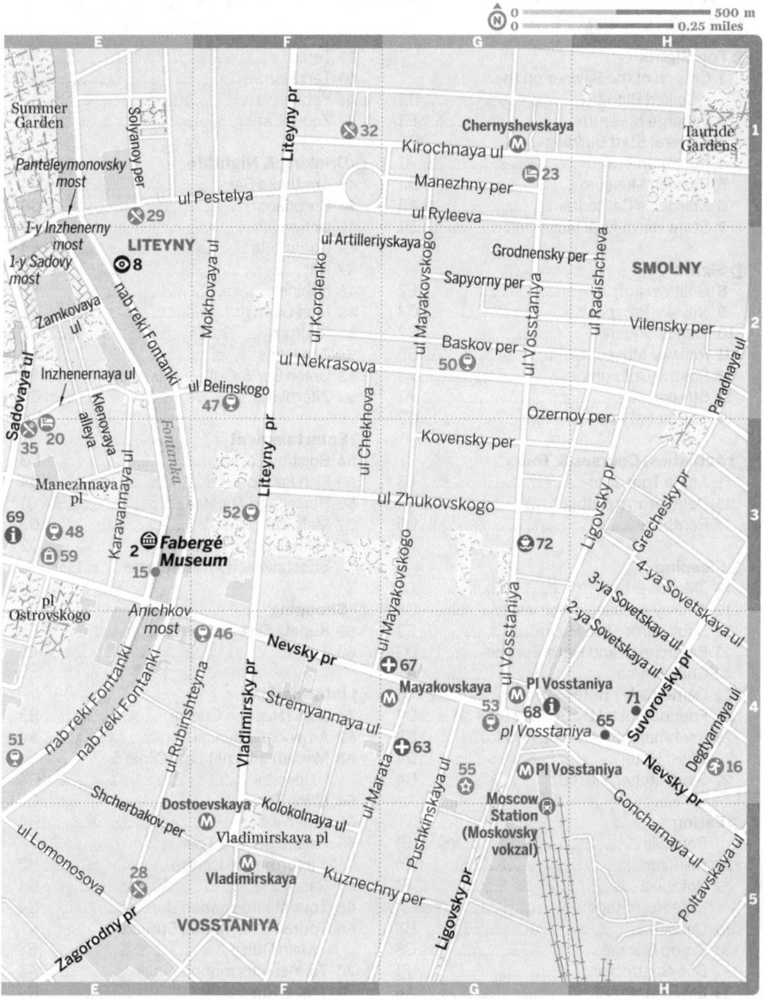

★ St Isaac's Cathedral MUSEUM

(Исаакиевский собор; Map p92; ☎812-315 9732; www.cathedral.ru; Isaakievskaya pl; cathedral adult/student ₽250/150, colonnade ₽150; ⏲cathedral 10.30am-10.30pm Thu-Tue May-Sep, to 6pm Oct-Apr, colonnade 10.30am-10.30pm May-Oct, to 6pm Nov-Apr; Ⓜ Admiralteyskaya) The golden dome of St Isaac's Cathedral dominates the St Petersburg skyline. Its obscenely lavish interior is open as a museum, although services are held in the cathedral throughout the year. Most people bypass the museum to climb the 262 steps to the *kolonnada* (colonnade) around the drum of the dome, providing superb city views.

★ Fabergé Museum MUSEUM

(Музей Фаберже; Map p92; ☎812-333 2655; http://fabergemuseum.ru; nab reki Fontanki 21; ₽450, incl tour ₽600; ⏲10am-8.45pm Sat-Thu; Ⓜ Gostiny Dvor) The magnificently restored Shuvalovsky Palace is home to the world's largest collection of pieces manufactured by the jeweller Peter Carl Fabergé (including nine imperial Easter eggs) and fellow master craftspeople of pre-revolutionary Russia.

Historic Centre

Top Sights
1 Church of the Saviour on the Spilled Blood ... D2
2 Fabergé Museum ... E3
3 General Staff Building ... C2
4 Kunstkamera ... A1
5 Russian Museum ... D2
6 St Isaac's Cathedral ... A3
7 State Hermitage Museum ... B1

Sights
8 Golitsyn Loft ... E2
9 Nevsky Prospekt ... D3
10 Palace Square ... B2
11 Railway Museum ... B5
12 Rostral Columns ... A1
13 Strelka ... A1
14 Triumphal Arch ... C2

Activities, Courses & Tours
15 Anglo Tourismo ... E3
16 Degtyarniye Baths ... H4
17 Rentbike ... C5

Sleeping
18 3MostA ... D1
19 Andrey & Sasha's Homestay ... C4
20 Baby Lemonade Hostel ... E3
21 Belmond Grand Hotel Europe ... D3
22 Chao Mama ... A5
23 Demetra Art Hotel ... G1
24 Friends Hostel by Gostiny Dvor ... D4
25 Rachmaninov Antique Hotel ... C3
26 Rossi Hotel ... D4
27 Soul Kitchen Hostel ... B4

Eating
Banshiki ... (see 16)
28 Bekitzer ... E5
29 Botanika ... E1
Cafe Hermitage ... (see 3)
30 Cococo ... B3
31 Co-op Garage ... C5
32 Duo Gastrobar ... F1
33 EM Restaurant ... A4
34 Gogol ... B3
35 Gräs x Madbaren ... E3
36 Idiot ... A4
Julia Child Bistro ... (see 22)
37 Marketplace ... C3
38 Severyanin ... B5
39 Teplo ... A4
40 Terrassa ... C3
41 Yat ... C2
42 Zoom Café ... C4

Drinking & Nightlife
43 Apotheke Bar ... D4
44 Borodabar ... C4
45 Coffee 22 ... C4
46 Commode ... F4
47 Hat ... F2
48 Kabinet ... E3
49 Mod Club ... D2
50 Redrum ... G2
51 Top Hops ... E4
52 Union Bar & Grill ... F3
53 Ziferblat ... G4

Entertainment
54 Bolshoy Zal ... D3
55 Fish Fabrique ... G4
56 Hermitage Theatre ... C1
57 Maly Zal ... D3
58 Mikhailovsky Theatre ... D2
Shostakovich Philharmonia ... (see 54)

Shopping
59 Kupetz Eliseevs ... E3
60 Taiga ... C1

Information
61 36.6 (Historic Centre) ... B3
62 American Medical Clinic ... A4
63 Medem International Clinic & Hospital ... G4
64 Milor-Tur ... C5
65 Ost-West ... H4
66 Palace Square Tourist Information Centre ... B2
67 Raduga ... G4
68 Tourist Information Bureau ... G4
69 Tourist Information Bureau Main Office ... E3
70 Tourist Information Kiosk ... A3
71 Travel Russia ... H4

Transport
72 Ferry Centre ... G3
73 Peterhof Express ... A2
74 Train Tickets Centre ... C3

Nevsky Prospekt STREET

(Map p92) Nevsky Prospekt is Russia's most famous street, running 4km from the Admiralty to Alexander Nevsky Monastery, from which it takes its name. The inner 2.5km to Moskovsky vokzal is the city's shopping centre and focus of its entertainment and street life. Walking Nevsky is an essential St Petersburg experience. If you're here on a holiday evening (such as 27 May – City Day), the sight of thousands of people pouring like a stream down its middle is one you'll not forget.

Petrograd & Vyborg Sides

★ **Peter & Paul Fortress** FORTRESS
(Петропавловская крепость; Map p96; www.spbmuseum.ru; grounds free, SS Peter & Paul Cathedral adult/child ₽450/250, combined ticket for 5 exhibitions ₽600/350; grounds 8.30am-8pm, exhibitions 11am-6pm Mon & Thu-Sun, 10am-5pm Tue; M Gorkovskaya) Housing a cathedral where the Romanovs are buried, a former prison and various exhibitions, this large defensive fortress on Zayachy Island is the kernel from which St Petersburg grew into the city it is today. History buffs will love it and everyone will swoon at the panoramic views from atop the fortress walls, at the foot of which lies a sandy riverside beach, a prime spot for sunbathing.

Museum of Political History MUSEUM
(Музей политической истории России; Map p96; 812-313 6163; www.polithistory.ru; ul Kuybysheva 4; adult/child ₽200/free, audio guide ₽200; 10am-6pm Sat-Tue, 10am-8pm Wed & Fri, closed Thu; M Gorkovskaya) The elegant Style Moderne Kshesinskaya Palace (1904) is a highly appropriate location for this excellent museum – one of the city's best – covering Russian politics in scrupulous detail up to contemporary times. The palace, previously the home of Mathilda Kshesinskaya, famous ballet dancer and one-time lover of Nicholas II in his pre-tsar days, was briefly the headquarters of the Bolsheviks, and Lenin often gave speeches from the balcony.

Sennaya & Kolomna

★ **Yusupov Palace** PALACE
(Юсуповский дворец; Map p96; 8-921-970 3038; www.yusupov-palace.ru; nab reki Moyki 94; adult/student incl audio guide ₽700/500, Rasputin tour ₽350/250; 11am-6pm; M Sadovaya) This spectacular palace on the Moyka River has some of the best 19th-century interiors in the city, in addition to a fascinating and gruesome history. The palace's last owner was the eccentric Prince Felix Yusupov, a high-society darling and at one time the richest man in Russia. Most notoriously, the palace is the place where Grigory Rasputin was murdered in 1916, and the basement where this now infamous plot unravelled can be visited as part of a guided tour.

★ **New Holland** ISLAND
(Новая Голландия; Map p96; www.newhollandsp.ru; nab Admiralteyskogo kanala; 9am-10pm Mon-Thu, to 11pm Fri-Sun; M Sadovaya) This triangular island was closed for the most part of the last three centuries, and has opened to the public in dazzling fashion. There's plenty going on here, with hundreds of events happening throughout the year. There are summertime concerts, art exhibitions, yoga classes and film screenings, plus restaurants, cafes and shops. You can also come to enjoy a bit of quiet on the grass – or on one of the pontoons floating in the pond.

Smolny & Vosstaniya

★ **Alexander Nevsky Monastery** MONASTERY
(Александро-Невская лавра; Map p96; www.lavra.spb.ru; Nevsky pr 179/2; cemetery ₽400, pantheon ₽150; grounds 6am-11pm summer, 8am-9pm winter, churches 6am-9pm, cemeteries 9.30am-6pm summer, 11am-4pm winter, pantheon 11am-5pm Tue, Wed & Fri-Sun; M Ploshchad Aleksandra Nevskogo) The Alexander Nevsky Monastery – named for the patron saint of St Petersburg – is the city's most ancient and eminent monastery. Peter the Great made a mistake when he founded the monastery on this spot at the far end of Nevsky pr, thinking wrongly that it was the site where Alexander of Novgorod had beaten the Swedes in 1240. Nonetheless, in 1797 the monastery became a *lavra,* the most senior grade of Russian Orthodox monasteries.

Vasilyevsky Island

★ **Erarta Museum of Contemporary Art** MUSEUM
(Музей современного искусства Эрарта; 812-324 0809; www.erarta.com; 29-ya Liniya 2; adult/under 21yr ₽500/350; 10am-10pm Wed-Mon; M Vasileostrovskaya) Erarta's superb hoard of 2300 pieces of Russian contemporary art trumps its somewhat far-flung location. Housed in an ingeniously converted neoclassical Stalinist building, the museum is spread over five floors, with the main galleries focused on the permanent collection. There are also installation spaces, plenty of temporary exhibitions, occasional shows, plus a good restaurant and gift shop.

Strelka LANDMARK
(Map p92; Birzhevaya pl; M Vasileostrovskaya) This eastern tip of Vasilyevsky Island is where Peter the Great wanted his new city's administrative and intellectual centre to be. In fact, it became the focus of the city's maritime trade, symbolised by the colonnaded Customs

Central St Petersburg

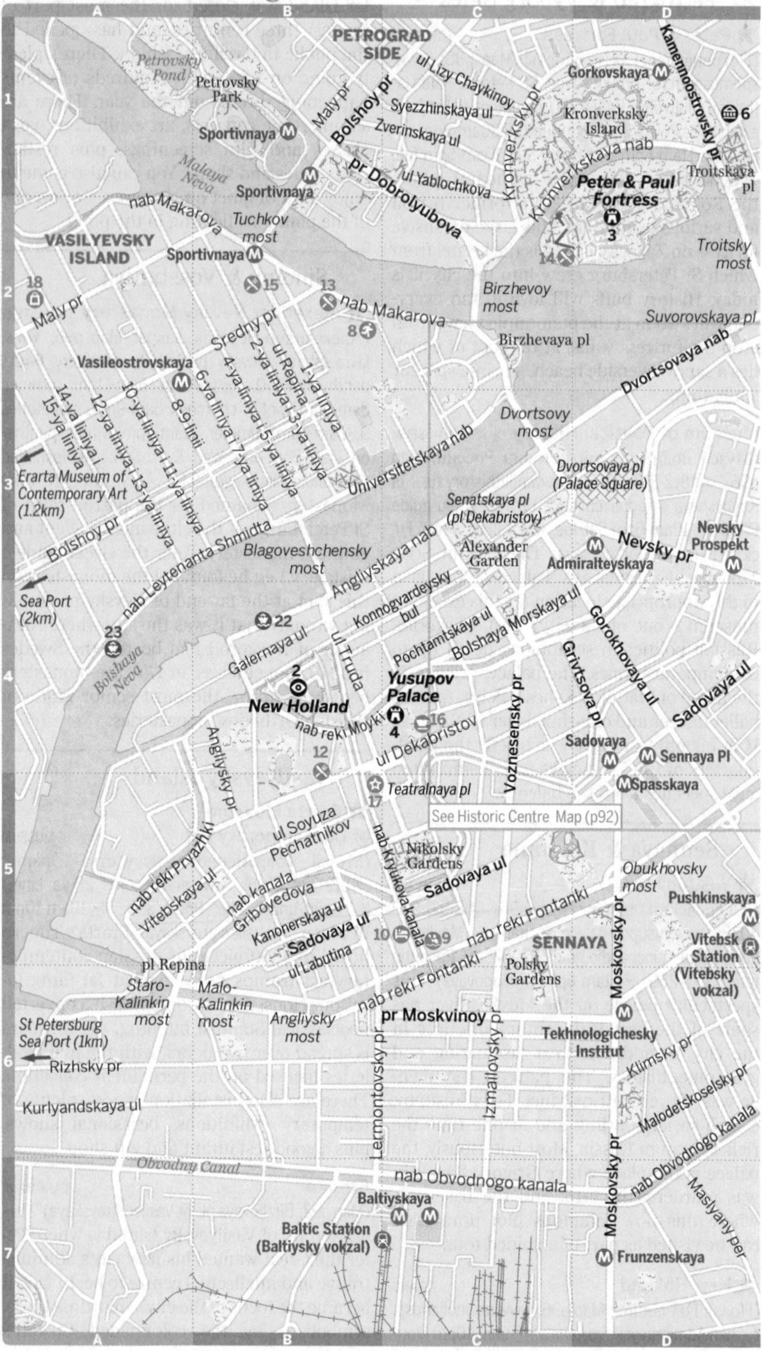

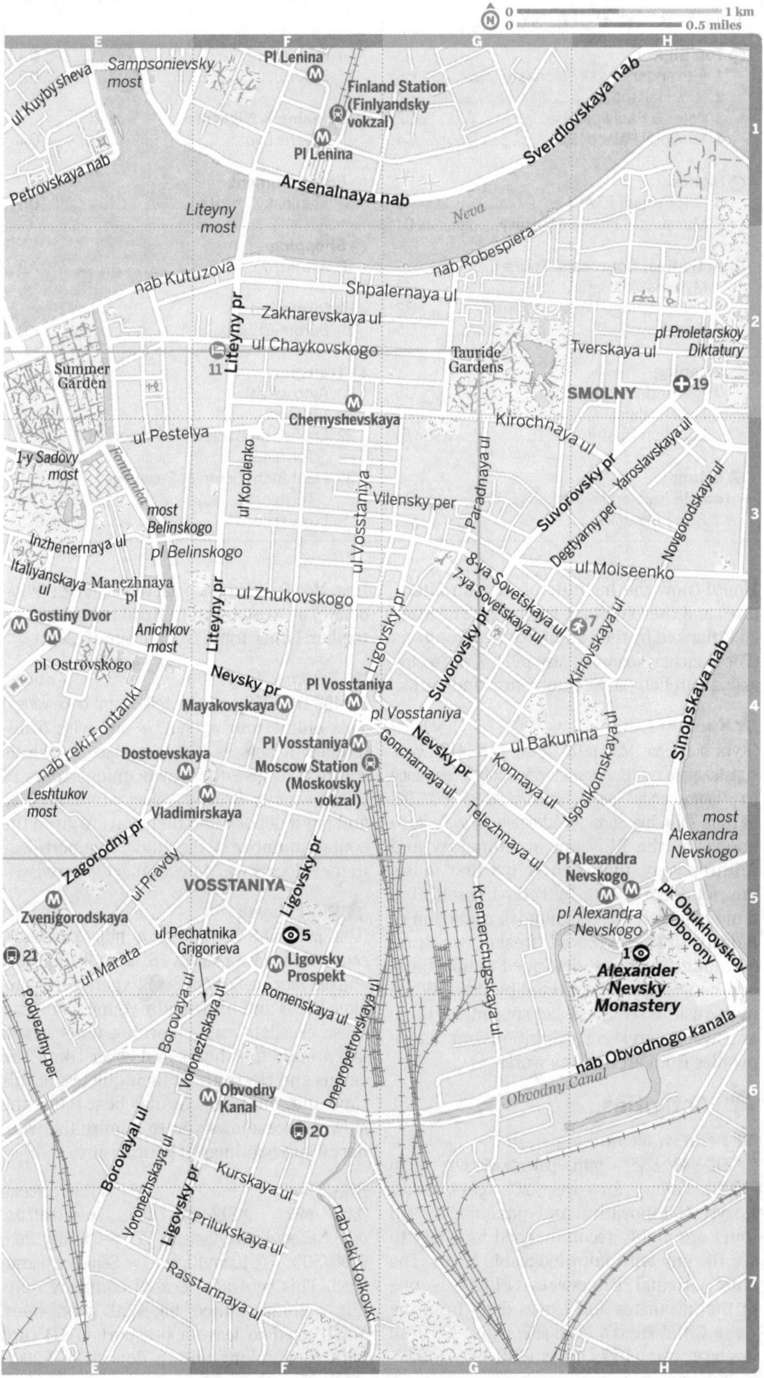

0 1 km
0 0.5 miles
E
F
G
H
1
2
3
4
5
6
7
ul Kuybysheva
Sampsonievsky most
Pl Lenina
Finland Station (Finlyandsky vokzal)
Pl Lenina
Sverdlovskaya nab
Petrovskaya nab
Arsenalnaya nab
Liteyny most
Neva
nab Robespiera
nab Kutuzova
Shpalernaya ul
Zakharevskaya ul
Liteyny pr
ul Chaykovskogo
11
Tauride Gardens
Tverskaya ul
pl Proletarskoy Diktatury
Summer Garden
SMOLNY
19
Chernyshevskaya
ul Pestelya
Kirochnaya ul
1-y Sadovy most
Fontanka
ul Korolenko
ul Vosstaniya
Vilensky per
Paradnaya ul
Suvorovsky pr
Yaroslavskaya ul
Novgorodskaya ul
most Belinskogo
Degtyarny per
Inzhenernaya ul
pl Belinskogo
8-ya Sovetskaya ul
7-ya Sovetskaya ul
ul Moiseenko
Italiyanskaya ul
Manezhnaya pl
Liteyny pr
ul Zhukovskogo
Ligovsky pr
Gostiny Dvor
7
Kirlovskaya ul
Anichkov most
Suvorovsky pr
pl Ostrovskogo
Nevsky pr
Pl Vosstaniya
Sinopskaya nab
Mayakovskaya
pl Vosstaniya
nab reki Fontanki
Pl Vosstaniya
Nevsky pr
ul Bakunina
Goncharnaya ul
Dostoevskaya
Moscow Station (Moskovsky vokzal)
Konnaya ul
Ispolkomskaya ul
Leshtukov most
Vladimirskaya
Telezhnaya ul
most Alexandra Nevskogo
Zagorodny pr
ul Pravdy
Pl Alexandra Nevskogo
VOSSTANIYA
Ligovsky pr
Kremenchugskaya ul
pr Obukhovskoy Oborony
Zvenigorodskaya
pl Alexandra Nevskogo
ul Pechatnika Grigorieva
5
21
1
Alexander Nevsky Monastery
ul Marata
Ligovsky Prospekt
Podyezdny per
Borovaya ul
Voronezhskaya ul
Romenskaya ul
Dnepropetrovskaya ul
nab Obvodnogo kanala
Obvodny Kanal
Obvodny Canal
Borovayal ul
20
Voronezhskaya ul
Kurskaya ul
Ligovsky pr
Prilukskaya ul
nab reki Volkovki
Rasstannaya ul

Central St Petersburg

Top Sights
1 Alexander Nevsky Monastery H5
2 New Holland B4
3 Peter & Paul Fortress D2
4 Yusupov Palace C4

Sights
5 Loft Project ETAGI F5
6 Museum of Political History D1

Activities, Courses & Tours
7 Mytninskiye Bani H4
8 Palace Bridge Wellness Club B2
9 Piter Kayak C5

Sleeping
10 Alexander House C5
11 Hotel Indigo F2
Location Hostel .... (see 5)

Eating
12 1818 Kafe and Bikes B4
13 Buter Brodsky B2
14 Koryushka C2
15 Stolle B2

Drinking & Nightlife
16 Solaris Lab C4

Entertainment
17 Mariinsky Theatre B5

Shopping
18 Artmuza A2

Information
19 Euromed H2

Transport
20 Avtovokzal F6
21 Ecolines E5
22 English Embankment Passenger Terminal B4
23 Lieutenant Schmidt Passenger Terminal A4
Lux Express .... (see 20)

House (now the Institute of Russian Literature) and the Old Stock Exchange. The Strelka is flanked by the pair of **Rostral Columns** (Ростральная колонна; Map p92; M Vasileostrovskaya), archetypal St Petersburg landmarks.

★Kunstkamera MUSEUM
(Кунсткамера; Map p92; ☎812-328 1412; www.kunstkamera.ru; Universitetskaya nab 3, entrance on Tamozhenny per; adult/child ₽300/100; ⊙11am-7pm Tue-Sun; M Admiralteyskaya) Also known as the Museum of Ethnology and Anthropology, this is the city's first museum, founded in 1714 by Peter himself. It is famous largely for its ghoulish collection of monstrosities, preserved 'freaks', two-headed mutant foetuses, deformed animals and odd body parts, all collected by Peter. While most rush to see these sad specimens, there are also interesting exhibitions on native peoples from around the world.

Activities

★Peterswalk Walking Tours WALKING
(☎812-943 1229; http://peterswalk.com; from ₽1320) Going for over 20 years, Peter Kozyrev's innovative and passionately led tours are highly recommended as a way to see the city with knowledgeable locals. The daily Original Peterswalk (₽1320) is one of the favourites and leaves daily from the **Julia Child Bistro** (Map p92; ☎812-929 0797; Grazhdanskaya ul 27; mains ₽310-490; ⊙9am-11pm Mon-Fri, from 10am Sat & Sun; 📶📝; M Sadovaya) at 10.30am from April to end of September. Other tours from around ₽2000.

★Sputnik Tours WALKING
(☎499-110 5266; www.sputnik8.com; price varies) This online tour agency is one with a difference: it acts as a marketplace for locals wanting to give their own unique tours of their own city. Browse, select a tour, register and pay a deposit and then you are given the contact number of the guide. A superb way to meet locals you'd never meet otherwise.

★Piter Kayak KAYAKING
(Map p96; ☎8-921-435 9457; http://piterkayak.com; nab Kryukova kanala 26; tours ₽1700-2500; ⊙tours 7am Tue-Sun Apr-Sep) Experienced kayaker Denis and his friendly young team lead these excellent early morning tours which last around four hours and cover 11km. The canals and rivers are at their quietest at this time and, unlike on regular boat tours, the slower pace allows you to admire the wonderful surroundings at your leisure.

Rentbike CYCLING
(Map p92; ☎812-981 0155; www.rentbike.org; Naberezhnaya fontanki 77; per hr/day from ₽100/500; ⊙10am-10pm; M Sennaya Ploshchad) This centrally located company rents out well-maintained bikes at good rates. You'll need to leave a passport or ID card with them, along with a deposit of ₽2000

per bike. The place is in a courtyard off Naberezhnaya fontanki.

★Palace Bridge Wellness Club SPA
(Map p96; ☎812-335 2214; www.pbwellnessclub.ru; Birzhevoy per 4a; before/after 4pm Mon-Fri ₽990/1390, 4hr/whole day Sat & Sun ₽1790/1990, children 3-12yr half-price, children under 3yr free; ⊙gym, sauna & pool 7am-11pm, spa 10am-10pm; Ⓜ Sportivnaya) Attached to the Sokos Hotel Palace Bridge, there's a good gym and a variety of spa treatments here, but the highlights are the giant swimming pool (with jet fountains to massage tired backs) and the many styles of sauna (including Finnish and Russian) in which to steam away all your stresses.

It's free for hotel guests. It's a mixed-sex spa, so wear your bathing costume; towels and slippers can be rented.

Degtyarniye Baths BATHHOUSE
(Дегтярные Бани; Map p92; ☎812-985 1983; www.d1a.ru; Degtyarnaya ul 1a; per hr ₽400-750, private banya ₽4500-17,500; ⊙8.30am-10pm; Ⓜ Ploshchad Vosstaniya) These modern baths are divided up into men's and women's sections, or you can book private unisex *bani* (hot baths) of varying degrees of luxury (these accommodate up to 14 people). Prices are cheaper before 1pm on weekdays. Minimum charge of two hours.

Mytninskiye Bani BATHHOUSE
(Мытнинские бани; Map p96; www.mybanya.spb.ru; ul Mytninskaya 17-19; per hr ₽200-350; ⊙8am-10pm Fri-Tue; Ⓜ Ploshchad Vosstaniya) Unique in the city, Mytninskiye Bani is heated by a wood furnace, just like the log-cabin bathhouses that are still found in the Russian countryside. It's actually the oldest communal *banya* (hot bath) in the city, and in addition to a *parilka* (steam room) and plunge pool, the private 'lux' *banya* (₽1000 to ₽2000 per hour) includes a swanky lounge area with leather furniture and a pool table.

★Anglo Tourismo BOATING
(Map p92; ☎8-921-989 4722; http://anglotourismo.com; 27 nab reki Fontanki; 1hr cruise adult/student ₽1900/900; Ⓜ Gostiny Dvor) There's a huge number of companies offering cruises all over the Historic Heart, all with similar prices and itineraries. Anglo Tourismo, however, is the only operator to run tours with commentary in English. Between May and September the schedule runs every 1½ hours between 11am and 6.30pm. From 1 June to 31 August there are also additional night cruises.

Festivals & Events

The city's biggest event is the **Stars of the White Nights Festival** (www.mariinsky.ru; ⊙late May–mid-Jul), which includes all kinds of arts events and performances across the city throughout June and into July, with the Mariinsky Theatre taking the lead. The climax is **Scarlet Sails** (Алые паруса; http://parusaspb.ru; ⊙Jun) when massed crowds line the banks of the Neva for a spectacular fireworks display and to see a magnificent red-sail Swedish frigate float by.

Sleeping

Historic Heart

★Baby Lemonade Hostel HOSTEL $
(Map p92; ☎812-570 7943; http://babylemonade.epoquehostels.com; Inzhenernaya ul 7; dm/d with shared bathroom from ₽600/2500, d from ₽3800; @📶; Ⓜ Gostiny Dvor) The owner of Baby Lemonade is crazy about the 1960s and it shows in the pop-art, psychedelic design of this friendly, fun hostel with two pleasant, large dorms and a great kitchen and living room. However, it's worth splashing out for the boutique-hotel-worthy private rooms that are in a separate flat with great rooftop views.

★Friends Hostel by Gostiny Dvor HOTEL $$
(Map p92; ☎812-740 4720; www.en.friendsplace.ru/druzya-na-lomonosova; ul Lomonosova 3; r from ₽5200; @📶; Ⓜ Gostiny Dvor) Sharing the top floor of a renovated historic building with a budget hotel, this is one of the best branches of the Friends chain. There are no dorms here and all the rooms have attached bathrooms, but the same cosy, quirky decorative charm is in place – complete with cuddly toys and flowery print curtains and linens.

★Rachmaninov Antique Hotel BOUTIQUE HOTEL $$
(Map p92; ☎812-327 7466; www.hotelrachmaninov.com; Kazanskaya ul 5; s/d from ₽6300/7500; @📶; Ⓜ Nevsky Prospekt) The long-established Rachmaninov still feels like a secret place for those in the know. Perfectly located and run by friendly staff, it's pleasantly old world, with hardwood floors and attractive Russian furnishings, particularly in the breakfast salon, which has a grand piano.

DON'T MISS

RAILWAY MUSEUM

A must for train fans is the **Railway Museum** (Музей железнодорожного транспорта; Map p92; www.cmzt.narod.ru; Sadovaya ul 50; adult/student Mon-Fri ₽300/150, Sat & Sun ₽400/200; ⌚10.30am-5.30pm; Ⓜ Sadovaya). It houses a collection of scale locomotives and model railway bridges, often made by the engineers who built the real ones. The oldest such collection in the world, the museum dates to 1809, 28 years before Russia had its first working train!

Come on weekends for the free Russian-language tours of the museum (held at 11am and 2pm), when guides raise little drawbridges, ring station bells and operate mechanized trains along various tracks in the galleries.

Look out for the fantastic map of Russia hanging above the main museum staircase showing all the train lines in the country, which almost makes up for the total lack of signage in English.

3MostA HOTEL $$
(Map p92; ☎812-611 1188; www.3mosta.com; nab reki Moyki 3a; s/d from ₽5000/9000; ❄📶; Ⓜ Nevsky Prospekt) Near three bridges over the Moyka River, this 26-room property is surprisingly uncramped given its wonderful location. Even the standard rooms are of a good size, with tasteful furniture, minibars and TVs. Some rooms have great views across to the Church of the Saviour on the Spilled Blood, and all guests have access to the roof for the panoramic experience.

★**Belmond Grand Hotel Europe** HERITAGE HOTEL $$$
(Map p92; ☎812-329 6000; www.belmond.com/grand-hotel-europe-st-petersburg; Mikhailovskaya ul 1/7; s/d from ₽26,500/31,270; ❄@📶🏊; Ⓜ Nevsky Prospekt) Since 1830, when Carlo Rossi united three adjacent buildings with the grandiose facade we see today, little has been allowed to change in this heritage building. No two rooms are the same at this iconic hotel, but most are spacious and elegant. It's worth paying extra for the terrace rooms, which afford spectacular views across the city's rooftops.

★**Rossi Hotel** BOUTIQUE HOTEL $$$
(Map p92; ☎812-635 6333; www.rossihotels.com; nab reki Fontanki 55; s/d/ste from ₽9740/9830/15,230; ❄@📶; Ⓜ Gostiny Dvor) Occupying a beautifully restored building on one of St Petersburg's prettiest squares, the Rossi's 65 rooms are all designed differently, but their brightness and moulded ceilings are uniform. Antique beds, super-sleek bathrooms, exposed brick walls and lots of cool designer touches create a great blend of old and new.

Sennaya & Kolomna

★**Soul Kitchen Hostel** HOSTEL $
(Map p92; ☎8-965-816 3470; www.soulkitchenhostel.com; nab reki Moyki 62/2, apt 9, Sennaya; dm ₽1500-2400, d ₽5700-9000; @📶; Ⓜ Admiralteyskaya) Soul Kitchen blends boho hipness and boutique-hotel comfort, scoring perfect 10s in many key categories: private rooms (chic), dorm beds (double-width with privacy-protecting curtains), common areas and kitchen (all beautifully designed). The lounge is a fine place to hang out, with a record player, a big screen projector (for movie nights) and an artful design.

★**Andrey & Sasha's Homestay** APARTMENT $$
(Map p92; ☎8-921-409 6701, 812-315 3330; asamatuga@mail.ru; nab kanala Griboyedova 51, Sennaya; r ₽5800-7300; 📶; Ⓜ Sadovaya) Energetic Italophiles Andrey and Sasha extend the warmest of welcomes to travellers lucky enough to rent out one of their three apartments (by the room or in its entirety). All are centrally located and eclectically decorated with lots of designer touches and an eye for beautiful furniture, tiles and mirrors. Bathrooms are shared, as are kitchen facilities.

★**Alexander House** BOUTIQUE HOTEL $$
(Map p96; ☎812-334 3540; www.a-house.ru; nab kanala Kryukova 27, Kolomna; s/d/apt incl breakfast from ₽9000/12,200/14,600; 🚭❄📶; Ⓜ Sadovaya) This historic building opposite the Nikolsky Cathedral dates back to 1826, and contains a beautifully designed guesthouse. Each of the 14 spacious rooms are named after a city (Kyoto, Marrakesh, Venice) and contain artwork and crafts from there. Beautifully polished floors, warm colours and beamed ceilings are common throughout. There's also a lovely fireplace-warmed lounge and a vine-laden courtyard, plus a guests-only restaurant.

Chao Mama HOTEL $$

(Map p92; ☎812-570 0444; www.chaomama.ru; Grazhdanskaya ul 27; d ₽3600-7500; ❄📶; Ⓜ Sadovaya) In an excellent location, Chao Mama has nine stylish rooms, each boasting a unique design, and offers excellent value for money. The best rooms have small kitchenettes and ample natural light, while the 54-sq-metre Gagarin Room has two balconies and sleeps up to four. For something a little cosier, opt for the artistically designed Jacqueline, which also boasts a fireplace.

Smolny & Vosstaniya

Location Hostel HOSTEL $

(Map p96; ☎812-329 1274; http://en.location-hostel.ru; Ligovsky pr 74, Vosstaniya; dm/r from ₽700/1600, design r ₽9000; 📶; Ⓜ Ligovsky Prospekt) Come and stay in St Petersburg's coolest art gallery and cultural space – the 3rd floor of Loft Project ETAGI is given over to this super-friendly hostel. Some of the dorms here are enormous (one has 20 beds in it!), but the facilities are spotless, and include washing machines and a small kitchen.

Hotel Indigo HOTEL $$

(Map p96; ☎812-454 5577; www.indigospb.com; ul Chaykovskogo 17, Smolny; r from ₽10,700; ❄@📶; Ⓜ Chernyshevskaya) A total overhaul of the original building – a pre-revolutionary hotel in its day – paved the way for the sleek and stylish Hotel Indigo, a big step up from many St Petersburg offerings with its excellent service and handsomely designed guest rooms. The incredible atrium makes even the interior-facing rooms light filled, and touches such as rain showers and free minibars in rooms are also very welcome.

Demetra Art Hotel BOUTIQUE HOTEL $$$

(Map p92; ☎812-640 0408; www.demetra-art-hotel.com; ul Vosstaniya 44; r ₽16,000-24,000, ste ₽36,000; ❄📶; Ⓜ Chernyshevskaya) In a grand art nouveau building dating from 1913, the Demetra Art Hotel has plush rooms with oak flooring, richly patterned drapes and duvets, and touches of artwork throughout (reproductions of works from the celebrated Erata Museum). Some rooms can be on the small side, though the top-notch service, stylish bar and restaurant, and great location add to the appeal.

Eating

Historic Heart

★ **Zoom Café** EUROPEAN $

(Map p92; ☎812-612 1329; www.cafezoom.ru; Gorokhovaya ul 22; mains ₽350-550; ⌚9am-midnight Mon-Fri, from 11am Sat, from 1pm Sun; 📶; Ⓜ Nevsky Prospekt) A perennially popular cafe (expect to wait for a table at peak times) with a cosy feel and an interesting menu, ranging from Japanese-style chicken in teriyaki sauce to potato pancakes with salmon and cream cheese. Well-stocked bookshelves, a range of board games and adorable cuddly toys (each with its own name) encourage lingering.

Cafe Hermitage INTERNATIONAL $

(Кафе Эрмитаж; Map p92; ☎812-703 7528; General Staff Bldg, 8 Dvortsovaya pl; mains ₽250-450; ⌚11am-11pm Tue, Thu, Sat & Sun, until 8pm Wed & Fri; Ⓜ Admiralteyskaya) When the east wing of the General Staff Building was turned into a new branch of the Hermitage, they at least made sure it had a decent place to eat (unlike in the Winter Palace). It's a self-serve cafe for drinks, appealing sandwiches and hot dishes and can be visited whether or not you go into the museum itself.

Marketplace RUSSIAN, INTERNATIONAL $

(Map p92; http://market-place.me; Nevsky pr 24; mains ₽200-300; ⌚8am-5.30am; 📶; Ⓜ Nevsky Prospekt) The most central branch of this minichain that brings a high-class polish to the self-serve canteen concept, with many dishes cooked freshly on the spot to order. The hip design of the multilevel space is very appealing, making this a great spot to linger, especially if you indulge in one of the desserts or cocktails served on the 1st floor.

★ **Gräs x Madbaren** FUSION $$

(Map p92; ☎812-928 1818; http://grasmadbaren.com; ul Inzhenernaya 7; mains ₽420-550, tasting menu ₽2500; ⌚1-11pm Sun-Thu, until 1am Fri & Sat; 📶; Ⓜ Gostiny Dvor) Anton Abrezov is the talented exec chef behind this Scandi-cool meets Russian locavore restaurant where you can sample dishes such as a delicious corned beef salad with black garlic and pickled vegetables or an upmarket twist on ramen noodles with succulent roast pork. The connected cocktail bar Madbaren is equally inventive, offering libations such as Siberian Penicillin (horseradish vodka, pollen syrup and rhubarb).

★Yat RUSSIAN $$

(Ять; Map p92; 812-957 0023; www.eatinyat.com; nab reki Moyki 16; mains ₽370-750; 11am-11pm; ; M Admiralteyskaya) Perfectly placed for eating near the Hermitage, this country-cottage-style restaurant has a very appealing menu of traditional dishes, presented with aplomb. The *shchi* (cabbage-based soup) is excellent, and there is also a tempting range of flavoured vodkas. There's a fab kids area with pet rabbits for them to feed.

★Gogol RUSSIAN $$

(Гоголь; Map p92; 812-312 6097; http://restaurant-gogol.ru; Malaya Morskaya ul 8; mains ₽350-690; 9am-3am; ; M Admiralteyskaya) Like its sibling restaurant Chekov, Gogol whisks diners back to the genteel days of pre-revolutionary Russian home dining. The menu comes in a novel, with chapters for each of the traditional courses. Salads, soups, dumplings and classics such as chicken Kiev are all very well done and served in charming, small dining rooms.

Terrassa EUROPEAN $$

(Map p92; 812-640 1616; http://ginza.ru/spb/restaurant/terrassa; Kazanskaya ul 3a; mains ₽600-1000; 11am-1am, from noon Sat & Sun; ; M Nevsky Prospekt) Sleek and buzzing, Terrassa is centred on its namesake terrace, which boasts unbelievable views (open only in warmer months). Inside you can watch the chefs, busy in the open kitchen, preparing fresh fusion cuisine that exhibits influences from Italy, Asia and beyond.

★Cococo RUSSIAN $$$

(Map p92; 812-418 2060; www.kokoko.spb.ru; Voznesensky pr 6; mains ₽650-1300; 7-11am & 2pm-1am; ; M Admiralteyskaya) Cococo has charmed locals with its inventive approach to contemporary Russian cuisine. Your food is likely to arrive disguised as, say, a small bird's egg, a can of peas or a broken flowerpot – all rather gimmicky, theatrical and fun. The best way to sample what it does is with its tasting menu (₽2900). Bookings are advised.

Petrograd & Vyborg Sides

Koryushka RUSSIAN, GEORGIAN $$

(Корюшка; Map p96; 812-640 1616; www.ginza.ru/spb/restaurant/korushka; Petropavlovskaya krepost 3, Zayachy Island; mains ₽650-2400; noon-1am; ; M Gorkovskaya) Lightly battered and fried smelt *(koryushka)* is a St Petersburg speciality every April, but you can eat the small fish year-round at this relaxed, sophisticated restaurant beside the Peter & Paul Fortress. There are plenty of other very appealing Georgian dishes on the menu to supplement the stunning views across the Neva.

Sennaya & Kolomna

Co-op Garage PIZZA $

(Map p92; www.cooperativegarage.com; Gorokhovaya 47; pizzas ₽260-390; noon-midnight Sun-Thu, to 2am Fri & Sat;) Tucked into an unmarked courtyard off Gorokhovaya, this sprawling restaurant and drinking den is the go-to spot for creatively topped thin-crust pizzas and craft beers. The industrial setting draws a chatty crowd of tatted-up hipsters and style mavens, with a mostly rock soundtrack playing in the background. On warm days you can take a table in the courtyard.

1818 Kafe and Bikes INTERNATIONAL $

(Кафе и Велосипеды; Map p96; www.cafe1818.ru; ul Dekabristov 31; mains ₽240-420; 10am-11pm Mon-Fri, from 11am Sat & Sun; ; M Sadovaya) Combining a love of bicycles and street food from around the globe, Kafe and Bikes serves up delicious cooking amid upbeat grooves, exposed bulbs and those slate grey walls so prevalent in St Petersburg. *Shawarmas* (grilled meat and salad wrapped in flat bread), wok-fried buckwheat noodles with vegetables, pizzas, *khachapuri* (Georgian cheese bread) and *syrniki* (sweet cheese fritters) are all served up in a hurry by friendly staff.

★Severyanin RUSSIAN $$

(Северянин; Map p92; 8-921-951 6396; www.severyanin.me; Stolyarny per 18; mains ₽620-1300; noon-midnight; ; M Sennaya Ploshchad) An old-fashioned elegance prevails at Severyanin, one of the top choices for Russian cuisine near Sennaya pl. Amid vintage wallpaper, mirrored armoires and tasselled lampshades, you might feel like you've stepped back a few decades. Start off with the excellent mushroom soup or borsch (beetroot soup), before moving on to rabbit ragout in puff pastry or Baltic flounder with wine sauce.

WORTH A TRIP

PETERHOF

Hugging the Gulf of Finland, 29km west of St Petersburg, Peterhof was the palatial estate of Peter the Great. The **Grand Palace** (Большой дворец; www.peterhofmuseum.ru; ul Razvodnaya; adult/student ₽700/400, audio guide ₽600; 10.30am-6pm Tue-Sun, closed last Tue of month) and other buildings are surrounded by leafy gardens and a spectacular ensemble of gravity-powered fountains, the centrepiece of which is the **Grand Cascade** (11am-5pm Mon-Fri, to 6pm Sat & Sun May-Oct).

The lovely **Upper Garden** is free. Admission to the **Lower Park** (Нижний парк; www.peterhofmuseum.ru; adult/student May-Oct ₽750/400, Nov-Apr free; 9am-7pm) is payable at the cash booths on the jetty and outside the gates leading to the Grand Cascade.

To get here take *marshrutka* 300, 424 and 424A (₽80) from outside the Avtovo metro station, or *marshrutka* minibus 103 from outside Leninsky Prospekt station. Tell the driver you want to go *'vo dvaryéts'* ('to the palace') and you'll be let off near the main entrance to the Upper Garden, on Sankt-Peterburgsky pr.

Alternatively, take a train (₽60, 40 minutes) from Baltic Station (Baltiysky vokzal) to Novy Peterhof, from where you can walk (around 30 minutes), or take any bus except 357 to the fifth stop, which will take another 10 minutes.

From May to September, the **Peterhof Express** (Map p92; www.peterhof-express.com; single/return adult ₽800/1500, student ₽600/1000; 10am-6pm) hydrofoil departs from the jetty in front of the Admiralty every 30 minutes from 9am. The last hydrofoil leaves Peterhof at 7pm, and the trip takes 30 minutes.

★Teplo MODERN EUROPEAN $$
(Map p92; 812-570 1974; www.v-teple.ru; Bolshaya Morskaya ul 45; mains ₽360-940; 9am-midnight Mon-Fri, from 11am Sat & Sun; ; M Admiralteyskaya) This much-feted, eclectic and original restaurant has got it all just right. The venue itself is a lot of fun to nose around, with multiple small rooms, nooks and crannies. Service is friendly and fast (when it's not too busy) and the peppy, inventive Italian-leaning menu has something for everyone. Reservations are usually required, so call ahead.

Idiot RUSSIAN $$
(Map p92; 8-921-946 5173; www.idiot-spb.com/eng; nab reki Moyki 82; mains ₽300-1000, brunch ₽690; 11am-1am; ; M Sennaya Ploshchad) Something of an expat favourite, the Idiot is a charming place that has been serving up high-quality Russian fare for years now. The friendly basement location is all about atmosphere, relaxation and fun (encouraged by the complimentary vodka coming with each meal). You can't go wrong here, whether opting for bliny (wheat pancakes) with caviar, grilled trout or *pelmeni* (Russian-style ravioli) with mushrooms and sour cream.

EM Restaurant EUROPEAN $$$
(Map p92; 8-921-960 2177; http://emrestaurant.ru; nab reki Moyki 84; set menu ₽3500; 7-11pm Tue-Sun; ; M Admiralteyskaya) Bookings are essential for this superb restaurant where the chefs calmly prepare seven beautifully presented courses in an open kitchen. Be prepared for such exotic elements as reindeer, smoked perch, red cabbage sorbet and fois gras coloured with squid ink. Individual food preferences can be catered to and every Sunday they work their culinary magic on a vegan menu.

Smolny & Vosstaniya

★Duo Gastrobar FUSION $
(Map p92; 812-994 5443; www.duobar.ru; ul Kirochnaya 8a; mains ₽350-500; 1pm-midnight; M Chernyshevskaya) Boasting a minimalist Scandinavian design scheme, Duo Gastrobar has wowed diners with its outstanding cooking that showcases quality ingredients with global accents in delectable plates such as crab bruschetta, duck breast with smoked cheese and tomato, and rich French onion soup. There's an excellent wine list (over a dozen by the glass) as well.

Bekitzer ISRAELI $
(Бекицер; Map p92; 812-926 4342; www.facebook.com/bktzr; ul Rubinshteyna 40; mains ₽180-450; noon-6am Mon-Fri, from noon Sat & Sun; ; M Dostoyevskaya) Always crowded and spilling out into the street, this Israel-themed eatery and drinking den lures hip

and joyful people with its creative cocktails, Israeli Shiraz and the best falafel wraps this side of the Baltic Sea. Other culinary temptations include sabich salad (with eggplant, egg, hummus and tahini), appetiser spreads with baba ghanoush and pitas, and rather imaginative matzah pizzas.

Botanika VEGETARIAN $
(Ботаника; Map p92; ☎812-272 7091; www.cafebotanika.ru; ul Pestelya 7; mains ₽360-650; ⏱11am-midnight; 📶✍; Ⓜ Chernyshevskaya) This vegetarian charmer lives up to its green-minded name, with zesty fresh salads, vegie curries and ingredient-rich soups, plus a menu that takes in Russian, Indian and Italian dishes, all of which are handsomely executed. It's a friendly space, with plants and flower vases sprinkled about, and there's even a playroom and menu for the kids.

★ **Banshiki** RUSSIAN $$
(Банщики; Map p92; ☎8-921-941 1744; www.banshiki.spb.ru; Degtyanaya 1; mains ₽500-1100; ⏱11am-11pm; 📶; Ⓜ Pl Vosstaniya) Although it opened in 2017, Banshiki has already earned a sterling reputation for its excellent Russian cuisine, serving up a huge variety of nostalgic dishes with a contemporary touch. Everything is made in-house, from its refreshing *kvas* (fermented rye bread water) to dried meats and eight types of smoked fish. Don't overlook cherry *vareniki* (dumplings) with sour cream, oxtail ragout or the rich borsch.

Vasilyevsky Island

Stolle RUSSIAN $
(Map p96; www.stolle.ru; 1-ya liniya 50; pies from ₽90; ⏱8am-10pm; Ⓜ Vasileostrovskaya) This cosy pie shop and cafe was the first in this now nationwide chain. Aptly enough for a cafe that sells Saxon-style pies, it's located in the heart of St Petersburg's old German neighbourhood.

★ **Buter Brodsky** EUROPEAN $$
(Бутер Бродский; Map p96; ☎8-911-922 2606; https://vk.com/buterbrodskybar; nab Makarova 16; mains ₽260-780; ⏱noon-midnight; 📶; Ⓜ Sportivnaya) Shabby chic has never looked so good as it does at this cafe-bar dedicated to the poet Joseph Brodsky (the name is a pun on *buterbrod*, the Russian word for sandwich), a super-stylish addition to Vasilyevsky Island's eating and drinking scene. The menu runs from excellent *smørrebrød* (open sandwiches; from ₽260) to various set meals of salads and soup.

WORTH A TRIP

CREATIVE CLUSTERS

Occupying either old buildings or former industrial complexes across the city are a series of 'creative clusters', home to a vibrant mix of artists, creative businesses, boutiques, bars and restaurants. The following are the best ones:

Loft Project ETAGI (Лофт проект ЭТАЖИ; Map p96; ☎812-458 5005; www.loftprojectetagi.ru; Ligovsky pr 74; rooftop ₽100; ⏱9am-11pm; Ⓜ Ligovsky Prospekt) This five-floor former bakery includes exhibition spaces, eye-catching shops, a hostel, a bar and a cafe. In the yard, converted shipping containers house yet more pop-up clothing shops, record sellers, cafes and eateries whipping up affordable street food.

Taiga (Тайга; Map p92; http://taiga.space; Dvortsovaya nab 20; ⏱1-9pm; 📶; Ⓜ Admiralteyskaya) The warren of rooms in the ancient building near the Hermitage are worth exploring to find cool businesses ranging from a barber to fashion and books.

Golitsyn Loft (Map p92; nab reky Fontanki 20; Ⓜ Gostiny Dvor) Offers the usual mix of businesses as well as a hostel with capsule-style bunks. Enter via the archway into a large courtyard, which is spread with outdoor eating and drinking spots in the summer, then head up any of the stairwells into the five buildings for a bit of urban exploration.

Artmuza (Артмуза; Map p96; ☎812-313 4703; http://artmuza.spb.ru; 13-ya liniya 70-72; ⏱11am-10pm; Ⓜ Sportivnaya) With around 13,000 sq metres of space over several floors this is one of St Petersburg's largest creative clusters. Also come here to see exhibitions and theatre, and to enjoy the view from its large rooftop terrace (where there's also a cafe).

Drinking & Nightlife

Historic Heart

★Coffee 22 CAFE

(Map p92; https://vk.com/coffeeat22; ul Kazanskaya 22; ⏲8.30am-11pm Mon-Thu, until 1am Fri, 10am-1am Sat, 10am-11pm Sun; 📶; Ⓜ Nevsky Prospekt) In an area heavily saturated with hipster cafes, Coffee 22 – with its tattooed baristas and service staff, arty decor (piercing portrait of Joseph Brodsky, a rustic wall of dried mosses) and fashion-forward customers – is perhaps the hippest of them all. Listen to its DJs via its mixcloud.com/coffee22 soundtrack.

★Top Hops CRAFT BEER

(Map p92; ☎8-966-757 0116; www.tophops.ru; nab reki Fontanki 55; ⏲4pm-1am Mon-Thu, 2pm-2am Fri-Sun; 📶; Ⓜ Gostiny Dvor) One of the nicer craft-beer bars in town, this riverside space with friendly staff serves up a regularly changing menu of 20 beers on tap and scores more in bottles. The tasty Mexican snacks and food (go for nachos and chilli) go down exceptionally well while you sample your way through their range.

★Apotheke Bar COCKTAIL BAR

(Map p92; ☎812-337 1535; http://hatgroup.ru/apotheke-bar; ul Lomonosova 1; ⏲8pm-6am Tue-Sun; Ⓜ Gostiny Dvor) The antithesis of the nearby dive bars, Apotheke is a calm, cosy cocoon for cocktail connoisseurs. Its slogan is 'think what you drink', so there's no official menu but a friendly young bartender, most likely in a white jacket and sporting a hipster moustache, to make suggestions or simply surprise you.

★Kabinet COCKTAIL BAR

(Map p92; ☎8-911-921 1944; www.instagram.com/kabinet_bar; Malaya Sadovaya ul 8; ⏲8am-6pm; Ⓜ Gostiny Dvor) Bookings are essential for this speakeasy cocktail bar styled as a secret poker joint and hidden beneath the Grill Brothers burger restaurant. It's a fun, sophisticated place with the waiters dealing sets of cards to determine your choice of cocktail.

★Borodabar COCKTAIL BAR

(Map p92; ☎8-911-923 8940; www.facebook.com/Borodabar; Kazanskaya ul 11; ⏲5pm-2am Sun-Thu, to 6am Fri & Sat; 📶; Ⓜ Nevsky Prospekt) Boroda means beard in Russian, and sure enough you'll see plenty of facial hair and tattoos in this hipster cocktail hang-out. Never mind, as the mixologists really know their stuff – we can particularly recommend their smoked Old Fashioned, which is infused with tobacco smoke, and their colourful (and potent) range of shots.

★Mod Club BAR, CLUB

(Map p92; www.modclub.info; nab kanala Griboyedova 7; cover ₽150-350; ⏲6pm-6am; Ⓜ Nevsky Prospekt) A popular spot for students and other indie types who appreciate the fun and friendly atmosphere and a cool mix of music both live and spun. Laid-back and great fun, this is a solid choice for a night out.

Sennaya & Kolomna

Solaris Lab CAFE

(Map p96; www.facebook.com/solarislab11; per Pirogova 18, 4th fl; ⏲1pm-midnight; Ⓜ Sadovaya) Set inside a glass, semi-spherical dome, Solaris Lab has magnificent views over the russet rooftops of St Petersburg to the glittering dome of St Isaac's. It draws a mixed crowd of families and hipsters, who linger over pots of high-quality tea and tasty desserts (try the lemon tart). On warm days, there's outdoor seating on the rooftop.

Smolny & Vosstaniya

★Redrum BAR

(Map p92; ☎812-416 1126; www.facebook.com/redrumbarspb; ul Nekrasova 26; ⏲4pm-1am Sun-Thu, to 3am Fri & Sat; Ⓜ Mayakovskaya) One of St Petersburg's best drinking dens, Redrum hits all the right notes. It has a cosy, white brick interior, a welcoming, easygoing crowd, and a stellar selection of craft brews (some two dozen on tap). There's also good pub fare on hand to go with that creative line-up of Session Indian Pale Ales, sour ales, Berliner Weisse and porters.

★Commode BAR

(Map p92; www.commode.club; ul Rubinshteyna 1, 2nd fl; per hr ₽180; ⏲4pm-2am Sun-Thu, to 6am Fri & Sat) Stopping in for drinks at Commode feels more like hanging out in an upper-class friend's stylish apartment. After getting buzzed up, you can hang out in various high-ceilinged rooms, catch a small concert or poetry slam, browse books in the quasi-library room, play a round of table football, or chat with the easygoing crowd that have fallen for the place.

★**Hat** BAR
(Map p92; ul Belinskogo 9; 7pm-5am; M Gostiny Dvor) The wonderfully retro-feeling Hat is a serious spot for jazz and whiskey lovers, who come for the nightly live music and the cool cat crowd that makes this wonderfully designed bar feel like it's been transported out of 1950s Greenwich Village. A very welcome change of gear for St Petersburg's drinking options, but it can be extremely packed at weekends.

★**Union Bar & Grill** BAR
(Map p92; www.facebook.com/barunion; Liteyny pr 55; 6pm-4am Sun-Thu, to 6am Fri & Sat; ; M Mayakovskaya) The Union is a glamorous and fun place, characterised by one enormous long wooden bar, low lighting and a New York feel. It's all rather adult, with a serious cocktail list and designer beers on tap. The hip 20- and 30-something crowd packs in on weekends to catch live bands, but it's generally quiet during the week.

★**Ziferblat** ANTICAFE
(Циферблат; Map p92; 8-981-180 7022; www.ziferblat.net; 2nd fl, Nevsky pr 81; per min ₽3, per min after 1st hr ₽2; 11am-midnight; ; M Ploshchad Vosstaniya) A charming multiroom 'free space' that has started a worldwide trend, Ziferblat is the original anticafe in St Petersburg. Coffee, tea, soft drinks and biscuits are included as you while away your time playing chess and other board games, reading, playing instruments (help yourself to the piano and guitar) or just hanging out with the arty young locals who frequent its cosy rooms.

Entertainment

★**Mariinsky Theatre** BALLET, OPERA
(Мариинский театр; Map p96; 812-326 4141; www.mariinsky.ru; Teatralnaya pl 1; tickets ₽1200-6500; M Sadovaya) St Petersburg's most spectacular venue for ballet and opera, the Mariinsky Theatre is an attraction in its own right. Tickets can be bought online or in person; book in advance during the summer months. The magnificent interior is the epitome of imperial grandeur, and any evening here will be an impressive experience.

★**Mikhailovsky Theatre** PERFORMING ARTS
(Михайловский театр; Map p92; 812-595 4305; www.mikhailovsky.ru; pl Iskusstv 1; tickets ₽500-5000; M Nevsky Prospekt) This illustrious stage delivers the Russian ballet or operatic experience, complete with multitiered theatre, frescoed ceiling and elaborate productions. Pl Iskusstv (Arts Sq) is a lovely setting for this respected venue, which is home to the State Academic Opera & Ballet Company.

Shostakovich Philharmonia CLASSICAL MUSIC
(Санкт-Петербургская филармония им. Д.Д.Шостаковича; Map p92; www.philharmonia.spb.ru; tickets ₽800-2500; M Nevsky Prospekt) Under the artistic direction of world-famous conductor Yury Temirkanov, the Philharmonia represents the finest in orchestral music. The **Bolshoy Zal** (Большой зал; Map p92; 812-240 0180; Mikhailovskaya ul 2; M Nevsky Prospekt) is the venue for a full program of symphonic performances, while the nearby **Maly Zal** (Малый Зал; Map p92; 812-571 8333; Nevsky pr 30; M Gostiny Dvor) hosts smaller ensembles. Both venues are used for numerous music festivals.

Fish Fabrique LIVE MUSIC
(Map p92; http://fishfabrique.ru; Ligovsky pr 53; noon-4am daily, concerts from 8pm Thu-Sun; ; M Ploshchad Vosstaniya) There are St Petersburg institutions and then there's Fish Fabrique, the museum of local boho life that has been going for over two decades. Here, in the dark underbelly of Pushkinskaya 10, artists, musicians and counter-culturalists of all ages meet to drink beer and listen to music.

Shopping

★**Kupetz Eliseevs** FOOD & DRINKS
(Map p92; 812-456 6666; www.kupetzeliseevs.ru; Nevsky pr 56; 10am-11pm; ; M Gostiny Dvor) This Style Moderne stunner is St Petersburg's most elegant grocery store, selling plenty of branded goods from blends of tea to caviar and handmade chocolates as well as delicious freshly baked breads, pastries and cakes. Kids will love watching the animatronic figures in the window display and there are pleasant cafes on the ground floor and in the former wine cellar.

★**Udelnaya Fair** MARKET
(Удельная ярмарка; Skobolvesky pr, Vyborg Side; 8am-5pm Sat & Sun; M Udelnaya) This treasure trove of Soviet ephemera, pre-revolutionary antiques, WWII artefacts and bonkers kitsch from all eras is truly worth travelling

WORTH A TRIP

TSARSKOE SELO

The grand imperial estate of Tsarskoe Selo is next to the town of Pushkin, 25km south of St Petersburg. Its highlight is the vast baroque **Catherine Palace** (Екатерининский дворец; www.tzar.ru; Sadovaya ul 7; adult/student ₽1000/350, audio guide ₽150; ⏲10am-4.45pm Wed-Sun), built between 1752 and1756, but almost destroyed in WWII. The exterior and 20-odd rooms have been expertly restored; the Great Hall and famous **Amber Room** are particularly dazzling.

From Moskovskaya metro station, take the exit marked 'Buses for the airport', and then pick up *marshrutka* 286, 299, 342 or K545 towards Pushkin (₽40). Look for Пушкин or Дворец on the buses.

Suburban trains run from Vitebsk Station (p108) but they're infrequent except for weekends. For Pushkin, get off at Detskoe Selo (Детское село; ₽47, 30 minutes). From Detskoe Selo station, *marshrutky* (₽25) frequently run the 500m or so to Tsarskoe Selo.

for. Exit the metro station to the right and follow the crowds across the train tracks. Continue beyond the large permanent market, which is of very little interest, until you come to a huge area of independent stalls, all varying in quality and content.

Information

DANGERS & ANNOYANCES

- Foreigners tend to find Russians quite brusque and even unfriendly. Remember, this is a cultural thing, and try not to be offended by it. Russians take a while to warm up, but when they do they're exceptionally friendly.
- There has been an ongoing epidemic of racist attacks in St Petersburg. If you look very obviously non-Russian, it's a good idea to avoid the suburbs and take taxis at night.
- Due to legislation criminalising the 'promotion of homosexuality' to minors, levels of homophobia are higher now than they have been for some time. Gay travellers are advised to remain discreet.

EMERGENCY

Ambulance	☎03
Fire Department	☎01
Police	☎02

INTERNET ACCESS

Internet access is excellent and practically universal. Nearly all hotels have free wireless internet. Many restaurants, cafes, bars and clubs also have wi-fi. You may have to ask for a password *(parol)* to get online, and also input your mobile phone number. Sometimes this will need to be a Russian number (ie one starting with 7); if you don't have one, ask a local if you can use their number.

MEDICAL SERVICES

Clinics

These private clinics have facilities of an international standard and are pricey, but generally accept major international insurance policies, including direct billing.

American Medical Clinic (Map p92; ☎812-740 2090; www.amclinic.ru; nab reki Moyki 78; ⏲24hr; Ⓜ Admiralteyskaya)

Euromed (Map p96; ☎812-327 0301; www.euromed.ru; Suvorovsky pr 60; ⏲24hr; Ⓜ Chernyshevskaya)

Medem International Clinic & Hospital (Map p92; ☎812-336 3333; www.medem.ru; ul Marata 6; ⏲24hr; Ⓜ Mayakovskaya)

Pharmacies

Look for the sign АПТЕКА *(apteka)* or the usual green cross to find a pharmacy.

A chain of 24-hour pharmacies called **36.6 Pharmacy** (www.366.ru) has many branches around the city, including in the **Historic Heart** (Map p92; ☎812-324 2666; Gorokhovaya ul 16; ⏲9am-9pm Mon-Fri, 10am-9pm Sat & Sun; Ⓜ Admiralteyskaya). Other convenient pharmacies include Raduga, with branches in the **Petrograd Side** (Радуга; Bolshoy pr 62; ⏲9am-10pm Mon-Fri, from 10am Sat & Sun; Ⓜ Petrogradskaya) and **Smolny** (Map p92; ☎812-275 8189; Nevsky pr 98; ⏲24hr; Ⓜ Mayakovskaya).

MONEY

ATMs are everywhere and debit and credit cards are accepted in most places. Still, it's always a good idea to carry some cash.

POST

To send parcels home, head to the elegant **main post office** (Map p92; Pochtamtskaya ul 9; Ⓜ Admiralteyskaya). Smaller post offices may refuse to send parcels internationally; most importantly, your package is more likely to reach its destination if you send it from the main post office. You will need to provide a return address in St Petersburg – your hotel name will be fine.

TOURIST INFORMATION

Tourist information is halfway decent in St Petersburg, and in addition to the Tourist Information Bureau's **main office** (Map p92; ☎812-303 0555, 812-242 3909; http://eng.ispb.info; Sadovaya ul 14/52; ⏰10am-7pm Mon-Sat; Ⓜ Gostiny Dvor), just off Nevsky pr in the Historic Heart, there is an office in **Smolny** (Map p92; pl Vosstaniya; ⏰10am-7pm; Ⓜ Ploshchad Vosstaniya), and kiosks at **Palace Square** (Map p92; ☎8-931-326 5744; Dvortsovaya pl; ⏰10am-7pm; Ⓜ Admiralteyskaya), **St Isaac's Cathedral** (Map p92; Isaakievskaya pl; ⏰10am-7pm; Ⓜ Admiralteyskaya) and **Pulkovo Airport** (⏰9am-8pm).

TRAVEL AGENCIES

Milor-Tur (Map p92; ☎812-982 7489; www.milor-tour.spb.ru; Spassky per 14/35; Ⓜ Sennaya Ploshchad)

Ost-West (Map p92; ☎812-327 3416; www.ost-west.com; office 306, ul Vosstaniya 7; ⏰10am-6.30pm Mon-Fri; Ⓜ Ploshchad Vosstaniya)

Ost-West Kontaktservice (Map p92; ☎812-327 3416; www.ostwest.com; ul Vosstaniya 7, office 306; ⏰10am-6.30pm Mon-Sat; Ⓜ Ploshchad Vosstaniya)

Travel Russia (Map p92; ☎812-407 2015; www.travelrussia.su; Office 206, Suvorovsky pr 2b; ⏰9am-7pm Mon-Fri; Ⓜ Ploshchad Vosstaniya)

Getting There & Away

TRAIN

For information on trains to/from Moscow see p83.

Trans-Siberian Routes

There is a far wider choice of trains continuing east from Moscow. If you wish to bypass Moscow, take train 72 from the Ladoga Station to Yekaterinburg (₽5523 *kupe*, 35 hours). From Yekaterinburg you can connect to all Trans-Siberian services. Other services that take you from St Petersburg towards Siberia, and which go via Moscow, include the 145A train from Moscow Station to Chelyabinsk and the 74 train from the Ladoga Station to Tyumen.

Stations

➡ **Moscow Station** (Moskovsky vokzal; Московский вокзал; www.moskovsky-vokzal.ru; Nevsky pr 85; Ⓜ Ploshchad Vosstaniya) The most commonly used terminal where trains arrive from and depart to Moscow. Also services to the rest of western Russia and the Caucasus.

➡ **Finland Station** (Финляндский вокзал; Finlyandsky vokzal; www.finlyandsky.dzvr.ru; pl Lenina 6; Ⓜ Ploshchad Lenina) Express trains from Helsinki arrive and depart from here.

➡ **Ladoga Station** (Ladozhsky vokzal; Ладожский вокзал; http://lvspb.ru; Zanevsky pr 73; Ⓜ Ladozhskaya) Trains from Helsinki to Moscow stop en route in St Petersburg here; there's also a direct service to Yekaterinburg.

➡ **Vitebsk Station** (Vitebsky vokzal; Витебский вокзал; Zagorodny pr 52; Ⓜ Pushkinskaya) Serviced trains to the Baltic countries.

Tickets

Buying train tickets in person can be done at any train station (even at a different terminus from where your train departs), although waiting time can be long if you buy them at a counter. Far quicker are the ticket machines, which all work in English and where you can usually pay in both cash and by credit card. Another option is the centrally located **Train Tickets Centre** (Кассы ЖД; Map p92; nab kanala Griboyedova 24; ⏰8am-8pm Mon-Sat, until 6pm Sun; Ⓜ Gostiny Dvor), where there are also ticket machines, which makes waiting in line unnecessary.

International Destinations

From Helsinki there are four daily Allegro express trains that speed to St Petersburg in an impressive 3½ hours; see www.vr.fi for prices and timetables.

St Petersburg is well connected by train to lots of cities throughout Eastern Europe, including Berlin, Budapest, Kaliningrad, Kyiv, Prague and Warsaw, but all trains pass through Belarus, for which you're required to hold a transit visa.

AIR

Most travellers arrive in St Petersburg at **Pulkovo International Airport** (LED; ☎812-337 3822; www.pulkovoairport.ru; Pulkovskoye sh), 23km south of the city. This terminal building, which opened in 2014, and is confusingly still referred to as Terminal 1, handles all domestic and international flights and is St Petersburg's only airport.

BOAT

Cruise ships dock at one of the following:

English Embankment Passenger Terminal (Map p96)

Lieutenant Schmidt Passenger Terminal (Map p96)

Marine Facade Terminal (Пассажирский Порт Санкт-Петербург Морской Фасад; ☎812-303 6740; www.portspb.ru; 1 Bereg Nevskoy gubi; Ⓜ Primorskaya)

River Passenger Terminal (Речной вокзал; 812-262 6321, 812-262 0239; Obukhovskoy Oborony pr 195; M Proletarskaya)

Sea Port (Морской вокзал; 812-337 2060; www.mvokzal.ru; pl Morskoy Slavy 1)

St Petersburg Sea Port (Морской порт Санкт-Петербурга; www.seaport.spb.ru; Mezhevoy kanal 5)

You can buy ferry tickets for nearly all boats at the **Ferry Centre** (Паромный центр; Map p92; 812-327 3377; www.paromy.ru; ul Vosstaniya 19; 10am-7pm Mon-Fri; M Ploshchad Vosstaniya), a short walk from the Moscow Station. Alternatively, it's possible to buy ferry tickets in the Sea Port, as well as online.

BUS

St Petersburg's main bus station, **Avtovokzal** (Автобусный вокзал; Map p96; 812-766 5777; www.avokzal.ru; nab Obvodnogo kanala 36; M Obvodny Kanal), has bus connections to cities all over western Russia, including Veliky Novgorod, but most travellers won't use it. If you do happen to arrive here, it's a short walk along the canal to the metro station Obvodny Kanal (Line 5).

International buses are offered by a number of companies, including the following.

Lux Express (Map p96; 812-441 3757; www.luxexpress.eu; nab Obvodnogo kanala 36; 9am-9pm; M Baltiyskaya) runs buses from both Avtovokzal and from outside the Baltic Station (Baltiysky vokzal). Its buses run to Tallinn (from ₽1950, seven daily, seven hours), Rīga (from ₽2275, four daily, 11 hours) and Helsinki (from ₽1650, three daily, 7½ hours).

Ecolines (Map p96; 812-409 9410; www.ecolines.ru; Podezdny per 3; 8am-10pm; M Pushkinskaya) runs daily buses from the Vitebsk Station to Tallinn (₽1210, five daily, seven hours), Rīga (₽2240, four daily, 11 hours), Minsk (₽2130, three daily, 14 hours), Prague (₽6130, two to three daily, 36 to 38 hours) and Berlin (₽6840, two to three daily, 34 hours).

Transgold (812-995 0605; www.transgold.ru) runs door-to-door *marshrutky* (minibuses) to and from Helsinki and other destinations in Finland from ₽1300.

Getting Around

TO/FROM THE AIRPORT

Outside Pulkovo International Airport you'll find an official taxi dispatcher who will ask you for your destination's address, indicate which taxi to go to and write you a price on a slip of official paper that you can then give to your driver. Prices vary, but expect between ₽800 to ₽1000 to the centre, depending on where exactly you're headed. Drivers usually won't speak much English, but just hand over the money on arrival – you don't need to tip. It's also possible to book a trip into the city via a taxi app for around ₽700.

For those on a budget, *marshrutka* (minibuses) K39 shuttles you from outside the terminal building to the nearest metro station, Moskovskaya (₽35, every five minutes, from 7am to 11.30pm). The bus terminates at the Moskovskaya metro station, so you don't need to worry about where to get off, and you can connect to the rest of the city from there.

There's also bus 39 (₽40, every 15 minutes, from 5.30am to 1.30am) that runs the same route over longer hours, but trundles along somewhat.

KEY TRANSPORT ROUTES

Metro line 1 Worth getting out at every stop between pl Vosstaniya and Avtovo to admire the very handsomely decorated stations.

Tram 6 Great for travelling between areas north of the river without going through the centre: connects Vasilyevsky Island with the Petrograd Side and the Vyborg Side.

Trolleybus 7 Goes from Smolny along Nevsky pr, over the river, along the Strelka and to the Petrograd Side.

BUS, MARSHRUTKA & TROLLEYBUS

Buses, and particularly *marshrutky* (minibuses), are a very handy way to get around the city and they tend to cover routes that the metro doesn't, making them essential for certain parts of town. Most travellers find taking them a bit daunting, however, as there's little signage in English. On both buses and trolleybuses, you get on and then pay a conductor; the fare is ₽40.

Marshrutky can be flagged down anywhere along their route (there are no bus stops for *marshrutky*). Open the door yourself and jump in, then once you've taken your seat you pay the driver (pass the money via your fellow passengers if you're not sitting within reaching distance); the rates are usually posted on the inside of the bus near the driver. You'll also need to request the stop you want – usually announcing to the driver the name of the street or the place you're going to shortly before you get there. Alternatively, when you want to get off, simply say (or shout!): *'AstanavEEtye pazhalsta!'* ('Stop please!') and the driver will pull over as soon as possible.

METRO

The St Petersburg **Metro** (☎8-800- 350 1155; www.metro.spb.ru; ⏰6am-12.45am) is a very efficient five-line system. The network of some 70 stations is most usefully employed for travelling long distances, especially connecting the suburbs to the city centre. New stations are being added and it's possible that the one at Teatralnaya, next to the Mariinsky Theatre, will be operational by 2020.

Look for signs with a big blue 'M' signifying the entrance to the metro. The flat fare for a trip is ₽45; you will have to buy an additional ticket if you are carrying a significant amount of baggage. If you wish to buy a single journey, ask for *'adin proyezd'* and you will be given a *zheton* (token) to put in the machine.

If you are staying more than a day or two, however, it's worth buying a smart card (₽60), which is good for multiple journeys to be used over the course of a fixed time period – for example, 10 trips in seven days for ₽355. Their main advantage is that you won't have to line up to buy tickets – the ticket counters can have very long lines during peak hours.

The metro system is fully signed in English, so it's quite easy to use, even for first-timers in Russia.

Moscow to Yekaterinburg

Includes ➡

Route Info

- Distance: 1814km
- Duration: 26 hours
- Time zones: Moscow, Moscow +2

Best Places to Stay

- Surikov Guest House (p122)
- Smile (p127)
- Eva Hotel (p131)
- Kuptsov Dom (p118)

Best Places to Eat

- Restaurant Panorama (p117)
- Chaynaya (p124)
- Restoratsia Pyatkin (p127)

Why Go?

For travellers, this section of the journey across European Russia will often be accompanied by the excitement of the journey ahead. It is a relatively densely populated section with three main routes. One veers northeast via Yaroslavl and a second (used by the flagship *Ural* train 16) goes southeast via multicultural Kazan. The more usual route, however, passes through the ancient town of Vladimir. Then at Nizhny Novgorod it crosses the Volga – a geographic highlight of this leg – before continuing to Perm, which has several good cultural sights and access to the Perm-36 former prison camp. The train will pass through Kungur, set in rolling hills with a spectacular ice cave, and finally rattle sublimely across the Europe–Asia border and into Yekaterinburg. Note that if you're planning to stop at Golden Ring towns, it's only worth booking a sleeping compartment from Nizhny Novgorod onwards.

When to Go

Nizhny Novgorod

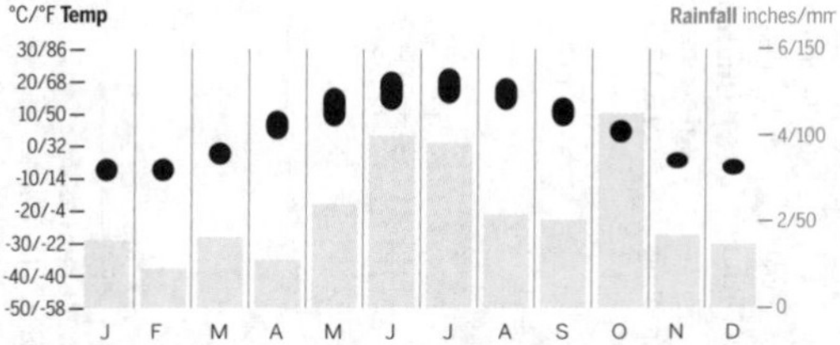

Feb Much of the Volga River will be frozen over and draped in a winter landscape.

Late Apr–late May A spring sun warms the air and life moves onto the streets.

Late Jul–Sep It's navigation season on the Volga and hiking is excellent in the Urals.

Moscow to Yekaterinburg Highlights

1. **Cable Car** (p125) Enjoying spectacular views over the Volga River in Nizhny Novgorod.
2. **Suzdal** (p119) Rambling through bucolic beauty while church bells sigh in the distance.
3. **Church of the Intercession on the Nerl** (p116) Admiring the stunning simplicity of this tiny white church in Bogolyubovo.
4. **Kazan Kremlin** (p123) Exploring the historic heart of Tatarstan's dynamic capital.
5. **PERMM** (p129) Inspecting the collection at Perm's museum of modern and contemporary art.
6. **Perm-36** (p133) Taking a tour through the haunting Gulag camp memorial.
7. **Kungur Ice Cave** (p133) Marvelling at grottoes adorned with ice formations.

The Route

MOSCOW TO NIZHNY NOVGOROD

0km from Moscow

Gradually the train slips away from the station and sets a course between the streets, backyards and apartment buildings of the capital towards provincial Russia. Most likely you will see signs warning Muscovites against taking shortcuts across the tracks. Everywhere, Muscovites will be taking shortcuts across the tracks, some of them carrying plastic shopping bags or rushing to work.

13km

A short distance beyond **Los** the train crosses the Moscow Ring Road. This stretch of track through outer Moscow has been immortalised by the Soviet underground writer Venedikt Yerofeyev in his novel *Moscow to the End of the Line*. The main character travels to **Petushki** on a whistle-stop *elektrichka* (suburban train) at the time of Gorbachev's liquor ban, philosophising on the virtues of alcohol and the evils of the Soviet lifestyle while toasting every station. He consumes mind-boggling cocktails, such as the 'Tear of a Young Communist League Girl', which consists of three brands of cheap Soviet eau de toilette, mouth rinse, nail polish and lemonade. Don't try to repeat this fictional experience, or you'll never get anywhere, let alone to Siberia.

190km (210km)

About three hours after departing, the train reaches Vladimir (p115), where most trains pause for about 20 minutes. Approaching the city, look for the golden spires and domes of the Assumption Cathedral high on the embankment to the north. Vladimir has some of the oldest churches in Russia and it was here that in 1157 Prince Andrei Bogolyubsky established his capital and shaped the town with architecture based on Kyivan and Western traditions. Almost 20 years later a plot was hatched to get rid of him and on one fateful night his flunkies burst into the chamber while he slept and finished him off with an axe.

200km (220km)

Just beyond Vladimir you pass the small town of **Bogolyubovo** (p114), another of the historic highlights of the region and the place where Prince Andrei built his palace. Today it is largely a monastery complex dating from the 18th century, which you can glimpse if you look north as the train approaches. East of it is the Church of the Intercession – the paragon of Russian church architecture, sitting in splendid isolation at the confluence of the Nerl and Klyazma Rivers.

Moscow to Yekaterinburg

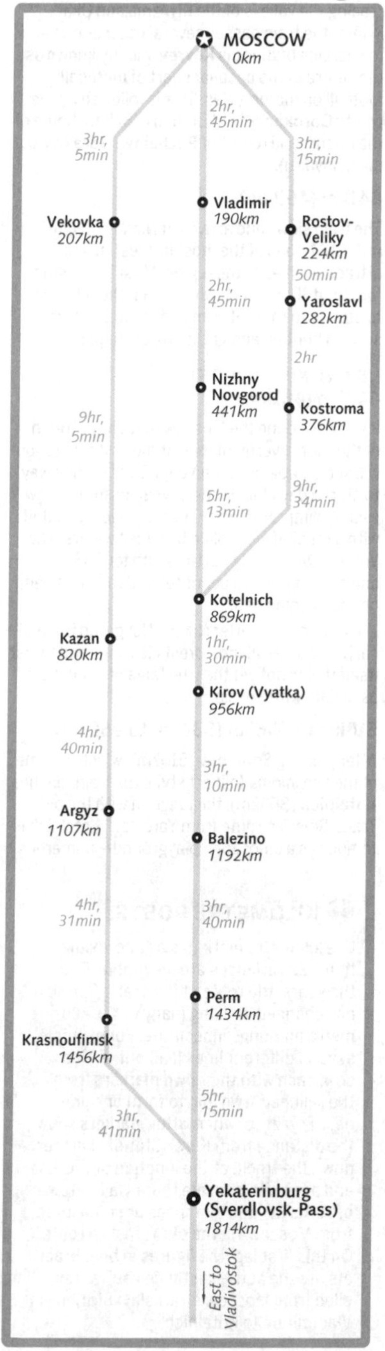

254km (274km)

Tracing the valleys of the Klyazma and Oka Rivers, the train passes several other ancient towns. One of these is **Kovrov**, mostly known as the centre of the peculiar sport of motoball – football on motorcycles. This is followed by the pretty **Gorokhovets** at 363km (382km), home of the popular ski resort of **Puzhalova Gora** (www.puzhalova.ru).

441km (460km)

The train slows and arrives at Nizhny Novgorod (p124), one of the most interesting and attractive cities in the region. Most trains stop for about 10 minutes, which is another chance to step onto the platform and engage in some serious hunting and gathering of supplies.

NIZHNY NOVGOROD TO PERM

442km (461km)

If you have done the Moscow to Nizhny stretch of the route overnight, one of the first things you will see on waking is the Volga River – a fine way to start a day at any time of year. In spring, however, it's impressive because the river is coated with a crust of ice broken by bluish waters. The Volga flows roughly north–south for 3530km and culminates in a beautiful wetland at its delta on the Caspian Sea.

The landscape after Nizhny Novgorod is a typical blend of farmland, forest clearings and forest itself that is not yet the true taiga of conifer we associate with Russia.

510km to 956km (530km to 956km)

After passing **Semenov** (510km), which is home of the *khokhloma* folk-art style, the train reaches **Kotelnich** (869km), the junction with the old Trans-Siberian route from Yaroslavl. Kotelnich is famous as a dinosaurs' playground – numerous Permian-period giant-lizard fossils have been discovered here. Just outside Kotelnich the train crosses the Vyatka River, a meandering 1367km waterway that accompanies the railway route to **Kirov** (956km), which is better known by its old name: Vyatka, same as the river. Most trains stop here for about 15 minutes. Not a lot of meaningful activity can be fit into the stopover at Vyatka, but you can celebrate having reached the northernmost point of your whole Trans-Siberian journey.

KILOMETRE POSTS

Use kilometre markings as approximations, as variances are inevitable. Over the years, the route of the Trans-Siberian has changed, making many of the kilometre markings inaccurate. For example, several different lines lead out of Moscow, each with their own markers from the railhead. Two join to form one line near Fryazevo, whereafter markers show the distance from Kursk Station. Further down the track, at the junction of this line and a former mainline route via the town of Yaroslavl, the distances are measured from Moscow via the old Yaroslavl route. On this first leg, the figures in bold brackets are the actual distance you've travelled from Moscow's Yaroslavl Station via Vladimir up to Kotelnich.

1126km

Yar is the first town you'll pass through in the Udmurt Republic, home to the Udmurts, one of Russia's four major groups of Finno-Ugric people. In contrast to Tatarstan further south, Udmurtia is a poor region which, unlike Tatarstan, never seriously considered independence when the Soviet Union collapsed, and has therefore received less money from Moscow than its Tatar neighbour. Around here the countryside becomes picturesque, with plenty of pretty painted log cabins.

1192km

At **Balezino** there's a change of locomotive during the roughly 20-minute halt.

1221km to 1314km

After crossing the Cheptsa River, the train enters the town of the same name. **Cheptsa** (1223km) is the junction with the line that runs between Perm and Kazan. About 40km further east, you'll cross into Perm Region and reach the foothills of the **Ural Mountains**, which stretch about 2000km from Kazakhstan to the Arctic Kara Sea. However, the Urals rarely break 500m above sea level in these parts, prompting the Russian academician Peter Pallas to drily note in 1770 on one of his journeys that the middle section of the Urals were particularly inconspicuous. Nevertheless, as the landscape unfolds you will have glimpses of verdant rolling hills and pine and birch forests, and this is one of the more attractive sections of the route before Kungur. In Perm Region (by the time you reach **Vereshchagino**; 1314km), local time is two hours ahead of Moscow time.

PERM TO YEKATERINBURG

1434km

The train rolls across the wide Kama River into the industrial city of Perm (p129), where most trains stop for 20 minutes. On the northern side of the train is a steam locomotive and the station itself has a small railway museum on the 2nd floor.

1535km

The railway turns southeast after Perm and reaches Kungur (p133), the centre of the Stroganov patrimony. This industrial family virtually ruled the Urals from the time of Ivan the Terrible to the reign of Peter the Great, and with the implicit agreement of Ivan the Terrible it also financed Yermak's campaign across the Urals into Siberia. From Kungur, the railway follows the meandering course of the Sylva River, which on a fine day is dotted with anglers casting lines into the shallows, behind them a picturesque backdrop of low mountains. This stretch, in fact, offers the entertaining contrast of scenery and anglers beyond the window, the creaking of fittings inside the train as it struggles around the curves, and – if you are in *platskart* (3rd class) – the likely interior scenario of weary travellers huddling over crosswords on their bunks, mentally ticking off the kilometres. The best scenery is on the left, which in this direction you will have to admire from the corridor in *kupe*.

1777km

The landscape recedes to unremarkable upland once the train leaves the valley of the Sylva River, and the next major point is the one-dog station of **Vershina** (6km after Pervouralsk) at the **border between Europe and Asia**, marked by a white monument. You will need to have your wits about you to catch it; it is located on the south (right-hand, heading east) side of the line.

1814km

The train travels along the Chusovaya River as it approaches Yekaterinburg, through a valley that was long the heart of the mining industry in the Urals. The first major station in Asian Russia – but still 260km short of the official beginning of Siberia – is Yekaterinburg (p139), where you can expect a 15- to 20-minute stop.

Vladimir Владимир

4922 / POP 345,380 / TIME MOSCOW

Founded at the dawn of the 12th century on a bluff over the Klyazma River, Vladimir became the cradle of Russian history when Prince Andrei Bogolyubsky moved his capital there from Kyiv in 1169. Thus began Vladimir's Golden Age, when many of the beautifully carved white-stone buildings for which the area is renowned were built by Bogolyubsky and his brother, Prince Vsevolod the Big Nest. After a Mongol invasion devastated the town in 1238, power shifted some 200km west to a minor settlement called Moscow. Though Vladimir eventually rebounded from the ruins, it would never regain its former glory.

Today this bustling city is the administrative centre of Vladimir Oblast. Although not as charmingly bucolic as nearby Suzdal, Vladimir's easy access from Moscow, its cluster of centrally located Unesco-listed sights and its stunning river-valley panoramas make it an ideal starting point for a Golden Ring tour.

MOSCOW TO YEKATERINBURG ROUTE PLANNER

The following is a suggested itinerary for covering the main sites of the area:

Day 1 Leave Moscow; 2½-hour train to Vladimir; stay Suzdal

Day 2 Tour Suzdal; return to Vladimir; train to Nizhny Novgorod

Day 3 Explore Nizhny Novgorod

Day 4 Continue exploring Nizhny Novgorod; night train (14½ hours) from Nizhny Novgorod to Perm

Day 5 Look around Perm

Day 6 Visit Perm-36 Gulag camp or do a day trip to Kungur

Day 7 Train (six hours) to Yekaterinburg

Sights

★Assumption Cathedral CHURCH

(Успенский собор; 4922-325 201; www.vladmuseum.ru; Sobornaya pl; adult/child ₽100/free; visitors 1-4.45pm Tue-Sun) Set dramatically high above the Klyazma River, this simple but majestic piece of pre-Mongol architecture is the legacy of Prince Andrei Bogolyubsky, the man who began shifting power from Kyiv to northeastern Rus (which eventually evolved into Muscovy). A white-stone version of Kyiv's brick Byzantine churches, the cathedral was constructed from 1158 to 1160, though it was rebuilt and expanded after a fire in 1185. It was added to Unesco's World Heritage List in 1992.

The seat of the Vladimir and Suzdal diocese, the cathedral has held services for its entire history except from 1927 to 1944. The cool, hushed interior is a riot of gold leaf – the baroque iconostasis was constructed with a donation from Catherine the Great. A few restored 12th-century murals of peacocks and prophets can be seen about halfway up the inner wall of the outer north aisle (originally an outside wall); the real treasures, though, are the *Last Judgement* frescoes by Andrei Rublyov and Daniil Chyorny, painted in 1408 in the central nave and

DON'T MISS

CHURCH OF THE INTERCESSION ON THE NERL

Bogolyubovo, just 12km northeast of Vladimir, is the location of the **Church of the Intercession on the Nerl** (Церковь Покрова на Нерли; Bogolyubovo; ⌚10am-6pm Tue-Sun), the gold standard of Russian religious architecture. Apart from ideal proportions, its beauty lies in a brilliantly chosen waterside location (floods aside) and the sparing use of delicate carving.

Legend has it that Prince Andrei Bogolyubsky had the church built in memory of his favourite son, Izyaslav, who was killed in battle against the Bulgars. As with the **Cathedral of St Dmitry** in Vladimir, King David sits at the top of three facades, the birds and beasts entranced by his music. The interior has more carvings, including 20 pairs of lions. If the church is closed (from October to April the opening hours are more sporadic), try asking at the house behind.

From Vladimir's Golden Gate or Sobornaya pl take bus 152 (₽20) and get off by the massive, blue-domed Bogolyubsky Monastery. Walk past the monastery to Vokzalnaya ul, the first street on the right, and follow it down to the train station. Cross the pedestrian bridge over the railroad tracks and follow the stone path for 1km across the meadow.

inner south aisle (under the choir gallery towards the western end).

Comply with the standard church dress code (no shorts for men; covered head and long skirts for women) at all times and be especially mindful of people's sensitivities outside the designated 'tourist time'. Tickets can be purchased at the small kiosk in the courtyard to the right of the cathedral.

★Old Vladimir Museum VIEWPOINT, MUSEUM
(Музей 'Старый Владимир'; www.vladmuseum.ru; ul Kozlov; adult/child ₽100/free; ⌚10am-6pm Mon-Thu, to 8pm Fri-Sun) This red-brick former water tower contains a multistorey exhibit of everyday objects from Vladimir's history (no English signage); the display of old clocks and stopwatches is among the most interesting. But follow the curving staircase all the way up to find the real draw here: the **observation deck**, which offers magnificent 360-degree views of Vladimir, with the Klyazma River curling lazily off into the distance and gold church domes set against the surrounding blue sky and green fields.

Georgievskaya Ulitsa STREET, VIEWPOINT
This pedestrian-only street curving southwest from the main strip was lovingly recreated in 2015 as a brick-paved thoroughfare from the old days, dotted with souvenir stores, whimsical bronze statues of 19th-century locals and working water pumps; at its far end is the former water tower. It's a lovely place for a stroll – don't miss the broad **viewing terraces** at the eastern end, which offer stunning views of Assumption Cathedral (p115) (especially gorgeous floodlit at night).

Cathedral of St Dmitry CHURCH
(Дмитриевский собор; www.vladmuseum.ru; Bolshaya Moskovskaya ul 60; adult/child ₽100/free; ⌚10am-6pm Mon-Thu, to 8pm Fri-Sun May-Sep, 11am-5pm Wed-Mon Oct-Apr) Built between 1193 and 1197, this exquisite, Unesco-listed whitestone cathedral represents the epitome of Russian stone carving. The attraction here is the cathedral's exterior walls, which are covered in an amazing profusion of images. At their top centre, the north, south and west walls all show King David bewitching the birds and beasts with music.

History Museum MUSEUM
(Исторический музей; ☎4922-322 284; Bolshaya Moskovskaya ul 64; adult/child ₽100/free; ⌚11am-6pm Mon-Thu, 10am-7pm Fri-Sun) This museum displays many remains and reproductions of the ornamentation from Vladimir's two cathedrals as part of an extensive exhibition covering the history of the town from Kyivan princes to the 1917 revolution. Particularly interesting are the artefacts upstairs, including a remarkable keyboardless typewriter from 1905. The redbrick edifice was purpose-built in 1902.

Sleeping

Given the proximity of the much more idyllic Suzdal, you may prefer to overnight there (unless you need to catch an early morning train to Moscow or Nizhny Novgorod).

Nice Hostel HOSTEL $

(Найс Хостел; ☎4922-421 231, 8-902-888 5004; www.nicehostel33.ru; Manezhney t 1; dm/d from ₽510/1500; 📶) This brand-new hostel won't win any design awards, but it's spotless and offers a free breakfast in the common kitchen. Dorm rooms (male-only, female-only and mixed) have four, six or eight beds; five doubles are available (three with private bathrooms), as well as a four-bed family room (₽2600). There's a washing machine and iron for guest use.

Rus HOTEL $$

(Русь; ☎4922-322 736; www.rushotel33.ru; ul Gagarina 14; s/d incl breakfast from ₽3000/3600; ❄📶) Occupying a large old house on a quiet corner just two blocks from Bolshaya Moskovskaya ul, this hotel offers nicely appointed and comfortable (if rather beige) rooms with extra towels and bathrobes. Reception staff are helpful and speak some English. Breakfast is included.

Voznesenskaya Sloboda HOTEL $$$

(Вознесенская слобода; ☎4922-325 494; www.vsloboda.ru; ul Voznesenskaya 14b; d ₽4800; P❄📶) Perched on a bluff with tremendous views of the valley, this hotel has one of the most scenic locations in the area. Outside is a quiet neighbourhood of old wooden cottages and villas dominated by the elegant Ascension Church, whose bells chime idyllically throughout the day. The new building's interior is tastefully designed to resemble art nouveau style c 1900.

Eating & Drinking

Bolshaya Moskovskaya ul and its surrounding streets between Sobornaya pl and the **Golden Gate** (Золотые ворота; ☎4922-322 559; www.vladmuseum.ru; Bolshaya Moskovskaya ul 1; adult/child ₽100/free; ⏲9am-6pm) are dotted with cafes and restaurants, though don't expect an exciting culinary adventure. You can also grab a cheap bite at the small food court on the top floor of the **shopping centre** (Торговые Ряды; Bolshaya Moskovskaya ul 19a; ⏲10am-10pm).

Salmon & Coffee INTERNATIONAL $$

(Лосось и кофе; www.losos-coffee.ru; Bolshaya Moskovskaya ul 19a; mains ₽340-790; ⏲11am-1am Sun-Thu, to 8am Fri & Sat; 📶) Salmon is yet to be found in the Klyazma, and coffee is not exactly what medieval princes had for breakfast. But instead of hinting at the city's past, this DJ cafe serving Asian and European dishes aims for a cosmopolitan touch in an ancient town. Lots of dark wood, dim lights and magenta-coloured metal railings create a cool, intriguing atmosphere.

★ **Restaurant Panorama** RUSSIAN $$$

(Ресторан Панорама; ☎4922-464 746; Bolshaya Moskovskaya ul 44b; mains ₽380-1260; ⏲noon-midnight Sun-Thu, to 2am Fri & Sat) This upscale restaurant, hidden down a lane off the main street, offers perhaps the fanciest meal in town, with attentive service, an elegant atmosphere and – true to its name – great views over the river valley from your table. The menu features the usual salads, pasta and meat dishes, including a rabbit confit the restaurant insists is worth the wait.

★ **Four Brewers Pub** CRAFT BEER

(Паб Четыре Пивовара; www.4brewers.ru; Bolshaya Moskovskaya ul 12; ⏲2pm-midnight Sun-Thu, to 2am Fri & Sat) This pocket-sized pub offers 20 brews on tap and dozens more in bottles – porter, IPA, stout, ale, you name it – all from the brewers' own vats or other Russian microbreweries, with such unforgettable names as 'Banana Kraken', 'Santa Muerte', 'Roksana and the Endless Universe' and (our personal favourite) 'Black Jesus, White Pepper'. Bartenders happily offer recommendations and free tastes.

Kofein CAFE, COFFEE

(Кофеин; Gagarina ul 1; ⏲8.30am-11pm Sun-Thu, to midnight Fri & Sat; 📶) This smart cafe in the town centre offers a variety of delicious desserts and espresso-based coffees (as well as a full food menu). Vegans, rejoice – there's soy milk, too. Free wi-fi.

Information

Russian Agricultural Bank (РоссельхозБанк; Bolshaya Moskovskaya ul; ⏲9.30am-5.30pm Mon-Fri, ATM 24hr)

Sberbank (Сбербанк; Bolshaya Moskovskaya ul 27; ⏲9am-7pm Mon-Fri, to 5pm Sat, ATM 24hr) Has exchange facilities.

Post Office (ul Podbelskogo 2; ⏲8am-10pm) Also has an ATM.

Vladimir Tourist Information (☎4922-377 000; www.invladimir.ru/en; Sobornaya pl; ⏲10am-6pm Tue-Sun) Located in a small house on the western side of Sobornaya pl.

Vladimir Region Tourist Information (www.tourism33.ru)

Getting There & Away

Vladimir is on the main trans-Siberian line between Moscow and Nizhny Novgorod and on a major highway leading to Kazan.

TRAIN

There are nine services a day from Moscow's Kursk Station (Kursky vokzal), with modern Strizh and slightly less comfortable Lastochka trains (₽600 to ₽1600, 1¾ hours). Both of these

WORTH A TRIP

YAROSLAVL ЯРОСЛАВЛЬ

In Soviet times most Trans-Siberian trains went via Yaroslavl, 266km northeast of Moscow, rather than via Vladimir and Nizhny Novgorod, as they do today. This is still a viable alternative that allows you to reunite with the main route shortly before the Urals.

The largest city on the Golden Ring, Yaroslavl was founded in 1010 by its namesake Kyivan prince, who – as legend goes – came to the place then known as Bear's Corner and axed the local tribe's totem bear, which now appears on the city's coat of arms.

Sights

Monastery of the Transfiguration of the Saviour (Спасо-Преображенский монастырь; ☎4852-303 869; www.yarmp.yar.ru; Bogoyavlenskaya pl 25; joint ticket adult/child ₽700/300; ⊙grounds 8am-8pm May-Sep, 9am-6pm Oct-Apr, exhibits 10am-5.45pm) Founded in the 12th century, this Unesco-listed monastery was one of Russia's richest and best-fortified by the 16th century. A bird's-eye view of Yaroslavl and its rivers can be had by climbing up to the top of the cathedral's bell tower.

John the Baptist Church at Tolchkovo (Церковь Иоанна Крестителя в Толчково; www.yarmp.yar.ru; 2-ya Zakotoroslnaya nab 69; adult/child ₽80/40; ⊙10am-5pm Wed-Sun May-Oct, closed rainy days) Yaroslavl's largest and most unique church features on the 1000-rouble currency note. Protected by Unesco, the red-brick structure (built 1671–87) boasts a staggering 15 green-coloured cupolas and some of the most extensive series of frescoes in the Orthodox world. It's located on the southern bank of the Kotorosl, by the second bridge, some 3km from the centre.

Church of Elijah the Prophet (Церковь Ильи Пророка; ☎4852-304 072; www.yarmp.yar.ru; Sovetskaya pl 7; adult/child ₽100/50; ⊙8.30am-7pm May-Oct, by appointment Oct-Apr, closed rainy days) This exquisite church has some of the Golden Ring's brightest frescoes – by the ubiquitous Gury Nikitin of Kostroma and his school – and detailed exterior tiles. The church is closed on rainy days to protect the frescoes from moisture.

Music & Time (Музыка и время; ☎4852-328 637; Volzhskaya nab 33a; adult/child ₽250/150; ⊙10am-7pm) Every object has a voice in this little house containing the late magician John Mostoslavsky's impressive collection of clocks, musical instruments, bells and antique gramophones. Guides (some of whom speak English) turn each tour into a concert by playing many of these items, which have been preserved in working condition.

Sleeping & Eating

Kuptsov Dom (Купцовъ дом; ☎4852-207 788; www.kdhotel.ru; ul Trefoleva 21; s/d incl breakfast ₽3250/3850; P ❄ 📶) A central location and elegantly decorated rooms with white furniture and light floral wallpaper make this new hotel in a historic building hard to beat for value. Helpful reception staff speak English and a generous buffet breakfast is included. Save some money by opting for one of the slightly cheaper attic rooms.

Buffet No 1 (Буфет № 1; ☎4852-646 401; ul Nakhimsona 23/55; mains ₽100-250; ⊙8am-11pm; 📶) With an art nouveau exterior and an upscale dining room, this self-serve buffet – which offers a large and inexpensive selection of tasty salads, omelettes, meat mains with side dishes, Italian pastas, Asian noodle dishes, and desserts – is a great place for a cheap meal in pleasant surrounds.

Getting There & Away

The main station is **Yaroslavl Glavny** (Ярославль-Главный; ul Svobody), 3km west of the centre.

There are 14 daily trains from Moscow's Yaroslavl Station bound for northern Russia and Siberia that stop at Yaroslavl (₽545 to ₽886, four hours). Eastbound trains go to Perm (₽2422 to ₽3414, 19 hours, three daily) and beyond the Urals.

To get to the station from the centre, take *marshrutky* (minibus) 45, 76 or 81, or buses 6, 8, or 72.

continue to Nizhny Novgorod (Strizh ₽1000 to ₽1750, Lastochka ₽800, two hours).

All long-distance trains heading towards Tatarstan and Siberia also call at Vladimir.

BUS

The bus is a poor option from Moscow or Nizhny Novgorod – the train (p118) is much faster and more reliable. Conveniently for those heading on to Suzdal, the **bus station** (автовокзал; Vokzalnaya pl) is right across from Vladimir's **train station** (Владимир; ul Vokzalnaya 2).

Buses run to Suzdal (₽95, 45 minutes, several times per hour) and Yaroslavl (₽610 to ₽699, five hours, 7.15am and 4.30pm).

TAXI

A one-way **taxi** (☎4922-555 555) to Suzdal costs approximately ₽600 (or download the Gett app from www.gett.com to order from your smartphone).

Getting Around

Trolleybus 5 from the train and bus stations runs along Bolshaya Moskovskaya ul.

Suzdal Суздаль

☎49231 / POP 10,535 / TIME MOSCOW

The sparkling diamond in the Golden Ring is undoubtedly Suzdal – if you have time for only one of these towns, this is the one to see. With rolling green fields carpeted with dandelions, a gentle river curling lazily through a historic town centre, sunlight bouncing off golden church domes and the sound of horse clops and church bells carrying softly through the air, you may feel like you've stumbled into a storybook Russia.

Suzdal served as a royal capital when Moscow was still a cluster of cowsheds, and was a major monastic centre and an important commercial hub for many years as well. But in 1864, local merchants failed to get the Trans-Siberian Railway built through here (it went to Vladimir instead). Suzdal was thus bypassed both by trains and 20th-century progress, preserving its idyllic character for future visitors.

Sights

★**Kremlin** FORTRESS

(Кремль; ☎49231-21 624; www.vladmuseum.ru; ul Kremlyovskaya; joint ticket adult/child ₽350/free; ⏲exhibitions 9am-6pm Sun-Thu, to 9pm Fri & Sat, grounds to 9pm) The grandfather of the Moscow Kremlin, this citadel was the 12th-century base of Prince Yury Dolgoruky, who ruled the vast northeastern part of Kyivan Rus (and, among other things, founded a small outpost that would eventually become the Russian capital). The 1.4km-long earthen ramparts of Suzdal's kremlin enclose a few streets of houses and a handful of churches, as well as the main cathedral group on ul Kremlyovskaya.

The Unesco-listed **Nativity of the Virgin Cathedral** (Церковь Казанской иконы Божьей Матери; Suzdal kremlin, ul Kremlyovskaya; adult/child ₽100/free; ⏲9am-7pm Sun-Thu, to 9pm Fri & Sat), its deep blue domes spangled with gold stars, was built in 1225 (only its richly carved lower section is original white stone, though, the rest being 16th-century brick). The inside is sumptuous, with 13th- and 17th-century frescoes and 13th-century damascene (gold on copper) west and south doors.

Within the kremlin, the **Archbishop's Chambers** (Архиерейские палаты) house the **Suzdal History Exhibition**, which includes the original 13th-century door from the cathedral, photos of its interior and a visit to the 18th-century **Cross Hall** (Крестовая палата), which was used for receptions. The tent-roofed 1635 kremlin **bell tower** (Звонница), directly across the yard from the cathedral, contains additional exhibits, including the 17th-century **Jordan Canopy** (Иорданская сень), the only one of its kind left in Russia; every January on Epiphany Day, this 28m-tall painted wooden structure would be placed over a cross-shaped hole in the ice on the Kamenka for the annual rite of blessing the river water.

To the southwest, between the cathedral and the river, is the 1766 **Nikolskaya Wooden Church** (Никольская деревянная церковь), which was moved to Suzdal from a nearby village in 1960. Other rural wooden buildings were subsequently moved for preservation to the excellent **Museum of Wooden Architecture & Peasant Life** (Музей деревянного зодчества и крестьянского быта; www.vladmuseum.ru; ul Pushkarskaya; adult/child ₽300/free; ⏲9am-7pm Sun-Thu, to 9pm Fri & Sat; 👪), across the river.

If you don't want to see all of the exhibitions, you can pay for admission to the cathedral separately; to walk around the grounds only costs ₽50 (children get in free).

★**Saviour Monastery of St Euthymius** MONASTERY

(Спасо-Евфимиев монастырь; ☎49231-20 746; ul Lenina; adult/child ₽400/free; ⏲10am-

Suzdal

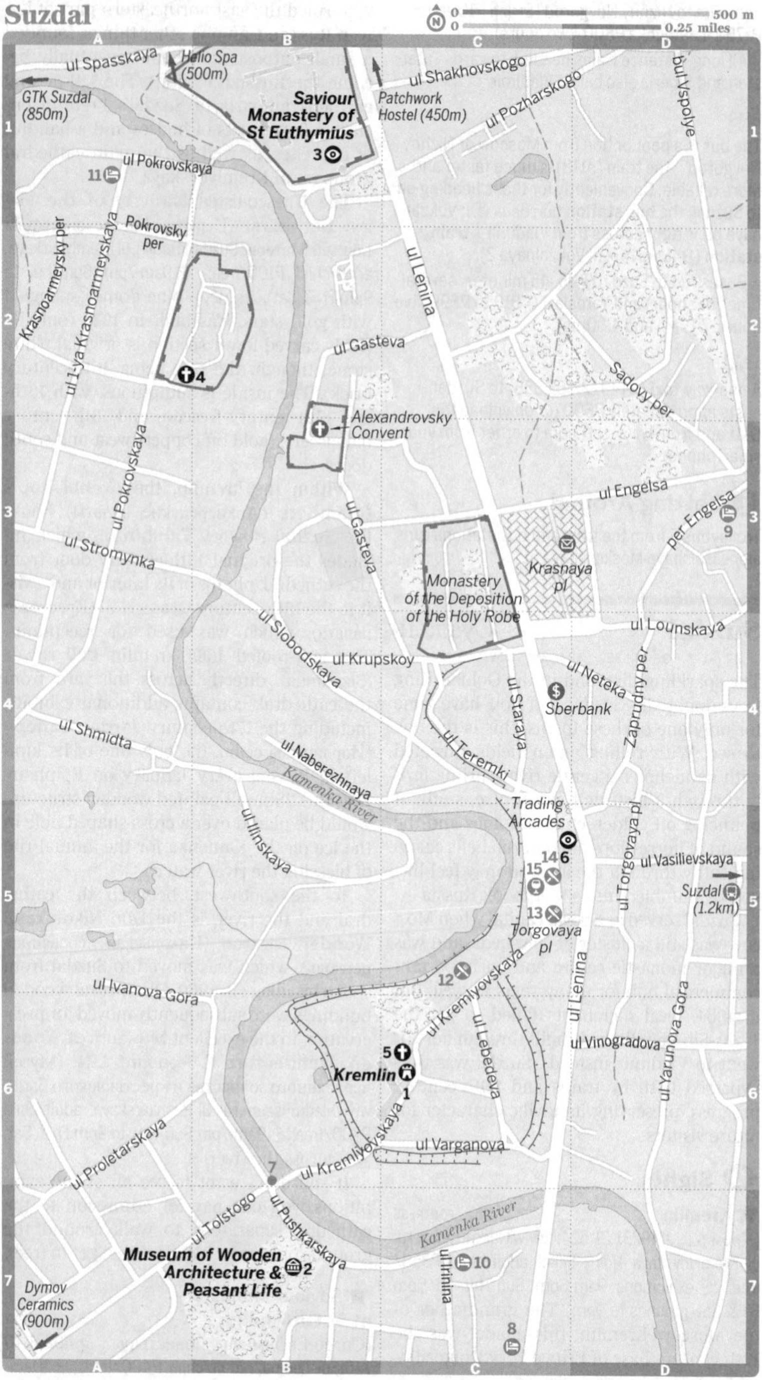
0
500 m
0
0.25 miles
Helio Spa (500m)
GTK Suzdal (850m)
Patchwork Hostel (450m)
Saviour Monastery of St Euthymius
3
11
4
Alexandrovsky Convent
Monastery of the Deposition of the Holy Robe
Krasnaya pl
9
Sberbank
Trading Arcades
6
14
15
13
Torgovaya pl
12
Suzdal (1.2km)
5
Kremlin
1
7
Museum of Wooden Architecture & Peasant Life
2
Dymov Ceramics (900m)
10
8
ul Spasskaya
ul Shakhovskogo
ul Pozharskogo
bul Vspolye
ul Pokrovskaya
Pokrovsky per
Krasnoarmeysky per
ul 1-ya Krasnoarmeyskaya
ul Pokrovskaya
ul Lenina
ul Gasteva
Sadovy per
ul Engelsa
per Engelsa
ul Stromynka
ul Gasteva
ul Slobodskaya
ul Krupskoy
ul Lounskaya
ul Neteka
Zaprudny per
ul Staraya
ul Teremki
ul Shmidta
ul Naberezhnaya
Kamenka River
ul Ilinskaya
ul Torgovaya pl
ul Vasilievskaya
ul Kremlyovskaya
ul Lebedeva
ul Lenina
ul Vinogradova
ul Yarunova Gora
ul Ivanova Gora
ul Varganova
ul Proletarskaya
ul Kremlyovskaya
ul Tolstogo
ul Pushkarskaya
Kamenka River
ul Irinina

7pm Sun-Thu, to 9pm Fri & Sat) Founded in the 14th century to protect the town's northern entrance, Suzdal's biggest monastery grew mighty in the 16th and 17th centuries after Vasily III, Ivan the Terrible and the noble Pozharsky family funded impressive new stone buildings and made large land and property acquisitions. It was girded with its great brick walls and towers in the 17th century.

Right at the entrance, the **Annunciation Gate Church** (Благовещенская надвратная церковь) houses an interesting exhibit on Dmitry Pozharsky (1578–1642), leader of the Russian army that drove the Polish invaders from Moscow in 1612.

A tall 16th- to 17th-century cathedral **bell tower** (Звонница) stands before the seven-domed **Cathedral of the Transfiguration of the Saviour** (Спасо-Преображенский собор); every hour on the hour from 11am to 5pm a short concert of chimes is played on its bells. The cathedral was built in the 1590s in 12th- to 13th-century Vladimir-Suzdal style. Inside, restoration has uncovered some bright 1689 frescoes by the school of Gury Nikitin from Kostroma. The tomb of Prince Dmitry Pozharsky is by the cathedral's east wall.

The 1525 **Assumption Refectory Church** (Успенская церковь), facing the bell tower, adjoins the old **Father Superior's chambers** (Палаты отца-игумена), which house a display of Russian icons and an excellent naive-art exhibition showcasing works by local amateur painters from the Soviet era.

The old **Monastery Dungeon** (Монастырская тюрьма), set up in 1764 for religious dissidents, is at the north end of the complex. It now houses a fascinating exhibit on the monastery's prison history, including displays of some of the better-known prisoners who stayed here. The Bolsheviks used the monastery as a concentration camp after the 1917 revolution. During WWII, German and Italian officers captured in the Battle of Stalingrad were kept here.

To the northeast of the main cathedral group, the combined **Hospital Chambers & St Nicholas Church** (Больничные кельи и Никольская церковь) feature a rich collection of gold church treasures.

Torgovaya Ploshchad SQUARE

(Торговая Площадь) Suzdal's Torgovaya pl (Market Sq) is dominated by the pillared **Trading Arcades** (Торговые ряды; 1806–11) along its western side. There are several churches in the immediate vicinity, including the 1739 **Kazan Church** (Казанская церковь) and the 1720 **Resurrection Church** (Воскресенская церковь) right on the square; the latter's hours are irregular but if it's open you can take the precarious climb to the top of the bell tower to be rewarded with wonderful views of Suzdal's gold-domed skyline.

Across ul Lenina, the five-domed 1707 **Tsar Constantine Church** (Цареконстантиновская церковь) in the square's northeastern corner is a working church with an ornate interior; next door is the 1750 **Church of Our Lady of Sorrows** (Скорбященская церковь).

Holy Intercession Convent CONVENT

(Свято-Покровский монастырь; www.spokrovmon.ru; Pokrovskaya ul; ⏲7am-7pm) FREE It's a classic Suzdal picture: the whitewashed beauty of monastic walls surrounded by green meadows on the banks of the lazily meandering river. Inside are beds of brightly coloured flowers tended by the nuns, who live in wooden cottages left over from a rustic hotel built here when the convent was

Suzdal

Top Sights
1 Kremlin ... C6
2 Museum of Wooden Architecture & Peasant Life ... B7
3 Saviour Monastery of St Euthymius ... B1

Sights
4 Holy Intercession Convent ... A2
5 Nativity of the Virgin Cathedral ... C6
6 Torgovaya Ploshchad ... C5

Activities, Courses & Tours
7 Boat Trips ... B6

Sleeping
8 Guesthouse Usadba Surikova ... C7
9 Petrov Dom ... D3
10 Pushkarskaya Sloboda ... C7
11 Surikov Guest House ... A1

Eating
12 Chaynaya ... C5
13 Gostiny Dvor ... C5
14 Salmon & Coffee ... C5

Drinking & Nightlife
15 Graf Suvorov & Mead-Tasting Hall ... C5

closed after the revolution (it was revived in 1992). Founded in 1364, this convent was originally a place of exile for the unwanted wives of tsars.

Activities

The gentle hills and attractive countryside around Suzdal are ideal for cycling, with bicycles available for rent at many hotels, including **GTK Suzdal** (ГТК Суздаль; ☎49231-23 380, 49231-20 908; www.gtksuzdal.ru; ul Korovniki 45; ⏲10am-6pm). **Gnezdo Pekarya** (Гнездо пекаря), a small bakery on the river side of the **Trading Arcades**, also has a stand of bikes outside the shop with a price list in English.

Helio Spa BATHHOUSE
(☎49231-23 939; www.suzdal.heliopark.ru; ul Korovniki 14) Cleanse body and soul with a visit to a Russian *banya*. Beautiful lakeside *bani* can be rented at Helio Park Hotel for ₽1600/1800 per hour on weekdays/weekends (minimum two hours) for up to six to eight people; attendant services, such as a gentle thrashing with *veniki* (birch branches), are available at extra cost. Advance booking is necessary.

Boat Trips CRUISE
(☎8-916-423 2541; ul Pushkarskaya, at ul Tostogo; adult/child ₽350/free; ⏲hourly noon-7pm) Once an hour a boat takes tourists on a 40-minute cruise up and down the Kamenka River, leaving from the bridge by the Museum of Wooden Architecture (p119). It's a good chance to look at and take pictures of Suzdal's many monasteries and churches from a different perspective. Call to enquire about evening charters. Children under 10 ride for free.

Sleeping

Suzdal is a popular destination for both domestic and international tourists, which means there are plenty of accommodation choices around town, from vast holiday resorts to quaint two- or three-room guesthouses. You can save some money if you avoid staying over at weekends and holidays.

Patchwork Hostel HOSTEL $
(☎8-930-831 3958; www.vk.com/hostel_patchwork; ul Gogolya 59; dm incl breakfast ₽600-700; P 📶) With just two dorm rooms (a six-bed mixed and a four-bed women-only), this new hostel is pocket-sized but spotless, and a short walk from the St Euthymius Monastery (p119). Thoughtful touches include free tea and coffee in the common room and USB charging ports at each bed. The staff speak excellent English, too. Bikes are available for rent.

★**Petrov Dom** GUESTHOUSE $$
(Петров дом; ☎8-919-025 6884; www.petrovdom.ru; per Engelsa 18; r from ₽2000; P 📶) Vlad and Lena offer three nicely furnished rooms in their wooden dacha-style house with a lovely garden on a quiet side street. It's a great option for travellers with children. A sumptuous breakfast costs just ₽200; self-caterers can use the kitchen and garden grill. There's also a private *banya* (hot bath) built by Vlad himself, available for guest rental.

★**Surikov Guest House** GUESTHOUSE $$
(Гостевой дом Суриковых; ☎8-915-752 4950, 49231-21 568; ul Krasnoarmeyskaya 53; d incl breakfast ₽2500; P 📶) This 11-room boutique guesthouse is positioned at a particularly picturesque bend of the Kamenka River across from the walls of the St Euthymius Monastery (p119). It has modestly sized but comfortable rooms equipped with rustic-style furniture (some made by the owner himself) and a Russian restaurant (for guests only) on the 1st floor. Visitors rave about this place.

Guesthouse Usadba Surikova B&B $$
(Гостиница Усадьба Сурикова; ☎8-920-910 7477; ul Lenina 35; r incl breakfast ₽2500; P ❄ 📶 🐾) This little B&B a few minutes' walk south of the kremlin (p119) is neat as a pin and cute as a button. Attentive host Alexander provides a filling, homemade breakfast each morning (including delicious Russian pancakes). Comfortable, spacious rooms come with minifridges.

Pushkarskaya Sloboda RESORT $$$
(Пушкарская слобода; ☎49231-23 303; www.pushkarka.ru; ul Lenina 45; d from ₽4950; P ❄ 📶 🏊) This attractive riverside holiday village has everything you might want for a Russian idyll, including accommodation options in traditionally styled log cabins (from ₽7900). It has three restaurants (including a rustic country tavern and a formal dining room) and a spa centre with pool. The staff can also arrange all sorts of tours and classes around Suzdal.

KAZAN КАЗАНЬ

The main appeal of the route across European Russia to Yekaterinburg via Kazan is that it allows you to stop over in the fascinating capital of the Tatarstan Republic.

Kazan (meaning 'cooking pot' in Tatar) is where Europe and Asia curiously inspect each other from the tops of church belfries and minarets. It is about 150 years older than Moscow and was founded as a northeastern outpost of Volga Bulgaria around AD 1000. After the Tatar Mongols flattened Great Bulgar, it became the capital of the region and was incorporated into the Golden Horde. The independent Kazan khanate was created in 1438. It was ravaged in 1552 by Ivan the Terrible's troops and Tatar allies; the collapse also cleared the way for Slavic Russians to move into the Urals region around Perm.

Tatar autonomy is strong in this oil-rich region. Moscow has pumped vast sums into the republic to persuade it to remain a loyal part of Russia – the city is even one of the locations for the 2018 World Cup.

Sights

The excellent **Kazan Tourist Information Centre** (Казанский туристско-информационный центр; ☎843-292 9777; http://kazantravel.ru/en; Kremlyovskaya ul 15/25; ⏰9.30am-6.30pm Mon-Fri, to 3.30pm Sat) has a good sheet map of town (also available in many hotels). Head first to the striking **Kremlin** (Казанский Кремль; ☎843-567 8001; www.kazan-kremlin.ru; ⏰8am-10pm, to 8pm in winter) FREE inside of which you'll find the beautiful **Kul Sharif Mosque** (Мечеть Кул Шариф; ☎843-567 8125; www.kazan-kremlin.ru; kremlin; museum ₽200; ⏰9am-7.30pm) named after the imam who died defending the city against the troops of Ivan the Terrible in 1552.

Located inside the former cadet school building, the **Hermitage Kazan** (Эрмитаж-Казань; ☎843-567 8032; www.kazan-kremlin.ru; kremlin; adult/concession ₽200/100; ⏰10am-6pm Tue-Thu, Sat & Sun, 11am-8pm Fri) has top-flight rotating exhibitions; many are from the collection of St Petersburg's Hermitage.

National Museum of the Republic of Tatarstan (Национальный музей Республики Татарстан; ☎843-292 8984; www.tatmuseum.ru; Kremlyovskaya ul 2; ₽150; ⏰10am-6pm Sat-Wed, 1pm-9pm Thu, 10am-5pm Fri; Ⓜ Kremlevskaya) occupies an ornate 1770 building. It has a large archaeology collection as well as jewellery, weapons and exhibits on the history of the Tatar people and its literary figures.

Also allow time to walk around and soak up the multicultural atmosphere of the city.

Sleeping & Eating

Hotel Giuseppe (Гостиница Джузеппе; ☎843-292 6934; www.giuseppe.ru; Kremlyovskaya ul 15/25; incl breakfast s ₽2900-5300, d ₽3900-7000, ste ₽6600-14,000; ❄📶) Run by a family with Italian ancestry, the charming place has spacious, comfortable rooms, with corridors decorated tastefully to give the atmosphere of a Venetian villa.

Tatarskaya Usadba (☎8-987-225 0433; http://tatusadba.ru; ul Mardzhani 8; mains ₽500; ⏰11am-1am; 📶) Dig into a full range of Tatar classics, including several dishes with horse-meat and lamb, as well as hearty soups and stews, other mains and desserts.

Kazan Askhane-Chai Yorty (Дом чая, кафе 'Казанская ашхане'; ☎843-292 5654; ul Baumana 64; mains ₽90, pastry ₽50; ⏰9am-8pm) Central, self-serve canteen offering delicious Russian and Tatar foods at reasonable prices.

Getting There & Away

The main station for trains to Moscow, as well as southern destinations along the Volga, is on ul Said-Galieva in the centre. It's variously known as Kazan-1 or Kazan-Pass (passenger) on timetables.

Kazan-2 (also known as Vosstanie-Pass on timetables) is located north of the centre and easily reached by metro. Many Siberia-bound trains go through this station, so check your ticket carefully.

Frequent trains connect Kazan with Moscow (from ₽2800, 12 hours) and Nizhny Novgorod (from ₽2600, nine hours).

Eating

★Chaynaya RUSSIAN $

(Чайная; www.tea-suzdal.ru; ul Kremlyovskaya 10g; mains ₽130-450; ⊙10am-9pm) It's hidden behind a kitsch crafts market, but this place is a gem. Russian standards – bliny, *shchi* (cabbage soup), mushroom dishes and pickles – are prominently represented, but it's all the unusual (and rather experimental) items on the menu that make Chaynaya so special. Red-buckwheat pancakes, anyone?

★Gostiny Dvor RUSSIAN $$

(Гостиный дворъ; ☎49231-021 190; www.suzdal-dvor.ru; Trading Arcades, Torgovaya pl; mains ₽450-550; ⊙10am-10pm Mon-Thu, 9am-11pm Fri-Sun;) There are so many things to like about this place: eclectic decor of rustic antiques and warm wood; outside terrace tables offering river views; hearty Russian dishes (chicken, pike, *pelmeni* dumplings) prepared with modern flair; and friendly, attentive service, to start. Finish up with a tasting set of house-made *medovukha* (honey ale) while the kids amuse themselves in the playroom.

Salmon & Coffee INTERNATIONAL $$

(Лосось и кофе; www.losos-coffee.ru; Trading Arcades, Torgovaya pl; mains ₽340-590; ⊙noon-11pm Mon-Thu, to midnight Fri, 11am-2am Sat, 11am-11pm Sun;) With its whitewashed wood interior and rustic-style decor, this rather quaint cafe on Torgovaya pl (p121) is one of the best places in town for an unhurried lunch or a cup of coffee. Despite the name, salmon is not really prominent on the menu, which includes inventive fusion European dishes and sushi.

Graf Suvorov & Mead-Tasting Hall BEER HALL

(Граф Суворов и зал дегустаций; ☎8-905-734 5404, 49231-20 803; Trading Arcades, Torgovaya pl; tasting menu ₽300-500; ⊙10am-6pm Mon-Fri, to 8pm Sat & Sun) Sit beneath vaulted ceilings and contemplate kitsch murals of Russian military hero Count Suvorov's exploits in the Alps as you make your way through a tasting set (10 samples) of the few dozen varieties of locally produced *medovukha*, a mildly alcoholic honey ale. Flavours also include berry and herb infusions. Located on the back (river) side of the Trading Arcades.

Information

Sberbank (Сбербанк; ul Lenina 73a; ⊙8am-4.30pm Mon-Fri) Exchange office and ATM.

Post Office (Krasnaya pl 3; ⊙8am-8pm Mon-Fri, to 6pm Sat, 9am-2pm Sun)

Getting There & Away

The **bus station** (Автовокзал; ☎49231-020 147; Vasilievskaya ul 44; ⊙4.30am-8pm) is 2km east of the centre on Vasilievskaya ul. Some long-distance buses pass the central square on the way.

There is no bus service to Suzdal from Moscow; you'll need to take a train to Vladimir and then switch to a Suzdal-bound bus there. Buses run very regularly throughout the day to and from Vladimir (₽95, 45 minutes).

For Plyos, take a bus to Ivanovo (₽150, 1½ hours, hourly 8am to 7.30pm) and change there for service to Plyos (₽173, two hours, 10 daily).

Getting Around

Saturn Taxi (Такси 'Сатурн'; ☎8-930-033 0373, 49231-26 061)

Taxi Max (☎8-962-090 0906, 49231-26 026; http://taxi-max.ukit.me)

Nizhny Novgorod Нижний Новгород

☎831 / POP 1.25 MILLION / TIME MOSCOW

Russia's fifth-largest city – sometimes referred to as the country's 'third capital' – would likely go unnoticed by most travellers if not for its arresting hilltop kremlin, overlooking the confluence of two wide rivers: the Volga and Oka. This is the locale where merchant Kuzma Minin and Count Dmitry Pozharsky (men commemorated in a monument in front of Moscow's St Basil's Cathedral) rallied a popular army to repel the Polish intervention in 1612. It's also the city (then known as 'Gorky') where late Soviet scientist-dissident Andrei Sakharov was banished in the 1980s as punishment for opposing the Soviet Union's 1979 invasion of Afghanistan.

Aside from stirring views out over the river (including the possibility of a high-altitude cable-car ride), 'Nizhny' offers several very good museums, and Sakharov's former apartment is home to a quirky exhibition on the great man's life. The port offers the possibility of river excursions to nearby towns.

Sights

Kremlin

Built on remnants of an earlier settlement, Nizhny Novgorod's magnificent **kremlin** (Нижегородский Кремль; ☎831-422 1080; www.

ngiamz.ru; ⌚10am-8pm) FREE dates to 1500–15 when Italian architect Pyotr Fryazin began work on its 13 towers and 12m-high walls. Most of the buildings are government offices, though the city's two most important museums are here, as well as the 17th-century **Cathedral of the Archangel Michael** (Собор Михаила Архангела; ☎831-439 1094; kremlin, building 2a; ⌚10am-8pm) and a striking **Monument to Heroes of WWII** (kremlin). You can walk the walls from May to November and take in riverside views.

★Arsenal/National Centre of Contemporary Art — GALLERY

(Государственный центр совеременного искусства; ☎831-422 4554; www.ncca.ru/nnovgorod; kremlin, building 6; ₽150; ⌚noon-8pm Tue-Sun) Situated in the former kremlin arsenal, on the right after you enter the main gate, this top-ranking national gallery has changing exhibitions of international and Russian contemporary artists. The refurbished space also houses a cafe-restaurant and a concert venue.

Nizhegorodsky State Art Museum — MUSEUM

(Нижегородский государственный художественный музей; ☎831-439 1373; www.artmuseumnn.ru; kremlin, building 3; ₽150; ⌚11am-6pm Wed-Mon) The former governor's house inside the kremlin houses the Russian collection of the vast Nizhegorodsky State Art Museum. Exhibits range from 14th-century icons to 20th-century paintings by artists such as Nikolai Rerikh and Vasily Surikov.

Dmitry Tower — MUSEUM

(Дмитриевская башня; ☎831-422 1080; www.ngiamz.ru; kremlin; museum ₽130, kremlin wall walk incl other towers Russian/foreigner ₽130/200; ⌚10am-5pm Tue-Sun, kremlin wall walk May-Nov) Squat Dmitry Tower, topped in green, is the main entrance to the kremlin and is visible for the length of pedestrianised Bolshaya Pokrovskaya ul. The tower has changing exhibitions on local history and is the starting point for a 1.2km walk along the kremlin walls.

Other Sights

★Cable Car — CABLE CAR

(Kazanskaya naberezhe; one-way ₽90; ⌚6.45am-10pm Mon-Sat, from 9am Sun, closed 11am-1pm Mon & Thu) Connecting Nizhny Novgorod with the unattractive settlement of Bor across the Volga, this cable car offers a spectacular 13-minute ride. In winter there are views of dot-sized figures fishing on Volga ice below, and in summer there's swamp, lush greens and gentle blues. The ride peaks at over 80m and is 3.6km long. The base station is located along the embankment, 2km east of the Kremlin. Take any bus to Sennaya bus station and walk back towards the mosque.

★Rukavishnikov Mansion — MUSEUM

(Усадьба Рукавишникова; ☎831-422 1050; www.ngiamz.ru; Verkhne-Volzhskaya nab 7; Russian/foreigner ₽80/200, tours ₽200/300; ⌚10am-5pm Tue-Thu, noon-7pm Fri-Sun) This exhibition space is located inside a 19th-century mansion once belonging to the Rukavishnikov merchant family. You can wander through the rooms on your own or join one of the hourly 40-minute tours in Russian and (less frequently) in English. Furniture and the illustrious interior of the unusual mansion are the threads running through the tours or a visit, and these are complemented by changing exhibitions – often with a focus on household furnishing and objects.

★Memorial Apartment of Andrei Sakharov — MUSEUM

(Музей Сахарова; ☎831-462 6125; pr Gagarina 214; ₽100; ⌚10am-5pm Sat-Thu) The nondescript flat where dissident scientist Andrei Sakharov, father of Russia's hydrogen bomb, spent seven years in exile after protesting the 1979 Russian invasion of Afghanistan. The Nobel laureate was held incommunicado until 1986, when Mikhail Gorbachev finally released him. Exhibits include background on Sakharov's life as well as the apartment itself. It's located 10km south of the centre. To get there, take a taxi or bus 1 from pl Minina i Pozharskogo or pl Gorkogo (stop: Muzey Akademika Sakharova).

Western European Art Collection — GALLERY

(Собрание Западноевропейского искусство; ☎831-439 1373; www.artmuseumnn.ru; Verkhne-Volzhskaya nab 3; ₽150; ⌚11am-6pm Wed & Fri-Mon, noon-8pm Thu) The Nizhegorodsky State Art Museum's collection of Western European art is exhibited a short walk from the kremlin along Verkhne-Volzhskaya nab, an attractive street lined with restored 19th-century buildings. Inside the art gallery you'll find a collection of mostly anonymous or lesser-known European painters who, despite their modest credentials, produced some remarkable works.

Nizhny Novgorod

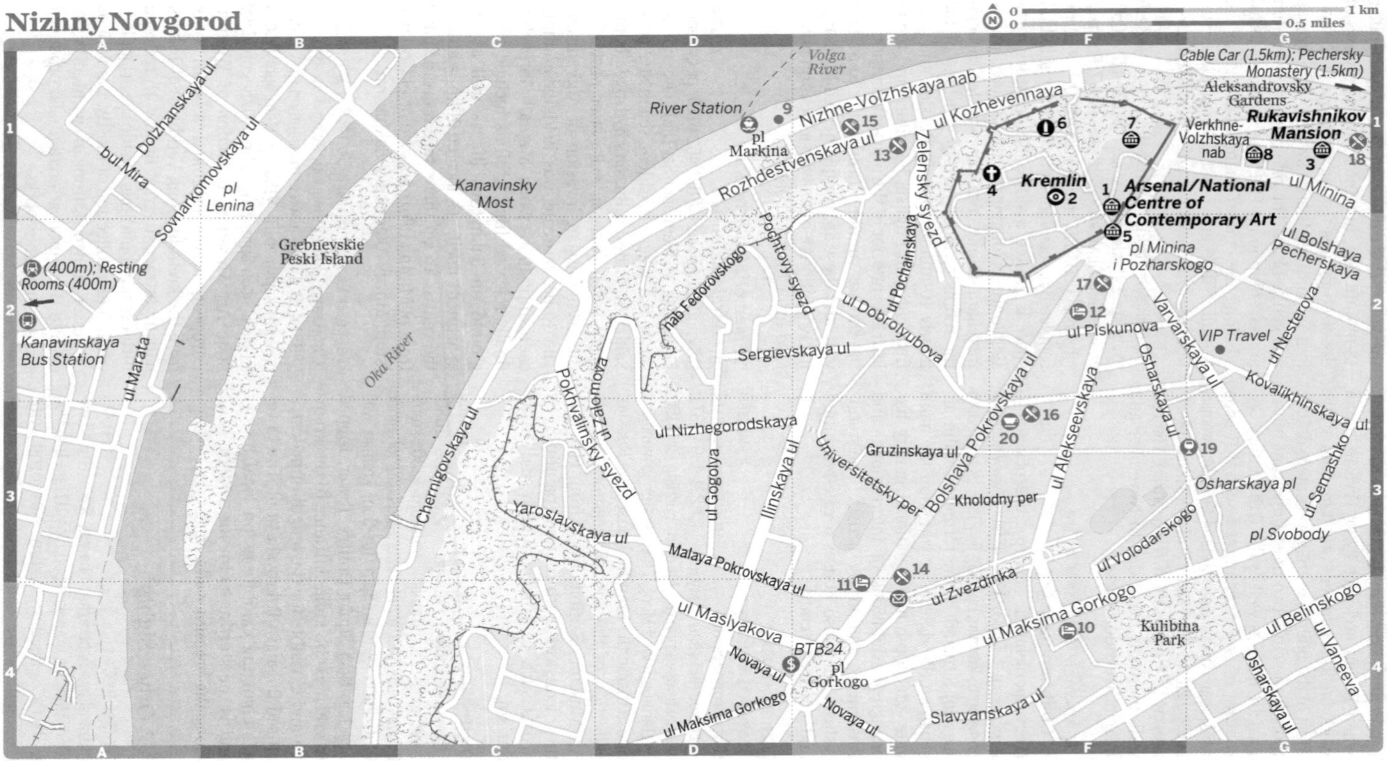

Pechersky Monastery MONASTERY

(☎831-436 1715; www.pecherskiy.nne.ru; Privolzhskaya sloboda 108; ⏰7am-8pm) This 17th-century monastery, overlooking the Volga, is perfect for a tranquil stroll in small but picturesque grounds. It's located about 500m east of the cable-car base station and around 2.5km east of the kremlin. Take any *marshrutka* or bus from pl Minina i Pozharskogo to pl Sennaya.

Sleeping

★ **Smile** HOSTEL $

(☎831-216 0222; www.smilehostel.net; Bolshaya Pokrovskaya ul 4; dm/d ₽450/1590;) Bright, friendly and efficient, this centrally located hostel has two doubles with twin beds that can be booked as a single, and five-, six- and eight-bed dorms. There's free tea and coffee, separate male and female bathroom facilities and a nice communal area.

Ibis Hotel HOTEL $$

(Ибис Отель; ☎831-233 1100; www.ibishotel.com; ul Maksima Gorkogo 115; r from ₽3100;) Nizhny's Ibis offers a high standard of rooms and comforts, with the advantage that it's large enough to cope with busy periods.

★ **Jouk-Jacques** BOUTIQUE HOTEL $$$

(Жук-Жак; ☎831-433 0462; www.jak-hotel.ru; Bolshaya Pokrovskaya ul 57; incl breakfast s ₽3000-4000, d/ste ₽4500/6000;) This cosy boutique hotel is one of the best in town. Rooms are modern and decorated in soft tones, some facing the yard. The cheapest are a bit cramped but they're neat and breakfasts are superb.

Eating

Salyut BURGERS $

(САЛЮТ; ☎8-952-788 8558; www.salutburgers.ru; ul Oktyabrskaya 9a; burgers ₽250; ⏰11.50am-10pm;) Just what Nizhny Novgorod needed to pull it into the 21st century: a trendy, artisanal burger bar that's a nice break from Russian sit-down meals. Get in line with everyone else, order at the counter, grab a seat on the terrace and wait for your number to be called. Classic hamburgers, along with vegetarian and vegan options. Excellent chips.

Stolle RUSSIAN $

(☎831-439 1460; www.stolle.ru; pl Minina i Pozharskogo 2/2; pastries ₽250; ⏰9am-9pm;) This one-trick pony does its one thing exceedingly well: making fresh-baked pastries

Nizhny Novgorod

that are stuffed with meat, mushrooms or fruit. Make your selection at the counter and carry your pie and cup of tea to your table. Perfect for lunch or a snack.

Biblioteka ITALIAN $

(Библиотека; ☎831-433 6934; www.biblioteca-nn.ru; Bolshaya Pokrovskaya ul 46; mains ₽250; ⏰11am-10pm;) Upstairs from the Dirizhabl bookshop with generic but tasty Italian dishes in an informal, quirky atmosphere. There's a nice range of salads and pastas, with a special selection of summertime cocktails. The cosy interior is meant to recall – not surprisingly, given the location – a bookshop.

★ **Restoratsia Pyatkin** RUSSIAN $$

(Ресторация Пяткин; ☎831-430 9183; www.pir.nnov.ru/pyatkin; Rozhdestvenskaya ul 25; mains ₽500; ⏰noon-midnight;) Pyatkin makes you feel like a merchant back in his mansion after a great trading day at the fair. The menu is full of Volga fish specialities; it brews the unusual apple *kvas* (fermented rye bread water) for ₽75 and has a children's menu.

Bezukhov RUSSIAN, INTERNATIONAL $$
(Безухов; ☎831-433 8763; www.bezuhov.ru; Rozhdestvenskaya ul 6; mains ₽600; ⏲24hr; 📶✍) This literary cafe with antique furnishings, stucco ceiling and the feel of a living room is part of a Nizhny Novgorod project called 'Eda i Kultura' (Food and Culture), which brings food and culture together into a delicious whole. The menu is overflowing with salads, pastas and fish, poultry and red-meat dishes, and is augmented by good breakfasts.

Tiffani INTERNATIONAL $$
(Тиффани; ☎831-419 4101; www.tiffanibar.ru; Verkhne-Volzhskaya nab 8; mains ₽600; ⏲noon-2am; 📶✍) This upmarket all-rounder is a restaurant during the day and evening, a cafe at any time, and has well-known DJs some nights. The views across the Volga to the forest are spectacular.

Drinking & Nightlife

★**Bufet** BAR
(Буфет; ☎831-218 0338; www.ekproject.ru; Osharskaya ul 14; ⏲noon-2am; 📶) Descending the steps of this hidden art bar is to step into a bohemian world of monkey-motif wallpaper. The ambience is relaxed and alternative. There's a good range of teas and alcoholic beverages as well as a rotating menu of light bites, such as pasta and hummus. Find the entrance at the far southern end of a long building.

Traveler's Coffee CAFE
(☎831-216 0078; www.travelerscoffee.ru; Bolshaya Pokrovskaya ul 20b; ⏲8am-midnight; 📶) One of several American chain-style coffee bars along pedestrianised Bolshaya Pokrovskaya ul, the main difference being that the coffee is particularly good. Order a well-crafted double espresso and sit in or take away. There's a small selection of cakes and pastries as well.

Information

BTB24 (ВТБ24; pl Maksima Gorkogo 4/2; ⏲24hr) ATM; accepts major cards.

Central Post Office (Центральный почтамт; Bolshaya Pokrovskaya ul 57; ⏲8am-8pm Mon-Fri, 10am-5pm Sat & Sun) Just off central pl Gorkogo.

Getting There & Away

VIP Travel (Вип Трэвел; ☎831-202 1271; www.viptravelnn.ru; Kovalikhinskaya ul 8; ⏲9am-6pm Mon-Fri, to 4pm Sat) can help book air or rail tickets as well as plan excursions to nearby sights or around Russia.

TRAIN

Nizhny Novgorod train station is still sometimes known as Gorky-Moskovsky vokzal, so 'Gorky' appears on some timetables. It's on the western bank of the Oka River, at pl Revolyutsii 2a. The service centre at the train station is helpful for buying rail tickets.

The train station is conveniently located above metro station Moskovskaya (Московская). From the station, take the metro one stop to Gorkovskaya (Горьковская), the main square on the eastern bank of the Oka River that's close to major sights.

Westbound

The high-speed Sapsan/Lastochka runs to Moscow's Kursky vokzal (seat ₽2400, four to five hours, two daily). More than a dozen other trains also serve Moscow (₽1300, seven hours) via Vladimir (₽800, three hours). The Volga (059) runs to/from St Petersburg (₽2800, 14½ hours, daily).

Eastbound

Trans-Siberian flagships run to Perm (₽3600, 14½ hours, daily) and beyond, but lesser trains do the trip for ₽2450 – for Kazan (₽2600, nine hours, daily) the 41 is a top-flight (and only) choice. Other trains go to Yekaterinburg (₽4300, 20 hours, several daily) and beyond.

AIR

Nizhny Novgorod International Airport (Международный аэропорт Нижний Новгород;GOJ; ☎831-261 8080; www.nnov-airport.ru/eng) is 15km southwest of the city centre. The airport has several flights daily to Moscow and a handful of flights to other large cities around Russia, including to Kazan. To get to the airport, take the metro to the southern terminus at Park Kultury (Парк культу́ры) and then bus 11 or 20.

BOAT

The **river station** (Речной вокзал; Nizhne-Volzhskaya nab) is below the kremlin. All services on the Volga are cruise, day-excursion or tourist boats. Unfortunately, there are no short-hop ferries between major towns. Hydrofoils to Gorodets leave from their own pier at the river station.

BUS

Buses to Vladimir (₽600, four hours, eight daily), Kostroma (₽1000, nine hours, daily) and Gorodets (₽200, two hours, about every half-hour) depart from the small **Kanavinskaya bus station** (Автостанция Канавинская; ☎831-246 2021; www.nnov.org/transport/busm/kanavinskaya; Sovetskaya ul 20a). Private operators run minibuses to Moscow (₽800, six hours, at least six daily), which depart across the road from the train station; others leave from the bus station.

WORTH A TRIP

GORODETS

The Volga river town of Gorodets, 60km north of Nizhny Novgorod, makes for a fun day trip and, in summer, a chance to get out on the water. The town is the oldest in the region and is famous for its distinct style of folk art. The local museum quarter has been attractively preserved and can be toured in under half a day.

Gorodets earned its reputation for folk art starting around the time of the schism in the Russian Orthodox Church (1660). The town became home to a population of Old Believers seeking religious sanctuary. They became skilful craftsmen, artists and wealthy tradesmen.

In a largely illiterate society, Gorodets oil-on-wood paintings played the role of glossy magazines about lifestyle and current events. Today you can buy pictures (from ₽200) or a whole piece of furniture, painted in Gorodets style. The town's other speciality is *pryaniki* – hard, honey-rich cakes sold in most shops.

Several hydrofoils leave daily for Gorodets from Nizhny Novgorod's river station (₽200, one hour) from late May to September. **Vodokhod Tour Office** (Водоходъ; ☎831-461 8030; https://volga-vodohod.ru; Nizhne-Volzhskaya nab; ⊙10am-9pm Mon-Fri, to 7pm Sat & Sun) in Nizhny Novgorod runs excursions for around ₽1000. Out of sailing season, Gorodets is accessible by bus from Nizhny Novgorod's bus station (₽180, two hours, about half-hourly).

Getting Around

Central Nizhny Novgorod is compact enough to walk around, and a car-free pedestrian zone, ul Bolshaya Pokrovskaya, links the main square, pl Gorkogo (пл Горького), to busy pl Minina i Pozharskogo (пл Минина и Пожарского), near the kremlin.

Both the bus and train stations are located on the western side of the Oka River, about 3km from main sights (which are all situated on the eastern side). Buses and *marshrutky* run from the train station to both hubs on the eastern side: pl Gorkogo and pl Minina i Pozharskogo. The metro has a useful link between pl Gorkogo and the train station.

Uber ride-share service (www.uber.com) operates in Nizhny and rates are significantly cheaper than standard taxis.

Perm — Пермь

☎342 / POP 1.05 MILLION / TIME MOSCOW +2HR

'Perm' once referred to a mysterious Finno-Ugric land encompassing most of the northwestern Ural Mountains, colonised by Russians since the early medieval ages. But the city is relatively new, founded by the lieutenants of Peter I in 1723.

It is believed that Chekhov used Perm as the inspiration for the town his Three Sisters were so desperate to leave, and Boris Pasternak sent his Doctor Zhivago to a city clearly resembling Perm.

Located on the Kama River, Perm has long welcomed passers-by from various regions. Consequently, today's Perm is a cultural hotpot; the residents are welcoming and many of them speak English.

Perm has some interesting museums and cultural attractions, and is also the base from which to visit a great wooden architecture museum, located in Khokhlovka; the famous ice cave in Kungur; and a grim reminder of Soviet-era political persecution – the Perm-*36* labour camp.

Sights

Perm was one of the first cities in Russia to introduce the tourist-line concept and has two tourist trails, both around 5km in length with signposts in English. The green line tracks the main architectural sights, while the red line has more of a romantic focus, with local life and love stories interlaced into the city's history. The Tourist Information Center (p132) has a free, multilingual *Green Line* booklet for self-guided city walks.

There are a number of good museums in town and every third Wednesday of the month entrance to most of them is free.

★Museum of Contemporary Art PERMM MUSEUM

(Музей современного искусства PERMM; ☎342-254 3552; www.permm.ru; bul Gagarin 24; ₽150; ⊙noon-9pm Tue-Sun) This museum was opened in 2009 with the aid of gallery dealer Marat Gelman. At that time it was housed in the historic Perm River Station Hall. It moved in 2014 and today continues to play a pivotal role in the Perm contemporary-arts scene, with changing exhibits that attract a diverse crowd.

Perm

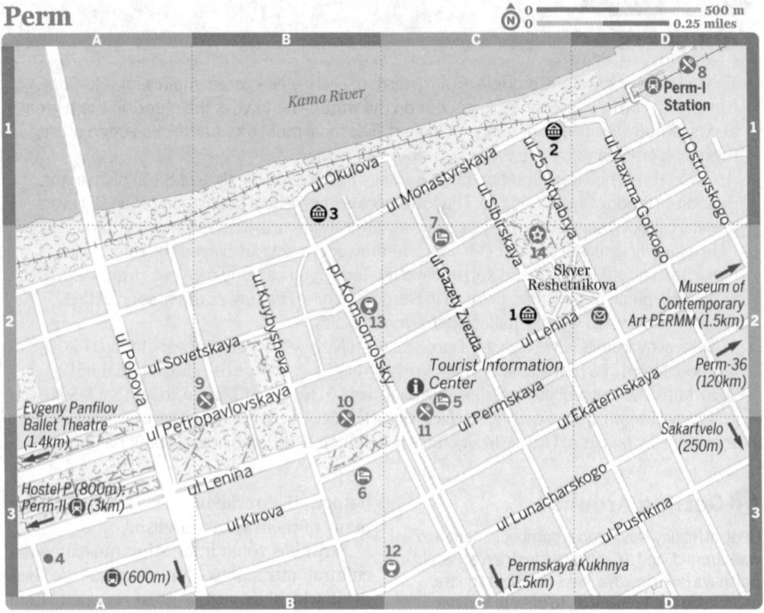

Perm

Sights

1 Museum of Perm Prehistory C2
2 Perm Regional Museum C1
3 Perm State Art Gallery B1

Activities, Courses & Tours

4 Krasnov A3
Permturist .... (see 6)

Sleeping

5 Eva Hotel C2
6 Hotel Ural B3
7 Vicont Hotel C2

Eating

8 Expedicia Restaurant D1
9 Mishka Food B2
10 Pelmennaya No 2 .... B3
11 Sister's Bar C2

Drinking & Nightlife

12 Molotov Bar & Beer Shop C3
13 Old Moose Pub B2

Entertainment

14 Tchaikovsky Theatre of Opera & Ballet C2

Transport

Aviakassa .... (see 6)
Railways Booking Office .... (see 6)

Museum of Perm Prehistory MUSEUM
(Музей пермских древностей; ☎342-212 5657; www.museum.perm.ru/filiali/muzey-permskih-drevnostey; ul Sibirskaya 15; ₽120; ⏱10am-7pm Fri-Sun, Tue & Wed, noon-9pm Thu) The archaeological collection here encompasses over 2000 antiques, many from the Perm region. The highlight is a skeleton exhibit, where visitors will find a number of original and replica skeletons of dinosaurs and animals from prehistoric times. There is a big focus on the Permian period and animals unique to the area. Many of the explanations are in English.

Perm State Art Gallery GALLERY
(Пермская Государственная Художественная Галерея; ☎342-212 2395; www.permartmuseum.ru; pr Komsomolsky 4; ₽120; ⏱10am-7pm Tue, Wed, Fri & Sat, noon-9pm Thu, 11am-7pm Sun) Housed in the grand Cathedral of Christ Transfiguration on the banks of the Kama, the Perm State Art Gallery is renowned for its collection of Permian wooden sculpture. Take

trolleybus 1 to the stop Galereya, or trolleybus 5 to the stop Sovetskaya, or trams 3, 4, 7 and 11 to the stop Tsum.

Perm Regional Museum MUSEUM
(Пермский Краеведческий Музей; www.museum.perm.ru; ul Monastyrskaya 11; ₽130; ⊙10am-7pm Tue, Wed & Fri-Sun, noon-9pm Thu) Located inside the imposing Meshkov House, this regional museum only gets really interesting when you see the small collection of intricate metal castings of the 'Perm animal style' used in the shamanistic practices of ancient Finno-Ugric Permians.

Tours

★ **Evrasia** ADVENTURE
(☎342-249 8222; www.permtours.com; ul Timiryazeva 50; ⊙10am-7pm Mon-Fri) Perm's oldest tourism company specialises in custom-made tours of Perm and beyond, with everything from city and Perm-36 tours to outdoor rafting, cycling and hiking trips. English-, German-, Italian- and Spanish-speaking guides are available by request and service from the Evrasia team is impeccable. The Evrasia office stocks maps and the *Green Line* booklet.

Krasnov ADVENTURE
(Краснов; ☎342-238 3520; www.uraltourism.ru; ul Borchaninova 4; ⊙10am-6.30pm Mon-Fri, by arrangement Sat) Offers active and adventure tourism such as rafting or cross-country skiing in the Urals, beginner Russian courses, river cruises and many more activities. The Russian version of the website has a wider and sometimes less expensive choice.

Permturist ADVENTURE
(Пермтурист; ☎342-218 6999; www.turizm-ural.ru; Hotel Ural, office 219, ul Lenina 58; ⊙10am-7pm Mon-Fri, by arrangement Sat) Located inside the Hotel Ural, Permturist organises excursions (in Russian and English) to places like the Kungur Ice Cave, and also does city tours in Perm.

Festivals & Events

★ **Diaghilev Festival** PERFORMING ARTS
(www.diaghilevfest.ru) Perm is said to be the third ballet mecca, following Moscow and St Petersburg. Every two years the Diaghilev Festival (named after the famous Russian ballet star Sergei Diaghilev) attracts arts fans with its rich ballet and opera program.

Kamwa Festival CULTURAL
(www.kamwa.ru) The annual 'ethno-futuristic' Kamwa Festival held in summer in Perm and Khokhlovka brings together ancient ethno-Ugric traditions and modern art, music and fashion. Dates vary considerably each year – see the website.

Sleeping

Hostel P HOSTEL $
(☎342-214 7847; www.permhostel.ru; ul Lenina 67; dm ₽400-700; ❄📶) Nine clean and pleasant rooms make up this friendly hostel, located close to Perm-II railway station, about 15 minutes' walk to the centre of town. There's a bright kitchen where guests can cook their own food, and there are laundry facilities (for an additional fee).

★ **Eva Hotel** BOUTIQUE HOTEL $$
(☎342-212 5858; www.eva-hotel.ru; ul Permskaya 63/1; incl breakfast s ₽3100-3800, d ₽3500-4200; P❄📶🐾) Located in the centre of town on a quiet street, Eva Hotel is a delightful boutique stay with just 10 light-filled rooms. Staff are courteous and will serve tasty breakfasts (with a changing weekly menu) in your room.

Vicont Hotel BOUTIQUE HOTEL $$
(☎342-215 5670; www.hotelvicont.ru; ul Sovetskaya 40; incl breakfast s ₽3200-5000, d ₽3600-5300; ⊖❄📶) A pleasant boutique hotel located close to all the city attractions, Vicont Hotel has nine double rooms, with continental breakfasts served in-room or in the on-site cafe.

Hotel Ural HOTEL $$$
(Гостиница Урал; ☎342-218 6262; www.hotel-ural.com; ul Lenina 58; incl breakfast s ₽2700-7200, d ₽3600-12,400; ⊖@📶) This one-time Soviet monolith rising up in the heart of the city has adapted to the age and boasts a shimmering, high-tech lobby and modern, reasonably sized rooms.

Eating

Pelmennaya No 2 RUSSIAN $
(Пельменная No. 2; ☎342-212 3895; ul Lenina 47; pelmeni ₽160-340) Designed to depict a typical Russian *dacha* (summer countryhouse), Pelmennya No 2 is where the masses come for *pelmeni* (Russian-style dumplings stuffed with meat). There's a wide selection of the famous Russian dumplings, with everything from chicken to pork to fish. Pelmennaya No 1 – part of the same chain and located a

few blocks from the city centre – is a quieter option.

Sister's Bar CAFE $
(☎342-259 2515; ul Lenina 54a; mains ₽240-440; ⊙11am-midnight Sun-Thu, to 1am Fri & Sat) Sisters Alaya and Ksenia opened this cafe in 2013 wanting to break away from their corporate jobs. The sisters enjoy Cantonese cuisine and food from the Basque region of Spain, so they serve a selection of dishes that are a bit of a mishmash. The indoor space is light and airy and there's a balcony that fills up in summer.

Mishka Food CAFE $
(☎342-203 0352; ul Osinskaya 19; mains ₽160-380; ⊙10am-10pm; 📶) Craving poached eggs? At Mishka Food there's a decent selection of modern cafe breakfast items available until 4pm. Breakfast, lunch or dinner, all the options are based on seasonal ingredients and look ever so pretty – make your decision by checking out mishka.food on Instagram.

Permskaya Kukhnya RUSSIAN $$
(Пермская Кухня; ☎342-244 1355; ul Gazety Zvezda 75; mains ₽219-369; ⊙11am-11pm; ❄📶✍) You can try Bashkir, Tatar, Russian and Finno-Ugric cuisine at this quirky and newly refurbished restaurant-museum. The manager is passionate about sharing his love for regional cuisine and might pop over to see what you think of the (sometimes) unusual menu offerings. Try the green soup – it's made from a wild herb that's endemic to the region.

★ **Expedicia Restaurant** RUSSIAN $$$
(Ресторан Экспедиция; ☎342-205 5975; www.expedicia-perm.ru; ul Monastyrskaya 3a; mains ₽570-1680, business lunches from ₽350; ⊙noon-last guest leaves daily; ❄) If you're happy to splash out you'll find spectacular northern Russian cuisine served here, with wild game and local fish dishes highly recommended. There's also a *banya*, a hotel and a gift shop for those who want to stay awhile.

Drinking & Nightlife

★ **Molotov Bar & Beer Shop** BREWERY
(☎342-243 0326; ul Lunacharskogo 62b; ⊙6-11pm Tue-Thu, 5pm-1am Fri & Sat, to 11pm Sun) Molotov Brewery has been making its own Russian craft beers since 2012 – and in 2016 it opened a bar, which fills up with a beer-loving crowd most nights. The changing menu includes local and Russian beers, with at least five from Perm on sale at any one time. Usual pub fare, such as pizzas and burgers, is available.

Old Moose Pub PUB
(☎342-203 2014; pr Komsomolsky 14; ⊙2pm-1am Sun-Thu, to 3am Fri & Sat) Owner Illya set out to open a pub that served the best international beers in town. He succeeded and today attracts a diverse crowd with his wide selection of predominantly Belgian, English, Czech and German beers, both draft and bottled. There are two more locations in the city, with the same huge list of beer variants.

Entertainment

Evgeny Panfilov Ballet Theatre BALLET
(Балет Евгения Панфилова; ☎342-271 6101; www.balletpanfilov.ru; ul Petropavlovskaya 185; tickets usually ₽200-500) A wide range of dance performances are held here, some quite unique and memorable – such as performances by the 'Eugene Panfilov Ballet of the Fat' group.

Tchaikovsky Theatre of Opera & Ballet THEATRE
(Театр оперы и балета Чайковского; ☎ticket office 342-212 3087; www.arabesque.permonline.ru; ul Petropavlovskaya 25; tickets ₽100-1000; ⊙ticket office 10am-2pm & 3-7pm) Performances by students of one of Russia's top ballet schools. Ticket prices depend on seat and performance.

Information

Main Post Office (ul Lenina 28; ⊙8am-10pm Mon-Fri, 9am-6pm Sat & Sun)

Tourist Information Center (Туристский информационный центр; ☎342-241 1080; www.visitperm.ru; ul Lenina 39; ⊙9am-7pm Mon-Fri, 10am-6pm Sat & Sun) The Perm Region Tourist Centre has a wealth of information about Perm city and Perm region. There are plenty of information booklets in English and English-speaking staff members are happy to help with any queries. They are also responsive to emails and it is generally one of the most helpful tourist centres in the country.

Getting There & Away

Inside the Hotel Ural you will find a **railways booking office** (☎342-233 0203; ⊙8am-7pm Mon-Fri, to 6pm Sat & Sun) and an **Aviakassa** (☎342-233 2509; ⊙8.30am-8pm Mon-Fri, 10am-5pm Sat & Sun).

TRAIN

Perm-II, the city's major train station, 3km southwest of the centre, is on the trans-Siberian route. Many trains travel the route to/from Moscow, including all of the Trans-Siberian *firmeny*

DON'T MISS

PERM-36

Officially known as the Memorial complex of political repressions, **Perm-36** (Мемориальный комплекс политических репрессий; 342-212 6129; www.itk36-museum.ru; derevnya Kuchino, Perm Krai; strict regime entry ₽300, special regime entry ₽200, excursion ₽100; 9am-6pm Tue-Sun, tours in Russian at 10am, 11.30am, 1.30pm & 3pm), located some 125km east of Perm, was a labour camp for dissidents from 1946 to 1987. In 1994 it became a museum complex run by the international human rights organisation Memorial, which was founded by the dissident Andrei Sakharov. It's one of the only remaining Gulag camps in Russia and today acts as a museum, with exhibitions about the camp as well as changing displays that don't relate directly to life in the Gulag.

It's a haunting site, isolated and set deep in a landscape which in summer is verdant and filled with birdsong. Countless artists, scientists and intellectuals spent years in the cold, damp cells here, many in solitary confinement. They worked at mundane tasks such as assembling fasteners and survived on measly portions of bread and gruel.

It's worth hiring a guide for the day to learn about the regimes and history of the Gulag – and to get you there and back. The Gulag is located in the outskirts of the village of Kuchino, about 25km from the town of Chusovoy, which itself is 100km from Perm. You can take a bus bound for Chusovoy or Lysva, get off at Tyomnaya (₽200, two hours) station, walk back to the main road and backtrack to the Kuchino turn-off (also leading to (Makhnutino), then walk another 2.5km to the village.

(premium, long-distance) trains. If you're on a tighter budget, many cheaper trains do the route from ₽1890. Heading east, the next major stop on the trans-Siberian route is Yekaterinburg (*platskart/kupe* ₽1000/1444, six hours). For Kazan (₽1300, 19 hours) the most direct route is with an inconvenient change in Izhevsk. Buses can be better. Note that some trains depart from the *gornozavodskoe napravlenie* (mining track) on the north side of Perm-II, as opposed to the *glavnoe napravlenie* (main track). Trains to the east never depart from the mining track, only those to the north and west.

AIR

Several airlines fly to Moscow (from ₽4400, two hours, frequent).

BOAT

The river station (Речной вокзал) is at the eastern end of ul Monastyrskaya, in front of Perm-I station. Boats do short tours of the Kama in the navigation season. **Evrasia** (p131) and **Permturist** (p131) can organise tours.

BUS

From the **bus station** (Автовокзал; 342-236 4434; www.avperm.ru; ul Revolyutsii 68) numerous buses go to Kungur (₽258, 1¼ hours); there are frequent buses to Khokhlovka (₽118, 1½ hours) and two daily buses to Ufa (₽1300, 11½ hours). Buses to Kazan depart every two days, with some additional services Friday and Saturday (₽1500, 12 hours).

Getting Around

Bus 42 and *marshrutka* (fixed-route minibus) 1t go between the bus station and the airport. Trolleybus 5 connects Perm-II station with Hotel Ural, tram 7 connects Perm-II with the corner of ul Lenina and ul Maksima Gorkogo via ul Petropavlovskaya, and tram 11 connects ul Maxima Gorkogo with the central market (about 400m from the bus station) via ul Petropavlovskaya and ul Borchaninova.

Kungur Кунгур

34271 / POP 66,000 / TIME MOSCOW +2HR

Kungur's main attraction is the frozen magic of its ice cave, drawing a stream of curious visitors. The city itself is a little rundown and belies a skyline graced by a multitude of pretty church cupolas, including the 18th-century Tikhvinskaya Church in the centre and the Transfiguration Church on the other bank of the Sylva.

Sights

Kungur Ice Cave CAVE

(Кунгурская ледяная пещера; 342-716 2602; www.kungurcave.ru; Filippovka village, Kungur rayon; guided tour ₽600-700, with laser show ₽700-800, private tour ₽1500; 10am-4pm, extended hours in summer) The network of caves stretches for more than 5km, although only about 1.5km are accessible. The ancient Finno-Ugric

WORTH A TRIP

ARCHITECTURAL-ETHNOGRAPHIC MUSEUM

This **museum** (Архитектурно-этнографический музей; http://heritage.perm.ru/hohlovka/; ₽120; ⏲10am-6pm, closed last Mon in month) is located near Khokhlovka, about 45km north of Perm. Its impressive collection of wooden buildings includes two churches dating from the turn of the 18th century. Most of the structures are from the 19th or early 20th centuries, including an old firehouse, a salt-production facility and a Khanty izba (traditional wooden cottage).

A few buses a day serve Khokhlovka from Perm (₽118, 1½ hours), the best ones departing Perm at 9.55am and returning from Khokhlovka at 4.30pm.

inhabitants of the region believed the cave to be the home of an underground creature, and the grottoes are adorned with ice formations and frozen lakes, although these are best seen in winter as most grottoes have minimal ice at other times. The ice cave is about 5km out of town and you can enter only on guided tours.

Bring warm clothes. The cost of the tour includes admission to a small museum on the site with displays of rocks and fossils.

Regional Local Studies Museum MUSEUM
(Кунгурский краеведческий музей; ☎342-712 4394; ul Gogolya 36; ₽80; ⏲10am-5pm Wed-Sun) Founded in 1663 on the banks of the meandering river, Kungur was a copper-smelting centre during the 17th and 18th centuries, which is a key focus of the Regional Local Studies Museum.

Sleeping & Eating

Stalagmit Tourist Complex HOTEL $
(☎342-716 2602; www.hotel.kungurcave.ru; Kunger Cave; incl breakfast s ₽800-2000, d ₽1400-3000;) This popular complex is close to the cave entrance and offers excellent rooms with their own bathroom (the cheaper ones don't have fridges and TV). Take bus 9 from the train station to the last stop.

Hotel Iren HOTEL $$
(Гостиница Ирень; ☎342-713 2270; www.hotel.kungur.ru; ul Lenina 30; r without bathroom ₽830-1830, incl breakfast s ₽1300-1800, d ₽2200-2500;) In the centre of town, Hotel Iren is good value, but it doesn't have a lift. Even the rooms without bathrooms are pleasant enough, and the shared toilets and showers are very clean.

Tri Medvedya RUSSIAN $
(Три медведя; ☎342-713 6739; ul Vorovskaya 5; mains from ₽200; ⏲noon-2am Sun-Thu, to 3am Sat & Sun;) Across the bridge in the centre of town, the riverside cafe-disco Tri Medvedya has very decent food. Helpful staff can order a taxi for you back to the bus and train stations.

Getting There & Around

Kungur is served from Perm by frequent intercity trains (₽400 to ₽670, 1½ hours), suburban trains (₽175, 2¼ hours, four daily) and trains to/from Yekaterinburg (₽463 to ₽1358, four hours). Bus is the best option from Perm, however, with departures every one to two hours; the most convenient leaves Perm at 8.25am or 9.25am and returns from Kungur at 6.40pm or 7.55pm (₽214, 2½ hours). Buses to Ufa (₽840, one daily) depart at 10am.

The bus and train stations are located alongside each other. Bus 9 (every one to two hours) plies the route between Hotel Iren, the train and bus stations, and the Stalagmit complex.

Yekaterinburg to Krasnoyarsk

Includes ➡

Route Info

➡ Distance: 2287km

➡ Duration: 35 hours

➡ Time zones: Moscow +2, Moscow +3, Moscow +4

Best Places to Stay

➡ Red Star Hostel (p143)

➡ Hotel Sibir (p151)

➡ DoubleTree by Hilton (p157)

➡ Gogol Hotel (p162)

Best Places to Eat

➡ Pashtet (p144)

➡ Romanov Restaurant (p152)

➡ La Maison (p158)

➡ Slavyansky Bazar (p163)

Why Go?

This leg of the journey starts in the Urals with the historically important city of Yekaterinburg. The train then moves into Siberia and eventually on to its buzzing capital, Novosibirsk. Both cities are worth a stop but the main attractions of the region both require detours off the Trans-Siberian route. From oil-rich Tyumen, consider a trip to Tobolsk which has a picturesque kremlin. Further on, a branch line will take you to the friendly university town of Tomsk, peppered with gorgeous wooden architecture.

The scenery outside the train isn't the most visually exciting, with little more to see than endless miles of forest and farmland. Perhaps the best way to make the journey, then, is on a series of night trains which will help you save on hotels. If you do take day trains, there is admittedly a certain pleasure to be gained from the unchanging countryside and the opportunity it provides to reflect on Russia, life, or whatever takes your fancy.

When to Go

Novosibirsk

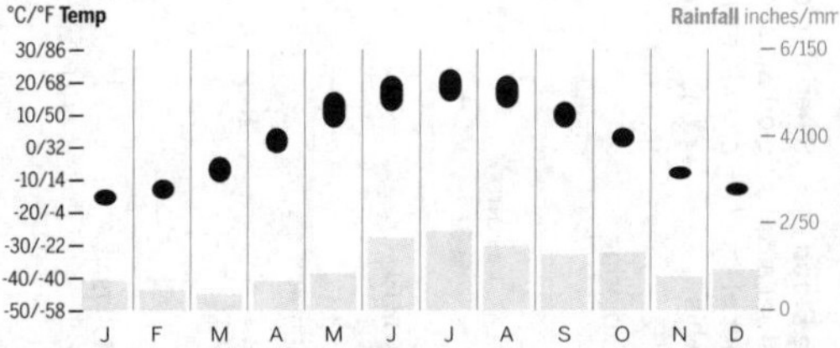

May & Jun Grand WWII Victory Day celebrations take place in Novosibirsk

Jul–Sep Travel across Siberia in glorious sunshine (just bring mosquito repellent)

Dec & Jan Tramp through Tomsk's winter wonderland and greet the New Year, Russian style

Yekaterinburg to Krasnoyarsk Highlights

1 **Church upon the Blood** (p141) Tracing the historical contours of the murder of Russia's last tsar and his family in Yekaterinburg.

2 **Tobolsk** (p149) Exploring Siberia's old capital with its glorious snow-white Kremlin and old town.

3 **Novosibirsk** (p153) Taking time out in Siberia's capital with its bustling bars and varied museums.

4 **Tomsk** (p159) Strolling through the Oxford of Siberia with its picturesque wooden homes and green-fingered gardens.

5 **Trinity Monastery** (p146) Walking along Tyumen's riverfront promenade en route to this striking complex.

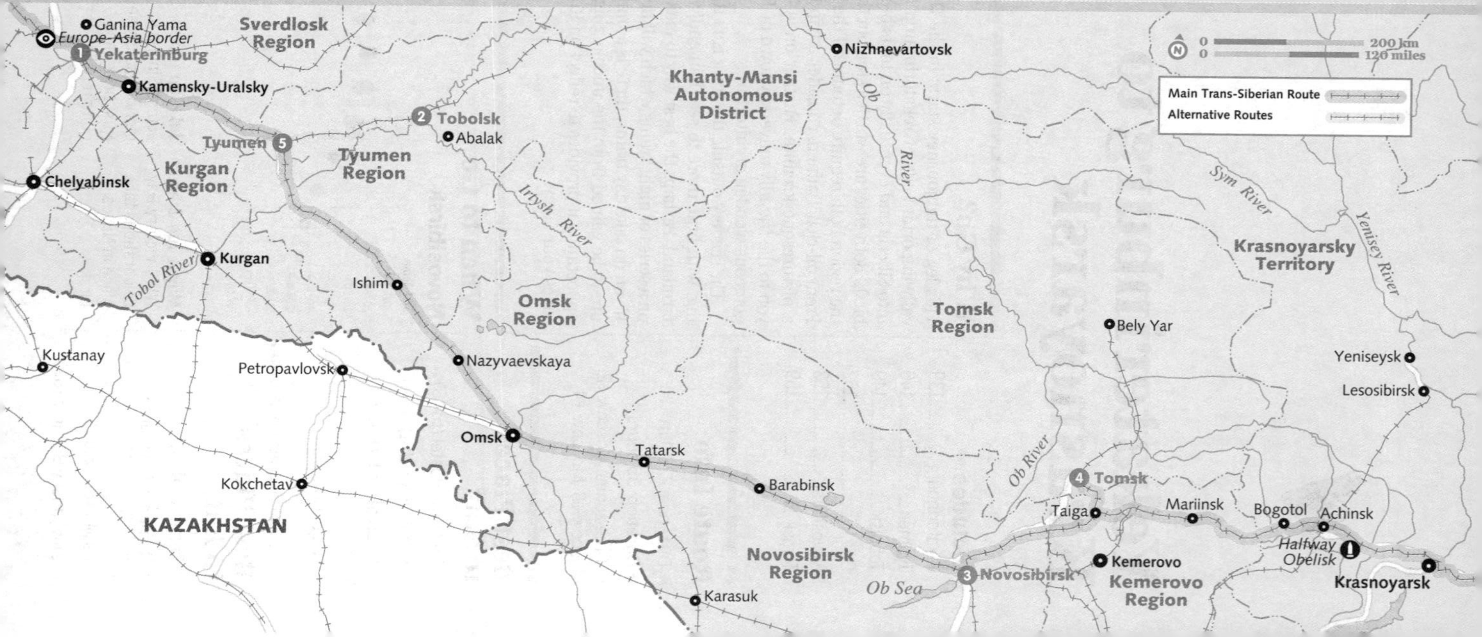

The Route

YEKATERINBURG TO OMSK

1814km from Moscow

Major trains halt at Yekaterinburg (p139) for 15 to 30 minutes. The cultural and economic capital of the Urals, the city is famous as the birthplace of Boris Yeltsin and as the place where Tsar Nicholas II and his family met their deaths at the hands of the Bolsheviks. Wander across the street for a look at the old train station, which now houses a railway museum.

2102km

This is where **Siberia** officially begins. Look out for the kilometre marker and celebrate the event in some way. After all, you are now in the famed land of snowstorms, Gulag camps and enthusiastic hospitality. Even for Russians, the word 'Sibir' – or 'Siberia' – is an evocative one, conjuring images of hardy Sibiryaki (Siberians), endless steppe and perpetual taiga. It's also where the influence of European Russia begins to visibly wane.

2138km

Trains stop for 15 minutes in Tyumen (p146), the region's oldest Russian settlement and now a dynamic oil-rich city. There's not much to see directly outside the train station, so you'd be better off stocking up on supplies, if necessary, from the station shop. From Tyumen our route detours 221km northeast off the official Trans-Siberian line to the old Siberian capital of Tobolsk (p149). Most of the route is fairly bland as the train slinks along the Tura and Tobol Rivers. From 210km to 216km, east-facing windows have pleasant if distant views of Tobolsk's kremlin. You cross the Irtysh River at 216km and pull into the train station 5km later. There's a picturesque market right on the platform, with stalls selling many varieties of dried and smoked fish, as well as beer and ubiquitous cheap Chinese noodles. As it's a long way into town, a good strategy – especially if you are arriving late – is to make use of the station's comfortable and clean resting rooms.

2428km

Back on the main Trans-Siberian route east, the next major stop is for 12 to 15 minutes at tiny **Ishim**, which was famous for its 19th-century Nikolskaya trade fairs (revived since 1991). This was the birthplace of the Russian fairytale writer Pyotr Yershov (1815–69), whose most famous work, *The Humpbacked Horse*, was banned for many years by the tsar's censors. Ishim has a striking, whitewashed 1793 cathedral. The Trans-Siberian reached this town of 65,000 in 1913 as the railway was extended from Tyumen to Omsk. At 2497km, local time becomes Moscow time plus three hours. Swampy land provides opportunities for birdwatchers, especially in warmer seasons.

Yekaterinburg to Krasnoyarsk

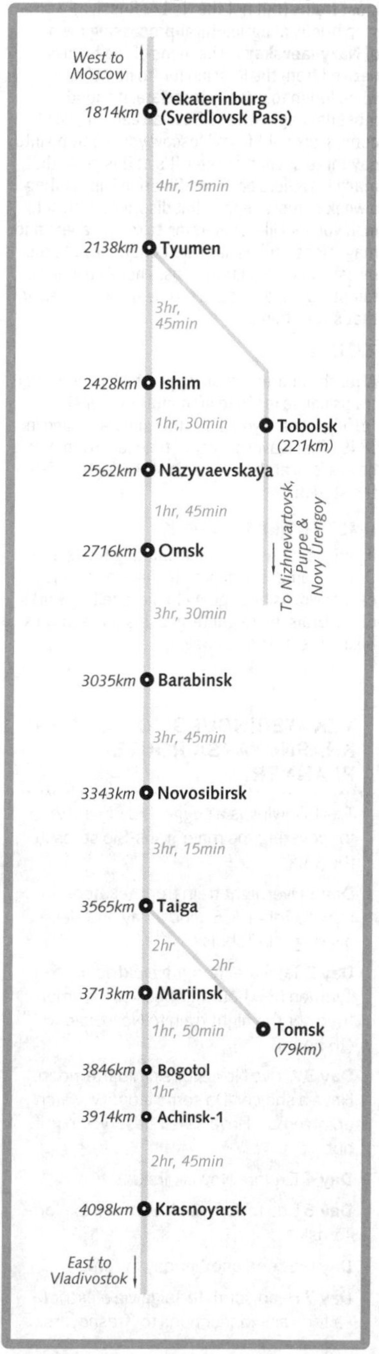

2562km

Most trains (but not the No 1/2 Rossiya) stop briefly at agricultural-processing town of **Nazyvaevskaya**. The name of the town is derived from the Russian for 'to name' and while tough to directly translate, it sounds most unimaginative to Russian ears. If you're coming straight from Moscow you'll now be into day three of your journey. It's at this point that many travellers on Trans-Siberian trips lasting a week or more report that disorientation sets in. If you feel like something to read, papers and magazines (in Russian) are continually offered by salespeople on the trains. There's usually a fair selection of sudoku puzzle books as well, if that's your thing.

2711km

After the impressive six-span Irtysh River bridge, trains pause for 15 to 40 minutes in Omsk (p152), where Fyodor Dostoevsky was exiled in 1849. That leaves plenty of time to nip out and have a look at the fine Lenin statue right outside the station.

OMSK TO KRASNOYARSK

If you notice an increase in passing trains after Omsk, blame it on coal from the Kuzbas Basin east of Novosibirsk going to the smelting works of the Urals. In freight terms, this is the world's busiest section of railway.

YEKATERINBURG TO KRASNOYARSK ROUTE PLANNER

The following is a suggested itinerary for covering the main Trans-Sib stops in the area.

Day 1 Overnight train from Yekaterinburg to Tobolsk. Spend a day and sleep overnight in Tobolsk.

Day 2 Take the morning *elektrichka* to Tyumen (3½ hours). Check out Tyumen, then get the night train to Novosibirsk (16 hours).

Day 3 Arrive Novosibirsk midafternoon. Have a shower. Do some laundry. Catch up on email. Have a well-deserved night out.

Day 4 Explore Novosibirsk.

Day 5 Bus to Tomsk (4½ hours). Explore Tomsk.

Day 6 Spend another day in Tomsk.

Day 7 Head south to Taiga via *elektrichka* for train connections to Krasnoyarsk.

3035km

Barabinsk was once a place of exile for Polish Jews. The surrounding Barabinsk Steppe is a boggy expanse of grassland and lakes that was formerly the homeland of the Kirghiz people. Many train engines and carriages that service the Trans-Siberian put in here for repairs at some point or other. There's usually a 30-minute stop here, plenty of time to grab provisions from the platform kiosks and vendors.

3330km

Get ready for the seven-span, 870m-long bridge across the **Ob**, one of the world's longest rivers. It's also extremely busy, with all manner of barges and cargo ships going about their business.

3336km

Some trains stop for up to 50 minutes in Novosibirsk (p153) (the Rossiya stops for 21 minutes). If you're not stopping over in the city, jump out the train and inspect the grand station interior, a real temple of the Trans-Siberian. Also try to have a quick look at the two WWII memorial statues on platform 1 depicting a family waving off soldiers to the front. The Nazis never got this far, but lots of Siberians left for the war from this station.

3565km

The 15-minute halt at the intriguingly named but entirely unspectacular town of **Taiga** provides plenty of time to wish you were heading 79km north up the branch line to Tomsk (p159). This is not a Womble (as Brits of a certain age may expect, from the kids TV program) but a charming old Siberian city that lost much of its regional importance when it was bypassed by the Trans-Siberian Railway. Myth says that the city fathers, fearing the dirt and pollution it would bring, declined the offer to have the town connected to the railway. However, the truth is rather more prosaic – swampland made the construction of a bridge over the river Ob problematic, so a decision was taken not to lay lines to the city. Its beautiful wooden buildings and lively café scene are well worth the short detour.

3713km

Spot another engine-repair yard to the south as you approach the station at **Mariinsk**, a 25-minute stop along the banks of the Kiya River. Originally named Kiysk, the town grew wealthy as the focus of a Siberian gold rush. It was renamed in 1857 to honour Tsar Alexander II's wife, Maria. Fifty years later, the town finally got round to unveiling a statue in her honour. Many of the furniture and metal factories that operated here in Soviet times are closed now, leaving few employment opportunities. Do your bit to help the local economy by buying a beer or *kvas* (fermented rye-bread water) and some dried fish from the women who meet the trains and offer all manner

SIBERIA – THE GRAPHIC NOVEL

Nikolai Maslov's graphic novel *Siberia*, released by the US-based Soft Skull Press, is one of the few recent works of art to portray everyday life in Soviet Siberia, as opposed to Solzhenitsyn-type Gulag camp tales. Drawn entirely in pencil on paper, Maslov's tale of a Soviet youth (the book's original title) spent in Siberia is bleak, bitter and beautiful.

Portraying with almost unbearable honesty the faces of the drunks and bullies he grew up with, Maslov had reportedly never actually read a graphic novel before he approached the French publisher of *Asterix* in Russia with the first pages of the book and asked him to finance the rest. The publisher agreed, allowing Maslov to quit his job as a night watchman and devote himself to his work. Maslov tells the story of his often brutal life with a complete lack of sentimentality, using matter-of-fact, almost crude frames to portray characters and everyday scenes in Western Siberian villages and towns.

of goods. We were tempted by a large fluffy toy, but common sense eventually prevailed.

3820km

The line enters vast **Krasnoyarsky Territory**, with enormous mineral and forest wealth. It covers 2.5 million sq km, stretching all the way to the Arctic coast. A journey through this stretch of the Trans-Siberian is particularly memorable around sunset, with sunlight flickering hypnotically through the branches of endless rows of trees. Time, perhaps, to get that dried fish out and reflect once more on Russia and its colossal territory.

3846km

The train makes a very brief stop at **Bogotol**, another example of a town being formed around the Trans-Siberian. A train station was opened here in 1893, but it was another 18 years before the subsequent settlement was awarded town status. Bogotol is today home to a locomotive-production factory, hence the tiny model train perched on top of the welcome-to-town sign.

3914km

Next up is **Achinsk**. This small town, built around an alumina refinery, has its origins in the founding of a fortress in the area in 1683. In the 19th century, soap made in Achinsk was famous all over Russia. The train stops here for just a minute or two before twisting through woodlands and over hills with yet more cinematic landscapes to enjoy.

3932km

A small, easily missed white obelisk south of the train line marks the halfway point between Moscow and Běijīng (via Ulaanbaatar).

4098km

Major services stop for 20 minutes at Krasnoyarsk (p170). That's just long enough to nip out and see a fine communist-era mural in red mosaics decorating a wall on the station square outside.

Yekaterinburg

Екатеринбург

☎343 / POP 1.5 MILLION / TIME MOSCOW +2HR

Gem rush, miners' mythology, the execution of the Romanovs, the rise of Russia's first president, Boris Yeltsin, and legendary gangster feuds of the 1990s – Yekaterinburg is not only Russia's fourth-largest city, it is like a piece of conceptual art with a fascinating historical subtext.

Bustling, but less than startling on the outside, the political capital of the Ural Mountains is overflowing with history and culture, while its economic growth is manifested in a thriving restaurant scene and, as in many other regional capitals, in atrociously trafficked avenues.

With one of the best international airports in Russia and quite a few agencies experienced in dealing with foreign travellers, Yekaterinburg is a good base camp for exploring the Ural Mountains.

History

Yekaterinburg was founded as a factory-fort in 1723 as part of Peter the Great's push to exploit the Ural region's mineral riches. The city was named after two Catherines: Peter's wife (later Empress Catherine I) and the Russian patron saint of mining.

The city is notorious, however, for being the place where the Bolsheviks murdered Tsar Nicholas II and his family in July 1918. Six years later, the town was renamed Sverdlovsk, after Yakov Sverdlov, a leading Bolshevik who was Vladimir Lenin's right-hand man until his death in the flu epidemic of 1919. The region still bears Sverdlov's name.

WWII turned Sverdlovsk into a major industrial centre, as hundreds of factories

Yekaterinburg

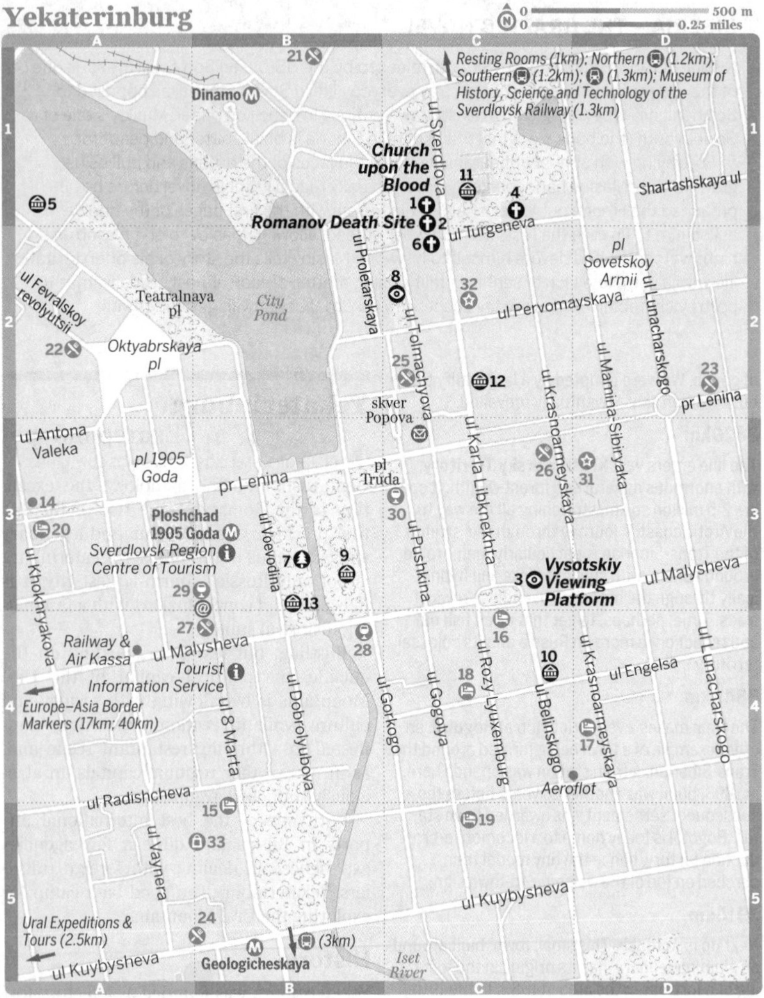

were transferred here from vulnerable areas west of the Ural Mountains. The city was closed to foreigners until 1990 because of its many defence plants.

During the late 1970s a civil engineering graduate of the local university, Boris Yeltsin, began to make his political mark, rising to become regional Communist Party boss before being promoted to Moscow in 1985. Several years later he was standing on a tank in Moscow as the leading figure in defending the country against a putsch by old-guard communists. He became the Russian Federation's first president in June 1991.

That year Yekaterinburg took back its original name. After suffering economic depression and Mafia lawlessness in the early 1990s, the city has boomed in recent years. Yekaterinburg is one of the very few cities in Russia governed by a mayor, Yevgeny Roizman, not from a party loyal to the kremlin.

Sights

Each summer, after the snow has cleared in May, Yekaterinburg paints a red line on the footpath to guide visitors past major sights. It's marked on the tourist office (p145) city map. There's also a second walking route

Yekaterinburg

Top Sights
1 Church upon the Blood ... C1
2 Romanov Death Site ... C1
3 Vysotskiy Viewing Platform ... C3

Sights
4 Ascension Church ... C1
5 Boris Yeltsin Presidential Center ... A1
6 Chapel of the Revered Martyr Grand Princess Yelizaveta Fyodorovna ... C2
7 Istorichesky Skver ... B3
8 Literary Quarter ... C2
9 Museum of Architecture and Design ... B3
10 Nevyansk Icon Museum ... C4
11 Rastorguev-Kharitonov Mansion ... C1
12 Yekaterinbrug History Museum ... C2
13 Yekaterinburg Museum of Fine Arts ... B3

Activities, Courses & Tours
14 Ekaterinburg Guide Centre ... A3

Sleeping
15 Hotel Chekhov ... B5
16 Hotel Tsentralny ... C4
17 Live Hotel ... D4
18 Novotel Yekaterinburg Centre ... C4
19 Red Star Hostel ... C5
20 Tenet Hotel ... A3

Eating
21 Cafe Kuznya ... B1
22 Cafe-Museum Demidov ... A2
23 Khmeli Suneli ... D2
24 Nigora ... B5
25 Pashtet ... C2
26 Pelmeni Club ... C3
27 Thank God It's Friday ... B4
Vertikal ... (see 3)

Drinking & Nightlife
28 Dr Scotch ... B4
29 New Bar ... B3
30 Rosy Jane ... C3

Entertainment
31 Opera & Ballet Theatre ... D3
32 Philharmonic ... C2

Shopping
33 Grinvich ... B5

available for English speakers. There's no line painted anywhere for this one; instead, visitors are advised to go to izi.travel (https://izi.travel/en) and download the English-language audio guide.

★ Romanov Death Site CHURCH, MEMORIAL
(Место убийства Романовых; ul Karla Libknekhta & ul Tolmachyova 34; ⏲dawn-dusk) The massive Byzantine-style **Church upon the Blood** (Храм на Крови; ☎343-371 6168; www.hram-na-krovi.cerkov.ru; ul Tolmachyova 34) dominates this site where Tsar Nicholas II, his wife and children were murdered by Bolsheviks on the night of 16 July 1918. Nearby, the pretty wooden **Chapel of the Revered Martyr Grand Princess Yelizaveta Fyodorovna** (Часовня в честь великой княгини Елизаветы и инокини Варвары; ul Tolmachyova 34b; ⏲8am-6pm Mon-Fri) honours the imperial family's great-aunt and faithful friend.

The executions took place in the basement of a local engineer's house, known as Dom Ipatyeva (named for its owner, Nikolai Ipatyev). During the Soviet period, the building housed a local museum of atheism, but it was demolished in 1977 by then governor Boris Yeltsin, who feared it would attract monarchist sympathisers, and for many years the site was a vacant block marked by a small cross and the wooden chapel to Grand Princess Yelizaveta Fyodorovna. Yelizaveta Fyodorovna was a pious nun who met an even worse end than the other Romanovs when she was thrown down a mine shaft, poisoned with gas and buried.

★ Vysotskiy Viewing Platform NOTABLE BUILDING
(Высоцкий небоскрёб; ☎343-378 4646; www.visotsky-e.ru; ul Malysheva 51, fl 52; viewing platform ₽250-300, museum free; ⏲noon-10pm Mon-Fri, 10am-10pm Sat & Sun) Take the lift up 52 floors to the viewing platform for one of Russia's best urban panoramas. Children under 15 years must be accompanied by an adult. The name of the tower is a pun on the Russian word for 'high' and the name of the singer Vladimir Vysotsky. A small museum is dedicated to 'Russia's raspy Dylan' here.

Yekaterinbrug History Museum MUSEUM
(Музей истории Екатеринбурга; ☎343-371 2111; www.m-i-e.ru; ul Karla Libknekhta 26; ₽200; ⏲10am-6pm Mon-Thu, to 8pm Fri, 11am-6pm Sat & Sun) At one of the more contemporary museums in town, most of the focus is on Yekaterinburg through the 18th and 19th centuries. Most exhibits are captioned in English and there are plenty of interactive displays.

Military Technology Museum MUSEUM
(☎343-684 7218, 343-684 6784; www.museum.elem.ru; ul Aleksandra Kozitsyna 2, Verkhnyaya Pyshma; exhibition hall ₽100, outdoor exhibition free; ⏰10am-6pm Wed-Sun) This vast indoor and open-air collection of tanks and armoured vehicles is located on the northern outskirts of Yekaterinburg in Verkhnyaya Pyshma. It's one of the largest of its kind in the world, with an extensive range of large military tanks and helicopters located outdoors, and smaller military craft and retro automobiles on display indoors.

Take bus 111 or *marshrutka* 111 or 111a from stop Kinotsentr Zarya (at Uralmash metro station) to Zavodskaya Stop.

Museum of Architecture and Design MUSEUM
(Музей истории архитектуры и дизайна; ☎343-372 0654; www.museumarch.com; ul Gorkogo 4a; ₽200; ⏰11am-7pm Wed-Sat) Situated on Istorichesky skver (Historical Sq), this museum is located on the grounds where the first ironworks was established in Yekaterinburg in 1723. In recent years the museum has had an overhaul, and today the former 19th-century factory and mint building houses a fascinating collection of miniature buildings depicting various historical eras throughout Yekaterinburg's history.

Ascension Church CHURCH
(Храм Вознесения Господня; www.voznesenka.cerkov.ru; ul Klary Tsetkin 11; ⏰dawn-dusk) The restored late-18th-century Ascension Church is the oldest in Yekaterinburg and rises up moodily alongside parkland that's perfect for a stroll.

Boris Yeltsin Presidential Center MUSEUM
(Президентский центр Бориса Ельцина; ☎495-729 5463; www.yeltsincenter.ru/yeltsin-presidential-center; ul Borisa Eltsina 3; ₽200; ⏰museum 10am-9pm Tue-Sun) Traffic was stopped the day the Boris Yeltsin Presidential Center was opened in 2015. The mammoth site includes a museum, a conference centre, an art gallery and a bookshop, although it's the museum that is of most interest to visitors. The museum depicts the former Russian prime minister's life through seven interactive zones designed to represent seven historical days during his ruling.

Most of the exhibit descriptions in the museum are in Russian, but there is an audio guide available for English-speakers. There are a number of tours that visitors can book and, although these are only available in Russian now, there are plans to introduce English-speaking options eventually.

Literary Quarter AREA
(☎343-371 0300; www.ompu.ur.ru) Located north of skver Popova, the Literary Quarter features restored wooden houses, some of them now museums about celebrated local writers such as Dmitry Mamin-Sibiryak and Pavel Bazhov; a full list of museums is on the website.

Istorichesky Skver PARK
The prettiest and most lively part of Yekaterinburg in summer is the landscaped park-

WORTH A TRIP

EUROPE–ASIA BORDER

The Ural Mountains have numerous monuments marking the border between Europe and Asia. Interestingly, the border was thought to be the Don River by the Ancient Greeks, but Yekaterinburg's founder Vasily Tatishchev drew it at the Ural Mountains in the mid-18th century, based on ideas of the day.

One of the more historic monuments is located 40km west of Yekaterinburg near Pervouralsk. It was erected in 1837 to commemorate a visit by Tsar Alexander II, who drank wine there and inadvertently began a favourite pastime of locals – drinking a glass in Europe and another glass in Asia (as if you needed an excuse!). To reach the monument, take a taxi (about ₽1000 return if you order in advance) to Pervouralsk. Expect to pay another ₽200 per hour for the driver to wait. Bus 150 leaves frequently from the Severny bus station to Pervouralsk (₽97; platform 9).

The city has erected a new border marker, more conveniently located just 17km out of Yekaterinburg and looking a little like a mini Eiffel Tower. This one is more kitsch, but a taxi will take you out there for about ₽600 return, with an hour at the monument.

Expect to pay ₽3600 to ₽4000 as an individual (less in groups) with reliable outfits such as **Ekaterinburg Guide Centre** (p143) or **Yekaterinburg For You** (p143).

land alongside the City Pond (Gorodskoy prud), where pr Lenina crosses a small dam. This was where Yekaterinburg began back in 1723.

Urals Military History Museum MUSEUM
(Уральский государственный военно-исторический музей; ☎343-246 5080; http://ugvim.ru; ul Krylova 2a; ₽180; ⏲10am-8pm Wed, to 6pm Thu, to 5pm Fri-Sun) Worthwhile for buffs, this military museum has two halls, one dedicated to the Urals Volunteer Tank Corp. Entry price is for both halls, but you can pay and visit only one if you wish. In the yard there's a collection of tanks and planes.

Yekaterinburg Museum of Fine Arts MUSEUM
(Екатеринбургский музей изобразительных искусств; ☎343-371 0626; www.emii.ru; ul Voevodina 5; ₽250; ⏲11am-8pm Tue-Thu, to 7pm Fri-Sun) The star exhibit of the Museum of Fine Arts is its elaborate Kasli Iron Pavilion, which won prizes in the 1900 Paris Expo. The museum has a good collection of icons, paintings and decorative art.

Nevyansk Icon Museum MUSEUM
(Музей Невянская икона; ☎343-220 6650; ul Engelsa 15; ₽150; ⏲11am-8pm Wed-Sun) FREE Excellent icons from the 17th to the 20th centuries, from the local Nevyansk school.

Rastorguev-Kharitonov Mansion HISTORIC BUILDING
(Усадьба Расторгуевых-Харитоновых; ul Karla Libknekhta 44) Situated across the road from the site where the Romanov family was executed, this mansion dates from the late 18th and early 19th centuries and was one of the most significant buildings of the era. Today people come to admire the pretty angular facade and relax in the pleasant park behind it.

Museum of History, Science and Technology of the Sverdlovsk Railway MUSEUM
(Музей истории, науки и техники Свердловской железной дороги; ☎343-358 4222; www.volzd.ru/museum-ekaterinburg.html; ul Vokzalnaya 14; ₽100; ⏲10am-6pm Tue-Sat) Railway buffs will enjoy the good collection here, housed in and around the old train station, dating from 1881. Exhibits highlight the history of the railroad in the Urals, including a re-creation of the office of the Soviet-era railway director.

Tours

Ekaterinburg Guide Centre ADVENTURE
(Екатеринбургский центр гидов; ☎343-384 0048; www.ekaterinburgguide.com; office 12, pr Lenina 52/1; ⏲10am-6pm Mon-Fri) Organises English-language tours of the city and trips into the countryside, including Nevyansk, Tobolsk and Nizhnyaya Sinyachikha, as well as winter activities and summer hiking and rafting expeditions. Day trips cost anything between ₽1800 and ₽8800, depending on destination and numbers. It also books hotel and hostel accommodation, often at discount rates.

Yekaterinburg For You TOURS
(☎912-280 0870; www.yekaterinburg4u.ru) Experienced guide and journalist Luba Suslyakova offers a range of city and regional tours, including Nevyansk and the pottery town of Tavolgi, winter dog sledding, and the eclectic Mafia Tour, which takes visitors into the graveyards where Yekaterinburg's rival Uralmash and Central gangsters of the 1990s rest in peace.

Ural Expeditions & Tours ADVENTURE
(☎961-762 2863; http://welcome-ural.ru; office 4, ul Baumana 6; ⏲11am-5pm Mon-Fri) This group of geologists, who graduated from the Sverdlovsk Mining Institute, leads trekking, rafting and horse-riding trips to all parts of the Ural Mountains, including Taganay and Zyuratkul National Parks. English-speaking guides.

Sleeping

★ **Red Star Hostel** HOSTEL $
(☎343-383 5684; www.redstarhostel.ru; ul Gorkogo 65; 6–12-bed dm ₽290-650, d ₽1600; ⊝📶) This excellent hostel opened in 2014 and has quickly established itself as a comfortable, very professionally run place, with 44 beds divided among male, female and mixed dorms, and a double with a large bed. It can do registration. Take trolleybus 1 or 9 from the train station to stop Kuybsheva.

Resting Rooms HOSTEL $
(Комнаты отдыха; ☎343-358 5783; 4th fl, Yekaterinburg train station; 12/24hr from ₽500/1250; ⊝) Book ahead as these fill fast.

★ **Hotel Chekhov** BOUTIQUE HOTEL $$
(☎343-282 9737; http://chekhov-hotel.ru; ul 8 Marta 32; incl breakfast s ₽4500-5500, d ₽5000-6000; ⊝📶) Hotel Chekhov offers modern, stylishly furnished rooms that make good use of exposed brick in a historic building. Take bus 23 from the train station to TRTs Grinvich.

Tenet Hotel BUSINESS HOTEL $$
(☎343-385 8582; www.tenethotel.ru; ul Khokhryakova 1a; d incl breakfast ₽3500-9000;) Opened in 2016, this hotel is conveniently located in the centre of town and attracts a mostly business crowd. The design is contemporary with nods to the city's history through black-and-white photographs spread throughout the building. The restaurant, too, draws on this concept, with old classic Russian dishes vamped up with a modern twist.

Live Hotel HOSTEL $$
(☎343-239 6969; www.live-ekb.ru; ul Krasnoarmeyskaya 72; dm/r from ₽600/2600;) A newcomer to Yekaterinburg, this large and modern complex includes a hotel, a hostel, a communal work space and a conference centre. Rooms in both the hostel and hotel are clean and comfortable, with pops of colour freshening up the design.

★**Hotel Tsentralny** HISTORIC HOTEL $$$
(Отель Центральный; ☎343-350 1004; www.hotelcentr.ru; ul Malysheva 74; incl breakfast s ₽2300-5000, d ₽3500-7000;) Opened in 1928, this historic hotel is housed in a grand art nouveau building in the heart of town and has seen its fair share of celebrity guests. It has 98 excellent business-class and standard rooms and eating and nightlife options are never far away. Trolleybuses 1 and 9 are among the many going to the hotel from the train station.

The hotel also acts as a museum, with photo displays on floors three to five. Guests and visitors can book a historical excursion through the hotel grounds, which costs ₽200 and takes approximately 30 minutes.

Novotel Yekaterinburg Centre HOTEL $$$
(☎343-253 5383; www.novotel.com; ul Engelsa 7; incl breakfast s ₽5900-7700, d ₽6900-8100, ste ₽11,000;) This excellent four-star chain hotel in the centre has variable rates and good deals online. Rooms are clean and comfortable and service always comes with a smile. The easiest way from the station is trolleybus 1 or 9 to ul Rozy Lyuksemburg stop.

Eating

Ul 8 Marta between pr Lenina and ul Malysheva has plenty of eating and drinking options, and ul Vaynera, which is partly pedestrian only, has a moderate choice of eateries. Whatever your food preference, there's a lot of choice, with everything from local fare to international cuisine to modern cafe nosh.

Pelmeni Club RUSSIAN $
(Пельмени Клаб; ☎343-271 3330; www.pelmeni-club.ru; ul Krasnoarmeyskaya 2; mains ₽190-470;) There's a great variety of *pelmeni* here, but what makes this restaurant stand out is the fact that you can learn to make your own. There is a second location on ul Lunacharskogo 82.

Nigora UZBEK $
(Нигора; ☎343-295 1417; http://nigora.ru; ul Kuybysheva 55; mains ₽200; noon-midnight) Yekaterinburg has several of these inexpensive Uzbek restaurants, all with young staff attired in Uzbek caps serving delicious Uzbek specialities. *Manti* (steamed, palm-sized dumplings), soups, sausages and shashlyk feature on the menu, including a very worthy lamb shashlyk. There are two other Nigora locations in town.

★**Pashtet** RUSSIAN $$
(☎343-228 0059; www.rest-pashtet.ru; ul Tolmacheva 23; mains ₽390-1550, business lunches ₽400; 11am-11pm Sun-Thu, to midnight Fri & Sat;) Reinvented Russian classics served in rooms designed to depict a traditional Russian summer dacha. Both the food and wine menus are extensive and the restaurant's house-made pâtés (*pashtet* in Russian) are definitely worth trying.

Cafe Kuznya RUSSIAN $$
(Кафе Кузня; ☎343-286 2925; www.gorn66.ru; ul Melkovskaya 3; mains ₽215-625; noon-11pm;) A fascinating cafe with wooden interiors crafted by one woodwork artist – Alexander Andreevich Lysyakov – and his students. The menu spans all the Russian classics with no surprises.

Khmeli Suneli GEORGIAN $$
(Хмели Сунели; ☎343-350 6318; www.hmeli.ru; pr Lenina 69/10; mains ₽450; noon-midnight Sun-Thu, to 2am Fri & Sat;) This large Georgian restaurant has a relaxed feel and is currently the best of its ilk in Yekaterinburg, serving a large range of soups, salads, fish and red-meat dishes and delicious shashlyk.

Cafe-Museum Demidov RUSSIAN $$
(☎343-371 7344; www.demidov-ural.ru; ul Fevralskoy revolyutsii 9; mains ₽510-1200) A quirky cafe-museum spread over two storeys, where guests are encouraged to touch the random collection of exhibits. The food is simple Russian fare; there are no elaborate descriptions and the meals come presented as if grandma was serving at home.

Thank God It's Friday INTERNATIONAL, BAR $$
(☎343-222 2902; http://ekb.tgifridays.ru; ul 8 Marta 8d; burgers ₽339-615, steaks ₽615-1300; ⊙noon-midnight Mon, to 2am Tue-Thu, to 7am Fri & Sat; 📶) 'TGIF' is loud and boisterous, has staff who introduce themselves by name before they take your order, and kitsch decoration many will know from other branches. The food's capably prepared but it's the atmosphere that draws people here for drinks and meals.

Vertikal INTERNATIONAL $$$
(Вертикаль; ☎343-200 5151; www.vertical51.ru; ul Malysheva 51, fl 51; mains ₽320-2000; ⊙noon-midnight Sun-Thu, to 2am Fri & Sat; ❄) Located on the 51st floor of the Vysotsky tower, Vertikal offers a formal, upmarket experience of pan-European dishes and some steaks, and its trump card: sensational views over town. Reserve ahead.

Drinking & Nightlife

★**New Bar** BAR
(☎953-058 4455; www.new-bar.ru; ul 8 Marta 8; ⊙6pm-6am; 📶) Relaxed art-scene cafe and cocktail bar on the top floor of Mytny Dvor mall. One storey below the same company restaurant serves Russian soul food and has a decent cocktail list. The restaurant is open noon to midnight daily.

Rosy Jane PUB
(☎343-317 1855; www.rosyjane.ru; pr Lenina 32/34; ⊙7am-6am Mon-Thu, to 7am Fri, 9am-7am Sat, to 6am Sun; 📶) This English-style pub aims at the New Russian drinking and eating crowd, who grace the bar and perch at polished wood tables gourmandising on steak and other very well-prepared Russian and international dishes (mains ₽550 to ₽1900). Steaks are top of the range. It serves decent breakfasts too, for early risers or those still out from the night before. Entry is off ul Gorkogo.

Dr Scotch PUB
(☎343-371 4363; www.doctorscotch.ru; ul Malysheva 56a; ⊙noon-2am) Doc Scotch is one of the liveliest pubs in town and has the advantage of being very central. Inside, expect lots of wood and even more beer.

Entertainment

Philharmonic CLASSICAL MUSIC
(Филармония; ☎tickets 343-371 4682; www.sgaf.ru; ul Karla Libknekhta 38; tickets from ₽200) Yekaterinburg's top venue for the classical performing arts often hosts visiting directors and soloists, as well as regular performances by the acclaimed Ural Mountains academic orchestra.

Opera & Ballet Theatre OPERA, BALLET
(Театр оперы и балета; ☎tickets 343-350 8057; www.uralopera.ru; pr Lenina 46a; tickets from ₽150) This ornate baroque theatre is a lovely place to see the Russian classics at a high standard.

Shopping

Grinvich MALL
(☎343-222 2525; www.grinvich.com; ul 8 Marta 46; ⊙10am-10pm) This enormous shopping complex near the ul Vaynera pedestrian zone is an oasis away from the traffic.

Information

Main Post Office (Почтамт; pr Lenina 39; ⊙8am-10pm Mon-Fri, 9am-6pm Sat & Sun)

Sverdlovsk Region Centre of Tourism (Центр развития туризма Свердловской области; ☎343-350 0525; www.gotoural.com; ul 8 Marta 13, 2 fl) Helpful city office with English-speaking staff. There are maps and brochures about Yekaterinburg as well as the whole Sverdlovsk Region.

Tourist Information Service (TIS; ☎343-222 2445; www.its.ekburg.ru; ul 8 Marta 21; ⊙10am-7pm Mon-Fri, 11am-4pm Sat & Sun) Helpful official city tourist office, with free maps of town showing the Red Line walking trail to major sights.

Tourist Information Service (☎343-222 2445; www.its.ekburg.ru; terminal b, fl 2; ⊙10am-7pm Mon-Fri) Airport branch of the city tourist office.

Traveller's Coffee (☎922-177 0201; ul 8 Marta 8d; ⊙8am-midnight; 📶) Free internet with an order.

Getting There & Away

TRAIN

Yekaterinburg – sometimes still called 'Sverdlovsk' on timetables – is a major rail junction with connections to all stops on the Trans-Siberian route. All trains to Moscow stop at either Perm (₽800, 5½ hours) or Kazan (₽1180, 14½ hours). Frequent trains to/from Moscow include the Ural (₽1700 to ₽3777, 26 hours, every couple of days) via Kazan. Heading east, the next major stops are Omsk (₽1380, 14 hours) and Novosibirsk (₽2134, 22 hours). You can buy tickets at outlets throughout the city, including the convenient **Railway & Air Kassa** (ЖД и Авиа кассы; ☎343-371 0400; www.bilet-vsegda.ru; ul Malysheva 31d; ⊙24hr).

The main airport is **Koltsovo** (☎800-100 0333; www.koltsovo.ru), 15km southeast of the city

WORTH A TRIP

GANINA YAMA

After the Romanov family was shot in the cellar of Dom Ipatyeva, their bodies were discarded in the depths of the forests of Ganina Yama (Ганина Яма), 16km northeast of Yekaterinburg. In their honour, the Orthodox Church has built the exquisite **Monastery of the Holy Martyrs** (☎343-217 9146) at this pilgrimage site. Expect to pay from ₽3600 to ₽4200 as an individual (less in groups) on tours conducted by Ekaterinburg Guide Centre or Luba Syuslakova.

The nearest train station to Ganina Yama is Shuvakish, served by elektrichki (suburban trains; ₽56, 30 minutes, every one to two hours) from the central station. Buses from the Northern Bus Station (Severny) run out here at 3.30pm Saturday and 10am Sunday (platform 11), returning at 8pm Saturday and 11.30am Sunday.

centre. Frequent services include Moscow, Novosibirsk, Krasnoyarsk, Irkutsk, Khabarovsk, Ufa, St Petersburg, Samara, Vladivostok and a host of Black Sea hubs. International services include Frankfurt am Main (Germany), Beijing (China), Prague (Czech Republic) and Astana (Kazakhstan). **Aeroflot** (☎343-356 5570; www.aeroflot.ru; ul Belinskogo 41; ⏲9am-7pm Mon-Fri) has offices here.

BUS

The **main bus station** (Южный автовокзал; Yuzhny avtovokzal; ☎343-257 1260; www.autovokzal.org) is 3km south of the city centre, but most buses also stop at the **Northern Bus Station** (Северный автовокзал; severny avtovokzal; ul Vokzalnaya 15a), conveniently located by the train station. Here you can catch frequent buses to Chelyabinsk (₽550, four hours) and Alapaevsk (₽380, three hours, five daily). There is also a bus station at Koltsovo airport serving destinations in the Sverdlovsk region and Chelyabinsk (₽550, 3½ hours, frequent). Touts sell tickets for minibuses to Chelyabinsk (₽700, 2½ hours, about every hour) at the main bus station.

Getting Around

Bus 1 links the Sverdlovsk-Passazhirskaya train station and Koltsovo airport (one hour) from 6.30am to 11.30pm. Bus 039 goes from the airport to metro pl 1905 Goda. *Marshrutka* 39 goes to metro Geologicheskaya.

Many trolleybuses such as 1, 3 and 9 and *marshrutky* (pay on board) run along ul Sverdlova/ul Karla Libknekhta between the train station and pr Lenina. Marshrutka 21 connects the train station with pl 1905 Goda, continuing along ul 8 Marta to the Grinvich shopping centre. Bus 024 runs along ul 8 Marta to the Northern Bus Station alongside the train station. Trams 13, 15 and 18 cover long stretches of pr Lenina.

A single metro line runs between the northeastern suburbs and the city centre, with stops at the train station (Uralskaya), pl 1905 Goda and ul Kuybysheva near the synagogue (Geologicheskaya).

Tyumen Тюмень

☎3452 / POP 581,000 / TIME MOSCOW +2HR

Founded in 1586, Tyumen was the first Russian settlement in Siberia. These days the city is the youthful, business-oriented capital of a vast, oil-rich *oblast* (region) stretching all the way to the Yamal and Gydansky Peninsula on the Arctic Kara Sea. Don't let mention of oil-hungry businesspeople leave you thinking that this is a dull, money-focused city though. The city has a buzzing street life in summer and a couple of worthwhile sights that, taken together, will keep you entertained for a day or so. Tyumen is also the stepping stone to the gorgeous old town of Tobolsk, a few hours' bus or train ride away.

Sights

If the weather is good, the best way to experience the city is by taking a stroll in central **City Park** (Городской Парк; ul Lenina), or by walking along the riverside promenade. You'll be in the company of masses of happy locals.

A number of curiously twisted old wooden houses can be found on the tree lined Beregovaya ul.

★**Trinity Monastery** MONASTERY
(Троицкий монастырь; ul Kommunisticheskaya 10) Riverside Trinity Monastery is undoubtedly Tyumen's most appealing architectural complex. Its kremlin-style crenellated outer wall is pierced by a single gate tower. Behind, gold domes top the striking Troitsky Church in the centre of the courtyard and, next to the black-turreted main gate, the 1727 Peter & Paul Church. In summer the flower beds of the complex burst with colour. The monastery is a pleasant 30-minute walk northwest from the city centre.

★**Riverside Promenade** AREA
(Набережная) Tyumen's sleek riverside promenade runs northwest from the centre almost all the way to Trinity Monastery. The

Tyumen

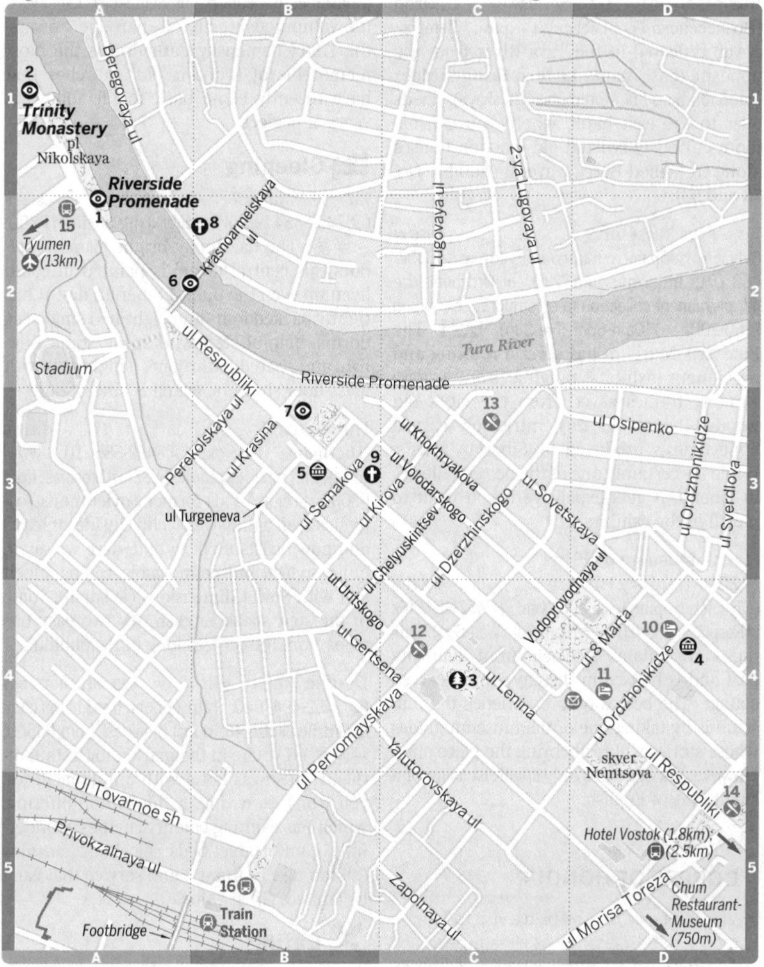

Tyumen

Top Sights

1 Riverside Promenade A2
2 Trinity Monastery A1

Sights

3 City Park C4
4 Fine Arts Museum D4
5 House-Museum of 19th- & 20th-Century History B3
6 Lovers Bridge A2
7 Selskhoz Academy B3
8 Voznesensko Georgievskiy Church B2
9 Znamensky Cathedral B3

Sleeping

10 Double Tree by Hilton D4
11 Muesli Mini Hotel D4

Eating

12 Berlusconi C4
13 In Da USA C3
Malina Bar .... (see 12)
14 Schaste D5

Transport

15 Buses to Centre A2
16 Buses to Centre from Train Station B5

promenade offers great views of the **Voznesensko Georgievskiy Church** (Вознесенско-Георгиевский храм; Beregovaya ul) reflected in the Tura River from the opposite (east) bank. **Lovers Bridge** (Мост влюблённых; ul Kommunisticheskaya) leads over to the east bank, where you can explore curiously twisted old wooden houses along tree-lined Beregovaya ul (notably No. 73 and 53).

Fine Arts Museum MUSEUM
(Музей изобразительного искусства; ☎3452-468 071; http://museum-72.ru; ul Ordzhonikidze 47; permanent collection free, temporary exhibition ₽150-200; ⊙10am-6pm Tue-Sun) FREE The Fine Arts Museum has several rotating and permanent exhibits ranging from ornate window frames saved from the city's old wooden houses to tiny, intricately carved bone figures produced by Siberian artists. While it's certainly one of the better galleries in Siberia, it gets expensive if you want to see all of the exhibits.

House-Museum of 19th- & 20th-Century History MUSEUM
(Музей истории дома XIX-XX вв; ☎3452-464 963; ul Respubliki 18; ₽200; ⊙10am-6pm Wed-Sun) This museum contains artefacts from Tyumen's past and is housed in the city's finest carved cottage. The best way to experience the museum is by taking one of the museum guides whose stories will really bring the place alive. However, most guides only speak Russian or a smattering of English.

CORPSE OF HONOUR

Vladimir Lenin himself paid a visit to Tyumen – in 1941. Yes, he was already dead. The Soviets evacuated his body (just the body – his brain remained in Moscow) to Tyumen to keep it safe from the invading Germans. The body was kept under a veil of secrecy in the **Selskhoz Academy** (сельскохозяйственная академия; ul Respubliki 7), an attractive early-20th-century brick building that still stands today, before being shipped back to Moscow in 1945. Throughout it all, the citizens of Tyumen remained blissfully unaware of the presence of a distinguished guest in their midst. Indeed, until after the war, few Russians had any idea the corpse had ever been transferred out of its mausoleum on Red Square!

Znamensky Cathedral CHURCH
(Знаменский собор; ul Semakova 13) With its voluptuously curved baroque towers, the 1786 Znamensky Cathedral is the most memorable of a dozen 'old' churches that have recently come back to life following years of neglect.

Sleeping

Muesli Mini Hotel HOSTEL $
(☎3452-464 191; ul Respubliki 49; dm from ₽800;) The dazzlingly bright primary colours this central hostel is painted in could liven up even the dullest Siberian day. It has tightly packed four- and eight-bed single-sex dorms, helpful staff who speak some English, and shared bathrooms (single sex) with glass-door showers, which is kind of odd!

Hotel Vostok HOTEL $$
(Гостиница Восток; ☎3452-686 111; www.vostok-tmn.ru; ul Respubliki 159; r incl breakfast from ₽3000; @) This former Soviet monstrosity has seen a massive facelift (inside, at least) and now boasts modern and, dare we say it, quite stylish and comfortable rooms, albeit still with Soviet dimensions (ie small). Some of the staff speak English. It's two easy bus stops from the centre along ul Respubliki.

Double Tree by Hilton BUSINESS HOTEL $$$
(☎3452-494 040; http://doubletree3.hilton.com; ul Ordzhonikidze 46; d incl breakfast from ₽4500;) If you're in the market for a state-of-the-art business hotel with ample facilities, you won't go wrong at this Hilton offering, which has calming colour schemes, wonderfully comfortable beds, blackout curtains (all too rare in Russia) and service that can't be faulted. Great value.

Eating

Schaste GEORGIAN $$
(Счастье; ☎3452-666 111; http://happyrest.ru; ul Respubliki 65, Kalinka Trade Centre; mains ₽300-700; ⊙11.45am-1am;) Funky, glass-fish-bowl-shaped restaurant and bar with leafy plants and bicycles mounted on the walls. There's a menu of Russian, international and some Georgian specialities such as fried *suluguni* (Georgian cheese), *kharcho* (beef stew) and *khinkali* (dumplings). If you're travelling with children, they are sure to enjoy the kids play area inside a train carriage.

In Da USA AMERICAN $$
(Ин Да Юса; ☎3452-070755; http://indausa.ru; ul Chelyuskintsev 10; mains ₽300-450; ⊙noon-

2am Sun-Thu, noon-6am Fri & Sat;) In Da USA is, naturally, festooned with Americana and serves Tyumen's best burgers along with Tex-Mex and a host of bar appetisers. It becomes a club famous for table-top dancing at weekends as well as live music and disco-coloured cocktails with sexy names.

Malina Bar CAFE $$
(Малина Бар; ul Pervomayskaya 18; meals ₽200-600; 24hr;) The city slicker Malina Bar has a huge menu of Russian and European food, overly fluffy cakes, filling breakfasts, real coffee, fast wi-fi and cosy seating in grand leather couches. Upstairs is sister Italian restaurant–steak house **Berlusconi** (ul Pervomayskaya 18; mains ₽300-1200; 11am-3am Mon-Thu, 11am-6am Fri-Sat).

★ **Chum Restaurant-Museum** RUSSIAN $$$
(Ресторан-музей Чум; 3452-621 660; http://maxim-rest.ru; str Maligina 59/12; mains ₽600-900; 11am-2am) Inside a faux Siberian hunters cabin lined with furs and skis, this unusual restaurant specalises in the cuisine of northern Siberia. Dishes include salted fish, elk, reindeer tongues and wild boar. However, whereas the average Siberian hunter probably just munches on a great hunk of meat, here the dishes are given a totally modern touch and presented with arty flamboyance.

Information

City maps and bus-route plans are sold at newspaper kiosks in the train station and throughout the city.

Main Post Office (Почтамт; ul Respubliki 56; 8am-10pm Mon-Fri, 9am-6pm Sat & Sun)

Getting There & Away

TRAIN

Several day and overnight trains go to Omsk (*platskart/kupe* ₽1708/2538, 8½ hours, 10.19pm) and points east along the Trans-Siberian main line, and dozens of westbound trains serve Yekaterinburg and beyond.

There are many daily trains to Tobolsk (from ₽600, 3½ hours). If you're looking to explore the Arctic, trains continue beyond Tobolsk all the way to Novy Urgenoy (at least twice daily). Other useful trains serve Barnaul (₽3141/4056, 29 hours, daily at 4.41am) and Tomsk (₽3423/4942, 23 hours, even-numbered days at 6.52am).

AIR

Tyumen's **Roshchino Airport** is 13km west of the centre. S7 and Aeroflot are among airlines with daily flights to Moscow (three hours), while regional carrier **Yamal Airlines** (http://yamal.aero) serves Novosibirsk (two hours, daily) and arctic hubs Novy Urengoy (daily) and Salekhard (daily) among many other destinations in Tyumen Oblast and beyond. Note that foreigners usually need a special permit to visit most Arctic Circle destinations. A second regional carrier, **UTAir** (www.utair.ru), serves Khanty-Mansiysk among other remote destinations in Tyumen Oblast.

BUS

From the **bus station** (ul Permyakova), 3km east of the centre, buses to Tobolsk (₽580, four hours, seven daily) travel via Rasputin's home town of Pokrovskoe (₽250, 1½ hours).

Getting Around

To get to Roshchino Airport, 13km west of the centre, catch marshrutka 35 or bus 141 anywhere along ul Respubliki (30 minutes). Taxis from the city centre cost ₽300 if ordered by phone through your hotel.

From the train station, bus 27 serves Hotel Vostok and passes near the bus station – hop off at the Krosno stop, and cross ul Respubliki. Several other bus lines also link the train station with the city centre. Buses also run from the eastern end of ul Lunacharskogo up and down ul Respubliki to the city centre. Taxis around town cost ₽200.

Tobolsk Тобольск

3456 / POP 100,000 / TIME MOSCOW +2HR

Siberia's former capital Tobolsk is one of the region's most historic cities and one of the nation's most beautiful, sporting a magnificent snow-white kremlin and a charmingly decrepit old town. It is off the Trans-Siberian main line but is well worth the short diversion from Tyumen.

The centre of the Russian colonisation of Siberia, Tobolsk was founded in 1587. Its strategic importance started to wane in the 1760s, when the new Great Siberian Trakt (post road) took a more southerly route. However, until the early 20th century it remained significant as a centre for both learning and exile. Involuntary guests included Fyodor Dostoevsky en route to exile in Omsk and deposed Tsar Nicholas II and his family, who spent several months here in 1917 before being taken to Yekaterinburg and executed.

Sights

Buses from the inconvenient train station give visitors a dismal first impression. Tobolsk's glories begin 3km further south around the splendid kremlin. Immediately beyond and below the kremlin, the old town sinks into the Irtysh's boggy floodplain.

★**Kremlin** HISTORIC BUILDING
(⏲grounds 8am-8pm) The centrepiece of the tower-studded, white-walled, 18th-century kremlin is the glorious 1686 **St Sofia Cathedral** (Софийский собор; Krasnaya pl 2). Less eye-catching from the outside, but with splendid arched ceiling murals, is the **Intercession Cathedral** (Покровский собор; kremlin). Between the two is a 1799 **bell tower** (kremlin), built for the Uglich bell, which famously signalled a revolt against Tsar Boris Godunov. The Kremlin prison is now the **Castle Prison Museum** (Тюремный замок; ☎3456-222 776; www.tiamz.ru; Krasnaya pl 5;

Tobolsk

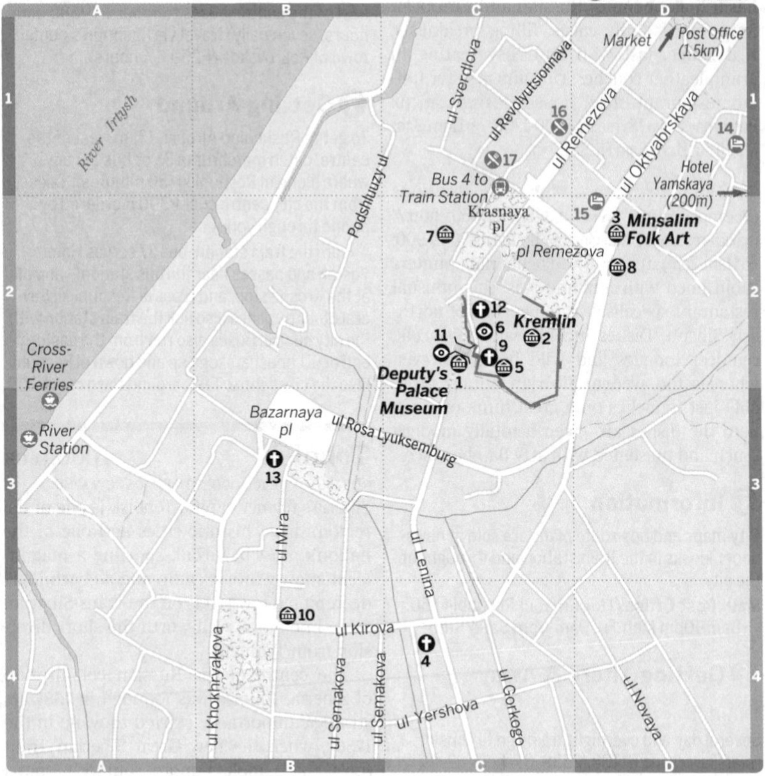

Tobolsk

Top Sights
1 Deputy's Palace Museum C2
2 Kremlin C2
3 Minsalim Folk Art D2

Sights
4 Archangel Mikhail Church C4
5 Arkhiereysky Mansion C2
6 Bell Tower C2
7 Castle Prison Museum C2
8 Gubernsky Museum D2
9 Intercession Cathedral C2
10 Kornilov Mansion B4
11 Pryamskoy Vzvoz C2
12 St Sofia Cathedral C2
13 Zachary & Elisabeth Church B3

Sleeping
14 Hotel Georgievskaya D1
15 Hotel Sibir D2

Eating
16 Kofeynya u Ershova C1
17 Ladeyny C1

₽300; ⏲10am-6pm Tue-Sun), where you can get a sense of the grim life behind bars in both tsarist and Soviet times.

The elegant **Arkhiereysky Mansion** (Архиерейский Дом; kremlin) was closed for renovations when we visited and will eventually be reopened as an Orthodox history museum.

Wooden stairs lead beneath the kremlin's **Pryamskoy Vzvoz** (Прямской Взвоз) (gatehouse) to the wonderfully dilapidated old town full of weather-beaten churches and angled wooden homes sinking between muddy lanes.

★Deputy's Palace Museum MUSEUM
(Дворец наместника; www.tiamz.ru; Krasnaya pl 1; admission ₽600; ⏲10am-6pm Tue-Sun) Tobolsk's best museum, and indeed one of the best museums in Siberia, occupies a beautiful 18th-century former administration on the southwestern edge of the Kremlin. The Romanovs called in here during their brief stint in Tobolsk in 1917, and a section of this remarkably modern museum is devoted to their time here. Tactile multimedia exhibits profile the characters who shaped Siberia before the Bolshevik revolution, as well as hometown heroes such as Dmitry Mendeleyev, who created the first periodic table.

Most exhibits have English placards. The space-age multimedia displays are in Russian only but are fun to play with regardless. Visitors really emerge from here with a sense of Tobolsk's importance in the 18th and 19th centuries, when it was the capital of all Siberia. There's an impressive collection of local art up on the 3rd floor.

★Minsalim Folk Art GALLERY
(Мастерская Минсалим; ☎3456-246 993; www.minsalim.ru; ul Oktyabrskaya 2; ⏲9am-6pm) FREE Minsalim is a master bone-carver who turns mammoth tusks and antler fragments into detailed figurines related to myths and legends of the local brand of shamanism. With a long mustache and flowing mane, eccentric Minsalim is something of a shaman himself and will gladly lead you on a tour of his workshop behind the gallery (phone in advance). His son and some members of staff speak English.

Gubernsky Museum MUSEUM
(Губернский музей; www.tiamz.ru; ul Oktyabrskaya 1; ₽200; ⏲10am-6pm Tue-Sun) Built in 1887 for the 300th anniversary of the founding of Tobolsk, the Gubernsky Museum has displays on the history of Tobolsk, a hugely impressive and near-complete mammoth skeleton and a display of bone carvings.

Archangel Mikhail Church CHURCH
(Церковь Архангела Михаила; ul Lenina 24) The attractive Archangel Mikhail Church has a colourfully restored interior. The character of Tatiana Larina in Pushkin's epic *Eugene Onegin* is said to have been modelled on Natalya Fonvizina, a Decembrist wife who prayed here.

Zachary & Elisabeth Church CHURCH
(Церковь Захария и Елизаветы; Bazarnaya pl 8) The 1759 Zachary & Elisabeth Church, with its soaring black-tipped spires, is extremely photogenic.

Kornilov Mansion MUSEUM
(Дом Корнилова; ul Mira 9) The grand Kornilov Mansion, named after a 19th-century statesman and philanthropist, is closed while being converted into a museum dedicated to the Romanovs, but is still worth a look for its lavish exterior.

Sleeping

Resting Rooms HOSTEL $
(komnaty otdykha; ☎3456-62 522; train station; dm 12/24hr from ₽600/800, s/d from ₽1400/2000; 📶) Clean and friendly. The location is utterly impractical for visiting the city, but ideal if you're arriving late or waiting for an early-morning connection.

★Hotel Sibir HOTEL $$
(Гостиница Сибирь; ☎3456-220 901; www.hotel-siberia.com; pl Remezova 1; s/d incl breakfast from ₽2100/3900; 📶) Sibir's rooms are comfortable, spacious and festooned with fading old photos, dark-wood furnishings and old-fashioned wallpaper, which gives it an enjoyably historical vibe. Another huge plus is that it's the closest to the kremlin of all Tobolsk's hotels. The breakfast is tasty and filling and the in-house restaurant is reliably good. A good-value spot.

★Hotel Yamskaya HOTEL $$
(Гостиница Ямская; ☎3456-226 177; yamskaya-tobolsk@mail.ru; ul Bolshaya Sibirskaya 40; r incl breakfast ₽3300; 📶) With cosy rooms, friendly service, a perfect location near the kremlin and a warm and inviting overall atmosphere, this 12-room hotel borders on boutique. The prices are extremely reasonable for what you get.

Hotel Georgievskaya HOTEL $$
(Гостиница Георгиевская; ☎3456-220 909; www.hotel-georgievskaya.ru; ul Lenskaya 35; s/d incl breakfast from ₽2700/3700;) Right behind a Dostoyevsky statue, this large hotel has spacious rooms that are a tad overdone with velvet curtains, satin bedspreads and the like, but at least that gives it a bit more character than many a Siberian hotel.

Eating

While Tobolsk has seen a modest tourist boom in recent years, there is still no restaurant scene to speak of.

Kofeynya u Ershova CAFE $
(Кофейня у Ершова; ☎3456-246 808; ul Remezova 7; mains ₽150-450; 10am-11pm) An easy stop near the kremlin for relatively quick and cheap Russian eats – think lunch standards such as *bishteks* (Russian-style hamburger), *solyanka* (pickled vegetables and potato soup) and stuffed *bliny* (pancakes). Portions tend to be on the small side so if you're hungry it might be worth ordering two dishes.

Ladeyny RUSSIAN $$
(Ладейный; ☎3456-222 111; ul Revolutsionnaya 2; mains ₽250-500; 11am-2am;) This place, an extra-large Siberian *izba* (wood house) that simply feels warm and welcoming, is a revolution as far as Tobolsk is concerned. Specialities include Siberian fish and home-made *pelmeni* (ravioli) and *varenyky* (dumplings). Nights sometimes bring live music. The English menu is extremely rare for these parts.

★**Romanov Restaurant** RUSSIAN $$$
(Ресторан Романов; ☎3456-399 139; ul Microrayon 1, Hotel Slavyanskaya; mains ₽1000-1500; noon-10pm) Housed in the Hotel Slavyanskaya, the very refined Romanov restaurant is in a class above everything else in Tobolsk. Dress sharp and tuck into a menu that features succulent 19th-century Russian dishes. Also has a family portrait of Russia's last tsar and his family on the ceiling and can count ex-presidents among its clientele.

Information

Post Office (Почта; Komsomolsky pr 42; 8am-6pm)

Getting There & Away

There are frequent trains to Tyumen (from ₽600, four hours).

Train 125 trundles to Novosibirsk on odd-numbered days at 9.21am (from ₽4696, 24 hours) via Omsk, while the 115 is a late-night option to Omsk on odd-numbered days (platskart/kupe ₽2598/3197, 13¼ hours, 1.26am).

Buses are another option to Tyumen (₽580, four hours) via Pokrovskoe (₽300, 2½ hours), Rasputin's home village. Eight buses per day to various destinations pass through nearby Abalak, site of an interesting monastery.

In the warm months ferries leave from the river station and cruise the Irtysh north to Salekhard (1st-/2nd-/3rd-class ₽3000/1200/900, five days, about six monthly) via Khanty-Mansiysk (two days), and south to Omsk (₽2200/1000/850, three days, about three monthly).

Getting Around

Bus 4 and *marshrutka* (fixed-route minibus) 20 link the train station, new town and kremlin. Taxis to/from the station cost around ₽250.

There are small ferry boats crisscrossing back and forth over the River Irtysh throughout daylight hours and into the early evening. They leave from just **north** of the river station and further **south**.

Omsk Омск

☎3812 / POP 1.15 MILLION / TIME MOSCOW +3HR

With its modest sights hidden behind busy roads and endless kilometres of drab concrete, this big industrial city is not worth a special detour. However, you may find it a convenient stopover to break up long journeys.

If you have time to kill, the **Fine Arts Museum** (☎3812-200 047; www.vrubel.ru; ul Lenina 3; ₽150; 10am-7pm Tue-Sun) displays a lot of fussy decorative arts but the rectilinear 1862 building is a historical curiosity in itself. It was built as the Siberian governor's mansion and hosted passing tsars: note the original Kalmykian throne with its ebony elephant armrests and 7kg of beaten silver. In 1918–19, however, the building was home to Admiral Kolchak's counter-revolutionary government and was the heart of White Russia before the Reds eventually claimed the city.

Other buildings to look out for include the ornate **Drama Theatre** (Омский театр драмы; www.omskdrama.ru; ul Lenina 8a) built in the early 20th century and the massive **Assumption Cathedral** (Успенский собор; Sobornaya pl) rebuilt after the collapse of the USSR.

Sleeping & Eating

Resting Rooms HOSTEL $
(komnaty otdykha; ☎3812-442 347; train station; 12/24hr from ₽900/1600) Spacious and with en suites, these are some of the best train station rooms we've seen in Siberia.

Ibis Sibir HOTEL $$
(☎3812-311 551; www.ibishotel.com; ul Lenina 22; r from ₽3400;) The always-reliable Ibis shuns Soviet dimensions and has the classic bright and cheery look the Ibis chain is known for. Staff are efficient and all up it's probably the best value in Omsk. Breakfast (which is fairly average) is ₽450.

Hotel Mayak BUSINESS HOTEL $$$
(Гостиница Маяк; ☎3812-330 303; www.hotel-mayak.ru; ul Lermontova 2; s/tw incl breakfast ₽3400/4800;) In the eye-catching rounded end of the vaguely ship-shaped art-deco river station, the Mayak has small, modish rooms with artistic lines and good bathrooms. Popular with Western business travellers. Friendly staff and an impressive breakfast buffet.

★ **Lapshichnaya Noodle Shop** VIETNAMESE $$
(Little Flower in Big Window; ☎3812-208 028; ul Lenina 20; 11am-11pm) The fresh, healthy and slightly spiced soups and curries of Southeast Asia are a rare treat in Siberia, so it's worth making a special effort to eat at this light, bright and modern noodle bar. We particularly enjoyed the beef in a spicy soya sauce.

Tamada GEORGIAN $$
(Тамада; ☎3812-200 127; ul Gagarina 3; meals ₽450-800; 10am-midnight;) It won't just be the food you remember at this Georgian restaurant. The setting, in a bizarre cave-like basement filled with fake ponds and palm trees, will live long in the memory too. The *khachapuri* (bread baked with cheese filling) and *lobiyo* (spicy red beans stewed in vegetables) are recommended. It's just off ul Lenina.

Information

Post Office (Почтамт; ul Gertsena 1; 8am-10pm Mon-Fri, 9am-6pm Sat & Sun)

Getting There & Away

Omsk is on the Trans-Siberian main line, which means numerous connections both east toward Novosibirsk (*platskart/kupe* from ₽1622/2700, about 7½ hours) and west toward Yekaterinburg. Destinations off the main line served from Omsk include Abakan (₽3183/5412, 30 hours, daily), Barnaul (₽2924/3549, 16 hours, one or two daily), Tomsk (₽3167/4391, 14 hours, even-numbered days) and Tobolsk (₽3547/4382, 12 hours, odd-numbered days at 8.30pm, even-numbered days at 10.16am).

An *elektrichka* (suburban train) serves Novosibirsk Tuesday, Thursday and Sunday at 2.55pm (1st-/2nd-/3rd-class ₽1623/1287/711, 6¾ hours).

Getting Around

The main streets, Ul Lenina and pr Marksa, run parallel to each other through the centre of town and cross the Om River just north of central pl Lenina. From the train station, trolleybus 4 and bus 69 are among many options that go to the centre along pr Marksa.

Novosibirsk Новосибирск

☎383 / POP 1.5 MILLION / TIME MOSCOW +4HR

Novosibirsk might be Russia's third-largest city, but you wouldn't know it. The city centre is compact and – thanks to lots of parks and tree-lined avenues – it has a quiet, green-fingered air to it, which makes it an ideal city for strolling about. And there's a lot here worth strolling for, including a slew of quirky museums and monuments, some impressive galleries, a good theatre and entertainment scene and some memorable places to eat. All this means it's hard not to like Novosibirsk and, sitting as it does on the main rail line, it makes a worthwhile Trans-Siberian pit stop. You can also jump off from here to architecturally splendid Tomsk, some 4½ hours away by bus.

Novosibirsk grew up in the 1890s around the Ob River bridge built for the Trans-Siberian Railway, and the city is festooned with original examples of the wood-lace architecture that prevailed at the time before the Soviets took over and started chucking concrete everywhere. Named Novo-Nikolaevsk until 1925 after the last tsar, it grew rapidly into Siberia's biggest metropolis, a key industrial and transport centre exploiting coalfields to the east and mineral deposits in the Urals.

Sights

Despite its daunting scale, Novosibirsk has a manageable centre focused on pl Lenina. The city's main axis, Krasny pr, runs through this square linking most points of interest.

Novosibirsk

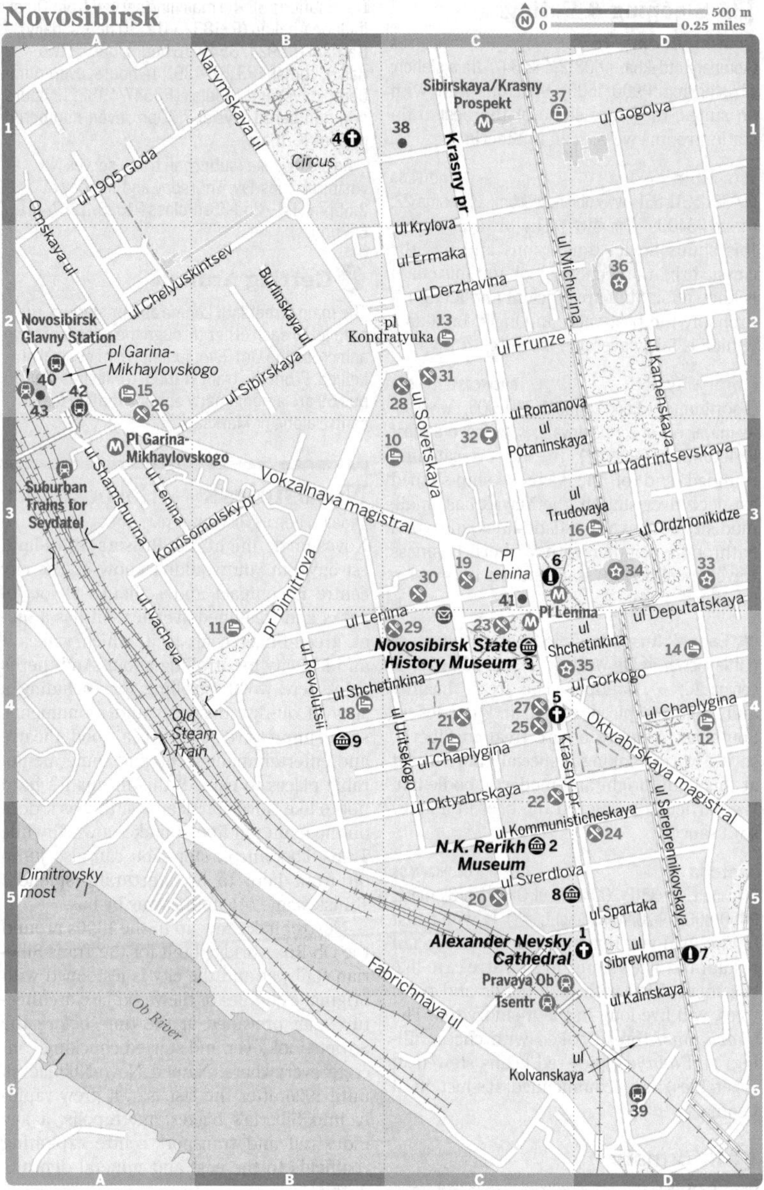

★N.K. Rerikh Museum MUSEUM

(Музей Н.К. Рериха; www.sibro.ru; ul Kommunisticheskaya 38; ₽200, free every 2nd Sat; ⏲11am-7pm Fri-Mon & Wed, 1-8pm Thu) This museum is dedicated to the works and life of the painter Nikolai Rerikh (Nicholas Roerick), beloved in these parts because of his life-long passion for Altai. While the many paintings on display are reproductions, they provide a thorough synopsis of his life's work, and you can buy affordable prints in the excellent gift shop.

Novosibirsk

Top Sights
1 Alexander Nevsky Cathedral D5
2 N.K. Rerikh Museum C5
3 Novosibirsk State History Museum C4

Sights
4 Cathedral of the Ascension B1
5 Chapel of St Nicholas C4
6 Lenin Statue C3
7 Monument to First Traffic Light D5
8 State Art Museum C5
9 USSR Museum B4

Sleeping
10 Avenue Hotel C3
11 Azimut Hotel Siberia B4
12 DoubleTree by Hilton D4
13 FunKey Hostel C2
14 Hostel Dostoevsky D4
15 Marins Park Hotel Novosibirsk A2
16 Novosibirsk Marriott Hotel D3
17 Provence Hostel C4
18 Zokol Hostel B4

Eating
19 Baranzhar C3
20 Goodman Steak House C5
21 La Maison C4
22 Nikolaevskaya Pelmennaya C4
23 Park Cafe C4
24 People's Bar & Grill D5
25 Puppen Haus C4
26 Shashlikoff A2
27 Shashlikoff C4
28 Tiflis C2
29 Trattoria la Trenta C4
30 Universam Avangard C3
31 Vilka-Lozhka C2

Drinking & Nightlife
Friends Cocktail Bar .... (see 24)
32 Rock City C3
Truba .... (see 31)

Entertainment
33 Brodyachaya Sobaka D3
34 Opera & Ballet Theatre D3
35 Philharmonia C4
36 Spartak Stadium D2

Shopping
37 Book Look C1

Transport
38 Aviakassa C1
39 Bus Station D6
40 Bus Stop for Airport A2
41 Central Travel Bureau C3
42 Marshrutky A2
43 Novosibirsk Glavny A2

Rerikh was also a writer, a philosopher, a scientist, an archaeologist, a statesman – and a traveller. An epic five-year expedition around Central Asia (including Altai) and the Himalayas in the 1920s provided fodder for many of his paintings and philosophies. That journey is explored in depth here, making the museum an inspiring spot for modern-day vagabonds. Incredibly, the expedition traversed 35 mountain passes of more than 14,000ft! There is a 15-minute movie in English on the artist's life, and rooms dedicated to the works of his wife and two sons – talented artists, writers and/or thinkers in their own right.

If you can, try to time your visit to the museum to coincide with one of the beautiful classical music concerts (free with entry) on 3rd floor at 3pm every Thursday and on the second Saturday of each month.

★ Alexander Nevsky Cathedral CHURCH
(Собор Александра Невского; Krasny pr 1a) The 1898 Alexander Nevsky Cathedral is a red-brick Byzantine-style building with gilded domes and colourful murals. The cathedral was originally built as a monument in honour of Tsar Alexander III who had initiated the construction of Novosibirsk. It was shut by the Soviet authorities in 1937 and only re-opened in 1989.

★ Novosibirsk State History Museum MUSEUM
(Краеведческий музей; Krasny pr 23; ₽200; 10am-6pm Wed-Fri, 11am-7pm Sat-Sun) In an elegant mansion, the State History Museum has recently re-opened after renovations and is now by far the best museum in Novosibirsk. The well-thought-out collection traces the history of Siberia and Novosibirsk from birth up to today. The highlights are the displays on nomadic life and shamanism (in the basement). The regular temporary exhibitions are a more hit-and-miss affair and can include anything from collections of posh frocks to delicate-faced dolls and puppets.

Unusually most displays are also labelled clearly in English.

Cathedral of the Ascension CHURCH
(Вознесенский собор; ul Sovetskaya 91) The gold-domed 1914 Cathedral of the Ascension

has a wonderful, colourful interior with a soaring central space that's unexpected given its fairly squat exterior appearance.

USSR Museum MUSEUM
(Музей СССР; ☎383-223 0266; ul Gorkogo 16; ₽200; ⊙noon-6pm Tue-Sat) While the collection of '70s Soviet bric-a-bric in this museum isn't particularly original, you get free rein over the place, which means photo-ops galore. Dress yourself up (don't worry, it's allowed!) as a Soviet apparatchik, country *dyevushka* (girl) or Great Patriotic War soldier and snap away. The museum is housed within a ramshackle wooden building.

Lenin Statue MONUMENT
(Памятник Ленину; pl Lenina) This is a particularly dashing statue of Lenin wearing a flapping coat. He's flanked by waving partisans vainly trying to direct the chaotic traffic.

Monument to First Traffic Light MONUMENT
(cnr ul Serebrennikovskaya & ul Sibrevkoma) This humorous monument portraying a stumpy little man staring up at a bendy traffic light is based at the rumoured site of the city's first ever traffic light. It's worth a quick diversion if you're in the southern part of town.

State Art Museum MUSEUM
(Художественный музей; Krasny pr 5; ₽200; ⊙noon-8pm Tue-Fri, 1-9pm Sat & Sun) The highlight is the museum's collection of 65 original paintings by Nikolai Rerikh on the 2nd floor, mostly mountainscapes from the celebrated drifter's time in the Himalayas. The 2nd floor also has a room of 17th-century European (mostly Dutch) masters, a collection of icons and several rooms dedicated to 18th-to-19th-century Russian art. The 3rd floor has some wonderful pieces from the Soviet era.

Chapel of St Nicholas CHURCH
(Часовня Святителя Николая; Krasny pr) The pretty little Chapel of St Nicholas was said to mark the geographical centre of Russia when it was built in 1915. Demolished in the 1930s, it was rebuilt in 1993 for Novosibirsk's centenary. Today it is an oasis of calm in the bustling city centre.

Sleeping

★ **FunKey Hostel** HOSTEL $
(☎383-263 6503; www.funhostel.ru; ul Frunze 5/2; dm ₽490-700, d ₽1700; ⊖❄📶) 'Funkey' indeed. It backs up its quirky name with one of Siberia's most creative hostel spaces. Bright colours and eye-catching photos enliven walls, extra-tall bunk beds penetrate soaring ceilings and guests kick back in a delightfully wide-open kitchen and common area. Staff are helpful, traveller savvy and speak good English. Easily the best hostel in town.

Provence Hostel HOSTEL $
(Хостел Прованс; ul Chaplygina 45; dm ₽650-700, d ₽2200; @📶) Occupying the 2nd floor of an attractive century-old brick building, the Provence is a large hostel and one that comes across as a little more 'grown-up' than the town's other hostels. Gone are the chalk graffiti walls so common at the competition and in are subtle whites and a hint of the Mediterranean. Capable, English-speaking staff.

Zokol Hostel HOSTEL $
(☎383-223 3611; www.zokolhostel.ru; ul Shchetinkina 34; dm ₽600, d ₽2000; ⊖📶) With down-to-earth English-speaking staff, a superb sightseeing map and an ideal location within walking distance of the train station, the Zokol is a solid bet. It's an intimate basement space with 19 beds in mostly windowless triples and quads, plus two cosy kitchen/common areas.

Hostel Dostoevsky HOSTEL $
(HD Hostel; ☎8-983-510 7583; www.hdhostel.com; ul Gorkogo 85, 3rd fl; ⊙dm ₽350-450; ⊖📶) The apparently only half-finished concrete steps leading up to this hotel, which is located in a tower block, are a little off-putting, but otherwise this is an arty, bustling space with predominantly large (8- to 12-bed) dorms and an airy, open common area.

Azimut Hotel Siberia HOTEL $$
(☎383-217 6970; www.azimuthotels.com; ul Lenina 21; s/d incl breakfast from ₽2750/2904; ⊖❄📶) Big changes have been afoot at this large former Soviet-era hotel. It's been given a good revamp and the rooms (though remaining Soviet size challenged) are clean, plain, quiet and functional. The staff are very efficient and the included breakfast is a veritable feast. A very good deal.

Marins Park Hotel Novosibirsk HOTEL $$
(Конгресс-Гостиница Новосибирск; ☎383-364 0101; www.hotel-novosibirsk.ru; Vokzalnaya magistral 1; r incl breakfast from ₽2500; ⊖❄@📶) Boasting awesome views of the city centre from its upper floors, this formerly glum

Soviet-era tower has been transformed into a plush modern hotel with fantastic service and prime rooms. The live python in a huge cage beside the reception desk is a novel touch. Great weekend and online deals are often available.

Avenue Hotel HOTEL $$
(Авеню Отель; ☎383-227 0534; ul Sovetskaya 57; r from ₽2400; 📶) The five rooms in the main wing of this quiet minihotel are huge and exceptionally well-appointed – a welcome change from the standard renovated Soviet fare. Cheaper rooms are in a neighbouring annexe. Very little English spoken. It's a little tricky to find but both buildings are in a quiet residential courtyard behind ul Sovetskaya 55.

★ **DoubleTree by Hilton** HOTEL $$$
(☎383-223 0100; www.novosibirsk.doubletreebyhilton.com; ul Kamenskaya 7/1; s/d incl breakfast weekday from ₽10,300/11,400, weekend from ₽5300/6400;) Has all the amenities you would expect, highlighted by luscious beds, mood lighting, ginormous plasma TVs, rain showers and (separate) extra-long bathtubs, although we'd like to see a bit more space in the standard rooms. Online booking can sometimes mean big discounts. The service is unusually good.

Novosibirsk Marriott Hotel BUSINESS HOTEL $$$
(☎383-230 0300; www.marriott.com; ul Ordzhonikidze 31; incl breakfast r Mon-Fri from ₽9751, Sat & Sun ₽7100;) Architecturally speaking, the city's new Marriott Hotel, straight opposite the opera theatre and in a pleasingly renovated old building with huge windows, blends nicely into the townscape. The decor is fairly cookie-cutter-luxury business class, though it's undeniably comfortable and well run.

Eating

Vilka-Lozhka CAFE $
(ul Frunze 2; meals ₽150-250; ⏲9am-10pm; 📶) This upmarket *stolovaya* (cafeteria) is popular for a reason – hip and cool with groovy tunes and piping-hot Russian staples like *bliny* (pancakes) and borsch at dirt-cheap prices. It even has beer on tap. Good place for a simple and fun meal.

Shashlikoff RUSSIAN $
(www.shashlikoff.com; Krasny pr 17; mains ₽250-300; ⏲9am-1am; 📶) This popular chain is fantastic value. Its signature shashlyk (kebabs) come in meat and fish varieties, accompanied by a full complement of Russian soups and salads, washed down with home-brewed beer (from ₽85). There's another branch opposite the **train station** (www.shashlikoff.com; Vokzalnaya magistral 1; mains ₽250-300; ⏲9am-1am; 📶).

NOVOSIBIRSK'S WOODEN HOUSES

While it can't quite match the wood-lace architecture of nearby Tomsk, Novosibirsk has some fine tsar-era houses hidden among the hulking Soviet structures of the centre. Photogenic streets include **ul Kommunisticheskaya** (check out Nos 3, 13, 19, 21, 23, 25 and 36), **ul Oktyabrskaya** (Nos 5, 9, 15 and 47), **ul Chaplygina** (Nos 25, 27 and 29) and **ul Gorkogo** (Nos 18, 20, 40, 81 and the brick No 26a).

Universam Avangard SUPERMARKET $
(Универсам Авангард; ul Lenina 10; ⏲24hr) Centrally located and well-stocked supermarket.

Nikolaevskaya Pelmennaya RUSSIAN $
(Николаевская Пельменная; Krasny pr 13; mains ₽130-250; ⏲10am-10.30pm) Cheap and simple *pelmeni* (Russian-style ravioli) with meat and fish fillings in an equally modest cafe located beneath a sex shop.

★ **Park Cafe** INTERNATIONAL $$
(☎383-310 9070; www.parkcafensk.com; Kransy Prospekt 25/1; mains ₽400-800; ⏲7.30am-1am Mon-Fri, 9am-1am Sat & Sun) Bulbous lights, arty fairy colours, shelves of books and beautifully created and presented dishes mean that this very central restaurant has a loyal local fan club. After you've finished tucking into one of their yummy soups, salads, fish cakes or some delicately prepared macarons, take a walk through the pretty neighbouring park.

Trattoria la Trenta ITALIAN $$
(☎383-223 9291; http://latrenta.ru; ul Uritsekogo 9; pizzas around ₽440, mains ₽350-500; ⏲noon-11pm Sun-Thu, noon-midnight Fri & Sat;) You could almost imagine this cute little trattoria has been magically transported straight from a honey-coloured Tuscany village to big old Novosibirsk. The walls are lined in paintings and dried pasta and there's a shaded terrace

for summer evenings. The menu lists all the Italian classics, but also includes a few local touches such as black buckwheat pizza bases.

Goodman Steak House STEAK $$
(☎383-289 2525; ul Sovetskaya 5; mains ₽540-720; ⏲noon-midnight) There's a busy, British-style pub atmosphere at the Goodman Steak House. Although plenty of people stop by after work for just a beer, it's renowned for having some of the best steaks in the city, as well as other pub favourites like chicken curry and homemade sausages.

Baranzhar CENTRAL ASIAN $$
(☎383-209 0902; www.baranjar.ru; ul Sovetskaya 18; mains ₽300-550; ⏲noon-midnight; ⓦ) With a warm, relaxed atmosphere and a creatively decorated dining room, it's no wonder that this central restaurant, which serves up an exotic flavour of Central Asia (although there's a fair few Russian staples as well), is currently one of Novosibirsk's favourites. The emphasis here is on kebabs, but the stuffed eggplant starter is delicious.

Tiflis GEORGIAN $$
(Тифлис; ☎383-222 8181; www.tiflisnsk.ru; ul Sovetskaya 65; mains ₽400-600; ⏲11am-11pm; ✎) This atmospheric tavern-cavern down in a basement offers the most authentic Georgian cuisine in town. The filling and delicious *khachapuri po-adzharski* (Georgian cheese bread with a raw egg swimming in the middle) is well worth a try. There's an English menu and the staff speak good English and will happily give menu suggestions.

People's Bar & Grill CAFE $$
(Krasny pr 22; mains ₽350-800; ⏲24hr) Trendy sister restaurant to Friends Cocktail Bar (p158), which is in the same building. Specialises in grilled meat.

★**Puppen Haus** RUSSIAN $$$
(☎383-251 0303; www.puppenhaus-resto.ru; ul Chaplygin 65/1; full meal around ₽2000; ⏲noon-midnight) The Puppen Haus (Puppet House), which specialises in refined traditional Siberian dishes, is both eccentric and divine. It consists of numerous little dining rooms and alcoves crammed with stony-eyed wooden puppets. The food is as memorable as the setting and if you've never tried elk steaks, Kamchatka lobster or – get this – boiled bear (!) then now is the chance.

Advance bookings are wise in the evening.

★**La Maison** EUROPEAN $$$
(☎383-209 0010; ul Sovetskaya 25; mains ₽600-1500; ⏲10am-midnight) In a beautiful former theatre dating to 1908, this is Novosibirsk's most sumptuous restaurant. The French- and Russian-leaning menu features quail, rabbit, rack of lamb and octopus along with upmarket versions of *solyanka* (soup from pickled vegetables and potato) and other Russian country faves. Also has an extensive wine list and rich desserts such as mille-feuille.

It's a place where people come if they want to impress so dress appropriately.

Drinking & Nightlife

★**Friends Cocktail Bar** BAR
(Krasny pr 22; ⏲6pm-6am) With bearded bartenders whipping up some of Siberia's best (and strongest) cocktails and a convivial crowd, this is unquestionably Novosibirsk's best spot to warm up for a night out. Indeed you may elect to not go anywhere else. Reliably action-packed on weekdays as well as weekends, and you can eat at equally trendy People's Bar & Grill (p158) in the same building.

Truba BAR
(Труба; www.vk.com/truba_nsk; ul Frunze 2; ⏲7pm till late; ⓦ) It bills itself as a jazz bar but the line-up runs the gamut from jazz and blues to trash rock and grunge. Whatever is playing, this underground institution is well worth checking out.

Rock City CLUB
(Рок Сити; ☎383-227 0108; www.rockcity.ru; Krasny pr 37; cover ₽150-350) Everything from Latin dancing to DJs to heavy-rock concerts. Thursday is ladies' night and Tuesdays feature two-for-one cocktails.

☆ Entertainment

★**Brodyachaya Sobaka** LIVE MUSIC
(Бродячая Собака; ☎383-218 8070; www.sobaka.su; Kamenskaya ul 32; ⏲5pm-1am Sun-Thu, 5pm-3am Fri & Sat; ⓦ) Weekends usually see live music performing at this grungy cabaret bar, while weekdays bring all manner of performing arts and other events ranging from clowns to quiz nights. Check the website for the schedule.

To find it look for the discreet rust-red carved metal sign and then head down the stairs to the basement.

★ Opera & Ballet Theatre THEATRE
(Театр оперы и балета; ☎383-222 6040; http://novat.nsk.ru; Krasny pr 36; tickets ₽500-5000; ⏲Oct-Jun, most shows at 6.30pm) For classical culture don't miss an evening at this gigantic silver-domed theatre. Built in 1945, it's the largest theatre in Russia – bigger even than Moscow's Bolshoi. The grand interior alone makes performances here one of the city's highlights. Ticket prices depend on seats and performances.

Philharmonia CLASSICAL MUSIC
(Филармония; ☎383-223 4141; www.philharmonia-nsk.ru; Krasny pr 32; tickets ₽200-1500; ⏲most shows 7pm) Classical music concerts as well as a little jazz and other musical strains.

Spartak Stadium SPECTATOR SPORT
(Стадион Спартак; http://fc-sibir.ru; ul Frunze 15; tickets ₽100-300) This 12,500-capacity venue is the home of local football team Sibir. Games are usually played on Saturday or Sunday.

Shopping

Book Look BOOKS
(ul Gogolya 13; ⏲10am-10pm) Has the best selection of maps in town, including maps of all Western Siberia *oblasti* (regions).

Information

Main Post Office (Главпочтамт; ul Sovetskaya 33; ⏲8am-10pm Mon-Fri, 9am-6pm Sat & Sun)

Getting There & Away

The well-located **Central Travel Bureau** (Центральное Бюро путешествий; Krasny pr 25; ⏲9am-8pm) is one of dozens of places to buy rail and air tickets, and also sells bus tickets (commission ₽100 to ₽200). Another such place is **Aviakassa** (Авиакасса; ul Gogolya 3; ⏲8.30am-8pm).

TRAIN

The city's huge main train station, **Novosibirsk Glavny** (ul Shamshurina 43), sits right on the Trans-Siberian main line and there are plentiful trains west to Moscow (48 to 55 hours) via Omsk, Tyumen and Yekaterinburg, and east to Irkutsk and beyond via Krasnoyarsk.

Train 117 is a direct service to Tobolsk (*platskart/kupe* ₽4300/6400, odd-numbered days, 1.04am, 21¾ hours); you'll be better off transferring in Tyumen.

For Tomsk try trains 144 or 142 (seat/*kupe* ₽479/1569, daily, 4½ hours) or connect to an *elektrichka* at Taiga; many travellers use the more frequent direct buses.

AIR

Novosibirsk's **Tolmachyovo Airport** (www.tolmachevo.ru), 30km west of the city, is well connected to Moscow (four hours) and various other domestic destinations. International destinations served by direct flights from Novosibirsk include Beijing, several cities in Central Asia, plus seasonal flights to destinations in Thailand, Turkey and Greece.

BUS

From the **bus station** (Автовокзал; www.nsk-avtovokzal.ru; Krasny pr 4) buses depart every hour or so for Tomsk (₽740, 4½ hours). For roughly double the price, shared taxis shave at least an hour or more off those times but can take a while to fill up. Taxi drivers stand outside the station trying to entice customers.

Getting Around

From the bus station, bus 111z (111з) goes to Tolmachyovo airport every 30 minutes from 4am to 10.30pm, stopping at the **bus stop** by the train station on the way. Allow an hour to get there (more during Novosibirsk's infamous rush hour). A taxi to the airport costs ₽800 (30 minutes, or one hour during rush hour). Going the other way drivers will often ask for ₽1200.

The metro has a major north–south line running beneath Krasny pr and across the river to ul Studencheskaya and pl Karla Marksa. For the main train station you'll need metro stop Ploshchad Garina-Mikhaylovskogo, which is on a second three-stop line that intersects with the major line at Sibirskaya/Krasny Prospekt.

Generally, buses and *marshrutky* (minibuses; ul Shamshurina; 📶) are handier than the metro within the centre. Buses 8, 21 and 37 link the train station with the river station via pl Lenina, Krasny pr and the bus station.

Tomsk Томск

☎3822 / POP 524,000 / TIME MOSCOW +4HR

Magnificent in snow, but fun to be in at any time of the year, the university city of Tomsk boasts numerous examples of fine wooden buildings and has an animated cafe and art scene. The city has enjoyed the reputation as the 'cultural capital of Siberia' since the 1960s, when artists, writers and theatre and film directors were invited to take up residence here.

One of Siberia's oldest cities, Tomsk was founded in 1604 and was a major trade outpost before the founding of Novosibirsk (then Novo-Nikolaevsk) and the subsequent relocation of the Trans-Siberian Railway line. With a huge and grand university,

Tomsk

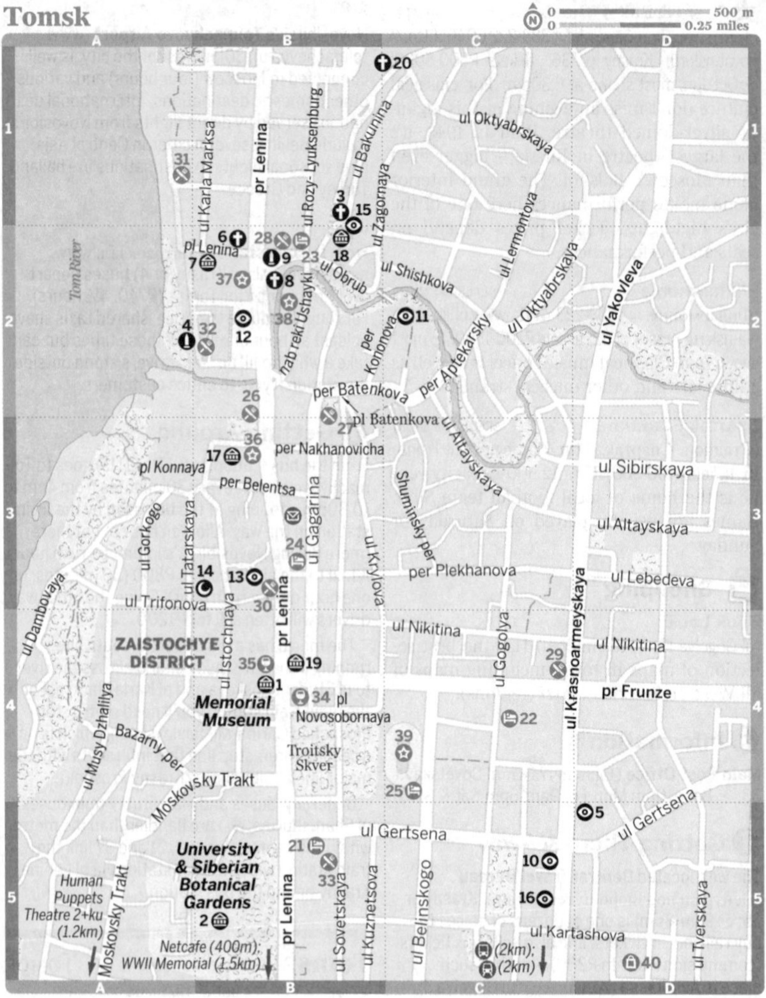

this is above all a city of learning, and today around one in every five residents is a student – hence the youthful, intellectual atmosphere.

Sights

★University & Siberian Botanical Gardens HISTORIC BUILDING
(Томский Государственный Университет; ☎3822-529 816; greenhouses ₽250; ⏲greenhouses 10am-noon & 1-3pm Tue, Thu & Sat) The classically colonnaded main buildings of the university lie in resplendently leafy grounds, giving Tomsk the sobriquet 'Oxford of Siberia'. Most of the buildings themselves are closed to the public, but the grounds are open to all. However, the **Siberian Botanical Gardens**, at the southern edge of the grounds, are the real highlight of a visit. The exterior gardens contain samples of many Siberian plant species while the enormous greenhouses (guided tour only) get all tropical and steamy.

★Memorial Museum MUSEUM
(Мемориальный музей 'Следственная тюрьма НКВД'; pr Lenina 44; ₽50, camera ₽100, tours in Russian/English ₽200/400; ⏲10am-6pm)

Tomsk

Top Sights
1 Memorial Museum B4
2 University & Siberian Botanical Gardens B5

Sights
3 Catholic Church B1
4 Chekhov Statue A2
5 Dragon House D5
6 Epiphany Cathedral B2
7 Former Trading Arches B2
8 Iverskaya Chapel B2
9 Lenin Statue B2
10 Peacock House C5
11 Per Kononova 2 .... C2
12 Ploshchad Lenina B2
13 Prospekt Lenina 56 .... B3
14 Red Mosque B3
15 Resurrection Hill B1
16 Russian-German House C5
17 Tomsk Art Museum B3
18 Tomsk Historical Museum B2
19 Tomsk Regional Museum B4
20 Voznesenskaya Church C1

Activities, Courses & Tours
Tomskturist .... (see 25)

Sleeping
21 Bon Apart Hotel B5
22 Gogol Hotel C4
23 Hotel Magistrat B2
24 Hotel Siberia B3
25 Hotel Sputnik C4

Eating
26 Bulanzhe B2
27 Coffee House Leto Cafe B2
28 Marle Bua B2
Obzhorni Ryad .... (see 21)
29 People's Bar & Grill C4
30 People's Bar & Grill B3
31 Reka 827 .... A1
32 Slavyansky Bazar B2
33 Vechny Zov B5

Drinking & Nightlife
34 Sibirsky Pub B4
35 Underground Jazz Cafe B4

Entertainment
36 Aelita Theatre B3
37 Drama Theatre B2
Organ Hall .... (see 19)
38 Philharmonia B2
Tom Tomsk FC .... (see 39)
39 Trud Stadium C4

Shopping
40 Dzerzhinskogo Market D5

The gloomy basement of this former NKVD (proto-KGB) building is now a museum dedicated to the unspeakable horrors that took place here. Look out for the Gulag map, the system of Soviet labour camps depicted as an uncountable mass of red dots across the territory of the former USSR.

Prisoners who passed through here included Gulag chronicler Eufrosinia Kersnovskaya and the family of the purged Kazakh writer Akhmet Baytursinuli. Outside the museum are two monuments to victims of Stalinist repression – the larger to local victims, the second to Poles slaughtered by Uncle Joe and his cronies.

Tours are recommended, but the English-language ones should be booked in advance. If you go it alone and don't read Russian, you'll miss out on a lot; but, as they say, 'A picture is worth a thousand words', and the pictures on display here are just screaming out.

Ploshchad Lenina HISTORIC SITE

Central pl Lenina isn't really a square so much as a jumbled collection of beautifully restored historic buildings interspersed with banal Soviet concrete lumps. The frustrated **Lenin statue** (pl Lenina), now relegated to a traffic circle, points at the ugly concrete of the Drama Theatre (p164), apparently demanding 'build more like that one'. Fortunately, nobody's listening. Topped with a golden angel, in a second circle beside Lenin, is the **Iverskaya Chapel** (Иверская часовня; pr Lenina; 10am-6pm), whose celebrated icon is dubbed 'Tomsk's Spiritual Gateway'.

The drama theatre is flanked by the splendid 1784 **Epiphany Cathedral** (Богоявленский собор; pl Lenina 7), the former **trading arches** (Гостиный Двор; ul Lenina), and the elegant 1802 Hotel Magistrat (p162).

Tomsk Regional Museum MUSEUM

(Краеведческий музей; 3822-512 935; www.tomskmuseum.ru; pr Lenina 75; ₽200; 10am-6pm Tue-Sun) Housed in the splendid Atashev Palace, this modest museum has a 2500-year-old bear amulet and an interesting exhibit on the Great Tea Trail. But it's the building, commissioned in 1842 by the gold-mining entrepreneur Ivan Atashev, that's the main attraction. It was once used as a church, hence the incongruous steeple tower and wonderful organ hall.

Tomsk Historical Museum MUSEUM
(Исторический музей Томска; Resurrection Hill; museum/temporary exhibitions/viewing tower ₽60/80/50; ⏲10am-7pm Tue-Sun) Up on Resurrection Hill, this museum's moderately interesting collection of old artefacts, clothing and recreations of old homes is well-presented, with placards in English. Climb the observation tower and try to spot Tomsk's seven historic churches from the top. For ₽50 you can rent historical costumes for silly photo-ops. The stone just outside the museum entrance marks the founding of the city.

Resurrection Hill HISTORIC SITE
This dimple-sized hill was the location of Tomsk's original fortress, and the replica of its central wooden *spasskaya bashnya* (savior's tower), which stands here today, was built in 2004 for the city's 400th anniversary celebrations. Next to the tower, the Tomsk Historical Museum has spouted its own wooden observation tower; try to spot the seven historic churches from the top. The stone just outside the museum entrance marks the founding of the city.

Also up on Resurrection Hill is a pretty **Catholic church** (ul Bakunina 4) dating to 1883.

WWII Memorial MONUMENT
A Tomsk landmark, this moving mother-and-son monument is at the very southern end of pr Lenina. The beautiful birch-tree park (Лагерный сад) here is a local favourite for strolls, not least for its fine views across the Tom River.

Tomsk Art Museum MUSEUM
(Художественный музей; ☎3822-514 106; http://artmuseumtomsk.ru/page/1; per Nakhanovicha 3; ₽150; ⏲10am-6pm Tue-Sun) Well worth popping into for its wide range of permanent and temporary exhibits. The highlight is the collection of 19th- and early 20th-century Russian art; there's also a small exhibit of 12th- to 13th-century religious icons.

Tours

Tomskturist TOURS
(Томсктурист; ☎3822-532 121; www.tomskturist.ru; ul Belinskogo 15, Hotel Sputnik; ⏲9am-7pm Mon-Fri, 11am-4pm Sat) Tomskturist can arrange two-hour walking tours of the city, with English-, French- and German-speaking guides, although the price (₽4500) makes this more of a group option. Can also help sort out Altai border-zone permits, arrange regional excursions and sell plane and train tickets. The offices are inside the Hotel Sputnik.

Sleeping

Bon Apart Hotel HOTEL $$
(☎3822-534 655; www.bon-apart.ru; ul Gertsena 1a; s/d incl breakfast from ₽4700/5900; 📶) The large rooms here have comfortable, good-sized beds and polished-tile bathrooms, but are otherwise very plain. The walk-in rates (quoted here) aren't worth bothering with – by booking online you'll likely pay 60% less, which makes the place more tempting.

Hotel Siberia HISTORIC HOTEL $$
(Гостиница Сибирь; ☎3822-527 225; www.hotelsibir.tomsk.ru; pr Lenina 91; s/d/ste incl breakfast from ₽3500/4500/5000; 🚭📶) This centrally located old hotel is popular, despite its largely unimaginative singles and doubles. It does, however, offer great suites with real fireplaces for ₽5500. Dinner is available on top of complimentary breakfast for ₽600 extra, but you'd be better off eating elsewhere.

Hotel Sputnik HOTEL $$
(Гостиница Спутник; ☎3822-526 660; www.sputnik.tomskturist.ru; ul Belinskogo 15; d with/without bathroom ₽3100/1600; 🚭@📶) The winner of Tomsk's first hotel competition in the 1990s, the Sputnik may have lost its 'town's best hotel' status, but it remains decent value if rather insipid. The breakfast is hardly worth getting up for.

★ **Gogol Hotel** BOUTIQUE HOTEL $$$
(☎3822-909 709; http://gogolhotel.ru; ul Gogol 36a; s/d with breakfast from ₽3600/4800; 🚭❄📶) Bordering on boutique, this classy 19-room property has quickly become Tomsk's most sought-after address. Rooms are spacious, with muted grey tones, and the walls are emblazoned with photos of old Tomsk. You can swim in the king-sized beds and the breakfast is fantastic.

Hotel Magistrat HISTORIC HOTEL $$$
(Гостиница Магистрат; ☎3822-511 111; www.magistrathotel.com; pl Lenina 15; s/d incl breakfast from ₽6900/8900; ❄📶) Dating back to 1802, this hotel has an air of gravitas. At least, that's the case on the outside. Inside, there's lots of marble and a bit too much self-importance. The position, though, is prime and the rooms are truly enormous – a real rarity in Russia. No lift.

Eating

Obzhorni Ryad RUSSIAN $
(Обжорный ряд; ul Gertsena 1, Bon Apart Hotel; mains ₽200-250; 11am-10pm;) For penny-pinchers in search of good-value Russian fare, look no further than this *stolovaya* (cafeteria), whose name translates to Guzzler's Row. Travelling children will appreciate the in-house play centre – and parents will appreciate the five minutes of peace it brings them. It's inside the Bon Apart Hotel.

Bulanzhe CAFE $
(Буланже; pr Lenina 80; mains ₽200-350; 10am-11pm;) Fantastic cafe – bright and cheery with an exciting menu of international food, fresh salads, great coffee and a wide tea selection. The Belgian waffles are highly recommended. It's a place to chat and chew rather than work on a laptop.

★ **Marle Bua** ITALIAN $$
(3822-998 888; www.marlebua.ru; pl Lenina 11; mains ₽260-500; 8am-midnight Mon-Fri, 11am-2am Sat, 11am-midnight Sun) For over 150 years this basement restaurant has been keeping the tummies of Tomsk full. In its latest incarnation it's an Italian restaurant and grill. As you'd expect from a place with such maturity, they know what they are doing in the kitchen, with dishes such as rabbit ragout, pasta and pizza. Service is smart and prices are low, considering the quality of food.

Vechny Zov RUSSIAN $$
(Вечный Зов; 3822-528 167; www.vechzov.tomsk.ru; ul Sovetskaya 47; mains ₽200-800; noon-2am;) Named after a popular Soviet TV serial, this is the place to sample Siberian specialities like *stroganina* (frozen raw *chyr*, a white fish common in Arctic rivers, *muksun* (an Ob River white fish) and, perhaps morally questionable, bear meat. Carnivores can even go for a four-meat (bear, deer, pork, beef) *pelmeni* (Russian-style dumplings stuffed with meat). It boasts a mock Siberian ranch outside and a cosy antique-filled home feel inside.

Coffee House Leto Cafe CAFE $$
(Кофейная Лето; ul Gagarina 2; meals ₽300-500; 8am-10pm;) A trippy, yellow vegetarian and glutton-free cafe decorated like a circus with kites and glass mobiles. The menu features food with hard-to-get (in Siberia) ingredients such as pumpkin, pesto and real feta cheese. Also has proper ground coffee.

People's Bar & Grill INTERNATIONAL $$
(pr Lenina 54; mains ₽250-550; noon-2am;) This trendy bar-and-grill embraces pop culture with movie-star photos, music videos and Hollywood-inspired dishes – Big Lebowski (beef steak with potatoes) and Pulp Fishion (salmon steak). There's another branch just off **pr Frunze** (ul Krasnoarmeyskaya 31; mains ₽250-550; noon-2am;).

★ **Reka 827** SEAFOOD $$$
(3822-902 020; www.reka827.ru; ul Kooperativnyy 2; mains ₽700-900; noon-midnight Sun-Thu, noon-1am Fri & Sat) If it's summer, sit out on one of the sun loungers on the deck of this sophisticated restaurant and eat great seafood while watching the locals swim in the river below. The fish dishes here are prepared with verve, which means you can look forward to tastes such as whole fried octopus and little fishy tapas-style dishes.

★ **Slavyansky Bazar** RUSSIAN $$$
(Славянский Базар; 3822-515 553; pl Lenina 10; mains ₽500-1200; noon-midnight Mon-Thu & Sun, noon-2am Fri & Sat;) Slavyansky Bazar, Tomsk's fanciest restaurant, is housed in a 19th-century building with an interior like something from a period drama. Chekhov

CHEKHOV ON TOMSK – 'BORING CITY, DULL PEOPLE'

Not everyone falls in love with Tomsk. Playwright Anton Chekhov – who visited the city on his way to Russia's Far East – certainly didn't. 'Tomsk isn't worth a damn,' he wrote in his diary. 'A boring city...with dull people.' He also described it as 'a drunken city' where there were 'no beautiful women at all'. He also complained that a waitress had wiped a spoon 'against her backside' before handing it to him. But then, as legend has it, he did almost drown while crossing the Tom River, so maybe he was feeling grumpy. The city had its revenge, though. In 2004, on Tomsk's 400th anniversary, a caricature of the famous writer was unveiled, in the form of a bronze **statue** entitled 'Anton Pavlovich [the writer's patronymic] through the eyes of a drunk lying in a ditch'. The statue is on the riverbank opposite Slavyansky Bazar restaurant. Rubbing its well-polished nose is said to bring good luck.

ate at an earlier incarnation of this establishment in 1890. The food was one of the few things he liked about the city and if he ate here today, he would still approve. Expect refined takes on classic Russian dishes.

Drinking & Nightlife

★Underground Jazz Cafe BAR

(☎3822-516 319; www.jazzcafe.tomsk.ru; pr Lenina 46; cover charge weekends ₽250-400; ⏲6pm-midnight; 📶) A hip and literally underground basement with live jazz, including frequent US guests, most weekends. Also has an extensive drinks and food menu and old black-and-white films play in the background.

Sibirsky Pub PUB

(Сибирский Паб; pl Novosobornaya 2; Guinness pints ₽360; ⏲1pm-1am; 📶) Siberia's first Irish pub was founded over a century ago by a certain Mr Crawley, an Anglo-Egyptian albino who'd gotten stuck in Tomsk after touring with a circus freak show. There are fewer freaks today, but as compensation there is live music at weekends.

Entertainment

★Human Puppets Theatre 2+ku PUPPET THEATRE

(Театр живых кукол 2+ку; ☎3822-420 486; www.2ky.tomsk.ru; Yuzhniy per 29; tickets ₽200-500) Housed in a quaint log cabin near the WWII memorial (take ul Savinykh all the way down until you can go no further), this one-man, homey 'robotic puppet' theatre is a real experience, and one you don't need to understand Russian to appreciate. Check the website for performance details.

Organ Hall CLASSICAL MUSIC

(pr Lenina 75; tickets ₽200-500; ⏲concerts 7pm, noon on Sun) Beautiful organ concerts are held several times a month upstairs in the Atashev Palace. The acoustics are brilliant.

Drama Theatre THEATRE

(Драматический театр; ☎3822-906 837; www.tomskdrama.ru; pl Lenina 4) The drama theatre might be housed in a huge ugly slab of concrete on pl Lenina, but the performances are far from ugly.

Philharmonia CONCERT VENUE

(Филармония; ☎3822-515 186; http://bkz.tomsk.ru; pl Lenina 1) Classical music and

DON'T MISS

WOODEN HERITAGE ARCHITECTURE

Much of Tomsk's appeal lies in its well-preserved late-19th- and early-20th-century 'wooden-lace' architecture – carved windows and tracery on old log and timber houses. There are a few streets to home in on if touring the city on foot.

Ul Tatarskaya has perhaps the richest concentration of such houses. It's reached via the steps beside a lovely old house at **prospekt Lenina 56** (пр Ленина 56). The best examples are on the block north of ul Trifonova, where you'll also find the modest **Red Mosque** (Красная Мечеть; ul Tatarskaya 22), which dates from 1904. It was used as a vodka factory by the atheist Soviets, but was reopened to worshippers in 1997. Over on the east side of pr Lenina, **ul Gagarina** is similarly endowed with graceful heritage houses.

A few blocks east of ul Belinskogo, near the corner of ul Krasnoarmeyskaya and ul Gertsena, look out for the spired, bright-turquoise **Russian-German House** (Российско-Немецкий Дом; ul Krasnoarmeyskaya 71), built in 1904; the late 19th-century **Dragon House** (Дом Дракона; ul Krasnoarmeyskaya 68) which is home to a clinic; and the fan-gabled early-20th-century **Peacock House** (Дом Павлина; ul Krasnoarmeyskaya 67a). **Ul Dzerzhinskogo**, one block east of ul Krasnoarmeyskaya, is worth a wander as well for wood houses and the colourful outdoor **Dzherzhinskogo Market** (p165), which sprawls for a full block south of ul Kartashova, providing photo-ops as well as fuel in the form of local fruits and nuts.

Other streets worth strolling are **per Kononova** – look for **No 2** (per Kononova 2), where the doomed communist mastermind Sergei Kirov lodged in 1905 – and nearby **ul Shishkova**. Finally, if you walk from **Resurrection Hill** (p162) to the **Voznesenskaya church** (Вознесенская церковь; ul Oktyabrsky Vzvoz 10), you will find yourself on a delightful, quiet road lined with timber log houses and lots of trees and plants. It's so much quieter than surrounding streets that it's easy to think you are in the countryside rather than a large town.

great big-band jazz. Hosts the Tomsk International Jazz Festival in the first week of June.

Aelita Theatre THEATRE

(Театр Аэлита; ☎3822-514 436; www.aelita.tom.ru; pr Lenina 78) Eclectic offerings, from rock concerts to Indian dance to experimental plays.

Trud Stadium STADIUM

(ul Belinskogo 15/1) Home stadium of local football side Tom Tomsk. There's a shop selling Tomsk scarves and T-shirts. It's open 11am to 7pm Monday to Friday, and on weekends on home-match days.

Tom Tomsk FC SPECTATOR SPORT

(Томь Томск ФК; tickets from ₽300) Trud Stadium is the home of Siberia's top football club. Since 2004 Tom Tomsk has spent a number of years in the Russian Premier League, making it Europe's most easterly top-flight football club. Unfortunately the team was relegated to the second flight in 2014 and it's stayed there since.

Shopping

Dzerzhinskogo Market MARKET

(Рынок Дзержинского; ul Dzerzhinskogo) This market sprawls for a full block south of ul Kartashova, providing photo-ops as well as fuel in the form of local fruits and nuts.

Information

Main Post Office (Почтамт; pr Lenina 95; ⏲8am-10pm Mon-Fri, 9am-6pm Sat & Sun) Stamps, but no postcards of Tomsk (find postcards in most museums).

All the hotels have wi-fi otherwise there's **Netcafe** (pr Lenina 41; per hr ₽50; ⏲9am-11pm) south of the university.

Getting There & Away

TRAIN

From Tomsk 1 (main) train station, there's a train on even-numbered days to Barnaul (*platskart/kupe* ₽1100/2000, 15½ hours, 9.20pm) via Novosibirsk. There are trains on odd-numbered days to Novokuznetsk (₽1100/1530, 12½ hours, 7.33pm) and Moscow (₽7350/11,060, 56 hours), and a train every 4th day to Vladivostok.

For more frequent connections east (toward Irkutsk) and west (toward Novosibirsk), take an *elektrichka* (suburban train) to Taiga (₽112, two hours, 9.06am and 4.15pm) or a bus to Yurga (₽210, two hours, four daily); most main-line Trans-Siberian trains stop at both stations. *Elektrichki* from Taiga to Tomsk depart at 7.07am and 4.15pm.

AIR

Bogashevo Airport (www.tomskairport.ru), 22km southeast of Tomsk, has several daily flights to Moscow plus a few seasonal charters. The choice is much wider from Novosibirsk.

BUS

For Novosibirsk, buses (₽740, 4½ hours, every hour) depart from the central **bus station** (Автовокзал; https://avtovokzal.tomsk.ru), which is right next to the main train station.

Getting Around

The bus station and Tomsk 1 (main) train station sit together about 2km southeast of the centre. Good maps are available in the train station and at street kiosks. A taxi to the city centre is around ₽150.

Buses 4, 12 and 12a run from pl Lenina to the train station via pr Lenina and pr Kirova. Hop on and off trolleybuses 1 and 3, or bus 17, which all go along pr Lenina.

Tomsk's antiquated and atmospheric trams are a great way to take a cheap (₽15) city tour. Tram 2 runs the length of ul Sovetskaya before connecting with the train station via pr Kirova. Tram 1 trundles all the way to the city's northern outskirts via ul Sovetskaya and ul Bolshaya Podgornaya.

Lake Baikal: Krasnoyarsk to Ulan Ude

Includes ➡

Why go?

If you've made it this far from Moscow or Běijīng, this 1500km ribbon of rail and sleeper is where things get interesting. This is arguably the most varied stretch of the line, so bid farewell to your *provodnitsa* (carriage attendant) along its length for some of the most memorable experiences Siberia has to offer.

Most travellers making only a single stop on their Trans-Sib odyssey do so in Irkutsk, surely Siberia's most engaging city. Only a smidgen over 350 years old, this grand city packs in heaps of history. When you tire of ornate facades, stuccoed palaces and streets of traditional timber dwellings, then glorious Lake Baikal, the unrivalled highlight of any rail trip across Russia, is just a short bus ride away.

When the tracks finally peel away from Baikal's mind-boggling vistas, Trans-Sibbers find themselves in the Republic of Buryatiya, an exotically Asian retreat of Buddhist temples and shamanist traditions, increasingly coming under the gravitational pull of southern neighbour Mongolia.

Route Info

- Distance: 1544km
- Duration: 24 hours
- Time zones: Moscow +4, Moscow +5

Best Places to Stay

- Iris (p174)
- Belka Hostel (p189)
- Nikita's Homestead (p191)

Best Places to Eat

- 0.75 Please (p175)
- Rassolnik (p184)
- Kochevnik (p183)
- Shenekhenskiye Buuzy (p200)

When to Go

Irkutsk

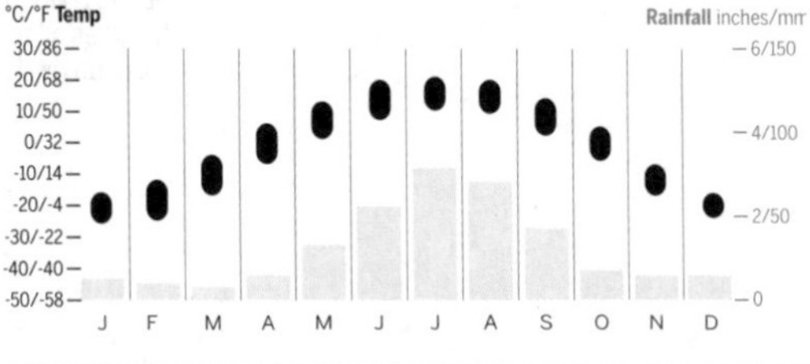

Nov–Mar Snuggle into a Russian Railways blanket and watch the snowbound Siberian landscapes

Mar Go ice fishing on Lake Baikal when Siberia's harsh winter turns its surface hard as steel

Jul & Aug Join holidaying Russians on the sandy beaches of Lake Baikal's eastern shore

Krasnoyarsk to Ulan-Ude Highlights

1. **Lake Baikal** Gazing at its blue waters or getting active on or around the Pearl of Siberia.
2. **Circumbaikal Railway** (p193) Taking a turn around Baikal's rocky southern shore.
3. **Irkutsk** (p177) Wandering boulevards of haughty 19th-century architecture.
4. **Ivolginsk (Ivolga) Datsan** (p203) Communing with the monks at this revived Buddhist monastery.
5. **Great Baikal Trail** (p188) Hiking a section of the trail between Listvyanka and Bolshie Koty.
6. **Olkhon Island** (p191) Enjoying a couple of days in midst of Lake Baikal.
7. **Stolby Nature Reserve** (p171) Climbing up to the volcanic rock fingers protruding above Krasnoyarsk.

Lake Baikal: Krasnoyarsk to Ulan-Ude

ℹ The Route

KRASNOYARSK TO TAYSHET

4098km from Moscow

Heading east out of Krasnoyarsk your fellow travellers may not have even fathomed there's a foreigner in their midst before the train crosses the 1km-long **Yenisey River bridge**, whose 1898 original won a gold medal at the 1900 Paris Expo (along with the Eiffel Tower). The Yenisey traditionally marks the unofficial border between Eastern and Western Siberia.

4229km

There's no stop for the Rossiya, but most other trains do shudder to a halt at **Uyar**, where you can admire the cream-and-green art nouveau–style station. Understandably the town is rarely referred to by its full name, Uyarspasopreobrazhenskoye.

4344km

The Rossiya makes its first stop after Krasnoyarsk at **Kansk-Yeniseysky**, which serves the settlement of Kansk. Founded in 1636, this historic town boasts a scattering of century-old buildings, a Trinity Cathedral whose spire can be seen for miles around, an impressive bronze war memorial and an illuminated victory arch. With ample time, this is possibly the only place on this entire stretch worth getting off to see (just). If you are confined to the platform, there's always the obligatory steam train to marvel at, this time mounted on an impressive marble plinth.

4377km

Ilanskaya has a small museum in the 100-year-old, red-brick locomotive depot at the western end of the station, and a freshly painted locomotive and water tower behind the wooden station building. The *provodnitsa* allows passengers to roam for 20 minutes here. The last exciting thing to happen here was when an LP author was detained by the police for taking photographs on the platform. Better leave the camera in your compartment.

4474km

The train passes into Irkutsk Region; local time becomes Moscow time plus five hours.

4501km

If you're heading from Moscow to Běijīng via Chita, you're halfway there.

4515km

The Rossiya stops for just two minutes at Tayshet (p237); other trains can loiter here for 20 minutes, giving you time to photograph yet another beached steam loco, a large, renovated station building and an incongruously attractive, Italian-built water tower behind. This is the Trans-Siberian's westernmost junction with the BAM (the Baikal-Amur Mainline or Baikalo-

Amurskaya Magistral), and many travellers and locals find themselves waiting here for connections to Severobaikalsk and Tynda. Tayshet was once an infamous transit point for Gulag camp prisoners. The town even gets a less-than-complimentary mention in Aleksandr Solzhenitsyn's *The Gulag Archipelago* (not recommended reading on a trip to Russia, believe us). Surprisingly, English-speaking help is available here, making the town worth an overnight stay.

TAYSHET TO IRKUTSK

4515km to 4600km

If riding straight through from Moscow, you're now on day three but only halfway to the Pacific. As the railway skirts the foothills of the **Sayany Mountains**, endless taiga and a real sense of wilderness set in.

4644km

Now you can crack open a celebratory tub of instant porridge or sachet of three-in-one coffee – you've made it halfway from Moscow to Vladivostok.

4649km

Welcome to UK; no, not Blighty, but the station of Ук, which may just have the shortest name of any Trans-Sib station. No stop for the Rossiya, though.

4678km

There's a 13-minute stop at mildly historical **Nizhneudinsk**. Cossacks first built a small fortress here in 1649 and for more than two centuries the town served as an important centre for gold and fur traders. The St Nicholas Church and the regional museum entice few off the rails, but an 18km hike along the Uda River to the 20m-high Ukovsky waterfalls could make for an adventurous side trip. Further east the landscape flattens out and you'll find that the forests have been extensively logged.

4795km

The next stop is timber **Tulun**, where you'll have just two minutes to contemplate the merits of the architecturally confident station building. From here a road heads 225km north to Bratsk on the BAM. The town has a far-flung Decembrist Museum but very few visitors.

4934km

There's an overgenerous 30-minute break in proceedings at the former exile town of **Zima**, which translates ominously as 'winter'.

5087km

(No stop for the Rossiya.) More translation is required at **Polovina**, whose name means roughly 'halfway' (between Moscow and Vladivostok), which it was in the early 20th century before the line was rerouted in many places.

5118km

From Polovina the train heads southeast and is joined by the Angara River around **Usole-Sibirskoe**, where a shuddering stop may jolt you from your slumber but hopefully not from your bunk altogether. The town supplies much of Russia's salt and many of its matches.

5145km

By the time you reach oil-rich **Angarsk**, where there's a clock museum if you really want to get off, it's probably time to start collecting your belongings scattered around the compartment if you're alighting at Irkutsk.

5178km

Heading west on some services originating in Irkutsk, you may rejoice at having a compartment all to yourself – that is until hordes of locals board at Irkutsk Sortirovka, a marshalling yard on the city's western outskirts.

5185km

The train crosses the Irkut River 3km before Irkutsk (p177) station. Once nicknamed the 'Paris of Siberia', Irkutsk is the most popular Siberian stop for most transcontinental travellers, notably as a launching point to reach Lake Baikal, 70km further southeast.

IRKUTSK TO ULAN-UDE

5185km to 5321km

Moving on from Irkutsk, the line takes a sharp right where the tracks once continued along the Angara River to Port Baikal, a stretch flooded by the Angara Dam project. The early 1950s rerouting includes the tightest twists and the steepest descent on the entire line (providing

KRASNOYARSK TO ULAN-UDE ROUTE PLANNER

Here's a suggested itinerary for continuing from Krasnoyarsk to Ulan-Ude:

Day 1 Take an overnight train from Krasnoyarsk to Irkutsk (18 hours).

Day 2 Arrive Irkutsk, then head out for a tour of the city.

Day 3 Bus to Taltsy Museum of Wooden Architecture then on to lakeside Listvyanka for one night.

Day 4 Return to Irkutsk; catch train for short hop to Slyudyanka for more lake views or go for a ride on the Circumbaikal Railway from Port Baikal.

Day 5 Skirt around the picturesque southern shore of Lake Baikal on a day train to Ulan-Ude.

great opportunities for photos of the train) just before **Kultuk**, where passengers get their first tantalising glimpse of **Lake Baikal**.

5311km

The first stop after Irkutsk for the Rossiya is at Slyudyanka (p192) where Baikal is so close it's tempting to dash down for a quick dip. However, the scheduled stop here – usually no longer than two minutes – means that you could run the very real risk of being stranded in Siberia as the train chugs off without you. If that prospect doesn't appeal, stay on the platform and snap up a snack of smoked *omul* (a fish native to Lake Baikal) from the countless hawkers instead. If the *provodnitsa* won't let you off, perform the transaction through a window (if one will open). For the next 200km or so the stuffy carriages fill with a fishy aroma, especially on hot days. If you've not bought any *omul*, fellow travellers are certain to offer you some.

5352km

There's no stop for the Rossiya between Slyudyanka and Ulan-Ude as it rattles around the southern shores of Lake Baikal. The Rossiya is not the best service to take on this stretch of the line as it does the journey either side of midnight.

5352km

The town of **Baikalsk** was once home to a cellulose plant, the biggest polluter of Lake Baikal. Thankfully it was closed down in 2013. Many come to ski at a big resort just above the town.

5352km to 5561km

Bag a left-facing window for this stretch (right-facing if you're travelling west), considered by most seasoned Trans-Sibbers as the most scenic on the entire line. The tracks run just metres from the lake at some points and delves into thick forest at others. The views across Baikal are superb at any time of year, but especially on crisp sunny days in late winter when the entire lake freezes into one mammoth block of white ice. If you're stuck on the 'wrong' side of the train, don't despair – the views of the Khamar Daban Mountains are equally impressive. Imagine the 18th- and 19th-century tea caravans from China emerging over the ridges to catch their first glimpse of Lake Baikal below.

5391km

Some trains make a two-minute halt at the lakeside fishing village of **Vydrino**. You've now entered the fascinating Republic of Buryatiya, which is in the same time zone as Irkutsk Region. This stretch of the Trans-Siberian is possibly the most worthwhile place to leave the comfort of your compartment. Some 5km to the south lie the Teplye Lakes, wonderful bodies of water cupped by steep wooded hills. The name 'Teplye' means warm and comes from the fact that the water is kept above freezing year-round by thermal springs. There's a cheap *turbaza* (holiday camp) nearby.

5420km

Just after another Baikal fishing settlement called **Tankhoi**, the train rumbles over a bridge spanning the fast-flowing Pereyomnaya River, one of 300 rivers feeding Lake Baikal. The village is home to the headquarters of the Baikal Biosphere Reserve in which you now find yourself.

5477km

The village of **Babushkin** (for Mysovaya) is a blur from the Rossiya, but in the early 20th century, before the line around the south of Lake Baikal was built (and occasionally afterwards), this was where the icebreakers *Angara* and *Baikal* – carrying their cargoes of wagons and passengers from Port Baikal – would dock. Both of the ships were built in Newcastle-upon-Tyne and the *Angara* survives as a museum in Irkutsk. The *Baikal* went to the bottom of Lake Baikal during the Russian Civil War, though no one is sure exactly where it lies.

5530km

The Trans-Sib waves farewell to Lake Baikal's bluer-than-blue waters just before the village of **Posolskaya**. A road from here heads to Lake Baikal and the village of Posolskoe, where a renovated and very picturesque monastery looks out across the water.

5561km

Around half an hour after Posolskaya, the Rossiya zips through **Selenga** (for Selenginsk), the nearest stop on other trains to the incredible Selenga Delta (p194).

5561km to 5641km

At Selenga the Trans-Sib joins up with the Selenga River carrying its load of silt (and Mongolian pollution) to Lake Baikal. The line hugs the left riverbank as far as Tataurovo, after which it crosses to the right bank, just in time to arrive at Ulan-Ude (p196).

Krasnoyarsk Красноярск

391 / POP 1.08 MILLION / TIME MOSCOW +4HR

Orderly and affluent, Krasnoyarsk reflects in the blueish-grey surface of the mind-bogglingly wide Yenisey River, which marks the border between the swampy west and the mountainous east of Siberia. Uniquely, the million-strong city boasts a hugely popular national park located within city boundaries. The other prominent urban feature is unfortunately a giant aluminium plant, which contributes to some serious air pollution in the centre. With outstanding museums, a lively restaurant scene and some exquisite timber mansions popping up here and there amid the Soviet-era concrete, Krasnoyarsk is an agreeable place to break the long journey between Tomsk (612km west) and Lake Baikal.

The city centre's grid layout, which makes Krasnoyarsk look a bit like US cities, is easy to navigate. The zoo, ski resort and Stolby Nature Reserve are over 10km west along the Yenisey's south bank.

Sights

Dotted about Krasnoyarsk are some very fine wooden houses, notably ul Lenina 88 and 67 and ul Karla Marksa 118. There are also many art nouveau facades such as pr Mira 76, ul Lenina 62 and ul Parizhskoy Kommuny 13.

★Stolby Nature Reserve NATURE RESERVE
(www.stolby.ru) FREE Russia's most visited national park is located right across the river from Krasnoyarsk's city centre. Its highlight are the fingers of volcanic rock called **stolby** poking above gently sloping wooded mountains. To reach the most spectacular of them (as well as the newly opened visitors centre), follow the track (7km long) near Hotel Snezhnaya Dolina (bus 50). Alternatively, you can take the year-round **chairlift** (Фуникулёр; ₽250) at Bobrovy Log Ski Resort and hike about the same distance through the park.

New paths and steps mean going it alone is not the daredevil experience it once was, but English-language tours with SibTourGuide (p174) are a much more pleasant and entertaining affair. Be aware that infected ticks are dangerous between May and July, and tick protection or predeparture encephalitis jabs are essential at this time.

Regional Museum MUSEUM
(Краеведческий музей; www.kkkm.ru; ul Dubrovinskogo 84; ₽150; ⏲10am-6pm Tue-Sun) Housed in an incongruously attractive 1912 art nouveau Egyptian temple, this is one of Siberia's better museums. Arranged around a Cossack explorer's ship, surprisingly well-presented exhibitions across the two floors examine every facet of the region's past, from Cossacks and gentlemen explorers to the Tunguska explosion, local fauna, prerevolution institutions and religious art.

Highlights include the 20th-century 'nostalgia' section on the upper level and the 4m-tall mammoth skeleton looking like something straight off a Hollywood museum movie set. There are touchscreen games for kids throughout and a decent cafe to look forward to at the end.

★Ploshchad Mira MUSEUM
(Площадь Мира; www.mira1.ru; pl Mira 1; adult/child ₽150/70; ⏲11am-7pm Tue, Wed & Fri-Sun) Krasnoyarsk's Lenin museum was opened on the occasion of the October Revolution's 70th anniversary in 1987, only to see the entire communist system collapse four years later. But, in a true revolutionary spirit, it has reinvented itself as a beautifully eclectic art venue that fuses elements of the original communist-era exhibitions with top-quality contemporary art and photography. An installation dedicated to Afghan and Chechen wars, which mixes naive art with photographs and personal belongings of deceased soldiers, is especially poignant.

Ploshchad Mira also serves as the venue of Krasnoyarsk's art biennale, held in 2018 and 2020. The museum's old library has now been converted into what Russians call 'open space' – a wi-fi hotspot lounge, where you can comfortably spend time checking emails, reading a book or chatting with friends over a cup of coffee. Called Okna, it also runs lectures and public discussions.

Literature Museum MUSEUM
(Литературный музей; www.kkkm.ru/filialy-muzeya/literaturnyj-muzej; ul Lenina 66; ₽100; ⏲10am-6pm Tue-Sun) Occupying a glorious 1911 merchant's mansion, this wonderfully restored museum highlights various aspects of Siberian life that inspired authors who wrote about it – from cold and gloom to multicoloured gems and shaman dances. Of special note is the exhibit dedicated to Agafia Lykova, a member of the famous Old Believer hermit family.

Revolution Square SQUARE
(pl Revolyutsii) The city's vast central square showcases Soviet-era architectural classics in all their Stalinist glory – complete with colonnaded government buildings and a statue of Lenin, who extends one hand as if inviting visitors for a stroll in **Dubrovinsky Park of Culture and Leisure**, another compulsory element of any Soviet city. Untouched by Moscow-style gentrification, the park is dotted with tacky 1990s funfair attractions and abuts in pleasantly revamped Levobereznaya nab – a riverside promenade, great for both walks and cycling.

A Ferris wheel is useful for photographers keen to snap a winning shot of the Yenisey and the foothills of Sayan mountains beyond it.

Krasnoyarsk

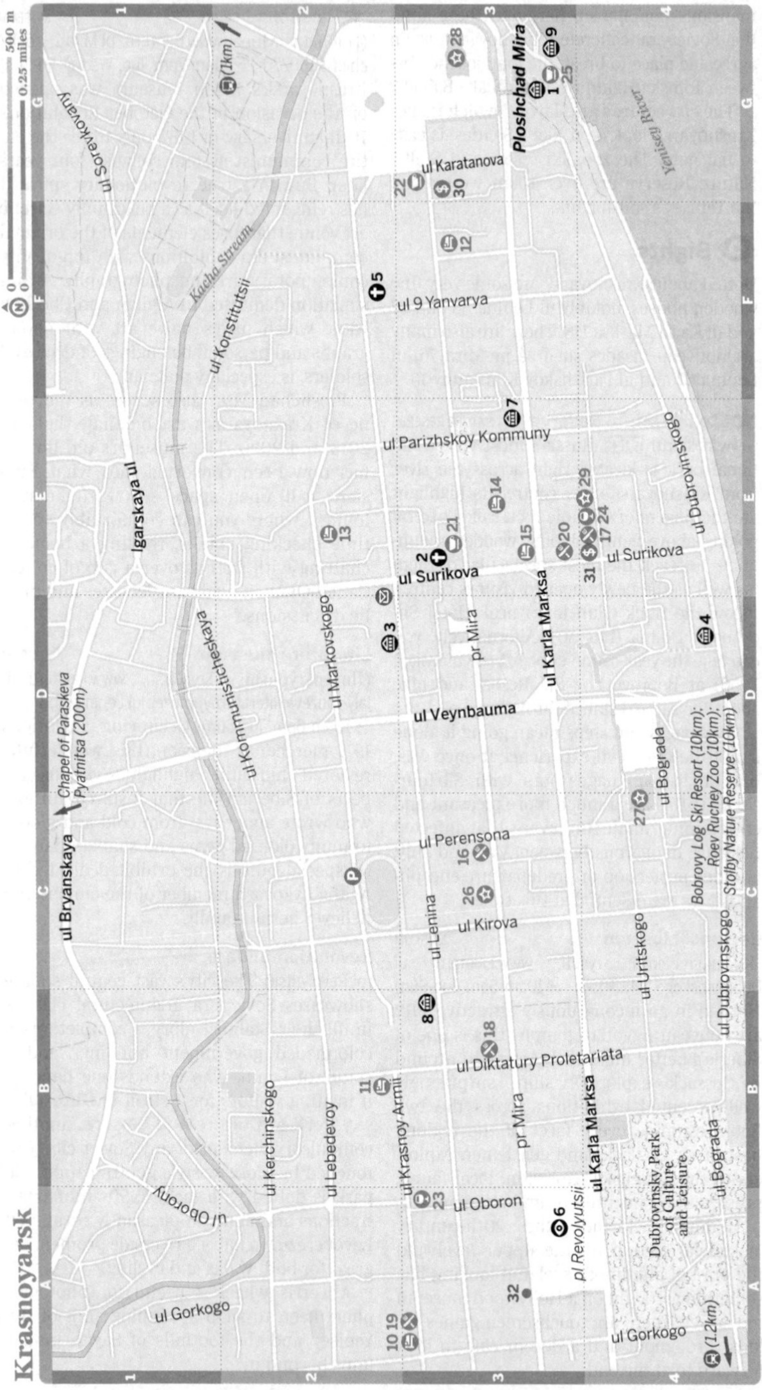

Krasnoyarsk

Surikov Art Museum MUSEUM
(Художественный музей Сурикова; ul Parizhskoy Kommuny 20; ₽150; ⌚10am-6pm Tue, Wed & Fri-Sun, 1-9pm Thu) The cute Surikov Art Museum displays works by Russian 19th-century artist Ivan Surikov and his contemporaries. Its affiliate at **ul Mira 12** houses a small but impressive collection of Russian vanguard art, including Kandinsky, Malevich and Rodchenko.

Chapel of Paraskeva Pyatnitsa NOTABLE BUILDING
(Часовня Параскевы Пятницы; top of Karaulnaya Hill) For some spectacular city views, climb Karaulnaya Hill (there's no bus) to the little chapel that features on the Russian 10-rouble banknote (now slowly being replaced with a coin). It was designed in 1855 by Konstantin Thon, the architect behind Moscow's Christ the Saviour Cathedral. At midday a deafening one-gun salute is fired from just below the chapel.

Roev Ruchey Zoo ZOO
(Зоопарк Роев ручей; www.roev.ru; adult/child ₽300/100; ⌚9am-9pm) Take bus 50 or 50A to this animal-friendly zoo near the Bobrovy Log Ski Resort to see numerous Siberian species.

Intercession Cathedral CHURCH
(Покровский собор; ul Surikova) This pleasingly small old church dating from 1795 has an interior of unusually glossed and intricately moulded stucco framing haloed saints.

SV Nikolai MUSEUM
(Святой Николай; ₽70; ⌚10am-8pm Tue-Sun) Permanently docked below Ploshchad Mira art centre is the SV *Nikolai*, the ship that transported future revolution leader Vladimir Lenin to exile in Shushenskoe in 1897 and the future Tsar Nikolai II across the Yenisey in 1891.

Resurrection Church CHURCH
(Благовещенская церковь; ul 9 Yanvarya) The top-heavy but elegant Resurrection Church (1804–22) was decapitated in the 1930s but given a new tower in 1998–99. Its icon-filled interior billows with incense.

Surikov Museum-Estate MUSEUM
(Музей-усадьба Сурикова; www.surikov-dom.com; ul Lenina 98; ₽200; ⌚10am-6pm Tue-Sun) The Surikov Museum-Estate preserves the house, sheds and vegetable patch of 19th-century painter Vasily Surikov (1848–1916). The heavy-gated garden forms a refreshing oasis of rural Siberia right in the city centre.

More of Surikov's work is on show at the old-school Surikov Art Museum.

WORTH A TRIP

DIVNOGORSK & OVSYANKA

From Krasnoyarsk, a popular day trip by bus follows the Yenisey River 27km to Divnogorsk (Дивногорск) town through a wide, wooded canyon. Some 5km beyond Divnogorsk's jetty is a vast 90m-high **dam**. Turbine-room visits are not permitted, but if you're lucky you might see ships being lifted by a technologically impressive inclined plane to the huge Krasnoyarsk Sea behind. A few kilometres beyond you can observe ice fishing from December to March or, in the summer, boats and yachts can be hired.

The Krasnoyarsk–Divnogorsk road has a panoramic overlook point at km23 and passes quaint Ovsyanka village (Овсянка). From the main road walk 100m (crossing the train tracks) to Ovsyanka's cute wooden **St Inokent Chapel** (ul Shchetinkina, Ovsyanka) then 50m right to find the **house-museum** (ul Shchetinkina 26, Ovsyanka; ₽100; 10am-6pm Tue-Sun) of famous local writer Victor Astafiev, who died in 2001. Directly opposite in Astafiev's grandma's cottage-compound is the more interesting **Last Bow Museum** (ul Shchetinkina 35, Ovsyanka; ₽100; 10am-6pm Tue-Sun) giving a taste of rural Siberian life.

Regular *marshrutky* (₽100) leave from Krasnoyarsk's bus station. Ask the *marshrutka* driver to drop you off at Ovsyanka, 30km away from Krasnoyarsk. **SibTourGuide** in Krasnoyarsk offers various tailored excursions in English or will include the Divnogorsk loop as part of its 'Ten-Rouble Tour'.

Activities & Tours

Bobrovy Log Ski Resort SNOW SPORTS
(Лыжный курорт Бобровый Лог; www.bobrovylog.ru; ul Sibirskaya 92; ski pass per hour/day ₽350/1300, ski hire from ₽450) Below the Stolby the slap and swish of skis and snowboards can be heard at the Bobrovy Log Ski Resort. Snow cannons keep the slopes going well into May, and in the summer months the Roedelbahn (a kind of downhill forest roller coaster), a pool and regular sports events keep the fun level high.

Cable car provides access to Stolby Nature Reserve (p171) observation point and hiking trails. The resort is also the location of one of the city's finest restaurants, Khozyain Taygi. To get here, catch bus 37 that runs from the train station direct to the resort via pr Mira and Predmostnaya pl. An Uber ride from the centre costs ₽140.

SibTourGuide TOURS
(391-251 654, 8-913-534 2654; www.sibtourguide.com) Experienced tour guide Anatoly Brewhanov offers personalised hiking trips into the Stolby, imaginative tours around Krasnoyarsk and general travel assistance. He also provides authentic 'rural experiences' at his dacha (summer country house), organises cruises along the Yenisey and leads trips to the site of the Tunguska Event, all while maintaining an info-packed website.

Festivals & Events

Zelyony Festival MUSIC
(Зелёный фестиваль; http://gorodprima.ru; Jun) Usually held in June on Tatyshev island, this giant picnic celebrates modern art and street food in addition to lots of good music.

Sleeping

★**Hovel Hostel** HOSTEL $
(Хостел Ховел; 8-929-309 4020; www.hovel24.ru; ul Lenina 52 (enter from ul Markovskogo); dm/d without bathroom from ₽400/1400, q ₽2200;) A sparkling oasis for budget travellers who have made it all the way here through Siberia's snowy wilderness, this boutique hostel features a large kitchen, a common area with comfy couches, and a range of rooms from dorms and cosy doubles to an airy two-level studio, ideal for a family with children.

★**Iris** BOUTIQUE HOTEL $$
(Ирис; 391-227 2292; www.iris-apart-hotel.ru; pr Mira 37; s/d ₽3600/4000;) Housed in a 19th-century former religious school for girls, the romantic French theme and impeccable personal service set the Iris apart from most Siberian hotels. The 10 rooms are done out in soothing beiges and light browns but the *pièces de résistance* here are the two romantic design suites, all period wallpaper, belle époque furniture and mock chateau elements.

Dom Neo HOTEL $$

(Дом Нэо; ☎391-223 9360; www.dom-hotel24.ru/hotel/neo; ul Krasnoy Armii 10 str 5; r from ₽2800; ❄📶) Definitely the brightest-coloured building in central Krasnoyarsk, this progressive hotel achieves an optimal value for money ratio by cutting out optional amenities, such as minibars, and focusing entirely on the essentials – the bed, the bathroom and the light. Everything is sparkling new and designed in a futuristic style. A filling set-menu breakfast is an extra ₽350 at Cafe Benedikt downstairs.

Dom Hotel HOTEL $$$

(☎391-290 6666; www.dom-hotel24.ru; ul Krasnoy Armii 16a; s/d from ₽4200/5900; @📶) Centred around a rather characterless courtyard, the 81 light-filled rooms at Krasnoyarsk's top business hotel are immaculately maintained and have become a firm favourite among foreigners looking for Western comforts. Staff are courteous and there is an inexpensive on-site restaurant. Breakfast costs extra.

Hotel Oktyabrskaya HOTEL $$$

(Гостиница Октябрьская; ☎391-223 0808; www.hoteloctober.ru; pr Mira 15; s/d from ₽3800/4200; 📶) Comfortable and professionally run with rooms approximating Western standards, albeit without air-conditioning. Satellite TV includes Western channels and some English is spoken. The trendy lobby area has a stylish juice bar. Includes breakfast.

Soft Hotel HOTEL $$$

(☎391-228 2700; www.softhotel.ru; ul Surikova 16; s/d from ₽3900/4600; ❄📶) With its European business-standard facilities, waxy antique-style furniture, 21st-century bathrooms (with bidets!) and high-flying ceilings, taking the soft option might be the way to go now in Krasnoyarsk. Efficient service and good value for money – only the views and the nonbuffet breakfast disappoint slightly.

Eating

Vinegret Bufet CAFETERIA $

(Буфет Винегрет; ☎391-2311 989; https://vk.com/vinegretbufet; ul Surikova 12; mains ₽100-150; ⏲10am-10pm) A vast and modern rustic-themed cafeteria, Vinegret lures white-collar workers with a large salad bar and a grill station. Pancakes with a variety of fillings make a good breakfast option.

★0.75 please RUSSIAN $$

(☎391-215 2913; www.facebook.com/075please; pr Mira 86; mains ₽480-640; ⏲noon-2am) This gem is two in one – a wine bar and an Arctic-themed restaurant that upgrades traditional Siberian staples to near-Michelin levels. *Nelma stroganina* (a kind of frozen ceviche) quite literally melts in your mouth. Reindeer steak with cheese and pear makes a star duo with homemade chokeberry liquor. Crème brûlée with sea buckthorn sorbet is nothing short of Elysian.

Bar Bulgakov FUSION $$

(Бар Булгаков; ☎391-272 8778; http://barbulgakov.ru; ul Surikova 12; mains ₽250-700; ⏲noon-2am; 📶🖉) This delightfully bizarre space decorated with Soviet vanguard art and presided over by a Soviet-era female rower statue that holds a giant fork instead of an oar is best for late-night alcohol-infused dinners. The inventive fusion menu is permeated with Caucasian motifs and includes such wondrous concoctions as lamb and aubergine stew cooked in a clay pot with a rye bread cap.

Svinya i Biser EASTERN EUROPEAN $$

(Свинья и бисер; ☎391-290 4040; http://bellinigroup.ru/rest/pig-and-beads; ul Krasnoy Armii 16a; mains ₽250-600; ⏲7am-1am) Its wood-rich interior strives to convey the ambience of old Europe. The menu at 'Pig & Beads' is carnivore concerto grosso, with pork playing the first violin. Sausages, shashlyk (meat kebabs), burgers, steaks, schnitzels – the menu seems to cover every existing method of preparing meat. Excellent buffet breakfasts are served from 7am (₽450).

Mike & Molly ITALIAN $$

(www.mikeandmollycafe.ru; ul Diktatury Proletariata 32a; mains ₽200-500; ⏲11am-midnight) The stylishly unassuming interior of this Italian job suggests the focus is firmly on the food, and that assumption would be right. Possibly Krasnoyarsk's best lasagnes, pastas, salads and proper starters land promptly on your table as you kick back on the black-cloth wall sofas with a glass of Chianti.

Khozyain Taygi RUSSIAN $$$

(Хозяин Тайги; ☎391-256 8649; www.bobrovylog.ru; ul Sibirskaya 92; mains ₽560-1100; ⏲noon-midnight) Siberian taiga, in the form of Stolby Nature Reserve (p171), begins right outside this refined restaurant, entirely dedicated to the kind of food one can catch or forage in the world's largest forest. A sample menu could include mousse made of, well, moose for starters, *nelma* (Arctic salmon) as second course and terrific frozen red whortleberries mixed with cedar nut for dessert.

Drinking & Nightlife

★Chaynaya Yurta TEAHOUSE

(Чайная юрта; ☎391-297 6037; https://vk.com/yurtea; pl Mira 1; ⊙noon-midnight) Literally a yurt occupying a prime riverside spot next to the city's best museum, this place celebrates the tea culture of Siberian nomads. Try Orlan Sagaan tea, which contains the *sagaan-dalya* (a ubiquitous East Siberian herb rhododendron) or Tuvan tea with *talgan* (barley flour), milk and butter. The food menu is equally exotic.

Kofeynya Kultura COFFEE

(Кофейня Культура; https://vk.com/culture_krsk; pr Mira 56; ⊙8am-10pm) As the name suggests, this is a den of coffee nerds who see the dark brew as an agent of cultural revolution and who perpetually experiment with brewing techniques and equipment. Besides that, it is a pleasant modern environment to spend some time in the company of a friend or a gadget.

Tovarishch CRAFT BEER

(Comrade; ☎8-913-836 5949; https://vk.com/clubtkbkrsk; ul Oborony 2a; ⊙1pm-midnight) A few dozen brands of Russian and international beers, both draft and bottled, are on offer in this dim-lit bar with crypto-Maoist subtext ciphered in the decor. Zolotoy Yarlyk lager and Black Jack stout are among the most popular brews.

Zalech na Dno v Gamburg BEER HALL

(Lying Low in Hamburg; ☎391-286 3355; http://berrywoodfamily.ru/blog/zalech-na-dno-v-gamburg; ul Surikova 12 k6; ⊙noon-2am) A vast vaulted cellar contains a German *biergarten* with a Siberian twist. There is a good dozen German, Czech and Belgian beers on tap, which you can top up with wurst and sauerkraut, or – more experimentally – with *suguday* (frozen raw fish with onion) served in a jar.

Krem CAFE

(☎391-258 1538; pr Mira 10; ⊙24hr; 📶) One of Krasnoyarsk's classiest coffee houses has black-and-white photography, dark-wood furniture, a belt-stretching dessert menu and reasonably priced lattes and espressos.

☆ Entertainment

Dom Kino CINEMA

(Дом кино; ☎391-227 2637; www.filmshouse.ru; pr Mira 88) A place to watch sophisticated art-house cinema, often shown in the original language, with Russian subtitles.

Mod's Bar LIVE MUSIC

(http://themodsbar.ru; ul Aviatorov 19; ⊙6pm-morning) This new and smarter-than-usual nightlife venue, located inside Grand Hall Siberia in Vzlyotka area (east of the centre), runs DJ and live-music events, as well as dance and art performances during weekends. Thursday karaoke night features a live band that can smooth out even the lousiest singing.

Burton Bar LIVE MUSIC

(☎391-214 0224; https://vk.com/burtonbar; ul Televizornaya 1 str 26) A far-flung indie rock and 'intellectual hip-hop' (whatever that is!) venue run by fans of the film director Tim Burton.

Opera-Ballet Theatre THEATRE

(Театр оперы и балета; ☎391-227 8697; www.opera.krasnoyarsk.ru; ul Perensona 2) The architecturally nondescript Opera-Ballet Theatre has daily performances of productions such as *Carmen, Swan Lake* and *Romeo and Juliet* starting in the early evening, October to June.

Rock-Jazz Kafe LIVE MUSIC

(Рок-Джаз Кафе; ☎391-252 3305; https://vk.com/rockjazzcafe; ul Surikova 12; ⊙4pm-6am Tue-Sun) This dark venue showcases live bands around an upturned motorcycle from 10pm most days.

Philharmonia LIVE MUSIC

(Филармония; ☎391-227 4930; www.krasfil.ru; pl Mira 2b) The Philharmonia has three concert halls showcasing folk, jazz and classical music.

ℹ Information

Rosbank (pr Mira 7; ⊙9am-6pm Mon-Thu, 9am-4.45pm Fri) Currency exchange and 24-hour indoor ATM.

Sberbank (Сбербанк; ul Surikova 15; ⊙10am-7pm Mon-Sat) Currency-exchange window and ATM.

Post Office (ul Lenina 62; ⊙8am-8pm Mon-Fri, 9am-6pm Sat)

Prospekt Mira (https://prmira.ru) is a Russian-only online publication that covers upcoming cultural events.

ℹ Getting There & Away

TSAVS (ЦАВС; www.krascavs.ru; ul Mira 112; ⊙8am-8pm) is a centrally located one-stop shop for all bus, train and air tickets.

TRAIN

Krasnoyarsk has the following rail connections:

Irkutsk *platskart/kupe* from ₽1600/₽3300, 18 hours, up to nine daily

Moscow *platskart/kupe* from ₽7200/₽11,000, 64 hours, up to seven daily

Novosibirsk *platskart/kupe* from ₽2000/₽2600, 12 hours, up to 11 daily

Severobaikalsk *platskart/kupe* ₽3250/₽6700, 27 to 35 hours, three daily

Tomsk *platskart/kupe* ₽1900/3250, 18 hours, every other day

AIR

A new sparkling **Yemelyanovo Airport** (☎391-255 5999; www.yemelyanovo.ru) terminal was about to open at the time of writing. Services to almost anywhere in Siberia and the rest of Russia are available. International destinations include Bangkok and several Chinese airports. Local flight connections include:

Irkutsk from ₽8000, two daily

Moscow from ₽7500, up to seven daily

Novosibirsk from ₽5600, two daily

BUS

The main **bus station** (Автовокзал; www.kras-avtovokzal.ru; ul Aerovokzalnaya 22) is to the northeast of the city centre and is best reached by Buses 49, 24 and 53 from ul Karla Marksa. Destinations include Tomsk (₽1300, 11 hours, daily).

Getting Around

There is no public transport between the airport and the city, except for rare and inconvenient buses stopping on the way between Cheremshanka and Krasnoyarsk bus station (one hour, ₽82, four to six daily). Taxis charge between ₽600 and ₽1000 for the ride into town.

Within the city centre, almost all public transport runs eastbound along ul Karla Marksa or pr Mira, returning westbound on ul Lenina. Frequent, if slow, trolleybus 7 trundles from the train station through the city centre via ul Karla Marksa. Useful bus 50 starts beyond the zoo, passes the Turbaza Yenisey and comes through the centre of town.

All major taxi app services – Gett, Uber, Yandex Taxi and Maxim – are represented. A typical Uber ride within the centre costs ₽80.

Irkutsk Иркутск

☎3952 / POP 3952 / TIME MOSCOW +5HR

The de facto capital of Eastern Siberia, pleasantly historic Irkutsk is by far the most popular stop on the Trans-Siberian Railway between Moscow and all points east. With Lake Baikal a mere 70km away, the city is the best base from which to strike out for the western shoreline. Amid the 19th-century architecture, revived churches, classy eateries and numerous hostels, plentiful English-speaking agencies can help you plan anything from a winter trek across the lake's ice to a short walking tour through the city.

In recent years Irkutsk has seen something of a tourist boom, spawning a municipally funded information centre, detailed city maps planted at strategic points and a handful of freshly conceived museums, as well as the blockbuster 130 Kvartal project, an entire neighbourhood given over to typical Siberian timber buildings housing new restaurants, bars, cafes and the odd museum.

History

Founded in 1661 as a Cossack garrison to extract the fur tax from the indigenous Buryats, Irkutsk was the springboard for 18th-century expeditions to the far north and east, including Alaska – then known as 'Irkutsk's American district'.

As Eastern Siberia's trading and administrative centre, Irkutsk dispatched Siberian furs and ivory to Mongolia, Tibet and China in exchange for silk and tea. Constructed mostly of local timber, three-quarters of the city burnt down in the disastrous blaze of 1879. However, profits from the 1880s Lena Basin gold rush swiftly rebuilt the city's most important edifices in brick and stone.

Known as the 'Paris of Siberia', Irkutsk did not welcome news of the October Revolution. The city's well-to-do merchants only succumbed to the red tide in 1920, with the capture and execution of White Army commander Admiral Kolchak, whose controversial statue was re-erected in 2004. Soviet-era planning saw Irkutsk develop as the sprawling industrial and scientific centre that it remains today.

Sights

Irkutsk's centre can be easily explored on foot – you'll only need to hop aboard a bus or *marshrutka* to see the Angara Dam and the Znamensky Monastery.

Volkonsky House-Museum MUSEUM

(Дом-музей Волконского; ☎3952-207 532; per Volkonskogo 10; ₽200, with Trubetskoy House-Museum ₽300; ⏰10am-6pm Tue-Sun) The duck-egg-blue and white home of Decembrist Count Sergei Volkonsky, whose wife Maria Volkonskaya cuts the main figure in Christine Sutherland's unputdownable book *The Princess of Siberia*, is a small mansion set in a scruffy courtyard with stables, a barn and servant quarters. Renovated in the late

Irkutsk

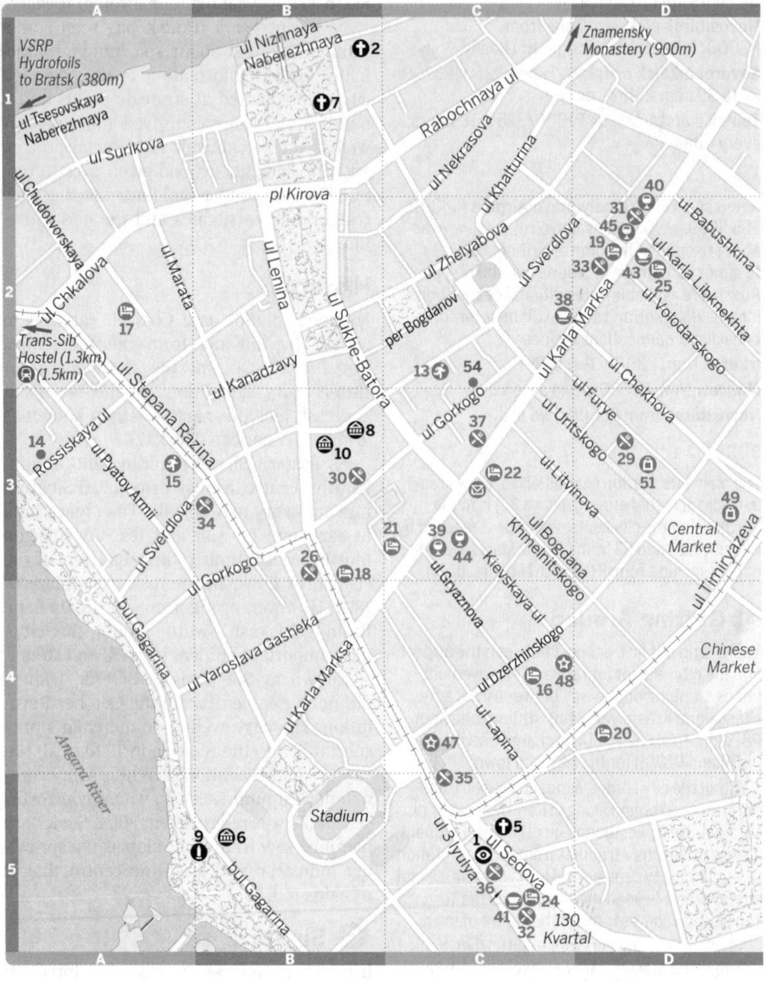

1980s, the house is now a museum telling the story of the family's exile in Irkutsk.

In the decade leading up to the Volkonskys' return to St Petersburg in 1856, the house was the epicentre of Irkutsk cultural life, with balls, musical soirées and parties attended by wealthy merchants and high-ranking local officials. A tour of the building, with its big ceramic stoves and original staircases, takes visitors from the family dining room, where governor Muravyov-Amursky once feasted on fruit and veg grown by Volkonsky himself in the garden out back, to the upstairs photo exhibition including portraits of Maria and other women who romantically followed their husbands and lovers into exile.

Emotionally charged items on show include Maria's pyramidal piano, a browsable book of images collected by fellow Decembrist wife Ekaterina Trubetskaya of the various places the Decembrists were imprisoned, and Maria's music box sent from Italy by her sister-in-law.

Znamensky Monastery MONASTERY

(ul Rabochego Shtaba) **FREE** Stranded on the wrong side of a thundering roundabout, the 1762 Znamensky Monastery is 1.9km

northeast of Skver Kirova. Echoing with mellifluous plainsong, the wonderful interior has muralled vaulting, a towering iconostasis and a gold sarcophagus holding the miraculous relics of Siberian missionary St Inokent. Celebrity graves outside include the nautically themed tomb of Grigory Shelekhov, the man who claimed Alaska for Russia, and a much humbler headstone belonging to Decembrist wife Ekaterina Trubetskaya (directly in front of you as you enter).

White Russian commander Admiral Kolchak was executed by Bolsheviks near the spot where his statue was controversially erected in November 2004 at the entrance to the monastery grounds; the plinth is exaggeratedly high enough to prevent diehard communists from committing acts of vandalism. Trolleybus 3 trundles this way.

130 Kvartal AREA

(130th Block; btw uls Sedova & 3 Iyulya) What does a city boasting some of Siberia's most impressive original timber architecture do to improve the visitor experience? Yes, that's right, recreate an entire quarter of yet more wooden buildings, some transported here from other locations, some fake. The unromantically named 130 Kvartal south of the Raising of the Cross Church is nonetheless a pleasant place to stroll, packed with restaurants, cafes and commercial museums, and culminating in Eastern Siberia's only real 21st-century (and quite impressive) shopping mall.

Guarding the entrance to this timber theme park is a monster bronze *babr,* the mythical beast that features on Irkutsk's municipal coat of arms. The spot has become a popular place to have that 'I've been to Irkutsk' photo taken.

Trubetskoy House-Museum MUSEUM

(Дом-музей Трубецкого; ul Dzerzhinskogo 64; ₽200, with Volkonsky House-Museum ₽300; ⏲10am-6pm Wed-Mon) Irkutsk's second Decembrist house-museum emerged from a recent renovation with English-language information, touchscreens and tinkling background music. This pleasingly symmetrical minimansion was actually built for the daughter of Decembrist Sergei Trubetskoy – the original Trubetskoy house near the Znamensky Monastery burnt down in 1908. The lower level tells the Decembrists' story, from failed coup to arrival in Irkutsk, while the upper floor displays personal items belonging to Ekaterina Trubetskaya, Trubetskoy's French wife who died in Irkutsk.

Usadba Sukacheva MUSEUM

(www.sukachoff.ru; ul Dekabrskikh Sobyty 112; ₽150; ⏲10am-6pm Tue, Wed & Fri-Sun, noon-8pm Thu) A small park on the edge of the historical centre contains a smattering of beautiful wood-lace buildings and arbours. These house exhibitions dedicated to the family of 19th-century benefactor Vladimir Sukachev, who lived here until the October Revolution. The collection includes period furniture and paintings by old Spanish and Dutch masters. Perhaps the most touching bit is the recreated 'winter garden' – an indoor greenhouse filled with exotic tropical plants.

Irkutsk

Sights

1	130 Kvartal	C5
2	Bogoyavlensky Cathedral	B1
3	Bronshteyn Gallery	E1
4	Museum of City Life	F2
5	Raising of the Cross Church	C5
6	Regional Museum	B5
7	Saviour's Church	B1
8	Sculpture Gallery	B3
9	Statue of Tsar Alexander III	B5
10	Sukachev Regional Art Museum	B3
11	Trubetskoy House-Museum	E2
12	Volkonsky House-Museum	F2

Activities, Courses & Tours

13	Basninskiye Bani	C2
14	Krugobaikalsky Ekspress	A3
15	Tu-tu Baikal	A3

Sleeping

16	52°17' Travel Center	C4
17	Admiral Hostel	A2
18	Baikaler Hostel	B3
19	Best Hostel	D2
20	Hostel Katyusha	D4
21	Hotel Sayen	C3
22	Hotel Viktoria	C3
23	Hotel Yevropa	F5
24	Kupechesky Dvor	C5
	Marussia	(see 24)
25	Rolling Stones Hostel	D2

Eating

26	Baikal Love Cafe	B3
27	Design Bar	E1
28	Dom Rybaka	F4
29	Govinda	D3
30	Kochevnik	B3
31	La Boulangerie & Patisserie	D2
32	Mamay	C5
33	Mamochka	D2
34	New Zealand Pies	B3
35	Poznaya na Lenina	C5
36	Rassolnik	C5
37	Slata	C3

Drinking & Nightlife

38	Belaya Vorona	C2
39	Bierhaus	C3
40	Brasserie BBB	D2
41	Castro Cafe	C5
42	Cheshskaya Pivovarnya	F2
43	Engineria Coffee	D2
44	Kwak Inn	C3
45	Library Bar	D2

Entertainment

46	Benzin	E2
47	Philharmonic Hall	C4
48	Rock'n'Roll Pub	C4

Shopping

49	Central Market	D3
50	Karibu	E3
51	Prodalit	D3

Information

52	Tourist Office	F2

Transport

53	Bus Station	F1
54	Central Air Agency	C2

Sculpture Gallery GALLERY
(Галерея скульптуры; ☎3952-487 054; www.museum.irk.ru; ul Sverdlova 16; ₽50; ⏰10am-6pm Tue-Sun) Opened in 2016, this lovely gallery puts in the spotlight Russian and Soviet sculpture previously kept in the city's main art museum and private collections, but the true highlights here are the whimsical creations of modern artists working with multicoloured Siberian gems.

Bronshteyn Gallery GALLERY
(Галерея Бронштейна; ☎3952-209 208; www.vbgallery.ru; ul Oktyabrskoy Revolyutsii 3; adult/child ₽150/50; ⏰11am-8pm) A large and sparkling new modern-art venue that most prominently features a collection of Dashi Namdakov's sculptures inspired by Buddhist prayer dolls used by Buryats. Also clearly inspired by Dalí. Very competently curated temporary exhibitions of local artists.

Statue of Tsar Alexander III MONUMENT
(Памятник Александру III) Adorning the Angara embankment, a recast statue of Alexander III (a copy of the 1904 original) has the only tsar ever to visit Siberia looking as though he's holding an invisible balloon on a string.

Sukachev Regional Art Museum MUSEUM
(Иркутский областной художественный музей имени В. П. Сукачёва; www.museum.irk.ru; ul Lenina 5; ₽150; ⏰10am-6pm Tue-Sun) The grand old art museum has a valuable though poorly lit collection ranging from Mongolian *thangkas* (Tibetan Buddhist religious paintings) to Russian Impressionist canvases. However, the main reason for coming here may be to see a top-notch temporary show (extra charge).

Museum of City Life MUSEUM
(ul Dekabrskikh Sobyty 77; ₽120; ⏰10am-6pm Thu-Tue) This small museum filling six rooms of a former merchant's house illustrates just

why 19th-century Irkutsk was nicknamed the 'Paris of Siberia'. Changing exhibitions of everyday and decorative items such as lamps, dolls, tableware and porcelain are donated free of charge by the people of Irkutsk and are displayed against a background of period wallpaper, elegant double doors and high ceilings. The ticket is also valid for the tiny **Tea Museum** above the tourist office opposite.

Raising of the Cross Church CHURCH
(Krestovozdvizhenskaya tserkov; ul Sedova 1) The 1758 baroque Raising of the Cross Church has a fine interior of gilt-edged icons and examples of intricate brickwork in a rounded style that's unique to Irkutsk and the Selenga Delta village of Posolskoe.

Saviour's Church CHURCH
(Спасская церковь; www.spashram.irk.ru; ul Sukhe-Batora 2) Constructed in 1706, this is the oldest stone-built church in Eastern Siberia and has remnants of the original murals on its facade. Until the late 1990s it housed a museum, hence the rather bare interior.

Regional Museum MUSEUM
(Краеведческий музей; ☎3952-333 449; www.museum.irkutsk.ru; ul Karla Marksa 2; ₽200; ⏲10am-7pm Tue-Sun) Irkutsk's rapidly ageing Regional Museum occupies a fancy 1880s brick building that formerly housed the Siberian Geographical Society, a club of Victorian-style gentlemen explorers. The highlights here are the downstairs ethnographical exhibitions and the nostalgic display of 20th-century junk upstairs, as well as the small gift shop selling birch-bark boxes, jewellery made from Baikal minerals and other interesting souvenirs.

Bogoyavlensky Cathedral CHURCH
(Богоявленский собор; ul Sukhe-Batora 1a) This fairytale ensemble of mini onion domes atop restored salmon, white and green towers first appeared on the Irkutsk skyline in 1718, but during the Soviet decades it served as a dormitory and a bakery. The interior is a fragrant riot of aureoled Byzantine saints with no surface left plain.

Activities

Denis Sobnakov TOURS
(http://baikaltour.net) Sharing his time between Irkutsk and Ulan-Ude, one of Siberia's best guides offers tours to Olkhon and the southwestern shores of Baikal, as well as elsewhere around the region. Contact by email.

Basninskiye Bani BATHHOUSE
(☎3952-722 832; http://basninskiebani.ru; ul Sverdlova 35; before/after 4pm ₽900/1100; ⏲noon-11pm Mon-Fri, 10am-11pm Sat & Sun) Come to this renovated bathhouse to steam off railway slime and fatigue. There are separate departments for men and women, to enjoy Turkish hammam in addition to traditional Russian *banya*. Foam massage is available in both departments.

Baikal Secrets TREKKING
(☎8-914-949 1462; www.baikalsecrets.com) English-speaking Ivan and Yekaterina run summer and winter trekking tours on Baikal and in Tunka Valley.

Baikal Adventure ADVENTURE SPORTS
(☎8-902-768 0505; www.baikal-adventure.com) Energetic agency specialising in adventurous trekking, biking, climbing and caving trips, and full-blown expeditions.

Tours

Local tour companies are useful not only for organising excursions but also for booking hotels and most kinds of tickets. All of Irkutsk's hostels can arrange Baikal tours.

Baikaler TOURS
(☎3952-336 240, 8-908-663 3142; www.baikaler.com) Imaginative Jack Sheremetoff speaks very good English and is well tuned to budget-traveller needs. Original personalised tours, two great hostels and a friendly welcome.

BaikalComplex TOURS
(☎3952-461 557; www.baikalcomplex.com) Well-organised operation offering Lake Baikal accommodation and trips tailored for international travellers.

Baikalinfo TOURS
(☎3952-707 012; www.baikalinfo.ru) Baikal tours as well as transfers, hikes and fishing trips.

BaikalExplorer TOURS
(☎8-902-560 2440; www.baikalex.com) Baikal cruises, fishing and diving trips, treks in Tunka Valley.

Green Express TOURS
(☎3952-734 400; www.greenexpress.ru) Professional outfit specialising in outdoor activities.

Sleeping

Irkutsk is struggling to catch up with the ever-increasing flow of Chinese and Russian tourists. Hostels are mushrooming, but there is a serious shortage of quality midrange options, so try to book in advance, especially if you are travelling during the high summer season or in February and March.

★Baikaler Hostel HOSTEL $
(☎3952-336 240; www.baikaler.com; ul Lenina 9, apt 11; dm ₽600, d with shared bathroom ₽1500; ❄@📶) Experienced tour guide Jack Sheremetoff had a super-central apartment hostel in Irkutsk long before the word even entered the Russian language. Despite competition, the city's original backpacker haven is still *the* place to meet travellers and organise trips. The spotless, air-conditioned dorms are spacious, but beds are limited so book ahead. The entrance is at the rear of the building.

52°17' Travel Center HOSTEL $
(☎3952-725 217; https://5217.co; ul Gryaznova 15a; dm/tw ₽700/1800) The stated goal of opening sister hostels in every major city of the world is yet to be achieved, so for now this hyper-ambitious project is confined to a section of a quaint wooden cottage and has just one dorm sleeping 10. But it's a cosy place run by avid travellers, who also offer a variety of Baikal tours.

Best Hostel HOSTEL $
(☎3952-242 091; www.hostel-irkutsk.com; ul Karla Marksa 41; dm ₽65-850, d ₽1700-4000) Yet to live up to its immodest self-description, this airy modern place stands out in the long list of Irkutsk's claustrophobic converted-flat hostels. Orthopaedic mattresses and a large, well-equipped kitchen area are among other virtues.

Hostel Katyusha HOSTEL $
(☎8-914-899 9011; www.katyusha.club; ul Timiryazeva 6; dm from ₽450, d ₽1800) Freshly opened when we visited, this brightly coloured hostel occupies a new building and has lots of common space, unlike its labyrinthine competitors in Irkutsk old town. Breakfast is available for an extra ₽150.

Rolling Stones Hostel HOSTEL $
(☎8-950-050 2888; www.vk.com/hostelrs; ul Karla Libknekhta 6; dm ₽600, d with/without bathroom ₽2400/1600; 📶) This fashionably designed (think lots of wood and bare brick surfaces), if slightly cavernous, hostel is run by two young travel enthusiasts, who can help with trips to Baikal and elsewhere in the region. Bunk beds with orthopaedic mattresses are built in the manner of pigeon holes, so you can hide in your private little world protected from outside views.

Trans-Sib Hostel HOSTEL $
(☎8-904-118 0652; www.irkutsk-hostel.com; per Sportivniy 9a, apt 8; dm/d from ₽750/1000; @📶) Well-established, cosy backpacker hostel around a 10-minute walk from the train station offering a kitchen, washing machine, a high bathroom-to-bed ratio and one of the best ranges of owner-led tours in town. Rates include a light breakfast.

Admiral Hostel HOSTEL $
(☎8-902-560 2440; www.irkutskhotel.irk.ru; ul Cheremkhovsky 6, apt 1; dm ₽500-600, d with shared bathroom ₽1500-1600; @📶) With its Kolchak-inspired name, this cosy 13-bed apartment hostel has become well-established digs for Trans-Siberian wanderers. The lower bunks sport privacy curtains, staff sell bus tickets to Olkhon Island, there's a free (light) breakfast and you can even get your washing done. Enter from the rear of the building.

Hotel Yevropa HOTEL $$
(Гостиница Европа; ☎3952-291 515; www.europe-hotel.ru; ul Baikalskaya 69; s/d from ₽3600/4300; ❄📶) Behind nine Doric columns, immaculate rooms are realistically priced at this gleaming four-star favourite. Reception staff speak English and the Western-style breakfast is reportedly the best in town.

Hotel Sayen HOTEL $$$
(☎3952-500 000; www.sayen.ru; ul Karla Marksa 13b; r from ₽9300; ❄📶) Described by some as the finest luxury sleep east of the Urals, this very central Japanese hotel gets rave reviews and justifiably so. The 24 rooms enjoy design-mag decor, big baths and gadgets galore, going beyond the standards of many Western hotels. Twenty-four-hour room service, two pricey restaurants and a celebrated Japanese spa provide additional ways to lighten your wallet of roubles.

Kupechesky Dvor HOTEL $$$
(☎3952-797 000; www.kupecheskyhotel.ru; ul Sedova 10; d/tw ₽5400/6200; 📶) Rising high above the 130 Kvartal, this professionally run, freshly minted timber hotel mixes traditional wooden architecture with boldly contemporary design features. The 14 rooms come with big colour-swirl carpets, retro light switches, revolving TV towers and some of the best bathrooms in the city. The English-speaking service is top-drawer and breakfast in the tiny reception area is included.

Marussia BOUTIQUE HOTEL $$$

(3952-500 252; www.marussiahotel.ru; ul Sedova 12; s/d ₽4900/5600;) This timber-built 14-room boutique hotel in the 130 Kvartal has an unpretentious feel with a brown-beige colour scheme and stripped wooden floors sporting rustic rugs but with 21st-century bathrooms. Breakfast is taken in the hotel's first-rate cafe and receptionists speak your lingo.

Hotel Viktoria HOTEL $$$

(3952-986 808; www.victoryhotel.ru; ul Bogdana Khmelnitskogo 1; s ₽3600-4000, d ₽4200-4600;) Just a few steps off ul Karla Marksa, the 30 rooms at this purpose-built tower hotel remain stylish and unfrumpy despite the antique-style furniture and flowery wall coverings. If you've been in Russia a while, the courteous staff, baths in every room and online booking could feel almost eccentric. Lower rates from September through to May.

Eating

Slata SUPERMARKET

(Слата; ul Karla Marksa 21; 24hr) Supermarkets are surprisingly rare in central Irkutsk so this centrally located, open-all-hours store is a godsend. Stocks a lot of ready-to-eat meals (meatballs, steaks, salads), ideal for long train journeys.

Poznaya na Lenina BURYAT $

(ul Lenina 25; mains ₽120-180; 9am-11pm) With a stylishly dark interior and Buryat-themed modern paintings on the walls, this otherwise unpretentious cheapie is possibly the best place to sample *pozy* (₽40 per person) and other Buryat-Mongolian fare in the city. The picture menu helps to break the language barrier.

Baikal Love Cafe BURYAT $

(8-964-112 3181; www.instagram.com/baikallove_irkutsk; ul Lenina 32; mains ₽150-250; 10am-10pm) For a quick introduction to native Siberians' food, check out this little eatery that serves Buryat *buuzy* dumplings, *bukhlyor* meat broth and *suguday* (Siberian version of ceviche) as well as Russian bliny pancakes and Central Asian noodle dishes. You'll be confronted by a bear skin hanging on the wall as you enter – because Siberia.

New Zealand Pies PASTRIES $

(3952-940 054; https://vk.com/nzpies; ul Sverdlova 8; pies ₽80; 8am-8pm) Blown into central Eurasia by Pacific winds (along with myriad secondhand Japanese cars), this tiny joint churns out delicious pies with unusual fillings, from Pacific salmon and giblets in sour cream sauce to strawberries and cherries. Something worth stocking up on before boarding your Trans-Siberian train.

Mamochka CAFE $

(Мамочка; ul Karla Marksa 41; mains ₽80-100; 10am-9pm) With its menu of imaginative salads, filling soups and (almost) healthy mains, this is no ordinary point-and-eat canteen. Swab the decks with a Slovak lager then sit back and admire the interior, a mishmash of old newspapers and Soviet bric-a-brac.

Govinda VEGETARIAN $

(3952-933 101; 2nd fl, ul Furye 4; mains ₽50-100; 11am-8pm;) Irkutsk's only meat-free restaurant is a small self-service affair with a half-hearted Indian theme and a menu of soya sausages, basmati rice, spicy soups, mild curries, quorn chilli con carne, imaginative desserts and whole plantations of tea.

★ **Kochevnik** MONGOLIAN $$

(Кочевник; 3952-200 459; http://ресторан-кочевник.рф/; ul Gorkogo 19; mains ₽300-1200; 11am-midnight) Take your taste buds to the Mongolian steppe for some yurt-size portions of mutton, lamb and steak as well as filling soups and *buuzy* dumplings, sluiced down with a bottle from the decent foreign wine list. Smiley service, a picture menu, low prices and an exotically curtained summer terrace make this one of the most agreeable places to dine in town.

WORTH A TRIP

TALTSY MUSEUM OF ARCHITECTURE & ETHNOGRAPHY

About 47km southeast of Irkutsk, 23km before Listvyanka, **Taltsy Museum of Architecture & Ethnography** (Архитектурно-этнографический музей Тальцы; http://talci-irkutsk.ru; ₽250; 10am-5pm, to 4pm in winter) is an impressive outdoor collection of old Siberian buildings set in a delightful riverside forest. Amid the renovated farmsteads are two chapels, a church, a watermill, some Evenki graves and the eye-catching 17th-century Iliminsk Ostrog watchtower. Listvyanka–Irkutsk buses and marshrutky stop on request at Taltsy's entrance (look out for the roadside 'Музей' sign), and the ticket booth is a minute's walk through the forest.

★**Rassolnik** RUSSIAN $$
(www.rassolnik.su; 130 Kvartal, ul 3 Iyulya 3; mains ₽300-700; noon-midnight) Arguably the best eating addition in the 130 Kvartal, this retro restaurant serves up a 100% Soviet-era menu (think upmarket *pelmeni, okroshka, shchi, kvas* and grandmother's pickles) in a plush Stalinist banqueting hall bedecked in nostalgia-inducing knick-knackery. Classic Soviet-era films are projected onto one wall, the menu is designed like a 1960s scrapbook and waiting staff are dressed for the occasion.

La Boulangerie & Patisserie BAKERY $$
(3952-432 339; ul Karla Marksa 41/1; set menu breakfast ₽350; 9am-noon) This is the kind of place Siberia's earliest Francophones, the Decembrists, must have dreamed would emerge in Irkutsk one day. Believe us, no freshly baked croissant feels more invigorating than the one consumed straight after disembarking from a train in the middle of Siberia. A variety of breakfast sets is on offer, including a not fully authentic Full English.

Mamay ASIAN $$
(Мамай; 3952-500 560; https://vk.com/mamai_club; 130 Kvartal, ul Sedova 16; mains ₽350-550; noon-1am) Like a nomad galloping through the steppe, the menu of this large modern restaurant carries goodies poached from all over Asia, from authentic tom yum and East Asian noodles to Siberian specialities, like *muksun* (white Arctic fish) fillet and Mongolian lamb grilled on charcoal.

Design Bar INTERNATIONAL $$
(3952-403 399; www.facebook.com/ilovedesignbar; ul Karla Marksa 40; mains ₽400-500; noon-midnight) On the 2nd floor of a large interior design store and decorated with a multitude of red Chinese lamps, this intimate eatery-cum-bar serves inventive fusion food as well as cocktails. A great place for lunch (set menu ₽300 to ₽350), though getting a table is sometimes tricky.

Dom Rybaka SEAFOOD $$$
(Дом рыбака; 3952-484 000; ul Partizanskaya 47; mains ₽400-1100; noon-midnight) You might have already been introduced to Siberian fish, but for fundamental ichthyology head to this upmarket restaurant on the outskirts of the old town. *Nelma, chir, taymen* and a dozen other fish varieties are served fried, stewed, grilled, as well as fresh – in the form of *suguday,* the Siberian version of ceviche. No English menu.

Drinking & Nightlife

★**Belaya Vorona** CAFE
(Белая ворона; ul Karla Marksa 37; 9am-10pm Mon-Fri, 10am-11pm Sat & Sun;) Disciples of the bean should definitely head to the 'White Crow', a relaxing cellar-based coffee hang-out hiding from view in the cellar of a flower shop on the main drag. A funky soundtrack provides background for caffeine or a late breakfast as you catch up on emails or browse in the small book exchange, wishing you could read the Cyrillic paperbacks.

Brasserie BBB PUB
(https://vk.com/brasseriebbbirk; ul Karla Marksa 41/1; 9am-midnight) Belgian Benoit de With ended his career as beer plant manager and set up this great beer place. It has its own beer (cheap) and dozens of kinds of Belgian and other international beers. Belgian and French food is good, but expensive. Quiz shows and football broadcasts are both regular features.

SOMETHING FISHY

No trip to Baikal is complete without tasting **omul**, a distant relative of salmon that's delicious when freshly hot-smoked. There are over 50 other varieties of Baikal fish, including perch, black grayling, ugly frilly-nosed bullheads and tasty *sig* (lake herring). While the lake isn't Russia's greatest place for anglers, from February to April it offers the unusual spectacle of **ice fishing**. There are two forms: individuals with immense patience dangle miniature hooked lines through Inuit-style ice holes; elsewhere, especially in shallow waters, whole teams of villagers string long, thin nets beneath the ice and pull out *omul* by the hundred.

You can get beneath the ice yourself with Irkutsk-based scuba-diving outfit **Baikal Tek** (www.baikaldiving.ru). But the lake's greatest divers are the unique **nerpa seals**. Indigenous to Lake Baikal, they are the only seal in the world to spend its entire existence in a freshwater environment. They thrive in many locations on the lake's shore, but usually (and wisely) stay away from human populations.

Castro Cafe CAFE
(https://vk.com/castrocafe; 130 Kvartal, ul 3 Iyulya 7; ⏲8.30am-11pm) This place is cleverly divided into two areas – the downstairs bar for those who want a quick cup of brew, and a brightly coloured upstairs lounge zone with comfy couches and cushions.

Engineria Coffee COFFEE
(Инженерия кофе; ☎3952-580 404; https://vk.com/engineeriacoffee; ul Karla Libknekhta 2; ⏲8am-8pm) These guys are nerdishly serious about the brew and if you share their passion, you can spend half an hour talking about percolate, immersion and AeroPress in barely comprehensible industry slang. But the bottom line is they just make great coffee.

Library Bar BAR
(☎3952-926 925; ul Kalandarashvili 9; ⏲6pm-3am) Russian literary celebrities stare at you from every wall, so after a few pints of Smolensk craft beer or a selection of great cocktails, you might be treating Mayakovsky as your buddy. But you can find better company than dead poets as the place is located next to three popular hostels, so English-speaking travellers are in no short supply.

Kwak Inn BEER HALL
(☎3952-201 141; http://kwakinn.ru; Kievskaya ul 2; ⏲noon-1am) There is a bit of an American-diner feel about this supposedly Belgian place that belongs to Estonians. But crucially, it has a very good vibe, with friendly service and indeed lots of Belgian beer on tap.

Cheshskaya Pivovarnya PUB
(Чешская пивоварня; ul Krasnogvardeyskaya 29; ⏲5pm-2am Tue-Thu, from 4pm Fri & Sat, to midnight Sun & Mon) You'll smell this place before you see it: Irkutsk's unpretentious microbrewery-pub creates its own Pilsner Urquell lager, pumping out a pungent hop aroma in the process.

Bierhaus PUB
(☎3952-550 555; www.bier-haus.ru; ul Gryaznova 1; ⏲noon-2am Mon-Thu, to 4am Fri & Sat, to midnight Sun; 📶) Upmarket Bavarian-style *bierstube* (beer hall with heavy wooden furniture) serving Newcastle Brown and Guinness as well as German beers and sausages. Enter from ul Karla Marksa.

☆ Entertainment

Rock'n'Roll Pub LIVE MUSIC
(www.vk.com/rocknrollpub; Kievskaya ul 24) Head to this cheap no-frills pub and diner to check what Siberian and indie music are about.

Benzin LIVE MUSIC
(Бензин; ☎3952-204 205; https://vk.com/club-benzin; ul Fridrikha Engelsa 8b) A slick entertainment centre with four bars, frequent live gigs and DJ parties.

Philharmonic Hall LIVE MUSIC
(Филармония; ☎3952-242 968; www.filarmoniya.irk.ru; ul Dzerzhinskogo 2) Historic building staging regular children's shows and musical programs from jazz to classical.

🛍 Shopping

Central Market MARKET
(☎3952-667 545; ul Chekhova 22; ⏲8am-7pm) Very central indeed, Irkutsk's well-maintained and perfectly authentic market is the place to stock up on cedar nuts, taiga herbs and Siberian fish, notably the famous Baikal *omul*, which can be packed in hermetic cellophane for transportation by air.

Prodalit BOOKS
(Продалитъ; ul Furye 8; ⏲10am-7pm Mon-Fri, to 6pm Sat & Sun) This large bookstore on the 2nd floor of a small shopping centre sells regional and city maps, Baikal- and Irkutsk-themed coffee-table books and Lonely Planet guides in Russian.

Karibu CLOTHING
(ul Timiryazeva 34; ⏲10am-7pm Mon-Sat, noon-5pm Sun) Tiny shop selling beautifully furry *unty* (traditional deerskin cowboy boots) made on-site and typically costing around ₽10,000. Some English spoken.

ℹ Information

Post Office (ul Karla Marksa 28; ⏲8am-8pm Mon-Fri, 9am-6pm Sat & Sun)

Tourist Office (☎3952-205 018; www.irkvisit.info; ul Dekabrskikh Sobyty 77; ⏲9am-8pm; 📶) Municipally funded tourist office with English-speaking staff, free wi-fi, free city maps and lots of well-produced brochures and booklets on Irkutsk and Lake Baikal. Between June and August staff are posted at strategic points around the city handing out info.

www.irk.ru Local city info.

www.irkutsk.org Bags of information on every aspect of the city.

ℹ Getting There & Away

TRAIN

Irkutsk has the following rail connections:

Běijīng *kupe* ₽18,200, 70 hours, twice weekly

Chita *platskart/kupe* from ₽2600/2900, 16 hours to 20 hours, up to six daily

Khabarovsk *platskart/kupe* ₽6600/10,000, 57 to 65 hours, two daily

Krasnoyarsk *platskart/kupe* from ₽2600/4600, 18 hours, up to nine daily

Moscow *platskart/kupe* from ₽13,000/₽16,000, three days and three hours to five days and 18 hours, up to seven daily

Severobaikalsk *platskart/kupe* ₽3800/₽5600, 34 hours, daily

Slyudyanka *elektrichka* ₽180, four hours, four daily

Ulaanbaatar *kupe* ₽7200, 27 hours, daily

Ulan-Ude *platskart* ₽1600, *kupe* ₽1900 to ₽2300, 6½ hours to 8½ hours, up to nine daily

Vladivostok *platskart/kupe* ₽5350/10,700, 72 hours, three daily

AIR

Irkutsk's antiquated little 'international' **airport** (www.iktport.ru) is handily placed near the city centre. Foreign destinations include Bangkok, Běijīng, Seoul, Tokyo and Ulaanbaatar. Direct flights to Germany were scrapped in 2011 but might restart in the coming years.

For Moscow, there are direct flights with S7 Airlines, Aeroflot and some dodgier airlines (from ₽15,000, three daily). Irkutsk also enjoys direct air links to dozens of other domestic destinations, with tickets for all services sold through the convenient **Central Air Agency** (Центральная авиакасса; ☎3952-500 703; http://ikt.moyreys.ru; ul Gorkogo 29; ⊙8am-7pm).

BOAT

In summer hydrofoils buzz along the Angara River to Listvyanka and up Lake Baikal to Bolshie Koty, Olkhon Island, Ust-Barguzin and Nizhneangarsk. Departures are from the **Raketa Hydrofoil Station** (Речной вокзал; Prichal Raketa) beyond the Angara Dam in Solnechny Mikro-Rayon, two minutes' walk from bus 16 stop 'Raketa'. Timetables are posted by the quay. Services in the other direction to **Bratsk** leave from a separate jetty in the city centre.

All services are operated by **VSRP** (☎3952-287 115; www.vsrp.ru). Check the English-language website for all times and prices.

THE EASY WAY TO OLKHON ISLAND

To Khuzhir on Olkhon Island, convenient door-to-door transfers (₽800) can be arranged through any of Irkutsk's hostels. Minibuses pick up from any hostel in the morning and drop off passengers at any guesthouse in Khuzhir midafternoon. Hostels sell tickets even to nonguests.

BUS

From the partially renovated **bus station** (https://avtovokzal-on-line.ru; ul Oktyabrskoy Revolyutsii; ⊙5.30am-8pm), book tickets at least a day ahead in summer for Arshan (₽400, four to five hours, two daily), Listvyanka (₽110, 1¼ hours, hourly) via Taltsy (₽90), Bratsk (₽1050, 11 hours, eight daily) and Ust-Kut (on the BAM railway; ₽1800, 16 hours). The station has a left-luggage office.

Minibuses to Ulan-Ude (₽1000, seven hours) and Slyudyanka (₽200, two hours) depart throughout the day from the train station forecourt, where you can also catch a minibus to Arshan, if more convenient.

Getting Around

Within the central area, walking is usually the best idea as one-way systems make bus routes confusing.

Frequent trolleybus 4 and bus/*marshrutka* 20, 80, 90 and countless others connect the city centre with the airport. A taxi to/from the airport costs around ₽110 with Gett or Maxim.

From the train station, trams 1, 2 and 4A run to ul Lenina and ul Timiryazeva, 4A continuing on to the bus station. Tram 4 links the central market with the bus station.

Gett and Maxim taxi app services are available. A typical fare for a ride in the centre is ₽90.

LAKE BAIKAL

ОЗЕРО БАЙКАЛ

One of the world's oldest geographical features (formed 25 to 30 million years ago), magnificent Lake Baikal is the highlight of Eastern Siberia. Summer travellers enjoy gobsmacking vistas across waters of the deepest blue to soaring mountain ranges on the opposite shore; rarer winter visitors marvel at its powder-white surface, frozen steel-hard and scored with ice roads. Whether they swim in it, drink its water, skirt its southern tip by train, cycle or dog sled over it in winter, or just admire it from 2000km of shoreline, most agree that Siberia doesn't get better than this.

Banana-shaped Baikal is 636km from north to south and up to 1637m deep, making it the world's deepest lake, containing nearly one-fifth of the planet's unfrozen fresh water. Despite some environmental concerns, it's pure enough to drink in most places, but use common sense. Fed by 300 rivers, it's drained by just one, the Angara near Listvyanka.

Foreign tourists typically visit Baikal from Listvyanka via Irkutsk, but approaching via

Baikal

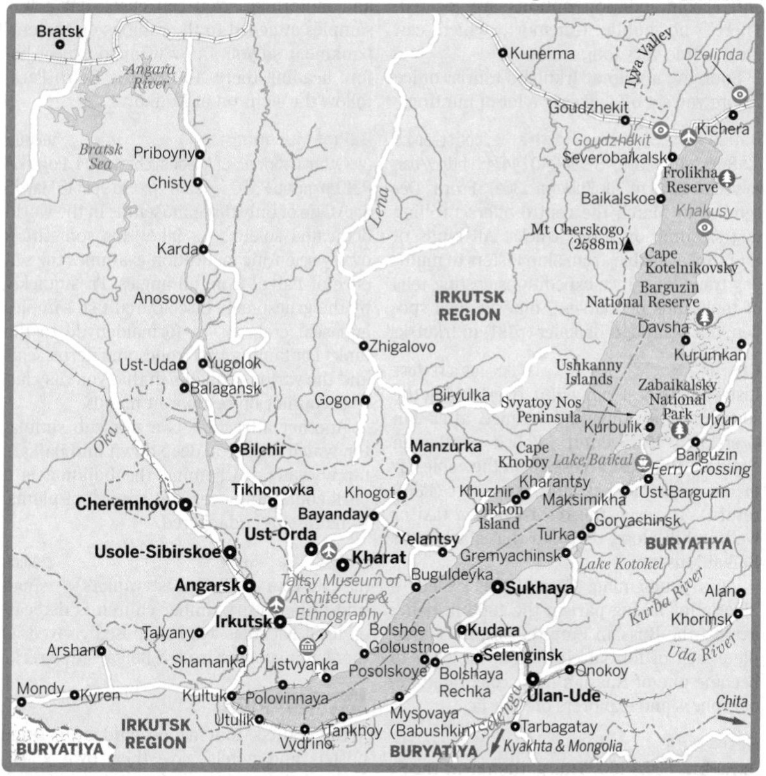

Ulan-Ude (for eastern Baikal) produces more beach fun and Severobaikalsk (p239) (on the BAM railway) is best for accessing wilderness trekking routes. Choosing well is important as there's no round-lake road and the northern reaches are in effect cut off by land from the southern shores. Not even the Great Baikal Trail (p188) will create a complete loop as some stretches of shoreline are just too remote. Hydrofoil connections are limited to summer services in the south plus the Irkutsk–Olkhon–Nizhneangarsk run. Inexplicably, there are virtually no scheduled boat services linking the east and west shores.

Listvyanka Листвянка

☎3952 / POP 1970 / TIME MOSCOW +5HR

As the closest lakeside village to Irkutsk, Listvyanka – aka the 'Baikal Riviera' – is the touristy spot where most travellers go to dunk their toes in Baikal's pure waters. Having picked at *omul*, admired the hazy views of the Khamar Daban mountains on the opposite shore and huffed their way from one end of the village to the other, most are on a *marshrutka* back to Irkutsk late afternoon. But there's more to Listvyanka: stay longer to hike the Great Baikal Trail, discover more about the lake at the Baikal Museum and chill out at one of Siberia's most eco-friendly sleeps.

If you're looking for beach fun, the eastern shore (Buryatiya) is the place to build sandcastles. However, what the Buryat shore doesn't have is Listvyanka's range of activities: from short boat trips to diving and jet-skiing in the summer and ice mountain biking to lake treks and ice sculpting in the winter.

Sights & Activities

The village extends 4.5km from Rogatka at the mouth of the Angara to the market area. A single road skirts the shore, with three valleys running inland where most of

Listvyanka's characterful timber dwellings and accommodation options are located. There's no public transport, which can mean some very long walks.

Sourcing a map at Irkutsk's tourist office before you set off will save a lot of hunting.

Baikal Dog Sledding Centre DOG SLEDDING
(☎8-983-412 2694, 8-914-940 4474; http://baikalsled.blogspot.ru; ul Kulikova 136a) From December to March the centre offers thrilling dog sledding on forest tracks. All kinds of tours are available, from 5km tasters to multiday trans-Baikal ice expeditions costing tens of thousands of roubles. Some English spoken. Book through Baikaler (p181) in Irkutsk.

Chersky Rock NATURAL FEATURE
Listvyanka's best viewpoint, overlooking the source of the Angara, is named after Jan Czerski, a 19th-century Polish gentleman explorer. It is best accessed via the cable car of the mediocre Eastland ski resort (₽300 return). To reach the resort, take a taxi or walk uphill along the road that starts near Baikal Museum.

As a young man, Czerski was exiled to Siberia for taking part in the 1863 uprising against the Russian Empire. Despite a complete lack of formal education, he grew to become one of Russia's most celebrated geographers and explorers of Siberia.

Retro Park GARDENS
(ul Kulikova 62b; ₽100) This garden near the St Nicholas Church is full of wacky sculpture pieces fashioned from old Soviet-era cars and motorbikes. You can check out a few samples attached to the railings on the embankment so you know what to expect before heading there. To find the Retro Park, follow the signs on ul Kulikova.

Baikal Museum MUSEUM
(www.bm.isc.irk.ru; ul Akademicheskaya 1, Rogatka; ₽310, minisub ₽500; ⏲9am-7pm, to 9pm 15 May-15 Sep) One of only three museums in the world dedicated solely to a lake, this sometimes overly scientific institution examines the science of Baikal from all angles. Pass quickly by the gruesomely discoloured fish samples and seal embryos in formaldehyde to the tanks containing two frolicsome nerpa seals and the various Baikal fish that you may later encounter on restaurant menus.

Another attraction is a minisub simulator, which takes you deep down into Baikal's nippy waters. Adjoining the building is a park containing over 400 species of plants, some rare or endangered.

St Nicholas Church CHURCH
(ul Kulikova 90) Listvyanka's small mid-19th-century timber church is dedicated to St Nicholas, who supposedly saved its merchant sponsor from a Baikal shipwreck.

Sleeping

Many Irkutsk tour agents and even some hostels and hotels have their own guesthouse or homestay in Listvyanka. For turn-

THE GREAT BAIKAL TRAIL

Inspired largely by the Tahoe Rim Trail (a hiking path encircling Lake Tahoe in California and Nevada), a small band of enthusiasts began work in summer 2003 on the first section of what was grandly named the Great Baikal Trail (GBT; in Russian, Bolshaya Baikalskaya Tropa, BBT). Every summer since has seen hundreds of volunteers flock to Lake Baikal's pebbly shores to bring the GBT organisation's stated aim – the creation of a 2000km-long network of trails encircling the whole of Lake Baikal – closer to fruition. This lofty ambition may still be a far-off dream, but the GBT is nonetheless the first such trail system in all Russia.

These rudimentary bits of infrastructure, the GBT organisation hopes, will attract more low-impact tourists to the region, thus encouraging eco-friendly businesses to flourish and providing an alternative to industrial and mass-tourism development. Volunteers and local activists are also involved in raising awareness of environmental issues among local people, visiting schools and fundraising. Nomination as a finalist in *National Geographic*'s 2008 Geotourism Challenge is arguably the GBT's greatest achievement to date and has greatly raised its profile in the world of ecotourism.

Many Baikal explorers simply enjoy trekking the 540km of trails created thus far, but every year young and old from around the world join work crews for a few enjoyable weeks of clearing pathways, cutting steps, creating markers and building footbridges. Those eager to volunteer should visit the GBT website (www.greatbaikaltrail.org) for more details.

up-and-hope homestays, the best street to try first is ul Chapaeva.

★ Belka Hostel HOSTEL $

(☎8-952-626 1251; www.baikaler.com; ul Chapaeva 77a; dm/tw ₽600/1500; @) This purpose-built hostel located at the far end of ul Chapaeva provides top-notch digs for backpacker prices, leaving Listvyanka's other flat-footed accommodation in its green wake. From the energy-saving light bulbs and basalt-foam insulation to the solar-heated water and solar-generated electricity, owner Jack Sheremetoff has crafted a low-impact haven with lots of personal touches.

Start the day with a bit of sun worship on the yoga deck and breakfast on the forest-facing chill-out area; end it with a scramble up the mini climbing wall and a scrub-down in the *banya* before snuggling up in a handmade timber bed (no bunks) in an en-suite dorm. Two guest kitchens, 24-hour reception and many other features you won't find anywhere else. Booking well ahead is essential.

No fibre-optic cable laid in this part of Listvyanka, so sadly no wi-fi.

Gavan Baikala GUESTHOUSE $$

(☎3952-500 620; www.gavanbaykal.com; ul Gudina 84; d/q ₽3000/4500) This chalet-styled log house has a large common balcony with a distant view of the lake, and pine-scented rooms with soft mattresses and good shower cabins. Breakfast is served in the Chekhovian dining room. Conveniently located on the road leading up to the Great Baikal Trail.

Baikal Chalet GUESTHOUSE $$

(☎8-914 895 1961, 3952-462 244; www.baikalcomplex.com; ul Gudina 75; tw ₽3200) The 13 comfortable twin rooms in this timber guesthouse around 800m back from the lake are a good deal. Its sister guesthouse in Bolshie Koty offers similar rates and standards. Breakfast included.

Derevenka HOTEL $$

(☎8-914-877 5599; www.baikal-derevenka.ru; ul Gornaya 1; s/d from ₽1500/2000, tent pitch ₽200; 📶) On a ridge behind the shore road, cute little wooden huts (named after Baikal's winds) with stove-heaters, private toilets and hot water (but shared showers) offer Listvyanka's most appealing semibudget choice. Behind the complex is Listvyanka's only official camp site. Rates include breakfast.

Dream of Baikal Hotel HOTEL $$

(☎3952-496 888; www.dreamofbaikal.ru; ul Gorkogo 105; s ₽3500-5500, d ₽3800-5600; 📶) Set just an endemic species' throw from Baikal's lulling waves/crumbly ice, this newish, clumsily named, purpose-built hotel by the market is a step up from Listvyanka's usual timber guesthouses. Rooms bedecked in generous drapery are packed with faux-antique furniture. The reception works 24 hours, apart from when the receptionist dozes off just after lunch.

Priboy HOTEL $$

(☎3952-496 725; http://hotel-priboy.ru; upper fl, ul Gorkogo 101; r from ₽3500) Spitting distance from the lake in the port area, this glass-and-steel hunk of incongruity has seen renovation in recent years, rendering the four lake-view rooms some of the best deals in town. The other 15 chambers are less spectacular but rates include breakfast taken in the downstairs cafe.

Krestovaya pad HOTEL $$$

(☎3952-496 863; www.krestovayapad.ru; ul Gornaya 14a; tw & d from ₽6500; 📶) This stylishly upmarket complex, with very comfortable international-standard pine-clad rooms, dominates the hillside above Krestovka.

U Ozera HOTEL $$$

(У Озера; ☎3952-496 777; www.listvjanka-baikal.ru; Irkutsk Hwy km3; d ₽4000-5000, cottages ₽5500; 📶) Just 10m from the shoreline, it's not surprising that all nine rooms (doubles only) at this small hotel have wonderful lake views. Rooms are a little too intimate but have balconies where you can stretch out. The cottages sleeping two lack the views but offer more space. Located between Krestovka and Rogatka.

Eating

Near the port, the large fish and souvenir market is the best place to buy smoked *omul* and is surrounded by greasy spoons offering cheap *plov* and shashlyk.

Café Podlemore CAFE $

(ul Gorkogo 31; mains ₽200-300; ⊙9am-midnight) The Podlemore has porridge and oven-fresh pastries, but rather flummoxed serving staff. Early opening makes it a popular breakfast halt.

Listvyanka Club RUSSIAN $$

(☎3952-496 739; ul Sudzilovskogo 2; mains ₽300-500; ⊙10am-11pm) This new airy lakeside place focuses on Baikal fish, with *omul* cooked in cedar-seed juice (Russians call it cedar milk), bringing together the two most iconic local staples. There is also an ample list of meat dishes, including a good variety of homemade *pelmeni* dumplings.

Proshly Vek RUSSIAN **$$**
(Прошлый век; ul Lazo 1; meals ₽460-700; ⌚noon-midnight) Listvyanka's most characterful eatery has a nautical theme, a fish-heavy menu and Baikal views. The upper floor is filled with fascinating old junk, which you can admire while tucking into *omul* done any which way you please.

ℹ Information

ATMs can be found in the Mayak and Priboy hotels.

Post Office (ul Gorkogo 49; ⌚8am-1pm & 2-8pm Mon-Fri, 9am-6pm Sat)

Tourist Office (☎3952-656 099; hydrofoil quay; ⌚10am-6pm) Located at the *marshrutka* terminus (there are several imposters), this surprisingly useful office hands out free maps as well as providing bus, ferry and hydrofoil timetables and offering imaginative Baikal boat trips. Bike rental available.

ℹ Getting There & Away

Hourly *marshrutky* (₽120, luggage ₽50, 1¼ hours) leave for Irkutsk from outside the tourist office (where tickets are bought). The last service departs at 9pm.

From mid-May to late September, hydrofoils stop at Listvyanka between Irkutsk and Bolshie Koty three times a day.

A tiny, battered car ferry lumbers across the never-frozen Angara River mouth to Port Baikal from Rogatka four times a day mid-May to mid-October, and just twice a day in the winter months.

Contact **VSRP** (p186) in Irkutsk for details of all these boat services.

Port Baikal Порт Байкал

☎3952 / POP 1960 / TIME MOSCOW +5HR

You'd be excused for dismissing Port Baikal as a rusty semi-industrial eyesore when seen from Listvyanka across the unbridged mouth of the Angara River. But it has a melancholic appeal, with a pretty train station teleported here from somewhere in Central Europe and a port where derelict vessels are laid to rest. A kilometre southwest of the port, Baranchiki is a ramshackle 'real' village with lots of unkempt but authentic Siberian cottages and a couple of accommodation options. Awkward ferry connections mean that Port Baikal remains largely uncommercialised, lacking Listvyanka's attractions but also its crowds. It's thus popular with more meditative visitors, but the main draw is that it's both the beginning and terminus of the Circumbaikal Railway.

Sleeping & Eating

Apart from *turbazy* restaurants, a couple of poorly stocked grocery kiosks are the only other sources of sustenance.

U Starogo Mayaka HOTEL **$$**
(☎3952-643 994, 3952-645 915; Port-Baikal; dm ₽800, d from ₽2200) Not too busy with its main occupation, Port Baikal's pretty railway station is part-timing as a hotel. Clean and bland in an almost nostalgically Soviet

WORTH A TRIP

BOLSHIE KOTY

Tiny and roadless, this serene Baikal village is what the great Siberian escape is all about. But things weren't always this quiet: in the 19th century Koty experienced a mini gold rush and boasted soap and candle factories, a glassworks, churches and a school. Today all that's long over, leaving Irkutsk bourgeoisie to assemble their lakeside dachas in peace.

A section of the Great Baikal Trail runs between Koty and Listvyanka, and is a fabulous full- or half-day hike (around 20km). Take plenty of food (drink from the lake) as there's none en route.

Two-day guided treks from Listvyanka to Bolshie Koty with **Baikaler** (p181) cost ₽7000 person (provided there are at least two people to form a group), including accommodation and food.

The only other way to reach Bolshie Koty (unless you hike from Listvyanka) is aboard one of the three hydrofoils a day from Irkutsk (via Listvyanka). Check **VSRP** (p186) for times and ticket prices. Winter ice roads briefly unite the village with the outside world.

Three minutes' walk from the hydrofoil quay is the **Lesnaya 7 Hostel** (☎8-904-118 7275; www.lesnaya7.com; ul Lesnaya 7, Bolshiye Koty; dm ₽700; ⌚summer only; @).

way, the rooms on the station's 2nd floor are perfect for spending a night, if you are late for the last ferry to Listvyanka.

Fort Baikal GUESTHOUSE $$
(☎3952-242 415, 8-908-668 73 91; www.fortbaikal.ru; Shcholka pad; cabins per person ₽1200;) Around 2km away from Port Baikal and geared primarily for domestic tourists, this modern *turbaza* has summer-only rustic log houses with funky wooden fixtures, traditional wooden stoves and authentic samovars. Mountain bikes and horses available for hire. Staff can pick you up at the port, if you let them know in advance.

Getting There & Away

The ferry to Rogatka (₽62) near Listvyanka's Baikal Museum runs five times daily between mid-June and mid-September (at 8.15am, 11.15am, 4.15pm, 6.15pm and 8.15pm), but less frequently out of season and only twice in winter. Check the schedule beforehand. From mid-June to August there are direct hydrofoils to/from Irkutsk. All services are operated by **VSRP** (p186).

One or two trains a day come via the slow Circumbaikal route from Slyudyanka.

Olkhon Island Остров Ольхон

POP 1670 / TIME MOSCOW +5HR

Halfway up Lake Baikal's western shore and reached by a short ferry journey from Sakhyurta (aka MRS), the serenely beautiful Olkhon Island is a wonderful place from which to view the lake and relax during a tour of Siberia. Considered one of five global poles of shamanic energy by the Buryat people, the 72km-long island's 'capital' is the unlovely village of Khuzhir (Хужир), which has seen quite a serious tourist boom over the last few years, improbably triggered by a song about Baikal winning a TV contest in China.

Sights

Escaping Khuzhir's dusty, dung-splattered streets is the key to enjoying Olkhon. Every morning tours (from ₽900 per person) leave from Khuzhir's guesthouses to the north and south of the island, the most popular a seven-hour bounce in a UAZ minivan to dramatic **Cape Khoboy** at Olkhon's very northern tip, where Baikal seals sometimes bask.

Driver-guides cook fish soup for lunch over an open fire, but few speak any English. Between January and March, UAZ vans drive at least half the way on ice roads around the island. See the Nikita's Homestead (p191) website (www.olkhon.info) for details of this and other excursions (boat and even airplane trips are on offer in summer). Otherwise, rent a bike and strike out on your own.

In winter, bikes with studded tyres, as well as skates, are available for hire at Nikita's, but take all food and water with you as there's none outside Khuzhir.

Shaman Rocks LANDMARK
The unmistakable Shaman Rocks are neither huge nor spectacular, but they have become the archetypal Baikal vista found on postcards and travel-guide covers. A long strip of sandy beach lines the Maloe More (Little Sea) east of the rocks.

Museum MUSEUM
(ul Pervomayskaya 24; ₽100; 10am-6pm) Khuzhir's small museum displays a random mix of stuffed animals, Soviet-era junk, local art and the personal possessions of its founder, Nikolai Revyakin, a teacher for five decades at the school next door.

Sleeping

Khuzhir has an ever-growing range of places to stay, though the vast majority of independent travellers bunk down at Nikita's Homestead (p191). If all 50 rooms at Nikita's are full, staff can arrange homestays costing around ₽850, with meals taken at the Homestead canteen. Booking ahead anywhere in Khuzhir is only necessary during July and August.

★**Nikita's Homestead** GUESTHOUSE $
(☎8-914-895 7865; www.olkhon.info; ul Kirpichnaya 8; r incl breakfast & dinner with/without bathroom from ₽2200/1800; reception 8am-11pm) Occupying a sizeable chunk of Khuzhir, this intricately carved timber complex has grown (and continues to grow) into one of Siberia's top traveller hang-outs. The basic rooms in myriad shapes and sizes are attractively decorated with petroglyphs and other ethnic finery and heated by wood-burning stoves – but only a select few have showers (put your name down for the *banya*).

The organic meals are served two times a day in the large canteen near reception and two other (paid) eateries stand behind. There's a small cycle-hire centre and a packed schedule of excursions and activities. Note there is no alcohol for sale at Nikita's and consumption on the premises is frowned upon.

U Olgi GUESTHOUSE $
(☎8-908-661 9015; ul Lesnaya 3-1; full board per person ₽1300) This well-liked option has nine rooms, three in a typical village house and six in a purpose-built, pine-fragrant building opposite. New showers and flushing toilets plus scrumptious Siberian fare cooked by Olga herself make this a winner every time. Book through Baikaler (p181) in Irkutsk.

Solnechnaya GUESTHOUSE $
(Солнечная; ☎3952-683 216; www.olkhon.com; ul Solnechnaya 14; half-board per person ₽1300-1600; @) A pleasant place to stay offering a good range of activities. Accommodation is in two-storey cabins and tiny single-room shacks with verandahs. Enter from ul Solnechnaya or from near the relay station at the top of the hill.

Voskresenie GUESTHOUSE $$$
(Воскресенье; ☎8-904-117 7526; olhonsng@gmail.com; ul Pushkina 16; r ₽4200) The owners, a former Soviet table-tennis champion and his polyglot wife, indulge in interior design passion, as you will immediately notice when you move into one of only four individually designed rooms that sleep up to three people. Newer ones display a significant progress in both skill and material supply.

The incredibly nice and well-informed hosts also run a cute coffee shop in the premises.

Baikal View RESORT $$$
(☎8-983-698 9460; www.baikalview.com; ul Rossiyskaya 17; s/d incl breakfast from ₽9000/9850) Looking from the outside like a research station in Antarctica, this upmarket establishment has rooms with laconic Scandinavian-style interior design featuring many light-coloured wooden surfaces. In summer there is an outdoor swimming pool. Available all year is a nice restaurant and spa that offers bath treatment in a *taban-arhan* wooden barrel.

Information

There's no ATM on the island, so you'll need to bring enough cash to cover your stay.

Getting There & Away

The simplest way to reach Olkhon is aboard the morning *marshrutka* that leaves Irkutsk's hostels around 8.30am. Many other services run in July and August but can be impossible to track down in Irkutsk.

With a little warning, agencies or hostels can usually find you a ride in a private car to/from Irkutsk (5½ hours) for ₽2500 per seat, ₽10,000 for the whole car. Prices include the short ferry ride to/from MRS – from mid-January to March an ice road replaces the ferry. When ice is partly formed or partly melted, the island is completely cut off for motor vehicles, but there is an ad hoc minihovercraft service operated by locals.

In summer a hydrofoil service operates from Irkutsk to Olkhon, dropping passengers near the ferry terminal, from where it's possible to hitch a paid lift into Khuzhir. See **VSRP** (p186) for times and prices.

Slyudyanka Слюдянка

☎39544 / POP 18,240 / TIME MOSCOW +5HR

The lakeside railway town of Slyudyanka provides a grittier alternative to Listvyanka for those eager to get up close to Lake Baikal's waves/groaning ice and the Trans-Siberian Railway, which hugs the lake's pebbly shore either side of town. Most alight from a train at the glittering, solid-marble train station, which is a mere five-minute walk from Lake Baikal.

Sights & Activities

A rather strenuous trail heads up **Pik Cherskogo** (aka Mt Chersky) along the former post road to Mongolia, which once formed a part of the Silk Route. **Turbaza Pik Cherskogo** (☎8-902-543 6795; https://vk.com/turbazapik; tent pitch/dm ₽150/500) provides accommodation at the top of the mountain, but book in advance.

The annual **Peak Chersky race**, usually held around 20 August, involves participants running either a section of or the entire 44km distance to the top. Inquire at Delight (p194) or Slyudyanka Hostel (p194) about dates and participation.

A popular picnic excursion is to **Cape Shaman**, an easy 4km stroll north towards Kultuk along Baikal's gravelly shore. Owners of the Slyudyanka Hostel (p194) run guided trips there and to the former marble and mica (*slyud* in Russian, hence the town's name) mines southeast of the town.

Baikal Mineral Museum MUSEUM
(ul Slyudyanaya 36; ₽300; ⏲10am-7pm) Geology buffs should consider heading to the privately run Baikal Mineral Museum, which claims to exhibit every mineral known to man.

East Siberian Railway Museum MUSEUM
(ul Zheleznodorozhnaya 22; ₽100; ⏲8am-noon & 1-5pm Mon-Fri) Amid the nearby railway repair sheds and admin buildings you'll find

WORTH A TRIP

CIRCUMBAIKAL RAILWAY

From 1900 to 1904 the Trans-Siberian Railway tracks from Irkutsk came to an abrupt halt at Port Baikal. They continued on Lake Baikal's far-eastern shore at Mysovaya (Babushkin), and the watery gap was plugged by ice-breaking steamships, including the **Angara** (www.angara.gavailer.ru; ul Marshala Zhukova 36a; ₽150; ⏰10am-9pm), now restored and on view in Irkutsk. Later, the tracks were pushed south and around the lake. This Circumbaikal line required so many impressive tunnels and bridges that it earned the nickname 'The Tsar's Jewelled Buckle'. With the damming of the Angara River in the 1950s, the original Irkutsk–Port Baikal section was submerged and replaced with an Irkutsk–Kultuk shortcut (today's Trans-Siberian). That left poor little Port Baikal to wither away at the dead end of a rarely used but incredibly scenic branch line. The nicely restored train station houses a new and informative **exhibition** (Port Baikal railway station; ₽30; ⏰opens by request) about the railway. Toy-train buffs will be delighted by the vintage scaled models of main tunnels.

Riding the Railway

Excruciatingly slow train ride or a great social event? Opinions are mixed, but taking one of the four-per-week Slyudyanka–Port Baikal trains along the scenic, lake-hugging Circumbaikal Railway remains a popular tourist activity. The most picturesque sections of the route are the valley, pebble beach and headland at Polovinnaya (around halfway), and the bridge area at km149. Note that most trains *from* Port Baikal travel by night and so are useless for sightseeing. Another thing to remember: if you travel outside summer season, you won't be able to catch a ferry to Listvyanka when you arrive in Port Baikal, so you'll have to overnight there. In summer, the last ferry departs at 8.45pm, so you'll be all right even if your Matanya train arrives late.

The old stone tunnels, cliff cuttings and bridges are an attraction even for non-train buffs who might drive alongside sections of the route on winter ice roads from **Kultuk**. Hiking the entire route or just sections of the peaceful track is also popular, and walking a couple of kilometres from Port Baikal leads to some pleasant, if litter-marred, beaches. Or get off an Irkutsk–Slyudyanka *elektrichka* at Temnaya Pad three hours into the journey and hike down the stream valley for about an hour. You should emerge at km149 on the **Circumbaikal track**, from where you can continue by train to Port Baikal if you time things well.

At the time of research, Matanya trains departed from a side platform at Slyudyanka 1 station at 1.20pm on Monday, Thursday, Friday and Sunday – check timetables carefully. An additional but more expensive tourist train direct from Irkutsk departs at 8.20am on Wednesday and Saturday, reaching Slyudyanka at 10.30am. Except in high summer season, Matanya trains arrive in Port Baikal in the evening after the last ferry for Listvyanka has departed, so organising accommodation in advance is advisable.

An expensive alternative to Matanya is the retro-train tour run by **Tu-tu Baikal** (☎3952-500 849; http://tutubaikal.tilda.ws; ul Stepana Razina 26; tour with/without Baikal view seat ₽5000/4500). An early-20th-century steamer pulls modern comfortable carriages, departing from Irkutsk train station twice a week at 8am and reaching Port Baikal in the evening. From there, people are ferried back to Irkutsk. Make sure you pay ₽500 extra for a Baikal-view seat, otherwise the trip may turn into a disappointment.

Yet another, fun way of exploring the Circumbaikal Railway is by high-speed boat, which takes people from Listvyanka to Polovinnaya, where it stops for a picnic before returning. Tours run by **Krugobaikalsky Ekspress** (☎3952-202 973; www.krugobaikalka.ru; bul Gagarina 68g; tours adult/child ₽4700/4000) include transfers to/from Irkutsk.

this fascinating little museum housed in an ornate wooden building set back from ul Zheleznodorozhnaya. There are exhibitions on the Circumbaikal Railway, the history of Slyudyanka and Lake Baikal, plus heaps of railway paraphernalia.

Sleeping & Eating

Self-catering is your best bet in Slyudyanka, unless you are staying at Delight (p194), where every meal is a feast.

Slyudyanka Hostel HOSTEL $
(☎39544-53 198, 8-902-576 7344; www.hostel-s.com; ul Shkolnaya 10, apt 7; dm ₽600; @) Six-bed hostel-homestay at the southern end of town providing a great opportunity to experience small-town Siberian family life. A fully equipped kitchen, heaps of outdoorsy tours and hikes and evenings of authentic Baikal hospitality await those who make the effort to find the place. It's a 20-minute walk, five-minute *marshrutka* ride (No 1) or ₽120 taxi journey along ul Parizhskoy Komuny.

Booking ahead is pretty much essential.

Delight HOMESTAY $$
(☎8-902-178 1788; rufenok@gmail.com; ul Kapotina 14; r ₽1800) Trekking and cycling enthusiasts Rufina and Yevgeny run this cosy and well-equipped homestay with just two rooms and a large shared bathroom, which contains a Trans-Siberian traveller's ultimate delight – a full-sized bathtub. For a small extra fee, Rufina cooks excellent dinners as well as breakfasts that by far surpass most served in multistarred hotels.

English-speaking Yevgeny is a wealth of info on Chersky Peak and Tunka Valley hikes, Munku-Sardyk climbs and ice treks on Baikal.

Spar SUPERMARKET
(ul Lenina 118; ⏲9am-10pm) The Spar supermarket opposite the bus station is the place to stock up on enough fruit, cheese, bread and instant porridge to keep you going all the way to the Urals.

Sputnik RUSSIAN $
(☎39544-755 77; ul Sovetskaya 46a; mains ₽100-120) A little tidy cafe by the bus station serves ordinary, but well-prepared *stolovaya*-type food.

ℹ Getting There & Away

Elektrichki (₽70, four daily) from Irkutsk take three hours to arrive at Slyudyanka 1 station; ordinary passenger trains (*platskart* ₽850, up to eight daily) take just two hours. Slyudyanka is also the usual starting point for the Circumbaikal Railway trip. From the bus station *marshrutky* run to Irkutsk (₽190, two hours, every 30 minutes). For Arshan, change at nearby Kultuk, reachable by local *marshrutka* (₽36, 20 minutes).

Eastern Baikal

Backed by the snow-capped Khamar-Daban mountains in the south and providing a gateway to the dramatic Barguzin Valley in the north, the eastern coast of Baikal is no less interesting than its western, which gets the bulk of visitors. That said, it is popular with local urbanites, from both Irkutsk and Ulan-Ude, so guesthouses or *turbazy* holiday camps can be found anywhere along the coast. There is plenty to do, from skiing or surfing in the south to birdwatching in the delta of the Selenga River and some serious hiking on Svyatoy Nos peninsula.

Selenga Delta

Some 300 waterways feed Lake Baikal, but none compare in size and volume to the Selenga River. One of only 80 rivers around the world to form a delta, the Selenga dumps its load of sand (and pollution from Mongolia) on Baikal's eastern shore in a huge fan of islands, reed beds and shallow channels measuring 35km across. Over 200 bird species draw spotters from all over the world; motorboat trips can be arranged through Ulan-Ude agencies.

Between birdwatching sessions many bed down in the village of Posolskoe, immediately south of the delta, where the Western-standard **Sofiya Hotel** (☎8-914-638 9521; full pension ₽1800) shares a lakeside location right beside a beautifully renovated monastery. Posolskoe is also the venue of regular water-sports competitions, usually held in August, and ice boat races held in March. **Sergei Klimov** (www.facebook.com/sergey.klimov.7146) is the best person to contact, if you are interested in watching or participating.

Immediately north of the delta, a road bound for Zarechye passes several classic Baikal villages of unpainted log houses with sea-blue window shutters. The popular sandy beach at Enkhaluk fills up with Ulan-Ude residents in the hot months. **Baikalskaya Solianka** (☎8-902-565 3951, 3012-297 499; http://baikalmix.ru/; ul Lesnaya 17, Novy Enkhaluk; d/q with full board from ₽6000/10,000, yurts per person with full board from ₽1400) is a funky-looking and popular place to stay. Around 10km further on, the **Zagza thermal spring** (₽200; ⏲9am-9pm) provides a welcome alternative to Baikal's icy waters. A couple of kilometres beyond it, at Sukhaya, there is a good Buryat restaurant that also has rooms.

South of the Selenga

East of Slyudyanka, the Trans-Siberian Railway and the parallel motorway skirt the coast up to Selenga Delta, where they both take a sharp turn east towards Ulan-Ude. Here, the snow-peaked Khamar-Daban Mountains rise steeply from the lake shore, leaving just a narrow strip of flat alluvial plain dotted with villages, where Irkutsk residents buy holiday homes to escape the city on hot summer weekends.

There are plenty of accommodation options, all of which are primarily geared to domestic tourists. Russians rave about **Ryzhaya Sova** (Рыжая сова, Red Owl; ☎8-914-006 4407; https://vk.com/copper_owl; ul Mira 15, Mangutay; per person from ₽750) at Mangutay (19km from Slyudyanka) and **Baikal Yeti** (☎8-904-150 0000; www.baikalyeti.com; ul Beregovaya 12, Utulik; dm/s/d from ₽500/1200/2000) in Utulik (32km from Slyudyanka).

Further north, 6km from Utulik, the unlovely **Baikalsk** is home to the now-defunct Baikal Pulp and Paper Plant, which once was the lake's main polluter. However, it's swarming with visitors in winter, thanks to **Sobolinaya Gora** (Соболиная гора; www.baikalski.com) ski resort, which has been tested and approved by one avid skier, Vladimir Putin.

More adventurous skiers head to **Mamay Mountain**, near Vydrino, at the border of Irkutsk Region and Buryatiya. It has turned into a mecca for off-piste skiers, thanks to the efforts of Extreme Sports Federation, an informal group of adventure-sports fans led by Sergei Klimov (p194) and based in Ulan-Ude. He is the best person to contact for details on access and conditions.

North of the Selenga

Access to the coast is across a forested pass from Ulan-Ude via tiny **Baturino** village, with its elegantly renovated Sretenskaya Church.

After around 2½ hours' drive, the newly paved road first meets Lake Baikal at pretty little **Gremyachinsk** (Гремячинск), a popular trip out of Ulan-Ude for hurried Trans-Siberian travellers with a day to spare; the village also has **Baykalskaya Riviera** (☎8-983-531 2313; http://baikalriviera.ru; ul Lesnaya 36, Gremyachinsk; summer cabins s/d incl breakfast ₽1800/2400, with full board ₽2800/4400, standard incl breakfast s/d ₽4200/4600, with full board ₽5200/6600), a fully-fledged resort that's good value for money, with simple though tastefully decorated summer-only wooden cabins and hotel-style accommodation available all year round. Buses stop at a roadside cafe from which Gremyachinsk's sandy but litter-strewn beach is a 15-minute walk up ul Komsomolskaya. *Marshrutky* back to Ulan-Ude are often full so consider prebooking your return.

Approximately 5km from Gremyachinsk, at least 10 large tourist camps are strung around **Lake Kotokel**, whose thermal springs keep it warm year-round. At the northern end of the lake rises **Monastyrsky Island**, once home to an isolated hermitage and a church.

The main road offers surprisingly few Baikal views until the fishing port of **Turka**, from where there are pleasant walks to several secluded bays in either direction. Bigger **Goryachinsk** (Горячинск), around 3km from the lake, is centred on a typically institutional hot-springs *kurort* (spa) with cheap cottage homestays in the surrounding village.

Further north through the uninhabited taiga lies the quaint little fishing hamlet of **Maksimikha** (Максимиха), where picturesque Baikal beaches stretch northwest. From here the blacktop bends before zipping through the forest to Ust-Barguzin.

Ust-Barguzin Усть-Баргузин

Low-rise Ust-Barguzin has sandy streets of traditional log homes with blue-and-white carved window frames. These are most attractive towards the northern end of the main street, ul Lenina, where it reaches the Barguzin River ferry. From here, views are magical towards the high-ridged peaks of the Svyatoy Nos Peninsula. Travelling in this remote area would be hard if not for the eminent Aleksander Beketov, who runs **Beketov Homestay** (☎30131-91 574; per Bolnichny 9, Ust-Barguzin; full board per person ₽1550, tent pitch ₽100) and **Banya Museum** (☎30131-91 574; per Bolnichny 9, Ust-Barguzin; ⏲by appointment only).

Daily *marshrutky* from Ust-Barguzin to to Ulan-Ude (₽430 to ₽510, five hours) run twice a day and will pick you up from your accommodation if you book ahead. In July and August a daily hydrofoil links Ust-Barguzin with Irkutsk and Khuzhir on Olkhon Island; check out VSRP (p186) for details. In February and March the ice drive across Lake Baikal to Severobaikalsk takes around five hours.

Buy tickets ahead for Ulan-Ude–Barguzin *marshrutky* (₽700, seven hours, three daily) and services to Kurumkan (₽900, nine hours, two daily). From Barguzin public transport to Ust-Barguzin, Uro and Kurumkan is rare, though there's usually at least one service early morning and in the afternoon. Hitchhike or arrange a tour through the Beketovs in Ust-Barguzin.

Svyatoy Nos Peninsula

Rising almost vertically out of shimmering waters, dramatic Svyatoy Nos is one of Lake Baikal's most impressive features. It's within the mostly impenetrable **Zabaikalsky National Park** and joined to Ust-Barguzin by a muddy 20km sandbar that's possible but painful to drive along (there's also a toll). Guides can be hired at the **national park offices** (per Bolnichny 9, Ust-Barguzin) in Ust-Barguzin for all-day trek-climbs to the top of the peninsula, more than 1800m above Lake Baikal. The views from the summit are truly awe-inspiring.

Nerpa seals are particularly abundant off the peninsula's west coast around the **Ushkanny Islands**, accessible by charter boat from Ust-Barguzin. Contact Aleksander Beketov at the national park headquarters. Prices begin at around ₽6000.

ULAN-UDE

3012 / POP 414,000 / TIME MOSCOW +5HR

With its smiley Asian features, cosy city centre and fascinating Mongol-Buddhist culture, the Buryat capital is one of Eastern Siberia's most likeable cities. Quietly busy, welcoming and, after Siberia's Russian cities, refreshingly exotic, it's a pleasant place to base yourself for day trips to Buddhist temples and flits to eastern Lake Baikal's gently shelving beaches, easily reachable by bus. For some travellers UU is also a taster for what's to come in Mongolia.

Founded as a Cossack *ostrog* (fort) called Udinsk (later Verkhneudinsk) in 1666, the city prospered as a major stop on the tea-caravan route from China via Troitskosavsk (now Kyakhta). Renamed Ulan-Ude in 1934, it was a closed city until the 1980s due to its secret military plants (there are still mysterious blank spaces on city maps).

UU's small city centre is divided into two districts: the communist-era upper city centred around pl Sovetov and the Lenin Head; and the riverside former merchant quarter,

OFF THE BEATEN TRACK

BARGUZIN & THE BARGUZIN VALLEY

The road north from Ust-Barguzin emerges from thick forests at Barguzin, a low-rise town of wooden cottages that dates back to 1648. Walking from the bus station, you can see its handful of dilapidated historic buildings in about 20 minutes by heading along ul Krasnoarmeyskaya past the cursorily renovated old **church** to pl Lenina. Opposite the quaint little post office, the wooden-colonnaded **Former Uezdny Bank** (ul Krasnoarmeyskaya 54, Barguzin) was once the grand home of Decembrist Mikhail Kyukhelbeker. Other exiles to make a home in Barguzin were Jews from Poland and European Russia who arrived here in the 1830s and 1860s. The last signs of the Jewish community can be seen in the crumbling old **cemetery** (a block northeast of the church), where crooked Hebrew-inscribed graves stand to the left and Orthodox headstones, including that of Decembrist Mikhail Kyukhelbeker, to the right. Hidden in the village school and difficult to access, the small **museum** (8-924-391 3126; https://vk.com/muzej_barguzin; ul Kalinina 51a, Barguzin; ₽100) has some interesting Decembrist-related exhibits as well as the usual dusty rocks and mammoth bones.

Barguzin's real interest is as a launch pad for visiting the stunningly beautiful **Barguzin Valley** as it opens out into wide lake-dotted grassland, gloriously edged by a vast Toblerone of mountain peaks. These are most accessibly viewed across the meandering river plain from **Uro** village. Similarly inspiring panoramas continue for miles towards the idyllic village of **Suvo**, overshadowed by rock towers of the **Suvo Saxony** (Suvinskaya Saksoniya), so-called for its similarity to rock formations on the Czech–Saxony border. A few kilometres beyond Suvo, the roadside **Bukhe Shulun** (Byk), a huge boulder resembling a bull's hoof, is considered to have miraculous powers. Heading north you'll pass through widely scattered, old-fashioned villages where horse carts and sleighs outnumber cars. Way up on the valley's mountainous west side, **Kurumkan** (411km northeast of Ulan-Ude) has a small but photogenic peak-backed *datsan* (Buddhist temple). The valley tapers to a point 50km north of Kurumkan at **Alla**, where a tiny *kurort* (spa) can accommodate guests in the summer months.

half of which still serves as the commercial hub extending from the 19th-century trading rows (pl Revolutsii). Dusty streets of crooked timber dwellings make up the other half.

Sights

You can take in pretty much all that matters in Ulan-Ude by walking down ul Lenina from pl Sovetov to Odigitria Cathedral. The newly pedestrianised part of the route, locally known as Arbat (after its Moscow equivalent), features a statue of Russian writer Anton Chekhov, who spent one night here and noted in his diary that Ulan-Ude is a 'pleasant little town'. He didn't elaborate any further.

Lenin Head MONUMENT
(pl Sovetov) Ulan-Ude's main square is entirely dominated by the world's largest Lenin head that creates an ensemble with the grey constructivist government building behind it. The 7.7m-high bronze bonce was installed in 1970 to celebrate Lenin's 100th birthday. Oddly, UU's bird population never seems to streak Lenin's bald scalp with their offerings – out of respect for the great man's achievements, bark diehard communists (but perhaps due to the barely visible anti-bird spikes, groan the rest).

Rinpoche Bagsha Datsan BUDDHIST TEMPLE
(www.yelo-rinpoche.ru; ul 1ya Dzerzhinskaya) Roosting high above the city's far north, the inside of this new and unexpectedly modern Tibetan temple looks like a kind of Buddhist-themed bus terminal, though the 6m-high gilt Buddha is pretty impressive. However, the real show-stealer here is the panoramic view, the smog-hazed city ringed by rumpled dust-bare peaks.

Take *marshrutka* 97 from outside the Hotel Baikal Plaza on pl Sovetov to the last stop (right by the temple entrance).

If you catch the monks doing their thing with drums, cymbals and chanting, the atmosphere can be electric. An extra feature is the circular walk around the temple featuring pavilions with grotesque, man-size representations of the Chinese signs of the zodiac.

Ulitsa Sobornaya STREET
(Соборная улица; ul Sobornaya (Linkhovoina)) The pedestrianised street abutting Odigitria Cathedral preserves the spirit and the wooden lace architecture of the old downtown, populated by merchants and intelligentsia. Original inhabitants suffered badly from Bolshevik violence. A grim reminder of those violent times is the white stone building at the cathedral end of the street, which housed the NKVD – Stalin's secret police, responsible for torture and mass executions. You'll find a touching **monument to the victims of oppression** at the other end of the street.

Tragedy and comedy often walk hand in hand, as evidenced by the hilarious gilded statues on top of a house that stands right in front of the sombre monument. The house contains **Lev Bardanov art gallery**, the brainchild of a local businessman, and the statues depict four of his favourite local cultural figures. Locals say the collection is no less eccentric, but the gallery had still not been opened for the public, when we hung around.

Ethnographic Museum MUSEUM
(www.ethnomuseum03.ru; Verkhnyaya Berezovka; ₽200; ⏲9am-5.30pm Wed-Fri, 10am-6.30pm Sat & Sun) In a forest clearing 6km from central Ulan-Ude, this outdoor collection of local architecture plus some reconstructed burial mounds and the odd stone totem are worth the trip. The collection is divided into seven areas, each devoted to a different nationality, tribe or ethnic group. There are Hun-era standing stones, Evenki *chumy,* traditional Buryat yurts, timber European town houses and a whole strip of Old Believers' homesteads, all brimming with period furniture and inhabited by costumed 'locals' giving craft demonstrations.

Marshrutka 37 from outside the Hotel Baikal Plaza on pl Sovetov passes within 1km and drivers are used to detouring to drop off tourists.

Opera & Ballet Theatre THEATRE
(Бурятский государственный академический театр оперы и балета; ☎3012-213 600; www.uu-opera.ru; ul Lenina 51) UU's striking Stalinist-era theatre reopened after lengthy renovation in 2011 (the first performance was for a group of foreign tourists from the luxury Golden Eagle train). Visitors cannot fail to be impressed by the level of craftsmanship inside, though some might be slightly surprised at the new lick of paint and rub of polish given to all the Soviet symbols, including a couple of smirking Stalins. The trademark performance is *Angara* – a ballet inspired by Buryat folklore and traditional music.

Ulan-Ude

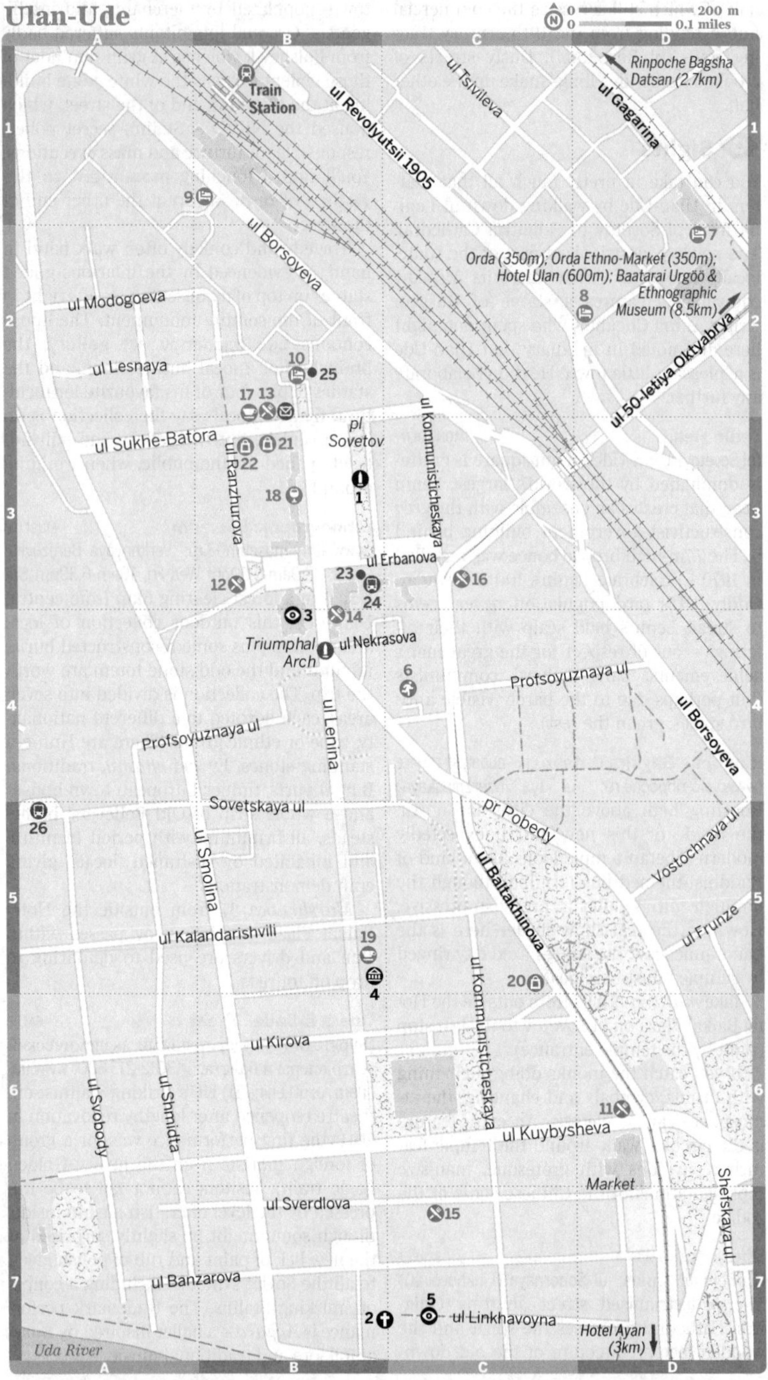

0 200 m
0 0.1 miles
Train Station
Rinpoche Bagsha Datsan (2.7km)
ul Revolyutsii 1905
ul Tsivileva
ul Gagarina
ul Borsoyeva
Orda (350m); Orda Ethno-Market (350m); Hotel Ulan (600m); Baatarai Urgöö & Ethnographic Museum (8.5km)
ul Modogoeva
ul Lesnaya
ul 50-letiya Oktyabrya
ul Sukhe-Batora
pl Sovetov
ul Kommunisticheskaya
ul Ranzhurova
ul Erbanova
Triumphal Arch
ul Nekrasova
Profsoyuznaya ul
ul Lenina
Sovetskaya ul
pr Pobedy
Vostochnaya ul
ul Smolina
ul Baltakhinova
ul Kalandarishvili
ul Frunze
ul Kirova
ul Svobody
ul Shmidta
ul Kuybysheva
Market
Shefskaya ul
ul Sverdlova
ul Banzarova
ul Linkhavoyna
Hotel Ayan (3km)
Uda River
A
B
C
D
1
2
3
4
5
6
7
1
2
3
4
5
6
7
8
9
10
11
12
13
14
15
16
17
18
19
20
21
22
23
24
25
26

Ulan-Ude

Sights

1	Lenin Head	B3
2	Odigitria Cathedral	B7
3	Opera & Ballet Theatre	B4
4	Ulan-Ude City Museum	B5
5	Ulitsa Sobornaya	C7

Activities, Courses & Tours

6	Baikal Naran Tour	C4
	Denis Sobnakov	(see 10)

Sleeping

7	Hotel Sagaan Morin	D2
8	Hotel Shumak	D2
9	Mergen Bator	B1
10	Ulan-Ude Travellers House	B2

Eating

11	Chay Khana	D6
12	Modern Nomads	B3
13	Myasoroob	B2
14	Shashlykoff	B4
15	Shenekhenskiye Buuzy	C7
16	Sputnik Supermarket	C3

Drinking & Nightlife

	Bar 12	(see 9)
17	Bisquit	B2
18	Churchill	B3
19	Macondo Coffee & Store	B5

Shopping

20	Central Market	C5
21	Dombo	B3
22	Zam	B3

Transport

23	Central Ticket Office	B3
24	Marshrutka Stop for Ethnographic Museum & Rinpoche Bagsha Datsan	B3
25	S7 Airlines	B2
26	Selenga Bus Station	A5

Ulan-Ude City Museum MUSEUM
(www.uumuseum.ru; ul Lenina 26; ₽60; ⏰9am-6pm) Occupying the merchant's house where imperial heir Nicholas II stayed in 1891, this small but progressive museum has exhibits examining Verkhneudinsk's role in the tea and fur trades, the huge fairs that took place at the trading arches and several other aspects of the city's past.

Odigitria Cathedral CHURCH
(ul Lenina 2) Built between 1741 and 1785, UU's largest church was also the first stone structure to appear in the city. Used as a museum store from 1929 until the fall of communism, its exterior has been renovated in a chalky white and the domes are once again tipped with gold, but the interiors are plain whitewash, awaiting their Byzantine decoration.

Activities

Ulan-Ude has several agencies happy to sell you Buryatiya and Baikal tours. English is often spoken.

★**Baikal Naran Tour** TOURS
(☎3012-215 097; www.baikalnaran.com; Office 105, Hotel Buryatiya, ul Kommunisticheskaya 47a) There's nothing director Sesegma (aka Svetlana) can't arrange for travellers in Buryatiya. An award-winning tour company and by far the best folks to approach if you want to see the republic's more remote corners, Old Believers' villages, the Selenga Delta, the Barguzin Valley and the region's Buddhist and shamanist heritage.

Denis Sobnakov TOURS
(☎8-950-391 6325; www.burtour.com; ul Lenina 63) English-speaking Denis and his deputy Ivan run the city's best hostel as well as fun-packed walking tours of UU and many other Buryatiya-wide trips, including those to famous *datsany*, Old Believers' villages and beauty spots on Baikal. Denis has also started guiding groups along the entire Trans-Siberian route and in European Russia.

Sleeping

★**Ulan-Ude Travellers House** HOSTEL $
(☎8-950-391 6325; www.uuhostel.com; ul Lenina 63, apt 18; dm ₽500-650; 📶) So central is this high-ceilinged apartment hostel, you might even catch a glimpse of Lenin's conk from one of the windows. The 14 beds are divided between two spacious, ethnically themed dorms (Russian and Buryat), there's a small kitchen where a free light breakfast is laid out daily, and heaps of UU information is pasted on the walls.

There's also a washing machine for guests to use. The exceptionally friendly owner, Denis Sobnakov, is in and out of town these days, but the place runs like a well-oiled machine and his staff are just as helpful in setting up trips to Baikal and around Buryatiya.

Hotel Ulan HOTEL $$

(☎3012-551 110; ul 50-letiya Oktyabrya 32; s/d ₽1400/2100) This tiny hotel, with 10 comfortable rooms on the 1st floor of a Soviet apartment block (entrance at the back of the building), is good value for money. The location is not central, but a short tram ride from the main square. Receptionists put on funny folk costumes when they serve breakfast in your room in the morning.

Hotel Shumak HOTEL $$

(☎8-902-160 8181; http://гостиницашумак.рф/; ul Revolyutsii 1905 goda 32; s/d ₽2000/2300) Sleeping on a comfy bed amid a wood-dominated interior, you may very well forget it's just another apartment-block hotel in a not-so-pretty location. But being so close to both the train station and the centre makes it good value for money.

Hotel Ayan HOTEL $$

(Отель Аян; ☎3012-415 141; www.ayanhotel.ru; ul Babushkina 164; s/d ₽850/1700; ❄📶) The inconvenient location 2km south of the city centre is more than recompensed by pristine international-standard rooms, some with air-conditioning. The cheapest singles are a good deal and every room has its own water heater. There's also a tiny cafe should you get peckish from all the stair climbing you'll do here – incredibly, this six-storey new-build has no lift.

A taxi from the train station costs around ₽170 or arrange a ₽300 private transfer with the hotel.

Mergen Bator HOTEL $$$

(Отель Мэргэн Батор; ☎3012-200 002; www.mergen-bator.ru; ul Borsoyeva 19b; tw/d ₽6200/7000; ❄📶) UU's only 21st-century hotel is a swish pad indeed and completely on a par with any Western four-star establishment. From the trendy retro-veneered corridors to the commendably equipped fitness centre, the modern-as-tomorrow bathrooms to the impeccable service, this place is worth splashing out on. Breakfast is included and can be served in your room free of charge.

Hotel Sagaan Morin HOTEL $$$

(Отель Сагаан Морин; ☎3012-444 019; www.sagaan-morin.ru; ul Gagarina 25; s/d from ₽3800/4800; 📶) The gleaming 17-storey, 89-room 'White Horse' offers spacious, crisply designed, almost understated rooms, lots of amenities and a 14th-floor restaurant (Panorama) with look-while-you-eat city vistas.

Eating

Ul Kommunisticheskaya, ul Sverdlova and the surrounding streets are packed with (sometimes very) basic dumpling canteens. For a fascinating insight into traditional Buryat life, Baikal Naran Tour (p199) can arrange dinner in a yurt with a local family out in the suburbs of Ulan-Ude.

Sputnik Supermarket SUPERMARKET

(Супермаркет Спутник; ul Kommunisticheskaya 48; ⏲24hr) A convenient but pricey supermarket stocking foreign groceries.

Shenekhenskiye Buuzy BURYAT $

(☎8-902-565 2862; www.vk.com/shenexen; ul Sverdlova 20; mains ₽120-200; ⏲8.30am-8pm) This heritage wooden *izba* painted in a rather psychedelic shade of green is a local

BURYAT CULTURE

Indigenous ethnic Buryats are a Mongol people who comprise around 30% of Buryatiya's population, as well as 65% of the former Agin-Buryat Autonomous District southeast of Chita. Culturally there are two main Buryat groups. During the 19th century, forest-dwelling western Buryats retained their shamanic animist beliefs, while eastern Buryats from the southern steppes mostly converted to Tibetan Buddhism, maintaining a thick layer of local superstition. Although virtually every Buryat *datsan* was systematically destroyed during the communists' antireligious mania in the 1930s, today Buryat Buddhism is thriving. Many *datsany* have been rebuilt and seminaries for training Buddhist monks now operate at Ivolga and Aginskoe.

The Buryat language is Turkic, though very different from Tuvan and Altai. Dialects vary considerably between regions but almost everyone speaks decent, if heavily accented, Russian. Mongolians claim some Buryat dialects resemble their medieval tongue.

For the predeparture lowdown, check out Buryatiya's official English-language tourism website (www.visitburyatia.ru) and the government website (http://egov-buryatia.ru/eng/), which has English-language tourist information.

institution run by Buryats who have been returning from Chinese exile in recent decades. They are widely considered as keepers of the *buuzy* golden standard. Order at the counter telling how many dumplings you want. Korean fern salad is our preferred side dish.

Shashlykoff GRILL $
(Шашлыкофф; ☎3012-222 288; http://shashlikoff.com; ul Lenina 52; mains ₽200-250; ⏰10am-3am) A nationwide chain run by a national culinary show celebrity, Shashlykoff wins the battle for the hearts and stomachs of young Buryatians with the simple barbecue+beer formula, with homemade brew going as cheap as ₽73 per pint. The place is always heaving and getting a table can be challenging at dinner time.

Myasoroob BURGERS $
(Мясоруб; ☎8-983-438 5386; www.facebook.com/myasoroob03; ul Sukhe-Batora 7; burgers ₽250-350; ⏰11am-11pm) Lumbersexual butchers seduce Buryatiya with nine kinds of gourmet burgers, craft beer and their trademark ginger *mors* (berry drink). A nice place for a quick lunch in the company of gadget-wielding hipsters.

Orda BURYAT $$
(Орда; ☎3012-403 838; www.orda03.ru; ul Pushkina 4a; mains ₽500-1300; ⏰noon-2am) An aspiring centre of Buryat cultural renaissance, the 'Horde' elevates coarse nomad cuisine to haute levels. Yes, it is largely meat with more meat and some onions, but the chef knows how to make lamb and even horse meat pieces as tender as spring artichokes. Frequent dinnertime concerts by famous Buryat musicians, including throat-singing artists, cost an extra ₽500 to ₽1000.

Baatarai Urgöö BURYAT $$
(www.baikalkhan.ru; Barguzinsky Trakt, Verkhnyaya Berezovka; mains ₽300-450; ⏰11am-11pm; 📶) This yurt complex in the Verkhnyaya Berezovka suburb is a great lunch spot after a visit to the Ethnographical Museum. Take a seat in the main tent and give your taste buds the Buryat treatment in the form of *buuzy* (meat-filled dumplings), *bukhuler* (meat broth) and a glass of *airag* (fermented mare's milk). Take *marshrutka* 37 from pl Sovetov to the yurt stop.

The dining space is decorated with suits of Mongol armour, traditional *buryat* furniture and folk costumes, and the serving staff are also dressed the part.

Modern Nomads MONGOLIAN $$
(ul Ranzhurova 1; mains ₽400-700; ⏰11am-11pm) Clean-cut and very popular Mongolian place, good for a quick snack and a beer or for a full-blown dinner splurge costing thousands. Meat features heavily on the menu, but there are many veggie-friendly salads and other dishes with a contemporary twist to choose from, too.

Chay Khana UZBEK $$
(Чай Хана; Evropa Business Centre, ul Baltakhinova; mains ₽250-590; ⏰11am-midnight Mon-Thu, to 2am Fri, 1pm-2am Sat, to midnight Sun) This high-perched Uzbek restaurant has a triangular cushion-scattered dining space, trendy oriental fabrics and a menu of exotic *plov*, grilled meats and imaginative salads. But it's the spectacular views of UU and the Selenga valley that are the real showstopper here, best enjoyed from the summer terrace. Take the lift to the 9th floor, then the stairs.

The business centre building is nicknamed 'the toilet' – you'll soon see why.

Drinking & Nightlife

Bar 12 BAR
(12th fl, Mergen Bator Hotel, Ul Borsoyeva 19b; ⏰24hr) Capping off the Mergen Bator (p200) hotel, this bar probably offers the best views of any in Russia: the entire Buryat capital and the surrounding mountainscape are laid out dramatically below you. The bar's party piece is to rotate through 360 degrees every 30 minutes, meaning you see the entire panorama without leaving your seat.

Macondo Coffee & Store COFFEE
(ul Lenina 26) A bric-a-brac shop attached to the city museum comes with a hobbit-sized coffee bar that provides a welcome respite from dust, railway slime and instant coffee. It also brews by far the best latte this side of Khamar-Daban. Note the Gabriel García Márquez reference in the name.

Bisquit CAFE
(Бисквит; ul Sukhe-Batora 7; ⏰11am-midnight) A stylish coffee-shop-cum-bar with bare brick walls and leather couches serves as coffee ambassador to Asian tea lands. Food is also available. A giant mirror at the entrance is handy for morning arrivals to examine damage after days on the train.

Churchill PUB
(Черчилль; www.pubchurchill.ru; ul Lenina 55; ⏰noon-2am) A bekilted Scottish piper (well, a bagpiping dummy at least) greets you at

the door of this relatively upmarket British-themed pub. The Brit paraphernalia extends throughout the two stylishly finished halls, the food is tasty and there's an international draught beer menu at central London prices.

Shopping

Zam GIFTS & SOUVENIRS

(Зам; www.vk.com/zamspace; ul Sukhe-Batora, 16a; ⌚10am-7pm) This sparkling new shop doubles as a Buryat culture centre that runs lectures and masterclasses in traditional crafts. Goods include stylish jewellery by local artists, folk-themed clothes, locally produced leather bags and shoes. A little coffee bar attached to the counter comes as a bonus.

Orda Ethno-Market ARTS & CRAFTS

(☎3012-441 001; http://ordagallery.ru/; ul Pushkina 4a; ⌚10am-7pm) Sometimes moving, sometimes kitschy modern Buryat art, clothes and souvenirs. Buddhist-themed metal sculpture contains some of the most striking items.

Dombo GIFTS & SOUVENIRS

(Домбо; www.facebook.com/dombo.buryatia; ul Sukhe-Batora 16a; ⌚10am-1pm & 2-6.30pm Mon-Sat) Elegant artisanal ceramics by Ayuna Dorzhieva, who fuses Buryat motifs with modern art.

Central Market MARKET

(ul Baltakhinova; ⌚9am-8pm) Tidy, Soviet-era market selling unusual local produce such as pine nuts, reindeer meat, buckthorn juice, *salo* (raw pig fat) and seasonal fruit and veg. At the back of the building are several stores offering *unty,* beautifully decorated reindeer skin boots. Prices start from around ₽12,000 a pair.

ULAN-UDE TO ULAANBAATAR

With flights between the two capitals once again grounded, there are just two ways to travel from Ulan-Ude to Ulaanbaatar, Mongolia. The least comfortable way is by Trans-Mongolian train, which takes between 15 and 23 hours to complete the 657km trip. A much cheaper and convenient way to go is to hop aboard the daily coach (₽1500, 10 hours), which leaves from the main bus station in Ulan-Ude. Tickets can be bought from **Baikal Naran Tour** (p199) and the **Ulan-Ude Travellers House** (p199).

Information

Handy ATMs can be found in the Buryatiya hotel and at the train station.

Post Office (ul Lenina 61; ⌚8am-10pm Mon-Fri, 9am-6pm Sat & Sun; 📶)

Tourism Portal (www.uutravel.ru) Official tourism website with a smattering of interesting information in English.

Visit Buryatiya (☎3012-210 332; www.visit-buryatia.ru) Official tourist board, which runs a summertime-only yurt-based information office on pl Sovetov.

Getting There & Away

TRAIN

When travelling to Irkutsk, take a day train for superb views of Lake Baikal.

Ulan-Ude has the following rail connections:

Běijīng *kupe* ₽15,000 to ₽19,000, 43 to 61 hours, two weekly

Chita *platskart/kupe* ₽1800/₽2600, 10 to 12 hours, up to six daily

Irkutsk *platskart/kupe* ₽1600/₽2500, seven to nine hours, up to nine daily

Ulaanbaatar *kupe* ₽4900, 15 or 23 hours, daily

AIR

UU's **Baikal Airport** (www.airportbaikal.ru), 11km from the city centre, handles surprisingly few flights. Buy tickets at the **Central Ticket Office** (ul Erbanova 14; ⌚9am-7pm) or **S7 Airlines** (ul Lenina 63; ⌚9am-7pm). Ulan-Ude has the following flight connections:

Irkutsk ₽3400, five weekly

Moscow ₽16,000, at least two daily

BUS

Ulan-Ude's **Selenga bus station** (Автовокзал Селенга; http://03bus.ru; ul Sovetskaya 1) is a tiny but user-friendly affair located to the west of pl Sovetov. Buy all tickets at least a day in advance. The useful Russian-language website http://03bus.ru updates schedules and prices for destinations all over Buryatiya. Services include Barguzin (₽660, seven hours, three daily) and Ust-Barguzin (₽530, six hours, twice daily).

Additional *marshrutky* to Irkutsk (₽1000, eight hours) and Chita (₽1430, seven hours) run from the train-station forecourt, departing throughout the day when full.

Minibuses run from pl Banzarova to Ivolga, where you can change for Ivolginsk *datsan*.

Getting Around

From pl Sovetov *marshrutky* 28, 55 and 77 run a few times hourly to the airport, while *marshrutka* 37 passes the hippodrome, the **Ethnographic Museum** and Baatarai Urgöö restaurant.

Marshrutka 97 climbs to the Rinpoche Bagsha Datsan.

Around Ulan-Ude

You could spend a week making day trips out of Ulan-Ude to explore Buddhist temples, Old Believers' villages and forgotten border settlements. The main routes south are the scenic Ulan-Ude–Kyakhta road, which hugs the Selenga River for much of the way, and the Trans-Mongolian Railway, which crosses the border at the unremarkable railway town of Naushki. Note that both Naushki and Kyakhta are officially off limits to foreigners as they fall within the border zone. Permits to visit these places should be arranged through UU agencies at least two months before you travel.

DATSAN

Ivolginsk (Ivolga) Datsan TEMPLE

(Иволгинский дацан; ⏲premises dawn-dusk, temples 8am-5pm) The confident epicentre of Russian Buddhism owes its existence to none other than Josef Stalin, who reversed the Bolshevik policy of destroying temples and allowed it to be built, in a plot of marshy land 35km from Ulan-Ude, in gratitude to the Buryats for their sacrifices during WWII. The first temple was a modest affair, but today the *datsan* has grown large and is expanding fast. Pilgrims and tourists flock here on half-day trips from the Buryat capital.

The Ivolginsky *datsan* was one of only two working Buddhist temples in Soviet days (the other was at Aginskoe); most of what you see today has been built in the last two decades. A clockwise walk around the complex takes in countless monastery faculties, administrative buildings, monks' quarters and temples, but the most elaborate of all is the **Itygel Khambin Temple** honouring the 12th Khambo Lama, whose body was exhumed in 2002. To general astonishment, seven decades after his death his flesh had still not decomposed. Some 'experts' have even attested that the corpse's hair is still growing, albeit extraordinarily slowly. The body is displayed six times a year, attracting pilgrims from across the Buddhist world.

To reach the monastery, first take *marshrutka* 130 (₽45, 40 minutes, four hourly) from pl Banzarova to the last stop in uninteresting Ivolga. There, another *marshrutka* (₽25, no number, just a picture of the monastery or the word Дацан pasted to the front windscreen) waits to shuttle visitors the last few kilometres to the monastery compound. Otherwise contact agencies in Ulan-Ude, which offer private transfers and tours with well-informed guides.

The daily Gunrig Khural Ritual, which is said to protect participants from bad reincarnations and black magic, is held at 9am.

Tamchinsky Datsan TEMPLE

(Тамчинский дацан) First founded in 1741, this was Buryatiya's first Buddhist monastery and the mother ship of Russian Buddhism for two centuries. The original complex, 160km south of Ulan-Ude, was destroyed in the 1930s and the modern reconstruction is small scale and surrounded by the slowly dying village of Gusinoe Ozero (30km south of Gusinoozersk). View the newly renovated former school of philosophy, test out the amazing acoustics of the main temple and chat with the mobile-phone-toting head lama who, for a donation, may let you camp in the grounds and eat in the small refectory.

To get there, take the 7.24am Naushki train from Ulan-Ude (four hours) and alight at Gusinoe Ozero. A train runs back to Ulan-Ude late afternoon or you could hitch a lift to Gusinoozersk at the opposite end of the lake, from where there are regular *marshrutky* back to Ulan-Ude.

Ulan-Ude to Vladivostok

Includes ➡

Route Info

- Distance: 3648km
- Duration: Two days, 13½ hours
- Time zones: Moscow +5 to Moscow +7

Best Places to Stay

- Hotel Arkadia (p213)
- Hotel Bira (p217)
- Khabarovsk City Boutique Hotel (p220)
- Izba Hostel (p228)

Best Places to Eat

- Muscat Whale (p222)
- Kvartira 30 (p229)
- Food Like Food (p230)
- Cafe Simkha (p217)

Why Go?

The Trans-Siberian's last leg covers a staggering 3648km as it rolls into Russia's 'wild east'. This region has always lived by its own rules. 'Moscow is far' runs the local mantra. The people, like the countryside, are a bit wilder and more rugged than their Western brethren. Travelling this way before the Trans-Siberian was built, Anton Chekhov wrote that it 'seethes with life in a way that you can have no conception of in Europe'. And that's still apt.

Out the window, the taiga and Stalin-era housing blocks may seem similar to those found back west, but off the tracks lurk surprises such as Blagoveshchensk, a border town of tsarist-era buildings on the Amur River; Birobidzhan, Stalin's failed 'Zion'; and the charming riverside city of Khabarovsk. The railway ends at the stunning mountains-meet-ocean setting of Vladivostok, a once-closed navy port that today is Asia's uniquely Russian rising powerhouse.

When to Go

Vladivostok

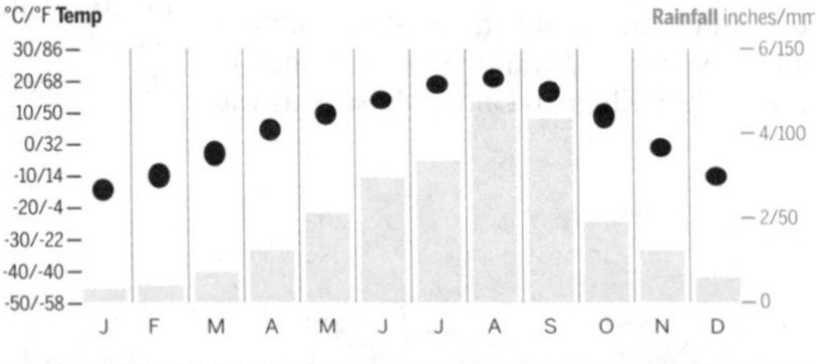

Feb–Mar Still the season for snowy delights, yet not too dark or too slushy.

Jun Essentially midspring, with all the beauty and climatic uncertainty that entails.

Sep–Oct Better weather, more square hectares of autumn foliage than anywhere on earth.

The Route

ULAN-UDE TO CHITA

5655km from Moscow

Trans-Mongolian trains bid farewell to the main Trans-Siberian route at **Zaudinsky**, virtually a suburb of Ulan-Ude. The main line then follows the wide Uda Valley with bare rolling hills visible across the plains. At an unmarked station about half an hour out of Ulan-Ude (before Onokhoi), a marshalling yard serves as a steam-loco graveyard. The scenery here is pretty, as the wide, flood-prone valleys continue, their rolling meadows backed distantly by trees on the north-facing slopes.

5771km

Quaint log-cabin settlements are scattered with patches of attractive woodland. You enter **Zabaikalsky Territory** 20km beyond Novoilyinsky. Local time becomes Moscow time plus six hours.

5784km

Petrovsky-Zavod is the station for Petrovsk-Zabaikalsky. The station name (and the old name of the town) means 'Peter's Factory', so called for the huge ironworks you may spot from the train. Decembrists jailed here from 1830 to 1839 are commemorated in a large mural on the station building. it's, worth getting off to take a snap if there's time (although the Rossiya makes only a two-minute stop here). There's also a good Decembrist Museum not far from the station, and if you're on the Decembrist trail through Siberia the town could make a good off-the-beaten-track day trip from Ulan-Ude. A few minutes out of Petrovsk-Zabaikalsky look out for a cemetery to the right of the tracks where some Decembrists are buried.

5800km to 6300km

The tracks now head northeast following the Khilok Valley, with the **Yablonovy Mountains** forming blue shadows in the distance.

5884km

At the small airbase town of **Bada**, look up from your instant noodles to admire a MiG-fighter monument.

5925km

The train slows as it leaves the valley and climbs into the mountains, affording inspiring views of the winding river and fields filled with wildflowers.

5932km

Khilok is the next major stop, and the station has some art-deco features. Some trains pause here for up to 20 minutes. There is a machine shop for repairing train engines here but little else, as the town is a product of the railway; it even has a yellow Trans-Siberian train hurtling across its coat of arms.

6130km

Soon after Mogzon you will reach the highest point (1040m) on the world's longest rail journey at **Yablonovaya**, where trains pass through a slender gap in the rock.

6198km

Most trains loiter for 25 minutes at Chita, long enough to explore the cathedral in the station forecourt. At the station, fans of the *Long Way Round* TV show will recognise the freight platform where Ewan McGregor et al struggled to heave their bikes aboard a Tynda-bound goods wagon.

CHITA TO MOGOCHA: 6198KM TO 6906KM

For the next 700km or so east the Trans-Siberian route follows the Ingoda and Shilka Rivers. Stay awake, as it's the most scenic part of this entire route. The best views are to the south, so if heading east grab an aisle seat in *platskart* for this part of the journey. But don't ignore the north side of the train with its rolling, colourful hills. Unfortunately, the Rossiya (and the similarly timed 7/8 train) trundles this way by night, so consider other options such as train 133/134, or (when the days are long) 392 from Chita to Blagoveshchensk.

6264km

River views open up around **Darasun**.

ULAN-UDE TO VLADIVOSTOK ROUTE PLANNER

Here's a suggested itinerary for finishing up the Trans-Siberian route from Ulan-Ude to Vladivostok:

Day 1 Take overnight train to Chita (10 hours).

Day 2 Spend the day seeing Chita's sights; night train to Blagoveshchensk (36 hours).

Day 3 On train to Blagoveshchensk.

Day 4 Tour Blagoveshchensk and spend the night.

Day 5 Return to the main Trans-Siberian line and continue to Birobidzhan. Take in the synagogue and riverfront. Later that day head to Khabarovsk by *marshrutka* or commuter train (three hours).

Day 6 Tour Khabarovsk and spend the night.

Day 7 Take an overnight train to Vladivostok (13 hours).

Day 8 Arrive in Vladivostok.

Ulan-Ude to Vladivostok Highlights

1 **Vladivostok** (p223) Discovering the Russian Far East's most interesting and cosmopolitan city.

2 **Khabarovsk** (p218) Enjoying a scenic riverside stroll, admiring grand architecture and then joining in the nightlife of this student town.

3 **Blagoveshchensk** (p215) Taking in exquisite tsarist buildings by the Amur River in this old Russian frontier town.

4 **Birobidzhan** (p217) Exploring the tiny capital of the world's only officially Jewish territory outside Israel.

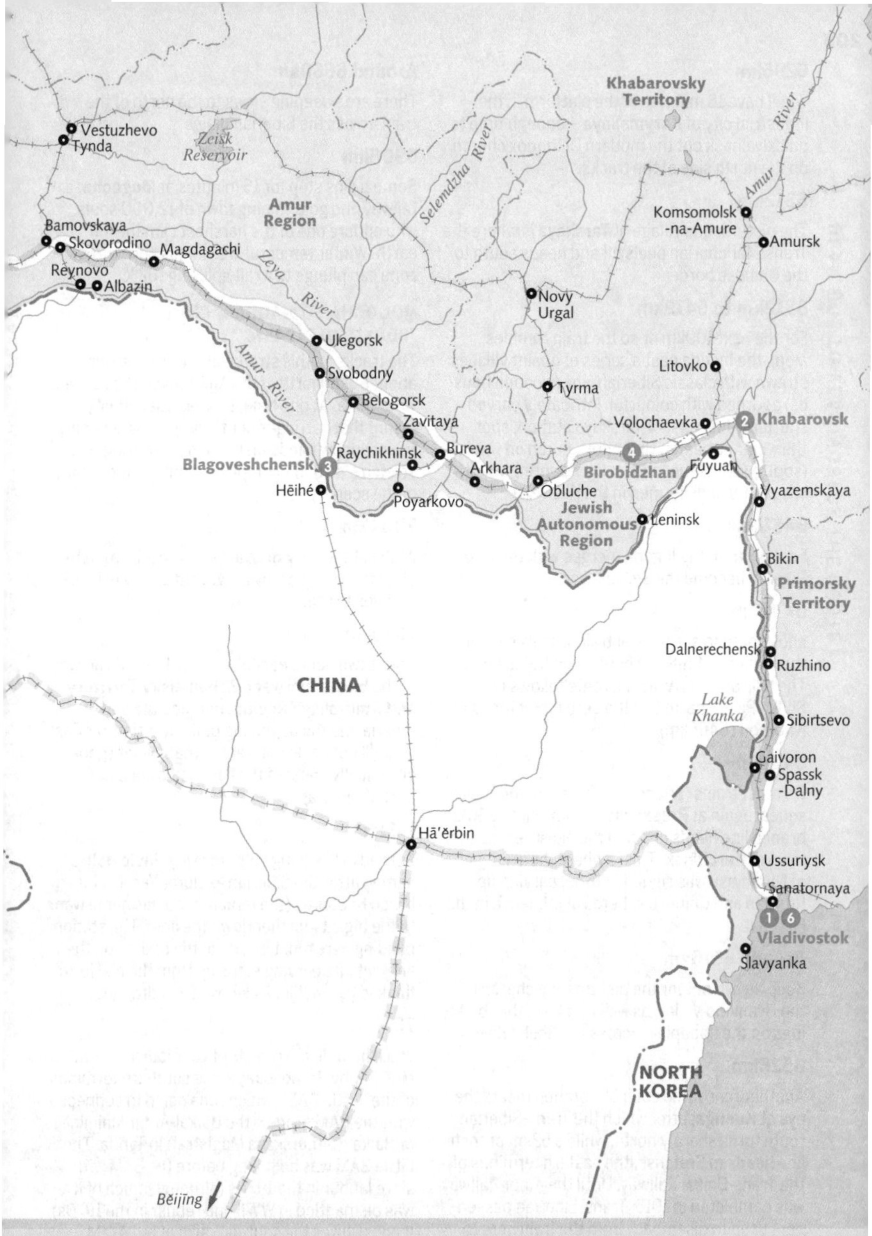

5 Decembrist Museum (p212) Researching banished 19th-century aristocrats at Chita's delightful museum.

6 Zarya Centre for Contemporary Art (p225) Checking out what's on at the Russian Far East's most avant-garde art institution.

7 Tsugol Datsan (p215) Spinning the prayer wheels at the Russian Far East's most impressive Buddhist temple.

6295km

You'll have 18 minutes at the platform in the industrial city of **Karymskaya** – enough time to quickly check out the modern Orthodox church on the north side of the tracks.

6312km

The picturesque village of **Tarskaya** is where the Trans-Manchurian peels off and heads south to the Chinese border.

6312km to 6412km

For the next 100km or so the train rumbles along the Ingoda past a series of quaint villages strewn with classic Siberian *izby* (wooden houses) adorned with colourful, intricately carved shutters. Just east of Tarskaya station, spot the weather-beaten Orthodox church on the far (south) side of the Ingoda. Come spring you'll see plenty of fishermen in the river.

6417km

East of **Onon** the Ingoda merges with the Onon River to become the Shilka River.

6445km

Look south to see piles of train wheels east of the station in **Shilka**, where some trains stop. The hills are pretty, as the route follows the Shilka River, marred by the derelict factories of **Kholbon** (6465km).

6489km

On most trains (but not the Rossiya), the brakes squeal again at **Priiskovaya**, from where a 10km branch line heads north to the old silver-mining town of **Nerchinsk**. This is where the Treaty of Nerchinsk was signed in 1689, carving up Russian and Chinese spheres of influence in the Far East.

Around 6510km

Keep an eye out for the picturesque church in the Byankino Valley, as well as a few other buildings on the floodplain across the Shilka River.

6526km

Another renovated cube of a station meets the eye at **Kuenga**, after which the Trans-Siberian route turns sharply north, while a 52km branch line heads to Sretensk, the eastern terminus of the Trans-Baikal Railway. Until the Amur Railway was completed in 1916, Trans-Siberian passengers used to disembark from the train here to board Khabarovsk-bound steamers.

6587km

Most train services take a lengthy breather at **Chernyshevsk-Zabaikalsky**, giving you time to stock up from the food and drink sellers (unless it's 3am). It's named after the 19th-century exile Nikolai Chernyshevsky, whose silver-painted statue is on the platform.

Around 6660km

There are sweeping views to the north of the train across the Siberian plains.

6906km

Some trains stop for 15 minutes at **Mogocha**, a railway and gold-mining town of 12,000 souls who endure one of the harshest climates on earth. Winter temperatures in this permafrost zone can plunge to a rail-splitting -62°C.

MOGOCHA TO MAGDAGACHI: 7000KM TO 7494KM

The tracks on this stretch of the line run only about 50km north of the Amur River, the border with China. At one time, strategic sensitivity meant that carriages containing foreigners had their window blinds fastened down during this stretch – so don't complain about the monotony of the scenery!

7004km

At the station in **Amazar**, you have a 16-minute stop; there's a nearby graveyard of steam locomotives to see.

7079km

About two hours east of Amazar the train arrives at the **border between Zabaikalsky Territory and Amurskaya Region**, marking the end of Siberia and the beginning of the Russian Far East – you'll notice no difference whatsoever (geographically, most of the Far East is considered part of Siberia).

7111km

Settled in low-lying hills, **Yerofey Pavlovich** is named after the Siberian explorer Yerofey Pavlovich Khabarov (the remainder of his name went to the big city further down the line). The station building here must be one of the oddest on the line, with its curving steps up from the platform flanked by what look like two Lego dragons.

7273km

You'll be well into day six of your journey from Moscow by **Bamovskaya**, the southern terminus of the 'Little BAM', which runs north to connect with the BAM proper (the Baikal-Amur Mainline or Baikalo-Amurskaya Magistral) in Tynda. The Little BAM was built long before the BAM with slave labour in the 1930s (although much of it was dismantled in WWII and rebuilt in the 1970s). It constitutes the southern arm of the AYaM (Amur-Yakutsk Mainline, or Amuro-Yakutskaya Magistral), which extends to Yakutsk in the Sakha Republic (although passenger services only reach Tommot).

7306km

If you plan to head north on the Little BAM, do not get off in Bamovskaya, as few Tynda-bound trains stop there. Instead, connect in **Skovorodino**,

Ulan-Ude to Vladivostok

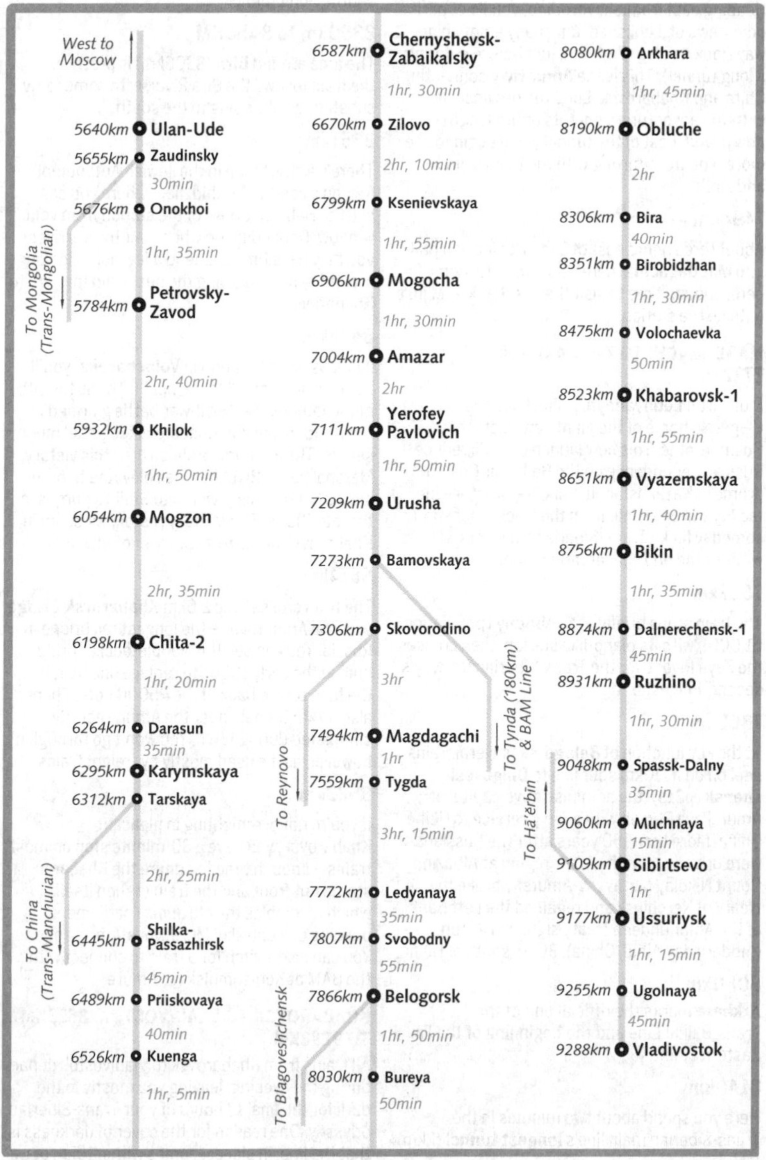

where an impressive Soviet steam locomotive holds court in front of a pretty pink station.

From Skovorodino, a spur line follows the Bolshoi Never River south to Dzhalinda (station name: Reynovo) near **Albazin**, an important Russian outpost on the Amur River in the 17th century and the site of key battles between Cossacks and Manchurians. The final Manchurian siege of the Albazin fort in 1686–87 claimed nearly 800 Russian lives, with only 66 survivors, and led to the signing of the Treaty of Nerchinsk. Colin Thubron writes about the bloodbath and his search for the remnants of the fort in his book *In Siberia*.

7306km to 7450km

Heading east from Skovorodino, you'll get periodic views of a polished, unusually empty highway (look north at 7342km, just before entering a long tunnel). This is the **Amur Hwy** connecting Chita and Khabarovsk. Long the province of extreme adventurers only, its entire length is now paved. East of the tunnel you'll begin to see more pine trees mixing with the taiga's birch and larch.

7494km

About three hours east of Skovorodino you pull into **Magdagachi**. There's a 15-minute stop here, enough time to visit the Sberbank ATM just outside the station.

MAGDAGACHI TO KHABAROVSK

7772km

From little **Lednyanaya**, a short spur goes to Ulegorsk, home of the giant new Vostochny Cosmodrome. This new launch pad will reduce Russian dependence on the Baikanur Cosmodrome in Kazakhstan. It's unclear whether the facility will be visible from the tracks, but surely someday lucky Trans-Siberian travellers will witness the odd spacecraft launch.

7807km

The train stops briefly at **Svobodny** (population 61,000), with its piano-like station, then crosses the Zeya River over the Trans-Siberian Railway's second-longest bridge.

7866km

At the key junction of **Belogorsk**, several trains peel off on a 110km spur line to **Blagoveshchensk** (p215), the administrative capital of Amurskaya Region with a ferry service to Hēihé, China. More than 150 years after the Russians were driven out of the Amur region at Albazin, Count Nikolay Muravyov-Amursky broke the treaty of Nerchinsk and regained the Left Bank of the Amur under a treaty signed in Argun (modern day Aihui, China), 30km south of Hēihé.

8080km

Arkhara marks the official end of the Trans-Baikal Line and the beginning of the Far Eastern Line.

8140km

Here you spend about two minutes in the Trans-Siberian main line's **longest tunnel** (2km).

8190km

Turn your clocks to Moscow plus seven hours in **Obluche**, where you leave the Amurskaya region and enter the Jewish Autonomous Region. Most trains stop for about 15 minutes here, time enough to admire the art-deco train station and stretch your legs in the leafy park next to the station. Fifteen minutes east of Obluche is another long tunnel.

8350km to 8450KM

The area around **Bira** (8306km) is pretty as the train follows the Bira River, with some fairly substantial hills rising to the south.

8351km

There's a short stop in the Jewish Autonomous Region's capital, Birobidzhan, where you can see the Hebrew letters of the station from your window. Depending on when your train arrives you may have time to spend a few hours looking around before boarding the next train through to Khabarovsk.

8475km

Just east of the station in **Volochaevka**, you'll notice a distinct hill to the north. This is the site of the famous 1922 civil-war battle glorified in the Birobidzhan and Khabarovsk regional museums. The man who orchestrated this victory, Marshal Vasily Blyukher, was elevated to hero status before falling victim to Stalin's purges in the late 1930s. The Military History Museum in Khabarovsk has a great portrait of Blyukher.

8514km

The train crosses the 2.6km **Khabarovsk Bridge** over the Amur River – the longest rail bridge in Russia. You can see this double-decker bridge, built in the early 1990s to replace one built by the tsar, on the back of the ₽5000 note. There's also a 7km tunnel under the Amur, secretly completed during WWII. You won't go through it, however, as it's used mostly by freight trains.

8523km

If you're not overnighting in pleasant Khabarovsk, you have a 30-minute stop on most trains – enough time to admire the Khabarov statue out front and the train station itself, which resembles the old *duma* (parliament) building on central ul Muravyova-Amurskogo. You can also switch for a train to connect with the BAM at Komsomolsk-na-Amure.

KHABAROVSK TO VLADIVOSTOK: 8523KM TO 9288KM

All trains from Khabarovsk to Vladivostok depart during the evening, leaving you mostly in the dark for the final 13 hours of your Trans-Siberian odyssey. One reason for the cover of darkness is that the line, in places, comes within 10km of the sensitive Chinese border.

8606km

Here you cross the **Khor River**, which flows into the Ussuri River on the border of China. The train shadows the Ussuri all the way to Lesozavodsk (8938km).

8651km

Most trains stop for 15 minutes at **Vyazemskaya**, where there will be plenty of people selling bread, salmon caviar, dried fish and pickles. From here the forests are dominated by deciduous trees, such as maple and elm, which briefly blaze in a riot of autumn colours during September.

8756km

You'll probably be settling down for some sleep by the time the train makes a brief stop in **Bikin**. The line crosses the Bikin River here and follows it south to the **border between Khabarovsky and Primorsky Territories** (8780km). The southern forests of the 165,900-sq-km Primorsky Territory are the world's most northerly monsoon forests and home to black and brown bears, the rare Amur (Siberian) tiger and the virtually extinct Amur leopard.

8931km

There's a 12-minute stop in the dead of night at **Ruzhino**.

9010km to 9080km

About 30km either side of **Spassk-Dalny** (9048km), you may be able to make out Lake Khanka, a 4000-sq-km, lotus-covered lake that straddles the China–Russia border.

9177km

At **Ussuriysk**, you can contemplate changing to the branch line west to Hā'ěrbīn (Harbin) in China; the train goes only twice a week and is monotonously slow. Ussuriysk, formerly named Nikolskoe in honour of the *tsarevitch's* 1891 visit, and home to a smattering of historic buildings, was once of greater size and importance than nearby Vladivostok.

9249km

After a week of travel from Moscow, you finally meet the **Pacific Ocean** – in the form of the **Amursky Gulf** – just south of the town of Prokhlodnaya. It should be dawn by now as the train travels south along the hilly peninsula that forms the eastern side of Amursky Gulf, passing a series of beach towns such as **Okeanskaya** (9266km), **Sanatornaya** (9269km) and **Sedanka** (9271km). Further south, Vladivostok rises in a series of concrete tower blocks on the hillsides.

9288km

Your epic journey ends (or begins) on the platform at the station in **Vladivostok** (p223). Before leaving, take a moment to admire the old locomotive on the platform beside the monument commemorating the completion of the great railroad you've just travelled along.

Chita Чита

☎3022 / POP 329,400 / TIME MOSCOW +6HR

Of all Eastern Siberia's major cities, Chita is the least prepared for visitors. It was literally put on the map by the noble-blooded Decembrists, one of whom designed its street-grid layout. Today there's nothing aristocratic about this regional capital where Soviet symbols still embellish Stalinist facades, shaven-headed conscripts guard pillared military headquarters and Chinese cross-border peddlers lug monster bales past a well-tended Lenin statue. Non-Chinese foreigners are still a rarity here; tourism is a thing that happens elsewhere.

Echoes of the Decembrist chapter in Chita's history make the city just worth visiting, and a number of attractive old timber merchants' houses grace its arrow-straight streets. It's also the jumping-off point for important Buddhist sights in the south of Zabaikalsky Territory.

History

Founded in 1653, Chita developed as a rough-and-tumble silver-mining centre until it was force-fed a dose of urban culture in 1827 by the arrival of more than 80 exiled Decembrist gentlemen-rebels – or more precisely, by the arrival of their wives and lovers who followed, setting up homes on what became known as ul Damskaya (Women's St). That's now the southern end of ul Stolyarova, where sadly only a handful of rotting wooden cottages remains amid soulless concrete apartment towers.

As gateway to the new East Chinese Railway, Chita boomed in the early 20th century, despite flirting with socialism. Following the excitement of 1905, socialists set up a 'Chita Republic', which was brutally crushed within a year. After the 'real' revolutions of 1917, history gets even more exciting and complex. Bolsheviks took over, then lost control to Japanese forces who possibly intercepted part of Admiral Kolchak's famous 'gold train' before retreating east. By 1920 Chita was the capital of the short-lived Far Eastern Republic, a nominally independent, pro-Lenin buffer state whose parliament stood at ul Anokhina 63. The republic was absorbed into Soviet Russia in December 1922 once the Japanese had withdrawn from Russia's east coast. Closed and secretive for much of the Soviet era, today Chita is still very much

Chita

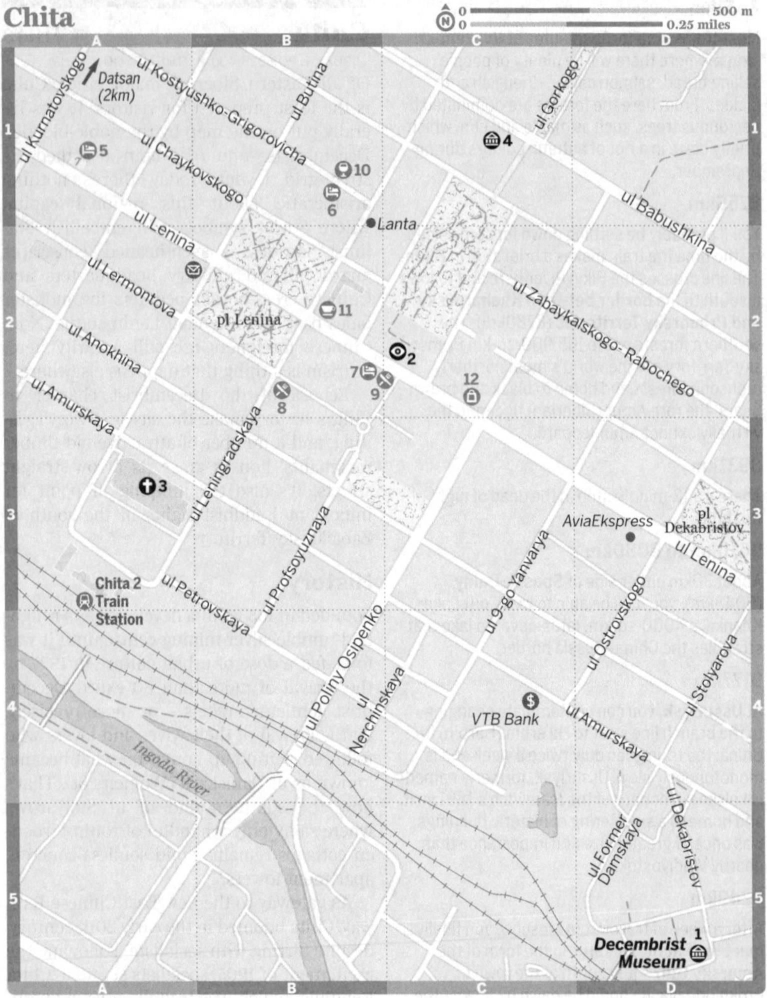

a military city and is once again flooded with Chinese traders.

Sights

★Decembrist Museum MUSEUM
(Музей Декабристов; www.museums75.ru/chitadekabr.htm; ul Selenginskaya; ₽130; ⏲10am-6pm Tue-Sun) If you're on the Decembrist trail through Siberia, this small but comprehensive museum is one of the best. It's housed in the 18th-century **Archangel Michael log church**, an unexpected sight amid the neighbourhood's shambolic apartment blocks. Inextricably linked to the Decembrist story, this was where they came to pray, where Annenkov married his French mistress Pauline Geuble and where the Volkonskys buried their daughter Sofia. Signs are in Russian only, but an English-language audio guide is available for ₽70.

The ground-level exhibition begins with the names of all the Decembrists picked out in gold on a green background, followed by interesting items such as the original imperial order sentencing the noble rebels to banishment in Siberia and oils showing their leaders' executions. The 2nd floor looks at the wives who followed their menfolk into

Chita

the Nerchinsk silver mines and the fates of all the Decembrists once they were allowed to settle where they pleased. Some of them lived long enough to feature as elderly, but rather stylish and optimistic-looking gentlemen, in black-and-white photographs displayed at the end of the exhibition.

Kuznetsov Regional Museum MUSEUM
(Забайкальский краевой краеведческий музей им. А.К. Кузнецова; ☎3022-260 315; www.museums75.ru/museum.htm; ul Babushkina 113; ₽140; ⊙10am-5.45pm Tue-Sun) The unexpectedly lively Kuznetsov Regional Museum has been around since 1895 and the imposing mansion it currently occupies was purpose-built to house it in 1914. The inevitable stuffed animals fill the 1st floor, but it is the collection of Buddhist art and exhibitions dedicated to indigenous Siberians and Russian settlers, both located on the 2nd floor, that attract most visitors. An interesting and politically neutral exhibition telling the gruesome story of Russian Civil War fratricide was added in 2017.

Datsan BUDDHIST TEMPLE
(ul Bogomyagkova 72; ⊙24hr) Chita's main Buddhist temple lies just outside the centre, a 15-minute walk or ₽150 taxi ride along Bogomyagkova from where it meets ul Babushkina. It's a recently built affair, but well-kept, with all its prayer wheels, butter lamps and yin-yang drums firmly in place. The tranquil grounds are home to a tiny *buuzy* (dumpling) joint.

House of Officers ARCHITECTURE
(ul Lenina 88) Striking gilded statues of soldiers adorn this landmark building that defines Chita as a military stronghold on the border with China. Walk through an archway to find yourself in ODORA Park, dotted with vintage military hardware.

Kazansky Cathedral CATHEDRAL
(Казанский кафедральный собор; train station forecourt) The train station reflected in its gilt onion domes, Chita's bright turquoise cathedral is the city's most impressive building, though inside it's lamentably plain. The original pre-Stalin cathedral stood on the main square, right on the spot where Lenin now fingers his lapels.

Sleeping

Chita has little budget accommodation and homestays are nonexistent. Hotels are often full, meaning many travellers who fail to book ahead often have no choice but to check into top-end hotels.

Hotel Arkadia HOTEL $$
(Гостиница Аркадия; ☎3022-352 636; www.arkadiyachita.ru; ul Lenina 120; s/d from ₽2450/3800; 📶) Chita's best deal has well-kept rooms, clean bathrooms, online booking, efficient staff and no-fuss visa registration. Often offers very good rates on popular booking websites.

Gostinny Dom GUESTHOUSE $$
(Гостинный дом; ☎8-914-521 7829; http://gostiniy-dom-chita.hoteloj.ru; ul Kirpichno-Zavodskaya 31a; d/tr from ₽1800/2300; 📶) This log house on the outskirts of Chita has developed a bit of a following with the international biker crowd, particularly Korean and Japanese overlanders. That's partly because the owner is an avid motorcyclist, but more importantly because the place is both quiet and comfortable, perhaps the best value for money in Chita.

No breakfasts served, but there is a kitchen, equipped with a multicooker and a microwave for self-caterers. The centre can be reached by taxi for ₽130 or by *marshrutka* 21 for ₽22.

Hotel Vizit HOTEL $$$
(Гостиница Визит; ☎3022-356 945; www.chitahotelvizit.ru; ul Lenina 93; s/tw ₽3400/6400; ❄📶) Occupying the 5th floor of a smoked-glass

THE DECEMBRIST WOMEN

Having patently failed to topple tsarist autocracy in December 1825, many prominent 'Decembrist' gentlemen revolutionaries were exiled to Siberia. They're popularly credited with bringing civilisation to the rough-edged local pioneer-convict population. Yet the real heroes were their womenfolk, who cobbled together the vast sleigh/carriage fares to get themselves to Siberia.

And that was just the start. Pauline Geubel, the French mistress of one aristocratic prisoner, spent so long awaiting permission to see her lover in Chita that she had time to set up a fashionable dressmakers shop in Irkutsk. By constantly surveying the prisoners' conditions, the women eventually shamed guards into reducing the brutality of the jail regimes, while their food parcels meant that Decembrists had more hope of surviving the minimal rations of their imprisonment. The Decembrist women came to form a core of civil society and introduced 'European standards of behaviour'. As conditions eventually eased, this formed the basis for a liberal Siberian aristocracy, especially in Chita and Irkutsk,where some Decembrists stayed on even after their formal banishment came to an end.

tower at the busy intersection of ul Lenina and ul Profsoyuznaya, this is Chita's best luxury offering with relaxing en-suite rooms, English-speaking receptionists and sparkling bathrooms. Some doubles have baths and the air-con provides relief from Chita's superheated summers.

Hotel Montblanc HOTEL $$$
(☎3022-356 945; www.montblanc.eldonet.ru; ul Kostyushko-Grigorovicha 5; r from ₽4900; ❄📶) A block away from the main square, this purpose-built business hotel has immaculately snazzy rooms, though at these prices the plumbing could be a touch more professional. The buffet breakfast is served in the Ukraine-themed restaurant and check-out time at reception provides an opportunity to witness just how badly Russian and Chinese businessmen can behave.

Eating & Drinking

Privoz CAFETERIA $
(Привозъ; ul Lenina 93; canteen mains ₽90-250; ⏰10am-midnight Sun-Wed, to 1am Thu-Sat) This clean and modern Odessa-themed service canteen serves well-cooked standard Russian fare and features a WWI machine gun on display in the middle of the premises.

Shchastye INTERNATIONAL $$
(Счастье; ☎3022-507 808; http://happiness75.ru; 2nd fl, ul Lenina 93; mains ₽380-580, set-menu lunch ₽350; ⏰1pm-11pm) Happiness (as the name translates) is when you find this oasis of neatness in the middle of a scruffy Siberian city. Soviet-style redneck patrons who inhabit this dollhouse of a place add a comic edge to the picture. The globalist menu includes several kinds of tasty shashlyk and a mean tom yum.

Mama Roma ITALIAN $$
(www.mamaroma.ru; ul Lermontova 9; mains ₽280-500; ⏰11am-10pm) Chequered tablecloths, glass divides, an English menu (!) and pleasant staff make this chain pizzeria an unexpectedly welcoming experience near the train station.

Harat's Pub PUB
(ul Leningradskaya 15a; ⏰noon-2am) Savour the slightly surreal experience of sipping a pint of Newcastle Brown in an Irish pub in Chita, while pondering just where the owners got all those Celtic flags, old US number plates and imitation Tiffany lamps. Friendly service.

Shokoladnitsa CAFE
(ul Leningradskaya 36; ⏰9am-midnight; 📶) This Europeanly stylish, peaceful oasis of a cafe is good for people-watching from the big windows while sipping coffee or tea and making full use of the free wi-fi.

Shopping

Zabaikalsky Khudozhestvenny Salon GIFTS & SOUVENIRS
(Забайкальский художественный салон; ul Lenina 56; ⏰10am-7pm Mon-Fri, to 6pm Sat, 11am-6pm Sun) This huge shop stocks every conceivable souvenir from across the entire Russian Federation, from Buryat dolls to Kostroma linen, Dzhgel plates to Chita fridge magnets. Local artists' work and the owner's photography are also available.

Information

VTB Bank (ВТБ Банк; ul Amurskaya 41; ⏰9am-6pm Mon-Fri) Has ATMs and currency-exchange window.

Main Post Office (ul Butina 37; ⌚8am-10pm Mon-Fri, 9am-6pm Sat & Sun) Quaintly spired wooden building.

Getting There & Away

TRAIN

Chita has the following rail connections:

Běijīng *kupe* ₽16,700, 53 hours, weekly

Blagoveshchensk *platskart/kupe* ₽3850/5200, 38 hours, two daily

Khabarovsk *platskart/kupe* ₽4900/6500, 43½ hours, two daily

Tynda *platskart/kupe* ₽3100/5000, 27 hours, every other day

Ulan-Ude *platskart/kupe* ₽1800/2500, 10 to 12 hours, up to six daily

Zabaikalsk *platskart/kupe* ₽1500/2600, 12 hours, daily

AIR

Kadala Airport (www.aerochita.ru) is 15km west of central Chita. Take bus 40 or *marshrutka* 12 or 14. **AviaEkspress** (АвиаЭкспресс; ☎3022-450 505; www.aviaexpress.ru; ul Lenina 55; ⌚8am-10pm) sells tickets for all flights, including the twice-daily service to Moscow (₽16,800).

BUS

The only two services you're likely to need are the *marshrutky* to Aginskoe (₽400, two hours, five daily) and the long-distance minivans to Ulan-Ude (₽1100, seven hours). Both leave from a stop on the train station forecourt.

Blagoveshchensk

Благовещенск

☎4162 / POP 225,000 / TIME MOSCOW +6HR

Located 110km south of the main Trans-Siberian Railway line and on the banks of the Amur River, Blagoveshchensk feels like a bit of a backwater – few visitors make it here. Those that do, find some charming tsarist architecture and a friendly local population who seem simultaneously puzzled and delighted to have visitors.

Across the massive river is modern China in the shape of Hēihé city. The cultural weight of its giant neighbour can be felt throughout Blagoveshchensk – Chinese restaurants, street signs, tourists and business people are ubiquitous and it's fair to say that the city looks far more to the south than it does towards Moscow.

Sights & Activities

Amur Regional Museum MUSEUM
(Амурский областной краеведческий музей; www.museumamur.org; ul Lenina 165; ₽300; ⌚10am-6pm Tue, Wed & Fri, 10am-9pm Thu, 10am-7pm Sat & Sun) Housed in a former tsarist-era trading house and Soviet-era HQ for the Communist Youth League (Komsomol), this impressive museum has 26 halls containing plenty of interesting photos, 1940s record players and a meteor that fell to earth in 1991 near Tynda. Russian-history buffs will enjoy the model of the 17th-century Cossack fortress in nearby Albazin and a painting depicting the Manchurian invasion of the fort in 1685. Signage is in Russian only.

At the regional museum, pick up the darling *Stary Blagoveshchensk* (Old Blagoveshchensk) map (₽10, in Russian) to plot your own walking tour of the dozens of glorious tsarist-era buildings on shady backstreets around the centre. The most impressive buildings are on ul Lenina within a few blocks of the museum and on and around nearby pl Pobedy.

Anton Chekhov came through Blagoveshchensk during his epic trip through the

OFF THE BEATEN TRACK

TSUGOL DATSAN

Important Buddhist sights are scattered south of Chita in an area that is predominantly populated by ethnic Buryats. Set just 2km from the 'holy' Onon River, **Tsugol Datsan** is surely the most memorable Buddhist temple in Russia. Located in the village of Tsugol, the almost 200-year-old building is extremely photogenic, with gilded Mongolian script-panels, wooden upper facades and tip-tilted roofs on each of its three storeys.

Unfortunately, getting to/from Tsugol is a pain – it lies 13km from Olovyannaya, reachable by a single morning bus from Chita. From Olovyannaya take a taxi (at least ₽500, more if asked to wait) or hike along the river. Alternatively contact Chita-based tour company **Lanta** (Ланта; ☎3022-353 639; www.lanta-chita.ru; ul Leningradskaya 56; ⌚9am-7pm Mon-Fri) who may be able to arrange a trip there for you, although there is no English spoken here.

Far East in 1890 (and headed straight to a Japanese prostitute, as recounted luridly in his later-published letters). A bust commemorating Chekhov's visit is on the facade of the lovely Institute of Geology and Wildlife Management building on pl Pobedy.

River Cruises BOATING
(ul Amurskaya; per person ₽250) One-hour daytime and evening river cruises leave from a pier at the east end of ul Amurskaya from mid-May through September.

Sleeping

Green Hostel HOSTEL $
(☎8-924-841 9008; www.green-hostels.ru; ul Ostrovskaya 65; dm ₽500-700;) This basic and not terribly friendly place has three dorm rooms with lino floors and a shared kitchen. It's just one block east of the bus station and centrally located. It's best to call ahead and let them know you're coming.

Hotel Strannik HOTEL $$
(Отель Странник; ☎4162-490 467; www.strannik-otel.ru; ul Teatralnaya 23; r from ₽3000;) This fun and friendly hotel has a range of fairly eccentrically furnished rooms that are nevertheless very comfortable and clean. Downstairs there's a rather cool restaurant open throughout the day – be sure to behold the wonderfully over-the-top toilets if you visit. There's a 5% reduction if you book via their website.

Hotel Gloria HOTEL $$
(Гостиница Глория; www.hotelamur.com; ul Amurskaya 221; r from ₽3500;) Definitely one of the city's best options, this smart business hotel has large rooms, modern bathrooms and all the creature comforts you'd expect at the upper midrange level. Staff are friendly and efficient, and you're a short walk from the main sights.

Hotel Armenia HOTEL $$
(Гостиница Армения; ☎4162-230 799; www.armeniablag.ru; ul Krasnoflotskaya 147; s/d incl breakfast from ₽2300/3800;) In an ideal location on the riverfront walkway, the flashy Armenia has modern carpeted rooms done up in earthy hues, with flat-screen TVs and luxurious bathrooms. The best rooms have river views. There are several restaurants on-site, including a patio pizza spot and an overdecorated dining room serving excellent Armenian dishes.

Eating

Mega INTERNATIONAL $
(Торгово-развлекательный центр Мега; ul 50 Let Oktyabrya; mains ₽150-400;) Across from the bus station, Mega has a top-floor food court with several cheap fast-food and canteen-style options.

Mandarin CHINESE $$
(Мандарин; ☎4162-331 751; ul 50 Let Oktyabrya 28; mains ₽400-800; 11am-midnight;) There are actually two Chinese restaurants sharing one kitchen here. Mandarin is the quieter and more sophisticated of the two in terms of decor and can be found around the back of the building; Panda, larger and noisier, is the better signposted and most visible from the main avenue.

SharLot Cafe INTERNATIONAL $$
(ul Lenina 113; mains ₽250-650; 9am-midnight;) Low lit and even a little bit stylish, SharLot Cafe has numerous menus, though sadly none of them are currently in English. However, many of them come with photos, so it's easy enough to point at what you want. Dishes range from salads, soups and pasta to meat and fish grills and various desserts.

Kofinya na Bolshoi CAFE $$
(Кофейня на Большой; ul Lenina 159; mains ₽350-750; 8am-1am;) Pleasant cafe with decent cappuccinos and a wide range of dishes including eggs and bliny for breakfast, and risotto and pizzas for later on.

Getting There & Away

Blagoveshchensk is 110km off the Trans-Siberian, reached via the branch line from Belogorsk. The **train station** (ЖД Вокзал; Stationnaya ul) is 4km north of the river on ul 50 Let Oktyabrya, the main north–south artery. Take bus 30 (unless it's heading to 'mikro-rayon') from outside the station down ul 50 Let Oktyabrya to reach the centre.

Trains heading east backtrack to Belogorsk on their way to Khabarovsk (*platskart/kupe* from ₽3050/3700, 13 hours, daily). Heading west, trains serve Chita (*platskart/kupe* ₽3500/4200, 38 hours, even-numbered days) and Tynda (*platskart/kupe* ₽2800/3300, 16¼ hours, odd-numbered days).

Additional options are available from Belogorsk to the north or Bureya to the east. *Marshrutky* connect Blagoveshchensk's **bus station** (автостанция; cnr ul 50 let Oktyabrya & ul Krasnoarmeyska) with the train stations in Belogorsk (₽350, two hours, at least hourly from 7am to 7pm) and Bureya (₽600, 3½ hours, three daily).

The **River Terminal** (Речной вокзал; ul Chaykovskogo 1) sends six daily boats to Hēihé, China (return ₽1650, 15 minutes), from where there's an evening train to Harbin. You'll need a Chinese visa and a multiple-entry Russian visa if you plan to return.

Birobidzhan Биробиджан

☎42622 / POP 74,500 / TIME MOSCOW +7HR

Quiet and shady, Birobidzhan is the rather unlikely capital of the Jewish Autonomous Region, a curious creation of Stalin designed to give Soviet Jews a homeland back in 1934 and which today remains the world's only officially Jewish territory outside Israel.

That the region failed to thrive is hardly surprising, given its swampy location, poor climate and the Stalin-sponsored waves of anti-Semitism that characterised the dictator's later years. But somehow, despite having just a tiny number of Jews living here, Birobidzhan retains a few hints of its Jewish heritage and is a pleasant and unusual place to get off and wander around on your way along the Trans-Siberian.

History

The Soviet authorities conceived the idea of a homeland for Jews in the Amur region in the late 1920s and founded the Jewish Autonomous Region in 1934, with its capital at Birobidzhan (named for the meeting place of the Bira and Bidzhan Rivers). Most of the Jews came from Belarus and Ukraine, but also from the US, Argentina and even Palestine. The Jewish population never rose above 32,000, and dropped to 17,500 by the end of the 1930s, when growing anti-Semitism led to the banning of Yiddish and synagogues.

The Jewish population rose gradually to about 22,000 by 1991, before Russia's Jews began emigrating en masse to Israel. The Jewish population has since dropped to around 3000 these days, and while there are a few monuments and some street names still given in Yiddish alongside Russian, there's otherwise almost no hint of Birobidzhan's fascinating and bizarre origins as you walk around the town. For further reading, Masha Gessen's account of the Jewish Autonomous Region's history *Where the Jews Aren't* is highly recommended.

Sights

Just a few vestiges of Birobidzhan's Jewish heritage remain. Note the Yiddish signs on the train station, the lively farmers market, and the post office on the riverfront at the southern terminus of ul Gorkogo. On the square in front of the train station a statue commemorates Birobidzhan's original Jewish settlers.

Freud SYNAGOGUE
(Биробиджанская еврейская религиозная община Фрейд; ☎42622-41 531, 8-924-642 8731; ul Lenina 19; ⌚9am-5pm Mon-Fri) A five-minute walk west from the centre on ul Lenina is a complex containing Birobidzhan's Jewish culture centre, Freud, and a synagogue with a small Jewish history museum inside. Call or ask around for Rabbi Roman Isakovich, who will give you a tour of the complex, talk about local history or find you a souvenir yarmulke (skullcap).

Regional Museum MUSEUM
(Областной краеведческий музей; ul Lenina 25; ₽100; ⌚10am-6pm Wed-Fri, 9am-5pm Sat) This museum has an excellent exhibit on the arrival of Jewish settlers to Birobidzhan in the 1930s, plus boars and bears and a mini-diorama of the Volochaevka civil war battle.

Sholem Aleichem Statue STATUE
(Памятник Шолом-Алейхему; ul Sholom-Aleykhema) Surrounded by trees on the pedestrian stretch of ul Sholom-Aleykhema is this quirky statue of Sholem Aleichem, whose much-loved Yiddish shtetl tales became the basis for *Fiddler on the Roof*.

Sleeping & Eating

Resting Rooms HOSTEL $
(Комнаты отдыха; ☎42622-91 605; train station; dm per 12-/24-hr from ₽660/1320, lyux ₽915) These simple train station rooms are probably the best option for a quick visit. It's an easy walk from the centre.

★**Hotel Bira** HOTEL $$
(Гостиница Бира; ☎42622-77 778; www.bira-hotel.ru; ul Sovetskaya 21; r from ₽2900; ❄📶) Easily the pick of the hotels in Birobidzhan, the Bira is modern, with large and comfortable rooms that have fridges and safes as well as the more standard appliances. There's a sauna on-site as well as a billiards room, and the location is good.

Cafe Simkha JEWISH $$
(Кафе Симха; ul Lenina 19; mains ₽300-600; ⌚10am-11pm; 📶) With its Star of David light fittings and multiple types of hummus on the menu, Cafe Simkha is in it to win it as

Birobidzhan's premier Jewish restaurant, even if much of its menu is Italian. It's also definitely the smartest place in town, bordering on the flouncy, but the food is tasty and good value.

Felicita CAFE $$

(ul Gorkogo 10; mains ₽250-750; ⏲10am-midnight; 📶) A short stroll from the train station, Felicita is an attractive, Italian-themed cafe, with coffee, salads, light meals and pizzas.

ℹ Getting There & Away

As a town on the Trans-Siberian, Birobidzhan is most commonly reached by train. It's just three hours from Khabarovsk or 10 hours from Blagoveshchensk. Coming from the west, you can easily stop off at Birobidzhan, have a look around and then grab a later train or bus for Khabarovsk.

While all Trans-Siberian trains stop at Birobidzhan **train station** (ЖД вокзал; Privokzalnaya pl), if you're heading to Khabarovsk, it's actually cheaper on the *elektrichka* (suburban train; ₽330, three hours, six daily).

You can also catch *marshrutky* to Khabarovsk (₽350, three hours, hourly until 6pm) from the small **bus station** (автостанция) beside the train station.

Khabarovsk Хабаровск

☎4212 / POP 607,000 / TIME MOSCOW +7HR

The Far East's most pleasant surprise, Khabarovsk boasts a dreamy riverside setting, vibrant nightlife, lots of greenery and boulevards lined with pretty tsarist-era buildings. It's something of a revelation if you're arriving on the train from Siberia to see such a pleasant and thriving place after days of relentless taiga.

Khabarovsk's trump card is its well-developed riverside park, which includes pleasant walkways through the trees, some lovely viewpoints and a popular town beach where people swim in the Amur River during the summer months.

It's hot in summer, but winter temperatures give it the unglamorous title of 'world's coldest city of over half a million people'. A dazzling display of ice sculptures occupies central pl Lenina from January until the spring thaw.

History

Khabarovsk was founded in 1858 as a military post by Eastern Siberia's governor-general, Count Nikolai Muravyov (later Muravyov-Amursky), during his campaign to take the Amur back from the Manchus. It was named after the man who got the Russians into trouble with the Manchus in the first place, 17th-century Russian explorer Yerofey Khabarov, of whom a statue stands outside the train station today.

The Trans-Siberian Railway arrived from Vladivostok in 1897 and quickly heralded the development of Khabarovsk from a small town to a medium-sized city. During the Russian Civil War (1917–22), the town was occupied by Japanese troops. The final Bolshevik victory in the Far East was at Volochaevka, 45km west.

In 1969 Soviet and Chinese soldiers fought a bloody hand-to-hand battle over little Damansky Island in the Ussuri River. Since 1984, tensions have eased. Damansky and several other islands have been handed back to the Chinese.

👁 Sights

Walking is the main activity in Khabarovsk: head to the fabulous riverfront and the green walkways that run up the middle of both Amursky bul and Ussuriysky bul, either side of ul Muravyova-Amurskogo. The busy main drag ul Muravyova-Amurskogo has impressive turn-of-the-20th-century architecture including the striking **Far Eastern State Research Library** (Дальневосточная государственная научная библиотека; ul Muravyova-Amurskogo 1), the mint-green painted **Tsentralny Gastronom** (ul Muravyova-Amurskogo 9) topped by a statue of Mercury, and the former **House of Pioneers** (Дом пионеров; ul Muravyova-Amurskogo 17), now a 'palace of childhood creation'.

Khabarovsk Regional Museum MUSEUM

(Хабаровский краевой музей; www.hkm.ru; ul Shevchenko 11; ₽350; ⏲10am-6pm Tue-Sun) Located in an evocative 1894 red-brick building, this museum contains an excellent overview of Russian and Soviet history, despite not having a single word of non-Russian signage. Galleries take you decade by decade through the past with fascinating propaganda posters, old film clips, audio snippets, black-and-white photos (like the sad crowds gathered at the announcement of Stalin's demise) and rooms with period furnishings and accoutrements that give a taste of what life was like.

There's even a small section devoted to the Gulag (fitting, since the nearby prison population was bigger than the city's in the

1930s). Another section has garments, sleds and carvings of native peoples. The less intriguing new building has a wing dedicated to the Amur River, with live fish in tanks, and more stuffed animals.

Assumption Cathedral CATHEDRAL
(Градо-Хабаровский Успенский собор; Komsomolskaya pl) Built in 2002 this striking cathedral rose on the site of a far older church that was knocked down by Stalin during his antireligious campaigns.

Transfiguration Cathedral CATHEDRAL
(Спасо-Преображенский собор; ul Lenina) This highly impressive church's golden domes dazzle you from all over the city, with its prime location overlooking the Amur River. The cathedral was built in the early 21st century and is the third tallest church in Russia, topping off at 96m. Inside there's one massive central iconostasis, but otherwise it's almost entirely bare.

Archaeology Museum MUSEUM
(Музей Археологии; ☎4212-24 177; ul Turgeneva 86; ₽250; ⊙10am-6pm Tue-Sun) Undergoing a full renovation in 2017, this five-room museum displays tools and living essentials from early peoples. Pottery, animal-skin huts, dugout canoes, a tiny model settlement and many early hand tools are all normally here, though it was unclear how much of the original exhibit would remain on display when the museum reopens.

WWII Memorial MONUMENT
(ul Lenina) This impressive brutalist memorial to the Soviet Army's losses during WWII stands on a hillside overlooking the river.

Far Eastern Art Museum MUSEUM
(Дальневосточный художественный музей; ul Shevchenko 7; Tue-Fri/Sat & Sun ₽250/300; ⊙10am-6pm Tue-Sun) This smart and imposing building hosts a moderately interesting collection of local art, including religious icons, Japanese porcelain and 19th-century Russian paintings.

Activities & Tours

The most popular area tour offered by travel agents is to the interesting Nanai village of **Sikachi-Alyan**, where you can view the Sikachi-Alyan petroglyphs – stone carvings supposedly dating back 12,000 years. Hunting and fishing opportunities abound in the wild and woolly Khabarovsk region.

Amur River Cruise BOATING
(river boat landing; cruises from ₽500) Vital to Khabarovsk's rise, the Amur River can be seen on (at times rollicking) party boats. Cruises on the *Moskva-81* depart every two hours from 12.30pm to 12.30am, provided enough customers show up.

Sergey Outfitter TOURS
(Туристическая компания Вэлком; ☎4212-735 990, 8-914-542 1331; www.sergoutfitter.com; Office 1, ul Dzerzhinskogo 24) Burly Sergei Khromykh is your man if you are looking to do some hunting or fishing in the vast wilderness of Khabarovsk Territory or elsewhere in the Far East. Call ahead to arrange for an English-speaking guide.

Portal Sezonov TOURS
(Портал Сезонов; ☎4212-389 288; www.dvtravel.ru; ul Leningradskaya 58) Located in the train station, the respected Portal Sezonov runs a wide range of tours, including hiking and fishing trips, as well as city tours. English-speaking guides available.

Sleeping

Like Hostel Khabarovsk HOSTEL $
(Лайк Хостел Хабаровск; ☎8-924-403 4194; www.likehostels.ru; flat 20, entrance 2, ul Muravyova-Amurskogo 50; dm/s/d ₽590/1500/2000; ❄📶) This pleasant place has a fantastic location on the main avenue and is housed in a large apartment now divided into male and female dorms and a couple of private rooms. There's a kitchen and small communal area, but no English-speaking staff. Enter the courtyard of the building from ul Sheronova, look for entrance 2 in the corner and dial '20'.

Kakadu Hostel HOSTEL $
(☎4212-788 095; www.kakaduhostel.ru; entrance 1, ul Sheronova 10; dm ₽650, d with/without bathroom ₽2200/1600; ❄📶) This friendly and colourful hostel has pleasant male and female dorms, cosy private rooms, helpful staff and a clear sign visible from the main road. There's a kitchen and communal lounge, free laundry and English is spoken. Get directions before setting out.

From the airport take *marshrukta* 80 to the Volocvhayevskaya stop. From the train station take trams 1, 2 or 6 to the Ussuriyskaya stop.

★ **Hostel Valencia** GUESTHOUSE $$
(☎8-914-172 7262; 3rd fl, ul Dzerzhinskogo 21a; s/d/tr/q with shared bathroom from ₽1600/1800/2400/2800; @📶) Named after

Khabarovsk

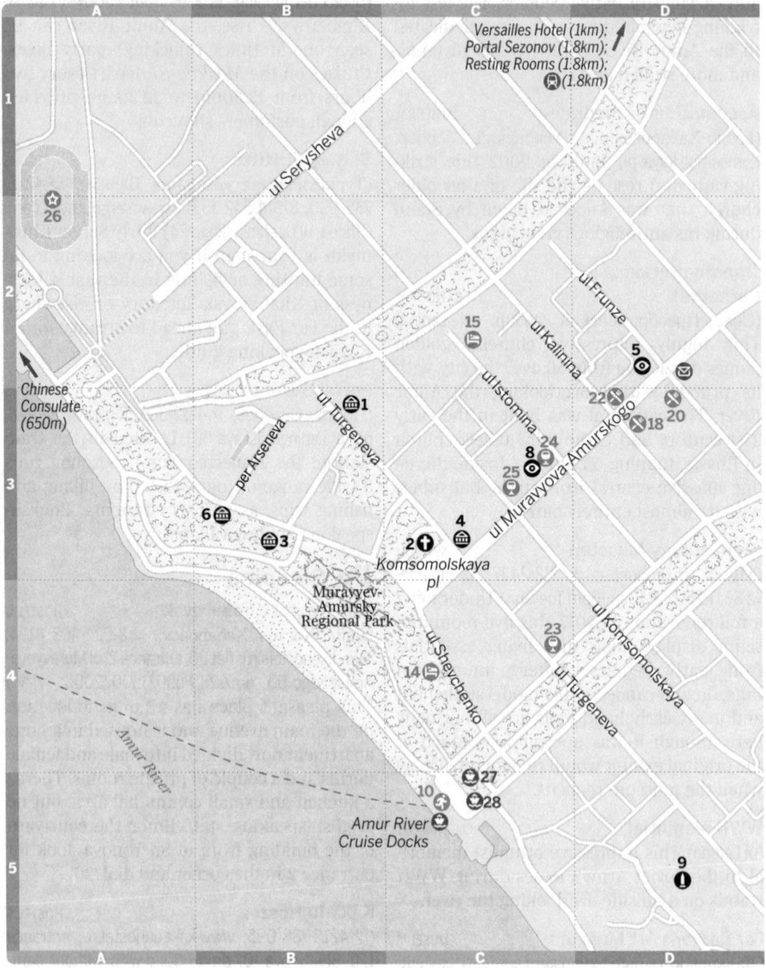

the city where the owners lived for many years, this friendly eight-room guesthouse has bright, attractively designed rooms that are kept sparkling clean. All rooms share bathrooms and toilets, but there's no kitchen and breakfast is not served. It remains a good deal though – find it in the last building in the yard, 75m back from the road.

★ Khabarovsk City Boutique Hotel BOUTIQUE HOTEL **$$$**
(Бутик-отель Хабаровск Сити; ☎4212-767 676; www.boutique-hotel.ru; ul Istomina 64; s/d incl breakfast from ₽3500/4500; ❄@🛜) Khabarovsk's most foreigner-friendly hotel has large, attractive rooms adorned with black-and-white photos from a bygone era. Throw in gorgeous bathrooms with rain showers, luxurious white bedspreads, a full complement of mod cons and a great location, and it's clear this is an excellent pick.

★ Hotel Parus HISTORIC HOTEL **$$$**
(Гостиничный комплекс Парус; ☎4212-335 555; www.hotel-parus.com; ul Shevchenko 5; s/d incl breakfast from ₽4950/6950; ❄@🛜) Part of a century-old brick building near the water, the 82-room Parus is definitely the smartest

Khabarovsk

Sights

1 Archaeology Museum B3
2 Assumption Cathedral C3
3 Far Eastern Art Museum B3
4 Far Eastern State Research Library C3
5 House of Pioneers D2
6 Khabarovsk Regional Museum B3
7 Transfiguration Cathedral E5
8 Tsentralny Gastronom C3
9 WWII Memorial D5

Activities, Courses & Tours

10 Amur River Cruise C5
11 Sergey Outfitter F3

Sleeping

12 Amur Hotel F4
13 Hostel Valencia E3
14 Hotel Parus C4
15 Khabarovsk City Boutique Hotel C2
16 Like Hostel Khabarovsk E2

Eating

17 Farsh E2
18 Muscat Whale D3
19 Plantacia E2
20 Satsivi D3
21 Trattoria Semplice F1
22 Vdrova D3

Drinking & Nightlife

23 Brozbar C4
24 Gatsby C3
25 Harley Davidson Bar C3

Entertainment

26 Lenin Stadium A2

Shopping

Tainy Remesla .... (see 5)

Transport

27 River Terminal C5
28 Sakhekspo C5

and most atmospheric top-end accommodation in Khabarovsk, with its chandeliers, iron staircase, riverside garden and reading room. Rooms are flouncy but sizeable and boast expensive Italian furniture and flat-screen TVs. Friendly, English-speaking service.

Amur Hotel HOTEL **$$$**
(Гостиница Амур; ☎4212-221 223; www.amurhotel.ru; ul Lenina 29; s/d incl breakfast from ₽4000/6000; ❄@📶) Having undergone an impressive renovation, this one-time Soviet place has begun a new life as a stylish and (almost) boutique hotel with a low-lit, arty reception and a totally overhauled restaurant downstairs. The rooms are not as smart as the lobby might suggest, but they are comfy, clean and have ornate moulded ceilings.

Eating

Plantacia CAFE **$**
(Плантация; ul Muravyova-Amurskogo 38; sandwiches ₽100-200; ⌚8am-midnight; 📶) On Khabarovsk's main avenue, this reliable and great-value subterranean spot serves good coffee, baked goods and sandwiches,

making it an ideal breakfast or lunch place. You'll also find local chains Tempo Pizza and Papa Wok, Mama Pasta in the same basement, giving you plenty of culinary variety. It's popular with a young, student crowd.

★**Muscat Whale** ITALIAN $$
(Мускатный кит; ul Kalinina 82; mains ₽400-800; ⏲10am-11.30pm; 📶) This gorgeous, chic, yet pleasantly unfussy, place is currently our top choice for a meal in Khabarovsk. The large and luminous space has white-tiled walls, painted brick and lots of wooden fittings, while its menu boasts wonderful fresh salads, scrumptious pizzas, innovative meat dishes and a huge dessert list.

Vdrova PIZZA $$
(ВДрова; ul Muravyova-Amurskogo 15; mains ₽300-500; ⏲11am-midnight; 📶) Vdrova comes with whimsically dressed Italian-style 'animators' who welcome you loudly, and sing, prance and shout throughout your meal in joyous waves of distraction perfect for anyone who doesn't have much to say to their dinner partner. The pizzas are some of the best in town though, and while many will hate the forced bonhomie, it can be a lot of fun.

Farsh FUSION $$
(Фарш; ul Sheronova 72; mains ₽300-800; ⏲10am-midnight; 📶) Another progressive place with an interesting and pleasingly unusual menu. Farsh dubs itself a gastrobar, but is really more of a fusion place with dishes such as Armenian tortillas filled with cheese, boiled pork salad with grapes in mustard sauce, and shrimp and squid wontons all on the menu. The stripped-down, white-painted walls give it a minimalist feel.

Satsivi GEORGIAN $$
(Сациви; ul Frunze 53; mains ₽200-450; ⏲noon-midnight, until 2am Fri & Sat; 📶📝👪) Despite its fairly unhelpful location in a rather sterile business centre, Satsivi is fiercely popular and puts on a good show of being a traditional Georgian restaurant. Named after a delicious chicken in walnut sauce dish popular in Georgia, Satsivi is a winner and boasts Khabarovsk's best Georgian cooking. The summer terrace is a great alternative to the rather dark main dining room.

Trattoria Semplice ITALIAN $$
(☎4212-206 051; ul Pushkina 54; mains ₽300-500; ⏲11am-11.30pm; 📝) White-painted plank walls, linen curtains and fresh-cut flowers brighten up this downstairs space near pl Lenina. The piping-hot thin-crust pizzas are among the city's best and even a small one can feed two (unless you're famished). The welcome is warm and friendly.

Drinking & Nightlife

Khabarovsk is most definitely a party town, with some of the best nightlife east of the Volga. Most of the action is concentrated along ul Muravyova-Amurskogo and in the side streets at its Amur River end.

★**Gatsby** LOUNGE
(☎4212-604 333; ul Istomina 49; ⏲noon-4am Mon-Thu, to 8am Fri & Sat, 5pm-4am Sun; 📶) Handsomely designed Gatsby has a main-level restaurant and lounge (with good food from ₽300 to ₽800). Downstairs is a swanky bar in one room, with big comfy seats around a horseshoe-shaped bar, and a small dance floor with DJ in another room. It draws a young stylish crowd, but the vibe overall is remarkably welcoming.

Brozbar CRAFT BEER
(Брозбар; ☎4212-204 230; ul Turgeneva 60; ⏲9am-midnight, to 2am Fri & Sat; 📶) With its industrial feel, this new edition to Khabarovsk's busy bar scene is definitely on the edgier side atmosphere-wise (well, at least by local standards). It has a good range of local and international craft beers on sale as well as a full food menu.

Harley Davidson Bar BAR
(ul Komsomolskaya 88; ⏲24hr) Features nightly shows (rock or country bands, cabaret), 10 brews on tap, tattooed bartenders and a long wooden bar. Upstairs is a veranda bar with street views. Cover charge runs ₽300 on weekends, when it's absolutely packed with the cream of Khabarovsk's rocker youth.

☆ Entertainment

Platinum Arena ICE HOCKEY
(Платинум Арена; ☎4212-313 502; www.platinumarena.ru; ul Dikopoltseva 12) This is the home arena for Khabarovsk's ice hockey team, the Amur Tigers, a hot ticket from October to March.

Lenin Stadium FOOTBALL
(Стадион Ленина; Riverfront Sports Complex; tickets from ₽150) Home to Khabarovsk's first-division football team, SKA-Energiya.

Theatre of Musical Comedy THEATRE
(Хабаровский краевой театр драмы и комедии; ☎4212-211 196; ul Karla Marksa 64; tickets ₽100-

1200) Funny operettas run from November to April; big musical acts run from May to October. There's also the occasional ballet.

Shopping

Tainy Remesla GIFTS & SOUVENIRS
(Тайны ремесла; ul Muravyova-Amurskogo 17; 10am-7pm) This is the best souvenir shop in town, located in the old House of Pioneers building.

Information

Post Office (Почта; ul Muravyova-Amurskogo 28; 8am-8pm Mon-Fri, 9am-6pm Sat & Sun)

Getting There & Away

TRAIN

Khabarovsk's **train station** (ЖД вокзал; ul Leningradskaya) is lovely, with a handy supermarket nearby (to the left of the station when exiting). Note that almost all trains to Vladivostok (*platskart/kupe* from ₽1900/2100; 11 to 15 hours, several daily) are overnight.

It's also worth bearing in mind that the westbound/eastbound 1/2 Rossiya train between Moscow and Vladivostok (*platskart* from ₽17,300) is significantly more expensive than all other trains (*platskart* from ₽11,300), and only slightly faster (five days and 12 hours versus six days and three hours). The 7/8 train between Novosibirsk and Vladivostok is also relatively expensive.

For Birobidzhan, take any westbound train or a cheaper *elektrichka* (₽330, three hours, six daily).

AIR

Khabarovsk Novy Airport (4212-262 006; www.airkhv.ru) is 7km east of the train station, and a taxi from the city centre costs around ₽300. This is the best connected airport in the Far East, with flights to cities throughout the region (including a daily service to Seoul and twice weekly to Běijīng), as well as to many other large cities in Russia.

BOAT

Many companies at the **river terminal** (Речной вокзал; Ussuriysky bul; 8am-7pm), such as **Sakhekspo** (Сахэкспо; 4212-656 668, 8-924-312 3019; 421624@mail.ru; Ussuriysky bul), offer morning and evening departures to Fŭyuán, China (90 minutes), which cost ₽4500 including tour and overnight lodging.

BUS

The **bus station** (Автовокзал; ul Voronezhskaya 19), 500m north of the train station (go by tram or bus 4), sends nine buses daily to Komsomolsk (₽600, 6½ hours) and hourly *marshrutky* to Birobidzhan (three hours, ₽350) until 6pm.

GETTING CHINESE VISAS IN THE FAR EAST

It's best to arrange Chinese visas in your home country, although foreigners with verve can attempt to obtain a Chinese visa on the road. In the Far East, only the **consulate** (p373) in Khabarovsk provides this service.

A one-month tourist visa for most costs from ₽2000 for five-day processing (expedited visas sometimes possible with a higher fee). Americans pay ₽9000 and Canadians pay ₽7300 (10-day processing only). You'll need a letter of invitation, application form and copies of your immigration card, latest hotel registration and Russian visa. All forms are in Russian, but travel agencies in Khabarovsk may be able to assist you with your application.

Getting Around

From Khabarovsk's **train station**, about 3.5km northeast of the waterfront, bus 4 goes to Komsomolskaya pl (board opposite the station and head southeast) and trams 1 and 2 go near pl Lenina. From the **airport**, 9km east of the centre, trolleybus 1 goes to Komsomolskaya pl along ul Muravyova-Amurskogo and bus 35 goes to the train station (25 minutes) and bus station. An official taxi to the centre from the airport is ₽500; usually ₽300 the other way.

Trolleybuses and trams cost ₽22.

Vladivostok Владивосток

4232 / POP 606,000 / TIME MOSCOW + 7HR

The unofficial capital of the Far East and one of Russia's most important commercial ports and naval bases, Vladivostok is a thoroughly charming city, with a gorgeous, hilly setting, striking architecture and numerous verdant islands and sandy bays along its Pacific coastline. Most notable of these is Golden Horn Bay (named for its likeness to Istanbul's), over which now soars a massive suspension bridge, one of two built in recent years that have hugely improved the city's lumbering Soviet-era infrastructure.

The cultural and social sides of Vladivostok have improved immeasurably in recent years,. New arts centres such as the Primorsky Stage, Hermitage Vladivostok and Zarya are attracting talent to the area and stand alongside excellent restaurants and great cocktail bars.

All up, it's a wonderful place to start or finish your Trans-Siberian adventure.

History

Founded in 1860, Vladivostok (meaning 'Master the East') became a naval base in 1872. *Tsarevitch* Nicholas (later Tsar Nicholas II) turned up in 1891 to inaugurate the new Trans-Siberian rail line. By the early 20th century, Vladivostok teemed with merchants, speculators and sailors of every nation in a manner more akin to Shànghǎi or Hong Kong than to Moscow. Koreans and Chinese, many of whom had built the city, accounted for four out of every five of its citizens.

After the fall of Port Arthur in the Russo-Japanese War of 1904–05, Vladivostok took on an even more crucial strategic role, and when the Bolsheviks seized power in European Russia, Japanese, Americans, French and English poured ashore here to support the tsarist counterattack. Vladivostok held out until 25 October 1922, when Soviet forces finally marched in and took control – it was the last city to fall.

In the years to follow, Stalin deported or shot most of the city's foreign population. Closed to foreigners from 1958 to 1992, Vladivostok opened up with a bang in the '90s – literally (Mafia shoot-outs were a part of early business deals). It quickly established itself as the most prosperous and dynamic city in the Far East as trade and transport links with its Asian neighbours blossomed.

Vladivostok's infrastructure was torn asunder and rebuilt for the big APEC summit on Russky Island in 2012. The most eye-catching developments include two giant suspension bridges: one across Golden Horn Bay to the previously difficult-to-access Cherkavskogo Peninsula, the other spanning more than 4km to Russky Island across the Eastern Bosphorus Strait. A brand-new university campus opened there in 2012, and it's here that the city's break-neck development continues apace.

Sights

Vladivostok's sights are rather spread out, so be prepared to get to grips with the public transport network or take plenty of taxis or tours. That said, the city centre is walkable.

Central Vladivostok

The main square in Vladivostok is portside pl Bortsov Revolyutsii, where a massive new **cathedral** (Спасо-Преображенский кафедральный собор) was under construction at the time of writing. The two main avenues are ul Aleutskaya and ul Svetlanskaya, which run perpendicular to one another and meet just west of pl Bortsov Revolyutsii. Ul Fokina (aka the Arbat) is a partially pedestrianised 'walking street' where locals stroll in the evening, running down to the cute Sportivnaya Harbour (p227), another lovely place to wander.

Arsenev Regional Museum MUSEUM

(Приморский Государственный Объединенный музей имени В. К. Арсеньева; ☎4232-413 977; ul Svetlanskaya 20; ₽400; ⏲10am-7pm) This recently redone museum dates from 1890 and offers three floors of galleries, although there's little in the way of English labelling. Exhibits delve into local history, covering early explorers of the region, Vlad's vibrant Chinatown from the early 1900s, and civil war (with a short silent film playing across a broken screen). English-speaking guides are sometimes available for free tours.

Hermitage Vladivostok MUSEUM

(www.hermitage.ru; ul Svetlanskaya 40) This gorgeous tsarist-era building in the centre of Vladivostok is the latest big cultural institution to open a Far Eastern campus. Once complete, the fully renovated building will host temporary exhibits from the Hermitage's vast collection in St Petersburg.

S-56 Submarine MUSEUM

(Подводная лодка С-56; ☎4232-216 757; Korabelnaya nab; ₽100; ⏲9am-8pm) Perched near the waterfront, the S-56 submarine is worth a look. The first half is a ho-hum exhibit of badges and photos of men with badges (all in Russian). Keep going: towards the back you walk through an officers' lounge with a framed portrait of Stalin and then onto a bunk room with Christmas-coloured torpedoes. Outside, note the '14', marking the WWII sub's 'kills'.

Vladivostok Fortress Museum MUSEUM

(Музей Владивостокская Крепость; ☎4232-400 896; ul Batareynaya 4a; ₽200; ⏲10am-6pm) On the site of an old artillery battery overlooking Sportivnaya Harbour, this museum has cannons outside, a six-room indoor exhibit of photos and many, many guns inside. There are English explanations, so it's quite accessible by Russian museum standards.

Primorsky Picture Gallery GALLERY
(Приморская государственная картинная галерея; ul Aleutskaya 12; ₽250; ⏲11am-7pm Tue-Sun) Vladivostok's main art museum on Partizansky pr has long been under renovation and shows no sign of reopening any time soon. In the meantime, some of its decent collection can be seen at rotating temporary shows held at this annex.

Funicular FUNICULAR
(Фуникулёр; ul Pushkinskaya; tickets ₽12; ⏲7am-8pm) Vladivostok's well-oiled funicular railway makes a fun 60-second ride up a 100m hill every few minutes (unless the old girl is experiencing one of her frequent 'technical breaks'). At the top, cross ul Sukhanova via the underpass to a great lookout over the bay. It's next to a statue of Sts Cyril and Methodius (inventors of the Cyrillic alphabet) on the campus of DVGTU.

The base of the funicular is about a 15-minute walk from the centre.

Outer Vladivostok

★Zarya Centre for Contemporary Art MUSEUM
(Центр современного искусства "Заря»; ☎4232-317 100; www.zaryavladivostok.ru; pr 100 let Vladivostoky 155; ⏲noon-8pm Mon-Thu, 11am-10pm Fri-Sun) FREE The full renovation and repurposing of a former clothing factory into a giant creative complex containing offices, studios, cafes and work spaces is one of Vladivostok's most interesting recent developments. Visitors will be most interested in the excellent Zarya Centre for Contemporary Art, which is divided into two exhibition halls where top-notch contemporary art and design exhibitions are held. Check out what's on via the website.

To get here from the centre, take bus 41 from outside **Clover House** (ul Semyonovskaya 15; ⏲10am-9pm) or bus 31 from outside the train station (p232) to the stop Fabrika Zarya and then cross the road using the bridge.

Russky Island ISLAND
(Остров Русский) A fully militarised zone for most of the past 150 years, this big island just offshore has been reinvented as a business and academic centre and is home to the sprawling Far Eastern Federal University campus and the new Oceanarium. There's great tourism potential here, not least for some excellent beaches as you go deeper and deeper into the island and away from the city, but at the moment Russky Island is very much a DIY attraction.

Access to the island is by bus over the suspension bridge. Take a northbound bus 29 or bus 15 from Okeansky pr or ul Aksakovskaya (p232). The more-frequent bus 15 takes you to the DVFU campus, from which you can transfer to a minibus 29, which makes a loop, stopping in Rynda and other spots on the island. Rynda has a couple of resorts and the best beaches (just hop out when you see one you like). There are many forts on the island, including the **Voroshilov Battery** (Музей Ворошиловская батарея; Russky Island; ₽200; ⏲9am-5pm Wed-Sun).

Primorsky Oceanarium AQUARIUM
(Приморский Океанариум; ☎423-223 9422; www.primocean.ru; ul Akademika Kasyanova 25; adult/child ₽700/400; ⏲10am-8pm Tue-Sun; 👪) This massive new development on Russky Island is one of Vladivostok's planned key attractions and opened with great fanfare in 2016. It's a vast space in a remote, purpose-built building, and while it has all the potential to be a great attraction, it actually had the feel of a place struggling on our last visit. The dolphinarium was closed, many tanks were empty and no food or drinks were available. Hopefully things will improve in time.

Fort No 7 FORTRESS
(Форт No 7; ₽300; ⏲10am-6pm Tue-Sun) Of Vladivostok's multiple, numbered defensive forts, No 7 (14km north of the centre) gets our vote. It has 1.5km of tunnels, pretty much untouched since the last 400 soldiers stationed here left in 1923, although the NKVD later used it as an execution chamber. Take a taxi here.

Antique Automobile Museum MUSEUM
(Музей автомотостарины; www.automotomuseum.vl.ru; ul Sakhalinskaya 2a; ₽200; ⏲10am-6pm Tue-Sun) If you're a bit of a car (or Soviet) nerd, the Antique Automobile Museum is an absolute classic. A room full of Sovietmobiles (motorcycles too) from the 1930s to 1970s includes a 1948 M&M-green GAZ-20 'Pobeda' (Victory). Take bus 31 along ul Svetlanskaya and get off after it reaches the end of ul Borisenko.

Popov Island ISLAND
(Остров Попова) Just beyond Russky Island, Popov Island is better regarded for its beaches and filled with many guesthouses and dachas. You'll probably need to stay overnight

Vladivostok

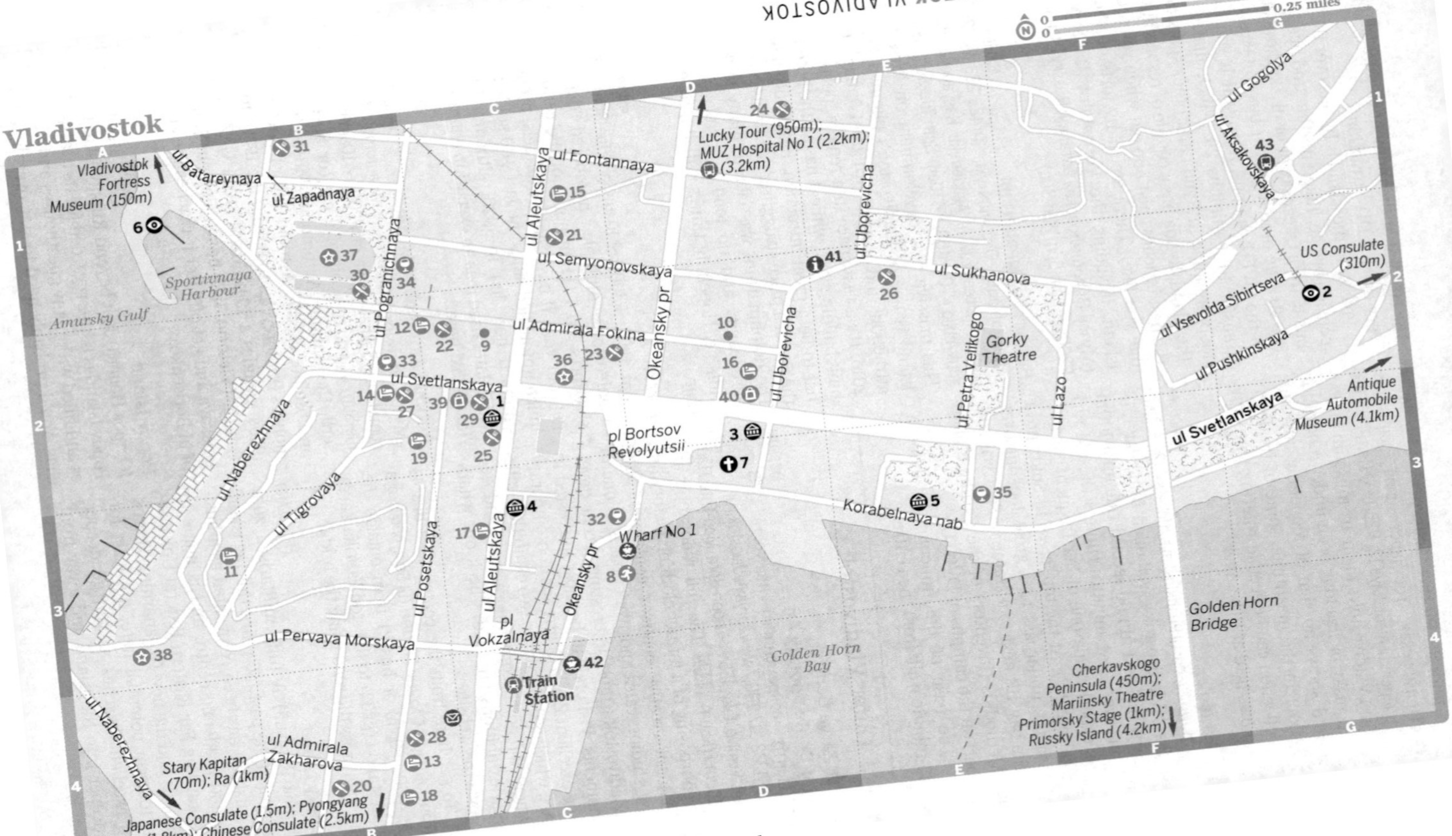

Vladivostok

Sights
1 Arsenev Regional Museum ... C2
2 Funicular ... G2
3 Hermitage Vladivostok ... D2
4 Primorsky Picture Gallery ... C3
5 S-56 Submarine ... E3
6 Sportivnaya Harbour ... A1
7 Transfiguration Cathedral ... D3

Activities, Courses & Tours
8 Bridges of Vladivostok ... C3
9 Dalintourist ... C2
10 Vladivostok Digger Club ... D2

Sleeping
11 Azimut Hotel ... A3
12 Gallery & More Guesthouse ... C2
13 Hotel Primorye ... B4
14 Hotel Versailles ... B2
15 Izba Hostel ... C1
16 Mattress, Sailor & Albatross Hostel ... D2
17 Optimum Hostel ... C3
18 Teplo ... B4
19 Vlad Marine Inn ... B2

Eating
20 Brothers Bar & Grill ... B4
21 Clover House ... C1
22 Five O'Clock ... C2
23 Food Like Food ... C2
24 Kvartira 30 ... D1
25 Mauro Gianvanni ... C2
26 Moloko & Myod ... E2
27 Ne Riday ... B2
28 Pizza M ... B4
29 Studio ... C2
30 Supra ... B1
31 Zuma ... B1

Drinking & Nightlife
32 Cuckoo Club ... C3
33 Moonshine ... B2
34 Mumiy Troll ... B1
35 Old Fashioned ... E3

Entertainment
36 Philharmonic Hall ... C2
37 Stadium Dinamo ... B1
38 Zabriskie Point ... A3

Shopping
39 Flotsky Univermag ... C2
40 GUM ... D2

Information
41 Primorsky Tourist Information Centre ... E2

Transport
InvestStroyTrest ... (see 42)
42 Marine Terminal ... C4
Storm Marine ... (see 42)
43 Ul Aksakovskaya Bus Stop ... G1

if you head out here, as there is only one boat per day (₽100, 1½ hours), departing in the early evening from Vladivostok's Wharf No 1 (1-й Причал).

Activities & Tours

Bridges of Vladivostok CRUISE
(Мосты Владивостока; ☎4232-999 590; Wharf 30, Okeansky pr; tickets ₽700-1000) This recommended outfit runs several daily cruises around the bays of Vladivostok. Departures at noon, 1pm and 2pm do an hour-long Bridges of Vladivostok tour, while a two-hour Sea Panorama tour leaves at 4.30pm, followed by a sunset cruise between 6.30pm and 8.30pm. All tours start and finish at Wharf 30.

Lotos Co TOUR
(☎4232-308 025; www.lotosco.ru; office 303, ul Dalzavodskaya 1; ⏰10am-6pm Mon-Fri) Offers a comprehensive assortment of tours, including visits to Russky Island, Popov Island and nature trips to the Primorsky Territory (waterfall visits, river rafting). One unique tour available is a three-hour bus tour of the new campus of the Far East Federal University on Russky Island, which is not possible to do on your own.

Lucky Tour TOURS
(☎4232-025 070; www.luckytour.com; ul Moskovskaya 1; ⏰9.30am-6pm Mon-Fri) Lucky Tour has over 20 years' experience leading tours in the Primorsky region, and its guides know Vladivostok backwards. There are dozens of city tours designed for all types of travellers and interests. English is spoken.

Vladivostok Digger Club TOURS
(Владивостокский диггер-клуб (ВДК); ☎4232-552 086; www.vladdig.org; office 303, ul Admirala Fokina 29a) This passionate outfit of fortress enthusiasts leads hour-long to full-day tours of Fort No 7 (p225), plus other forts, batteries and the tunnels that link them (some up to 3.5km long).

Dalintourist TOURS
(Дальинтурист; ☎4232-410 903; www.dalintourist.ru; ul Admirala Fokina 8a; ⏰9am-7pm Mon-Fri, 10am-3pm Sat) Runs professional tours of the

OFF THE BEATEN TRACK

A DAY AT THE BEACH

The **Sportivnaya Harbour** (Спортивная гавань) has a popular beach plus beer and shashlyk stands. You can hire paddle boats and rowboats here, and there's an amusement park just off the waterfront. Much of the water facing Vladivostok is quite polluted, but it gets cleaner as you go north. Sunbathers can get on a northbound *elektrichka* and hop off at any beach that looks good – try Sedanka, where there are a few resorts with services. You'll find even better swimming on Popov Island (p225) or Russky Island (p225).

Another easy trip to do by public transport is to **Nakhodka**, where you'll find some of Primorsky's best beaches. Ten daily express buses travel to Nakhodka from Vladivostok's bus station (₽400, three hours); the first is at 8am. Less frequent *elektrichkas* make the trip from the train station in around five hours (₽260). There are also six buses per day Monday to Friday only from outside the Aeroexpress terminal of the train station (₽420, three hours).

entire Primorsky region and can arrange English-speaking guides for Vladivostok city tours and beyond.

Festivals & Events

V-Rox MUSIC

(www.vrox.org/en; mid-Aug) The brainchild of local rock star Ilya Lagutenko of the famous Russian band Mumiy Troll, this massive rock festival is the biggest musical event in the Russian Far East. Held in mid-August, the four-day fest features some 70 different concerts around town (including in open-air venues), with performers from all over the world.

Pacific Meridian Film Festival FILM

(Меридианы Тихого; www.pacificmeridianfest.ru; Sep) One of Russia's most important film festivals, the Pacific Meridian has been held in Vladivostok every year since 2003. Screenings take place at the Gorky Theatre in the centre of town, and for a week in early September the city overflows with Russian movie stars.

Sleeping

★ **Izba Hostel** HOSTEL $

(Хостел Изба; 4232-908 508; www.izba-hostel.ru; ul Mordovtseva 3; dm ₽550-950, d from ₽2500;) It's quite a leap to believe you're in a 'traditional Russian hostel' given Izba's location in a thoroughly Soviet tower block, but the charming staff at this brand-new place make an impressive effort to help you. With lots of wood and *matryoshka* patterns throughout, there's a great kitchen, a comfortable common area and spotless bathrooms. The location is also excellent. The entrance is actually up a well-signed staircase on the ul Aleutskaya side of the building.

Gallery & More Guesthouse HOSTEL $

(8-914-325 5060; www.galleryandmore.ru; ul Admirala Fokina 4b; dm ₽700, r from ₽1900;) Enjoying a great location on the Arbat, this quirky and well-designed place combines an art gallery, cafe and small hostel. There's just one dorm with six beds, and several private rooms that are all extremely minimalist but rather funky and share bathrooms.

Mattress, Sailor & Albatross Hostel HOSTEL $

(Хостел "Матрас, Матрос и Альбатрос»; 8-914-661 3836; www.mattresshostel.ru; ul Svetlanskaya 33/5; dm/s/d from ₽600/1300/2800;) OK, so the name sounds much better in Russian, but this quirky place is a real winner for its superb location (in the trendy GUM courtyard, which is filled with bars, cafes and restaurants), its friendly staff and its new private rooms upstairs. The downside is the small kitchen and lack of hang-out space – you'll have to go outside.

Optimum Hostel HOSTEL $

(Barbados Hostel; 4232-729 111, 8-914-702 9111; www.hostel-optimum.ru; ul Aleutskaya 17; dm ₽600-800, d/tr ₽2200/2800;) Set in a grand eight-storey 1930s building topped with statues and in a perfect central location, Optimum Hostel offers wood-floored dorm rooms, free laundry, English-speaking staff and a guest kitchen. Ring the 'Optimum' buzzer. Out of hours, go round the left to Barbados Hostel, in the same building, which is run by the same people and has a reception desk.

Do note that Barbados Hostel only has dorms, while Optimum also has private rooms, although they all share bathrooms. There's no air-con in Barbados.

Vlad Marine Inn HOSTEL $

(☎4232-080 280; www.vlad-marine.ru; ul Posetskaya 53; dm ₽700, d with/without private bathroom ₽2100/1700;) In a cutely painted clapboard building on a hill in the centre of town, this inviting hostel has just five rooms, each with polished wood floors and ample natural light. Dorm beds have small individual flat-screen TVs, and the three doubles are pretty decent for the price. There's a basic kitchen for guests to use, but otherwise no food.

Teplo HOTEL $$

(☎4232-909 555; www.teplo-hotel.ru; ul Posetskaya 16; r from ₽2500;) Teplo brings a dash of style to Vlad's lodging options with a lounge-like lobby (with sofas and table football), and a white-brick corridor leading back to the small but appealing rooms. Each is equipped with TV, fridge and half bath (shower and sink only). There's free laundry and a guest kitchen, and the location on a quiet but central street is excellent.

Azimut Hotel HOTEL $$$

(☎4232-413 500; www.azimuthotels.com; ul Naberezhnaya 10; s/d from ₽6600/8250;) Formerly the Soviet-era Hotel Vladivostok, the Azimut group completely renovated this impressive hilltop property in 2015 and in doing so has led the charge to redevelop Vlad's rather unappealing beachfront. The vibe is sleek and stylish, with a fun approach to running a giant hotel. Highlights include an excellent restaurant, quiet rooms, professional staff and wonderful sea views.

Hotel Primorye HOTEL $$$

(Гостиница Приморье; ☎423-241 3040; www.hotelprimorye.ru; ul Posetskaya 20; s/d incl breakfast from ₽4900/5100;) Primorye has decent rooms with playful details such as funny artwork, though the design is rather dated and the beds are rockhard. The best rooms are two-room suites with views of the warships in Golden Horn Bay. An enticing bakery and cafe adjoins the lobby, while there's also an excellent pizzeria next door.

Hotel Versailles HOTEL $$$

(Гостиница Версаль; ☎4232-264 201; www.hotel-versailles.ru; ul Svetlanskaya 10; s/d incl breakfast ₽6300/7300;) The Versailles does a decent job of recapturing the imperial grace of a century-old hotel that reopened in the '90s, despite some bizarre decorative pairings in the lobby (think '70s lounge seats and tsarist-style chandeliers). Rooms are spacious, with some wonderful furniture and lavish bathrooms.

Eating

Ne Riday CAFETERIA $

(Не Рыдай; ul Svetlanskaya 10; mains ₽60-130; 9am-8pm;) This delightful cafeteria (whose name bizarrely means 'don't sob') is about as far from your Russian stereotyped *stolovaya* (canteen) as it's possible to get. With a large range of Russian cooking on offer and a smart, sleek space set in a historic building, it makes for a superb-value lunch spot.

Five O'Clock CAFE $

(ul Admirala Folkina 6; snacks ₽50-200; 8am-9pm Mon-Fri, 9am-9pm Sat, 11am-9pm Sun;) Russians so firmly believe that the British drink afternoon tea at 5pm each day that there's even a cafe named after this spurious assertion. The good news is that this much-loved local haunt on pedestrian ul Admirala Folkina serves muffins, cakes and quiche, all made fresh daily and sold for far less than you'll find elsewhere. Skip the coffee, though.

★**Studio** INTERNATIONAL $$

(☎4232-552 222; www.cafe-studio.ru; ul Svetlanskaya 18a; mains ₽300-900; 24hr;) In a courtyard in the heart of Vladivostok is this smart and appealing two-floor restaurant and lounge bar that attracts a young, well-heeled and in-the-know crowd. There's an enormous picture menu with everything from breakfasts and business lunches to seafood and pizzas; the elaborately gorgeous upstairs bar has to be seen to be believed.

★**Kvartira 30** EUROPEAN $$

(Квартира 30; ☎4232-974 483; ul Pologaya 65b; mains ₽400-600; noon-midnight;) This fantastic treasure is hidden away in an extremely unlikely location amid a hilltop housing estate. Run by the charming Olga Gurskaya, who also uses the space to run cookery classes, Kvartira 30 offers some of the most interesting and innovative Russian food in the city: the aubergines marinated in lemon juice and chilli with toasted rye bread were a revelation.

With only five tables, it's a good idea to reserve for the evenings. Don't miss the *zefir* dessert, a kind of local marshmallow made from blueberries. To find it, it's best to start from Okeansky pr, where the entrance to the street is just a staircase through some trees that becomes a residential street. Head up the road and look for the yellow neoclassical building on the left: the restaurant is to the left-hand side of that.

★**Zuma** ASIAN $$
(Зума; ☎4232-222 666; ul Fontannaya 2; mains ₽300-1400; ⊙11am-2am Sun-Thu; 📶🅿) A stylish welcoming place, this two-floor restaurant-lounge is decked out in an elaborate but classy Angkor Wat theme, replete with a massive black granite bar perfect for lingering with drinks. The real attraction here is the mouthwatering pan-Asian cooking (sushi, dumplings, stir-fries), plus creative salads, rack of lamb and a fabulous seafood selection.

★**Pyongyang** NORTH KOREAN $$
(Пхеньян; ul Verkhneportovaya 68b; mains ₽350-750; ⊙noon-midnight; 🅿) Staffed by waitresses from nearby North Korea who periodically break out into karaoke, this unique establishment is just strange enough to be considered a must-visit. You can pick from a photo menu of excellent food such as *bibimbap* (rice mixed with fried egg, sliced meat and other ingredients) and spicy fried pork with kimchi.

★**Food Like Food** RUSSIAN $$
(Еда как еда; ☎4232-240 4674; ul Admirala Fokina 16; mains ₽400-1000; ⊙11am-midnight, to 2am Fri & Sat; 📶) While it might sound like a fast-food joint, this charming little white-painted basement restaurant is anything but. The menu takes in classical Russian cooking, but presents dishes with an original twist, such as aubergines in oyster sauce or salmon in green pea purée. Staff are exceptionally engaged and knowledgeable, and cute Russian knick-knacks adorn the walls.

Supra GEORGIAN $$
(Супра; ☎4232-277 722; www.supravl.ru; ul Admirala Fokina 1b; mains ₽250-500; ⊙noon-midnight; 🅿) This bustling but charming spot has one of the best locations in town, meaning that it's always busy and you may well have to wait for a table. The traditionally clad staff work quickly in serving the various elements of a Georgian *supra* (feast) though, while the picture menu is huge and the realisation generally excellent.

Moloko & Myod INTERNATIONAL $$
(Молоко и Мёд; ul Sukhanova 6a; mains ₽400-750; ⊙10am-midnight Sun-Thu, to 2am Fri & Sat; 📶🅿) A trendy spot with a popular street-side terrace, 'Milk & Honey' has fabulous daily brunch offerings, great coffee, dangerously good cocktails and a menu that includes *salade niçoise,* assorted tapas and seafood risotto. Blankets warm terrace dwellers on chilly evenings.

Pizza M PIZZA $$
(Пицца М; ☎4232-413 430; ul Posetskaya 20; pizzas ₽300-650; ⊙24hr; 📶🅿) Classier than its name might suggest, the M is one of Vlad's coolest hang-outs, with two unique rooms setting their style sights higher than the humble slice. The pizzas are available as thin or thick crust and are delicious. Delivery is also available.

Mauro Gianvanni PIZZA $$
(Мауро Джанванни; ☎4232-220 782; www.mauro-gianvanni.ru; ul Aleutskaya 21; mains ₽220-700; ⊙noon-midnight Sun-Thu, to 2am Fri & Sat; 🅿) This little Italian-run brick-oven pizzeria has a modern interior and snappy service. The dozen-plus pizzas are crispy and arguably some of the best east of the Urals.

Brothers Bar & Grill INTERNATIONAL $$$
(☎4232-577 070; ul Bestuzheva 32; mains ₽400-1500; 📶) This rather stylish steak and grill house is worth seeking out for its excellent food, English menu and convivial staff. There's a lovely summer terrace and top-notch cocktail bar in the backyard, while the main dining room is distinctly dark and moody. There's an impressive selection of steaks, seafood, pizza and even a whisky-glazed burger to delight in.

Drinking & Nightlife

★**Moonshine** COCKTAIL BAR
(ul Svetlanskaya 1/2; ⊙6pm-2am; 📶) This exceptionally well-stocked and stylish place right by the seafront offers cocktails and a small but tantalising bar menu as well as wine by the glass. There's lots of exposed brickwork, distressed industrial fittings and rather love-it-or-hate-it lighting, but this is definitely a great spot to mix with Vladivostok's burgeoning creative classes.

★**Old Fashioned** COCKTAIL BAR
(☎4322-791 079; ul Petra Velikogo 4; ⊙noon-midnight, until 2am Fri & Sat; 📶) This fabulous cocktail lounge is a low-lit and beautifully set-out space, with a gorgeous wooden bar and gloriously comfortable sofas and chairs to lounge in. There's a meaty restaurant attached, where diners eat inside a glass atrium outside – but it's by far best used as a place to nurse wonderful cocktails from the large list.

Ra CLUB
(ul Nabarezhnaya 76; cover varies; ⊙1pm-5am) Where the cool kids can be found hanging out on the seafront boardwalk on summer evenings, this black-painted brick warehouse

is a simple bar with a pool table facing the beach during the day. Come nightfall the space becomes the setting for all kinds of parties, including techno, house and gay nights.

Mumiy Troll BAR
(Мумий Тролль; www.vvo.mumiytrollbar.com; ul Pogranichnaya 6; ⊙24hr) A fun and lively bar that draws a mix of locals and expats, rock-loving Mumiy Troll – set up by the nationally famous local band of the same name – has live acts most nights (from 10pm). There's rarely a cover, but guests must be 21 to enter.

Stary Kapitan PUB
(Старый Капитан; ☎4232-771 077; www.oldcaptainpub.ru; Leitenanta Shmidta 17a; ⊙noon-1am Sun-Thu, to 3am Fri & Sat) Facing the marina, the Old Captain has an excellent selection of draft beers, such as German Weihenstephan. The delectable seafood dishes (pan-seared tiger prawns and scallops) and appetisers (salted herring with black bread toast) go nicely with the brews. Reserve on weekends, when there's live music.

Cuckoo Club CLUB
(www.cuckooclub.ru; Okeansky pr 1a; cover ₽500-800; ⊙10pm-2am Mon-Thu, to 6am Fri & Sat) One of Vladivostok's fancier clubs, the dance floor here seethes at weekends and there's a lovely outdoor area that's the place to be seen in the summer months. Dress to impress to hurdle face control.

☆ Entertainment

Mariinsky Theatre Primorsky Stage CLASSICAL MUSIC
(Приморская сцена Мариинского театра; ☎4232-406 060; https://prim.mariinsky.ru; ul Fastovskaya 20; tickets ₽300-4000) This impressive new theatre is the Far Eastern stage of the venerable Mariinsky Theatre in St Petersburg and is the best place to see serious classical concerts, ballet and opera in the Russian Far East. The modern glass building contains both a big and small stage, as well as an outdoor summer stage.

Zabriskie Point LIVE MUSIC
(Забриски Пойнт; ☎4232-215 715; ul Naberezhnaya 9a; cover ₽500-1000; ⊙9pm-5am Tue-Sun) Zabriskie is Vladivostok's main rock and jazz club, drawing an older crowd to view live music acts. It doubles as a nightclub with dancing after performances are finished for the night. There's great sound and plenty of character.

Philharmonic Hall CLASSICAL MUSIC
(Филармония; ☎4232-264 022; www.primfil.ru; ul Svetlanskaya 15) Hosts classical music and jazz performances.

Stadium Dinamo SPECTATOR SPORT
(Стадион Динамо; ul Pogranichnaya; tickets ₽200-400) The popular local football team, Luch-Energiya, plays games at this bayside stadium from April to November.

Shopping

GUM GIFTS & SOUVENIRS
(ГУМ; ul Svetlanskaya 35; ⊙10am-8pm Mon-Sat, to 7pm Sun) This once deeply Soviet department store has recently undergone full refurbishment and is now Vladivostok's best place to shop. It's also housed in the Far East's most elegant art-deco building. You'll find traditional souvenirs on the 1st floor, as well as a range of restaurants, cafes and bars in its popular courtyard.

Flotsky Univermag SPORTS & OUTDOORS
(Флотский универмаг; ul Svetlanskaya 11; ⊙10am-7pm Mon-Fri, to 6pm Sat & Sun) For unusual souvenir turf, follow the navy – this outfitter has those cute blue-and-white-striped navy undershirts and other navy and military gear, as well as useful travel gear such as torches, knives, maps and toothpaste. There are also all kinds of kitschy pro-Putin T-shirts.

Information

Currency-exchange desks and ATMs are all over town; you'll never have to worry about finding either.

City Hospital No 1 (Городская клиническая Больница №1; ☎423-245 2682; ul Sadovaya 22)

Post Office (Почта; ul Aleutskaya; ⊙8am-10pm Mon-Fri, 9am-6pm Sat & Sun)

TOURIST INFORMATION

There are tourist information desks at the airport and the train station.

Primorsky Tourist Information Centre (Туристско-информационный центр Приморского края; ☎423-240 7120; ul Semyonovskaya 29; ⊙9am-6pm Mon-Fri) Tucked inside the Hyundai Hotel in the centre of the city.

www.tour.primorsky.ru Has information about the entire Primorsky Territory.

www.vladivostok-city.com Useful for pretrip city planning.

CONNECTING TO CHINA

Catching a train from Vladivostok to Harbin (Hā'ěrbīn) is a headache, with many stops and a long border check. Departures are early evening on Mondays and Thursdays, but the first night you only go as far as Ussuriysk, where they detach your car from the 351. You stay overnight in Ussuriysk and depart the next day for the border and Harbin. It's much quicker and easier to take a flight to Harbin (₽4700, 1¼ hour, daily except Wednesday & Saturday).

If you're ultimately headed to Běijīng, you'll need to go to Harbin first and transfer there. Or you can fly directly from Vladivostok (₽6300, 2½ hours, Tuesday, Saturday & Sunday).

Getting There & Away

Vladivostok is one of the Russian Far East's biggest transport hubs. In addition to serving as the terminus of the Trans-Siberian Railway, the airport has a large number of national and international flights, which makes it easy to get here from from almost anywhere in Russia and neighbouring countries.

TRAINS

Vladivostok's magnificent art nouveau **train station** (ЖД вокзал Владивосток; pl Voksalnaya; ⏲24hr) is located right in the centre of the city by the waterfront, and marks the terminus of the main Trans-Siberian Railway line.

Save money by avoiding the No 1 Rossiya train to Moscow, which is massively overpriced due to its perceived prestige (in fact it's fairly similar to less excitingly named and numbered trains).

AIR

Vladivostok has an excellent modern **airport** (Международный аэропорт Владивосток; ☎423-230 6909; www.vvo.aero; Artyom) located in Artyom (50km from the centre), with convenient if irregular, rail access to the city. A speedy rail link, the plush Aeroexpress (50 minutes, ₽230) connects Vladivostok's train station with the airport. However, with just five trains daily, you'll be lucky if there's one leaving at a convenient time for your flight.

Buses and marshrutka 107 (₽100 to ₽150) also connect the train station and airport, departing at least hourly throughout the day.

A taxi booth in the arrivals area charges ₽1500 for trips to the centre (45 minutes to one hour), and is the easiest way to connect to the city. A taxi from the city to the airport is around ₽1000.

BOAT

Vladivostok's ferry services depart from the **Marine Terminal** (Морской вокзал; Okeansky pr) in the centre of town. There is a weekly **Storm Marine** (☎423-230 2704; www.parom.su; office 124, Marine Terminal; ⏲9am-1pm & 2-6pm Mon-Fri) passenger-only ferry to Donghae in South Korea (from US$205 one way, 20 hours), which continues to Sakaiminato in Japan (from US$265 one way, 43 hours). It leaves Vladivostok at 2pm every Wednesday.

There is also a new weekly ferry, the Man Gyong Bong, to Rajin in North Korea run by **InvestStroyTrest** (ИнвестСтройТрест; ☎423-249 6560; www.rajin-investstroytrest.ru; Marine Terminal). This passenger and cargo ferry leaves Vladivostok each Friday at 8pm and returns to Vladivostok on Thursday at 7am (from ₽5300, eight hours). However, you will need a visa for North Korea to take this service.

BUS

Buses to Suífēnhé, the border town with China, depart at 6.20am (₽2850, four hours, Monday to Saturday) from the **bus station** (автовокзал; ul Russkaya), 3km north of the centre. There are no buses all the way to Harbin, but you can pick up transport on the other side of the border. There are also frequent departures for other destinations in the region, though do be aware that some southbound destinations may be off limits to foreigners without a permit.

Getting Around

Much of Vladivostok's relatively compact centre can be covered on foot as long as you don't mind lots of steep ascents and descents.

Alternatively, buses are your best bet to get around. From in front of the train station, buses 23, 31 and 49 run north on ul Aleutskaya then swing east onto ul Svetlanskaya to the head of the bay. Bus 15 heads to the Primorsky Aquarium from the **ul Aksakovskaya bus stop**.

For trips of more than 5km, you'll save money ordering a taxi (most easily done using the apps Yandex Taxi or Taxi Maxim).

The Baikal-Amur Mainline (BAM)

Includes ➡

Route Info

- Distance: 4287km
- Duration: Four days one hour
- Time zones: Moscow +5 to Moscow +7

Best Places to Stay

- Igor Shalygin (p238)
- Baikal Trail Hostel (p241)
- Biznestsentr (p245)
- Zolotaya Rybka (p241)
- Vremena Goda (p239)

Best Places to Eat

- Amrita (p239)
- Rialto (p241)
- Shinok Pervach (p245)

Why Go?

Most people know the Trans-Siberian Railway, but how many can say they've heard of the 'other' Trans-Sib, its poor country cousin, the BAM (Baikal-Amur Mainline or Baikalo-Amurskaya Magistral)? The branch line to end all branch lines, the BAM begins as a set of points at Tayshet and ends more than 4200 lonely kilometres further east at Sovetskaya Gavan, passing through some jaw-slackeningly off-the-map places en route. As great railway journeys go, this is a Soviet epic, a rail-clanging odyssey you'll never forget.

But it's a miracle the BAM was ever built at all. Costing billions of dollars and declared a 'Hero Project of the Century', construction was fraught with seemingly insurmountable difficulties. The line opened fully in 1991, just as the USSR collapsed. Today only a handful of trains ply the route.

Riding the BAM's snail-paced trains takes you to some very out-of-the-way places. Only Severobaikalsk on Lake Baikal is geared for visitors.

When to Go

Tynda

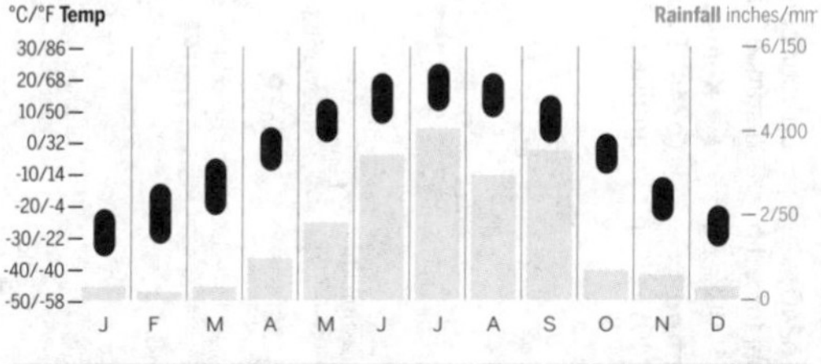

Mar Ponder the weird shapes into which Lake Baikal freezes from the shore at Severobaikalsk

Sep–Nov Avoid summer crowds and ticket shortages with an autumn trip along the BAM

Sep & Oct Larch trees around Lake Baikal's north fill the landscape with autumnal gold

BAM Highlights

1. **Khakusy Spa** (p240) Crossing Lake Baikal for a dip in this isolated hot spring.
2. **Frolikha Adventure Coastline Trail** (p240) Pulling on your boots for this long-distance Siberian hiking route.
3. **Komsomolsk-na-Amure** (p244) Touring the classical architecture and Soviet monuments of the BAM's nicest town.
4. **BAM Museum** (p243) Soaking up all things BAM at this varied and welcoming museum in Tynda.
5. **Bratsk Dam** (p238) Looking out across the Bratsk Sea from a BAM train window as you trundle across the top of the dam.
6. **Great Baikal Trail** (p188) Trekking the rugged section between Baikalskoe and Echo Turbaza.

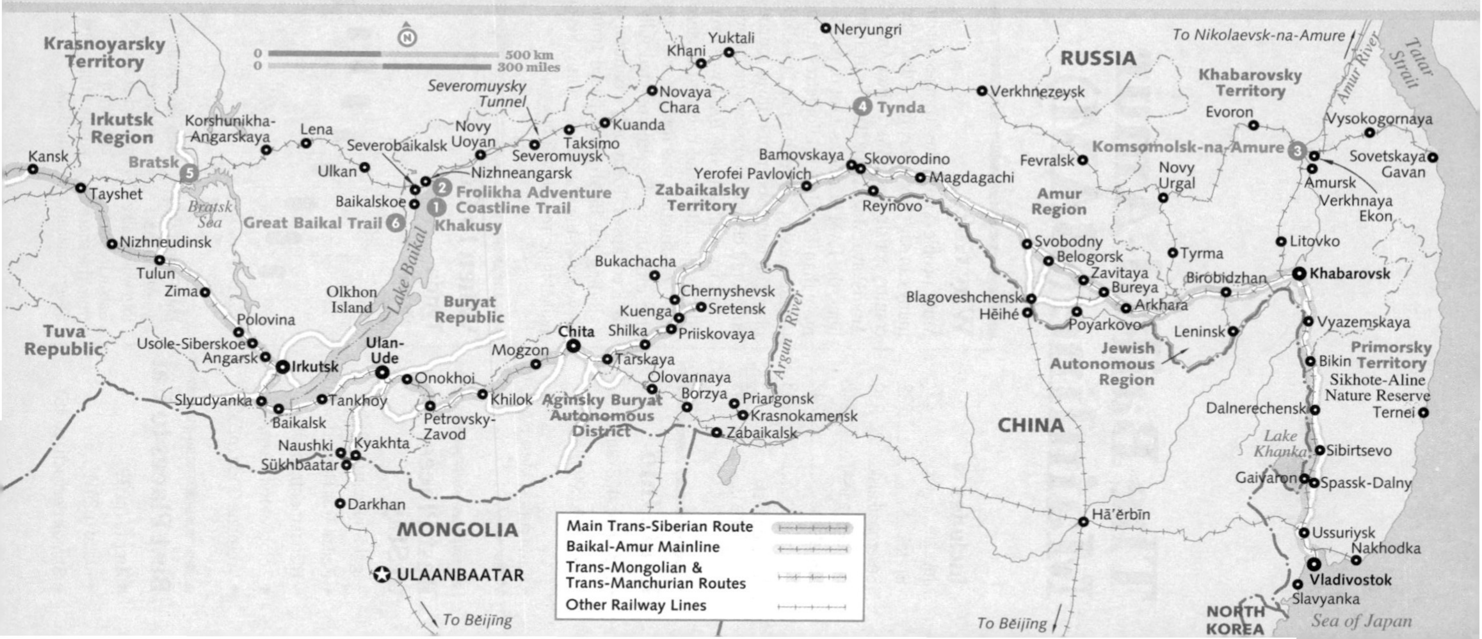

The Route

TAYSHET TO SEVEROBAIKALSK

0km from Tayshet

The junction with the Trans-Sib at Tayshet (p237) is the official start of the BAM (there's a monument recognising the fact). If you're a BAM purist you can start from here, but most pass directly through on daily services from Krasnoyarsk.

293km to 339km

The first major stops along the BAM are for **Bratsk** (p238), a sprawling city of almost 250,000 people on the edge of the Bratsk 'Sea', an artificial lake created in the 1960s by the building of the Bratsk Hydroelectric Station. The railway line actually crosses the top of the gigantic 1km-long dam at the 330km mark, presenting wide views on both sides.

552km

The taiga closes in on the line as you travel the next 600km towards the jagged mountains hemming in the northern end of Lake Baikal. **Korshunikha-Angarskaya** is the train station for the claustrophobic 1960s iron-ore processing town of Zheleznogorsk-Ilimsky.

573km

One of the few branch lines off the BAM veers north from Khrebtovaya to **Ust-Ilimsk**, a town of almost 100,000 people on the Angara River 215km away. The historic town of Ilimsk lies drowned at the bottom of the reservoir created by the Ust-Ilimsk Dam.

720km

A few kilometres after Lena the line swings across the **Lena River** on a single-track bridge with views down onto a large timber port to the north.

930km

At **Ulkan** station, a small but eye-catching metallic Lenin relief stands against a bright red 'flag' on the east end of the platform, but you'll only have three minutes to admire it.

982km

After **Kunerma** the track performs a full 180-degree loop. Hurry for the camera before you disappear into the 6km-long Daban tunnel.

1028km

Around half an hour before reaching Lake Baikal, some trains make a brief stop at picturesque **Goudzhekit**, once a village but now home only to a basic *turbaza* (no-frills holiday camp).

1063km

Severobaikalsk (p239) is by far the most interesting stop on the entire route. The surrounding area, which takes in the northern part of Lake Baikal, is beautiful and offers lots of opportunities for outdoor adventure. The *Thunderbirds*–style station, inspired, it is said, by the mayor's love of ski jumping, is one of the most striking along the line. Outside there's a steam train and a statue commemorating the workers from across the USSR who toiled on the BAM.

SEVEROBAIKALSK TO TYNDA

1090km

This is where the BAM gets serious. From Severobaikalsk to the fishing village of **Nizhneangarsk**, 30km north, the line skirts Lake Baikal, though views are often better from the road (unencumbered by tunnels). At **Nizhneangarsk 2** station, look out for the small airport, from where there are flights to Ulan-Ude and Irkutsk.

1105km

Only local *elektrichki* (suburban trains) stop at the Evenk village of **Kholodnaya** by the Verkhnyaya Angara River delta.

1142km

The tiny hot-springs resort at **Dzelinda** is also served by local slow trains.

BAM ROUTE PLANNER

Here's a suggested itinerary for the BAM:

Day 1 Take train from Krasnoyarsk to Tayshet, stay overnight at Igor's Homestay.

Day 2 Overnight hop to Severobaikalsk; keep an eye out for the Bratsk 'Sea' as you cross the top of the dam.

Day 3 Take a dip in Lake Baikal or a boat trip; chill out in Severobaikalsk.

Day 4 Excursion from Severobaikalsk to Baikalskoe, Nizhneangarsk or the hot spring at Khakusy. Catch the overnight train to Tynda.

Day 5 After spending most of the day on the train, stretch your legs with a walk to Tynda's BAM Builders Monument.

Day 6 Visit Tynda's BAM Museum before catching a sleeper to Komsomolsk-na-Amure.

Day 7 Arrive Komsomolsk-na-Amure; spend the day exploring. Overnight train to Sovetskaya Gavan.

Day 8 Arrive at BAM's end on the Tatar Strait.

Baikal-Amur Mainline (BAM)

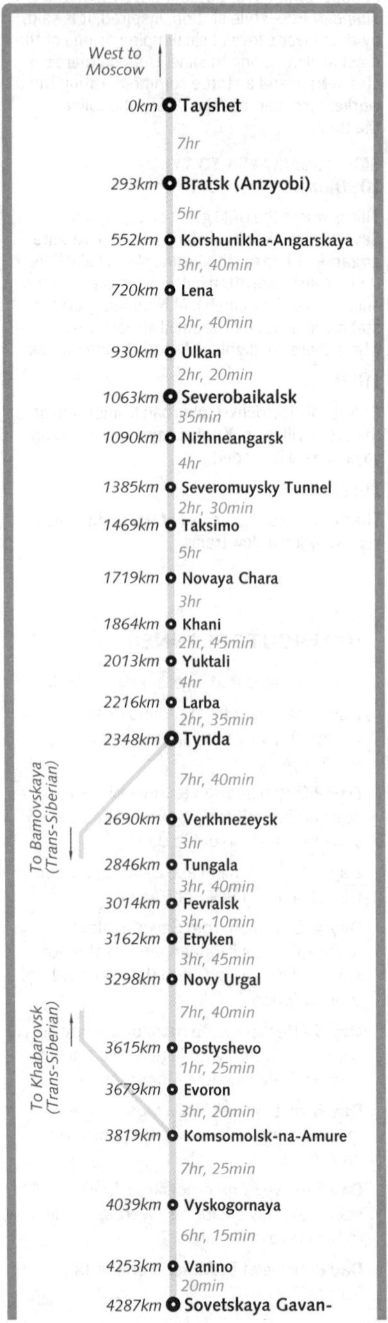

1150km to 2500km

The next 1300km or so give you ample time to appreciate the truly massive engineering achievement of the BAM. Many consider this the most interesting section of the line, as it climbs over densely forested, mountainous terrain along switchbacks and through several tunnels. But despite the region's remoteness, the train stops at least once an hour at communities established by BAM construction workers and their families in the 1970s and 1980s.

1242km

The first major halt on this section of the line is the low-rise ferroconcrete station belonging to **Novy Uoyan**, though there's no reason to get off here save to stretch your legs. Trains then snake across the flood plain of the Verkhnyaya Angara River until the line slams into the mountains again.

1385km

The 15.3km-long **Severomuysky Tunnel** is the longest in Russia and was only completed in 2004 after years of severe technical difficulties with the permafrost. The tunnel replaced more than 50km of track, which had steep gradients and was prone to avalanches.

1469km

The born-of-the-BAM town of **Taksimo** provides the next opportunity to escape the muggy air of *platskart* and take on a few provisions at the station kiosks. Get some much-needed exercise during the long stop (up to 50 minutes) by running to see the BAM Pioneer Monument. There are wilderness hiking possibilities in the surrounding mountains and along the River Muya.

1535km

Local time becomes Moscow time plus six hours.

1561km

At **Kuanda** look out for the Golden Link Monument commemorating the uniting of the two sections of the BAM in 1984.

1850km to 1950km

Shortly before **Khani** (1864km) you enter the Sakha Republic and continue along its border with the Zabaikalsky Territory and the Amur Region. Shortly beyond **Olyokma** (1918km) the train veers southeast and follows the Olyokma River into Tynda Region.

2000km to 2210km

The train leaves the Olyokma River, veers due east and rumbles into **Yuktali** (2013km), where there's a 35-minute stop. The next four hours are very scenic as you follow the Nyukzha River southeast until just before **Larba** (2216km).

2348km

Finally you roll into Tynda (p243), the unofficial BAM 'capital,' with a '70s train station that looks like a science-fiction film set. The main BAM trains all terminate in Tynda, so you'll have a layover if you are continuing east to Komsomolsk or west to Severobaikalsk or Moscow.

TYNDA TO SOVETSKAYA GAVAN

2348km to 2690km

Settle down for 36½ hours on train 364 heading east on the BAM to Komsomolsk. The route crosses the mighty Gilyuy River twice (at 2364km and 2409km). Night will fall as you cross several more rivers and enter the swamps leading into **Verkhnezeysk** (2690km) on the Zeysk Reservoir.

2779km to 2894km

The stretch from Ogoron to Dugda is about the prettiest the eastern BAM has to offer, with a range of snow-capped mountains to the northeast and patches of thick taiga near the tracks, but eastbound travellers will need to get up early. The best stretch is 10km either side of **Tungala** (2846km).

3015km

In **Fevralsk** (3014km) on the Byssa River, you get 35 minutes to contemplate the permafrost below, or gold mines and pulp mills outside town. It's a two-minute walk south to the little town centre, with food shops and a post office with internet access. The train station has an ATM.

3155km

You leave Amurskaya Region and enter Khabarovsky Territory between the station stops of Ulma (3149km) and Etryken (3162km).

3298km

After crossing the Bureya River (3292km), the train stops for 35 minutes in **Novy Urgal**, a coal-mining town near green hills and the white waters of the Akisma River. You can switch to train 663 here for a short cut to the Trans-Siberian line and Khabarovsk.

3382km

A couple of hours later, the train passes through the 2km **Dusse-Alin Tunnel**. Gulag camp labourers toiled (and died) over this during Stalin's watch, but it was only completed and put into use in 1982.

3615km

In **Postyshevo**, locals sell the town's famous red *ikra* (caviar) on the platform in late summer and autumn. The interesting station has socialist-realist bas-reliefs over both entrances, and a psychedelic, copper-toned, honeycombed ceiling inside.

3819km

Five hours east of Postyshevo, the 364 terminates in the BAM's loveliest city, Komsomolsk-na-Amure (p244). There are direct links here to Khabarovsk, on the main Trans-Siberian line.

3819km to 4253km

While most people get off in Komsomolsk, the BAM still has another 468km to go. Two night trains tackle this final 12-hour stretch. Some train mates may joke you're on an 'international route' as the train clanks through a couple of ho-hum villages passed on the way – **Kenada** (4080km) and **Toki** (4243km); they liken them phonetically with 'Canada' and 'Tokyo' (it's OK to fake a chuckle).

The BAM then pulls into view of a snaking Pacific bay lined with shipyards at **Vanino** (4253km; population 18,500), where boats leave for Sakhalin Island. Vanino's often foggy bay, looked over by two lighthouses, sees million tonnes of goods shipped in and out each year (including coal, lumber and gas).

4287km

The BAM terminates at **Sovetskaya Gavan-Sortirovochny** ('SovGavan' on train timetables; not to be confused with the city of Sovetskaya Gavan, about 25km further south).

Tayshet Тайшет

☎39563 / POP 35,500 / TIME MOSCOW +5HR

All Siberian roads, or railway lines at least, lead to Tayshet, a major rail junction where the Trans-Siberian, BAM and Tayshet–Abakan line collide. A child of the Trans-Sib, Tayshet had a difficult upbringing as the Gulag capital of Eastern Siberia. Between the late 1930s and the mid-1960s, numerous camps and prison colonies occupied bits of town, with everyone from 39,000 Japanese prisoners of war to well-known Moscow intellectuals passing through at various points. Not much remains of the camps today except for a few rows of prisoner-built wooden houses.

Tayshet is now becoming known as the gateway to fascinating Tofalaria – an excruciatingly remote land inhabited by Tofy, Russia's smallest ethnic group.

Sights

To learn more about the town's (dark) past visit the **Regional Museum** (ul Lenina 115; ₽20; ⏲10am-6pm Tue-Sat), where local historians are desperate to tell foreigners their story.

There are also some exhibits belonging to Tofalaria.

Tayshet's other main sight is its modernised **railway station**, where a huge L-series loco stands beached to the right of the building and an Italian-built water tower rises in architectural incongruity behind. **Kofeynya Paris** (Taishet railway station; ⌚9am-1am), a surprisingly metropolitan cafe inside the train station, serves good coffee and snacks till the last night train is gone.

A pretty macabre **Lenin monument** next to the station features the communist leader's gold-painted head placed on a podium made of reflective black stone.

Sleeping

Igor Shalygin HOMESTAY **$$**
(✆8-924-716 4004; www.facebook.com/pg/Trans-sib-baikal-transit-319120791457041; per person ₽1000) The best reason to get off at Tayshet is Igor Shalygin, an English- and German-speaking travel enthusiast who runs a cosy homestay in the old town, particularly popular with motorcycle overlanders. He can take you out to various beauty spots, romantically lost bits of the Trans-Sib and the old *trakt*, and give you a taste of authentic rural Siberian life.

The latter includes a superb *banya* (bathhouse), where the host performs the role of steam and twig master. In summer, Shalygin runs boat trips on the placid Biryusa River. In winter, when the river turns into an ice road, he can set up a trip to the reindeer herders and hunters of Tofalaria.

Getting There & Away

You may end up spending a whole day at the station waiting for connections. There are more services heading west towards Krasnoyarsk (*platskartny/kupe* ₽816/1845, 7½ hrs), than east towards Severobaikalsk (*platskartny/kupe* ₽1097/2112, 18 hrs).

Bratsk Братск

✆3953 / POP 234,150 / TIME MOSCOW +5HR

Bratsk is perhaps not worth leaving the 'comfort' of your carriage bunk, though it does neatly break up the journey from both Irkutsk and Krasnoyarsk to Severobaikalsk. The city's raison d'être is a gigantic **dam** (Братская ГЭС; www.irkutskenergo.ru) which drowned the original historic town in the 1960s. Slung between high cliffs and somehow holding back the mammoth Bratsk Sea, it's a striking spectacle, especially from the window of BAM trains that pass right across the top.

New Bratsk is a heavily polluted necklace of disconnected concrete 'subcities' and belching industrial zones, with the spirit-crushingly dull **Tsentralny** area at its heart.

HERO PROJECT OF THE CENTURY

The BAM is an astonishing victory of belief over adversity (and economic reason). This 'other' trans-Siberian line runs from Tayshet (417km east of Krasnoyarsk) around the top of Lake Baikal to Sovetskaya Gavan on the Pacific coast. It was begun in the 1930s to access the timber and minerals of the Lena Basin, and work stopped during WWII. Indeed, the tracks were stripped altogether and reused to lay a relief line to the besieged city of Stalingrad (now Volgograd).

Work effectively started all over again in 1974 when the existing Trans-Siberian Railway was felt to be vulnerable to attack by a potentially hostile China. The route, cut through nameless landscapes of virgin taiga and blasted through anonymous mountains, was built by patriotic volunteers and the BAM was labelled 'Hero Project of the Century' to encourage young people from across the Soviet Union to come and do their bit. But as cynicism began replacing enthusiasm in the late Brezhnev years, 'project of the century' turned into an ironic expression meaning a project that takes eternity to be completed. Building on permafrost pushed the cost of the project to US$25 billion, some 50 times more than the original Trans-Siberian Railway.

New 'BAM towns' grew with the railway, often populated by builders who decided to stay on. However, the line's opening in 1991 coincided with the collapse of the centrally planned USSR and the region's bright Soviet future never materialised. While Bratsk and Severobaikalsk survived, many other smaller, lonely settlements became virtual ghost towns. Today only a handful of passenger trains a day use the line.

Some 12km from Tsentralny is **Angara Village** (www.bratskmuseum.ru; ul Komsomolskaya; ₽150; ⊙10am-4.30pm Wed-Sun), an impressive open-air ethnographic museum containing a rare 17th-century wooden watchtower and buildings rescued from submerged old Bratsk. A series of shaman sites and Evenki *chumy* (tepee-shaped conical dwellings) lie in the woods behind. Take a taxi or arrange a visit through **Taiga Tours** (☎3953-416 513; www.taiga-tours.ru; 2nd fl, Hotel Taiga; ⊙10am-6pm Mon-Fri) who can also arrange permits and guides to visit Bratsk dam's turbine rooms.

Sleeping

Hotel Shvedka HOTEL $
(Гостиница Шведка; ☎8-902-179 0580; www.hotel-shvedka.ru; ul Mira 25; s/d from ₽1050/1400; 📶) Rooms here range from battered and cheap to almost design standard. Ask to see which you're getting before you commit. Breakfast is extra and is taken in the hotel's own cafe.

Vremena Goda HOTEL $$
(Времена года; ☎3953-414 777; www.hotelbratsk.ru; ul Podbelskogo 12; d from ₽3500) The city's most elegant hotel occupies an Alpine-styled wooden chalet with tastefully designed rooms, where the smell of natural wood all but suppresses the industrial odours that prevail outside. Paper-thin walls mean you can eavesdrop on neighbours' Skype calls and stay informed about the rest of their activities.

Hotel Taiga HOTEL $$
(Гостиница Тайга; ☎3953-414 710; www.hotel-taiga.ru; ul Mira 35; s/d from ₽2350/2900; 📶) This renovated Soviet hulk contains cramped rooms packed with tasteless furniture, but bathrooms are clean and modern. Some staff speak English, guest visas are registered and there's a decent hotel restaurant. Breakfast is extra.

Eating

Amrita VEGETARIAN $
(☎3953-454 097; www.amritacentr.ru; ul Pionerskaya 5; mains ₽80-120; ⊙noon-7pm; 🌶) In a gloomy macho town like Bratsk, this tidy vegetarian cafeteria comes as a pleasant surprise. Admittedly the lentil soup and samosas have lost any signs of their Indian roots, but perhaps it is the beginning of Siberia's own vegetarian cooking style.

Rock Garret EASTERN EUROPEAN $$
(Рок Гаррет; ☎3953-411 417; www.cherdak-bratsk.ru; ul Mira 43; mains ₽300-400; ⊙10am-2am) A restaurant, a pub and a rock-music venue – this all-in-one place is about the best option for an evening out in Bratsk. The menu is a carnivore's delight with a few Siberian elements, such as moose cutlets. Home-brewed lager, as well as English and Belgian ales, are on tap.

Getting There & Away

For Tsentralny, get off BAM trains at the Anzyobi (Анзеби) station and transfer by bus or *elektrichka* (suburban train). Bratsk has the following rail connections:

Irkutsk *platskart/kupe* ₽2500/2650, 16½ to 18½ hours, daily

Krasnoyarsk *platskart/kupe* ₽2000/2100, 12½ hours, up to four daily

Moscow *platskart/kupe* ₽8350/10,000, three days and three hours, one or two daily

Severobaikalsk *platskart/kupe* ₽2100/2300, 14 to 17 hours, up to four daily

Irkutsk can also be reached by Western-standard coach (₽1100, 10½ hours) from Tsentralny bus station (ul Yuzhnaya) and summer hydrofoil from a river station in southeast Tsentralny. Check **VSRP** (p186) for details of the latter.

Severobaikalsk

Северобайкальск

☎30130, 30139 / POP 23,900 / TIME MOSCOW +5HR

Founded as a shack camp for railway workers in the mid-1970s, Severobaikalsk has grown into the most engaging halt on the BAM, where travellers vacate stuffy railway compartments to stretch legs in the taiga or cool off in Lake Baikal. The town itself is a grid of soulless, earthquake-proof apartment blocks with little in between, but the mountainscape and nameless wildernesses backing the lake quickly lure hikers and adventurers away from the concrete. They discover a land more remote, less peopled and generally more spectacular than Baikal's south, a place where lazy bears and reindeer-herding Evenki still rule in timeless peace, despite the best efforts of *Homo sovieticus*.

Sights

Railway Station NOTABLE BUILDING
(pr 60 let SSSR; ⊙5am-midnight) The epicentre of SB's world is a striking construction with a nostalgically stranded steam locomotive standing guard to the right. The sweeping

architectural design of the brave-new-world station resembles a ski jump, but it's really meant to look like a ship. As with the rest of Severobaikalsk, it was designed by architects from Leningrad, who tried to convey the sense of both places being united by the nautical theme.

An overhead bridge to the right of the station leads across the tracks towards a scenic clifftop trail that skirts the coast.

BAM Museum MUSEUM

(Музей БАМа; per Proletarsky 5; ₽50; ⏲10am-1pm & 2-6pm Tue-Sat) Having moved into larger premises, the town's friendly museum has exhibits on BAM railway history (workers' medals, grainy black-and-white photos, 'old' BAM tickets), some Buryat artefacts and a few mammoth bones. An adjacent room houses an **art gallery** where local artists display their works. There is also a souvenir shop that peddles shaman drums amid kitschy bric-a-brac.

God's Mother of Kazan Cathedral CHURCH

(ul Mira 10) A strange sight in a town built by Komsomol (Youth Communist League) enthusiasts, the town's new Orthodox church sports two impressive onion domes in gleaming gold and a monster chandelier inside. It stands just beyond the town's grey-concrete **war memorial**.

Activities

Severobaikalsk is the base for trekking expeditions along the Great Baikal Trail on the ice in winter. These, along with visits to Evenki reindeer herders, can be organised with the help of local tourist agencies and hotel owners.

Frolikha Adventure Coastline Trail TREKKING

Part of the Great Baikal Trail, this incredible, relatively demanding 100km adventure trekking route runs between the delta of the Verkhnyaya Angara River and the spa hamlet of Khakusy on Baikal's eastern shore. You'll need a boat to find the start of the trail at the mouth of the river, from where it takes eight days to reach Khakusy via countless lonely capes and bays, wild camping by the lake all the way.

Exhilarating river crossings (including a biggie – the River Frolikha), deserted beaches and show-stopping Baikal vistas punctuate the trail, and from Ayaya Bay a return hike to remote Lake Frolikha beckons.

For more information and trail maps, contact Severobaikalsk tour agencies, the Baikal Trail Hostel (p241) or Dresden-based **Baikalplan** (www.baikalplan.de).

Tours

Rashit Yakhin/BAM Tour TOURS

(☎8-914-833 1646, 30139-21 560; www.gobaikal.com; ul Oktyabrya 16/2) This experienced full-time travel-fixer, guide and ex-BAM worker suffered an immobilising stroke in the mid-1990s, rendering his spoken English somewhat hard to follow. Nonetheless, Rashit is quick to reply to emails and able to set ice-cycling and skiing trips on Baikal in winter as well as catamaran trips in summer. Dacha (private summer cottage) visits are also on offer.

WORTH A TRIP

KHAKUSY SPA

Seismic activity in the northern Baikal area shakes free lots of thermal springs, around which tiny spas have sprouted. These are great places to soothe aching muscles after days of contortion in your BAM carriage bunk, though facilities are pretty basic. Costs are low for accommodation, food and bathing.

To land at **Khakusy Spa** (www.hakusy.com) , and idyllically isolated hot-spring *turbaza* (holiday camp) requires permits in summer (available through Severobaikalsk tour companies and hotels), but these are waived in February and March, when it takes about an hour to drive across the ice from Severobaikalsk. Bathing is fun in the snow and frozen steam creates curious ice patterns on the wooden spa buildings.

In summer, make sure you book the ferry well in advance as it's a popular trip among Russian holidaymakers. An alternative way to reach Khakusy is along the 100km **Frolikha Adventure Coastline Trail**.

Maryasov Family TOURS
(☎8-924-391 4514, 8-908-597 5988; www.baikaltrail.ru) The English-speaking family of Yevgeny Maryasov, a cofounder of the Great Baikal Trail, runs a homestay, information centre and tourism association, and also organises guided treks to Baikalskoe and Lake Frolikha, seal-spotting trips to Ayaya Bay and fascinating trips to the camps of Evenki reindeer herders.

Ecoland TOURS
(☎8-902-162 1623, 30130-36 191; www.ecoland-tour.ru) This award-winning tour agency specialises in horse-riding trips, Baikal boat excursions and trekking.

Sleeping

Baikal Trail Hostel HOMESTAY $
(☎30130-23 860, 8-924-391 4514, 8-924-779 2805; www.baikaltrailhostel.com; ul Studencheskaya 12, apt 16; tr per person ₽900; @ 📶) Run by the younger generation of the Maryasov family in their own flat, SB's original hostel is now reduced to a three-bed homestay. Kitchen, washing machine and a communal climbing wall are at visitors' disposal. It's one of the best places in town to arrange back-country treks and trips into the wilds around the northern end of Lake Baikal.

Dad's House HOSTEL $
(Папин дом; ☎8-983-430 9817, 8-950-060 7343; azubina@mail.ru; ul Promyshlennaya 17; dm ₽750) A pretty little cottage in an unpretty industrial neighbourhood, not far from the centre, this new hostel has eight bunk beds and offers sumptuous breakfasts for an extra ₽250.

★**Zolotaya Rybka** GUESTHOUSE $$
(Золотая Рыбка; ☎30130-21 134; www.baikalgoldenfish.ru; ul Sibirskaya 14; d from ₽2300; 📶) Well signposted from ul Olkhonskaya, SB's best guesthouse maintains immaculate and imaginatively designed rooms in three buildings, providing glimpses of Lake Baikal through the trees. There are spotless toilets and showers throughout, guests have access to kitchens and a cook prepares a restaurant-standard breakfast on request (₽300 extra). Owner offers trips to Evenki reindeer herders.

Dom u Baikala GUESTHOUSE $$
(Дом у Байкала; ☎30130-239 50, 8-950-119 7380; www.baikal-kruiz.narod.ru; pr Neptunsky 3; d with/without bathroom ₽2600/2200; 📶) Located in the pleasant lakeside residential area of Severobaikalsk, this cottage contains several clean and well-equipped if uninspiring rooms. The English-speaking owner runs tours of main northern Baikal attractions.

Hotel Olymp HOTEL $$
(Гостиница Олимп; ☎30130-23 980; www.hotelolymp.ru; ul Poligrafistov 2b; s/d from ₽2200/2600, with shared bathroom from ₽1200/1500; 📶) Severobaikalsk's smartest sleep has spotless, cool, airy rooms, though the plumbing could be more professionally screwed down. For this price you might expect breakfast and free wi-fi – you get neither.

Eating

For quick and cheap eats – *pozi* (dumplings), shashlyk, *plov* and beer – try makeshift Buryat and Kyrgyz eateries in the shop row east of the station on pr 60 let SSSR.

Bar Bison GRILL $$
(☎8-950-399 9359; www.vk.com/bizonsbk; Leningradsky pr 8; mains ₽200-600; ⏲11am-1am) There are all kinds of shashlyk and other grilled meat in this little restaurant-bar located in what looks like a construction-site cabin by the town's market. Local Tikhonov & Sons beer is on tap. Gets a little rowdy on weekends.

Rialto ITALIAN $$
(☎8-924-652 4151; ul Studencheskaya 8; mains ₽200-600; ⏲9am-9pm Mon-Thu, 10am-10pm Fri-Sun) Pizzas, pastas and really good coffee served in pleasant Italianesque premises, decorated with pictures of Venice and Rome. Sometimes closes for banquets on the weekend.

Shopping

Market MARKET
(Gorodskoy Rynok) Baikal fish, smoked and sun-dried, cedar pine nuts, *sagaan-dalya* and other local herbs – you'll find all of this in the small but bustling market located in the heart of town.

Information

There are ATMs at the railway station, in the Zheleznodorozhnik Culture Centre and at the Leningradsky pr branch of the VIST Supermarket.

Post Office (Почта; Leningradsky pr 6; ⏲9am-2pm & 3-7pm Mon-Fri, 9am-2pm Sat)

Warm North of Baikal (www.privet-baikal.ru; Leningradsky pr 5; ⏲10am-6pm) The local tourism association has turned the town's library into an informal hospitality centre, where – in theory – someone should always be available to help travellers with accommodation and local tours. It also runs an English-language website with tons of information and listings.

Getting There & Away

TRAIN

Severobaikalsk has the following rail connections:

Bratsk *platskart/kupe* ₽2100/3700, 14 to 16 hours, three daily

Irkutsk *platskart/kupe* ₽3800/7000, 38 hours, daily

Krasnoyarsk *platskart/kupe* ₽3300/5600, 28 hours, three daily

Moscow *platskart/kupe* ₽9300/10,080, three days 18 hours, one or two daily

Tynda *platskart/kupe* ₽3000/3200, 26 hours, daily

AIR

With hydrofoil services from Irkutsk and Olkhon suspended, two weekly flights from Irkutsk (₽3750) and Ulan-Ude (₽6500) operated by Angara airline provide the only fast option of getting into and out of Severobaikalsk.

BUS

Marshrutky cluster outside Severobaikalsk's train station and run to the following destinations:

Baikalskoe ₽70, 45 minutes, two daily

Goudzhekit ₽120, 45 minutes, three daily

Nizhneangarsk Airport ₽50, 50 minutes, half-hourly

Getting Around

Taxi drivers charge a standard fare of ₽80 before 10pm and ₽100 during the night for trips anywhere around town. **Taxi Milent** (☎30130-255 33) is a very reliable service.

Around Severobaikalsk

Nizhneangarsk Нижнеангарск

Until the BAM clunked into town, Nizhneangarsk had led an isolated existence for over 300 years, cobbling together its long streets of wooden houses and harvesting Baikal's rich *omul* (a type of fish) stocks. If truth be told, not much changed when the railway arrived, but despite the appearance of now larger Severobaikalsk 30km away, the 5km-long village remains the administrative centre of northern Baikal.

The **Regional Museum** (ul Pobedy 37, Nizhneangarsk; ₽100; ⏰10am-6pm Mon-Fri) chases the history of the region back to the 17th century and includes several Evenki exhibits. The museum often hosts performances by the local Evenki folklore collective **Siniga**, which can be arranged through the Maryasov family (p241) in Severobaikalsk.

To the east of the town, a long spit of land known as **Yarki Island** caps the most northerly point of Lake Baikal and keeps powerful currents and waves out of the fragile habitat of the Verkhnyaya Angara delta. You can walk along its length.

Scenic low-altitude flights cross Lake Baikal to Irkutsk and Ulan-Ude when weather conditions allow.

Marshrutky (₽70, 50 minutes) from Severobaikalsk run every 30 minutes along ul Pobedy then continue along the coast road (ul Rabochaya) to the airport.

Baikalskoe Байкальское

This timeless little fishing village of log-built houses 45km south of Severobaikalsk has a jaw-droppingly picturesque lakeside location backed by wooded hills and snow-dusted peaks. Your first stop should be the small, informal **school museum** (Baikalskoe; ₽100; ⏰10am-4pm). The only other sight is the wooden **Church of St Inokent**, which strikes a scenic lakeside pose.

Most visitors come to Baikalskoe on a day trip from Severobaikalsk, but if you do want to stay the night, arrange a homestay through tour agencies and fixers in Severobaikalsk. The Maryasov family (p241) in Severobaikalsk can put you up in the house of **Gertrude Freimane**, a Latvian deportee, who cooks excellent wild-berry cakes. There's no cafe in the village, just a couple of shops selling basic foodstuffs.

Marshrutky (₽100, 45 minutes) leave from outside Severobaikalsk train station every day early in the morning and in the early evening, returning an hour or so later.

A section of the Great Baikal Trail heads north from the fishing port 20 minutes up a cliff-side path towards the radio mast atop cape Ludar, from which there are particularly superb views looking back towards the village. Beyond that, Baikalskoe's shamanic **petroglyphs** hide in awkward-to-reach cliff-side locations and can only be found with the help of a knowledgeable local. The well-maintained trail continues another 18 scenic kilometres through beautiful cedar and spruce forests and past photogenic **Boguchan Island** to chilly **Lake Slyudyanskoe**, next to which stands the small **Echo** turbaza (holiday camp) – book through the Maryasov family.

The hike makes for a rewarding day trip and, with the path hugging the lake most of the way, there's little chance of getting lost. From the Echo *turbaza* head along a dirt track through the forest to the Severobaikalsk–Baikalskoe road to hitch a lift, or prearrange transport back to Severobaikalsk. Alternatively, some hikers tackle the day the other way round, catching the morning *marshrutka* to Echo *turbaza,* then timing the hike to make the evening *marshrutka* back to Severobaikalsk.

Tynda Тында

41656 / POP 35,500 / TIME MOSCOW +6HR

The king of the BAM, Tynda is a nondescript town flanked by low-lying pine-covered hills. Many stop here, as it's a hub for trains between Severobaikalsk, Komsomolsk-na-Amure and, on the Little BAM, Blagoveshchensk to the south, or, on the in-progress AYaM (Amuro-Yakutskaya Mainline), Neryungri and Tommot to the north.

Don't expect quaint. Tynda's fully Soviet – there was nothing but a few shacks before BAM centralised its efforts here in 1974. Liven up your visit by arriving during a festival. The Bakaldin Festival rotates between several nearby Evenki villages in late May or early June, with traditional song, dance, reindeer rides and plenty of reindeer shashlyki and other native delicacies. March sees the Reindeer Hunter and Herder Festival.

Sights

BAM Museum MUSEUM

(Музей истории Байкало-Амурской магистрали; http://muzbam.amur.muzkult.ru; ul Sportivnaya 22; ₽150; 10am-2pm & 3-6pm Tue-Fri, to 7pm Sat) Tynda's pride and joy has four rooms of BAM relics and photos – sadly all devoid of English labelling – as well as exhibits on native Evenki culture, WWII, local art and regional wildlife. Don't miss the 9m-long 'barrel of Diogenes' parked in the yard, where many BAM workers lived during the railroad's construction. After crossing the pedestrian bridge from the train station, take the first left, continue 200m and turn right up Sportivnaya, where you'll soon see it on your left.

One section covers the Little BAM and the Gulag prisoners who built it in the 1930s. They lived (and died) in 24 BAM labour camps between Tynda and Bamovskaya, and some moving photos chronicle the extreme hardships these prisoners endured. Two rooms are dedicated to the big BAM, sections of which were built in the 1930s, 1940s and 1950s before Stalin died and the project was mothballed. A final display covers the period between its relaunch in 1974 and final completion in 1984.

BAM Builders Monument STATUE

(Памятник строителям БАМа; ul Mokhortova) This iconic and rather aggressive looking statue is Tynda's most obvious sight. It's dedicated to the massive human effort (both voluntary and not) needed to build the extraordinary Baikal-Amur Magistral (BAM) railway line. Locals know the statue colloquially as *muzhchina s molotkom* – the guy with the hammer.

Tours

Alexey Podprugin TOURS

(8-985-205 0365; bamland@mail.ru) Feisty adventurer Alexey Podprugin knows the wilderness surrounding Tynda well and can arrange kayaking, hiking and cross-country skiing trips. He doesn't speak English, so email him if you don't speak Russian.

Sleeping & Eating

Resting Rooms HOSTEL $

(Комнаты отдыха; 41656-73 297; train station, Zarechnaya ul; bed per 6/12/24hr from ₽650/990/1650) Comfy and clean dorm rooms in the train station. Shower available for nonguests (₽150).

Hotel Yunost HOTEL $$

(Гостиница Юность; 41656-43 534; ul Krasnaya Presnaya 49; s/d from ₽3500/4000, s/d with shared bathroom ₽2000/3000;) Faded but fine option in centre; Dervla Murphy recuperated here while writing *Through Siberia by Accident*. You can get wi-fi literally on one sofa in the lobby: it's free, but you might need a while to do anything. Staff don't speak English and regard foreigners with a pleasing amount of suspicion, which seems correct after such a long journey.

Piv Bar Teremok PIZZA $$

(Пив Бар Теремок; ul Krasnaya Presnaya 59a; mains ₽300-600; noon-midnight;) Serves up palatable pizzas, Drakon draft beer (from Khabarovsk) and has seating on an open-sided veranda. To find it, turn left at the eastern end of Krasnaya Presnaya, and walk up 50m.

Information

The train station has an ATM and left-luggage office (₽140).

Getting There & Away

The **train station** (ЖД вокзал; Zarechnaya ul) – the city's most striking landmark – is across the Tynda River. A pedestrian bridge leads 1km north to ul Krasnaya Presnaya.

Train 75 heads via the BAM to Moscow (*kupe/platskartny* ₽20,800/10,000, five days) on even-numbered days, stopping in Severobaikalsk (*kupe/platskartny* ₽4600/2900, 27 hours), while trains 77, 97 and the 75 travelling in the other direction head to Novosibirsk (*kupe/platskartny* ₽11,600/6700, 67 hours), taking the Little BAM south on odd-numbered days to connect with the Trans-Siberian line at Skovorodino.

There are several daily departures to Neryungri, including the 325 (from ₽576, 5½ hours). Train 364 trundles to Komsomolsk daily (*kupe/platskartny* ₽5800/3000, 36 hours), and 325 heads daily to Khabarovsk at 2am via Skovorodino (*kupe/platskartny* ₽5500/3000, 28 hours).

Komsomolsk-na-Amure

Комсомольск-на-Амуре

☎4217 / POP 251,000 / TIME MOSCOW +7HR

After days of taiga and grey Soviet towns, Komsomolsk-na-Amure comes as a charming surprise with its attractive Stalin-era centre and pleasant Amur River setting. Built virtually from scratch in the 1930s as a vital cog in the Soviet Union's military industrial complex, Komsomolsk's name comes from the thousands of Communist Youth League volunteers who built the town alongside Gulag labourers.

Imitating the tsars, Stalin erected elaborate neoclassical buildings in the city centre and then festooned them with stars and statues of model Soviet citizens. Around town, factories sprouted up to produce ships, weapons, electricity and, most famously, Sukhoi (Su) fighter jets in a factory that still works today. Set along a few grand boulevards, the city is worth a night or more if you are getting on or off the BAM.

Sights

Just east of the river terminal is a **beach**, which is well attended on warm summer days.

Komsomolsk has a wealth of wonderful murals adorning the sides of apartment blocks and factories. Most were the creation of Khabarovsk-based artist Nikolai Dolbilkin, who lived here in the 1950s and '60s. Among the best are the double-triptych **WWII mosaic** (cnr pr Mira & alleya Truda) in the central grey *dom kultura* building near Sudostroitel Park (now inside a children's play space) and the **nauka (science) mosaic** (pr Lenina) at the Polytechnical Institute, a block east of Hotel Voskhod.

Municipal Museum of Regional Studies — MUSEUM

(Городской краеведческий музей; www.kmsgkm.ru; cnr alleya Truda & ul Kirova; ₽250; ⌚9.30am-5pm Tue-Fri, 10am-5pm Sat & Sun) This proud town museum has several rooms of photos and artefacts showing how Komsomolsk rose from a pioneer camp in 1932 to an industrial Soviet city. It also contains some old fish-skin jackets and other Nanai artefacts. It's expensive for the sure-to-be-quick visit, even more so as there's no labelling in English.

WWII Memorial — MEMORIAL

(ul Dzherzhinskogo) Just northwest of the river terminal is the impressive WWII memorial, which features stoic faces chipped from stone, with nearby pillars marking the years of WWII.

Japanese POW Memorial — MONUMENT

(ul Ordzhonikidze) This small monument is dedicated to the memory of the Japanese prisoners of war who were forced to work building the BAM after WWII.

Activities

Nata Tour — TOURS

(Ната-Тур; ☎Mikhail 8-914-189 1784, Vladimir 8-914-177 3724; komsomolsknata@mail.ru; office 110, ul Vasyanina 12; ⌚10am-6pm Mon-Fri) These local experts arrange three- to five-hour 'Stalin tours' of the city's communist sites (including a Gulag camp) from ₽1300 per person; adventure tours involving fishing, rafting or skiing; and day trips and/or homestays at Verkhnyaya Ekon. Mikhail speaks English.

River Cruises — BOATING

(River Terminal; ₽300) On summer weekends, you can hop aboard 90-minute cruises along the Amur River. Boats depart at 3pm Saturday and Sunday as well as 7pm Thursday and Saturday. Buy tickets on board.

Komsomolsk-na-Amure

Sights

1 Japanese POW Memorial B4
2 Municipal Museum of Regional Studies B3
3 Nauka Mosaic A2
4 WWII Memorial A4
5 WWII Mosaic B3

Activities, Courses & Tours

6 Nata Tour A2
7 River Cruises A4

Sleeping

8 Biznestsentr B4
9 Hotel Voskhod A2
10 Resting Rooms A1

Eating

11 Bistro B2
12 Kafema B2
13 Shinok Pervach A4

Sleeping

Resting Rooms HOSTEL $

(Комнаты отдыха; ☎4217-284 193; train station, pr Pervostroiteley; 12/24hr dm from ₽720/1100, s 12/24hr without bathroom ₽1040/1830) A clean and basic option inside the train station if you need a break from sleeping on trains.

★**Biznestsentr** HOTEL $$

(Гостиничный комплекс Бизнес-центр; ☎4217-521 522; bc@etc.kna.ru; ul Dzerzhinskogo 3; s/d incl breakfast from ₽2000/2500; ❄📶) Komsomolsk's most modern business-oriented hotel has bright, comfortably furnished rooms with modern bathrooms (including space-shuttle-like shower capsules). English-speaking receptionists are on hand too.

Hotel Voskhod HOTEL $$

(Гостиница Восход; ☎4217-535 131; www.hotel-voskhod.com; pr Pervostroiteley 31; s/d from ₽2200/2700; 📶) A 10-minute walk from the train station, this eight-storey Soviet-era beast has decently renovated rooms and surprisingly friendly staff.

Eating

In the summer, you can feast on *shashlyk* (₽200) and cold drinks along the riverfront overlooking the beach.

Kafema CAFE $

(Кафема; www.kafema.ru; Okyabrsky pr 39; pastries from ₽100; ⏲10am-8pm; 📶) This place does the best coffee in town, and the passionate, well-trained baristas will even sell you some of their delicious fresh beans to take with you on your travels. Cakes, pastries and other snacks are available.

Bistro RUSSIAN $

(Бистро; ul Lenina 19; mains ₽80-160; ⏲9am-10pm) Beside pl Lenina, this clean modern *stolovaya* serves tasty, affordable staples: baked dishes, roast meats and the usual beet or potato salads are all on offer.

Shinok Pervach UKRAINIAN $$

(Шинок Первач; www.shinok-pervach.ru; ul Dzherzhinskogo 34; mains ₽300-900; ⏲noon-3am; 📶) A local institution, Shinok Pervach is considered by locals to be the best restaurant in town. It serves up tasty grilled fish, roast meats and zingy salads (try the beetroot, walnut and prune for its subtle spice). The chunky wooden tables and circular dining

BAM ENDS, SAKHALIN BECKONS

BAM completists will end up in the grey Soviet port town of Vanino (actually the BAM ends 15 minutes beyond Vanino, in Sovetskaya Gavan-Sortirovka). From Vanino, there is a **Sakhalin Shipping Company** (SASCO; ☎42433-66 133, 42433-66 208; www.sasco.ru; ul Pobedy 18a, Kholmsk) ferry around three times a week leaving at varying times of day to Kholmsk on Sakhalin Island (tickets ₽1950 to ₽4200 depending on class, 18 hours). Do be aware that the two ferries working this route are very old, cramped and break down frequently. Despite this, your biggest obstacle is the unpredictable and fast-changing weather in the Strait of Tartary. Call the **ticket office** (SASCO; ☎42137-74 088; www.sasco.ru; Vanino) in Vanino the day before to reserve a seat and to check if the next day's ship is likely to sail, as it's far nicer to be stuck in Komsomolsk-na-Amure than Vanino.

room festooned maypole-style with ribbons bestow a certain peasant chic to the place.

Despite its address, it's actually located just off pr Internatsionalny.

Getting There & Away

TRAIN

From Komsomolsk's pink **train station** (ЖД вокзал; pr Pervostroiteley), the excruciatingly slow 351 leaves daily for Vladivostok (*kupe/platskartny* ₽5500/2600, 25 hours). There are also two daily services (trains 351 and 667) to Khabarovsk (*kupe/platskartny* from ₽2300/1300, 10 hours).

On the BAM, the daily 363 heads west to Tynda (*kupe/platskartny* ₽5800/3000, 38 hours); to reach Severobaikalsk, change in Tynda. The daily train 351 heads east to Vanino (*kupe/platskartny* ₽2200/1400, 13 hours). The BAM's first/last stop, 'Sovetskaya Gavan-Sortirovka', 15 minutes east of Vanino, is not to be confused with the city of Sovetsakaya Gavan, an hour away from Vanino by bus.

AIR

Komsomolsk-na-Amur's small **airport** (Аэропорт Хурба) has flights on Aurora to Vladivostok each Wednesday and Friday (₽3600, two hours).

BOAT

For a DIY adventure, head down the Amur River by hydrofoil to Nikolayevsk-na-Amure (from ₽4350, 11 hours). The boat departs three days a week from the **river terminal** (Речной вокзал) (currently on Monday, Wednesday and Friday mornings).

BUS

Local and long-distance buses leave from the **bus station** (автостанция; ☎4217-542 554; ⏲6am-10.30pm) near the river. Buses bound for Khabarovsk (from ₽640, six hours) leave every 90 minutes or so from 7am.

Getting Around

Within the city, handy tram 2 runs from the train station along ul Lenina and pr Mira to the river terminal (₽20).

The Trans-Mongolian Route

Includes ➡

Route Info

➡ Distance: 2217km

➡ Duration: Two days six hours

➡ Time zones: Moscow +4, Moscow +5

Best Places to Stay

➡ Zaya Hostel (p260)

➡ Lotus Guesthouse (p261)

➡ Urgoo Hotel (p261)

➡ Best Western Tuushin Hotel (p261)

Best Places to Eat

➡ Luna Blanca (p264)

➡ Hazara (p264)

➡ Bull (p264)

➡ Millie's Espresso (p263)

Why Go?

The Trans-Mongolian route is the most diverse leg of the cross-continental journey, cutting across three distinct cultures, landscapes and languages. It includes some of the most awe-inspiring sights of the long journey, not the least of which is the Gobi Desert, but also the vast Mongolian steppes and the stunning gorges outside Běijīng. The major jumping-off point is Ulaanbaatar (UB), where many travellers head for the colourful Naadam Festival, but any time of year reveals a surprisingly fast-paced city with great cultural attractions and heady nightlife.

Mongolia's real attraction lies in the untouched beauty of the countryside, its exhilarating wide open spaces and rich nomadic culture. Fortunately, these aspects are within reach on day trips or overnights from UB. The China leg is a relatively short hop but has its own unique character, highlighted by the beguiling Yúngāng Caves near Dàtóng.

When to Go

Ulaanbaatar

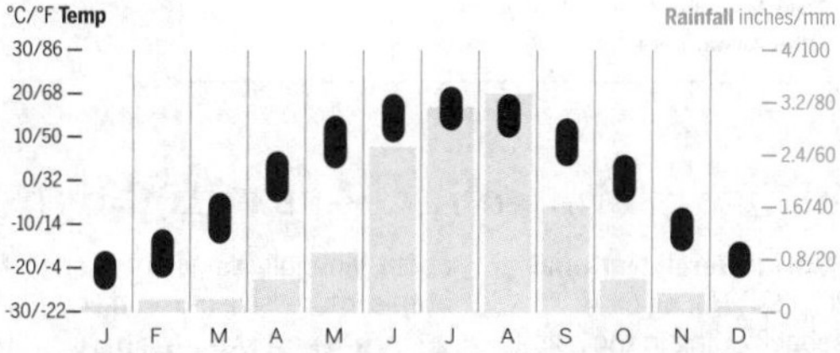

Mid-Jul Naadam grinds Ulaanbaatar to a halt to make way for wrestling, archery and horse racing.

Aug Prime time for lounging in Ulaanbaatar's open-air cafes, swapping travel stories.

Sep Autumn brings changing colours in forested areas and smaller tourist crowds.

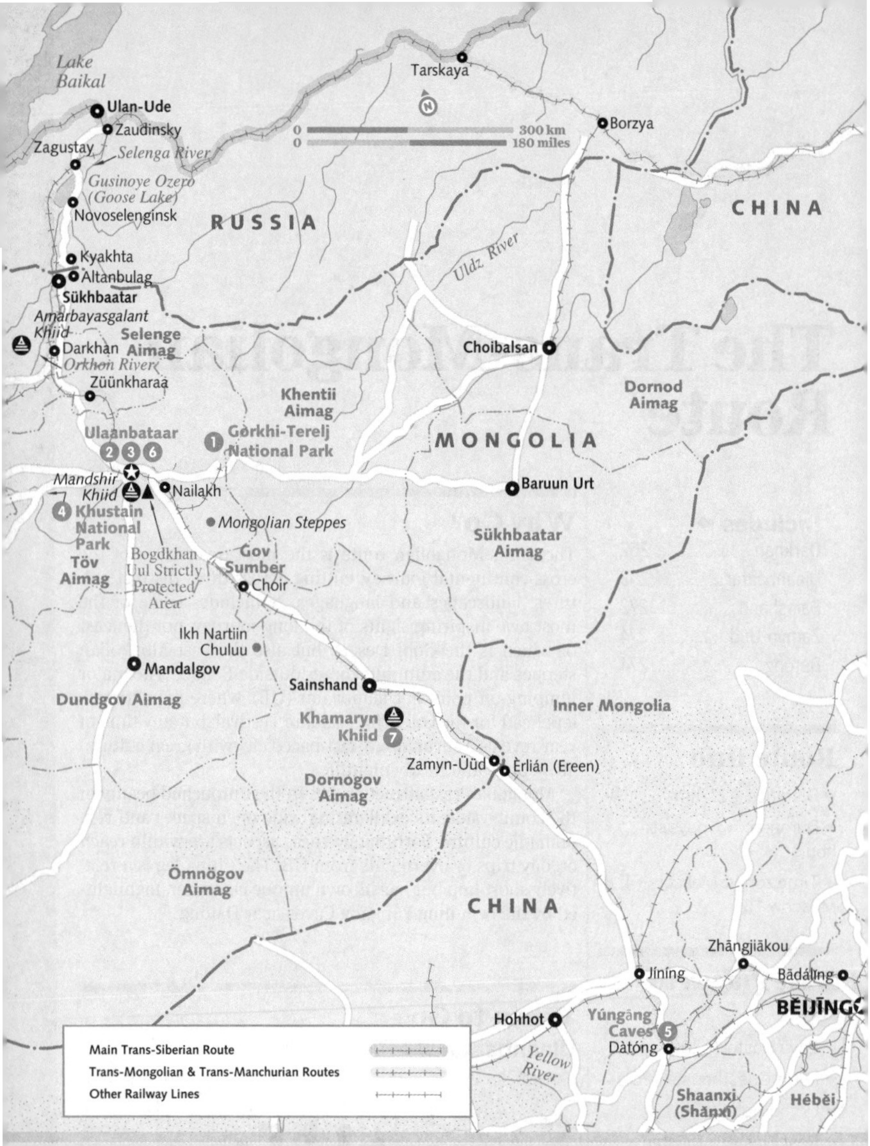

The Trans-Mongolian Route Highlights

1 **Gorkhi-Terelj National Park** (p271) Hiking or horseback riding in the hills and valleys near Ulaanbaatar

2 **Gandan Khiid** (p257) Walking the prayer circuit around the country's largest monastery in Ulaanbaatar.

3 **National Museum of Mongolia** (p258) Learning about Mongolia's ancient past at this impressive museum.

4 **Khustain National Park** (p272) Spotting the rare *takhi* (Mongolian wild horse) in this wildlife-rich park.

5 **Yúngāng Caves** (p278) Staring in wonder at the 51,000 Buddhist statues inside these caves near Dàtóng

6 **Naadam** Celebrating the midsummer festival, featuring Mongolia's best wrestlers, archers and race horses

7 **Khamaryn Khiid** (p274) Visiting this impressive ger-like structure then absorbing some of the earth's energy at nearby Shambhala.

The Route

The Trans-Mongolian line branches off from the main Trans-Siberian route at Zaudinsky, about 13km southeast of Ulan-Ude. Mongolia and China each have their own kilometre markers. In Mongolia, the markers measure the distance to the Russian–Mongolian border, so 0km is the border town of Naushki. Once in China, the markers measure the distance to Běijīng.

ZAUDINSKY TO NAUSHKI

5655km from Moscow

At **Zaudinsky** the branch line turns south and continues to follow the Selenge River, crossing at around 5701km. Here you'll see herds of cattle grazing across low, green hills beside a wide, lazy river, and villages of wooden houses with brightly painted window shutters and flourishing gardens that explode with fruits and flowers in summer.

5769km

After you pass the town of **Zagustay**, the train follows the shoreline of Gusinoe Ozero (Goose Lake), surrounded by thick woods of pine and birch that are usually prevalent further north.

5885km

Another crossing over the Selenge River.

5902km

The train arrives at **Naushki** (5902km in Russia but 0km for Mongolia), a small, uneventful town that serves as the Russian border post. The train hangs around the border for several hours for customs and passport checks.

SÜKHBAATAR TO ULAANBAATAR

21km from Naushki

Mongolia's chief border town, **Sükhbaatar** (population 19,700) is set at the junction of the Selenge and Orkhon Rivers. Founded in the 1940s, it's named after the revolutionary hero Damdin Sükhbaatar, who in 1921 famously rode his horse to Russia to enlist the aid of the Bolsheviks after Mongolia was invaded by White Russian troops. The train stops for an hour or two (depending on which train you're on), giving you time to stretch your legs and perhaps make the 10-minute walk to the tiny town center to pick up a snack at the convenience store.

63km

When you cross the **Erӧӧ River** look out for cranes, herons and other waterfowl in the marshy areas on the west side of the train. Having entered Mongolia you'll also sense a change of scenery: the forests thin out into the lush green pastures of the fertile Selenge River basin. You may also notice new scents (in the form of mutton) as the Mongolian dining car is attached after the train crosses the border.

123km

The rolling green hills of northern Mongolia break momentarily as the train pulls into **Darkhan** for a brief stop. You can buy some *buuz* (mutton-filled dumplings) from the ladies who sell them out of plastic containers.

274-290km

This is the most scenic stretch of the Trans-Mongolian route, a 15km ride through a pretty valley and alongside the Kharaa River.

355km to 365km

The train passes the area of **Hui Doloon Khutag**, where the Naadam horse races are held from 10 to 12 July. In the days before Naadam locals move out here en masse, creating a city of scattered gers. After another 20km the train curves around a valley towards Ulaanbaatar, where you'll get your first glimpse of the smokestacks and urban sprawl of the Mongolian capital.

404km

After a long march through the industrial outskirts the train pulls into **Ulaanbaatar**. If stopping off here, expect throngs of people on the platform offering tours, taxi rides or a bunk in a local guesthouse.

TRANS-MONGOLIAN ROUTE PLANNER

The following is a suggested itinerary for covering the main sites along the Trans-Mongolian route. This is a quick pace, so consider adding a few days to make the journey more leisurely:

Day 1 Leave Ulan-Ude and take an overnight train to Darkhan.

Day 2 Arrange a return taxi from Darkhan to Amarbayasgalant Monastery.

Day 3 Continue to Ulaanbaatar.

Days 4 & 5 Tour Ulaanbaatar and around.

Day 6 Travel to Ikh Nartiin Chuluu, overnight.

Day 7 Tour Ikh Nartiin Chuluu.

Day 8 Travel to Sainshand by road and train.

Day 9 Visit Khamaryn Khiid, continue on night train to Zamyn-Üüd.

Day 10 Cross border, continue by bus to Dàtóng.

Day 11 Tour Dàtóng and Yúngāng Caves.

Day 12 Train to Běijīng (seven hours).

Ulan-Ude to Běijīng

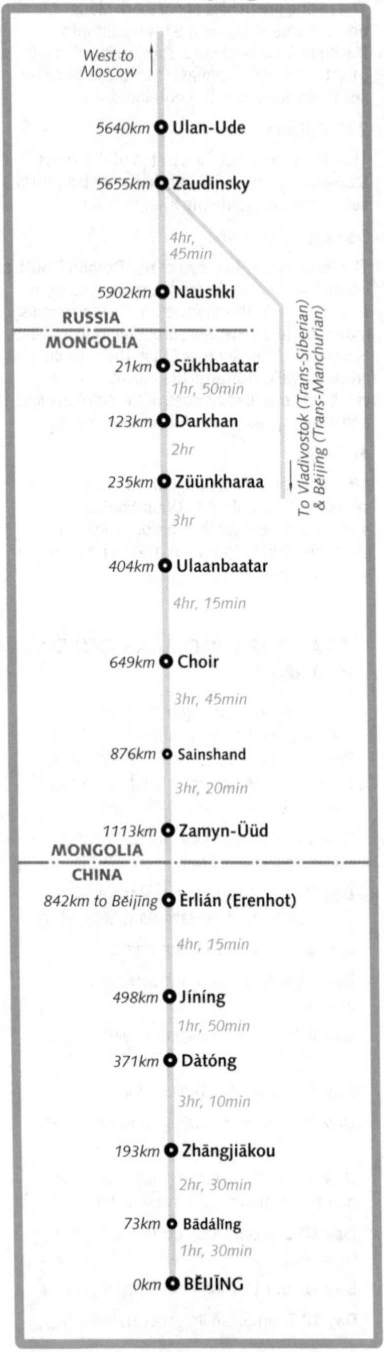

ULAANBAATAR TO ZAMYN-ÜÜD

415km to 440km

South of Ulaanbaatar, the railway winds through the gently swelling hills of the **Bogdkhan Uul** mountain range. Trees eventually disappear and the landscape becomes a 180-degree panorama of steppe, the only interruptions being grazing horses and the occasional ger.

649km

There's a 15-minute stop at **Choir**, where a statue of the first Mongolian cosmonaut stands in front of the station. During the Soviet era this neglected town of 13,000 people was home to Mongolia's biggest air base.

From Choir, it's possible to detour south for one hour to **Ikh Nartiin Chuluu**, an area of rocky outcrops that provide shelter for endangered argali sheep.

Continuing south, the train enters the flat, arid and sparsely populated **Gobi Desert**. Occasional stops at small outposts provide glimpses of dilapidated shacks and villagers hauling water or galloping alongside the train on horseback. Any small bodies of water attract livestock, and you'll probably spot horses, camels, sheep and goats (sorry, no yaks in this part of the country).

876km

The train stops for around 20 minutes at **Sainshand** (Good Pond). The vendors on the platform selling *buuz* run out of product quickly, so you'll need to act fast. The westbound Trans-Mongolian train (3/23) does not allow passengers to disembark. About 40km south of Sainshand is **Khamaryn Khiid**, one of the most important Buddhist monasteries in the Gobi.

1113km

The bleak, dusty landscape continues to the border town of **Zamyn-Üüd**. Travel writer Paul Theroux visited the town in the mid-1980s and commented that Zamyn-Üüd was 'a wreck of a town set on glaring sands and so lacking in events that when a camel went by everyone watched it'. Sadly, not much has changed since then. From here you can cross by road or rail over the border to China. If you're coming from China you'll have to wait around for the next local train heading north, or ask around for a share taxi.

Chinese and Mongolian railways run on different track gauges, so if you're on a local train, you'll have to change trains here. Travellers on international trains in either direction (including 3/23 or 4/24) can avoid this and roll on through, but prepare for at least two hours of thunks, thuds and clangs as the bogies are changed at Èrlián.

ZAMYN-ÜÜD TO BĚIJĪNG

842km from Běijīng

Compared to Zamyn-Üüd, the Chinese side of the border, **Èrlián**, is a veritable megalopolis.

From here it takes about 13 hours to get to Běijīng by direct train.

For the first several hours the train continues through the Gobi, now in the ostensibly autonomous region of **Inner Mongolia**. Mongolians make up only about 15% of the population here, and since 1949 China has done its best to assimilate them, eradicating their nomadic lifestyle, even though they have been permitted to keep their written and spoken language. Further south, the desert slowly gives way to grasslands and you'll spot Mongol shepherds tending their flocks.

It's a long journey between Zamyn-Üüd and Běijīng – especially if you are on the Trans-Mongolian train, which does not stop between these cities – so if you're getting a little antsy, go to the dining car, where most of the train's socialising takes place. The Chinese dining car is arguably the best on the entire trans-continental route – but we'll let you be the judge of that.

498km

At the main rail junction of **Jíníng**, vendors sell drinks, snacks and colourful balloons on the platform. This is where the Ulaanbaatar–Hohhot train breaks off the main line and heads west.

371km

Dàtóng is the centre of China's coal industry but the region remains an important centre of Chinese history and was the powerbase for the Tang dynasty (618–907). Slip off the train here for a trip to nearby Yúngāng Caves.

300km

From Dàtóng the line turns east, entering Héběi province. Héběi is characterised by its mountainous tableland where the Great Wall runs. There are good views of the Wall on the northern side of the tracks between 295km and 275km.

In addition, keep your eyes peeled for the occasional walled villages, typically composed of thick rammed-earth walls with traditional homes stuffed into their small interior. One example can be seen between the 264km and 263km markers on the south side of the tracks.

193km

Formerly known as Khaalga, which means 'door' or 'gate' in Mongolian, **Zhāngjiākou** was was where the ancient tea caravans crossed the Great Wall. From here the terrain becomes increasingly hilly and the scenery is quite dramatic as the train travels across a plateau punctuated by cropland and tree-filled gullies.

85km

From here the train begins its final approach to Běijīng, swiftly entering a mountainous zone that separates the Chinese capital from the northern plains. There are some 60 tunnels to pass through and while it can be difficult to spot the kilometre markers you can easily count down (or count up if you're heading west) the tunnel numbers, painted at the entrance of the tunnels (on the right side). The first number is the tunnel number, the second is the kilometre marker and the third is the length of the tunnel. Each time the train emerges from a tunnel there are stunning scenes of canyons, rivers and soaring rock towers.

0km

Make a toast with any leftover Russian vodka; you've reached **Běijīng**, the end of the line. If you're starting your journey in Běijīng, take a moment to wipe down the windows with a dust cloth; the photo opportunities are excellent outside Běijīng and you'll want a clear shot (heading west the best views are out the left side of the train).

RUSSIA–MONGOLIA BORDER CROSSING

Trans-Mongolian train travellers go in and out of Russia at the Naushki–Sükhbaatar train border crossing. Be prepared to be stranded for hours on the Russian side, spending much of the time locked inside the train wagons.

Procedures on the Ulaanbaatar–Moscow train are faster than on the local trains. Heading out of Russia, you will be asked to fill out a customs declaration form. You should note on the form how much currency you are taking out of the country.

Naushki You can have a look around Naushki, but there is little to see and the train border crossing usually takes place in the middle of the night. Surprisingly, you may have difficulty finding anyone at the Naushki station to change money, so wait until Sükhbaatar or Ulaanbaatar, or somewhere else in Russia. (Get rid of your tögrög before you leave Mongolia, as almost no one will want to touch them once you are inside Russia.)

Sükhbaatar The train may stop for one or two hours at the pleasant Mongolian border town of Sükhbaatar. You may be able to buy some Russian roubles or Mongolian tögrög from a money changer at the train station, but the rate will be poor. If there aren't any money changers, you can use US dollars to get by until you can change money elsewhere.

Darkhan

☎7037, 01372 / POP 97,700 / TIME MOSCOW + 5HR

Mongolia's second largest city sprawls across a few hills and dusty smatterings of steppe. It's not our first pick for must-see tourism destination of the 21st century, but it does make an appealing short stop en route to Amarbayasgalant Khiid or the Russian border.

The city was created by the Soviets in the 1960s as an industrial base for the north. Under communist rule it worked as a model urban cooperative of factory workers, tractor drivers, coal miners and government officials. The economy took a nosedive in the early 1990s following independence, but is slowly picking up again, thanks to grain production and coal mining.

Darkhan is divided into an 'old town' near the train station and a 'new town' to the south, with most hotels, restaurants and amenities located in the latter.

In the new town is the appealing little **Museum of Darkhan-Uul** (☎7037-3020; What3words: nearly.nests.caravans; admission T1500; ⌚9am-1pm & 2-6pm Mon-Fri) which contains a well-presented collection of archaeological finds, traditional clothing, religious artefacts and stuffed wildlife.

There's good-value midrange accommodation about 10 minutes' walk from the bus station at the **Kharaa Hote** (☎9147 0069; kharaa.hotel@yahoo.com; What3words: disarmed.afternoon.barmaid; r/lux incl breakfast from T40,000/60,000; @📶)l which has clean and comfortably furnished rooms. The bar on the ground floor adds a bit of spice to this compact hotel. Decent Western and better Mongolian cuisine can be found at **Texas Pub** (☎7037-4008; What3words: comply.clusters.tangling; meals T5000-24,000; ⌚8am-midnight Mon-Fri, from 11am weekends; 📶).

Darkhan is the only train junction in northern Mongolia: all northern trains to/from Ulaanbaatar, and all trains to/from Erdenet, stop here. The express service to Ulaanbaatar (hard seat/hard sleeper/soft sleeper T5500/13,500/15,300) leaves Darkhan at 2.10pm, arriving in Ulaanbaatar at 6pm.

From the main **bus station** (Авто Вокзал; What3words: walking.inactivate.ticket), buses depart hourly between 8am and 8pm for Ulaanbaatar (T10,100, 3½ hours). Also from here plenty of shared taxis (T15,200) do the three-hour run to UB.

> **ℹ MONGOLIAN ADDRESSES: WHAT THREE WORDS**
>
> In 2016 the Mongol post service adopted the What3words (https://what3words.com) address system. The system is slowly being used across the country as a means of navigation using its smartphone app. All the addresses in the listings in this chapter use the What-3words system.

Amarbayasgalant Khiid

Tucked up a remote valley 35km from any main road, **Amarbayasgalant Monastery** (Амарбаясгалант Хийд; What3words: picketing.inflicts.tourists; T5000; ⌚10am-7pm summer, hours vary at other times; 🅿) is one of the finest examples of Buddhist architecture in Mongolia. While not the easiest place to reach, it's worth considering if you have a particular interest in Buddhism or off-the-beaten-path sites.

The monastery was built between 1727 and 1737 by the Manchu emperor Yongzheng, and dedicated to the great Mongolian Buddhist lama and sculptor Zanabazar, whose mummified body was moved here in 1779. The design references Manchu style, down to the inscriptions, symmetrical layout, imperial colour scheme and roof guardians on every roof corner.

Despite extensive restoration by Unesco, there's a sense of genteel decay and a gradual takeover by nature that adds to the allure of the place. The monastery was largely spared during the 1937 purge, possibly because of sympathetic and procrastinating local military commanders. These days about 30 monks live here, compared with more than 2000 in 1936.

Most of the temples in the monastery are normally closed, so if you want to see any statues or *thangkas* (scroll paintings), you'll have to find the monks with the keys in the monks' quarters, the yellow concrete buildings on the right side (east) of the monastery. This isn't an uncommon request, so don't feel too awkward about asking. The main gates to the temple are supposed to be open from 10am to 7pm during the summer, although these times seem a little fluid in practice. During winter, you'll usually have to ask at the dorms for the keys.

Ceremonies are usually held at 10am, so arrive early or stay overnight to see them.

A couple of newer monuments – a golden Buddha statue and a stupa – are situated on the hills behind the monastery. You could continue hiking up the mountains for even better views of the valley.

IF Tour Ger Camp (☎9918 9981, 9119 0808; iftour@yahoo.com; What3words: siege.megabyte.scale; ger & r/cabin T50,000/60,000; ⊙May-Oct; P), furthest west from the temple complex, is the one with the best facilities. Choose between a cosy ger with electricity, an individual cabin or a bright room inside the lodge. It's clean, comfortable, offers hot showers and flushing toilets and serves hearty meals (dinner around T13,500). Some English and German spoken.

No regular public transport goes to the monastery, so you'll need to organise your own transport. From Ulaanbaatar, travel north to the T-intersection for Erdenet (just short of Darkhan). Take the Erdenet road for 90km and then turn right on to a dirt road; look for the sign (GPS: N 49°12.814', E 104°59.131'; What3words: medicating.protein.meandering) that says 'Amarbayasgalant 35km'. Altogether, the journey to/from Ulaanbaatar takes around five or six hours. If you don't have your own car you could charter one from Darkhan; if you bargain, you can negotiate a day rental for around T150,000.

Ulaanbaatar

☎011, 021, 051 / POP 1.4 MILLION / TIME MOSCOW + 5HR

If Mongolia's yin is its pristine countryside, then Ulaanbaatar (UB; Улаанбаатар) harmonises as its vibrant yang. It's a sprawling, industrialised city of pulsating commerce, wild traffic, sinful nightlife and bohemian counter-culture. The contrasts within the city are intriguing: Armani-suited businessmen rub shoulders with mohawked punks and *del*-clad nomads fresh off the steppes; one minute you're dodging the path of a Hummer H2 and the next you're entranced by chanting Buddhist monks at Gandan Khiid. As the coldest capital in the world, come summer the city bursts into life after slumbering through a long winter.

Ulaanbaatar is not always the easiest city to navigate, but with a little patience travellers can take care of all their logistical needs, visit world-class museums, watch traditional theatre, sample international cuisine and party till three in the morning. Indeed, this ever-changing city may be the biggest surprise of your Mongolian adventure.

History

The first recorded capital city of the Mongolian empire was created in 1639. It was called Örgöö and was originally located at the monastery of Da Khuree, some 420km from Ulaanbaatar in Arkhangai aimag (province). The monastery was the residence of five-year-old Zanabazar who, at the time, had been proclaimed the head of Buddhism in Mongolia. Because it consisted of felt tents, the 'city' was easily transported when the grass went dry. Some 25 movements were recorded along the Orkhon, Selenge and Tuul Gols (rivers). Throughout these movements the city was given some fairly unexciting official and unofficial names, including Khuree (Camp) in 1706.

ULAANBAATAR IN...

Two Days

On your first morning in town pay a visit to the **National Museum of Mongolia** (p258), then take a turn around **Sükhbaatar Sq** (p257). After lunch visit the **Choijin Lama Temple Museum** (p258). Watch a Mongolian cultural show in the evening. Rise early on day two to visit **Gandan Khiid** (p257) in time to catch the monks chanting. Head down to the **State Department Store** (p267) to shop for souvenirs. After lunch, head south to the **Winter Palace of the Bogd Khan** (p258). In the evening climb the steps to the **Zaisan Memorial** (p114) to watch the sun set over the city, then hit **Seoul St** (p266) for a night out on the town.

Four Days

On day three visit the **Zanabazar Museum of Fine Arts** (p258), then head over to **Naran Tuul Market** (p266). Celebrate your stay with a cocktail at rooftop **17 Sky Bar** (p265) or craft beer at **Hops & Rocks** (p265), before hitting **iLoft** (p265) nightclub. On day four take a day trip out of town to **Chinggis Khaan Statue Complex** (p115). Have a Mongolian feast at **Modern Nomads 2** (p264) or vegetarian at **Luna Blanca** (p264).

Central Ulaanbaatar

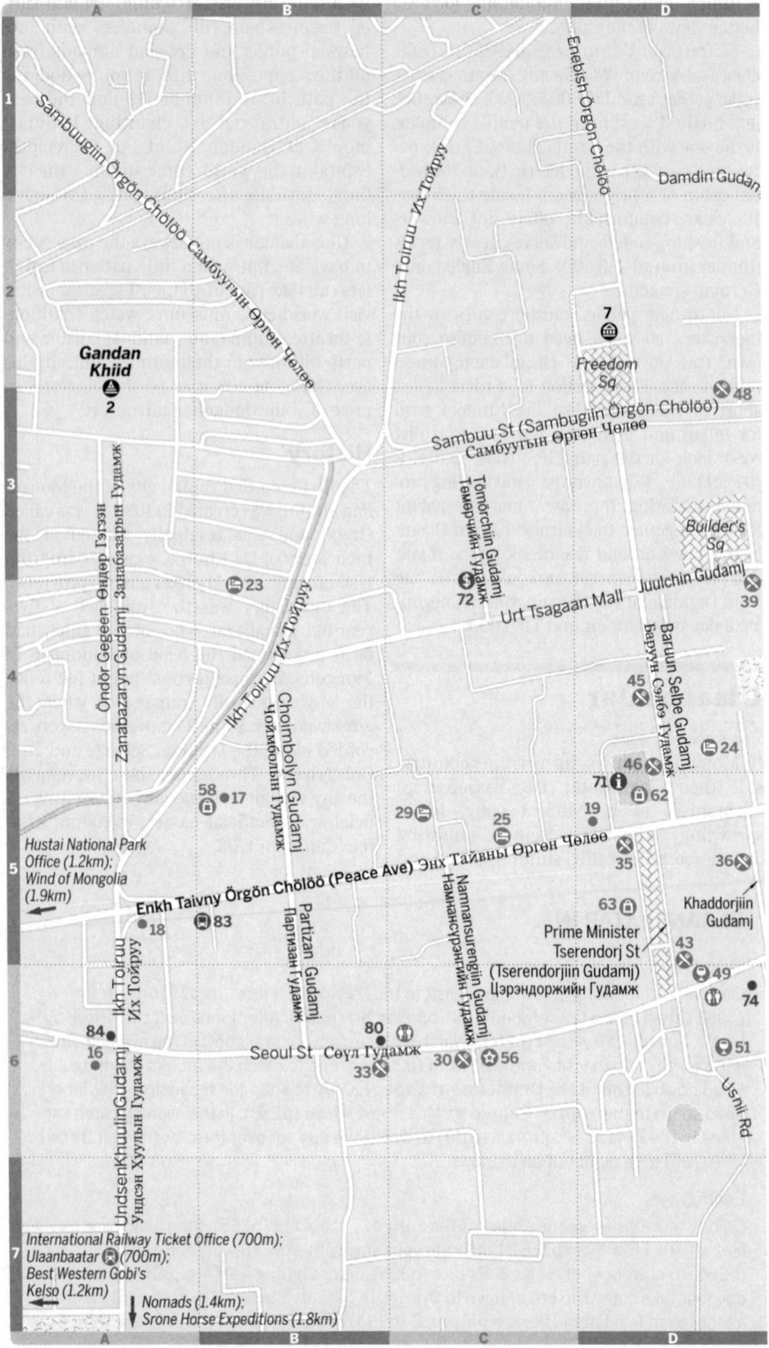

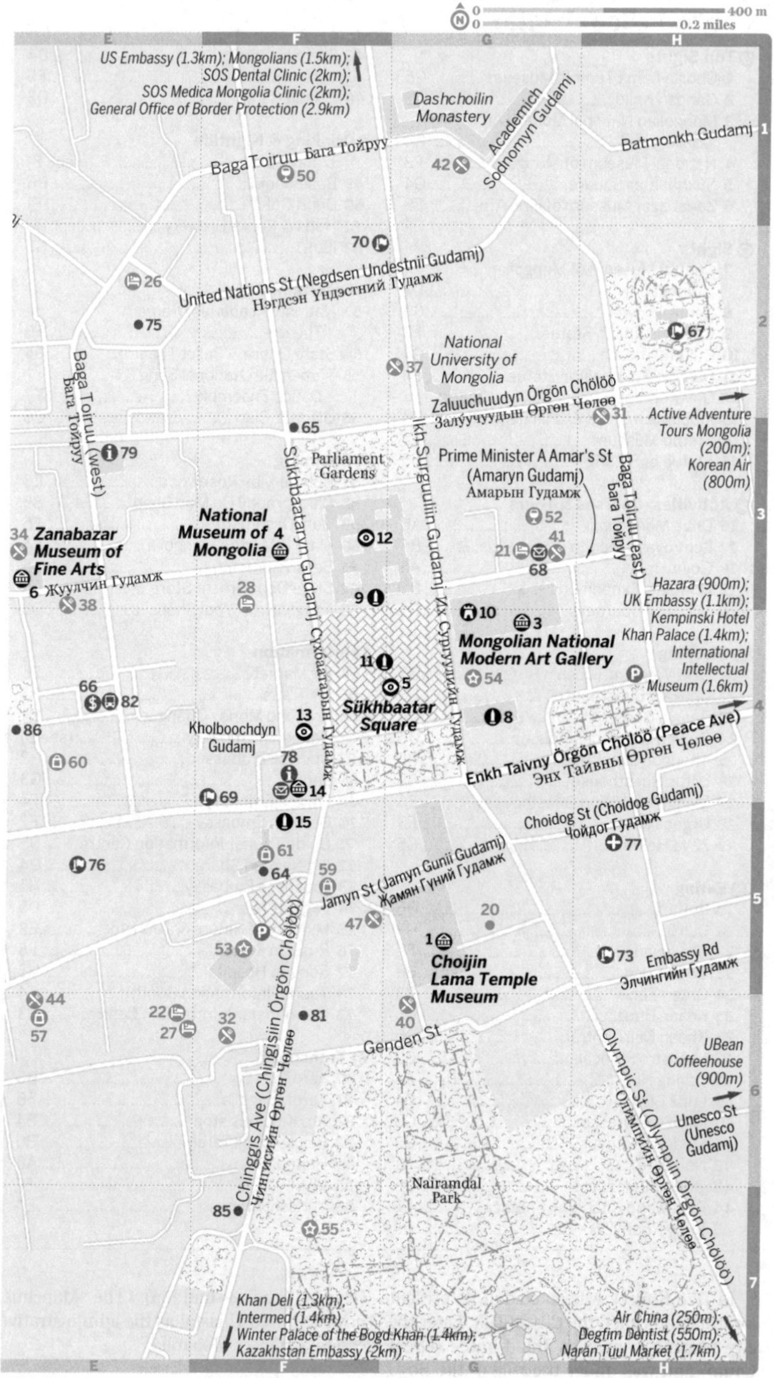

US Embassy (1.3km); Mongolians (1.5km); SOS Dental Clinic (2km); SOS Medica Mongolia Clinic (2km); General Office of Border Protection (2.9km)
Dashchoilin Monastery
Academich Sodnomyn Gudamj
Batmonkh Gudamj
Baga Toiruu Бага Тойруу
United Nations St (Negdsen Undestnii Gudamj) Нэгдсэн Үндэстний Гудамж
National University of Mongolia
Zaluuchuudyn Örgön Chölöö Залуучуудын Өргөн Чөлөө
Active Adventure Tours Mongolia (200m); Korean Air (800m)
Baga Toiruu (west) Бага Тойруу
Parliament Gardens
Sükhbaataryn Gudamj Сүхбаатарын Гудамж
Ikh Surguulin Gudamj Их Сургуулийн Гудамж
Prime Minister A Amar's St (Amaryn Gudamj) Амарын Гудамж
Baga Toiruu (east) Бага Тойруу
Zanabazar Museum of Fine Arts
National Museum of Mongolia
Жуулчин Гудамж
Hazara (900m); UK Embassy (1.1km); Kempinski Hotel Khan Palace (1.4km); International Intellectual Museum (1.6km)
Mongolian National Modern Art Gallery
Sükhbaatar Square
Kholboochdyn Gudamj
Enkh Taivny Örgön Chölöö (Peace Ave) Энх Тайвны Өргөн Чөлөө
Choidog St (Choidog Gudamj) Чойдог Гудамж
Jamyn St (Jamyn Gunii Gudamj) Жамян Гүний Гудамж
Choijin Lama Temple Museum
Embassy Rd Элчингийн Гудамж
Genden St
Chinggis Ave (Chingisiin Örgön Chölöö) Чингисийн Өргөн Чөлөө
Olympic St (Olympiin Örgön Chölöö) Олимпийн Өргөн Чөлөө
UBean Coffeehouse (900m)
Unesco St (Unesco Gudamj)
Nairamdal Park
Khan Deli (1.3km); Intermed (1.4km); Winter Palace of the Bogd Khan (1.4km); Kazakhstan Embassy (2km)
Air China (250m); Degfim Dentist (550m); Naran Tuul Market (1.7km)
400 m
0.2 miles

Central Ulaanbaatar

Top Sights
1 Choijin Lama Temple Museum G5
2 Gandan Khiid A3
3 Mongolian National Modern Art Gallery............G4
4 National Museum of Mongolia F3
5 Sükhbaatar Square............G4
6 Zanabazar Museum of Fine Arts............E3

Sights
7 Central Museum of Mongolian Dinosaurs D2
8 Central Tower............G4
9 Chinggis Khaan Statue............F3
10 Cultural Palace G4
11 Damdin Sükhbaatar Statue............F4
12 Government House............F3
13 Mongolian Stock Exchange............F4
14 Stamp Museum............F4
15 Statue of S Zorig F5

Activities, Courses & Tours
16 Drive Mongolia............A6
17 EcoVoyage Mongolie B5
18 Goyo Travel............A5
19 Nomadic Expeditions D5
20 Nomadic Journeys............G5

Sleeping
21 Best Western Tuushin Hotel............G3
22 Chuka's Guesthouse............E6
23 Gana's Guest House B4
24 Golden Gobi Guesthouse D4
25 Khongor Guest House C5
26 Lotus Guesthouse............E2
27 Mongolian Vision Guesthouse............E6
28 Urgoo Hotel............F3
29 Zaya Hostel............C5

Eating
30 Bull C6
31 Bull 3 ....H2
32 Chairman............F6
33 Good Price............B6
34 Green Zone E3
35 Khaan Buuz............D5
36 Khaan Deli Central D5
37 Le Bistro Français G2
38 Loving Hut............E3
39 Luna Blanca D4
40 Millie's Espresso............G6
41 Modern Nomads 2 ....G3
42 Namaste............G1
43 Oriental Treasure............D5
44 Rosewood Kitchen + Enoteca E6
45 Ruby Room UB D4
46 Shashlik Stands D4
47 Veranda............F5
48 Zochin Cafe D3

Drinking & Nightlife
17 Sky Bar ....(see 8)
49 Basement............D6
50 Dund Gol F1
51 Hops & Rocks Brewery D6
52 iLoft............G3

Entertainment
53 National Academic Drama Theatre............F5
54 State Opera & Ballet Theatre............G4
55 Tumen Ekh National Song & Dance Ensemble............F7
56 UB Jazz Club C6

Shopping
57 Butchery by Rosewood............E6
58 Cartography Co Map Shop............B5
59 Gobi Cashmere F5
60 Mary & Martha Mongolia E4
61 Seven Summits............F5
62 State Department Store D5
63 Tsagaan Alt Wool Shop............D5

Information
64 Air Market F5
65 Air Trans............F3
66 Ard Kino Money Changers............E4
Canadian Embassy............(see 8)
67 Chinese Embassy H2
68 FedEx............G3
69 French Embassy F4
70 German Embassy F2
71 Guide Tourist Information Centre D5
72 Ikh Naiman Sharga C4
73 Japanese Embassy............H5
74 Legend Tour D6
75 Ministry of Nature & Tourism E2
76 Russian Embassy............E5
77 Songdo Hospital H5
78 Tourist Information Booth............F4
79 Ulaanbaatar Information Centre E3

Transport
80 Aeroflot B6
81 AeroMongolia............F6
82 Ard Kino bus stop E4
83 Bus stop for Terelj B5
84 Hunnu Air............A6
85 MIAT F7
86 Turkish Airlines E4

In 1778 Khuree was erected at its present location and called the City of Felt. Later the city became known as Ikh Khuree (Great Camp) and was under the rule of the Bogd Gegeen (Living Buddha). The Manchus, however, used Uliastai as the administrative capital of Outer Mongolia.

In 1911, when Mongolia first proclaimed its independence from China, the city became the capital of Outer Mongolia and was renamed Niislel Khuree (Capital Camp). In 1918 it was invaded by the Chinese and three years later by the Russians.

Finally in 1924 the city was renamed Ulaanbaatar (Red Hero), in honour of the communist triumph, and declared the official capital of an 'independent' Mongolia (independent from China, not from the Soviet Union). The *khangard* (garuda), symbolising courage and honesty, was declared the city's official symbol. In 1933 Ulaanbaatar gained autonomy and separated from the surrounding Töv aimag.

From the 1940s the Soviets built the city in typical Russian style: lots of large, brightly coloured theatres and cavernous government buildings. Tragically, the Soviets also destroyed many old Russian buildings as well as Mongolian monasteries and temples. Today the city heaves with construction projects fuelled by Mongolia's mining boom. It has also enjoyed a cultural resurgence with many museums, galleries, theatre performances and clubs bringing out the best in 21st-century Mongolian culture.

Sights

Most sights are located within a 15-minute walk of Sükhbaatar Sq. The Winter Palace of the Bogd Khan and the Zaisan Memorial are a short bus or taxi ride south of the city. Gandan Khiid is about 2km to the west.

Sükhbaatar Square SQUARE
(Сүхбаатарын Талбай; What3words: indeed.strapped.unite) In July 1921 in the centre of Ulaanbaatar, Damdin Sükhbaatar (the 'hero of the revolution') declared Mongolia's final independence from China. A square later built on the spot now bears his name and features at its centre a **bronze statue** of the revolutionary astride his horse. In 2013 the city authorities changed the name of the plaza to Chinggis Khaan Sq, but in 2016 Sükhbaatar's descendants won a court battle to restore the original name.

Peaceful anti-communism protests were held here in 1990, which eventually ushered in the era of democracy. Today, the square *(talbai)* is occasionally used for rallies, ceremonies, rock concerts and festivals, but is generally a relaxed place where kids drive toy cars and teens whiz around on bikes. Near the centre of the square, look for a large **plaque** that lists the former names of the city – Örgöö, Nomiin Khuree, Ikh Khuree and Niislel Khuree. The large **warehouse** on the square houses temporary exhibits. Poke your head inside to see what's on.

The enormous marble construction at the north end was completed in 2006 in time for the 800th anniversary of Chinggis Khaan's coronation. At its centre is a seated bronze **Chinggis Khaan statue**. He is flanked by Ögedei (on the west) and Kublai (east). Two famed Mongol soldiers (Boruchu and Mukhlai) guard the entrance to the monument.

Behind the Chinggis monument stands Parliament House, which is commonly known as **Government House** (Засгын Газрын Ордон, Parliament House). An inner courtyard of the building holds a large ceremonial ger used for hosting visiting dignitaries.

To the east of the square is the 1970s Soviet-style **Cultural Palace** (Sükhbaatar Sq, What3words: nuzzling.facelift.crinkled), a useful landmark containing the Mongolian National Modern Art Gallery (p259) and several other cultural institutions. At the southeast corner of the square, the salmon-pinkish building is the State Opera & Ballet Theatre (p266). Just south of the opera house is the symbol of the country's new wealth, **Central Tower** (www.centraltower.mn; Peace Ave, Sükhbaatar Sq, What3words: shocks.daydreams.weddings), which houses luxury shops including Louis Vuitton and Armani.

The light-coloured colonnaded building to the southwest is the **Mongolian Stock Exchange** (Sükhbaatar Sq, What3words: pinch.scrubbing.keyboards), which was opened in 1992 in the former Children's Cinema. Across from the Central Post Office is a **statue of S Zorig** (Peace Ave, What3words: pity.post.shrugging), who, at the age of 27, helped to lead the protests that brought down communism in 1990 (and was tragically assassinated in 1998).

★**Gandan Khiid** BUDDHIST MONASTERY
(Гандан Хийд, Gandantegchinlen Khiid; Öndör Gegeen Zanabazaryn Gudamj, What3words: upstarts.gangs.shuffle; T4000; ⌚8.30am-7pm) Around the start of the 19th century more than 100 *süm* (temples) and *khiid* (monasteries) served a population of about 50,000 in Urga (the former name of Ulaanbaatar). Only a handful of these buildings survived the religious purges of 1937. It wasn't until the early 1990s that the people of Mongolia started to openly practise Buddhism again. This monastery is one of Mongolia's most important,

WORTH A TRIP

CHINGGIS KHAAN STATUE COMPLEX

Mongolia's most iconic landmark is a 40m-high glistening stainless-steel statue of **Chinggis Khaan** (What3words: backlashes.snakes.gremlin; GPS: N47°48.494', E107°31.860'; adult/child T8500/3500; 9am-8pm mid-May–mid-Oct; 10am-6pm mid-Oct–mid-May) on horseback. Built in 2008, it has a lift (elevator) rising up its tail, from where there are steps to the horse's head. It was built at Tsonjin Boldog, so the legend goes, because this was the spot where Chinggis Khaan found a golden whip.

The complex includes an impressive **museum** (with Hunnu artefacts and items from the Mongol empire), a cafe and a souvenir shop. A round trip in a taxi from Ulaanbaatar will set you back about T80,000.

Located 1km east of the Chinggis Khaan monument stands the **statue** (What3words: toward.prohibits.richly; T1000) of his mother, Hoelun, who gazes back towards her son. A restaurant and hotel complex was being developed here as of late 2017.

and also one of its biggest tourist attractions. The full name, Gandantegchinlen, translates roughly as 'the great place of complete joy'.

You can take photos (camera T7000, video T10,000) around the monastery and in Migjid Janraisig Süm, but not inside the other temples. Try to be there for the captivating ceremonies – they generally start at around 9am, though you may be lucky and see one at another time. Most chapels are closed in the afternoon.

★ **Winter Palace of the Bogd Khan** MUSEUM

(Богд Хааны Өвлийн Ордон; 11-342 195, 7000 1926; www.bogdkhaanpalace.mn; Bogd Javzandamda's St, What3words: dawn.elections.punctured; adult/student/child T8000/3000/1500, photography/video T50,000/70,000; 9am-7pm mid-Apr–mid-Sep, 9am-6pm Thu-Mon mid-Sep–mid-Apr) Built between 1893 and 1903, this palace is where Mongolia's eighth Living Buddha, and last king, Jebtzun Damba Hutagt VIII (often called the Bogd Khan), lived for 20 years. For reasons that are unclear, the palace was spared destruction by the Russians and turned into a museum. The summer palace, on the banks of Tuul Gol, was completely destroyed. There are six **temples** in the grounds; each now contains Buddhist artworks, including sculptures and *thangkas*.

★ **National Museum of Mongolia** MUSEUM

(Монголын Үндэсний Музей; 7011 0913; www.nationalmuseum.mn; cnr Juulchin Gudamj & Sükhbaataryn Gudamj, What3words: wonderful.successes.devoured; adult/child T8000/1000, photography T10,000; 9am-7pm, last entry 5.30pm mid-May–mid-Sep, 9am-6pm Tue-Sat, last entry 4.30pm mid-Sep–mid-May) Mongolia's wonderful National Museum sweeps visitors from the Neolithic era right to the present day. It's UB's only genuine blockbuster sight, offering an unparalleled overview of Mongolian culture, ranging from stone-age petroglyphs and exquisite gold ornamentation to, arguably the highlight, the full gamut of traditional ceremonial costume – which unmistakably inspired the look of characters from the *Star Wars* prequels.

★ **Choijin Lama Temple Museum** MUSEUM

(Чойжин Ламын Хийд-Музей; 11-324 788, 11-328 547; www.templemuseum.mn; Genden St, What3words: should.indulgent.surviving; adult/student/child incl audio guide T8000/3000/1500; 9am-5.30pm Tue-Sat) This temple museum smack in the middle of downtown Ulaanbaatar was the home of Luvsan Haidav Choijin Lama ('Choijin' is an honorary title given to some monks), the state oracle and brother of the Bogd Khan. Construction of the monastery commenced in 1904 and was completed four years later. It was closed in 1938 and probably would have been demolished had it not been saved in 1942 to serve as a museum demonstrating the 'feudal' ways of the past.

Zanabazar Museum of Fine Arts MUSEUM

(Занабазарын Уран Зургийн Музей; 11-326 060; www.zanabazarfam.mn; Juulchin Gudamj, What3words: aimed.fills.measuring; adult/student/child T8000/2500/1000, audio guide free, photography T45,000; 9am-5.30pm Apr-Sep, 10am-4.30pm Oct-Mar) This fine-arts museum has a superb collection of paintings, carvings and sculptures, including many by the revered sculptor and artist Zanabazar. It also contains other rare religious exhibits such as scroll *thangka* and Buddhist statues, representing the best display of its kind in Mongolia. A bonus is that most of the exhibit captions are in English, to go with a very comprehensive audio guide.

International Intellectual Museum MUSEUM
(Оюун Ухааны Олон Улсын Музей, Mongolian Toy Museum; ☎11-461 470; www.iqmuseum.mn; Peace Ave 10, What3words: overused.replays.dwelled; adult/child incl guide T8000/6000; ⊙10am-6pm Mon-Sat;) This museum contains an intriguing collection of puzzles and games made by local and international artists. One puzzle requires 56,831 movements to complete, says curator Zandraa Tumen-Ulzii. There are dozens of handmade chess sets and ingenious traditional Mongolian puzzles that are distant cousins to Rubik's cube. An enthusiastic guide will show you how the puzzles operate and will even perform magic tricks. A fascinating place for both kids and adults.

Mongolian National Modern Art Gallery GALLERY
(Монголын Уран Зургийн Үзэсгэлэн; ☎11-331 687; www.art-gallery.mn; Sükhbaatar Sq 3, Central Cultural Palace B, What3words: spells.competent. suggested; T2000; ⊙10am-6pm Jun-Sep, 9am-5pm Oct-May) Sometimes called the Fine Art Gallery, this place contains a large and impressive display of modern and uniquely Mongolian paintings and sculptures, with nomadic life, people and landscapes all depicted in styles ranging from impressionistic to nationalistic. The Soviet romantic paintings depicted in *thangka* style are especially interesting, but the most famous work is Ochir Tsevegjav's 1958 *The Fight of the Stallions* (aka *Horse Fighting*).

Central Museum of Mongolian Dinosaurs MUSEUM
(☎7000 0171; www.dinosaurmuseum.mn; Sambugiin Örgön Chölöö, Freedom Sq, What3words: instilled.diamonds.remix; adult/student/child T3000/1000/500, photography T5000; ⊙10am-7pm mid-May–mid-Sep, 9am-6pm mid-Sep–mid-May) Dinosaurs of all shapes, sizes and appetites once roamed the Gobi Desert. Their fossilised bones and eggs were first uncovered by American explorer Roy Chapman Andrews in the 1920s. Today you can come face-to-skull with some of the best examples of Mongolian dinosaur fossils in this museum. The centrepiece of the museum is the UV-lit 4m-tall, 3-tonne, flesh-eating Tarbosaurus bataar (a cousin of the Tyrannosaurus rex) and the smaller Saurolophus, with its distinctive cranial crest.

Activities & Tours

Most guesthouses offer their own range of tours, which tend to be unimaginative jeep trips that follow a standard route. Dedicated tour operators typically charge more, but you'll likely get better service, guides and food, as well as a more interesting itinerary.

Active Adventure Tours Mongolia CYCLING, HORSE RIDING
(☎11-354 662; www.tourmongolia.com; Erkhuu St, Macro Center Bldg, 5th fl, What3words: blending. bugs.unpainted) Good for bike and horse trips, this eco-conscious Mongolian-run outfit also runs traditional homestays (US$15 per night including full board) and employs sustainable tourism practices by hiring local guides rather than shipping them out from Ulaanbaatar.

Drive Mongolia TOURS
(☎9911 8257, 11-312 277; www.drivemongolia.com; Bayangol District, 3rd Khoroo 24-1, What3words: presuming.belief.insist) This unique company specialises in driving tours of the countryside, as in you drive the car. You can head off by yourself or bring along a guide. Motorbike tours are also available.

Goyo Travel TOURS
(☎11-313 050; www.goyotravel.com; Golomt Town, Peace Ave, tower A, door 1a, What3words: shirt.critic. stealthier; ⊙9.30am-6pm Mon-Fri) An experienced and reliable British-Mongolian outfit, Goyo offers a variety of countrywide trips and some unique tours that may include hot-air ballooning and kayaking on the Tuul Gol (Tuul River). Particularly good with film and media groups or high-end travel. Well-regarded for personal service and tailored trips.

EcoVoyage Mongolie TOURS
(☎English speaking 9901 5171, French speaking 9500 3242; www.ecovoyagemongolie.com; Apt 19A-D16, 2nd Khoroo, Chingeltei District, What3words: duke.fairness.resembles; ⊙8am-7pm Mon-Fri) French-run tour operator that specialises in horse and walking treks, Buddhism tours and visits to shamans. It can also organise food and cooking tours.

Nomadic Journeys ADVENTURE
(☎11-328 737; www.nomadicjourneys.com; Olympic St 7/3, Tselmeg Tower, 5th fl, What3words: widely. herds.snooping) A joint Swedish-Mongolian venture, this business concentrates on low-impact tourism, environmental protection and community development. It runs

DON'T MISS

Built by the Russians to commemorate 'unknown soldiers and heroes' from various wars, the **Zaisan Memorial** (Зайсан Толгой; Zaisan Hill, What3words: blanked.octagonal.blanking) features stirring socialist realism imagery with Soviet mosaics and reliefs, including that of Stalin and Lenin. Accessed via steep stairs, the monument sits atop the hill south of the city with wonderful views of Ulaanbaatar and the surrounding hills – but blighted by recent high-rise commercial development. Take bus 8 or 52 from Bayangol Hotel or Baga Toiruu.

fixed-departure yak, camel and horse treks and can also arrange rafting trips on the Tuul Gol. Its trip in Terelj is unique – you walk while yaks haul your own portable ger on a cart. Also good for taimen (a salmon-like fish) fishing trips.

Mongolia Canoeing CANOEING
(☎11-685 503, 9982 6883; www.mongoliacanoeing.com) A German-run tour company that offers canoe trips on several rivers across Mongolia, including the Tuul, Orkhon, Eg and Chuluut rivers. Day or overnight trips are possible from Ulaanbaatar.

Stone Horse Expeditions HORSE RIDING
(☎9592 1167; www.stonehorsemongolia.com; Chinggis Ave, Gutal Office, room 606, What3words: bonds.airbase.looked) Offers horse treks in the Khan Khentii Mountains (trips start from just one hour out of Ulaanbaatar) and Gorkhi-Terelj National Park. Professional outfit with well-tended horses and eco-conscious policies. Also offers reasonably priced homestay opportunities with herders near Ulaanbaatar.

Nomadic Expeditions TOURS
(☎11-313 396; www.threecamellodge.com; Peace Ave 76, What3words: inhaled.truckload.apricot) This is the Mongolian office of the US-based travel company. Runs countrywide tours, but is especially good for the Gobi, where it runs the excellent Three Camel Lodge. A leader in environmental conservation and work with Mongolian scientists to protect plant and animal species in the Gobi.

Nomads TOURS
(☎7011 9370; www.nomadstours.com; off Industrial St, What3words: lots.cupboards.hiked; ⏲9am-6pm Mon-Fri, 10am-4pm Sat Jun-Sep, 9am-5pm Mon-Fri Oct-May) In business since 1992, this is a well-established company known for its horse-trekking tours. It offers a wide range of fixed-departure trips, including popular horse treks in Khentii and through Terelj, visiting Günjiin Süm. Also good for hiking and trekking in western Mongolia. Has English-, French-, German- and Russian-speaking guides.

The office is located in Khan Uul District, 600m south of the train station.

Wind of Mongolia TOURS
(☎11-316 222, 9909 0593, 9898 0593; www.windofmongolia.mn; Dilav Khutagt Jamsranjav's St, 7th fl, apt 45, What3words: reckoned.shadows.abolish) This French-run tour operator offers creative and offbeat trips, including rock climbing, mountain-biking, kayaking and tours that focus on Buddhism, archaeology and botany. Owner Joel Rauzy is perhaps best known for his winter dog-sledding trips in Terelj and Khövsgöl. Call ahead before turning up as there is not always someone there.

Sleeping

There is a wide range of places to stay in the capital city, in particular budget guesthouses. There's some fantastic upmarket hotels, too, but quality midrange options are limited. During the week surrounding Naadam accommodation may be in short supply and prices are often higher; book well in advance if you're here in July.

★ **Zaya Hostel** GUESTHOUSE $
(☎11-331 575, 9908 9478; www.zayahostel.com; off Peace Ave, What3words: clustered.elder.reminds; s/d/tr without bathroom US$25/36/45, s/d with bathroom US$30/40; @ 📶) While most guesthouses in town are located in crumbling old Russian flats, this one is in a modern building with hardwood floors, sparkling bathrooms, a comfortable lounge, fresh paint and smart furnishings. Owner Zaya speaks English, enjoys a good conversation and is happy to help travellers. Eggs on toast and proper filter coffee are available for breakfast.

Zaya is not too keen on groups of noisy backpackers, however, so if you're looking for a party guesthouse, skip this one. The hostel is on the 3rd floor of an orange building, about 100m north of Peace Ave (behind the glass-fronted Peace Tower, and then a bit past the Seoul Hotel). It also has another branch on the other side of Peace Ave.

★Chuka's Guesthouse GUESTHOUSE $
(☎9422 5672, 9999 5672; chuka927@gmail.com; Bldg 33, entrance V, What3words: vibrating.pocket.chum; dm US$10-15, s/d US$25/35; 📶) This popular guesthouse enjoys a central location in a quiet courtyard set behind the National Academy Drama Theatre. It's pricier than some of its competitors, but the quality of the rooms stands out. Furnishings are modern and the bunk beds are soft and warm. It has a fully equipped contemporary kitchen and a cosy lounge.

Golden Gobi Guesthouse GUESTHOUSE $
(☎11-322 632, 9665 4496; www.goldengobi.com; off Peace Ave, What3words: upstarts.goodbye.flipping; dm US$7-10, r with/without bathroom from US$39/33; ❄📶) This family-run place has a fun, youthful vibe, with colourful noise-proof walls, homely lounges and lots of soft sofas. Dorms and private rooms are clean and comfortable, and the bathrooms are kept tidy. On the downside, it can get very crowded in summer. It's inside a courtyard about 100m east of the State Department Store.

It also has an adjoining apartment with equally nice rooms.

Lotus Guesthouse GUESTHOUSE $
(☎11-325 967, 9909 4943; www.lotuschild.org; off Baga Toiruu W, What3words: endearing.reforming.tiptoes; dm US$10-15, r US$30, apt US$50; @📶) This homely place almost feels more like a boutique guesthouse than a hostel. Rooms are individually styled, some with traditional Mongolian furniture. It has a cosy, traditional atmosphere, but some parts can be a little dim. The location is central and quiet. It's run by the Lotus Children's Centre, an NGO that helps orphaned children and employs Mongolians who used to live in the orphanage.

Khongor Guest House GUESTHOUSE $
(☎9925 2599, 11-316 415; www.khongor-expedition.com; Peace Ave 15, apt 6, What3words: pupils.humid.delivers; dm/s/d/f US$10/15/20/30; @📶) This popular guesthouse in an apartment block is run by a friendly, knowledgable team who work overtime to help guests with logistical matters, and remains one of the best to arrange countryside tours. The guesthouse is a basic affair with small private rooms and slightly larger dorms equipped with curtains, lamps and power points. There's a kitchen and a homely lounge with computers.

Khongor has a prime city location overlooking Peace Ave, and the entrance of the guesthouse is around the back of the third building west of the State Department Store. Credit cards are accepted.

Mongolian Vision Guesthouse GUESTHOUSE $
(☎9511 9399, 11-322 369; www.mongolianvisiontours.com; Bldg 33, door 65, What3words: forum.operating.baths; dm/r incl breakfast US$7/25; @📶) A fresh renovation in 2017 has given new life to this hostel, with sparkling, modern rooms, thick mattresses and a Western-style kitchen. Dorm beds are kitted out with power points and curtains. Rooms in the older wing are dated, but have more character. The friendly English-speaking staff keep the place tidy, and run a tour company with trips across Mongolia.

Gana's Guest House HOSTEL $
(☎011-319 325, 9911 6960; Gandan Khiid ger district, house No 22, What3words: joints.implanted.archduke; dm/s/d/tr incl breakfast US$6/15/20/25; ⏲Apr-Oct; @📶) One of UB's most unique sleeping options is this long-time backpacker hang-out where you can stay in a ger on the rooftop. Gana's also has private rooms inside a main block, but here it's all about the gers; otherwise it's a pretty ramshackle place. Centrally located, it's part of a ger district close to Gandan Khiid.

Urgoo Hotel BOUTIQUE HOTEL $$
(☎7011 6044; www.urgoohotel.com; Tourist St 6, M100 Bldg, What3words: proper.bashed.creatures; d/ste incl breakfast from T185,000/225,000; ❄📶) This boutique hotel has just 10 rooms, each one decked out in brown and beige furnishings, with flat-screen TVs and modern, albeit small, bathrooms. The prime selling point here is the location, overlooking a little park near the National Museum. There's a suave European restaurant downstairs.

Overall it's a nice place to stay if you're looking for something quaint, but keep expectations in check: the breakfast is a bit disappointing for the price and the air-con units in the back can be noisy at night.

★Best Western Tuushin Hotel HOTEL $$$
(☎11-323 162; www.bestwesternmongolia.mn; Prime Minister A Amar's St 15, What3words: grapevine.unto.duties; r incl breakfast from T562,000; ❄@📶) Ulaanbaatar's premier upscale hotel is this five-star gem with a prime location steps away from all the downtown museums and theatres. Spacious, tastefully decorated rooms have incredible city views, and

facilities include a spa, a fitness centre, a couple of restaurants and a cocktail lounge on the 25th floor with more epic views.

Best Western Gobi's Kelso HOTEL $$$
(☎7736 3636; www.bestwesternmongolia.com; Jasrai St 27/1, What3words: overpaid.viewing.whirlwind; s/d incl breakfast from US$90/100; P ⊖ ✻ ☎) A 10-minute walk from the train station, this Best Western is a smart choice for weary travellers stumbling off the Trans-Siberian Railway and looking for quality digs. Rooms are spacious, there's a substantial breakfast included and the management bends over backwards to ensure a pleasant stay. While conveniently close to the station, it's a good 30- to 40-minute hike to downtown, or a short cab ride.

Kempinski Hotel Khan Palace HOTEL $$$
(☎11-463 463; www.kempinski.com/en/ulaanbaatar; E Cross Rd, What3words: bridge.crank.perfect; s/d incl breakfast US$190/210; P ✻ @ ☎) This Kempinski-managed venture on the east end of Peace Ave is one of the best-run places in town. Rooms are plush, with a tasteful design and little niceties such as humidifier, robes and slippers. The hotel also has a fitness centre and sauna, upmarket restaurants (both Mongolian and Japanese) and a classy cocktail bar.

Eating

There are dozens of Mongolian budget restaurants *(guanz)* and they can be found on every block in the city. Some are chain restaurants and you'll start to recognise prominent eateries, including Zochin Buuz (Зочин Бууз), **Khaan Buuz** (Хаан Бууз; Peace Ave, What3words: moon.flops.guideline; mains T6000-8500; ⏲24hr) and **Zochin Cafe** (Зочин Кафе; ☎11-327 277; Sambugiin Örgön Chölöö, What3words: lend.trending.possible; mains T3000-14,900; ⏲9am-9pm). They serve up *buuz* (steamed mutton dumplings) and *tsuivan* (fried noodles) plus soups and various meat-based creations. They are often quite dire – think globs of mashed potatoes, chunks of fatty mutton, and rice topped with ketchup – so keep your expectations at ground zero. Some of the chains operate 24 hours. Meals cost T4500 to T8000.

Loving Hut VEGAN $
(☎11-321 396, 9101 8889; www.lovinghut.com/mg; Juulchin Gudamj, What3words: exchanges.grad.confined; mains T4500-12,500; ⏲11am-8.30pm Mon-Sat; ✎) This popular cafe's all-vegan menu offers a good variety of healthy and tasty dishes. Try the *mogul* (a veggie stir fry served on a sizzling platter), one of the half-dozen soups, the veggie gyoza or the *buuz*. Ask to see the special menu featuring fruit shakes and herbal teas.

Green Zone CAFE $$
(☎9553 9766; www.facebook.com/thegreenzoneub; Juulchin Gudamj, Builder's Sq, What3words: spirit.outgrown.jiffy; mains T6900-23,800; ⏲10am-midnight; ☎ ✎) Appropriately named Green Zone is a lush oasis, where plants seem to grow from walls and colourful, fresh ingredients appear in front of hungry diners. The cafe-style menu features sandwiches, burgers, quiche and soups. There's hummus, freshly baked bread, mini pizzas and salads with ingredients grown in the restaurant's hanging garden. Our go-to favourites are the broccoli soup, tuna melt and lasagne.

Khaan Deli Central AMERICAN $$
(☎8846 3354; www.khaandeli.com; Khaddorjiin Gudamj, bldg 31-44, What3words: collides.miracle.spelling; mains breakfast T5000-13,000, dinner T15,000-17,000; ⏲8am-8pm Sun-Thu, to 10pm Fri & Sat; ☎) Owner and Michigan native Darren has done his best to bring American heartland food to Ulaanbaatar. The speciality American breakfasts and bagels are the perfect cure for a hangover, or if you've come for lunch, there's a range of burgers, hot dogs, salads and pulled-pork sandwiches. It also serves some surprisingly good Mongolian dishes, including *tsuivan* and *khuitsai*, a beef and vegetable stew.

There's a second **branch** (Khan Uul District, Zuun Khoriin Myangat area, bldg 17, What3words: dull.twilight.clocking; ⏲8am-8pm Mon-Sat; ☎) about a five-minute walk north of the Winter Palace of the Bogd Khan.

Mongolians MONGOLIAN $$
(☎9909 7716; Ikh Toiruu 93, Barilga Mega Store, What3words: equity.remove.arena; mains T8600-30,000; ⏲11am-10pm; 👪) This upmarket Mongolian restaurant has walls lined with traditional antiques and old photos, and a menu of contemporary local cuisine. Expect stir-fried meats, dumplings and boiled mutton, along with some Russian and European influences and cold beer on tap. It's a bit out of the way, however.

If you want to go all out, order the *khorkhog* (T175,000) – meat chunks cooked in a metal steamer with scalding hot rocks added to the pot to aid cooking – enough for six to eight people (you must call and order six

DON'T MISS

THE NAADAM FESTIVAL

The high point of the Mongolian year is **Naadam** (11-15 Jul). In Ulaanbaatar the festival has all the trappings of a big sporting event, with jostling crowds, souvenir salespeople, traffic and screeching loudspeakers.

While Naadam officially kicks off on 11 July, other events get underway several days before. Uriankhai- and Buriat-style archery is held on 7 and 8 July while a children's archery tournament is held on 9 July. On 10 July, two horse races are held and the archery tournament officially begins, as does the ankle-bone shooting competition.

The festival officially begins at 9.30am on 11 July at Sükhbaatar Sq when an honour guard marches the nine horse-tail banners to the stadium. The **opening ceremony**, which starts at 11am at the Naadam Stadium, includes a speech from the president and a 40-minute show featuring traditional music, dancing and colourful costumes.

The **wrestling** starts in the stadium about 20 minutes after the ceremony and continues all day.

The **horse racing** is held about 40km west of the city on an open plain called Hui Doloon Khutag. Buses and minivans go there from the road north of the Naadam Stadium for around T1000. The races can be disappointing from a spectator's point of view because although the race lasts about two hours you can only see the finish. Be prepared for some traffic bottlenecks to and from the racecourse. What is nice about the event is not so much the race itself but the generally festive atmosphere around the horse-race grounds. A cultural area near the finish line shows off traditional Mongolian music and games.

Most people file out of the stadium after the opening ceremony to catch a little archery or ankle-bone shooting. Around the stadium are carnival games and rides for kids, as well as food tents. On the night of 11 July, a concert and fireworks display is held on Sükhbaatar Sq.

Quite a few events now happen on 13 July at the horse-race area. A mini-Naadam is held for the benefit of trainers; you'll see cultural performances and wrestling. You could even ride your own horse to the racing grounds. **Stepperiders** (9911 4245, 9412 5965; www.stepperiders.mn; What3words: buckled.open.buxom; GPS: N 47°43.649', E 106°47.418') does four-day trips from its base near Bogdkhan Uul.

To find out what is going on during the festival, look for the events program in the UB Post. The website http://naadam.viahistoria.com has pictures and historical information on Naadam and the associated sporting events.

Tickets

Admission to the stadium (except for the two ceremonies), and to the archery and horse racing, are free, but you'll definitely need a ticket for the opening ceremony and possibly the last round or two of the wrestling and the closing ceremony.

Cost Ticket costs vary per section; the north side of the stadium (which is protected from the sun and rain by a roof) is more expensive with tickets going for US$40 or more. The cheapest ones are around US$12.

Buying tickets Tickets are sold at the Naadam Stadium and at the **Cultural Palace** (p257). They usually go on sale on 6 July but can be nearly impossible to get on your own as locals stand in line for hours to scoop them all up. The guesthouses and hotels always manage to get a few for their guests and this is the best way to get one. You can try to buy one from a scalper outside the stadium before the opening ceremony, but the going price is around T50,000.

hours in advance). There's a museum downstairs, too.

Millie's Espresso AMERICAN $$
(11-330 338; Marco Polo Plaza, What3words: putts.start.backs; mains T10,000-18,000; 8am-8pm Mon-Sat, 9am-4pm Sun;) Since it first opened its doors in 1998, Millie's has been a favourite among expats seeking American comfort food. The owners – Daniel and Densmaa – warmly greet patrons to

their sunlit restaurant and promptly serve up tasty burgers, sandwiches and soups. Special treats include smoothies, lemon pie and a delicious chocolate cake (which sells out early). Don't miss Daniel's famous Cuban sandwich, only available on Tuesdays.

Ruby Room UB BURGERS **$$**

(☎8802 1125; Baruun Selbe Gudamj, What3words: bossy.crumbles.films; burgers from T13,000; ⏰11am-11pm; 📶✎) Ruby Room serves up what could be Ulaanbaatar's best burgers. The simple menu offers a choice of seven juicy, supersized burgers, all served with fries and three sauces. The Mexican burger is a good choice if you like spicy food, and there's a vegan/vegetarian option, too. The interior is clean, but a bit dark and sparsely furnished.

Oriental Treasure TAIWANESE **$$**

(☎7013 5055; Prime Minister Tserendorj St, Beatles Sq, What3words: plugged.screening.buffoon; mains T14,000-22,000; ⏰10am-midnight) Among the numerous Chinese-style restaurants in Ulaanbaatar, this is one of the cleanest and most welcoming. The speciality here is steamed dumplings stuffed with chicken, pork or shrimp – all are delicious and fresh. Glass windows allow you to peek into the kitchen to watch how the dumplings are expertly prepared. On the downside, prices are a tad high considering the small portions.

Modern Nomads 2 MONGOLIAN **$$**

(☎7012 0808; www.modernnomads.mn; Prime Minister A Amar's St, What3words: knots.jolt.regulate; meals T8600-30,000; ⏰10am-midnight Mon-Fri, to 11pm Sat & Sun) One of UB's best places to sample a feast of classic Mongolian dishes, try the *khorkhog* (lamb cooked on hot stone), *khuushuur* (meat pastries), *buuz* (steamed meat-filled dumplings), Mongolian soups or even sheep's head. Portions are insanely large. It's part of a chain of restaurants, but this branch seems to do slightly better than the others. A picture menu makes ordering easy.

Luna Blanca VEGAN **$$**

(☎11-327 172, 5515 9651; www.facebook.com/lunablancarestaurant; Juulchin Gudamj 16, FPMT Buddhist Centre, 1st fl, What3words: remarried.lighter.tools; dishes T6000-13,000; ⏰11am-10pm Mon-Fri, noon-9pm Sat & Sun; ✎👪) 🍃 Famous for being the first vegan restaurant in Mongolia, this place remains very popular for its consistently tasty and healthy food. The kitchen whips up classic Mongolian dishes such as the Flour Power *(tsuivan)* and Mongol Combo Plate (with *buuz* and *khuushuur*), as well as Asian- and European-inspired fare. The atmosphere is refreshingly clean, alcohol-free, kid-friendly and great value for money.

Bull HOTPOT **$$**

(☎7710 0060; Seoul St, What3words: avoid.whimpered.broth; per piece T4500-9000; ⏰10.30am-midnight Mon-Fri, 11.30am-midnight Sat & Sun; ✎) A local favourite, this hotpot place gets a steady stream of patrons at its three locations – two on Seoul St and another **branch** (Baga Toiruu E, Blue Mon Bldg, 3rd fl, What3words: amps.heads.harmony; ⏰11am-10pm; ✎) diagonally opposite the Chinese embassy.

★ **Hazara** INDIAN **$$$**

(☎9919 5007, 11-480 214; www.hazara.mn; Peace Ave 16, What3words: transmit.composts.spurned; dishes T17,700-26,200; ⏰noon-10pm; ✎) Tucked behind the Wrestling Palace, this North Indian restaurant has consistently been one of the best restaurants in Ulaanbaatar for over 15 years. Each table is cov-

SELF-CATERING

For self-caterers, there are many shops around the city that sell food imported from China, Korea, the US and Europe. Fresh fruit and vegies are also available; some items are home-grown in Mongolia, although most of what you'll find is imported from China. Some tasty local products include yoghurt, cheese, apples, berries, tomatoes and cream. Most markets are open from about 8am to 10pm daily. The supermarket on the ground floor of the **State Department Store** (☎11-319 292; Peace Ave 44, What3words: conductor.nearing.given; shashlik T7500; ⏰8.30am-10pm) has a well-stocked selection, while **Good Price** (Seoul St, What3words: mull.direction.drawn; ⏰9am-midnight) is good for imported international items.

Bread is available everywhere, but the best is found at small bakeries such as **Butchery by Rosewood** (☎9401 0561; www.facebook.com/thebutcheryub; off Seoul St, What3words: cone.keyboards.donates; ⏰11am-8pm) and **Le Bistro Français** (☎11-320 022; www.facebook.com/bistrotfrancaisUB; Ikh Surguuliin Gudamj 2, What3words: mildest.expectant.hint; mains T21,000-41,000; ⏰9.30am-11pm Mon-Fri, 11am-11pm Sat & Sun; 📶).

ered by a colourful Rajasthani tent, where you sit back and enjoy tandoori baked delights. Try the chicken tikka, *aloo gobi* (potato and cauliflower) or *raan-e-hazara* (lamb marinated in rum).

Chairman MONGOLIAN **$$$**
(☎11-334 411; off Chinggis Ave, Corporate Hotel, 2nd fl, What3words: trip.unpainted.depended; mains T12,000-30,000; ⏱11am-midnight) One the best places in town for Mongolian food. Try the excellent *khuushuur* or the *guriltei shuul* (flour soup).

Veranda MEDITERRANEAN **$$$**
(☎7710 2992; www.veranda.mn; Jamyngun St 5/1, What3words: overdone.scared.finishers; mains T17,000-39,000; ⏱noon-midnight;) While it's not particularly old, this fine-dining restaurant has an almost colonial air to it, with couch seating inside and a big porch overlooking the Choijin Lama Temple Museum. The food is surprisingly good, with a menu featuring an array of delectable main dishes that fuse Italian and French recipes served by bow-tie uniformed waiters. Reserve ahead if you want a patio table.

Namaste INDIAN **$$$**
(☎7555 2020; www.namaste.mn; Baga Toiruu, Khatan Suikh Bldg, what3words: nuzzled.confining.dish; dishes T12,200-25,000; ⏱11.30am–10pm;) Treat your taste buds to some gourmet Indian cuisine prepared by chefs from Uttarakhand. Try the delicious *saag gosht* (beef in spinach sauce) or *murg makhani* (butter chicken) with a garlic naan and rice. Vegetarian options are available, as well as classic street food such as *golgappa* (pastry with chickpeas).

Rosewood Kitchen + Enoteca ITALIAN **$$$**
(☎9402 0561; www.facebook.com/rosewoodkitchenenoteca; Seoul St, Mandal Bldg, What3words: guarded.prawn.defenders; mains T16,000-37,000; ⏱7.30am-10pm Mon-Sat;) Hidden behind an ugly facade is this popular bistro that does homemade pastas, pizzas, sandwiches and salads, all made with high-quality local and imported ingredients. Many items are made in-house, including the breads. The atmosphere is smart and businesslike and popular with expats.

It's tucked off the street in the ground floor of a five-storey grey building next to a large ger. There's also its Butchery (p264), a small grocery that sells its bread, locally sourced meats and gourmet treats.

Drinking & Nightlife

Take note that on the first day of the month UB is totally dry, with alcohol sales prohibited across the city's supermarkets, bars and clubs. So if you're looking for a celebratory or evening drink be sure to stock up the day before (though you're likely to find some on the sly in a karaoke club or the like). Otherwise it's a good excuse to give your liver a break...

17 Sky Bar BAR
(☎11-310 707; www.facebook.com/sky17barulaanbaatar; Sükhbaatar Sq 2, Central Tower, 17th fl, What3words: represent.coaching.wriggle; ⏱noon-2am;) One of UB's best spots for a cocktail is this ritzy rooftop bar atop the Central Tower, featuring wonderful views of the city and surrounding hills. Drinks are well made by friendly bar staff, though order off the menu if you're after something more classic. There's also bar food and international cuisine (mains from T17,000). DJs and live music on weekends.

iLoft CLUB
(☎9909 0528; off Prime Minister A Amar's St, What3words: shows.greyhound.tooth; cover T20,000; ⏱10pm-4am;) This multi-use venue transforms into a pulsing nightclub after dark. There's leather seating, a large dance floor, techno beats and a mature crowd. It's located behind the Best Western Tuushin Hotel.

Basement BAR
(☎9520 7050; www.facebook.com/basementhouze; Seoul St, What3words: impulses.yachting.hobbit; ⏱6pm-4am) Head downstairs to this cool, grungy basement club in Seoul St to hang out with the local indie kids. There's regular live bands and DJs, and it's a good place to meet a friendly, alternative crowd.

Dund Gol BAR
(☎8827 8017; www.facebook.com/dundgol; Baga Toiruu, What3words: schematic.liked.workforce; ⏱noon-midnight;) One for lovers of obscure, indie music, Dund Gol is a hip little bar that doubles as a record store, stocking an impressive collection of Soviet and post-communist vinyl. You'll come across some fascinating genres, from Polish psychedelic to Russian disco, all for purchase or to listen to. It's a cool place to hang out with retro lounge decor and an art-filled, front beer garden.

★**Hops & Rocks Brewery** CRAFT BEER
(☎8800 3506; www.facebook.com/hopsandrocksbrewery; Usnii St, What3words: purifier.flitting.staples; ⏱6pm-2am Tue-Sat) Mongolia's first

DON'T MISS

SEOUL STREET

On weekend evenings come summer, don't miss the revelry that takes place along Seoul St, when the strip is clear of traffic and is transformed into a boozy street party. Most folks have a drink in hand as they're entertained by live music and DJs, while food trucks line the street. Otherwise during the week it's also worth checking out, with plenty of lively pubs, bars and clubs.

genuine producer of craft beer is this bar set up by a team of locals who brew a Crazy Shaman IPA, a Two Rams pale ale and a Red Cheeks amber ale. There are also a few seasonal brews, along with bar food. It's in the same entrance as the Ikh Mongol beer hall, northeast of the circus.

★UBean Coffeehouse CAFE

(☎9638 2326; www.ubeanroasterie.com; Manlaibaatar Damdinsuren St, What3words: tastier.snap.skewed; ⏲8.30am-8pm Mon-Fri, to 2pm Sat; 📶) Ulaanbaatar's best spot for coffee, the stylish American-owned UBean specialises in pour-overs using single-origin beans sourced from farms from Ethiopia to Honduras. All coffee beans are roasted on-site, and prepared by knowledgable baristas; there's also 12-hour cold drip for summer. Food is another reason to drop by, with homemade bagels, doughnuts, BLT sandwiches and cakes on offer (mains from T8000).

☆ Entertainment

Both the *UB Post* and the *Mongol Messenger* English-language newspapers contain weekly events listings. Theatres and galleries sometimes post English ads outside or you could just buy a ticket and hope for the best. Also visit the EASYticket website (www.easyticket.mn) to see what's showing.

★Tumen Ekh National Song & Dance Ensemble TRADITIONAL MUSIC, DANCE

(☎11-322 238; www.tumenekh.wordpress.com; Nairamdal Park, State Youth & Children's Theatre, What3words: readily.wealth.squashes; tickets T25,000, camera/video T20,000/100,000; ⏲4pm & 6pm daily; 👪) The Tumen Ekh Song & Dance Ensemble at the State Youth & Children's Theatre is the most popular tourist cultural show in town, featuring traditional singers, dancers and contortionists. It's a great chance to hear *khöömii* (throat singing) and see some fabulous costumes. Shows last just over an hour, and are held daily other then winter months; check the ensemble's Facebook page for the schedule.

National Academic Drama Theatre THEATRE

(☎7011 8187, 7012 8999; www.drama.mn; cnr Seoul St & Chinggis Ave, What3words: converged.nurtures.satin; tickets T10,000-50,000; ⏲ticket sales 10am-7pm) During most of the year this large, red-hued theatre shows one of a dozen or so Mongolian-language productions by various playwrights from Mongolia, Russia and beyond. You can buy tickets in advance through Easy Ticket (www.easyticket.mn) or at the booking office, which is inside the small concrete guardhouse on the right-hand side of the theatre.

State Opera & Ballet Theatre OPERA, BALLET

(☎7011 0389, 9690 7010; www.opera-ballet.mn; Sükhbaatar Sq, What3words: media.congested.rock; tickets T8000-15,000; ⏲box office 10am-2pm & 3-6pm Wed-Sun) Built by the Russians in 1932 (look for the Soviet stars on the columns), the State Opera & Ballet Theatre is the salmon-pinkish building on the southeast corner of Sükhbaatar Sq. On Saturday and Sunday evenings throughout the year, and sometimes also on weekend afternoons in the summer, the theatre stages stirring ballet and Mongolian-language opera. It's closed in August.

UB Jazz Club JAZZ

(☎7700 0138; www.facebook.com/UbJazzClub; Seoul St, bldg 44, What3words: intruders.dampen.inherits; ⏲11am-4am) As the name suggests, this is a dedicated jazz club – the only one in Ulaanbaatar. There's live music nightly at around 9pm. A rotating group of bands play here (check the Facebook page for upcoming events). You don't need a ticket to get in, unless it's a special event. The unfiltered house beer is another reason to drop by.

Shopping

★Naran Tuul Market MARKET

(Наран Туул Зах; Narnii Rd, What3words: satin.liquid.impresses; ⏲9am-6pm Wed-Mon) Also known as the Black Market (Khar Zakh) is this must-see spot for those wanting to pick up traditional Mongolian clothing, carpets, horse-riding gear and souvenirs. It's notorious for pickpockets and bag slashers, so wear your backpack on your front and stash valuables in your money belt.

★State Department Store DEPARTMENT STORE
(Их Дэлгүүр; ☎1800 2888; www.nomin.mn; Peace Ave 44, What3words: bravo.hexes.steamed; ⏲8.45am-10pm Mon-Fri, 9am-10pm Sat, to 9.30pm Sun) Established in 1921, the State Department Store, known as *ikh delguur* (big shop), is a local institution and virtually a tourist attraction in itself. Here the best products from around the city are squeezed into one building, and it's the place to come for quality cashmere (2nd floor), Erdenet carpets (4th floor) and a wide range of souvenirs, traditional clothing and books about Mongolia (6th floor).

★Mary & Martha Mongolia GIFTS & SOUVENIRS
(☎9972 5297; www.mmmongolia.com; off Peace Ave, What3words: dust.goods.flamingo; ⏲10.30am-7pm) Fair-trade shop selling handmade traditional handicrafts, felt products, clothing (including men's and children's), toys, jewellery and modern Kazakh wall hangings. Has some innovative little products such as computer bags and mobile-phone cases made with traditional designs. As well as cashmere products, it has yak- and camel-wool products.

Tsagaan Alt Wool Shop GIFTS & SOUVENIRS
(☎11-318 591; www.mongolianwoolcraft.com; Prime Minister Tserendorj St, Beatles Sq, What3words: released.bystander.grandest; ⏲10am-7pm Mon-Sat, to 6pm Sun) This nonprofit store, which sends money directly back to the craftspeople, has all manner of wool products, including toys, clothes and artwork.

Gobi Cashmere CASHMERE
(☎11-329 202; www.gobi.mn; Chinggis Ave 3, What3words: unwound.ascendant.overruns; ⏲9am-10pm) This downtown outlet of the iconic brand shows off the latest fashions in cashmere and wool.

Information

DANGERS & ANNOYANCES

Ulaanbaatar is a fairly carefree and easygoing city, but there are a few concerns to keep in mind.

Pickpockets and bag slashers are still a problem, though the situation is not as dire as it was a few years ago. When it happens, robbery is seldom violent against foreigners, just opportunistic.

Be particularly vigilant on Peace Ave between the post office and the State Department Store, or other main streets where tourists wander. Pickpockets also target public buses and the Naran Tuul Market. Keep an eye on your bag when sitting in cafes. Be very careful around the stadium during Naadam.

Alcoholism is a big problem in Ulaanbaatar, especially among out-of-work middle-aged and older Mongolian men. It's worse around Naadam time, but drunks are usually more annoying than dangerous.

Probably the most dangerous thing you can do in Ulaanbaatar is cross the street. Pedestrians are given no special treatment, so expect that you could get run over at any given moment. A green man or a zebra crossing are not safe either because at some intersections the right-turn arrow turns green simultaneously, so as you step onto the road a car will come around the corner into your path. Look out!

EMERGENCY & IMPORTANT NUMBERS

It might take a few minutes to get hold of an English speaker for these numbers.

Emergency Aid/Ambulance ☎103

Fire ☎101

Police Emergency ☎102

INTERNET

Your hotel or guesthouse will most likely offer wi-fi, and nearly all cafes and restaurants in UB also offer free access. There are several public wi-fi hotspots, mainly in public squares and parks, as well as at the airport.

MAPS

Several maps of Ulaanbaatar are available; a good one is the 1:10,000 *Ulaanbaatar City Map*. The most extensive selection of maps is at **Seven Summits** (☎9942 9989, 11-317 923; www.activemongolia.com; btwn Peace Ave & Seoul St, What3words: absorb.inkjet.whisk; ⏲10am-7pm Mon-Fri, to 6pm Sat & Sun). The **Cartography Co Map Shop** (☎9115 6023; Ikh Toiruu, What3words: courtyard.studs.laugh; ⏲9am-1pm & 2-6pm Mon-Fri, 10am-4pm Sat) is another place to check.

MEDIA

That's Ulaanbaatar is a free magazine published yearly and packed with updated tourist information, available at hotels and tourist offices.

Ulaanbaatar's two English-language newspapers, *Mongol Messenger* (weekly) and *UB Post* (www.theubpost.mn; thrice weekly), are well worth picking up for local news and entertainment information.

MEDICAL SERVICES

For life-or-death emergencies you'll need to be sent to Seoul or Běijīng.

Pharmacies (*aptek;* Аптек) are common in Ulaanbaatar, stocking Mongolian, Russian,

Chinese and Korean medicine. Check expiry dates carefully. The US embassy website (https://mn.usembassy.gov) has an extensive list of medical services.

Degfim Dentist (☎9916 2930, 7733 1313; www.degfim.com; Unesco St, Union Bldg, 3rd fl, What3words: twkling.sank.chainsaw; ⏰9am-5pm Mon-Sat) A modern, recommended dentist office with some English-speaking staff.

Intermed (☎7701 1111; www.intermed.mn; Chinggis Ave 41, Khan-Uul District, What3words: stands.pushover.kickers; ⏰8am-5pm Mon-Fri, 8am-1pm Sat) Hospital with 24-hour emergency and specialist doctors trained in South Korea. Rates to see a specialist start from T38,000.

Songdo Hospital (☎7011 1163; www.songdo.mn; Choidog St, What3words: sampled.cool.submerge; ⏰8.30am-5pm Mon-Fri, 8am-noon Sat) Modern Korean-run hospital with examinations starting at T20,000.

SOS Dental Clinic (☎11-464 330; www.sos-medica.mn; Big Ring Rd, 4a Bldg, What3words: native.surround.trembles; ⏰9am-6pm Mon-Fri) The best place for dental work. In the same building as SOS Medica Mongolia Clinic.

SOS Medica Mongolia Clinic (☎11-464 325, emergency 9911 0335; www.sosmedica.mn; Big Ring Rd, 4a Bldg, What3words: native.surround.trembles; ⏰9am-6pm Mon-Fri) The best place for most of your health care needs with Western expat doctors. It's very expensive, though (consultations cost around US$200), so you'll need to ensure you have travel insurance.

MONEY

Banks, ATMs and moneychangers are widespread. Banks with the best services include Golomt, Khan Bank and Trade & Development Bank. ATMs (you'll find them in department stores, mini markets and hotel lobbies) dispense tögrög; you can get dollars or euros from a bank teller, with your debit card and passport (expect a fee of around 1% to 3% from your home bank). The moneychanger on the ground floor of the **State Department Store** (p267) is handy, but rates here are not the best. The moneychangers at Ard Kino and Ikh Naiman Sharga generally have the best rates:

Ard Kino Money Changers (Baga Toiruu W, What3words: laces.craft.vans; ⏰9am-7pm Mon-Fri, 11am-5pm Sat & Sun)

Ikh Naiman Sharga (Tömörchiin Gudamj, What3words: relies.tuck.slang; ⏰9am-7pm) This building contains several moneychangers on the ground floor. The sign on the building says: Их 8 Шарга.

POST

Central post office (CPO, Töv Shuudangiin Salbar; ☎11-313 421; cnr Peace Ave & Sükhbaataryn Gudamj, What3words: wicked.greet.conjured; ⏰7.30am-9pm Mon-Fri, 9am-8pm Sat & Sun) Located near the southwest corner of Sükhbaatar Sq. The Postal Counter Hall is the place to post mail, packages and check poste restante (counter 7). EMS express (priority) mail can also be sent from here. On Sunday, although it's open, most services are nonexistent. Express services such as FedEx are more reliable if sending important documents. There is also a good range of postcards, small booklets about Mongolia in English and local newspapers for sale. Upstairs is the small **Stamp Museum** (⏰9am-1pm & 2-6pm Mon-Fri).

FedEx (☎11-320 591; www.fedex.com/mn; Prime Minister A Amar's St 15, What3words: appoints.self.lads; ⏰9am-6pm Mon-Fri) Located next to the Best Western Tuushin Hotel is this local FedEx contractor, Tuushin (www.tuushin.mn/eng). A 500g letter to most Western countries costs around $45.

TOURIST INFORMATION

Guide Tourist Information Centre (☎7010 1011; www.touristinfocenter.mn; Peace Ave, State Department Store, 1st fl, What3words: bravo.hexes.steamed; ⏰9am-9pm Mon-Fri, 10am-9pm Sat & Sun May-Sep, to 6pm Oct-Apr) Privately run tourist information centre within the State Department Store; offers maps, brochures and tours. It's located up the stairs on the western side of the building.

Tourist Information Booth (Central Post Office, Peace Ave, What3words: wicked.greet.conjured; ⏰8am-8pm; 📶) Privately owned tour company has a tourist information booth within the GPO office. It offers brochures, maps, guesthouse booking, general info and wi-fi access.

Ulaanbaatar Information Centre (☎7010 8687; www.tourism.ub.gov.mn; Baga Toiruu W 15, What3words: float.unscathed.snippets; ⏰8am-5pm Mon-Fri) Located in the Ulaanbaatar Bank building (door is on the north side). This office (run by the city) has a rack of brochures, but the staff here seem pretty indifferent to visitors.

TRAVEL AGENCIES

Staff at backpacker guesthouses can help with visa registration and train tickets. For a small fee, some guesthouses even help visitors staying at other hotels.

Air Market (☎11-305 050; www.airmarket.mn; cnr Seoul St & Chinggis Ave, What3words: outright.composers.umbrellas; ⏰9am-10pm Mon-Fri, 10am-4pm Sat & Sun) Good for organising air tickets.

Air Trans (☎11-313 131; www.airtrans.mn; cnr Sükhbaataryn Gudamj & Sambuu St, What3words: stow.dare.branching; ⏰8am-8pm Mon-Fri, 10am-4pm Sat & Sun)

ℹ Getting There & Away

TRAIN

The very Soviet-looking **railway station** (Narny Gudamj, What3words: ethic.pursuing.baking) has a left-luggage office (T1000 per piece), an ATM, a foreign exchange, mobile phone companies, an information centre and a restaurant.

From Ulaanbaatar daily trains travel to northern Mongolia and on to Russia, via Darkhan and Sükhbaatar, and southeast to China, via Choir, Sainshand and Zamyn-Üüd. There are also lines between Ulaanbaatar and the coal-mining towns of Erdenet and Baganuur.

To buy a ticket you must show identification; a passport or driver's licence will do (student ID won't work).

Tourists seldom use the train in Mongolia to travel domestically as buses are faster, cheaper and more reliable.

The **domestic railway ticket office** (☎21-24109, 21-24137; www.ubtz.mn; Narny Gudamj, What3words: engrossed.veal.abacus; ⏲8am-9pm Mon-Fri, 9am-5pm Sat, 11am-5pm Sun) is located in the modern-looking building on the east side of the train station. Boards inside the office show departure times (in Cyrillic) and ticket prices. There's also a full timetable at the information desk on the station platform. Times and schedules are available at www.ubtz.mn (in Mongolian), however it's rarely updated, especially given timetables are always changing.

Tickets can be booked for a seat *(niitin obshe)*, hard sleeper *(untlagiin obshe)* or a soft sleeper *(tasalgat)*.

Upstairs from the domestic railway ticket office is the **International Railway Ticket Office** (☎2124 3848, 2124 4367; Narny Gudamj, 2nd Fl, What3words: engrossed.veal.abacus; ⏲8am-8.20pm). Here you can buy tickets to Irkutsk and Moscow in Russia, and to Běijīng, Èrlián and Hohhot in China. Timetables are listed in English.

AIR

Chinggis Khaan International Airport (☎1900 1980; http://en.airport.gov.mn; What3words: inspects.roaring.nags; 📶),16km southwest of the city, will remain Mongolia's main gateway until the full completion of the New Ulaanbaatar International Airport (www.nubia.mn). The airport has an ATM (though it's not always reliable), a post office, free wi-fi, mobile phone operators and car rental. A tourist booth operates inside the baggage hall when planes arrive.

Mongolia has two domestic carriers: **Hunnu Air** (☎7000 1111; www.hunnuair.com; cnr Ikh Toiruu & Seoul St, Rokmon Bldg, What3words: covenants.spoiler.outgoing; ⏲9am-6pm Mon-Fri, 10am-5pm Sat & Sun) and **AeroMongolia** (☎7010 3030; www.aeromongolia.mn; Chinggis Ave 15, Monnis Tower, 1st fl, What3words: echo.smuggled.alleyway; ⏲9am-6pm Mon-Fri, 10am-5pm Sat). On domestic routes with Hunnu Air and AeroMongolia you are allowed 10kg to 15kg of baggage (combined carry-on and check-in). You'll pay around T3000 per kilogram over the limit. Flight days always change, so check updated schedules. The airlines accept credit cards for international and domestic flights.

Aeroflot (☎11-320 720; www.aeroflot.ru; Seoul St 15, What3words: opponent.prank.crust; ⏲9am-5pm Mon-Thu, 8am-4pm Fri, 10am-1pm Sat)

Air China (☎7000 9933; www.airchina.com; Narny Gudamj 87, What3words: weekends.steady.hoping; ⏲9am-noon & 1-5pm Mon-Fri, 9am-noon & 1-3pm Sat & Sun)

Korean Air (☎11-317 100; www.koreanair.com; Tokyo St, Chinggis Khaan Hotel, 3rd fl, What3words: outs.mimed.bracelet; ⏲8.30am-12.30pm & 1.30-5.30pm Mon-Fri)

MIAT (Mongolian Airlines; ☎11-322 144; www.miat.com; 13 Chinggis Ave, What3words: cools.shelters.cashiers; ⏲9am-7pm Mon-Fri, 10am-3pm Sat & Sun)

Turkish Airlines (☎7585 9999; www.turkishairlines.com; Baga Toiruu-17, JJ Tower, 1st fl, What3words: swooned.viewer.guesswork; ⏲9am-6pm Mon-Fri)

At the time of writing, the **New Ulaanbaatar International Airport** (www.nubia.mn; What3words: loaves.clipping.ministers), 50km south of Ulaanbaatar near Zuunmod in Töv Province, was scheduled to begin operations in August 2018. It will service flights from Europe, North America and Asia.

BUS & MINIVAN

Two stations handle most bus traffic. **Bayanzürkh Bus Terminal** (Баянзүрх Авто Вокзал; Bayanzürkh Avto Vaksal; ☎9455 5009; What3words: fries.forever.certainly), is 6km east of Sükhbaatar Sq. **Dragon Bus Terminal** (Dragon Avto Vaksal; ☎1900 1234; www.eticket.transdep.mn; Peace Ave, What3words: outs.solve.enlarge; ⏲7.30am-7.30pm), is 7km west of Chinggis Khaan Sq.

In addition to buses, minivans run daily to many of the same destinations (at a similar price), departing when full. It's best to have a Mongolian friend call the bus station to inquire about the minivans, as schedules change frequently. An online schedule can be found at www.transdep.mn (in Mongolian), where you can book tickets online.

Buses are always full, so buy your ticket as early as possible; tickets can be bought up to one month in advance from the station.

International Buses

Vostok Trans (☎9906 0734; Dragon Station) runs a daily bus service from UB to Ulan Ude.

It departs Wednesday, Friday and Saturday at 7.30am, and Sunday at 7am. The journey takes 12 hours and costs T67,000. Buses leave from the Dragon Bus Terminal. Tickets are sold inside the domestic railway ticket office on the 1st floor. You can buy a ticket one week in advance. Tickets are also available online at teever.gov.mn, in Mongolian.

Getting Around

TO & FROM THE TRAIN STATION

It's a 25-minute walk from the train station to the State Department Store. International trains arrive early in the morning while the city is still quiet, so with a backpack it's easy to walk into town. Guesthouses and hotels may pick you up if contacted ahead of time (some hostel owners will be at the station anyway, trawling for guests).

The nearest bus stop is across the street from the station. Bus 29 or trolleybus 4 will get you to the State Department Store and Sükhbaatar Sq. To the train station, bus 29 takes Seoul St so you won't see it if waiting near the State Department Store. In this direction you should take trolleybus No 4.

Some taxi drivers at the station, like those at the airport, may agree on one price and then charge more once you reach the hotel. If this happens, stay calm and be patient and polite. Don't give in to their demands. Eventually they will get bored with trying to rip you off and will just accept a reasonable price. Keep your luggage with you in the car so they can't hold it hostage in the boot. If you must use a taxi, head out of the station and up the road to escape the sharks, then flag down a taxi and pay the standard rate of T800 per kilometre. Expect to pay around T10,000 for a ride into town.

TO/FROM THE AIRPORT

If it's your first visit to Mongolia, the best way to get into the city from Chinggis Khaan International Airport is to organise a pick-up from your hotel/guesthouse (just email them with your flight details). This may be free (usually if you book a few nights' accommodation) or cost around US$15 to US$20. Otherwise there are plenty of official taxis waiting at the terminal that charge a fixed price of around T20,000 into the city. Be certain to confirm the price before taking off as otherwise they will likely rip you off.

If you don't mind walking a little, you can use bus Ch-7 (T500) that connects with the city centre and the district of Nisekh, close to the airport. At the airport, go out of the terminal and across the parking lot to the main road (a 500m walk). At the main road turn right and walk about 400m, until you reach the bus turn-out (there is no sign, but you'll see others waiting). Only do this during daylight (for safety reasons). A bus comes by every 15 minutes or so until 8.30pm. You'll need to purchase a U Money card (T3600) before you embark, available from the small kiosk at the bus shelter. Once in the city you can get off at the bus stop near the main library (opposite the Drama Theatre).

To the airport, bus Ch-7 will stop at **Ard Kino** (Baga Toiruu, What3words: movies.stealthier.jump), and also near the Bayangol Hotel, but again it won't drop you at the terminal. You still have to haul your luggage 500m from the bus stop on the highway.

BUS

Local public transport is reliable and departures are frequent, but buses can get crowded. Cash payment is no longer accepted on board, so you'll need to purchase a **U Money** card (T3600), available from bus kiosks around town. Be sure to touch-on when boarding and touch-off upon exiting. Bus trips cost T500, and T300 for trolleybus.

Pickpockets and bag slashers occasionally ply their trade on crowded routes. Seal up all pockets, hold your bag on your chest and be careful when boarding.

The route number is next to the (Cyrillic) destination sign on the front of the trolleybus or bus. The route is often marked on the side of the bus. For short trips it's just as cheap to take a taxi, especially for two or more passengers.

TAXI

In Ulaanbaatar there are official and unofficial taxis. The official ones are noticeably labelled on the exterior and inside may or may not have a meter. The unofficial taxis are simply locals trawling for passengers.

All charge a standard T800 per kilometre (check the current rate, as it increases regularly). Don't agree to a set daily price because it will always be more than the standard rate per kilometre.

Before you get in the cab always have the driver reset the odometer to zero and agree on a per-kilometre rate before setting off. It also helps to have some idea of the route and the price.

To find a taxi, just stand by the side of a main street and hold your arm out with your fingers down. After dark, avoid using a private car – stick to an official taxi.

Help Cab & Tours (☎ 9965 2371; www.help-tours.com) Has an English-speaking dispatcher and a reputation for being reliable, safe and honest. Its main clients are expats and the prices are slightly higher than other companies. Booking fee is T1000 and flagfall is T5000 for the first 2km and then T1000 per kilometre. A ride to/from the airport to the city centre is T40,000. You can also hire a car for a half-/full-day city tour for T80,000/120,000.

Noyon Zuuch Taxi Company (☎ 1950) Reliable service with English-speaking dispatchers.

Around Ulaanbaatar

Mongolia's real attraction lies in the untouched beauty of the countryside, its exhilarating wide open spaces and rich nomadic culture. Fortunately, these aspects are within reach on day trips or overnights from Ulaanbaatar.

Mandshir Khiid Мандшир Хийд

For the 350 monks who once called the monastery **Mandshir Khiid** (Мандшир Хийд; What3words: passports.derives.stalling; GPS: N 47°45.520', E 106°59.675'; adult/child T1000/500, photography T2000; ⏲9am-1pm & 2-6pm Mon-Fri, 8am-noon & 1-7pm Sat & Sun) home, its gorgeous setting (elevation 1645m) must have been a daily inspiration. Like most monasteries in Mongolia, Mandshir Khiid was destroyed in 1937 by Stalin's thugs, but was partially restored in the 1990s.

The main temple has been restored and converted into a museum, but the other buildings remain in ruins. The monastery and museum are not amazing in themselves, but rather it's the beautiful forest setting that makes a visit worthwhile.

It's worth climbing up the rocks behind the main temple, where there are some 18th-century **Buddhist rock paintings**. The views from the top are even more beautiful, and you'll find yourself in the midst of a lovely pine forest.

The area around the monastery is one of the best camping spots near Ulaanbaatar. You should get permission from the caretaker at the monastery if you're camping nearby (per person T3000), or just hike off into the woods. Of the ger camps in the area the best one is **Ovooni Enger Ger Camp** (☎8313 2011; What3words: expenditure.recreations.potbelly; ger per person T60,000-100,000, r T80,000-240,000) but, unless you enjoy singing, avoid weekends, as it's popular with folk from UB who come for karaoke.

Located 46km from Ulaanbaatar, the monastery is a perfect half-day trip from the capital, or can be used as a starting point for hikes into the Strictly Protected Area. If you get here early enough, one possibility to return to UB is to hike back over the hills.

Terelj Тэрэлж

Only 55km northeast of Ulaanbaatar the Terelj (Тэрэлж) region makes up part of **Gorkhi-Terelj National Park** (What3words: embarrasses.envy.sphere; T3000), offering great opportunities for hiking, rock climbing, swimming (in icy-cold water), rafting and horse riding. At 1600m, the area is cool, and the alpine scenery magnificent, and for hardcore extreme-sports fanatics, there's skiing and dog-sledding in the depths of winter.

The most popular destination for hiking or horseriding is **Turtle Rock** (Melkhi Khad; What3words: luxuriously.balloon.packer; GPS: N 47°54.509', E 107°25.428'). It's easily spotted along the main road through the park. From here it's less than an hour's hike up to the picturesque Buddhist meditation retreat of Aryapala.

Terelj is a great place to go camping, or guesthouses can arrange accommodation in the park – sometimes staying in real gers with local families. Most of the tourist ger camps in Terelj offer similar facilities and prices – the pick are the offbeat **Ecotourism Ger Camp** (☎9973 4815, 9973 4710; bergroo@hotmail.com; What3words: displayed.insulate.proteins; GPS: N 47°58.722', E 107°28.907'; per person incl meals €35) run by an eccentric Dutchman named Bert and his lovely family; the secluded **Buuveit Camp** (☎9911 4913, 11-322 870; www.tsolmontravel.com/en/our-camps/buuveit-camp; What3words: leases.clenched.whoops; per person with/without meals from US$55/20) about 13km along the main road from the park entrance; and the luxurious American-built **Ayanchin Four Seasons Lodge** (☎9909 4539; www.ayanchinlodge.mn; What3words: woodwork.overcook.horns; ger/yurt/r incl breakfast from T250,000/300,000/300,000; wi-fi), which is also a great place to eat.

ℹ Getting There & Away

The road from Ulaanbaatar to Terelj Village, which goes through part of the national park, is in pretty good nick. A bus (T2500, 2½ hours) departs daily at 4pm, from a **stop** (Peace Ave, What3words: wins.energetic.interrupt) opposite the Narantuul Hotel. It then stops at every bus stop heading east along Peace Ave. Get there with 15 minutes to spare as they sometimes depart early. Going the other way, it leaves Terelj at 8am Monday to Friday and 11am on weekends; catch it near Hotel Terelj. You may have to pay an extra T2500 for a bike or heavy luggage.

Another option is to take one of the frequent buses between Ulaanbaatar and Nalaikh (T900, every 10 minutes), and then to hook up with one of the shared minibuses that shuttles between Nalaikh and Terelj Village (T1500, roughly every hour). A taxi to Terelj from Nalaikh costs about T25,000.

Khustain National Park

Хустайн Нуруу

Spanning over 506 sq km, this **national park** (Хустайн Нуруу; Khustain Nuruu, Birch Mountain Range; ☎9323 0169, 21-245 087; www.hustai.mn; What3words: fancy.hesitations.respond; T18,000, Mongolians free) was established in 1993 to protect Mongolia's wild horse, the *takhi*, as well as the reserve's steppe and forest-steppe environment. In addition to the *takhi*, there are populations of *maral* (Asiatic red deer), steppe gazelle, deer, boar, Pallas's cats, wolves, lynx, marmot and some 223 species of birds. Located about 100km southwest of Ulaanbaatar, a visit to the park is a popular overnight excursion from the capital.

The **information centre** (☎9323 0169, 21-245 087; www.hustai.mn; What3words: hike.topple.cardigan; ⏲7am-9pm) at the entrance to the park at **Hustain Tourist Camp** (☎21-245 087, 9323 0169; What3words: hike.topple.cardigan; per person incl meals & park entry T146,000, incl breakfast only T56,500) offers an excellent overview of the national park. Other places to stay either near or inside the park include **Moilt Camp** (☎21-245 087, 9323 0169; What3words: stipulating.plunking.swimmers; per person incl meals & park entry T136,000, incl breakfast only T46,500) and **Khustai Lunoba Resort** (☎9910 8840, 9950 7691; www.facebook.com/moltsog.els.khustai; r with/without bathroom incl breakfast T180,000/85,000; ⏲mid-May–Oct).

Horse riding (T12,000/70,000 per hour/day), hiking and jeep excursions (T2000 per kilometre, plus T65,000/100,000 for a guide per half/full day) are all good ways to explore the park. Park regulations require you to take a park guide (free within the park) who can direct your driver to the best spots. You must stick to the existing tracks, and keep 200m from the *takhi*.

ℹ Getting There & Away

To get to the park, travel 100km west from Ulaanbaatar, along the road to Kharkhorin, where there is a signpost pointing you 13km south to the park entrance.

If you don't have a car, there's a minivan (one-way US$15) that travels from the park to Ulaanbaatar and back twice a week, departing the park at about 10am on Friday and Sunday, and returning from Ulaanbaatar at 5pm on the same days. The van only has 10 seats, and is really for workers and volunteers, so you'll need to make an advance booking. In UB it leaves from the **Hustai National Park Office** (☎21-245 087; www.hustai.mn; Hustai Bldg, 2nd khoroo, Bayangol District, What3words: flux.exonerate.refrain; ⏲8.30am-5.30pm Mon-Fri).

Ikh Nartiin Chuluu

Их Нартын Чулуу

A splendid area of rocky outcrop in the desert, the 670-sq-km **Ikh Nartiin Chuluu Nature Reserve** (Ikh Nart, Их Нартын Чулуу; www.ikhnart.com; GPS: N 45°34' E108°38'; What3words: verge.confusedly.compounds), can give you a good taste of the Gobi without venturing too far off the Trans-Mongolian.

Several ancient **burial mounds** (GPS: N 45°75.546', E 108°65.454') and additional Tibetan **petroglyphs** (GPS: N 45°60.787', E 108°57.201'; N 45°60.237', E 108°55.959'; N 45°59.175', E 108°61.397') can be found throughout the park, but the reason it's on the tourist radar is the wildlife, specifically a healthy population of the globally threatened argali sheep.

Nomadic Journeys (p259) operates the splendid **IkhNart Wilderness Camp** (☎11-330 360; www.nomadicjourneys.com; GPS: N 45°39.830', E 108°39.204'; What3words: verge.confusedly.compounds; per night incl meals US$125-135; P) 🍃 in the reserve, about 50km drive from Shiveegobi train station. Guided wildlife walks, multiday camel treks and jeep tours are available to guests, and the main camp offers true glamping, with 15 gers supported by gorgeous hand-painted pillars, and furnished with a dung burning oven, a private sink and reading chairs.

You can access the reserve by taking a southbound train from Ulaanbaatar and getting off at Shiveegobi, Tsomog or Choir train stations. However, you'll have to arrange pick up, as there will be no taxis awaiting your arrival. The best plan is to book with IkhNart Wilderness Camp (p272). They will arrange for a local driver to meet you at the train station and escort you into the park.

Sainshand Сайншанд

☎01522, 7052 / POP 20,515 / TIME MOSCOW + 5HR

Sainshand is divided into two parts: a cluster of homes and businesses around the train station, and the more developed centre, 2km south, where you'll find most of the action. It is not a tourist town by any conceivable measure, but the nearby monastery Khamaryn Khiid and a couple of museums in town are worth a look. Plus, the sunsets ooze pastels.

The small but well-put-together **Museum of Danzan Ravjaa** (☎1522-23221; www.danzanravjaa.org; What3words: swirls.shavers.sackful; T2000; ⊙9am-8pm) honours the life of Noyon Khutagt Danzan Ravjaa (1803–56), a well-known Mongolian writer, composer, painter and medic who was born about 100km southwest of Sainshand. The well-appointed **Sainshand Natural History Museum** (☎1522-22657; What3words: curvature.capful.privileges; T2000; ⊙9am-1pm & 2-6pm) houses plenty of stuffed Gobi animals, and a collection of seashells and marine fossils (Dornogovi was once beneath the sea). There is also an impressive skeleton of a Protoceratops and a dinosaur egg.

Easily the best hotel in town, even if service is a bit sour, is **Lux Hotel** (☎9962 6152; What3words: annoyance.vendor.expensively; d T45,000-55,000; P ❄ 📶). Clean and friendly, **Best Restaurant** (☎9925 5579; What3words: puns.hollered.disdains; meals T5000-10,000; ⊙10am-11pm) is the local favourite for eating. It doles out excellent Mongolian dishes; they recommend the *bainshte shöl* (dumpling soup). Ask for the English menu.

Getting There & Away

At least two trains link Sainshand with Ulaanbaatar every day.

Departure times here are based on the summer schedule (May to September), and are subject to slight variations each year.

UB to Sainshand Train 286; departs 9.35am daily; arrives 8.15pm

Sainshand to UB Train 285; departs 9pm daily; arrives 8.05am

UB to Zamyn-Üüd Train 276; departs UB 4.30pm daily; arrives in Sainshand 1.38am

Zamyn-Üüd to UB Train 275; departs Sainshand 11pm daily; arrives in UB 9.25am

Tickets from Ulaanbaatar cost T9100/18,000/28,700 for hard seat/hard sleeper/soft sleeper. If you book your ticket more than a day ahead there is a T800 to T1200 fee, although we found it fairly easy to buy same-day tickets to Ulaanbaatar from here. If you want to guarantee a private compartment, you'll have to buy up all four seats.

The Trans-Mongolian Railway and the trains between Ulaanbaatar and Èrlián (Ereen; just over the Chinese border) and Hohhot (in Inner Mongolia) stop at Sainshand, but you cannot use these services just to get to Sainshand unless you buy a ticket all the way to China.

THE GOBI DESERT

The world's northernmost desert straddles the border between Mongolia and China, an immense, barren plateau the size of Western Europe. The Mongolians say that there are 33 different types of Gobi, but only about 2% of it is *Lawrence of Arabia*–style sand dunes. Most of the land is gravel plains, an occasional mountain range, and some sandstone cliffs.

The harsh climate sees the temperature shift from minus 30°C in winter to above 40°C in summer. Still, some hardy nomads manage to eke out an existence here, raising camels, goats and other livestock. They have recently been joined by an army of entrepreneurs, prospectors, geologists and others seeking to cash in on Mongolia's booming mining sector, based largely in the south Gobi.

The Gobi was brought into the consciousness of the Western world thanks largely to the explorations of Roy Chapman Andrews, the head of New York's Museum of Natural History. In the 1920s Andrews made five trips into the Gobi (with both camels and Dodge trucks sent across the Pacific), where he collected an enormous amount of dinosaur skeletons, fossils and dinosaur eggs.

Contrary to popular belief, the Gobi is home to a significant amount of wildlife, including *khavtgai* (wild camels), *khulan* (wild asses), *zeer* (gazelles), *argal* (argali sheep), *yangir* (ibex), *irbis* (snow leopards) and *mazaalai* (Gobi bears).

In the Gobi the locals have a lot of time on their hands, and can spin yarns about other legendary beasts of the desert, including the *allegorhoi horhoi* ('death worm'), which sprays poisonous venom from its mouth and discharges a powerful electric shock from its tail. Another Gobi resident is the Almas, a sort of Bigfoot or Yeti that locals describe as a 'marmot-eating half-ape.' Both creatures have inspired National Geographic–style search expeditions in recent years. So far both have remained elusive.

Around Sainshand

The area's highlights are **Khamaryn Khiid** (Хамарын Хийд; GPS: N 44°36.038', E 110°16.650'; What3words: misguided.likening.timely; ⌚9am-1pm & 2-6pm) and the nearby **Shambhala** (T5000) (also known as the Energy Centre). The monastery was founded by legendary poet- monk Danzan Ravjaa in the 1820s, and for decades after it flourished as a cultural institution. Danzan Ravjaa organised opera performances here, wrote poetry and music and practised traditional medicine. After he died his followers maintained the institutions he founded and tall tales spread about his magical feats.

The monastery was destroyed in 1937 but many of his possessions were hidden and protected. In 1990 a new monastery was founded here and it has been growing in popularity as a pilgrim destination.

About 2km from the monastery is Shambhala, where pilgrims arrive in large numbers to lay flat on the ground and absorb the energy of this sacred spot. The site is surrounded by 108 stupas and special ceremonies are held here on 10 September.

If you want to sleep out in the desert, **Gobi Sunrise Tavan Dohoi** (☎9908 0151; GPS: N 44°45.418', E 110°11.236'; with/without meals US$45/12; Ⓟ) is a well-maintained ger camp with flush toilets and hot showers. A taxi here from town costs around T20,000 to T30,000 one way.

A taxi from Sainshand to Khamaryn Khiid costs T50,000 to T60,000 return, including waiting time.

Zamyn-Üüd

☎02524, 7052 / POP 13,300 / TIME MOSCOW + 5HR

The last stop (or first depending on your direction) of the Trans-Mongolia line before it plunges into China is this small, otherwise insignificant border village in the Gobi Desert.

Most of the town's activity can be found around the square in front of the train station. The chief attractions here are the disused water fountain, some outdoor pool tables and grabbing a bite at one of the many eateries that cater to transit travellers killing time.

If you miss the train to UB and need to spend the night, **Jinchin Hotel** (What3words: tackling.unwinding.eraser; d shared/private bath T32,000/40,000; 📶) is good value, but the rooms have no air-con. It's that turquoise building on the east side of the train station.

Dàtóng

☎0352 / POP 3.4 MILLION / TIME MOSCOW + 5HR

Dàtóng (大同) today is fascinating, and charming to boot. Come nighttime, the old-town sensations – with red lanterns swinging in the breeze and wind chimes tinkling on the illuminated city walls – evoke Dàtóng's past glories as an ancient capital. No matter that most of this has

MONGOLIA-CHINA BORDER CROSSING

Most travellers end up in the Chinese border town of Èrlián (二连) in the middle of the night when passing through on an international train. Zamyn-Üüd, on the Mongolian side, is not an interesting place, so you aren't missing anything if you are on the overnight train.

Opening hours The Zamyn-Üüd–Èrlián crossing is open daily but note that on holidays only the train (not the road) crossing will operate. For vehicles the border is open 8am to 6pm.

Processing Mongolian customs and immigration officials take about two hours to process all the train passengers.

Walking It's not possible to walk across the border.

Change money If you have just come from Mongolia, change any remaining tögrög here or you'll be keeping it as a souvenir.

Onward travel Remember that if you are carrying on to the Chinese interior there is no need to go to Běijīng first. From Èrlián you can travel to the rail junction at Dàtóng and then catch trains or buses to Píngyáo, Xī'ān and points south. For western China and Tibet, get off at Jíníng where you can change to Hohhot, Lánzhōu and beyond. Read Lonely Planet's *China* guide for details on connections from these cities.

Dàtóng

Top Sights

1 China Sculpture Museum ... B3
2 Dàtóng City Wall ... B4
3 Nine Dragon Screen ... B3

Sights

4 Dàtóng Cathedral ... B3
5 Dàtóng Mosque ... B3
6 Huáyán Temple ... B3
7 Old Town ... B3
8 Shànhuà Temple ... B4

Sleeping

9 Garden Hotel ... B4
10 Green Island Youth Hostel ... B1
11 Hóngqí Hotel ... B1

Eating

12 Dōngfāng Xiāo Miàn ... A4
13 Fènglín Gé ... B3
Tónghé Dàfàndiàn ... (see 11)

Information

14 Agricultural Bank of China ... B4
15 Industrial & Commercial Bank of China ... B1
16 Public Security Bureau ... A4

been re-created from scratch by an over-ambitious mayor: a mountain of cash – an estimated ¥50 billion – has been ploughed into a colossal renovation of the old quarter. The city wall has been rebuilt in its entirety, enclosing a retinue of renovated (or newly built) sights, the paint still fresh on most. But it's beyond the wall where Dàtóng really comes into its own. The town is the gateway to the awe-inspiring Yúngāng Caves, one of China's most outstanding Buddhist treasures, as well as a launchpad to the photogenic Hanging Monastery, the world's oldest wooden pagoda, crumbling earthen sections of the Great Wall and onward trips to sacred Wǔtái Shān.

Sights

Much of Dàtóng's **old town** (老城区; Lǎochéngqū) has been re-created in an astonishingly ambitious program commenced by former city mayor Geng Yanbo, which aimed to restore its ancient grandeur and charm. While much, including the amazing **city wall** (大同城墙; Dàtóng Chéngqiáng; 5am-2am high season, 6am-midnight low season) FREE, is now largely finished, further re-creations have been dragging their feet, including the simply colossal and still unfinished Dài Wángfǔ palace. Generally the rebuild looks good, but it has unfortunately involved a huge and deliberate loss of the former city and its residents to re-create something better looking.

Buildings largely rebuilt from the ground up include the **mosque** (清真大寺; Qīngzhēn Dà Sì; Da Xi Jie; 大西街; ¥10; 8am-8pm), **Chunyang Taoist Temple**, **Guandi Temple** and many former courtyard houses, while portions of Huayan Jie, Da Beijie and Da Nanjie are now pedestrian-only shopping streets.

The vast cost of the old-town refit has been partially passed onto visitors, with admission prices to key sights increasing, although these have since been reigned in (the city wall is now free, for example). But more enduring costs include the resettling of tens of thousands of residents to accommodate the great rebuild. Mayor Geng Yanbo (nicknamed 'Geng Chai Chai', or 'Demolition Geng') was moved to a new position of Tàiyuán mayor in 2013, greatly slowing the pace of the program.

A 2015 documentary about Geng by Chinese filmmaker Hao Zhou, called *The Chinese Mayor,* paints a fascinating and nuanced picture of a man who set out to reverse the fortunes of this once blighted coal city, and is well worth tracking down.

★Bā Táizi RUINS
(八台子; Bā Táizicūn; 八台子村; ⊙24hr) FREE Alongside magnificently dilapidated earthen sections of the Great Wall that disappear over the top of Horsehead Hill (马头山; Mǎtóu Shān), a fabulous Gothic church ruin is quite a sight. All that remains of the **Holy Mother Church** (圣母堂; Shèngmǔ Táng), built in 1876, is its front gate and bell tower and lopped-off spire above it. No explanation for the church's demise is given in the blurb on the board alongside, nor how the church arrived in such a remote spot.

★Nine Dragon Screen WALLS
(九龙壁; Jiǔlóng Bì; Da Dongjie; 大东街; ¥10; ⊙8am-6.30pm) Emblazoned with nine coiling dragons picked out in coloured glazed tiles, this is one of the finest *yǐngbì* (影壁) spirit walls in China (it has two counterparts in Běijīng). It's also the largest, at 45.5m long, 8m high and 2m thick. Built in the Ming dynasty in 1392, the palace it once protected belonged to the 13th son of a Ming emperor and burnt down in 1644. Amazingly, the palace is being rebuilt in its entirety, covering a vast area of town.

★China Sculpture Museum GALLERY
(中国雕塑博物馆; Zhōngguó Diāosù Bówùguǎn; Da Beijie; 大北街; ⊙8.30-11.30am & 2.30-5.30pm Tue-Sun) FREE This cavernous museum is built within the north Wǔdìng Mén gate section of the restored city walls, with seemingly endless corridors of excellent contemporary sculpture by Chinese and foreign artists. When you get bored of looking at statues and photography, look out for uncovered sections of the original city walls at the very rear, dating from the Ming, Jin, Liao and Northern Wei dynasties. You will need your passport for admission.

Dàtóng Cathedral CHURCH
(大同天主堂; Dàtóng Tiānzhǔtáng; Lǐhuáijiǎo; 李怀角; ⊙hours variable) This working cathedral – also called the Cathedral of the Immaculate Heart of Mary – is an astonishing sight once you find it and stand before its twin bell towers. Built in 1891, the church was burned down on 13 July 1900 during the xenophobic and anti-Christian Boxer Rebellion, taking a few Catholics with it; it was rebuilt in 1906. Both bell towers were destroyed in 1966 during the Cultural Revolution, but the house of worship was repaired in 1982 and 2006.

Huáyán Temple BUDDHIST SITE
(华严寺; Huáyán Sì; Huayan Jie; 华严街; ¥65; ⊙8am-6.30pm; 🚌38) Built by the Khitan during the Liao dynasty (AD 907–1125), this temple faces east, not south (it's said the Khitan were sun worshippers) and is divided into two separate complexes. One of these is an active monastery (upper temple), while the other is a museum (lower temple). Dating to 1140, the impressive main hall of the **Upper Temple** (上华严寺; Shàng Huáyán Sì) is one of the largest Buddhist halls in China, with Ming murals and Qing statues within.

Shànhuà Temple BUDDHIST SITE
(善化寺; Shànhuà Sì; Nansi Jie; 南寺街; ¥50; ⊙8am-6pm) Originally constructed in AD 713 and today standing just inside the city walls, Shànhuà Temple was rebuilt during the Jin dynasty. The grand wooden-bracketed hall at the rear contains five beautiful central Buddhas and expressive statues of celestial generals in the wings. Look out for the impressive and quite colossal turquoise, yellow and ochre five-dragon screen (五龙壁; *wǔlóngbì*). It stands outside the current temple perimeter, so is free to admire.

Sleeping

★Green Island Youth Hostel HOSTEL $
(绿岛青年旅舍; Lǜdǎo Qīngnián Lǚshě; ☎158 3524 4211; www.facebook.com/datongyouthhostel; 5th fl, block A, Jinhu Guoji building, 1029 Weidu Dadao; 魏都大道1029号金湖国际A座5层; dm ¥50-55, d ¥160-210; ❄📶) This hostel in a huge tower block puts dorm beds and comfortable double rooms within an easy stroll of the train station, while numerous buses trundle into the walled city not far away. The main common area is a bit small, but everything is neat and Simon the owner is helpful and friendly. It has excellent coffee too.

Hóngqí Hotel HOTEL $$
(红旗饭店; Hóngqí Fàndiàn; ☎0352-536 6666, 0352-536 6111; www.hongqihotel.com; 11 Zhan-

qian Jie; 站前街11号; s & tw incl breakfast ¥380, ste incl breakfast ¥680-1288;) This classic place opposite the train station has excellent rooms, drinkable tap water, fully equipped shower rooms with regularly restocked toiletries, very friendly staff (in huge abundance) and prices that regularly dip to a very attractive ¥218. The included buffet-style breakfast is also excellent, with a Western option provided.

★ Garden Hotel HOTEL $$$
(花园大饭店; Huāyuán Dàfàndiàn; 0352-586 5888; www.gardenhoteldatong.com; 59 Da Nanjie; 大南街59号; d & tw incl breakfast ¥1080-1780, tw ¥1380-1580, ste ¥2880-3880;) The well-appointed rooms at this popular hotel feature down quilts, carved rosewood bed frames and excellent bathrooms. There's an attractive atrium with a cafe lounge and fake palms, Latin American and Chinese restaurants, plus excellent staff. The impressive breakfast spread includes decent espresso coffee. Significant discounts (even in high season) knock prices as low as ¥320: excellent value.

Eating

Dàtóng has several excellent dining options, from packed and popular noodle diners to elegant, traditional-style restaurants.

Fènglín Gé CHINESE $
(凤临阁; 0352-205 9799; near cnr Gulou Xijie & Huayan Jie; 鼓楼西街华严街路口; mains from ¥25; 6.30-9.30am, 11.30am-2pm & 5.30-9pm;) Exquisite and delectable *shāomai* (steamed dim-sum dumpling) is the star of the show at this traditionally styled restaurant at the heart of the old town. Order by the steamer (笼; *lóng*) or half steamer. The crab *shāomai* are succulent and gorgeous, but not cheap (¥15 each, half steamer ¥45); there's lamb too (¥7 each, half steamer ¥26) and other tempting fillings.

Dōngfāng Xiāo Miàn NOODLES $
(East Wheat; 东方削面; Yingze Jie; 迎泽街; noodles from ¥6; 7am-10pm) Forgive the chain-store decor and bear the long queues (always a good sign) and you'll soon be in noodle heaven at this popular local chain. Steaming bowls of the humble Shānxī speciality (削面; *xiāo miàn*) is the star here; have it with pork (¥7), beef or lamb (¥10) and pair it with a variety of side dishes such as spicy cucumbers. A beer will help top it all off.

Tónghé Dàfàndiàn CHINESE $
(同和大饭店; 1 Zhanqian Jie; 站前街1号; dishes ¥16-40; 11am-2pm & 6-9pm) This fantastic, bright and cheery spot alongside the Hóngqí Hotel (p277) and a short hop from the railway station can look a little intimidating with its big, round tables better suited to functions, but solo diners can pull up a chair no problem. There's a huge range of tasty, well-presented dishes on the picture menu, suiting all budgets.

Information

Agricultural Bank of China (ABC; 中国农业银行; Zhōngguó Nóngyè Yínháng; Da Nanjie; 大南街; 8.30am-5.30pm) ATM and money exchange.

Industrial & Commercial Bank of China (ICBC; 工商银行; Gōngshāng Yínháng; Weidu Dadao; 魏都大道; 8.30am-5.30pm)

Public Security Bureau (PSB; 公安局城区分局; Gōng'ān Jú Chéngqū Fēnjú; 0352-201 4927; Zhengfa Building, Xinkai Nanlu; 新开南路政法大楼; 9am-noon & 3-5.30pm Mon-Fri)

Getting There & Away

TRAIN

At time of writing a new high-speed train was expected to connect Běijīng with Dàtóng by 2019, cutting the journey time to two hours and bringing a huge influx of new visitors to the city. Until then, departures from Dàtóng include Běijīng (hard seat/sleeper ¥48/108, six hours, 11 daily) and Hohhot (hard seat ¥42, three to four hours, 12 daily).

If you're heading north to Mongolia your options are the K3 and K23 (running three days a week in summer), which can be purchased at the train station in Dàtóng. It's best if you can buy this ticket ahead of time at the CITS office in Běijīng, so that you can be assured of a ticket. If tickets are unavailable in Dàtóng, take a bus to Èrlián, cross the border and continue by rail to Ulaanbaatar.

AIR

Located 20km east of the city, Dàtóng's small airport has flights to several destinations including Běijīng (¥450, one hour), Shànghǎi (¥1450, 2½ hours), Guǎngzhōu (¥1650, 4½ hours), Chéngdū ((¥1200, 3½ hours), and Xī'ān (¥550, 1¾ hours). Buy tickets at www.ctrip.com or www.elong.net.

BUS

Buses from the **south bus station** (新南公路客运站; Xīn nán gōnglù kèyùn zhàn; 0352-502 5222; Weidu Dadao; 魏都大道), located 9km from the train station include Běijīng (¥128, four hours, hourly, 7:30am to 5.30pm).

Buses from the main bus station include Hohhot (¥80, 3½ hours, hourly, 7.20am to 4.20pm).

Getting Around

Bus routes are still being readjusted owing to the massive construction all around town, so expect changes. Buses 4 and 15 run from the train station to the main bus station. Bus 30 takes 30 minutes to run from the train station to the new south bus station. Buses 27 and 35 go to the old town from Weidu Dadao. Bus 603 runs to the Yúngāng Caves.

Taxi flagfall is ¥7. Most drivers will also try to sell you a package deal out to the Yúngāng Caves and the Hanging Monastery, which, with a bit of bartering, can be had for ¥250 to ¥300.

Around Dàtóng

★Yúngāng Caves CAVE

(云冈石窟; Yúngāng Shíkū; 0352-302 6230; Dec-Feb ¥80, Mar-Nov ¥125; 8.30am-5.30pm 1 Apr-15 Oct, to 4.50pm 16 Oct-31 Mar) One of China's most supreme examples of Buddhist cave art, these 5th-century caves are simply magnificent. With 51,000 ancient statues and celestial beings, they put virtually everything else in the Shānxī shade. Carved by the Turkic-speaking Tuoba, the Yúngāng Caves drew their designs from Indian, Persian and even Greek influences that swept along the Silk Road. Work began in AD 460, continuing for 60 years before all 252 caves, the oldest collection of Buddhist carvings in China, had been completed.

To get to the caves take bus 603 (¥3, 45 minutes) from Dàtóng train station to the terminus. Buses run every 10 to 15 minutes. A taxi from Dàtóng is around ¥40 each way. You will pass the rather less appealing Dàtóng Coal Mine en route.

Hanging Monastery BUDDHIST MONASTERY

(悬空寺; Xuánkōng Sì; ¥130; 8am-7pm summer, 8.30am-5.30pm winter) Built precariously into the side of a cliff, the Buddhist Hanging Monastery is made all the more stunning by its long support stilts. The halls have been built along the contours of the cliff face, connected by rickety catwalks and narrow corridors, which can get very crowded in summer. It's a sight to behold, but we hear that the access up into the monastery itself might (understandably) eventually be closed owing to the large number of visitors. Get here soon.

Buses travel here from Dàtóng's main bus station (¥31, two hours). Most will transfer passengers to the monastery into a free taxi for the last 5km from Húnyuán (浑源). Heading back, you'll be stung for ¥20 for a taxi (per person) to Húnyuán.

Déshèngbǎo VILLAGE

(得胜堡) A good place to see some raw sections of the Great Wall is Déshèngbǎo, a 16th-century walled fort almost on the border with Inner Mongolia that is now a small farming village. The fort's north and south gates are still standing, as are parts of its walls. Some of the site has been recently restored. Walk through the village (many of its houses are built out of Great Wall bricks) to the north gate and beyond it you'll see wild wall – 10m-high sections of it.

To get here, take a minibus to Fēngzhèn (丰镇; ¥19, one hour) from opposite Tónghé Dàfàndiàn, next to Dàtóng train station. The bus will drop you at the turn-off for Déshèngbǎo, from where it's a 1km walk to the south gate. Heading back, return to the highway and flag down any Dàtóng-bound bus.

The Trans-Manchurian Route

Includes ➡

Route Info

➡ Distance: 2790km

➡ Duration: Two days, eight hours

➡ Time zones: Moscow +7, Moscow +9

Best Places to Stay

➡ Shangri-La (p285)

➡ Lungmen Grand Hotel (p289)

➡ Kazy International Youth Hostel (p288)

➡ Sōngyuàn Hotel (p293)

Best Places to Eat

➡ Rubles Restaurant (p285)

➡ Orient King of Eastern Dumpling (p290)

➡ Burger Spice (p291)

Why Go?

For connoisseurs of obscure rail routes, the Trans-Manchurian Railway ranks high on wish lists. It's not on the main line to Vladivostok, nor does it take the 'tourist route' via Mongolia; rather, the weekly Vostok (train 19/20) chugs through China's rust belt, where foreign faces are few and far between.

From Chita the railway heads towards the Chinese border at Mǎnzhōulǐ, sweeps through the grasslands of Inner Mongolia and passes through Harbin (Hā'ěrbīn) before carrying on towards the megalopolis that is Běijīng. The highlight is fascinating Harbin, where elements of turn-of-the-century Russia still poke through the surface of a thoroughly modern Chinese city. Bullet trains speed south from Harbin to Běijīng, but there's plenty to see along the way. Jumping-off points include Chángchūn, one-time capital of Japanese-occupied Manchukuo; Shěnyáng, with well-preserved relics of the Manchu era; and Shānhǎiguān, where the Great Wall meets the sea.

When to Go

Harbin

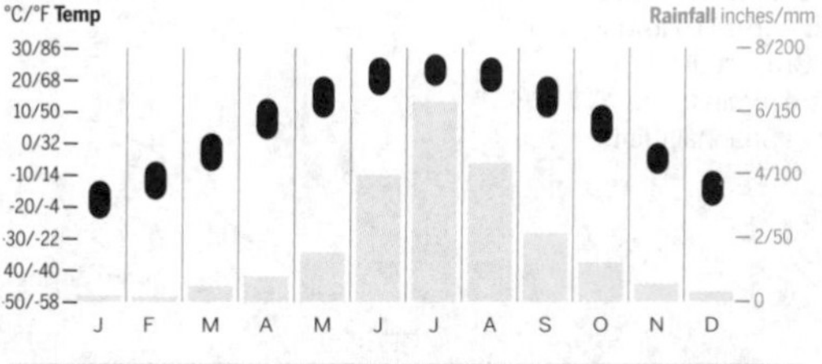

Jan Harbin hosts the dazzling Ice & Snow Festival.

Apr & May Avoid the summer hordes and the hot weather by visiting in the shoulder season.

Sep & Oct A good time to visit, after peak summer season and before the cold sets in.

The Trans-Manchurian Route Highlights

1 Russian Doll Park (p284) Snapping a selfie beside the giant *matryoshki* (nesting dolls) in this quirky park in the prosperous border town of Mǎnzhōulǐ.

2 Harbin Ice & Snow Festival (p287) Braving the cold to see the spectacular ice sculptures carved at Harbin's famous winter festival.

3 Church of St Sophia (p286) Contemplating Harbin's past at the largest Orthodox church in the Far East.

4 Harbin New Synagogue (p290) Delving into Harbin's Semitic past history at this museum recounting the experiences of 20,000 Jews on Chinese soil.

5 Imperial Palace of the Manchu State (p292) Exploring the home of Puyi, the last emperor of China, in Chángchūn.

6 Jiāo Shān Great Wall (p295) Following the Great Wall to where it meets the sea at Shānhǎiguān.

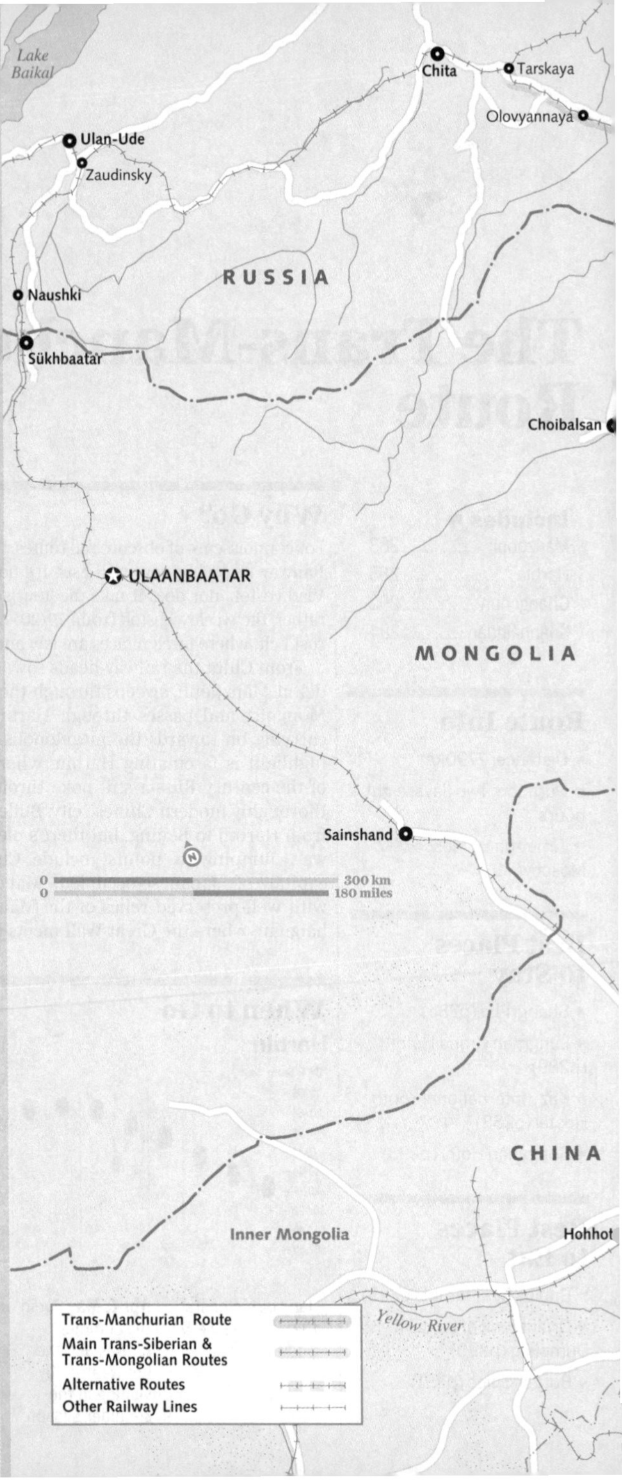

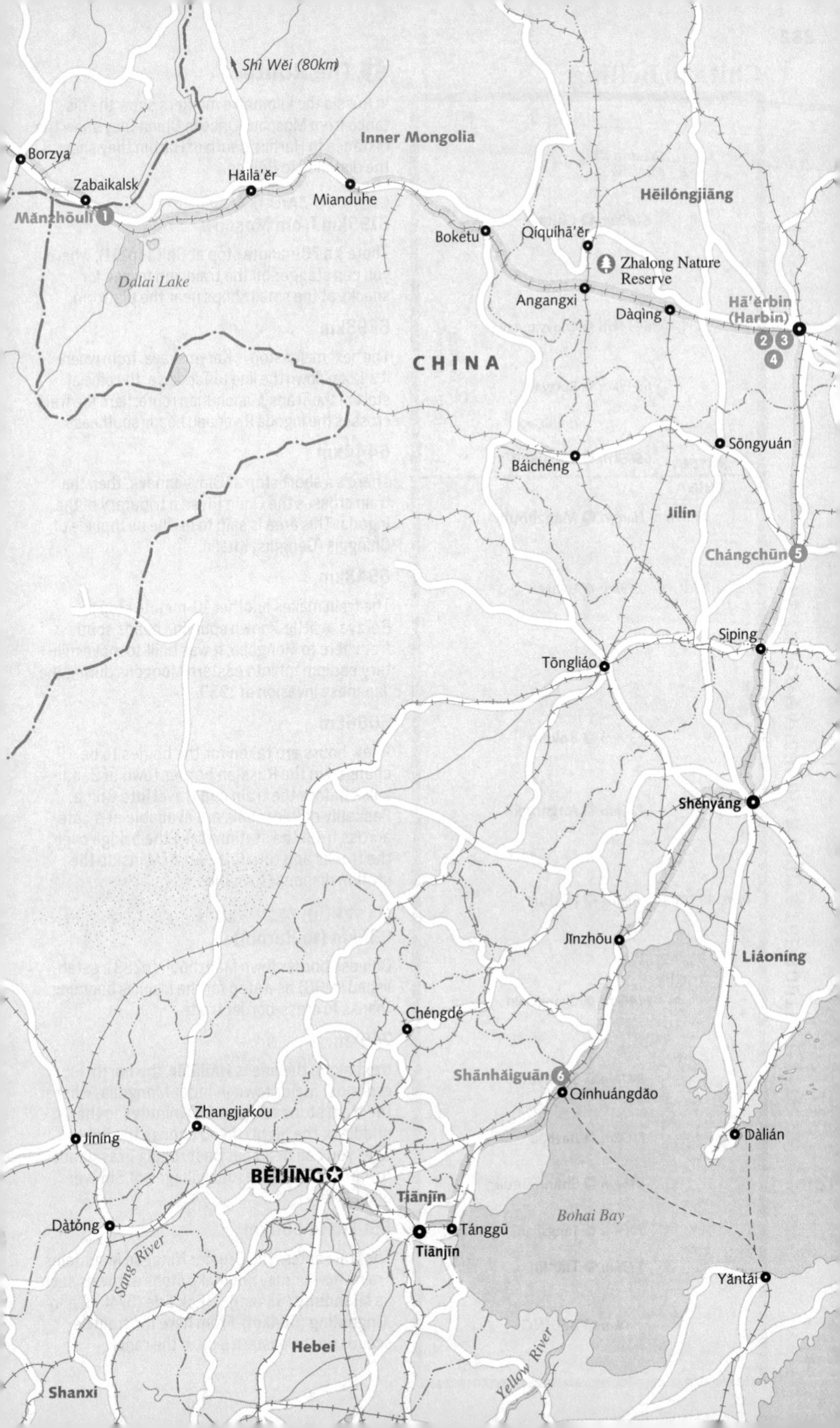

Shì Wěi (80km)
Inner Mongolia
Borzya
Zabaikalsk
Hǎilā'ěr
Mianduhe
Mǎnzhōulǐ 1
Dalai Lake
Boketu
Qíqiuhā'ěr
Hēilóngjiāng
Zhalong Nature Reserve
Angangxi
Dàqìng
Hā'ěrbīn (Harbin) 2 3 4
CHINA
Sōngyuán
Báichéng
Jílín
Chángchūn 5
Sìpíng
Tōngliáo
Shěnyáng
Jǐnzhōu
Liáoníng
Chéngdé
Shānhǎiguān 6
Qínhuángdǎo
Zhangjiakou
Jíníng
Dàlián
BĚIJĪNG
Tiānjīn
Dàtóng
Tánggū
Tiānjīn
Bohai Bay
Sang River
Yāntái
Hebei
Yellow River
Shanxi

Chita to Běijīng

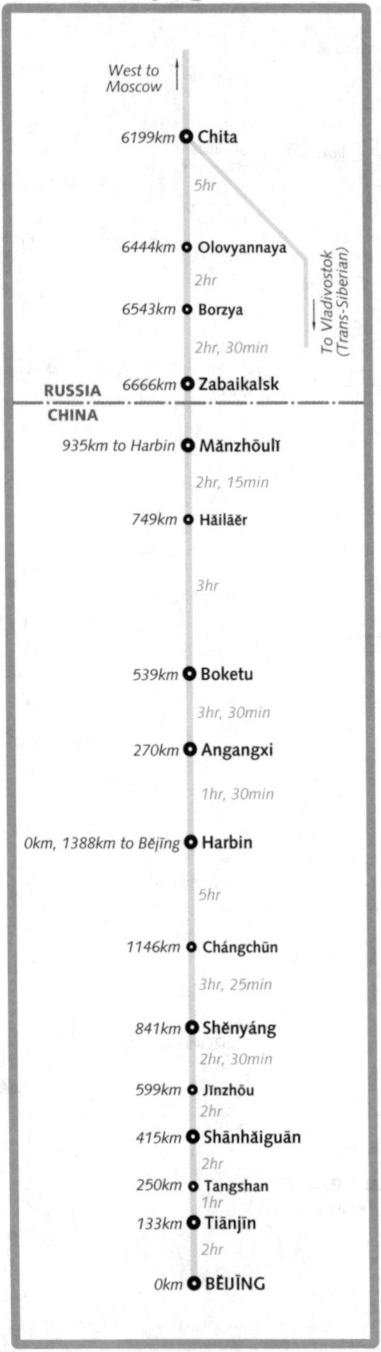

ℹ The Route

In Russia the kilometre markers show the distance from Moscow. Once in China they show the distance to Harbin; south of Harbin they show the distance to Běijīng.

CHITA TO ZABAIKALSK

6199km from Moscow

There's a 20-minute stop at Chita (p211), where you can stagger off the train and forage for snacks at the small shops near the platform.

6293km

The next major stop is Karymskaya, from where it's 12km down the line to Tarskaya, the official start of the Trans-Manchurian route; here the train crosses the Ingoda River and heads southeast.

6444km

There's a short stop at Olovyannaya, then the train crosses the Onon River, a tributary of the Ingoda. This area is said to be the birthplace of Chinggis (Genghis) Khaan.

6543km

The train makes another 10-minute stop at Borzya. A little-known spur line heads south from here to Mongolia; it was built to move military equipment into eastern Mongolia during the Japanese invasion of 1939.

6666km

A few hours are taken for the bogies to be changed in the Russian border town of Zabaikalsk before the train can travel into China. Passably edible meals are available at a cafe across from the station (take the bridge over the tracks and turn left). An ATM inside the station dispenses roubles.

MǍNZHŌULǏ TO HARBIN

935km (to Harbin)

Chinese border town Mǎnzhōulǐ (p283), established in1901 as a stop for the train, is booming thanks to cross-border trade.

749km

Next along the line is **Hǎilā'ěr**, the northern-most major town in Inner Mongolia, where the train stops for about 10 minutes in the middle of the night. If you choose to alight here you can head out past rolling grasslands towards the picturesque villages of Shì Wěi and Ēnhé.

650km to 560km

The train enters the Greater Hinggan Mountains. Trains may or may not make stops at towns such as **Mianduhe** (634km), **Yilick Ede** (574km) and **Xinganling** (564km). From here the train descends on the eastern side of the range.

539km

Shortly after the 8-minute halt at **Boketu**, the train leaves Inner Mongolia and enters the province of Hēilóngjiāng, meaning Black Dragon River. Known in Russian as the Amur River, it marks the border with Russia in northeastern China. At this point you can sense a changing climatic and topographic shift as you leave the steppes behind and enter the steamy Manchurian lowlands.

1388km (to Běijīng)

The final stretch before **Harbin** (p285), the capital of Hēilóngjiāng province, offers excellent views, especially as you cross the 1km-long bridge over the Sōnghuā River.

HARBIN TO BĚIJĪNG

1146km (to Běijīng)

The train stops for around 10 minutes in the industrial city of Chángchūn (p292), capital of Jílín province.

841km

Heading south, the train plies China's blighted rust belt towards **Shěnyáng**, where the Vostok halts for 15 minutes. This industrial city of 3.5 million people was a Mongol trading centre from the 11th century, becoming the capital of the Manchu empire in the 17th century. If you stop here, you can visit Shěnyáng's Imperial Palace, which resembles a small-scale Forbidden City.

841km to 500km

At around the 545km marker the train passes through an area of rice paddies and natural wetlands. Then at 528km there are some picturesque low mountains flanked by cornfields and small villages. The Vostok passes through this area at night, but if you are on a local day train you can watch the scenery pass by and grab some lunch. Cabin attendants push food carts up and down the aisles.

415km

At night, the train passes the Great Wall about 4km north of Shānhǎiguān (p294), where the Wall meets the sea. The small town has been tarted up for Běijīng day trippers and there are a number of sights worth visiting should you decide to alight.

250km

The train stops for 8 minutes at Tángshān, which, in 1976 mere months before Mao Zedong's death, was flattened by a deadly earthquake in which 250,000 people perished. Because of this, it's known as China's Brave City.

133km

The last stop before Běijīng is **Tiānjīn**, a sprawling metropolis of 9.6 million people. During the 19th century this port city attracted the interest of almost every European nation with a ship to put to sea. The evidence is that Tiānjīn is a living museum of early-20th-century European architecture. Note that many local trains will bypass Tiānjīn and travel direct between Běijīng and Shānhǎiguān.

0km

Blink into the glaring light of **Běijīng** (p297) as the masses pour off the train and into the chaotic Chinese capital.

Mǎnzhōulǐ 满洲里

0470 / POP 320,000 / TIME MOSCOW +5HR

This thriving border city, where the Trans-Siberian Railway crosses from China to Russia, is a pastel-painted boomtown of shops, hotels and restaurants catering to the Russian market. Unless you look Asian, expect shopkeepers to greet you in Russian. Mǎnzhōulǐ is modernising at lightning speed, but a few Russian-style log houses still line Yidao Jie.

Mǎnzhōulǐ is small enough to get around on foot. From the train station to the town centre, it's a 10-minute walk. Turn right immediately as you exit the station, then right again to cross the footbridge. You'll come off the bridge near the corner of Yidao Jie and Zhongsu Lu.

TRANS-MANCHURIAN ROUTE PLANNER

The following is a suggested itinerary for covering the main sights along the Trans-Manchurian route in the area:

Day 1 Leave Chita; overnight train to Zabaikalsk (10 hours); cross border, explore Mǎnzhōulǐ.

Day 2 From Mǎnzhōulǐ, take the overnight train to Harbin. (p285)

Day 3 Explore Harbin and overnight.

Day 4 See more of Harbin, then train to Chángchūn.

Day 5 Explore Chángchūn, then train to Shěnyáng.

Day 6 Tour Shěnyáng, then continue to Shānhǎiguān.

Day 7 Enjoy Shānhǎiguān, then travel to Běijīng.(p297)

CROSSING THE RUSSIA–CHINA BORDER

Train

Expect to spend at least half a day crossing from Zabaikalsk (后贝加尔, Hòubèijiāěr) to Mǎnzhōulǐ and vice versa, with time eaten up by customs procedures on the Russian side, and the need to change the bogies on the train to match the narrower gauge used in China. This will likely be the case for travellers on the Vostok (19/20) or the Mǎnzhōulǐ–Chita train (Friday and Sunday from Mǎnzhōulǐ, Thursday and Saturday from Chita). If you arrive in Zabaikalsk on the train from Irkutsk and it's Friday or Sunday morning, it may be possible to buy a ticket (₽80) for the Chita–Mǎnzhōulǐ train. However, this train is usually full by the time it gets to Zabaikalsk, so scoring a ticket at the station may be difficult.

In Mǎnzhōulǐ the international terminal is the yellow building next to the main station. This is where international travellers heading to Russia go through customs and passport control. However, international tickets are not sold here: you'll need to go to the **China International Travel Service** (CITS; 中国国际旅行社; Zhōngguó Guójì Lǚxíngshè; ☎0470 622 8319; www.cits.net; 35 Erdao Jie; 二道街35号; ⌚8-11.30am & 2-4pm Mon-Fri) branch at the Guójì Fàndiàn (International Hotel). Services to Chita leave on Monday at 7pm, Friday at 2pm and Sunday at 2pm; only *platskart* (3rd-class) tickets may be available (¥70).

There are daily overnight trains connecting Zabaikalsk and Chita (2nd class *platskart/kupe* ₽1855/2600, 12 hours); if these are full you can also take a train to Borzya and connect with a slower train to Zabaikalsk from there. Harbin and Mǎnzhōulǐ are also connected by four overnight trains (hard/soft sleeper ¥230/348, 12 to 16 hours), departing between 6pm and 9pm.

The train ride between Zabaikalsk and Mǎnzhōulǐ takes about 10 minutes. There's a sort of rivalry at the border: each country has built an enormous arch over the railway line as if they were trying to outdo each other. You'll need to be quick with your camera as the train does not linger on the border for long.

Bus

There are frequent buses travelling between the Zabaikalsk bus station and the Mǎnzhōulǐ bus station. From Zabaikalsk to China it costs ₽400 and from Mǎnzhōulǐ to Russia it's ¥92 (five hours, eight daily between 7.40am and 1.30pm). There's also one daily bus from Mǎnzhōulǐ to Chita (¥380), departing at 6.40pm.

The crossing in either direction is slow, taking up to five hours. Going from China to Russia usually takes longer because the Russian border guards spend a lot of time checking travellers for contraband. Private vehicles driven by Russians tend to get through faster, so one option is to negotiate a ride with a Russian driver either in town or at the border 9km from town.

At the Chinese border post you'll have to pay ¥10 departure tax: do this at the door to the left of the entrance and then give the receipt to the immigration officials as they stamp you out of the country. There's an exchange office in the Russian customs hall where your immigration card will be registered.

Sights

Hūlún Lake LAKE

(呼伦湖; Hūlún Hú; ¥20) Occupying an enormous 2339 sq km and one of China's largest freshwater lakes, Hūlún Lake, called Dalai Nuur (Ocean Lake) in Mongolian, unexpectedly pops out of the grasslands like a colossal inland sea. You can hire a horse (¥100 per 30 minutes) or a quad bike (¥100 per 20 minutes), take a boat ride (¥10 per 20 minutes) or simply stroll along the rocky lakeshore, taking in its magnificence. The lake is 47km southeast of Mǎnzhōulǐ. The only way to get to the lake is by hiring a taxi. Expect to pay about ¥200 return.

Russian Doll Park PARK

(套娃广场; Tàowá Guǎngchǎng; ☎0470 624 3499; 23 Huabu Dajie; 华埠大街23号; ⌚8am-6pm) FREE This bizarre and astonishing park is filled with giant Russian *matryoshki* (nesting dolls), some bearing portraits of famous historical figures. The largest doll of them all is a Russian-style restaurant. Next to the park is a **museum** of Russian art (admission ¥20; look for the blue building with gold onion-shaped domes).

Bus 10 runs along Huabu Dajie past the international bus terminal and the doll park before terminating at the Russian border area and scenic zone, **Guómén** (国门).

Sleeping

Mǎnzhōulǐ Volga International Youth Hostel HOSTEL $
(满洲里伏尔加河畔国际青年旅舍; Mǎnzhōulǐ Fú'ěrjiā Hépàn Guójì Qīngnián Lǚshě; ☎0470 281 5588; Entrance C, Yiwu Trade City, Wudao Jie; 五道街义务商贸城1期西侧大门C-16号; P ❄ @ 📶; 🚌10) Spotless, pine-clad dorms come with lockers and individual charging points, while the twin rooms – with their quirky, yurt-like styling – are potentially a nicer proposition than staying at one of Mǎnzhōulǐ's many business hotels. An excellent communal area makes up for the out-of-the-way location. Bus 10 goes here from outside the railway station, and continues on to the Russian Doll Park.

Fēngzéyuán Lǚdiàn GUESTHOUSE $
(丰泽源旅店; ☎139 4709 3443, 0470 225 4099; 8 Zhongsu Jie; 中苏街8号, near Yidao Jie; tw ¥200; @ 📶) Located inside a restored Russian log cabin (painted yellow and green), this friendly guesthouse offers large, clean and affordable rooms. Coming off the pedestrian bridge from the train station, it's on your left before you reach Yidao Jie.

Shangri-La HOTEL $$$
(香格里拉大酒店; Xiānggélǐlā Dàjiǔdiàn; ☎0470 396 8888; www.shangri-la.com; 99 Liudao Jie; 六道街99号; d ¥1388, ste ¥4588; ⊖ ❄ @ 📶 🏊) A byword for quality, style and service across Asia, the luxurious Shangri-La is Mǎnzhōulǐ's finest hotel. Lavish rooms offer views over the surrounding grasslands, and there are Chinese and open-kitchen international restaurants, a 20m swimming pool and a spa. Cocktails in the Lobby Lounge nicely round off the day. Prices are often discounted to around ¥850.

Eating

Qīnghuā Jiǎozi Guǎn DUMPLINGS $
(清花饺子馆; ☎133 9480 1166; Yidao Jie; 一道街; dumplings from ¥13; ⏲10am-10pm) This popular eatery just across the pedestrian bridge from the station serves up all manner of dumplings and cold beer, with a picture menu detailing a huge variety of Chinese dishes, including spicy grilled lamb skewers, if you want more choice.

Rubles Restaurant RUSSIAN $$
(卢布里西餐厅; Lúbù Lǐ Xī Cāntīng; ☎0470 281 3488; 178 Xisandao Jie; 西三道街178号; mains from ¥30; ⏲10am-11pm) The hottest Russian restaurant in town, Rubles packs them in for deliciously rustic fare like *syrniki* (西米丹奶酪饼; *xī mǐ dān nǎilào bǐng;* ¥12), traditional Russian pancakes filled with oozing cheese. And don't miss out on the unctuous beef pot pies (瓦罐俄式牛肉; *wǎ guàn é shì niúròu*). Wash it all down with frothy mugs of draught beer.

Information

China International Travel Service (p284) Sells train tickets for Chinese cities and one-day tours to the local sights, but isn't great for tourist information. Located on the 1st floor of Guójì Fàndiàn (国际饭店).

China Post (中国邮政; Zhōngguó Yóuzhèng; cnr Wenming Lu & Sidao Jie; 文明路四道街路口; ⏲9am-5pm)

Industrial & Commercial Bank of China (ICBC; 工商银行; Gōngshāng Yínháng; cnr Yidao Jie & Zhongsu Lu; 一道街中苏路的路口; ⏲8.30am-5.30pm)

Public Security Bureau (PSB; 公安局; Gōng'ānjú; cnr Sandao Jie & Shulin Lu; 三道街树林路的路口)

Getting There & Away

You can reach Mǎnzhōulǐ by train from Hǎilā'ěr (¥26 to ¥29, 2½ hours, eight daily) and Harbin (hard/soft sleeper ¥230/351, 13 to 15 hours, five daily). Two trains per day also roll to Běijīng (hard/soft sleeper ¥444/684, 32 hours, 9.18pm and 11.29pm).

Mǎnzhōulǐ Xījiāo Airport (满洲里西郊机场; Mǎnzhōulǐ Xījiāo Jīchǎng) is on the western edge of town, around 9km away; a taxi there will take about 15 minutes (¥40). There are daily flights to Běijīng (¥1150, 2¼ hours), five flights a week to Harbin (¥1150, 1½ hours), and in summer, daily to Hohhot (¥1150, 2½ hours). **Hunnu Air** (www.hunnuair.com) flies internationally five times a week to Ulaanbaatar (seasonal, 2½ hours).

There are 10 buses a day to Hǎilā'ěr (¥45, three hours, 6.30am to 5.30pm) from the **International Bus Station** (际客运站; Guójì Kèyùn Zhàn; ☎0470 622 0358; Huabu Dajie; 华埠大街).

Harbin 哈尔滨

☎0451 / POP 5.31 MILLION / TIME MOSCOW +5HR

For a city of its size, Harbin (Hā'ěrbīn) is surprisingly easygoing. Cars (and even bicycles) are barred from Zhongyang Dajie, the main drag of the city's historic quarter, where the densest cluster of Harbin's old buildings can be found. The leafy promenade lining the Sōnghuā River also provides sanctuary for walkers, as does Sun Island across the water.

Harbin

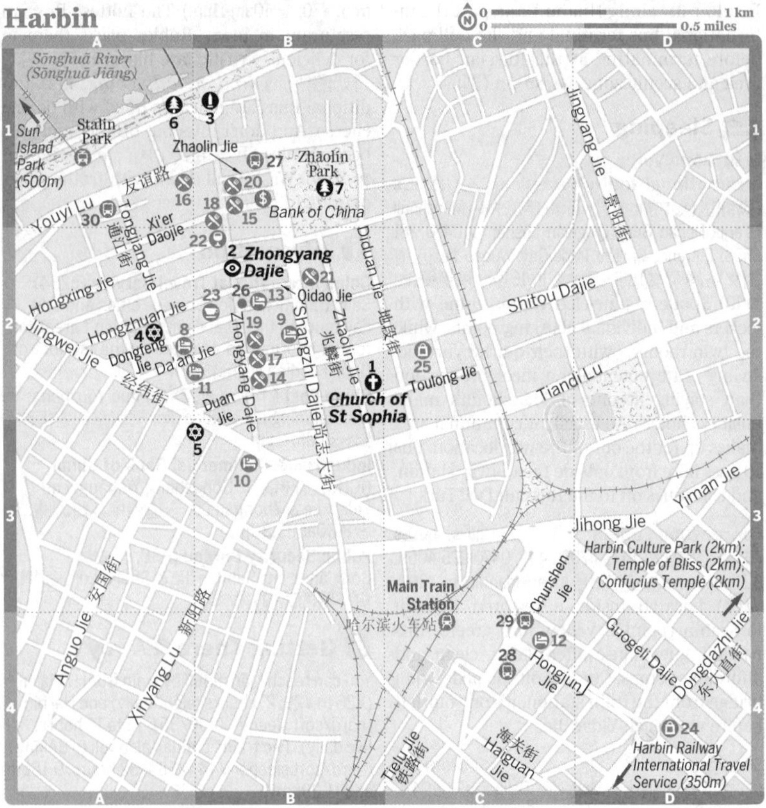

The city's sights are as varied as the architectural styles on the old street. Temples, churches and former synagogues coexist. Harbin's Russian and Jewish heritage is best explored during summer wanderings under blue skies, but winter is when Harbin really heats up, as host of the world-class Harbin Ice & Snow Festival (p287), centred around a neon-clad, subzero theme park created entirely from ice.

History

In 1896, to shorten journey times on the nascent Trans-Siberian Railway, Russia negotiated a contract to put a line through Chinese territory to Vladivostok. The new route passed through Harbin, then a sleepy fishing village on the Sōnghuā River. The subsequent influx of Russian railway workers turned Harbin into a Russian city in all but name. Russian Jews followed, then White Russians escaping the 1917 Russian Revolution.

These days, Harbin, whose name comes from a Manchu word meaning 'a place to dry fishing nets', is an ever-expanding, largely industrial city. While Chinese are the majority, foreign faces (especially Russian) are still common on the streets.

Sights

★Church of St Sophia CHURCH

(圣索菲亚教堂; Shèng Suǒfēiyà Jiàotáng; 88 Toulong Jie, cnr Zhaolin Jie; 透笼街88号; ¥20; ⏲8.30am-5pm) The red-brick Russian Orthodox Church of St Sophia, with its distinctive green onion dome and roosting pigeons, is Harbin's most famous landmark. Built in 1907 and expanded in 1932, it was the largest Orthodox church in the Far East and the centre of spiritual life for 100,000 Russian settlers. After surviving the Cultural Revolution it was used as a warehouse for a department store. Declared a protected landmark in the 1990s, the church was restored and the square cleared.

Harbin

Top Sights
1 Church of St Sophia B2
2 Zhongyang Dajie B2

Sights
3 Flood Control Monument B1
4 Harbin Main Synagogue A2
5 Harbin New Synagogue B3
6 Stalin Park A1
7 Zhāolín Park B1

Sleeping
8 7 Days Inn A2
9 Europa Hotel B2
10 Holiday Inn Harbin B3
11 Kazy International Youth Hostel B2
12 Lungmen Grand Hotel C4
13 Modern Hotel B2

Eating
14 Bomele 1931 Cafe B2
15 Burger Spice B1
16 Lài Biǎndan Chóngqìng Xiǎo Miàn A1
17 Lóngjiāng Xiǎochī Jiē B2
18 Old Chang's Spring Rolls B1
19 Orient King of Eastern Dumplings B2
20 Russia Coffee & Food B1
21 Sùxīn Shídù Vegetarian B2

Drinking & Nightlife
22 Carl Damo Bar B2
23 Luyu Coffee B2

Entertainment
Main Synagogue Concert Hall .... (see 4)

Shopping
24 Hóngbó Century Square D4
25 Tòulóng Shopping City C2

Information
26 Harbin Modern Travel Company B2

Transport
27 Flood Control Monument Bus Stop B1
28 Long-Distance Bus Station C4
29 Railway Station Bus Stop C4
30 Tonjiang Jie Bus Station A1

★ **Zhongyang Dajie** ARCHITECTURE
(中央大街; Central Street; Walking Street) The cobblestone avenue of Zhongyang Dajie is the most obvious legacy of Russia's involvement with Harbin. Now a pedestrian-only zone running from Jingwei Jie up to the Sōnghuā River, the street, and those nearby, are lined with buildings that date back to the early 20th century. Some are imposing, others distinctly dilapidated, but the mix of architectural styles is fascinating.

Stalin Park PARK
(斯大林公园; Sīdàlín Gōngyuán) This tree-lined promenade, dotted with statues, historic buildings, playgrounds and cafes, runs along part of the 42km-long embankment built to curb the unruly Sōnghuā River and is a pleasant spot to escape the hubbub of the city. The **Flood Control Monument** (防洪胜利纪念塔; Fánghóng Shènglì Jìniàntǎ) from 1958 commemorates the thousands of people who died in years past when the river overflowed its banks.

Boat rides along the river and to/from Sun Island also depart from various points along the park.

Sun Island Scenic Area PARK
(太阳岛公园; Tàiyángdǎo Gōngyuán; cable car single/return ¥50/80; cable car 8.30am-5pm) Across the water from Stalin Park is Sun Island, a 38-sq-km recreational zone with landscaped gardens, a 'water world', a 'Russian-style' town, and various small galleries and museums. It's a pleasant place to have a picnic, walk or bike (¥60 per hour), though as usual you need to pay extra to get into many areas (most people find these too kitsch and not worth the money).

Activities

Harbin Indoor Ski Resort SKIING
(哈尔滨万达娱雪乐园; Hā'ěrbīn Wàndá Yú Xuě Lèyuán; 0451 5556 6666; Shimao Dadao; 世茂大道; 2hr ¥288; 9.30am-9.30pm; 47) Billed as the world's largest indoor ski area, this resort was just opening at the time of writing. With an 80m vertical drop and two chairlifts, the ski hill is kept at -2°C year round. The site, called Harbin Wanda City, also has an ice rink, shopping mall and plans for several international hotels. Note that gear hire is extra on top of standard admission costs.

Bus 47 goes there (one hour) from the small bus station on Tongjiang Jie. A taxi should cost about ¥30.

Festivals & Events

★ **Harbin Ice & Snow Festival** ICE SCULPTURE
(冰雪节; Bīngxuě Jié; Harbin International Ice & Snow Sculpture Festival; 0451 8625 0068; day/evening ticket ¥150/300; 11am-9.30pm) Every

OFF THE BEATEN TRACK

EXPLORING THE CHINA–RUSSIA FRINGE

Travellers who choose to get off the main line will be rewarded with some of the more unsung sights along the Trans-Manchurian route. From **Hǎilā'ěr**, the northernmost major town in Inner Mongolia, head out past rolling grasslands towards Shì Wěi and Ēnhé. The former is a small Russian-style village of log cabins located right on the É'ěrgǔnà River, which marks the border with Russia. Spend some time gazing at the Russian village on the opposite bank. Look for wooden stages on both sides of the river: each country used to host performances for their neighbours!

The township of **Ēnhé** (恩河乡), located 70km north of Lābùdálín en route to **Shì Wěi** (室韦镇), is one of the area's unsung villages brimming with atmosphere. Surrounded by hills and hectares of lush grass, the village has recently opened to tourism and there's still a low-key vibe here. Many residents are of Chinese-Russian origin; some could easily pass for Russians. Here, herders milk their cows outside their properties when they aren't taking them out to pasture. Sample boiled milk at your accommodation. You can ride a horse for ¥60 (a bargain in Inner Mongolia!), hire a bicycle (¥10 per hour) or go for hikes. The mosquitoes are a killer in summer, so bring good repellent. You'll find plenty of homestays (rooms from ¥100) and local restaurants in both villages, and a couple of hostels in Ēnhé (summer only).

From Hǎilā'ěr, buses travel to Lābùdálín (拉布达林; ¥38, two hours, half hourly, 6.40am to 5.30pm). From Lābùdálín (sometimes called É'ěrgǔnà) there are two daily direct buses (¥44, four hours) at 9.30am and 3.30pm to Shì Wěi and direct buses (¥27, two hours) at 12.10pm and 2.30pm to Ēnhé. The Shì Wěi bound buses also stop on the main road leading to Ēnhé, from where it's a 1.5km walk into town. You can flag onward buses to Shì Wěi from the main road at around 11.15am and 5.15pm. From Shì Wěi, buses return to Lābùdálín at 8am and 1pm, but do buy your ticket in advance. From Ēnhé, buses return to Lābùdálín at 8.30am and 9.30am.

winter from early December to late February (officially the festival opens 5 January), Harbin dons a fur-lined, technicolour dreamcoat of ice, snow and neon and gets down, Narnia style – no matter that it's mind-numbingly cold and the sun vanishes by mid-afternoon.

The festivities are centred around the spectacular **Harbin Ice and Snow World** (冰雪大世界; Bīngxuě Dàshìjiè; Bingxue Dashijie Yuanqu; 冰雪大世界园区; ¥330, kids under 1.4m ¥200; 9am-9.30pm winter only; 47), a theme park built of ice 7.5km outside of town, complete with gargantuan recreations of world monuments and hair-raising ice slides, and the remarkable **Harbin International Snow Sculpture Art Expo** a few kilometres away on Sun Island Scenic Area.

In the centre of town, **Zhāolín Park** (照林公园; Zhàolín Gōngyuán; 377 Senlin Jie; 森林街377号; Ice Lantern venue ¥200) also has its own ice world, albeit on a smaller scale, featuring slides and fairy-tale castles for kids as well as ice lantern displays after dark (Harbin's ice fetish is said to originate from fishermen freezing pails of water to create candle-powered ice lanterns).

Admission prices to the various venues seem to go up every year as the festival commercialises, but public ice sculptures abound throughout the city all winter long, especially along Zhongyang Dajie up to the frozen Sōnghuā River, which also offers ice slides, skating and more. The Shangri-La Hotel opens an ice restaurant each winter, serving scalding hot pot in subzero surroundings, and there are usually figure skating and winter sports events scheduled around town, too.

Hotels and hostels can organise reasonably priced group transport to/from festival locations. Bus 47 goes to the main venue from Tongjiang Jie and the train station. Taxis are expensive and hard to flag down during the festival, but you can also reach the Harbin International Snow Sculpture Art Expo by horse carriage or on foot by crossing the Sōnghuā River.

Sleeping

★Kazy International Youth Hostel HOSTEL $
(卡兹国际青年旅舍; Kǎzī Guójì Qīngnián Lǚshě; 0451 8469 7113; kazyzcl@126.com; 27 Tongjiang Jie; 通将街27号; dm/s/tw without bathroom ¥40/60/80, d/tw ¥180/120; ; 13) The location couldn't be better, and after a recent spruce-up, the main area now boasts a bar

and adjoining library room, an ideal spot to warm up after icy escapades in winter. Friendly staff are a good source of travel information. The eight-bed dorms and private rooms have had a lick of paint, too. Popular, so book ahead. A taxi from Harbin station is ¥12.

7 Days Inn HOTEL $
(7天连锁酒店; 7 Tiān Liánsuǒ Jiǔdiàn; ☎0451 5882 5888; 55 Tongjiang Jie; 通江街55号; s & d from ¥179; @📶) A budget hotel with a superb location opposite the **Jewish Main Synagogue** (哈尔滨犹太会堂; Hā'ěrbīn Yóutài Huìtáng; 82 Tongjiang Jie; 通江街82号) FREE on leafy Tongjiang Jie and a few minutes from Zhongyang Dajie (p287), this branch of a popular Chinese chain even occupies a historic Harbin building (given the world's gaudiest paint job in the brand's circus-tent colours). Rooms are cheap, clean and identikit, and they sell ice creams in the lobby.

Holiday Inn Harbin HOTEL $$
(哈尔滨万达假日酒店; Hā'ěrbīn Wàndá Jiàrì Jiǔdiàn; ☎0451 8422 6666; www.ihg.com; 90 Jingwei Jie; 经纬街90号; tw & d from ¥550; P@📶) Rooms are spacious and pleasant, staff are cheerful and there's a cracking little noodle restaurant on the ground floor, next to a drowsy 'English' pub. But the best thing about this international midrange hotel is its perch facing the start of Zhongyang Dajie (p287). Check online for the cheapest deals.

Europa Hotel HOTEL $$
(欧罗巴宾馆; Ōuluóbā Bīnguǎn; Russia Europa Hotel; Europaer Hotel; ☎0451 8929 3333; www.russiaeuropahotel.com; 10 Xishidao Jie; 中央大街西十道街10号; tw & d from ¥250; ❄📶) This recently opened hotel seems too good to be true: perfect location between St Sophia church (p286) and Zhongyang Dajie (p287); handsome historic Russian building; great value, comfortable rooms. Unfortunately, broken showers, surly service and road noise means it falls well short of greatness, but it's still a serviceable, central option. The cheapest rooms are tiny.

★Lungmen Grand Hotel HISTORIC HOTEL $$$
(龙门贵宾楼酒店; Lóngmén Guìbīn Lóu Jiǔdiàn; Lóngmén Hotel; ☎0451 8317 7777; 85 Hongjun Jie; 红军街85号; d/tw ¥580/680; ❄@) With its turn-of-the-century old-world styling almost entirely intact (including marble staircase, dark wood-panelled hallways and copper revolving door), the Lungmen is one of the most atmospheric top-end options in town. Beds and rooms can feel a bit worn, however. South of the train station, the hotel lobby opens onto Hongjun Jie and its rows of heritage buildings.

Modern Hotel HISTORIC HOTEL $$$
(马迭尔宾馆; Mǎdié'ěr Bīnguǎn; ☎0451 8488 4000; www.madieer.cn; 89 Zhongyang Dajie; 中央大街89号; r incl breakfast from ¥980; ❄@📶🏊) Not 'modern' anymore, this 1906 construction halfway up Harbin's historic street features original marble, blond-wood accents and art nouveau touches, plus a category of somewhat faded 'European' rooms still with original fixtures. Even if you don't stay here, spend some time checking out the lobby bar's display of hotel memorabilia. Note that the entrance to the hotel is around the back. Discounts available.

✕ Eating

Local eateries specialise in Dōngběi (northeast) food: hearty dishes designed to fortify against the cold. Boiled dumplings (煎饺; *jiānjiǎo*) are ubiquitous and cheap; *guōbāoròu* (锅包肉) is a famous local dish of sticky-sweet battered pork; while 'three treasures' (地三鲜; *dì sān xiān*) is a moreish plate of fried potato, peppers and aubergine in a garlicky sauce. Questionably Russian restaurants selling beet-red borsch and steaks abound in Harbin's touristy districts.

WORTH A TRIP

TEMPLES & FERRIS WHEELS

Two temples and a former church are within walking distance of each other in the Nángàng district, connected by the less sacrosanct (but fun) Harbin Culture Park. The **Temple of Bliss** (极乐寺; Jílè Sì; 9 Dongdazhi Jie; 东大直街9号; ¥10; ⌚8.30am-4pm; 🚌53) sits off a pedestrian-only street reachable by bus 53 (¥1) or taxi (¥12) from the Zhongyang Dajie area 5km away. **Harbin Confucius Temple** (哈尔滨文庙; Hā'ěrbīn Wénmiào; 25 Wenmiao Jie; 文庙街25号; ⌚8.30am-3.30pm, closed Wed; 🚌53) is a 15-minute walk east along Wenmiao Jie, or you can cut through **Harbin Culture Park** (哈尔滨文化公园; Hā'ěrbīn Wénhuà Gōngyuán; 208 Nantong Dajie; 南通大街208号; ¥5, rides from ¥30; ⌚8.30am-5pm; 🚌53), and seek out the **Holy Dormition Church** en route, now a park attraction.

DON'T MISS

JEWISH HARBIN

The Jewish influence on Harbin was surprisingly long lasting; the last original Jewish resident of the city died in 1985. In the 1920s Harbin was home to some 20,000 Jews, the largest Jewish community in the Far East at the time. **Tongjiang Jie** was the centre of Jewish life in the city until the end of WWII and this is where you'll find the following sights.

Main Synagogue Concert Hall (哈尔滨犹太会堂; Yóutài Jiùhuìtáng; 82 Tongjiang Jie; 通江街82号) Harbin's Main Synagogue, dating back to 1909, has reopened as a delightfully intimate, well-priced concert venue for classical music performances, with four shows per week (7.30pm, ¥20 to ¥100, one hour). The ticket office, a star-shaped window around the north side of the synagogue, opens daily at 2pm. Seating is on the old wooden pews; even the cheapest tickets are decent.

Harbin New Synagogue (哈尔滨犹太新会堂; Hā'ěrbīn Yóutài Xīnhuìtáng; ☎0451 8763 0882; 162 Jingwei Jie; 经纬街162号; ¥25; ⏲8.30am-5pm) This synagogue was built in 1921 by the city's Jewish community, the vast majority of whom had emigrated from Russia. Beautifully restored and converted into a museum in 2004, the 2nd and 3rd floors present a fascinating exhibition (with detailed English captions) on the history and rich cultural life of Harbin's Jews.

Year-round, the streets off Zhongyang Dajie are abuzz with open-air food stalls (and beer gardens in summer), where you can slug a Hāpí (the famous Harbin beer), while munching on squid on a stick, *yángròu chuàn* (lamb skewers), roasted sweet potatoes and more.

Shops and stalls along Zhongyang Dajie hawk scarlet-skinned Russian sausages (ready to eat), Russian chocolate, bread and creamy ice-lollies branded to Harbin's Modern Hotel. In winter, everyone gnaws *bīngtánghúlu* (冰糖葫芦): frozen, candied fruit skewers.

Tongjiang Jie, towards the river end, is lined with small restaurants and hot pot joints that are less touristy (and consequently cheaper) than those on Zhongyang Dajie.

★Orient King of Eastern Dumplings DUMPLINGS $
(东方饺子王; Dōngfāng Jiǎozi Wáng; 81 Zhongyang Dajie; 中央大街81号; dumpling plates ¥13-38; ⏲10.30am-9.30pm; 📶📝) It's not just the freshly made *jiǎozi* (饺子; stuffed dumplings) that are good at this always busy and ever-expanding Harbin chain: there are also plenty of tasty vegie dishes and draught beer on tap. There's another location a few doors along at number 51. Picture menu available.

Lóngjiāng Xiǎochī Jiē FOOD HALL $
(龙江小吃街; Longjiang Snack St; Zhongyang Dajie; 中央大街; dishes ¥8-18; ⏲9am-6pm; ❄) This underground mall-style food court is part of a large shopping mall and is well-stocked with a variety of Chinese, Asian and Western food outlets. In winter, it makes a good refuge from the cold.

Bomele 1931 Cafe BAKERY $
(芭米莉咖啡; Bā Mǐ Lì Kāfēi; ☎0451 8768 0788; 45 Zhongyang Dajie; 中央大街45号; coffee from ¥20; ⏲8am-10pm; 📶) During Harbin's belle époque, Jewish bakeries were a fixture along Zhongyang Dajie. This one is resolutely Chinese, but they do a tasty bagel sandwich, decent (and cheap) coffee, plus a cornucopia of cakes and bread, made in-house. Best of all is the 2nd-floor terrace with delightful views over the cobbles (summer only, of course). Order upstairs for hot food.

Sùxīn Shídù Vegetarian VEGETARIAN $
(素心食度素食餐厅; Sùxīn Shídù Sùshí Cāntīng; ☎0451 8469 8934; 8 Qidao Jie; 七道街8号; buffet ¥18; ⏲11.30am-1.30pm & 5-6.30pm) For just ¥18 you can gorge on a healthy, meat-free buffet of filling dishes at this unadorned restaurant popular with elderly locals. For health reasons, no garlic or onion is used. Expect fare like yams, cauliflower, tofu, spinach and mung beans. You can also self-serve a variety of congee and mugs of sweetened soy milk.

Lài Biǎndan Chóngqìng Xiǎo Miàn SICHUAN $
(赖扁担重庆小面; ☎0451 8765 8375; 134-1 Youyi Lu; 友谊路134-1号; noodles ¥9-18; ⏲9am-10pm) A cute hole-in-the-wall eatery serving fiery Chóngqìng noodles to a steady stream of customers. Pull up a rustic wooden chair and slurp down sweat-inducing *xiǎo miàn* (小面; spicy soup noodles) plain or with *niú ròu* (牛肉; beef). If you can't take the heat, take the hit to your spice cred instead and order *qīng tāng* (清汤; clear soup noodles).

Old Chang's Spring Rolls CHINESE $
(老昌春饼; Lǎo Chāng Chūnbǐng; ☎0451 8468 5000; 180 Zhongyang Dajie; 中央大街180号; dishes ¥12-38; ⏰10.30am-9pm) *Chūnbǐng*, a northern Chinese speciality, are essentially DIY spring rolls. At this well-known basement shop, order a set of wheat roll skins (per roll ¥2), a few dishes of stir-fried meat, eggs and vegies, and then wrap your way to one enjoyable repast.

★ **Burger Spice** AMERICAN $$
(伯格斯餐厅; Bó Gé Sī Cāntīng; ☎0451 8768 1688; 2nd fl, Jīngǔ Hotel, 185 Zhongyang Dajie; 中央大街金谷大厦二楼; burgers from ¥45; ⏰11am-9.30pm; ❄📶) The dining room may be a little gloomy but the super-sized selection of burgers, salads and messy fries (including one stacked sandwich simply called OMG) is anything but. Perfect if you're craving a non-Chinese fix that doesn't involve borsch, caviar or potato salad. Spoil yourself; it's cheap, too.

Russia Coffee & Food RUSSIAN $$
(露西亚咖啡西餐厅; Lùxīyǎ Kāfēi Xī Cāntīng; 57 Xitoujiao; 西头到街57号; dishes ¥20-78; ⏰10am-midnight) Step back in time at this antique cafe-restaurant decorated with period furniture and possessions that once belonged to Nina, a Harbin resident from 1911 to her death in 2001. The owner purchased her estate (including portraits and photographs) and put it on display. It's a lovely spot for a tea (or vodka!), but the Russian offerings such as borsch and *pirozhki* (savoury pies) are so-so.

Drinking & Nightlife

Snack tents in and around Zhongyang Dajie (in summer) are fun spots to knock back jugs of draught Harbin, the local beer dating back to 1900. Modern Hotel has a big, touristy brewpub attached. For clubs and late-night drinking, catch a cab (¥15) to Qiaonan Jie (桥南街), a bar strip near the Harbin Institute of Technology (HIT).

★ **Carl Damo Bar** BAR
(卡尔大漠酒吧; Kǎ'ěr Dàmò Jiǔbā; ☎0451 8464 1258; 160 Zhongyang Dajie; 中央大街160号; cocktails from ¥35; ⏰2pm-2am) This alcohol-fuelled Aladdin's cave, crammed with curios, fairy-lights and arty nude photographs taken by eccentric Chinese owner 'Carl', is probably north China's, or at least Harbin's, quirkiest bar. With hidden nooks to take refuge in, bluesy music, strong drinks and a huge Alaskan hound prowling around, you'll soon realise you're not in Kansas anymore.

Luyu Coffee CAFE
(鹿鱼咖啡馆; Lù Yú Kāfēi Guǎn; ☎136 1364 4362; 43 Hongzhuan Jie; 红专街43号; cappuccino ¥28; ⏰10.30am-9.30pm) Cute spot set in the ground floor of a former Jewish hospital that brews excellent coffee and also has a bar menu.

Shopping

Shops along Zhongyang Dajie (and all over the city) flog Russian knick-knacks like *matryoshki* alongside vodka, cigarettes and children's toys. Big-brand Western clothing chains now occupy several of the heritage buildings.

Locals prefer to head to Dongdazhi Jie for their shopping needs, as well as the subterranean **Hóngbó Century Square** (红博世纪广场; Hóngbó Shìjì Guǎngchǎng; Dongdazhi Jie; 东大直街; ⏰6.30am-5pm), and **Tòulóng Shopping City** (透笼国际商品城; Tòulóng Guójì Shāngpǐn Chéng; 58 Shitou Dajie; 石头道街58号; ⏰9am-6pm) for 11 floors of bargains.

Information

ATMs are all over town. Most large hotels will also change money.

Bank of China (中国银行; Zhōngguó Yínháng; Xi'er Daojie; 西二道街; ⏰8.30am-5.30pm) Has a 24-hour ATM and will cash travellers cheques. Easy to spot on a side road as you walk up Zhongyang Dajie.

Many midrange and top-end hotels have travel services that book tickets and arrange tours throughout the province.

Harbin Modern Travel Company (哈尔滨马迭尔旅行社; Hā'ěrbīn Mǎdié'ěr Lǚxíngshè; 2nd fl, Modern Hotel, 89 Zhongyang Dajie; 中央大街89号) Offers one- and two-day ski trips to Yàbùlì and can handle flight tickets to Mòhé and other regions.

Getting There & Away

TRAIN

Harbin is a major rail transport hub with routes throughout the northeast and beyond. At the time of writing, Harbin's main **train station** (哈尔滨站; Hā'ěrbīn Zhàn; 1 Tielu Jie; 铁路街1号) was being rebuilt (due to be completed in 2019), and so in the meantime, fewer services are stopping here, with **Harbin West Station** (西站; Xīzhàn), 10km from town, picking up the slack. A taxi will cost ¥30 to ¥40.

By the time the station reopens, a new high-speed line between Běijīng and Shěnyáng should shorten journey times significantly between Harbin and the capital.

Běijīng Hard seat/sleeper ¥159/293, 10 to 16 hours, eight daily.

Běijīng (D/G train) Seat ¥307/542, seven to eight hours, six daily.

Chángchūn (D/G train) Seat ¥74/119, one to 1½ hours, regular.

Shěnyáng Seat ¥166/247, 2½ hours, regular.

AIR

Harbin Tàipíng International Airport (HRB; 哈尔滨太平国际机场; Hā'ěrbīn Tàipíng Guójì Jīchǎng) has flights to Russia, Japan, South Korea, Taiwan, Singapore, Malaysia and the US, as well as lots of domestic routes, including Běijīng (¥800, two hours).

BUS

The main **long-distance bus station** (长途客运站; Chángtú Kèyùn Zhàn) is a block southwest of the train station. Note that due to ongoing renovations of the train station, the immediate area is confusing to navigate.

Chángchūn ¥76, four hours, six daily (10am, noon, 1pm, 1.30pm, 3pm and 4pm).

Getting Around

TO/FROM THE AIRPORT

Harbin's **airport** is 46km from the city centre. From the airport, **shuttle bus route 1** (¥20) terminates at the Civil Aviation Building (99 Zhongshan Lu; around 6km southeast of the main train station), stopping near the railway station on route (¥20). To the airport, shuttles leave every 30 minutes from the Civil Aviation Building from 5.30am to 6.30pm. A taxi (¥100 to ¥125) takes 45 minutes to an hour. Drivers may ask you to change to another taxi for the final kilometre to save paying the airport expressway return toll.

PUBLIC TRANSPORT

Buses 47 and 13 run from a bus stop outside the train station to Tongjiang Jie, one block west of Zhongyang Dajie, Harbin's famous historic street; 47 continues on to the Harbin Ice and Snow World and the Indoor Ski Resort. Large-scale station renovations mean bus stops are being shifted around periodically.

Harbin's metro is currently of little use to tourists, but Line 2 (under construction at the time of writing) will connect the railway station with Zhongyang Dajie in Harbin's historic centre, continuing northwards to Zhāolín Park and on to Sun Island and Harbin North Station.

Taxi flag-fall is ¥8.

BORDER CROSSING: GETTING TO RUSSIA

Trains no longer depart from Harbin East Train Station to Vladivostok. Trains do run as far as Suífēnhé, however, from where you can make an onward connection to Vladivostok. There are now direct flights from Harbin to Vladivostok.

Travellers on the Trans-Siberian Railway to or from Moscow can start or finish in Harbin (six days). Contact the **Harbin Railway International Travel Service** (哈尔滨铁道国际旅行社; Hā'ěrbīn Tiědào Guójì Lǚxíngshè; ☎0451 5361 6718; www.ancn.net; 41 Xidazhijie; 西大直街41号; ⌚9am-5pm) for information on travelling through to Russia.

Chángchūn 长春

☎0431 / POP 7.79 MILLION / TIME MOSCOW +5HR

The Japanese capital of Manchukuo between 1933 and 1945, Chángchūn (长春) was also the centre of the Chinese film industry in the 1950s and '60s. Visitors expecting a Hollywood-like backdrop of palm trees and beautiful people will be disappointed, though. Chángchūn is now better known as China's motor city, the largest automobile-manufacturing base in the country.

But for people on the trail of Puyi, China's last emperor, it's an essential stop. Its cross-road position, linking three provinces on the high-speed railway, makes Chángchūn a useful stopoff.

Sights

There is a scatter of historic buildings dating back to the early 20th century, with several along Renmin Dajie, and another cluster on Xinmin Dajie heading south from **Culture Square** (文化广场; Wénhuà Guǎngchǎng), including the **Former Site of Manchukuo State Department**, which accepts visitors but was closed for renovation at time of writing. The red-brick **Former Military Department** across the street is now a hospital.

★ **Imperial Palace of the Manchu State** MUSEUM

(Puppet Emperor's Palace; 伪满皇宫博物院; Wěimǎn Huánggōng Bówùyuàn; 5 Guangfu Beilu; 光复北路5号; ¥80; ⌚8.30am-4.50pm, last entry 40min before closing; Ⓢ Line 4 to Weihuanggong) This is the former residence of Puyi, the Qing dynasty's final emperor, famously depicted in Bernardo Bertolucci's film *The Last Emperor* (1987). His study, bedrooms, temple, his wife's quarters and opium den, as well as his concubine's rooms, are all on show, but it's the exhibition on his extraordinary life, told in part with a fantastic collection of photos, that is most enthralling.

An English audio guide is well worth the extra ¥40.

In 1908, at age two, Puyi became the 10th Qing emperor. His official reign lasted just over three years until the old Imperial order was overthrown in 1911, but he was allowed to remain in the Forbidden City until 1924. He subsequently lived in Tiānjīn until 1932, when the Japanese installed him at this palace as the 'puppet emperor' of Manchukuo. After Japan's defeat in 1945, Puyi was captured by Russian troops. In 1950 he was returned to China, where he spent 10 years in a re-education camp before ending his days as a gardener in Běijīng. Puyi died in 1967.

While you're here, look out for the swimming pool (Puyi never used it as an emperor wasn't permitted to show his body in public), Puyi's horse track (now a riding school), and the chilly underground air-raid shelter where he retreated with his family when the bombs fell. Across the city at **Culture Sq**, a more permanent palace was being constructed for Puyi, but he never got to use it, and the buildings were later repurposed into the **Chángchūn Institute of Geology**.

Chángchūn World Sculpture Park SCULPTURE

(长春世界雕塑公园; Chángchūn Sijiè Diāodù Gōngyuán; Renmin Dajie; 人民大街; ¥30, shuttle vehicles per person ¥10; ⏲8am-5pm, to 4pm winter; 🚌66, Ⓢ Line 1 to Weixingguangchang) Nestled amid 90 hectares of neat parklands with an artificial lake in the far south of the city, the Chángchūn World Sculpture Park hosts an impressive array of sculptures from Chinese and international artists. The huge park is one of Chángchūn's unsung sights and worth sniffing out. A taxi from People's Sq will cost about ¥30.

Bānruò Temple BUDDHIST SITE

(般若寺; Bānruò Sì; 137 Changchun Lu; 长春路137号; ⏲9am-4pm; 🚌281, 256, Ⓢ Line 1 to Renmin Guangchang (People's Sq)) FREE One of the largest Buddhist temples in northeast China, Bānruò, built in 1931, is a lively place of worship for locals and pilgrims alike. After touring the inner grounds, wander the back alleys to observe the merchants peddling all manner of charms, statues, shrines and incense to the faithful.

Sleeping

Regent Hotel HOTEL $

(丽晶饭店; Lìjīng Fàndiàn; ☎0431 8117 0888; www.ljfdvip.com; 6 Renmin Dajie; 人民大街6号; r from ¥250; P ❄ @ 📶) This oval block, built in 2015, is a just a few hundred metres south of the station and a step-up in quality from the budget chains, while only costing marginally more. They certainly overdid it on the marble in the lobby, but the rooms are pleasant enough, and come with extras like complimentary fruit. The breakfast buffet, mostly Chinese, is bountiful.

Chūnyì Hotel HOTEL $$

(春谊宾馆; Chūnyì Bīnguǎn; ☎0431 8209 6888; 80 Renmin Daijie; 人民路80号; d & tw from ¥350; P ❄ @ 📶) Housed in an attractive low-rise building dating back to 1909, this charming hotel, directly opposite the railway station square, is a diamond in the rough. A marble staircase leads to wood-panelled corridors winding their way to rooms with high ceilings and period-style furnishings, while those in the newer annex have huge bathrooms. Prices dip to as low as ¥200 online.

★ **Sōngyuàn Hotel** HOTEL $$$

(松苑宾馆; Sōngyuàn Bīnguǎn; ☎0431 8272 7001; 1169 Xinfa Lu; 新发路1169号; d & tw ¥498-998; ❄ @ 📶) Nestled within its own park grounds, the Sōngyuàn was a former army commander's residence. Today, its heritage buildings host tourists in plush, well-decorated rooms. Friendly staff and several good in-house restaurants (Japanese and international) seal the deal. The downside is a slightly inconvenient location. A taxi from the train station costs ¥7.

Eating & Drinking

The area surrounding Tongzhi Jie between Longli Lu and Ziyou Lu is very popular and packed with inexpensive restaurants, music and clothing shops. Tree-lined Xikang Lu (west of Tongzhi Jie) is now an unofficial cafe street. Most of the dozen or so cafes have wi-fi and offer simple snacks. Guilin Lu (east from Tongzhi Jie) is lined with cheap eateries and street-food stalls.

Dong Teng DONGBEI $

(社会主义新农村; Shèhuì Zhǔyì Xīn Nóngcūn; ☎0431 8566 6600; 50-7 Yueyang Jie; 岳阳街50-7号; mains from ¥28; ⏲noon-9.30pm; Ⓢ Line 1 to Dongzhiwuyuan) Waitresses dressed as red guards dish up delicious Dōngběi (northeast) dishes amid trailing eaves of corn and bulbs of garlic at this Communist-themed restaurant. There's even a spicy fish dish named 'Cultural Revolution' (文化大革命; *Wénhuà Dàgémìng*) among the more proletariat pork knuckle stews and stir-fries.

Sānyú Zhúyuàn SICHUAN $$
(三俞竹苑; 0431 8802 8127; 2222 Tongzhi Jie; 同志街2222号; mains ¥32-88; 10am-10pm;) At this upscale chain, the decoration starts with the lovely faux-antique interior and continues with fistfuls of chilli adorning every platter – meat, seafood, even frog. In true Sìchuān style, mildly spicy can translate to very spicy. The picture English menu also contains lots of vegie and nonspicy options.

★**LR Lounge Bar** COCKTAIL BAR
(左右酒吧; Zuǒyòu Jiǔbā; 0431 8868 7688; Longli Hutong, 30m west of Baihui Jie; 隆礼路胡同与百汇街交汇西行30米; cocktails from ¥45; 6pm-2am;) If you can find Chángchūn's best speakeasy, you'll be rewarded with impeccable cocktails mixed by bow-tied bartenders, friendly locals propping up the intimate wooden bar, and some of the funkiest decor in the city. Look for a large industrial door 30m west of the intersection.

Information

There are 24-hour ATMs all over town.

China Post (中国邮政; Zhōngguó Yóuzhèng; 8 Renmin Dajie; 人民大街8号; 8.30am-6pm)

Police (长春市公安局; Chángchūn Shì Gōng'ān Jú; 2627 Renmin Dajie; 人民大街2627号)

Getting There & Away

TRAIN

Avoid getting tickets for Chángchūn's west station *(xī zhàn)*, 13km out of town. Instead use Chángchūn's **main railway station** (长春火车站; Chángchūn Huǒchē Zhàn), which serves the following destinations.

Běijīng (D/G trains) Seat ¥268, seven hours, eight daily.

Běijīng Hard seat/sleeper ¥129/252, eight to 16½ hours, nine daily.

Harbin (D/G trains) Seat ¥74 to ¥110, one to 1½ hours, hourly.

Shěnyáng (D/G trains) Seat ¥92 to ¥145, 1½ to two hours, 33 daily.

AIR

Chángchūn Lóngjiā International Airport (长春龙嘉国际机场; Chǎngchūn Lóngjiā Guójì Jīchǎng) has daily flights to major cities, including Běijīng (¥900, two hours) and Shànghǎi (¥1000, 2½ hours) and also Chángbái Shān (¥1000, one hour).

BUS

The **long-distance bus station** (长途汽车站; Chángtú Qìchēzhàn; 226 Renmin Dajie; 人民大街226号) is two blocks south of the train station behind the Regent Hotel. Buses to Harbin leave from the **North Bus Station** (客运北站; Kèyùn Běi Zhàn; 2088 Tiebei Er Lu; 铁北二路2088号) to the north of the train station, partially under construction at the time of writing. Facing the station, head left and take the underpass just past the 24-hour KFC (not to be confused with the non-24-hour KFC to the right of the train station, or the two across the street). Bus services include the following:

Harbin ¥76, 3½ hours, 8.30am, 10am and noon.

Shěnyáng ¥83, 4½ hours, 10am and 2pm.

Getting Around

TO/FROM THE AIRPORT

The airport is 35km east of the city centre. Shuttle buses to the airport (¥20, 50 minutes, every 30 minutes from 6am to 7pm) leave from the **Civil Aviation Administration of China** (CAAC; 中国民航; Zhōngguó Mínháng; 0431 8298 8888; 480 Jiefang Dalu; 解放大路480号) on the east side of town. Taxi fares to the airport are ¥80 to ¥100 for the 40-minute trip.

PUBLIC TRANSPORT

Buses heading south leave from the train station bus stop outside the south exit. Bus 6 follows Renmin Dajie all the way to the south part of town. Buses 62 and 362 run to the Chongqing Lu and Tongzhi Jie shopping districts.

The Chángchūn Metro connects **Chángchūn Railway Station** (p294) with the **Imperial Palace** (p292). Take Line 4, which starts just north of the train station two stops to Weihuanggang (2¥). Line 1 goes south from the train station along Renmin Dajie. Dongzhiwuyuan is a useful stop to get close to the bars and eateries around Tongzhi Jie. Get off at Renminguangchang for **Bānruò Temple** (p293).

Taxi fares start at ¥5.

Shānhǎiguān 山海关

0335 / POP 14,000 / TIME MOSCOW +5HR

The drowsy walled town of Shānhǎiguān (山海关) is the fabled point where the Great Wall snakes out of the hills to meet the sea.

The area holds real interest for Wall enthusiasts: in addition to its claim as the eastern end of the Ming Wall (in fact, the Hǔshān Great Wall, beside the North Korean border, is 380km further east), there's an excellent museum and plenty of opportunity to explore stretches of wild, unrestored Wall, climbing up and over the rugged, scrubland hills.

Bear in mind, however, that the town itself feels a bit soulless. With few residents remaining and no economy in the old town apart from tourism, what's left is something that feels mostly like a theme park, but without the rides.

History

Guarding the narrow plain leading to northeastern China, the Ming garrison town of Shānhǎiguān and its wall were developed to seal off the country from the Manchu, whose troublesome ancestors ruled northern China during the Jin dynasty (1115–1234). This strategy succeeded until 1644, when Chinese rebels seized Běijīng and General Wu Sangui opted to invite the Manchu army through the impregnable pass to help suppress the uprising. The plan worked so well that the Manchus proceeded to take over the entire country and establish the Qing dynasty.

Sights

★Jiǎo Shān Great Wall WALLS

(角山; ¥40, with chairlift ¥50; ⏲7am-sunset) Although a heavily restored section of the Great Wall, Jiǎo Shān nevertheless offers an excellent opportunity to hike up the Wall's first high peak – a telling vantage point over the narrow tongue of land below and one-time invasion route for northern armies. It's a steep 30-minute clamber from the base, or else the old chairlift (索道; *suǒdào*) can haul you up.

To leave behind the crowds, continue beyond the cable-car station to **Qīxián Monastery** (栖贤寺; Qīxián Sì) or even further to **Sweet Nectar Pavilion** (甘露亭; Gānlù Tíng). Better yet, climb up onto the closed section (accessed from paths on the side) and you'll be able to follow the crumbling Wall all the way up past several peaks. Explorers won't be able to resist – but use caution and don't go it alone.

To get here take tourist bus 5 from Shānhǎiguān station (high season) or hail a taxi (¥20 flat rate), but it's an easy 3km walk (or cycle) north of town. Just follow the road straight on from Shānhǎiguān's North Gate.

More fun than just following the road, though, is to approach Jiǎo Shān on an original, overgrown stretch of **Great Wall**, which still creeps its way through farmland from Shānhǎiguān to Jiǎo Shān. Most of its Ming brickwork has long since been pillaged, but there's still a scattering of bricks, including a couple of collapsed watchtowers. To take this route, walk straight on from North Gate and then take the first right on the main road to the Wall (you can't miss it). Turn left up the pathway beside the iron bridge and clamber up. You can walk on this earthen Wall all the way to Jiǎo Shān (it takes about an hour; you'll need to climb over onto a restored section across the highway); at the end, walk down to the ticket office to enter Jiǎo Shān.

First Pass Under Heaven HISTORIC SITE

(天下第一关; Tiānxià Diyī Guān; Dong Dajie; 东大街; ¥40; ⏲7am-5.30pm) The Great Wall's main gate as it snaked down the mountains and to the sea, the First Pass served as Shānhǎiguān's east gate and principal watchtower. Two storeys tall, with double eaves and 68 arrow-slit windows, it's a towering 13.7m high, with an enceinte extending east.

Old Dragon Head HISTORIC SITE

(老龙头; Lǎolóngtóu; 1 Longhai Dadao; 龙海大道1号; ¥50; ⏲7.30am-6.30pm) Famous across China (although a little overhyped if we're being honest), Old Dragon Head, 4km south of Shānhǎiguān, is where the Great Wall meets the sea. It's photogenic for sure, but bear in mind that what you see now was reconstructed in the late 1980s – the original wall crumbled away long ago. Bus 25 (¥2) goes here from Shānhǎiguān's South Gate, and its terminus in the other direction is Shānhǎiguān Railway Station.

Great Wall Museum MUSEUM

(长城博物馆; Chángchéng Bówùguǎn; Diyiguan Lu; 第一关路; ⏲9am-4pm Tue-Sun) FREE This impressive museum provides a thorough chronological history of the Wall, going into architectural features and including interesting scale models of the walled town and surrounding Great Wall locations. Plenty of photos and artefacts, as well as English captions.

Sleeping & Eating

Shānhǎiguān sleeping options are extremely limited. There are few hotels to begin with, and only a handful of those accept foreigners. For international options, stay in Qínhuángdǎo (秦皇岛), 18km away.

With few residents still living within Shānhǎiguān's walls, the town's eating options are fairly meagre and mostly revolve around noodles in myriad forms. Restaurants tend to close early unless there are lots of tourists. One snack you'll see everywhere is brittle, made from sesame, beans and peanuts (花生糕; *huāshēng gāo*). For a savoury bite, try *poluó yèbǐng* (桲椤叶饼), dumplings steamed in leaves and filled with prawn, egg and Chinese chives.

Shěnyáng Railway Bureau Shānhǎiguān Resort RESORT $$
(沈阳铁路局山海关疗养院; Shěnyáng Tiělù Jú Shānhǎiguān Liáoyǎngyuàn; Wànghǎi Vacational Village; 1 Wanghai Lu; 龙海大道望海路1号; r from ¥278; P ❄ @ ; 25) An alternative to sleeping within the old town walls, this place, set in private wooded grounds, is right beside Old Dragon Head (p295) (the Great Wall actually trundles around the edge of the hotel), and 100m from the beach. Rooms are nothing special, but the restaurant, in a plant-filled greenhouse, is good. Several period villas here charge upward of ¥4000 per night.

You can take bus 25 from the station or the south gate of Shānhǎiguān to the hotel; just get off at the Lǎolóngtóu stop.

Jìngshān Hotel HOTEL $$$
(景山宾馆; Jìngshān Bīnguǎn; 0335 513 2188/46; 1 Dong Dajie; 东大街1号; tw/tr from ¥580/680;) Housed in a pleasant, reconstructed, two-storey courtyard complex, the Jìngshān – the town's most agreeable hotel – is just steps from the First Pass Under Heaven (p295). Rooms here are airy and comfortable, though it was closed for a spruce-up when we last visited – hopefully they were fixing the dodgy hot-water pressure. Discounts can drop rates as low as ¥150. No English.

Shānhǎi Holiday Hotel HOTEL $$$
(山海假日酒店; Shānhǎi Jiàrì Jiǔdiàn; 0335 535 2888; www.shanhai-holiday.com; Bei Madao; 北马道; d & tw ¥880;) This traditional-style four-star hotel is housed in a large complex with several buildings, and is trying hard to impress, with staff dressed in traditional Manchu clothing. Unfortunately, the slightly musty rooms, though basically OK, are a let-down considering the exterior. Discounted rates hover around ¥270.

Èrtiáo Xiǎoxiàng Jiǎoziguǎn DUMPLINGS $
(二条小巷饺子馆; Ertiao Xiaoxiang, off Nan Dajie; 南大街二条小巷; dumplings ¥20; hours vary) Housed in a 200-year-old building, this one-woman show offers delicious, golden-fried dumplings (煎饺; *jiānjiǎo*) with a range of fillings, including pork and cabbage (白菜猪肉; *báicài zhūròu*) and egg and chives (韭菜鸡蛋; *jiǔcài jīdàn*). Walking south from the Drum Tower, look for the sign saying 'Alley Dumplings' in English down the second alley on the left. Unfortunately, opening hours are very sporadic. No English.

Information

Bank of China (中国银行; Zhōngguó Yínháng; Lao Longtou Lu; 老龙头路; 8.30am-5.30pm) Foreign-exchange facility.

China Post (中国邮政; Zhōngguó Yóuzhèng; Lao Longtou Lu; 老龙头路; 8.30am-6pm)

Industrial & Commercial Bank (ICBC; 工商银行; Gōngshāng Yínháng; Nan Dajie; 南大街) Has a handy ATM.

Public Security Bureau (PSB; 公安局; Gōng'ānjú; 0335 505 1163; Diyiguan Lu; 第一关路) On the corner of a small alleyway, opposite the First Pass Under Heaven gate.

Getting There & Away

TRAIN

Half a dozen D-class bullet trains link Běijīng Main Station with Shānhǎiguān (¥93, 2½ hours) throughout the day.

Alternatively, many more high-speed trains go from Běijīng to the nearby city of Qínhuángdǎo (秦皇岛; ¥88, 2½ hours), 18km from Shānhǎiguān.

Numerous trains also run to Qínhuángdǎo from Tiānjīn (¥122, 1¼ hours) and Shěnyáng (¥125, 2½ hours).

AIR

Shānhǎiguān's tiny airport closed in 2016, superseded by the new Qínhuángdǎo Běidàihé Airport (90km away), which has flights to Qīngdǎo, Nánjīng, Chéngdū, Shēnzhèn and Guǎngzhōu.

BUS

There's no long-distance bus station in Shānhǎiguān. Qínhuángdǎo's **bus station** (秦皇岛汽车站; Qínhuángdǎo qìchēzhàn), where the nearest long-distance buses arrive, is diagonally opposite its train station. Services from here include the following:

Běijīng (Bāwángfén) ¥105, 3½ hours, three daily (8am, 10am and 3.30pm)

Běijīng Capital Airport ¥140, four hours, hourly (6am to 5pm)

Getting Around

To get to Shānhǎiguān from Qínhuángdǎo's bus or train station, take bus 8 (¥1) from outside the train station for one stop – you can also walk it if you can communicate in Chinese – then cross the road and take bus 33 (¥2, 30 minutes) going the opposite direction to Shānhǎiguān's South Gate (南门; Nán Mén).

Consider hiring a bike from **Hēimǎ Chēxíng** (黑马车行; 12-1 Nan Dajie; 南大街12-1号; per day ¥10, fancier bike ¥50, deposit ¥100; 7am-6pm) to potter about the old town, head north to Jiǎo Shān Great Wall or south to Old Dragon Head.

Běijīng

Includes ➡

Best Places to Eat

- ➡ Dàlǐ Courtyard (p314)
- ➡ Crescent Moon Muslim Restaurant (p312)
- ➡ Little Yúnnán (p312)
- ➡ Sìjì Mínfú (p300)

Best Places to Stay

- ➡ Great Wall Box House (p322)
- ➡ City Walls Courtyard (p308)
- ➡ Courtyard 7 (p311)
- ➡ Orchid (p309)

Why Go?

For weary Trans-Siberian travellers, Běijīng (北京) will feel like the figurative pot of gold at the end of the rainbow. The 2008 Olympics were instrumental in transforming the Chinese capital, and perhaps for the first time since the Mongol invasion, Běijīng feels like a true international city, brimming with overseas business, cuisine of every kind, daring modern architecture and a thriving arts scene.

Despite its headlong rush into the future, though, the best of Běijīng lies in its links to the past. Magnificent historical sights such as the Forbidden City, Temple of Heaven Park, the Summer Palace and, of course, the Great Wall, will keep you busy for days. And ducking into the fast-disappearing *hútòng* (narrow alleyway) neighbourhoods is a magical experience, and the best way to discover Běijīng at its most intimate.

Come evening, choose from a million or so drinking spots and shout *'gān bēi!'* (bottoms up!) as you toast the end (or beginning) of your epic cross-continental journey.

When to Go

Běijīng

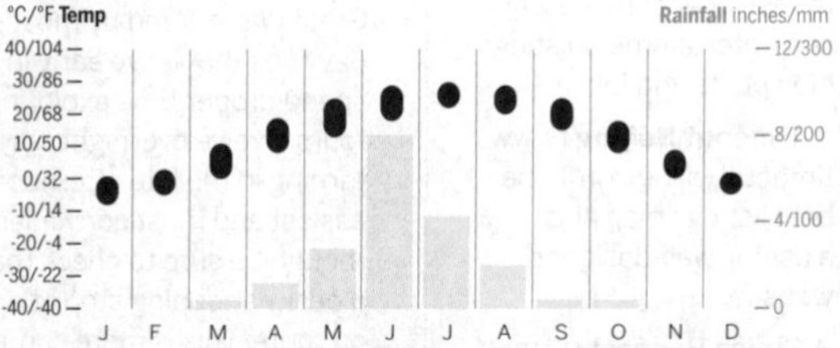

May Warming up after the winter freeze. Windy, but usually dry and clear.

Oct–Nov Gorgeously fresh after the scorching summer, with blue skies and fewer tourists.

Dec–Feb Dry as a bone and brutally cold, but the streets are pleasantly quiet.

NEED TO KNOW

Have the name and address of wherever you're going each day written down in Chinese characters before you go out. And always bring your hotel business card with you, so you can find your way home.

Fast Facts

- Telephone code: ☎ 010
- Population: 21.7 million
- Time Zone: Moscow +5hr

New in Běijīng

- **Bike-Sharing Scheme** Rent a bike for just ¥1 an hour.
- **Antismoking Law** Běijīng now has far more smoke-free venues than ever before.
- **WeChat** (www.wechat.com) Download China's most popular instant-messaging system to connect with locals you befriend.

Resources

- **Beijinger** (www.thebeijinger.com) Eating and entertainment listings, blog posts and forums.
- **Timeout Běijīng** (www.timeoutbeijing.com) The best listings mag and a useful, well-designed website.
- **Sinica Podcast** (http://popupchinese.com) Popular, uncensored current-affairs podcast based in Běijīng.

Arriving in Běijīng

Běijīng Capital International Airport The Airport Express (¥25, 30 minutes, 6.30am to 11pm) links up with the subway system (Lines 10 and 2). If taking a taxi (¥90 to ¥120), use the official taxi rank only.

Běijīng Train Station On subway Line 2.

Běijīng West Train Station On subway Line 9.

Běijīng South Train Station On subway Line 4.

Getting Around

Subway Easy to use and the quickest way to get around Běijīng. Trains start running from 5am to 6am and stop at around 11pm.

Bus Very cheap but crowded, slow and difficult for non-Chinese-speakers to use.

Taxi Cheap by Western standards, but often snarled in heavy traffic.

Cycling Běijīng is flat, making cycling easy, although the roads can be dangerous for cyclists.

Car and motorcycle Challenging and hazardous for foreigners unused to Chinese road conditions and driving.

Rickshaw Foreigners are routinely overcharged and we do not recommend using them.

GUIDED TOURS

There are a number of tour operators who can take you around Běijīng and/or the Great Wall. Tours can range from a half-day trip through the *hútòng,* to multiday tours taking in numerous locations that can be tailored to individuals or groups, so you only see what you are interested in. Tours can be done on foot, by bike, in cars and taxis, or even in a motorcycle sidecar.

Hútòng tours are especially useful because the best ones, like those run by the China Culture Center (p315) or Bike Běijīng (p315), will take you to places you're unlikely to stumble upon by just walking around on your own.

Popular with visitors are the numerous tours to the Great Wall offered by most hostels. Typically, they are day trips that leave early in the morning, allowing you to spend proper time exploring the Wall (although some tours involve overnight stays near the Wall), before returning in the late afternoon. These tours are often the easiest and most convenient way to get out to the Wall, though be sure to check that your tour doesn't include a pesky shopping stop at either a jade or silk factory on route. This is more common with Great Wall tours to Bādálǐng.

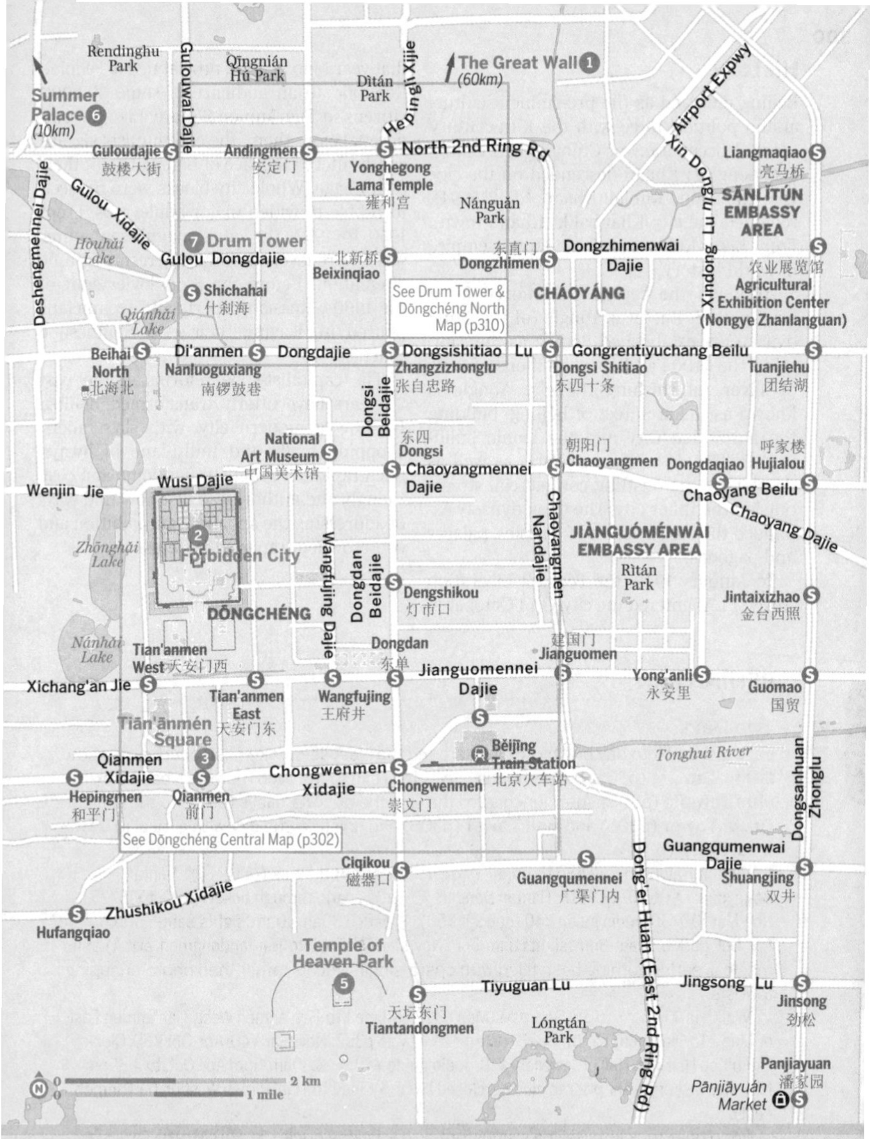

Beijing Highlights

❶ **Great Wall** (p321) Hiking along the wall, then bunking up for the night in a village guesthouse.

❷ **Forbidden City** (p300) Marvelling at the splendour of the world's largest palace complex.

❸ **Tiān'ānmén Square** (p300) Watching the flag-raising ceremony at this iconic square.

❹ **Běijīng hútòng** (p315) Exploring the historic alleyways that criss-cross the city centre.

❺ **Temple of Heaven Park** (p300) Experiencing a tranquil moment in this serene oasis of methodical Confucian design.

❻ **Summer Palace** (p307) Enjoying a taste of imperial high life amid sumptuous gardens and pavilions.

❼ **Drum Tower** (p305) Climbing this magnificent tower and looking over the grey-tiled rooftops in the alleys below.

History

Běijīng emerged as the pre-eminent cultural and political force with the 13th-century Mongol occupation of China, when Chinggis (Genghis) Khaan descended on the city. His grandson, Kublai Khaan (c 1215–94), renamed the city Khanbalik (Khan's town). From here, Kublai ruled the largest empire in world history.

Although the capital was moved for a brief period, Emperor Yongle (of the Ming dynasty) re-established Běijīng as the capital in the 1400s and spent millions of taels of silver refurbishing the city. Yongle is known as the architect of Běijīng, building the Forbidden City and the iconic buildings in Temple of Heaven Park, as well as developing the bustling commercial streets outside the inner city. The Qing dynasty expanded the construction of temples, palaces and pagodas.

In January 1949, the People's Liberation Army (PLA) entered the city. On 1 October of that year Mao Zedong proclaimed a 'People's Republic' to an audience of some 500,000 citizens in Tiān'ānmén Square. Like the emperors before them, the communists significantly altered the face of Běijīng to suit their own image. Whole city blocks were reduced to rubble to widen major boulevards. From 1950 to 1952, the city's magnificent outer walls were levelled in the interests of traffic circulation. Before the Sino-Soviet split of the 1960s, Russian experts and technicians poured in, leaving their own Stalinesque touches.

The capitalist-style reforms of the past 25 years have utterly transformed Běijīng. It's now a modern city, with skyscrapers, shopping malls and multi-lane highways. Such rapid development has come at a cost, though, and authorities must now find ways of addressing the appalling air pollution and overcrowded transport systems.

BĚIJĪNG IN...

Two Days

Ease yourself into day one by strolling around the incense-smoke-filled courtyards of the **Lama Temple** (p305) before hopping over the road to the even more laid-back **Confucius Temple** (p306). After lunch stroll through the **hútòng** alleys (p315) to the ancient **Drum Tower** (p305) and **Bell Tower** (p306) and finish off the day with a meal in **Dàlǐ Courtyard** (p314).

Rise at dawn on day two to enjoy **Temple of Heaven Park** (天坛公园; Tiāntán Gōngyuán; ☎010 6702 9917; Tiantan Donglu; 天坛东路; park/through ticket Apr-Oct ¥15/35, Nov-Mar ¥10/30, audio guide ¥40 (deposit ¥50); ⊙park 6.30am-10pm, sights 8am-5.30pm Apr-Oct, park 6.30am-8pm, sights 8am-5pm Nov-Mar; Ⓢ Line 5 to Tiantandongmen, exit A) at its magical, early-morning best: filled with opera-singing locals rather than photo-snapping tourists.

Walk via **Tiān'ānmén Square** (Map p302; Ⓢ Line 1 to Tian'anmen West, Tian'anmen East, or Line 2 to Qianmen) to the **Forbidden City** (Map p302; Nov-Mar ¥40, Apr-Oct ¥60, Clock Exhibition Hall ¥10, Hall of Jewellery ¥10, audio guide ¥40; ⊙8.30am-5pm Apr-Oct, to 4.30pm Nov-Mar, last entry 1hr prior to closing, closed Mon; Ⓢ Line 1 to Tian'anmen West or Tian'anmen East).

For dinner tuck into Běijīng's signature dish – Peking duck – at **Sìjì Mínfú** (p313).

Four Days

Get ready for the trip of a lifetime on day three; your journey to the **Great Wall** (p321). There are plenty of options; the adventurous could try hiking at **Gǔběikǒu** (p322) while **Mùtiányù** (p321) is a good option for families. Pack a picnic and don't expect to get back to the city until nightfall (or stay over at a nearby hotel).

Hop on the subway on day four to visit the **Summer Palace** (p307). You could spend the whole day here, or else save the afternoon for a trip to **798 Art District** (p307). Return to the city centre for an early evening meal so you have time to catch a show – **Peking Opera** (p316) or **acrobatics** (p316) – on your final evening.

Sights

Forbidden City 紫禁城

Ringed by 3.5km of scarlet citadel walls at the very heart of Běijīng, the Unesco-listed **Forbidden City** (紫禁城; Zǐjìn Chéng; Map p302; ☎010 8500 7114; www.dpm.org.cn; Nov-Mar ¥40, Apr-Oct ¥60, Clock Exhibition Hall ¥10, Hall of Jewellery ¥10, audio guide ¥40; ⊙8.30am-5pm Apr-Oct, to 4.30pm Nov-Mar, last entry 1hr prior to closing, closed Mon; Ⓢ Line 1 to Tian'anmen West or Tian'anmen East).) is China's largest and best-preserved collection of ancient buildings, and the largest palace complex in the world. Steeped in stultifying ritual and Byzantine regal protocol, this other-worldly palace was the reclusive home to two dynasties of imperial rule, sharing 900-plus buildings with a retinue of eunuchs, servants and concubines, until the Republic overthrew the last Qing emperor in 1911. So called because it was off limits to most people for 500 years, the Forbidden City is prosaically known as the Palace Museum (故宫博物馆; Gùgōng Bówùguǎn), although most Chinese people simply call it Gùgōng (故宫; Ancient Palace).

Tourists must enter the complex through the south gate, known as the **Meridian Gate** (午门; Wǔ Mén; Map p302), although you can exit via the south, east or north gates. Audio guides are available in several languages, and are usually preferable to one of the many actual guides who hustle for work by the entrance.

The complex is enormous – give yourself at least half a day here (there are cafes and restaurants) – and is made up of a series of courtyards, gateways and imperial halls, the largest and most impressive of which run along the central north–south axis. These were largely ceremonial, whereas the smaller, more intimate courtyards and buildings, in the east and west of the complex, were more commonly used in the everyday life of the imperial court. These side courtyards are usually quieter, so can be more fun to explore.

Many buildings inside the complex house museum exhibitions, showcasing priceless artefacts from imperial China (paintings, jade, porcelain etc). Some are extraordinarily impressive. Don't miss the **Nine Dragon Screen** (九龙壁; Jiǔlóng Bì; Map p302; Forbidden City; incl in through ticket) inside an area known as the **Treasure Gallery** (珍宝馆; Zhēn Bǎo Guǎn; Map p302; Forbidden City; ¥10), or the **Hall of Clocks & Watches** (钟表馆; Zhōngbiǎo Guǎn; Map p302; ¥10; ⊙8.30am-4pm summer, to 3.30pm winter), which you reach just before the Treasure Gallery entrance; both are in the eastern section of the complex, about halfway up.

The **Imperial Garden** (御花园; Yù Huāyuán; Map p302; Forbidden City) at the back of the complex leads to the north-gate exit, which pops you out opposite the south gate of Jǐngshān Park. Watch out for rickshaw and taxi touts here, who frequently cheat tourists with massively overpriced rides; instead, catch a bus (124 to the Drum Tower, or 专1 to Tiān'ānmén Sq), or walk a block and hail a passing cab.

Tiān'ānmén Square & Around 天安门广场

Flanked to the east and west by stern 1950s Soviet-style buildings and ringed by white perimeter fences that channel the hoi polloi towards security checks and bag searches, **Tiān'ānmén Square** (天安门广场; Tiān'ānmén Guǎngchǎng; Map p302; Ⓢ Line 1 to Tian'anmen West, Tian'anmen East, or Line 2 to Qianmen) FREE to the **Forbidden City** (紫禁城; Zǐjìn Chéng; Map p302; ☎010 8500 7114; www.dpm.org.cn; Nov-Mar ¥40, Apr-Oct ¥60, Clock Exhibition Hall ¥10, Hall of Jewellery ¥10, audio guide ¥40; ⊙8.30am-5pm Apr-Oct, to 4.30pm Nov-Mar, last entry 1hr prior to closing, closed Mon; Ⓢ Line 1 to Tian'anmen West or Tian'anmen East), the world's largest public square (440,000 sq metres), is a vast desert of paving stones at the heart of Běijīng.

It is also a poignant epitaph to China's hapless democracy movement, which got a drubbing from the People's Liberation Army (PLA) in June 1989. The stringent security and round-the-clock monitoring hardly makes it the most relaxing of tourist sights. Such, though, is its iconic status that few visitors leave Běijīng without coming here; and for Trans-Sib travellers, a visit is a ritual of sorts – it's fascinating to size up Tiān'ānmén against your experience in Moscow's Red Square.

If you get up early you can watch the **flag-raising ceremony** at sunrise, performed by a troop of PLA soldiers drilled to march at precisely 108 paces per minute, 75cm per pace. The same ceremony in reverse is performed at sunset. Ask at your hotel for flag-raising/-lowering times so you can get there early, as crowds can be intense.

Although the square is the symbolic centre of the Chinese universe, what you see today is a modern creation, conceived by Mao Zedong to project the enormity of the Communist Party. His giant portrait still hangs over the **Gate of Heavenly Peace** (天安门; Tiān'ānmén; Map p302; Xichang'an Jie; 西长安街; ¥15, bag storage ¥3-6; ⊙8.30am-

Dōngchéng Central

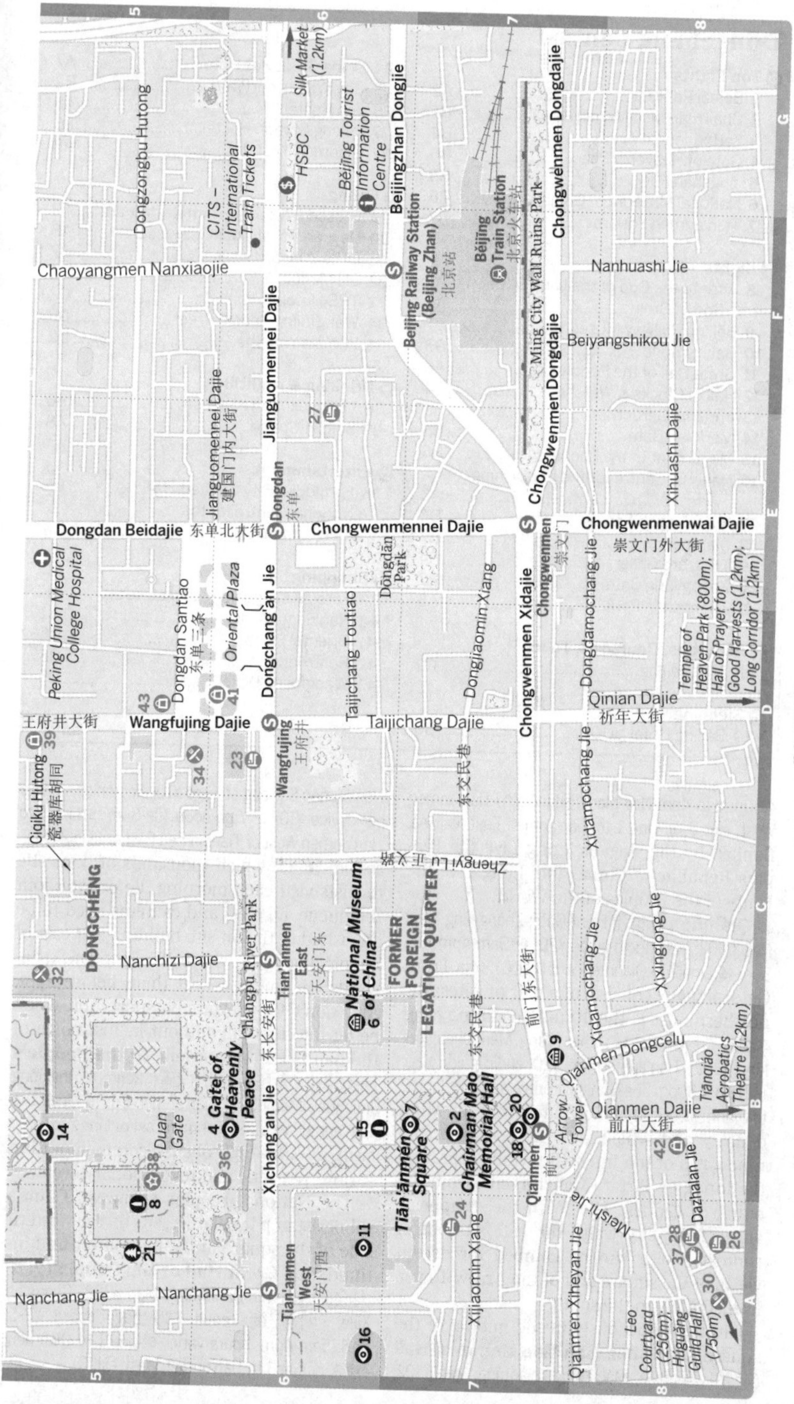

Dongzongbu Hutong
CITS – International Train Tickets
Silk Market (1.2km)
HSBC
Běijīng Tourist Information Centre
Beijingzhan Dongjie
Beijing Railway Station (Beijing Zhan)
北京站
Beijing Train Station
北京火车站
Ming City Wall Ruins Park
Chongwenmen Dongdajie
Chaoyangmen Nanxiaojie
Jianguomennei Dajie
Nanhuashi Jie
Beiyangshikou Jie
Jianguomennei Dajie
建国门内大街
27
Xihuashi Dajie
Dongdan
东单
Dongdan Beidajie
东单北大街
Chongwenmennei Dajie
Chongwenmen
Chongwenmenwai Dajie
崇文门外大街
崇文门
Peking Union Medical College Hospital
Dongdan Santiao
东单三条
Oriental Plaza
Dongchang'an Jie
Taijichang Toutiao
Dōngdān Park
Dongjiaomin Xiang
Chongwenmen Xidajie
Dongdamochang Jie
Qinian Dajie
祈年大街
Temple of Heaven Park (800m); Hall of Prayer for Good Harvests (1.2km); Long Corridor (1.2km)
王府井大街
Wangfujing Dajie
Wangfujing
王府井
Taijichang Dajie
43
41
39
34
23
Cigiku Hutong
瓷器库胡同
东交民巷
Xidamochang Jie
Zhengyi Lu 正义路
DŌNGCHÉNG
Nanchizi Dajie
Changpu River Park
Tian'anmen East
天安门东
National Museum of China
6
FORMER FOREIGN LEGATION QUARTER
Xidamochang Jie
Xingfong Jie
32
4 Gate of Heavenly Peace
东长安街
东交民巷
前门东大街
9
Qianmen Dongcelu
Tiānqiáo Acrobatics Theatre (1.2km)
14
Duan Gate
36
38
Xichang'an Jie
15
7
Tiān'ānmén Square
2
Chairman Mao Memorial Hall
20
18
Qianmen
前门
Arrow Tower
Qianmen Dajie
前门大街
42
Dazhalan Jie
8
21
11
24
Meishi Jie
Xijiaomin Xiang
37
28
26
Nanchang Jie
Tian'anmen West
天安门西
Qianmen Xiheyan Jie
30
16
Leo Courtyard (250m); Húguǎng Guild Hall (750m)

Dōngchéng Central

4.30pm, to 4pm Nov-Mar; S Line 1 to Tian'anmen West, exit B or Line 1 to Tian'anmen East, exit A), flanked by the slogans 'Long Live the People's Republic of China' and 'Long Live the Unity of the Peoples of the World'.

Qiánmén (前门; Front Gate; Zhèngyáng Mén; Map p302; ¥20, audio guide ¥20; 9am-4pm Tue-Sun; S Line 2 to Qianmen, exit B or C), aka Front Gate, actually consists of a pair of gates: the northernmost is the 40m-high **Zhèngyáng Gate** (正阳门城楼; Zhèngyáng Mén Chénglóu; Map p302; Tiān'ānmén Sq; ¥20, audio guide ¥20; 9am-4.30pm Tue-Sun, last entry 4pm; S Line 2 to Qianmen, exit A), which dates from the Ming dynasty and which was the largest of the nine gates of the Inner City Wall separating the inner, or Tartar (Manchu) city, from the outer, or Chinese city. With the disappearance of the city walls, the gate sits out of context, but it can be climbed for decent views of the square and of the Arrow Tower, immediately to the south.

Sitting innocuously in the middle of the square is the **Chairman Mao Memorial Hall** (毛主席纪念堂; Máo Zhǔxí Jìniàntáng; Map p302; Tiān'ānmén Sq; bag storage ¥10, electonics storage per device ¥10; 7am-noon Tue-Sun; S Line 1 to Tian'anmen West or Tian'anmen East or Line 2 to Qianmen) FREE, which thousands of domestic tourists visit each morning. Before you join the queue, all bags and cameras need to be deposited at the on-site building just east of Zhèngyáng Gate within Tiān'ānmén Sq towards Qiánmén; collect them before 2pm. And don't forget your passport. You won't be let into the hall without it. Just north of the hall is the **Monument to the People's Heroes** (人民英雄纪念碑; Rénmín Yīngxióng Jìniànbēi; Map p302; Tiān'ānmén Sq; S Lines 1 to Tian'anmen West, Tian'anmen East or Line 2 to Qianmen), a 37.9m-high obelisk commemorating various patriotic and revolutionary events.

The National People's Congress, China's rubber-stamp legislature, sits on the western side of the square in the monolithic and intimidating **Great Hall of the People** (人民大会堂; Rénmín Dàhuìtáng; Map p302; Chang'an Xijie; 西长安街; adult ¥30, bag deposit ¥2-5; 8.15am-4pm, hours vary; S Line 1 to Qianmen, exit A, or Line 1 to Tian'anmen West, exit C).

★**National Museum of China** MUSEUM
(中国国际博物馆; Zhōngguó Guójì Bówùguǎn; Map p302; http://en.chnmuseum.cn; Guangchangdongce Lu, Tiān'ānmén Sq; 天安门，广场东侧路; audio guide ¥30; ⏲9am-5pm Tue-Sun, last entry 4pm; Ⓢ Line 1 to Tian'anmen East, exit D) FREE Běijīng's premier museum is housed in an immense 1950s Soviet-style building on the eastern side of Tiān'ānmén Sq, and claims to be the largest in the world by display space. You could easily spend a couple of hours in the outstanding **Ancient China** exhibition alone, with priceless artefacts displayed in modern, low-lit exhibition halls, including ceramics, calligraphy, jade and bronze pieces dating from prehistoric China through to the late Qing dynasty. You'll need your passport to gain entry.

Zhōngshān Park PARK
(中山公园; Zhōngshān Gōngyuán; Map p302; 4 Zhonghua Lu; 中华路4号; adult ¥3, Spring Flower & Tulips Show ¥10; ⏲6am-9pm; Ⓢ Line 1 to Tian'anmen West, exit B) Named after Sun Zhongshan (Sun Yatsen), the father of modern China, this peaceful park sits at the southwest corner of the Forbidden City and partly looks out onto the palace's moat (you can rent pedal-boats here) and towering walls. A refreshing prologue or conclusion to the magnificence of the Forbidden City, the park was formerly the sacred Ming-style **Altar to the God of the Land and the God of Grain** (北京社稷坛; Shèjìtán; Map p302; Zhōngshān Park; Ⓢ Line 1 to Tian'anmen West, exit B), where the emperor offered sacrifices. The Square Altar remains, bordered on all sides by walls tiled in various colours.

North of the Forbidden City

★**Lama Temple** BUDDHIST TEMPLE
(雍和宫; Yōnghé Gōng; Map p310; www.yonghegong.cn; 12 Yonghegong Dajie; 北新桥雍和宫大街12号; ¥25, English audio guide ¥50; ⏲9am-4.30pm; Ⓢ Lines 2, 5 to Yonghegong-Lama Temple, exit C) This exceptional temple is a glittering attraction in Běijīng's Buddhist firmament. If you only have time for one temple (the Temple of Heaven isn't really a temple) make it this one, where riveting roofs, fabulous frescoes, magnificent decorative arches, tapestries, eye-popping carpentry, Tibetan prayer wheels, tantric statues and a superb pair of Chinese lions mingle with dense clouds of incense.

★**Drum Tower** HISTORIC SITE
(鼓楼; Gǔlóu; Map p310; Gulou Dongdajie; 鼓楼东大街; ¥20, Bell & Drum towers through ticket ¥30; ⏲9am-5pm, last entry 4.40pm; Ⓢ Line 8 to Shichahai, exit A2) Along with the more austere Bell Tower (p306), which stands behind

DON'T MISS

TEMPLE OF HEAVEN PARK

An oasis of peace and methodical Confucian design in one of China's busiest urban landscapes, the 267-hectare **Temple of Heaven Park** (p300) is absolutely unique. The largest of Běijīng's imperial parks, it not only assumes an important place in the history of China's capital, it's also a fabulous place in which to appreciate how Beijingers spend their free time.

It's impossible not to be bowled over by the architectural perfection of the **Hall of Prayer for Good Harvests** (祈年殿; Qínián Diàn; ¥20; ⏲8am-5pm) even though the one you'll see is an 1890 replica of the original Ming-dynasty structure, which burned down after being struck by lightning.

Immediately south of this is the **Imperial Vault of Heaven** (皇穹宇; Huáng Qióng Yǔ), enclosed within **Echo Wall** (回音壁; Huíyīn Bì) – so named because its unusual acoustic properties allow people standing at opposite ends of its circular courtyard to talk to each other without shouting – and the **Round Altar** (圜丘; Yuán Qiū), all of which played important roles in the winter solstice ceremony carried out by the emperor each year. He, and his enormous entourage, would travel in silent procession from the Forbidden City to the altars here, where animal sacrifices would be made as the emperor sought good harvests, divine clearance and atonement for the sins of the people.

The rest of the park is covered in groves of ancient cypresses, flower gardens and pleasant open spaces, including some well-tended lawns, where locals come to exercise, play music or just hang out. The area between the east gate and the north gate is prime kite-flying space. There's a huge exercise park in this area too, while nearby **Long Corridor** (长廊; Cháng Láng) is a popular spot for occasionally animated games of cards.

Tiantandongmen subway station is beside the park's east gate.

it, the magnificent red-painted Drum Tower used to be the city's official timekeeper, with drums and bells beaten and rung to mark the times of the day. Originally built in 1272, the Drum Tower was once the heart of the Mongol capital of Dàdū, as Běijīng was then known. It was destroyed in a fire before a replacement was built, slightly to the east of the original location, in 1420. The current structure is an 18th-century Qing-dynasty version of that 1420 tower.

Climb the steep inner staircase for views of the grey-tiled rooftops of the surrounding *hútòng*, and due south along the city's historic central axis to the pagoda that tops Jǐngshān Park (p307) (beyond this is the Forbidden City). Try to time your ascent to coincide with one of the regular drumming performances played out on reproductions of the 25 Ming-dynasty watch drums, which used to sound out across this part of the city. One of the original 25 drums, the **Night Watchman's Drum** (更鼓; Gēnggǔ), is on display, dusty, battered and torn. Also on display is a replica of a Song-dynasty water clock, which was never actually used in the tower, but is interesting nonetheless.

The times of the **drumming performances**, which only last for a few minutes, are at 9.30am, 10.30am, 11.30am, 1.30pm, 2.30pm, 3.30pm and 4.45pm.

★ Bell Tower HISTORIC SITE

(钟楼; Zhōnglóu; Map p310; Gulou Dongdajie; 鼓楼东大街; ¥20, Bell & Drum towers through ticket ¥30; ⏲9am-5pm, last tickets 4.40pm; Ⓢ Line 8 to Shichahai, exit A2) The restrained, grey-stone edifice of the Bell Tower is arguably even more charming than its resplendent other half, the Drum Tower (p305), after which this area of Běijīng is named. It also has the added advantage of being able to view its sister tower from a balcony.

Confucius Temple & Imperial College CONFUCIAN TEMPLE

(孔庙、国子监; Kǒng Miào & Guózǐjiàn; Map p310; 13 Guozijian Jie; 国子监街13号; ¥30, audio guide ¥30; ⏲8.30am-6pm May-Oct, to 5pm Nov-Apr, last entry 1hr before closing; Ⓢ Lines 2, 5 to Yonghegong-Lama Temple, exit C) An incense stick's toss away from the Lama Temple, China's second-largest Confucian temple has had a refit in recent years, but the almost otherworldly sense of detachment is seemingly impossible to shift. A mood of impassiveness reigns and the lack of worship reinforces a sensation that time has stood still. However, in its

DON'T MISS

CONTEMPORARY ARCHITECTURE

Běijīng is home to some of the world's most dazzling, state-of-the-art architecture:

CCTV Headquarters (央视大楼, Yāngshì Dàlóu; 32 Dongsanhuan Zhonglu, 东三环中路32号; Ⓢ Line 10 to Jintaixizhao, exit C) Shaped like an enormous pair of trousers, and known locally as Dà Kùchǎ (大裤衩; Big Pants), this astonishing tower is an architectural fantasy that appears to defy gravity.

National Centre for the Performing Arts (NCPA; 国家大剧院; Guójiā Dàjùyuàn; Map p302; ☎010 6655 0000; www.chncpa.org/ens; 2 West Chang'an Ave; 西长安街二号; admission ¥40, concert tickets ¥80-400; ⏲9am-4.30pm Tue-Sun; Ⓢ Line 1 to Tian'anmen West, exit C) Also known as the National Grand Theatre, this is a surreal yet spectacular location in which to catch a show. It looks like a giant mercury bead from another planet.

Galaxy Soho (银河Soho; Yínhé Soho; Map p302; Chaoyangmennei Dajie; 朝阳门内大街; Ⓢ Lines 2, 6 to Chaoyangmen, exit G) Designed by acclaimed British-Iraqi architect Zaha Hadid (1950–2016), the low-rise complex writhes and flows like an alien spaceship.

Bird's Nest (北京国家体育场; Běijīng Guójiā Tǐyùchǎng; Beijing National Stadium; http://cyvu.org/english; Beijing Olympic Park; 奥林匹克公园; ¥50; ⏲9am-6.30pm Apr-Oct, to 5pm Nov-Mar; Ⓢ Line 8 to Olympic Sports Center, exit B2) and **Water Cube** (Beijing National Aquatics Center; 国家游泳中心; Guójiā Yóuyǒng Zhōngxīn; www.water-cube.com/en; 11 Tianchen Lu, Olympic Park; 天辰东路11号; admission ¥30, swimming pool ¥60; ⏲9am-7pm, swimming 12.30-5.30pm Mon-Fri, 9am-5.30pm Sat & Sun; Ⓢ Line 8 to Olympic Sports Center, exit B2) The skeletal National Stadium, and its bubbly neighbour, the Water Cube, are particularly dazzling when lit up at night. However, walking around the desolate Olympic Sports Centre midweek is rather like being stuck in a zombie movie where humans have all but been wiped out.

tranquillity and reserve, the temple can be a pleasant sanctuary from Běijīng's often congested streets – a haven of peace and quiet.

★Běihǎi Park PARK

(北海公园; Běihǎi Gōngyuán; Map p302; ☎010 6403 1102; www.beihaipark.com.cn/en; high/low season ¥10/5, through ticket ¥20/15, audio guide ¥60; ⊙6.30am-8.30pm, sights to 5pm; Ⓢ Line 6 to Beihai North or Nanluoguxiang, or Line 4 to Xisi) Běihǎi Park, northwest of the Forbidden City, is largely occupied by the North Sea (Běihǎi), a lake fringed by willows that freezes in winter and blooms with lotuses in summer. Old folk dance together outside temple halls and come twilight, young couples cuddle on benches. It's a restful place to stroll around (come after 5pm in summer to beat the crowds), rent a rowing boat or watch calligraphers performing *dìshū* (地书), inscribing characters on the ground with brushes and water.

★Hòuhǎi Lakes LAKE

(后海; Hòuhǎi; Ⓢ Line 6 to Beihai North, exit B, or Line 8 to Shichahai, exit A1, or Line 2 to Jishuitan, exit B) FREE Also known as Shíchàhǎi (什刹海) but mostly just referred to collectively as Hòuhǎi, the Hòuhǎi Lakes are comprised of three lakes: Qiánhǎi (Front Lake), Hòuhǎi (Back Lake) and Xīhǎi (West Lake). Together they are one of the capital's favourite outdoor spots, heaving with locals and out-of-towners in the summer especially, and providing great people-spotting action.

★Jǐngshān Park PARK

(景山公园; Jǐngshān Gōngyuán; Map p302; Jingshan Qianjie; 景山前街; adult/child ¥10/5; ⊙6.30am-9pm; Ⓢ Lines 6, 8 to Nanluoguxiang, exit A) The dominating feature of Jǐngshān – one of the city's finest parks – is one of central Běijīng's few hills; a mound that was created from the loess excavated to make the Forbidden City moat. Called Coal Hill by Westerners during Legation days, Jǐngshān also serves as a feng shui shield, protecting the palace from evil spirits – or dust storms – from the north. Clamber to the top for a magnificent panorama of the capital and princely views over the russet roofing of the Forbidden City.

City Outskirts

★Summer Palace HISTORIC SITE

(颐和园; Yíhé Yuán; 19 Xinjian Gongmen; 新建宫门19号; Apr-Oct ¥30, through ticket ¥60, Nov-Mar ¥20, through ticket ¥50, audio guide ¥40; ⊙7am-7pm, sights 8am-5pm summer, 8.30am-4.30pm winter; Ⓢ Xiyuan or Beigongmen) As mandatory a Běijīng sight as the Great Wall or the Forbidden City, the Summer Palace was the playground for emperors fleeing the suffocating summer torpor of the old imperial city. A marvel of design, the palace – with its huge lake and hilltop views – offers a pastoral escape into the landscapes of traditional Chinese painting. It merits an entire day's exploration, although a (high-paced) morning or afternoon exploring the temples, gardens, pavilions, bridges and corridors may suffice.

★798 Art District GALLERY

(798 艺术新区; Qī Jiǔ Bā Yìshù Qū; cnr Jiuxianqiao Lu & Jiuxianqiao Beilu; 酒仙桥路; ⊙galleries 10am-6pm, most closed Mon; 🚌403, 909, Ⓢ Line 14 to Jiangtai, exit A) A formidable area of disused, Mao-era factories built with East German expertise, 798 Art District, also known as Dàshānzi (大山子), is Běijīng's main concentration of contemporary art galleries, art bookshops and cafes. The site first rose to prominence in the late 1990s, its Bauhaus-style former factory workshops ideally suited to ambitious art installations. The industrial complex celebrates its proletarian roots in the Communist heyday of the 1950s via the retouched red Maoist slogans decorating gallery walls and statues of burly, lantern-jawed workers dotting the lanes.

You could easily spend half a day wandering around the complex; look out for signboards with English-language maps to guide you around.

Galleries not to miss include **798 Art Factory** (798艺术工厂; 798 Yìshù Gōngchǎng; ☎186 1132 2248; 4 Jiuxianqiao Lu, 798 Art District; 酒仙桥路4号大山子艺术区; ⊙10am-6pm; Ⓢ Line 14 to Jiangtai, exit A) FREE, a hangar-like space with its concrete wall columns emblazoned in 1950s Maoist slogans, and industrial machinery scattered amid whichever Chinese or international art exhibition is currently in situ; **Faurschou Foundation Běijīng** (林冠基金会北京; Línguān Jījīn Huì Běijīng; www.faurschou.com; 2 Jiuxuanquao Lu, 798 Art District; 酒仙桥路2号798艺术区; ⊙10am-6pm; Ⓢ Line 14 to Jiangtai, exit A), hosting exhibitions by internationally acclaimed artists of the likes of Lucien Freud, Ai Weiwei and Andy Warhol; **Springs Centre of the Arts** (泉空间; Quán Kōngjiān; ☎010 5762 6373; www.springsart.com; 2 Jiuxianqiao Lu, 798 Art District; 酒仙桥路2号大山子艺术区; ¥10; ⊙10am-6pm Tue-Sun; Ⓢ Line 14 to Jiangtai, exit A), also exhibiting headliner artists from both China and abroad; and **UCCA** (Ullens Center for Contemporary Art; 尤伦

斯当代艺术中心; Yóulúnsī Dāngdài Yìshù Zhōngxīn; ☎010 5780 0200; www.ucca.org.cn/en; 4 Jiuxianqiao Lu, 798 Art District; 酒仙桥路4号大山子艺术区; ¥10-60; ⏲10am-7pm Tue-Sun; Ⓢ Line 14 to Jiangtai, exit A), another big-money gallery with immense, modern exhibition halls and an attached, funky design store.

Sleeping

Hostels offer the best all-round value, with traveller-friendly facilities and English-speaking staff, but bear in mind that you can find midrange hotels at a similar price point to hostel private rooms. Courtyard hotels are wonderfully atmospheric, but they lack the facilities (pool, gym etc) of top-end hotels in similar price brackets. Thanks to an excess of Olympics-era accommodation, Běijīng has rooms in international five-star hotels often going for under ¥1000.

Around the Forbidden City

★ City Walls Courtyard HOSTEL $

(城墙旅舍; Chéngqiáng Lǚshè; Map p302; ☎010 6402 7805; www.beijingcitywalls.com; 57 Nianzi Hutong; 碾子胡同57号; dm/s/tw ¥100/360/420; ❄@🛜; Ⓢ Lines 6, 8 to Nanluoguxiang, exit A) Hidden amid a maze of *hútòng* just north of Jǐngshān Park (p307) is this charming budget option offering a captivating sense of history. Rooms and dorms have private bathrooms; spacious four-bed dorms are especially great value. The main selling point is the sky-lit courtyard offering couches, cheap local beers and fresh coffee, and stuffed with pot plants and curios, including a full-sized Terracotta Warrior.

Peking Station Hostel HOSTEL $

(Map p302; 12 Babaolou Hutong, off Suzhou Hutong; 八宝楼胡同12号; dm ¥110-120, s & d ¥450; ⊖❄🛜; Ⓢ Line 2 to Beijing Railway Station, exit A) With only six tiny rooms and two dorms (one all-female), this delightful, boutique-styled hostel books out early, despite being one of the city's pricier backpacker digs. Nestled in a quiet alleyway a 10-minute walk from Běijīng Railway Station, it offers neat, white-walled rooms with towels and comfy beds and a bright, flower-strewn restaurant with a selection of wines and barista coffee.

China Great Hall Hotel HOTEL $$

(人民大会堂兵官; Rénmín Dàhuìtáng Bīngguǎn; Map p302; ☎010 6607 1188; 19 Xijiaomin Xiang; 西交民巷甲19号; Tiān'ānmén Sq viewing r ¥800; ❄@🛜🏊; Ⓢ Line 2 to Qianmen, exit C, or Line 1 to Tiananmen West, exit C) A little-known gem, this building attached to the Great Hall of the People (p304) was strictly cadres-only until it opened as a hotel in 2012. Functionally it's a typical four-star Chinese hotel, but geographically it's akin to staying in an annex of the Houses of Parliament, and quite simply the closest digs to Tiān'ānmén Sq without actually pitching a tent next to Mao's Mausoleum.

Běijīng Hotel NUO HOTEL $$$

(北京饭店莱佛士酒店; Běijīng Fàndiàn Láifóshì Jiǔdiàn; Map p302; ☎010 6526 3388; www.nuo-hotel.com/en; 33 Dongchang'an Jie; 东长安街33号; r from ¥1400; ⊖❄@🛜🏊; Ⓢ Line 1 to Wangfujing, exit C1) Sandwiched between two drab edifices (to the east, the 1970s lines of the Běijīng Hotel; to the west, a gawky Soviet-era facade), the seven-storey Běijīng Hotel NUO (formerly Raffles) oozes cachet and grandeur. Illuminated in a chandelier glow, the elegant lobby yields to a graceful staircase leading to immaculate standard doubles that are spacious and well proportioned, decked out with period-style furniture and large bathrooms.

WORTH A TRIP

RAILWAY MUSEUMS

Hard-core trainspotters should make tracks to the city's two railway museums.

The central **Běijīng Railway Museum** (北京铁路博物馆; Běijīng Tiělù Bówùguǎn; Map p302; ☎010 6705 1638; 2a Qianmen Dongdajie; 前门东大街2a号; ¥20; ⏲9am-5pm Tue-Sun; Ⓢ Qianmen) offers a fairly uninspired retelling of the development of the capital and China's railway system, with plenty of photos and models, but few English captions. The museum is based in the historic former Qiánmén Railway Station, which once connected Běijīng to Tiānjīn. Lack of space means there are few actual trains here, although there is a life-size model of the cab of one of China's high-speed trains to clamber into (¥10).

The **China Railway Museum** (中国铁道博物馆; Zhōngguó Tiědào Bówùguǎn; ☎010 6438 1317; north of 1 Jiuxianqiao Bei Lu, Chaoyang District; 朝阳区酒仙桥北路1号院北侧; ¥20; ⏲9am-4pm Tue-Sun; 🚌688), on the far northeastern outskirts of Běijīng, is vast and has far more loco action.

Around Tiān'ānmén Square

Leo Hostel HOSTEL $
(广聚园宾馆; Guǎngjùyuán Bīnguǎn; Map p302; ☎010 6303 1595, 010 6303 3318; www.leohostel.com; 52 Dazhalan Xijie; 大栅栏西街 52号; dm ¥55-90, r ¥240-380; ❄@📶; Ⓢ Line 2 to Qianmen, exit B or C) In a central location on this touristy pedestrianised strip close to Tiān'ānmén Sq and the surrounding sights, Leo Hostel is big, well-run and sociable, boasting a large communal bar with big-screen TV, Western food (including what must be Běijīng's only 'beans on toast') and plenty of cosy seating. Staff are friendly and mostly fluent in English.

Leo Courtyard HOSTEL $
(上林宾馆; Shànglín Bīnguǎn; ☎010 8316 6568; leocourtyard2015@outlook.com; 22 Shanxi Xiang; 陕西巷胡同 22号; dm/d/tr from ¥70/240/330; ❄📶; Ⓢ Line 7 to Hufangqiao, or Line 2 to Qianmen, exit B or C) It's a superb, historic warren of a building with a racy past featuring courtesans and the imperial elite, but the worn rooms and small dorms here are in desperate need of a little TLC. The attached bar-restaurant next door used to be a good place for a libation come sundown, but was closed on our most recent visit. It's down an alley off Dazhalan Xijie.

Qiánmén Hostel HOSTEL $
(前门客栈; Qiánmén Kèzhàn; Map p302; ☎010 6313 2370, 010 6313 2369; www.qianmenhostel.net; 33 Meishi Jie; 煤市街 33号; dm ¥60-80, r without/with bathroom ¥200/280; ❄@📶; Ⓢ Line 2 to Qianmen, exit B or C) A five-minute trot southwest of Tiān'ānmén Sq, this heritage hostel with an old-fashioned inner courtyard offers a relaxing environment with able staff. The rooms are simple and not big but, like the dorms, they are clean, as are the shared bathrooms. Despite the busy location, this is an easy place to switch off and appreciate the high ceilings, original woodwork and antique buildings.

North and West of the Forbidden City

Běijīng Downtown Backpackers HOSTEL $
(东堂客栈; Dōngtáng Kèzhàn; Map p310; ☎010 8400 2429; www.backpackingchina.com; 85 Nanluogu Xiang; 南锣鼓巷85号; dm incl breakfast ¥70-100, r ¥180-320; ❄@📶; Ⓢ Lines 6, 8 to Nanluoguxiang, exit E) Downtown Backpackers is Nanluogu Xiang's original youth hostel and it hasn't forgotten its roots. Rooms are basic, therefore cheap, but are kept clean and tidy, and staff members are fully plugged in to the needs of Western travellers. Dorms have curtains for added privacy, along with power sockets and lamps.

There's a rooftop terrace (complete with bench press and dumbbells) and a basement lounge to hang out in. The hostel rents bikes (per day ¥40) and runs recommended hiking trips to the Great Wall (¥280), plus a range of other city trips.

★**Orchid** COURTYARD HOTEL $$
(兰花宾馆; Lánhuā Bīnguǎn; Map p310; ☎010 5799 0806; www.theorchidbeijing.com; 65 Baochao Hutong; 鼓楼东大街宝钞胡同65号; r ¥805-1800; ❄@📶; Ⓢ Lines 2, 8 to Guloudajie, exit F, or Line 8 to Shichahai, exit A2) Opened by a Canadian and a Tibetan, the Orchid has transformed a dilapidated *hútòng* courtyard into a white-walled boutique sanctuary offering two tiers of rooftop terraces, the uppermost with views of the Drum and Bell Towers. Smallish rooms are doubles only, but are tastefully decorated and come with memory-foam mattresses, movies-on-demand, mobile phones, bike rental and an excellent local area map.

The Orchid also operates several self-contained apartments with cooking facilities close by, and serves excellent mezze-style dishes at **Toast** (Map p310; ☎010 8404 4818, 010 5799 0806; www.theorchidbeijing.com; 65 Baochao Hutong, Dulou Dongdajie, 鼓楼东大街宝钞胡同65号; mains from ¥88; ⏲10am-2.30pm & 6-10pm Wed-Mon; Ⓢ Lines 2, 8 to Guloudajie, exit F or Line 8 to Shichahai, exit A2), its popular in-house restaurant. Great Wall tours start from ¥1100 including lunch, admission and transport (or you can go bare bones and just book car and driver) and the hotel hosts a dumpling and wine party every Tuesday.

Nostalgia Hotel HOTEL $$
(时光漫步怀旧主题酒店; Shíguāng Mànbù Huáijiù Zhǔtí Jiǔdiàn; Map p310; ☎010 6403 2288; www.nostalgiahotelbeijing.com; 46 Fangjia Hutong; 安定门内大街，方家胡同46号; r from ¥428; ❄@📶; Ⓢ Line 5 to Beixinqiao, exit A) A good-value option if you don't fancy staying in a youth hostel, this large, funky hotel is housed in a small arts zone on trendy Fangjia Hutong. Simple rooms live up to its name and are decorated with a Chinese retro theme and knick-knacks, though thankfully the bathrooms are modern and generously proportioned.

Drum Tower & Dōngchéng North

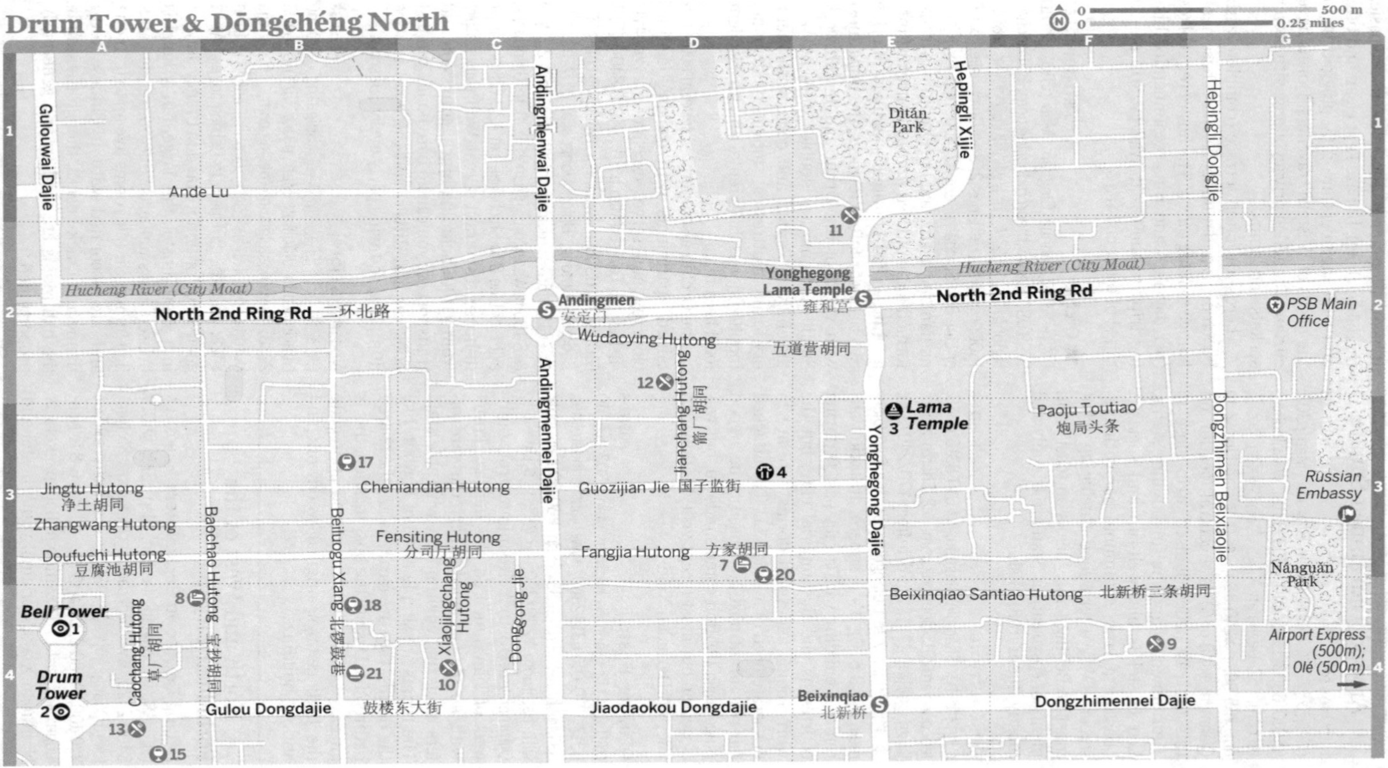

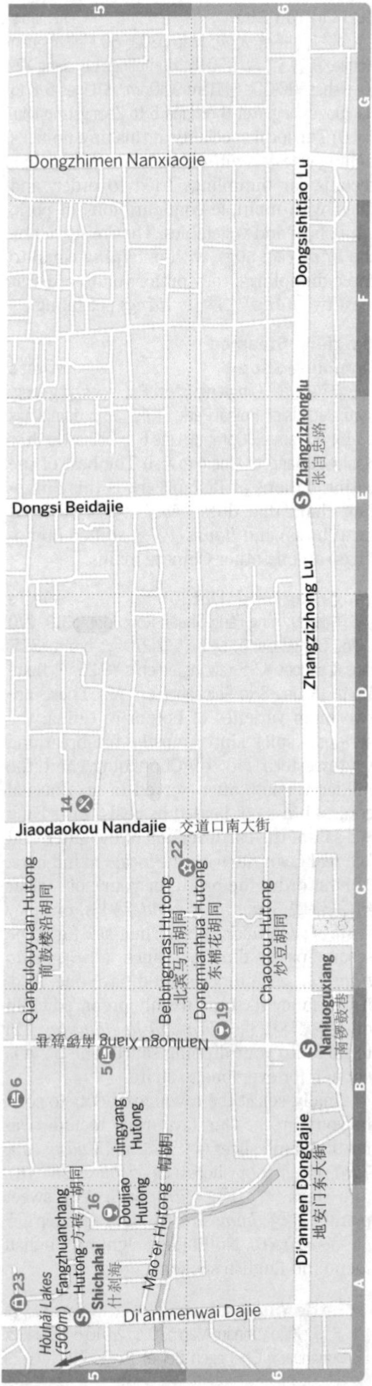

Drum Tower & Dōngchéng North

Courtyard 7 HUTONG HOTEL **$$$**

(四合院酒店; Sìhéyuàn Jiǔdiàn; Map p310; ☎010 6406 0777; www.courtyard7.com; 7 Qianguloyuan Hutong, off Nanluogu Xiang; 鼓楼东大街南锣鼓巷前鼓楼苑胡同7号; r incl breakfast ¥900-1200; ❄☎; S Lines 6, 8 to Nanluoguxiang, exit E) Period-style rooms with traditional Chinese furniture open onto a series of 400-year-old courtyard gardens, which over the years have been home to government ministers, rich merchants and even an army general. Despite the historical narrative and the impressively intact *sìhéyuàn* (quadrangle) layout, rooms still come with modern comforts such as underfloor heating, wi-fi and cable TV.

Standard rooms are less atmospheric, so upgrade to the superior rooms surrounding the courtyard. The *hútòng* location – down a quiet alley, but very close to hectic Nanluogu Xiang – is also a winner.

★**Rosewood Běijīng** BOUTIQUE HOTEL **$$$**
(北京瑰丽酒店; Běijīng Guīlì Jiǔdiàn; ☎010 6597 8888; www.rosewoodhotels.com/en/beijing; Jing Guang Centre, East 3rd Middle Ring Rd; 呼家楼京广中心; r from ¥2000; ; Ⓢ Line 10 to Jintaixizhao, exit A, or Lines 6, 10 to Hujialou, exit D) Opened in 2015, the Rosewood quickly staked its claim as Běijīng's most glamorous hotel, with serene public spaces, innovative restaurants and guest rooms strewn with designer furniture, arty curios, and automatic blinds that open to views of the iconic CCTV building.

Eating

Běijīng is a magnificent place for culinary adventures. With upwards of 60,000 restaurants here, you can enjoy the finest local dishes, as well as eating your way through every region of China. Some of your most memorable Běijīng experiences will take place around the dining table. So do as the locals do – grab those chopsticks and dive in.

★**Crescent Moon Muslim Restaurant** XINJIANG **$**
(新疆弯弯月亮维吾尔穆斯林餐厅; Xīnjiāng Wānwānyuèliàng Wéiwú'ěr Mùsīlín Cāntīng; Map p302; 16 Dongsi Liutiao Hutong, 东四六条胡同16号, 东四北大街; dishes from ¥18; ⏲11am-11pm; ; Ⓢ Line 5 to Zhangzizhonglu, exit C) You can find a Chinese Muslim restaurant on almost every street in Běijīng. Most are run by Huí Muslims, who are Han Chinese, rather than ethnic-minority Uyghurs from the remote western province of Xīnjiāng. Crescent Moon is the real deal – owned and staffed by Uyghurs, it attracts many Běijīng-based Uyghurs and people from Central Asia, as well as a lot of Western expats.

SELF-CATERING

For picnic supplies (or long train journeys) head to supermarkets such as **Olé** (Ole; 超市; Basement Ginza Mall, B1, 48 Dongzhimenwai Dajie; 东直门外大街银座百货; ⏲10am-10pm; Ⓢ Line 2 to Dongzhimen, exit C) and **Carrefour** (6b Beisanhuan Donglu; 北三环东路6b号; ⏲8.30am-10.30pm; Ⓢ Liufang). The deli **April Gourmet** (绿叶子食品店; Lûyèzi Shípǐn Diàn; 1st fl, Lianbao Mansion, Xingfucun Zhonglu; 三里屯幸福村中路联保公寓1层; ⏲8am-midnight; Ⓢ Line 2 to Dongsi Shitiao, exit B) caters for Westerners craving a taste of home.

Zuǒ Lín Yòu Shè BEIJING **$**
(左邻右舍褡裢火烧; Map p302; 50 Meishuguan Houjie; 美术馆后街50号; dumplings per liang ¥7-10, dishes ¥10-30; ⏲11am-9.30pm; Ⓢ Lines 6, 8 to Nanluoguxiang, exit B or Line 5 to Zhangzizhonglu, exit D) The local speciality at this tiny, no-frills Běijīng eatery is *dālián huǒshāo* (褡裢火烧), rectangular dumplings fried to order, and filled with multiple configurations of pork, lamb, beef and vegetables. They're served by the *liǎng* (两; 50g), with one *liǎng* equal to three dumplings; they prefer you to order at least two *liǎng* (二两; *èr liǎng*) per filling.

Qìngfēng Steamed Dumpling Shop DUMPLINGS **$**
(庆丰包子铺; Qìngfēng Bāozi Pù; www.qing-feng.com; Jade Islet, Běihǎi Park; 北海公园; dumplings ¥3-16; ⏲9am-6.30pm; Ⓢ Line 6 to Beihai North or Nanluoguxiang, or Line 4 to Xisi) The best of the eating options at Běihǎi Park is this dumpling chain that does *bāozi* (包子; steamed meat buns) and *jiǎozi* (饺子; stuffed dumplings) among other Chinese mains.

Yáng Fāng Lamb Hotpot HOTPOT **$**
(羊坊涮肉; Yáng Fāng Shuàn Ròu; Map p310; 270 Gulou Dongdajie; 鼓楼东大街270号; broth ¥8-15, dips & sauces ¥2-5, raw ingredients ¥6-25; ⏲11am-11pm; Ⓢ Line 8 to Shichahai, exit A2) There are two main varieties of hotpot in China: the seriously spicy kind from the fire-breathing southwestern city of Chóngqìng, and the milder version, often served in an unusual conical brass pot heated by coals. Yáng Fāng is a salt-of-the-earth version of the latter, and is a real favourite with the locals round here.

First order the broth for your pot – clear (清汤锅底; *qīng tāng guōde;* ¥15), or spicy (辣锅底; *là guōde;* ¥20). Then ask for some sesame-paste dipping sauce (小料; *xiǎo liào;* ¥5); each diner should have one. And, if you fancy it, some freshly prepared chilli oil (鲜榨辣椒油; *xiān zhá là jiāo yóu;* ¥2) to mix into your dipping sauce; one bowl is enough for everyone to share.

Finally, select the raw ingredients to cook in your broth. Our favourites include wafer-thin lamb slices (鲜羊肉; *xiān yǎng ròu;* ¥26), lotus root slices (藕片; *ǒu piàn;* ¥8), tofu slabs (鲜豆腐; *xiān dòufu;* ¥6), sweet potato (红薯; *hóng shǔ;* ¥6) and spinach (菠菜; *bō cài;* ¥6). No English sign; no English menu; no English spoken.

★**Little Yúnnán** YUNNAN **$$**
(小云南; Xiǎo Yúnnán; Map p302; ☎010 6401 9498; 28 Donghuang Chenggen Beijie; 东皇城根北街28

DON'T MISS

PEKING DUCK

The city's signature dish is Peking Duck – thes are among our favourite spots to sample it:

Déyuán Roast Duck (德缘烤鸭店; Déyuán Kǎoyā Diàn; Map p302; ☎010 6308 5371; 57 Dazhalan Xijie; 大栅栏西街57号; peking duck ¥138, dishes from ¥35; ⏰10am-2pm & 4.30-9pm; ❄📶; Ⓢ Line 2 to Qianmen, exit C) The locals' choice and affordable. Unlike Běijīng's more civilised duckeries, this is a spot to crack open a cold Yanjing beer or three, loosen your belt, and eat till you burst.

Sìjì Mínfú (四季民福; Map p302; ☎010 6526 7369; 11 Nanchizi Dajie, beside Forbidden City East Gate; 南池子大街11; peking duck whole/half ¥198/108; ⏰10.30am-10.30pm; ❄📶👪; Ⓢ Line 1 to Tiananmen East, exit B) Overlooking the Forbidden City's moat, this branch of the upscale chain boasts some of the best birds in town.

Duck de Chine (全鸭季; Quányājì; ☎010 6521 2221; Courtyard 4, 1949 Hidden City, off Gongrentiyuchang Beilu, 工体北路4号; mains ¥78-488; ⏰11am-2pm & 5.30-10pm; Ⓢ Line 10 to Tuanjiehu, exit A or D) A slick and stylish operation using both Chinese and French duck-roasting methods to produce some standout duck dishes.

号; mains ¥26-60; ⏰10am-10pm; Ⓢ Lines 6, 8 to Nanluoguxiang, exit B or Line 5 to Zhangzizhonglu, exit D) Run by friendly staff and housed in a cute courtyard conversion, Little Yúnnán is one of Běijīng's more down-to-earth Yúnnán restaurants. The main room has a rustic feel, with wooden beams, flooring and furniture. Dishes include classic southwest China ingredients, with tea-infused creations as well as river fish, mushrooms, fried goat's cheese and *là ròu* (腊肉; cured pork – south China's answer to bacon).

Zhāng Māma SICHUAN $$

(张妈妈特色川味馆; Zhāng Māma Tèsè Chuānwèiguǎn; Map p310; 76 Jiaodaokou Nandajie; 交道口南大街76号; mains ¥18-78; ⏰11am-10.30pm; Ⓢ Line 5 to Beixinqiao, exit A) The original Zhāng Māma, on nearby Fensiting Hutong, was such a hit that you had to wait up to an hour for a table. At this larger branch, they've more than halved the wait, and it's worth it. This is arguably Běijīng's best-value Sìchuān restaurant.

The speciality is *málà xiāngguō* (麻辣香锅; ¥48 to ¥58), a fiery, chilli-laced witches brew of either chicken (香锅鸡; *xiāngguō jī*), prawns (香锅虾; *xiāngguō xiā*) or ribs (香锅排骨; *xiāngguō páigǔ*) with a variety of tasty vegetables added into the mix. One bowl is enough for two or three people. The twice-cooked pork (回锅肉; *huíguōròu*) is another highlight: smoky bacon slices with green chilli, vegies and fried dough for crunch. Also worth a try is the *dàndàn miàn* (担担面; spicy dry noodles; ¥8). No English menu, so don't be shy about pointing to what fellow diners are eating. Chances are it'll be spicy, but delicious.

Stuff'd INTERNATIONAL $$

(塞; Sāi; Map p310; ☎010 6407 6308; www.stuff-d.com; 9 Jianchang Hutong, off Guozijian Jie; 国子监街, 箭厂胡同9号; sausages from ¥30, pies ¥68, pizzas ¥68; ⏰11.30am-9.30pm; 📶; Ⓢ Line 2 to Andingmen or Lines 2, 5 to Yonghegong-Lama Temple, exit D) Handmade sausages and home-brewed beer (from ¥40). What more could you want? Set up by Arrow Factory brewery (which has an adjoining taproom out the back), this rustic *hútòng* space has a genial ambience – like a tiny English gastro pub if it were housed within a restored Chinese *píngfáng* (bungalow).

Jīn Dǐng Xuān CANTONESE $$

(金鼎轩; Map p310; ☎010 6429 6699; 77 Hepingli Xijie; 地坛南门和平里西街77号; dim sum ¥15-30, mains ¥30-100; ⏰24hr; Ⓢ Lines 2, 5 to Yonghegong-Lama Temple, exit A) Girdled in red neon, this raucous Chinese restaurant by the south gate of Dìtán Park offers four bustling floors of great-value Cantonese, dim sum and family-style dishes around the clock. The menu is tome-like and service is regimented, and while the fare on offer isn't gourmet, you won't leave unsatisfied. Expect to take a number and wait in line at busy periods.

Bǎihé Vegetarian Restaurant CHINESE $$

(百合素食; Bǎihé Sùshí; Map p310; 23 Caoyuan Hutong; 东直门内北小街草园胡同甲23号; mains ¥35-80, tea per cup/pot from ¥25/45; ⏰11am-10pm; 🥕; Ⓢ Lines 2, 13 to Dongzhimen, exit A, or Line 5 to Beixinqiao, exit B) Though the decor has seen better days, this peaceful, courtyard restaurant, which also serves as a teahouse, has a pleasant air of serenity and an all-vegetarian menu (with English translations), which includes imaginative mock-meat dishes as well as more conventional vegetable dishes and a range of tasty noodles.

Dàlǐ Courtyard YUNNAN $$$

(大理; Dàlǐ; Map p310; ☎010 8404 1430; 67 Xiaojingchang Hutong, Gulou Dongdajie; 鼓楼东大街小经厂胡同67号; set menu ¥150; ⊙noon-2pm & 6-10pm; Ⓢ Line 2 to Andingmen, exit D, or Line 5 to Beixinqiao, exit A) The charming *hútòng* setting in a restored courtyard makes this one of Běijīng's more pleasant places to dine, especially in summer when the glass roof is removed (from mid-May). Specialising in the subtle flavours of Yúnnán cuisine, there's no menu; instead, you pay ¥150 per person (drinks are extra), and enjoy a greatest hits round-up of southwest Chinese fare.

TRB Hutong EUROPEAN $$$

(Map p302; ☎010 8400 2232; www.trb-cn.com; Sōngzhù Temple, 23 Shatanbei Jie, off Wusi Dajie; 五四大街沙滩北街23号, 嵩祝寺; 3/4/5/6 courses ¥388/488/588/688; ⊙11am-3pm & 5.30-11pm; ❄ 📶; Ⓢ Lines 6, 8 to Nanluoguxiang, exit B or Lines 5, 6 to Dongsi, exit E) Housed within the delightfully renovated grounds of a disused, centuries-old temple, this is Běijīng's most extravagant fine-dining experience for those seeking a special occasion splurge. Food is contemporary European fine dining with a French leaning – think lobster, poached scallops, slow-cooked veal and decadent desserts. TRB also boasts one of the most extensive wine lists in town and can mix a serious cocktail.

Drinking & Nightlife

Sānlǐtún is the best area for a wild night out, while the lakes at Hòuhǎi are lined with fun, but noisy, neon-lit bars.

★Great Leap Brewing BREWERY

(GLB #6; 大跃啤酒; Dàyuè Píjiǔ; Map p310; www.greatleapbrewing.com; 6 Doujiao Hutong; 豆角胡同6号; beers ¥25-50; ⊙2-11pm Sun-Thu, to midnight Fri & Sat; Ⓢ Line 8 to Shichahai, exit C) Běijīng's original microbrewery, this refreshingly simple courtyard bar, set up by American beer-enthusiast Carl Setzer, is housed in a hard-to-find, but beautifully renovated, 100-year-old Qing-dynasty courtyard and serves up a wonderful selection of unique ales made largely from locally sourced ingredients. Sip on familiar favourites such as pale ales, or sample China-inspired tipples like Honey Ma, brewed with lip-tingling Sìchuān peppercorns.

Voyage Coffee COFFEE

(Map p310; 80 Beiluogu Xiang; 北锣鼓巷80号; ⊙9am-9pm; 📶; Ⓢ Line 2 to Andingmen or Line 5 to Beixinqiao, exit C) Slotting in effortlessly along this happening strip is this chic third-wave coffee roaster decked out in exposed brick and blonde wood. Grab a stool to enjoy single-origin Chemex pour-overs, espressos or eight-hour cold brews. The VPN-enabled wi-fi makes it a good workspace.

Jing-A Brewing MICROBREWERY

(京A Brewing Co.; www.jingabrewing.com; Courtyard 4, 1949 Hidden City, off Gongrentiyuchang Beilu; 工体北路4号院; beers ¥40-60; ⊙5pm-1am Mon-Thu, 4pm-2am Fri, 11am-2am Sat, to midnight Sun; 📶; Ⓢ Line 10 to Tuanjiehu, exit A or D) Set within the classy red-brick 1949 precinct next door to posh Peking duck eatery Duck de Chine (p313), Jing-A has earned its reputation as a producer of some of Běijīng's best (and most experimental) craft beers, with a fantastic selection of ales using local ingredients. This location has around 20 beers on tap, featuring a mix of core and seasonal ales, and a few guest breweries.

★Tiki Bungalow COCKTAIL BAR

(Map p310; 101, Courtyard E, 46 Fangjia Hutong; 方家胡同46号院E 101; cocktails ¥60; ⊙7pm-1am Sun-Thu, 7pm-2am Fri-Sat; 📶; Ⓢ Line 5 to Beixinqiao, exit A) From the fake palms and Exotica soundtrack to the carved totem poles and Polynesian knick-knacks, this is your quintessential tiki bar down to the finest detail. Now across the alley from its original location, the bar is wider, the drinks list longer, and prices slightly higher than before. However, they still mix the most extravagant rum-based cocktails in Běijīng. You can only enter from Jiaodaokou Bei Santiao, one *hútòng* to the south.

★Dada CLUB

(达达; Dádá; Map p310; Bldg B, 206 Gulou Dongdajie; 鼓楼东大街206号; entry from ¥50, beers from ¥20; ⊙9pm-5am; 📶; Ⓢ Line 8 to Shichahai, exit A2) Since this zeitgeisty Shànghǎi club touched down in Běijīng in 2012, it's evolved into the capital's most credible spot for serious electronic-music fans, while remaining unpretentious and dive-y enough for the casual party-goer. By combining a thoughtfully left-field line-up of international performers at weekends with a commitment to keeping entry at around ¥50 or under, Dada delivers dance-floor fireworks week in, week out.

DON'T MISS

BĚIJĪNG'S HÚTÒNG

Běijīng's medieval genotype is most discernible down the city's leafy *hútòng* (胡同; narrow alleyways). The spirit and soul of the city lives and breathes among these charming and ragged lanes where a warm sense of community and hospitality survives.

After Chinggis (Genghis) Khaan's army reduced the city of Běijīng to rubble, the new city was redesigned with *hútòng*. By the Qing dynasty more than 2000 such passageways riddled the city, leaping to around 6000 by the 1950s; now the figure has drastically dwindled to somewhere above 1000.

Old walled *sìhéyuàn* (courtyards) are the building blocks of this delightful universe. Many are still lived in and hum with activity. From spring to autumn, men collect outside their gates, drinking beer, playing chess, smoking and chewing the fat. Inside, scholar trees soar aloft, providing shade and a nesting ground for birds. Flocks of pigeons whirl through the Běijīng skies overhead, bred by locals and housed in coops often buried away within the *hútòng*. More venerable courtyards are fronted by large, thick red doors, outside of which perch either a pair of Chinese lions or drum stones.

To savour Běijīng's courtyard ambience, enjoy a beer at **Great Leap Brewing** (p314) or a meal at **Dàlǐ Courtyard** (p314), before sleeping it all off at **Courtyard 7** (p311). Alternatively, **Bike Běijīng** (康多自行车租赁; Kāngduō Zìxíngchē Zūlìn; Map p302; ☎010 6526 5857; www.bikebeijing.com; 81 Beiheyan Dajie; 北河沿大街81号; ⏰8am-8pm; Ⓢ Lines 6, 8 to Nanluoguxiang, exit B, or Line 5 to Zhangzizhonglu, exit D) offers guided cycle tours of *hútòng* areas, or guides from the **China Culture Center** (Kent Center; ☎weekdays 010 6432 9341, weekends 010 8420 0671; www.chinaculturecenter.org; Victoria Gardens D4, Cháoyáng Gongyuan Xilu; 朝阳公园西路, 维多利亚花园D4; Ⓢ Line 14 to Zaoying or Line 10 to Tuanjiehu, exit C) can take you on foot.

Láijīnyǔxuān Teahouse TEAHOUSE
(来今雨轩茶社; Láijīnyǔxuān Cháshè; Map p302; ☎010 6601 9978; inside Zhōngshān Park; 中山公园, Zhōngshān Gōngyuán; tea per cup from ¥40; ⏰9am-9pm; Ⓢ Line 1 to Tian'anmen West, exit B) This 100-year-old teahouse, set in the east corner of the Forbidden City's Zhōngshān Park, has a large terrace and is a pleasant place to sample a cup of China's finest. A number of well-known writers, intellectuals and revolutionaries used to hang out here. These days it's mostly tourists, of course.

Soloist Coffee CAFE
(Map p302; www.soloistcoffee.com; 39 Yangmeizhu Xiejie; 杨梅竹斜街39号; coffee from ¥30; ⏰noon-8pm; Ⓢ Line 2 to Qianmen, exit B or C) Partway down a gentrifying *hútòng* is this classy coffee roaster and cafe, which started out here as a pop-up during the annual Běijīng Design Week in 2014. Supposedly once a public bathhouse (the building is decades old), it now deals out liquid relief of the caffeinated kind, hawking a gourmand's selection of single origin coffees, nitro lattes and cold brew.

Nina COCKTAIL BAR
(Map p310; ☎139 1111 0763; 66 Beiluoguxiang; 北锣鼓巷66号; cocktails from ¥40; ⏰6pm-2am Mon-Thu, 6pm-late Fri-Sat, noon-late Sun; 📶) Set up for *aperitivo* with a menu that boasts spritz, snacks and seven variations on the Negroni cocktail, this charmingly simple *hútòng* bar has Italian and Chinese owners, including one from Napoli, lending tasty credence to the bar's array of pizza bites. Also served are *cartoccio:* crispy fried seafood, gooey cheese balls and more, served in paper cones.

Pass By Bar BAR
(过客; Guòkè; Map p310; 108 Nanluogu Xiang; 南锣鼓巷108号; ⏰10am-2am; 📶; Ⓢ Lines 6, 8 to Nanluoguxiang, exit E) One of Běijīng's longest-running bars, Pass By is a local institution and offers respite from tourist-clogged Nanluogu Xiang. Run by common owners of NBeer, here you'll get a selection from six of their beers on tap, as well as 100-odd brands in the fridge. There's an old-school backpackers' menu of pizzas, burgers and local dishes served in its light- and plant-filled courtyard or rooftop terrace.

Mài Bar BAR
(麦; Mài; Map p310; 40 Beiluogu Xiang; 北锣鼓巷40号; cocktails from ¥45, beers from ¥30; ⏰6pm-2am; Ⓢ Lines 2, 8 to Guloudajie, exit G) An intimate affair, Mài Bar hides away in part of an old *hútòng* courtyard, comprising a worn wooden bar, a scatter of candlelit tables and a narrow strip of outdoor seating. Cocktails are competently concocted by bow-tied

bartenders, and come with crunchy nibbles and hot towels, or choose a craft bottled beer from the amply stocked fridge.

Bookworm CAFE
(书虫; Shūchóng; ☎010 6586 9507; www.beijingbookworm.com; Bldg 4, Nansanlitun Lu; 南三里屯路4号楼; ⏲9am-midnight; 📶; Ⓢ Line 10 to Tuanjiehu, exit A or D) A combination of a bar, cafe, restaurant, library and bookshop, the Bookworm is a Běijīng institution and a mainstay of the capital's cultural life. Much more than just a cafe, there are 16,000-plus books here you can browse while sipping your coffee. For freelancers, it's a popular workspace. The food is reasonably priced (mains from ¥60), if uninspired, but there's a decent wine list.

☆ Entertainment

Húguǎng Guild Hall PEKING OPERA
(湖广会馆; Húguǎng Huìguǎn; ☎010 6351 8284; www.theatrebeijing.com/theatres/huguang_guild_hall; 3 Hufang Lu; 虎坊桥路3号; tickets ¥180-680, opera museum ¥10; ⏲performances 6.30-7.30pm & 8-9pm, opera museum 9am-5.30pm; Ⓢ Line 7 to Hufangqiao, exit C) The most historic and atmospheric place in town for a night of Peking opera. The interior is magnificent, coloured in red, green and gold, and decked out with tables and a stone floor, while balconies surround the canopied stage. Opposite the theatre, there's a very small opera **museum** displaying operatic scores, old catalogues and other paraphernalia.

Tiānqiáo Acrobatics Theatre ACROBATICS
(天桥杂技剧场; Tiānqiáo Zájì Jùchǎng; ☎010 6303 7449; 95 Tianqiao Shichang Jie; 天桥市场街95号; tickets ¥180-380; ⏲performances 5.30pm; Ⓢ Line 7 to Zhushikou, exit D) West of the Temple of Heaven Park, this 100-year-old theatre offers one of Běijīng's best acrobatic displays, a one-hour show performed by the Běijīng Acrobatic Troupe. Less touristy than the other venues, the theatre's small size means you can get very close to the action. The high-wire display is awesome. The entrance is on Beiwei Lu, along the eastern side of the building.

National Centre for the Performing Arts CLASSICAL MUSIC
(国家大剧院, Guójiā Dàjùyuàn; Map p302; ☎010 6655 0000; www.chncpa.org/ens; 2 Xichang'an Jie; 西长安街2号; tickets ¥80-880; ⏲performances 7.30pm; Ⓢ Line 1 to Tian'anmen West, exit C) Sometimes called the National Grand Theatre, this spectacular Paul Andreu–designed dome, known to Beijingers as the 'Alien Egg', attracts as many architectural tourists as it does music fans. But it's *the* place to listen to classical music from home and abroad. You can also watch ballet, opera and classical Chinese dance here.

Forbidden City Concert Hall CLASSICAL MUSIC
(中山公园音乐堂; Zhōngshān Gōngyuán Yīnyuè Táng; Map p302; ☎010 6559 8285; www.fcchbj.com; Zhōngshān Park; 中山公园内; tickets ¥30-880; ⏲performances 7.30pm; Ⓢ Line 1 to Tian'anmen West, exit B) Located on the eastern side of Zhōngshān Park, this is a wonderfully romantic venue for performances of classical and traditional Chinese music, as well as highly rated musicians from abroad. It's also one of the city's best venues for acoustics.

★ **Jiāng Hú** LIVE MUSIC
(江湖酒吧; Jiāng Hú Jiǔbā; Map p310; 7 Dongmianhua Hutong; 东棉花胡同7号; live music performances ¥30-50; ⏲7pm-2am, closed Mon; Ⓢ Lines 6, 8 to Nanluoguxiang, exit F) One of the coolest places to hear Chinese indie and rock bands, Jiāng Hú, run by a trombone-playing, music-loving manager, is housed in a small courtyard and packs in the punters on a good night. Intimate, cool, and a decent spot for a *hútòng* drink, even when no bands are playing. Beers from ¥30.

🛍 Shopping

Cháoyáng district has some of the swankiest malls in town, many of which can be found in the eye-catching, ultra-modern shopping zone known as **Sānlǐtún Village** (三里屯太古里; 19 Sanlitun Lu; 三里屯路19号; ⏲10am-10pm; Ⓢ Line 10 to Tuanjiehu, exit A). Cháoyáng is also home to the popular (and crowded) **Silk Market** (秀水市场; Xiùshuǐ Shìchǎng; 14 Dongdaqiao Lu; 东大桥路14号; ⏲9.30am-9pm; Ⓢ Line 1 to Yonganli, exit A1), which will test your bartering skills, and your patience, to the full. The silk, sold on the 3rd floor, is one of the few genuine items on sale here.

Prestigious, but these days rather old-fashioned, the part-pedestrianised **Wangfujing Dajie** (王府井; Map p302; Ⓢ Line 1 to Wangfujing, exit C2 or B) boasts a strip of stores selling well-known, midrange brands, and a number of tacky souvenir outlets. At its south end, **Oriental Plaza** (东方广场; Dōngfāng Guǎngchǎng; Map p302; ☎010 8518 6363; 1 Dongchang'an Jie; 东长安街1号; ⏲10am-10.30pm; Ⓢ Line 1 to Wangfujing, exit B) is a top-quality, modern shopping mall. Further north, just before the pedestrianised section ends, is the well-stocked **Foreign Languages Bookstore** (外文书店; Wàiwén Shūdiàn; Map p302; 235 Wangfujing Dajie; 王府井大街235号; ⊙9.30am-9pm; S Line 5 to Dengshikou).

The old alley **Nanluogu Xiang** (南锣鼓巷; Map p302; Nanluogu Xiang; S Lines 6, 8 to Nanluoguxiang, exit E) is an insatiably hectic strip of shops, cafes, eateries and hotels (and a dwindling number of bars). It was given a complete makeover in 2016.

Ruìfúxiáng SILK, CLOTHING

(瑞蚨祥丝绸店; Ruìfúxiáng Sīchóudiàn; Map p302; ☎010 6303 5313; 5 Dazhalan Jie; 大栅栏街5号; ⊙9.30am-8pm; S Line 2 to Qianmen, exit B) Housed in a historic building on Dashilar, Ruìfúxiáng has been trading here since 1893 and is still one of the best places in town to browse for silk. There's an incredible selection of Shāndōng silk, brocade and satin-silk. The silk starts at ¥168 a metre, although most of the fabric is more expensive. Ready-made, traditional Chinese clothing is sold on the 2nd floor.

Ruìfúxiáng also has an outlet at **Dianmenwai Dajie** (瑞蚨祥; Ruìfúxiáng; Map p310; 50 Di'anmen Waidajie; 地安门外大街50号; ⊙10am-8.30pm; S Line A to Shichahai, exit A2).

Măliándào Tea Market TEA

(马连道茶城; Măliándào Cháchéng; ☎010 6343 8550; www.mldteamall.com; 11 Maliandao Lu; 马连道路11号; ⊙8.30am-6pm; S Lines 7 to Wanzi) Măliándào is the largest tea market in northern China and home to, if not all the tea in China, then an awful lot of it. There are brews from all over the country here, including *pŭ'ĕr* and oolong, while Maliandao Lu has hundreds of tea shops, where prices for tea and tea sets are lower than in tourist areas.

Sanfo SPORTS & OUTDOORS

(三夫户外; Sānfū Hùwài; ☎010 6201 5550; www.sanfo.com/en; 3-4 Madian Nancun; 北三环中路马甸南村4之3—4号; ⊙9am-9pm; S Line 10 to Jiandemen, exit D) With three shops grouped together in this location, Sanfo is the place to come for outdoor wear, climbing and camping gear, as well as surfboards, mountain bikes and other adventure-sports gear. It's something of a nexus for Běijīng's hikers and climbers – Sanfo organises weekend trips – and is a good place to pick up information, plus any supplies for walking the Great Wall.

Information

EMERGENCY

Ambulance ☎120

Fire ☎119

Police ☎110

Police / Emergency (English language hotline) ☎010 6525 5486

INTERNET ACCESS

Hotels Almost all hotels and guesthouses provide free wi-fi, with only a few charging a daily rate. Some older hotels have broadband wired internet. Youth hostels have free wi-fi as well as computer terminals, but usually levy a small internet charge (around ¥10 per hour) to use them.

Internet Cafes Internet cafes (网吧; *wăngbā*) are generally easy to find, although some are tucked away down side streets and above shops. They are generally open 24 hours. Standard rates are ¥3 to ¥5 per hour, although there are usually different priced zones within each internet cafe – the common area *(pŭtōng qū)* is the cheapest. Many internet cafes do not allow the use of a USB stick.

Internet cafes are required to see your passport before allowing you to go online, and a record of your visit may be made. You will be filmed or digitally photographed at reception by a rectangular metal box that sits on the counter of each licensed internet cafe in town. Usually you will then be given a card with a number *(zhèngjiànhào)*

DON'T MISS

PĀNJIĀYUÁN MARKET

Hands down the best place in Běijīng to shop for arts, crafts and antiques is **Pānjiāyuán Market** (潘家园古玩市场; Pānjiāyuán Gŭwán Shìchăng; west of Panjiayuan Qiao; 潘家园桥西侧; ⊙8.30am-6pm Mon-Fri, 4.30am-6pm Sat & Sun; S Line 10 to Panjiayuan, exit B). Some stalls open every day, but the market is at its biggest and most lively on weekends, when you can find everything from calligraphy and cigarette-ad posters to Buddha heads, ceramics, Qing dynasty–style furniture, Tibetan carpets and authentic Cultural Revolution propaganda posters.

Pānjiāyuán hosts around 3000 dealers and up to 50,000 visitors a day, all hunting for treasures. The market is chaotic and can be difficult if you find crowds or hard bargaining intimidating. Make a few rounds to compare prices and weigh it up before forking out for something.

To get here, come out of exit B at Panjiayuan subway station, then walk west for 200m to find the main entrance to the market.

and password (*mìmǎ* or *kǒulìng*) to enter into the on-screen box before you can start.

Wi-fi Cafes Almost all cafes and most Western-style bars offer free wi-fi. Be prepared for occasionally slow connections and the sudden disappearance of sites for periods of time.

Censorship Some politically sensitive websites and many of the most popular social-media websites, such as Twitter, Facebook and YouTube, are blocked in China, as is Gmail. To access such websites while here you will need to run your laptop or smartphone through a VPN (virtual private network). Bear in mind that some popular VPN services are themselves blocked, so ask around or check online before committing to a service.

MEDICAL SERVICES

Pharmacies (药店; *yàodiàn*) are identified by a green cross and are widespread.

Běijīng United Family Hospital (和睦家医疗; Hémùjiā Yīliáo; ☎4008 919191, 24hr emergency hotline 010 5927 7120; http://beijing.ufh.com.cn; 2 Jiangtai Lu; 将台路2号; ⏲24hr; Ⓢ Line 14 to Jiangtai, exit A or B) Can provide alternative medical treatments, along with a comprehensive range of inpatient and outpatient care. There is a critical-care unit. Emergency room staffed by expat physicians.

International SOS (国际SOS医务诊所; Guójì SOS Yīwù Zhěnsuǒ; ☎24hr alarm centre 010 6462 9100, clinic appointments 010 6462 9112, dental appointments 010 6462 0333; www.internationalsos.com; Suite 105, Wing 1, Kunsha Bldg, 16 Xinyuanli, off Xin Donglu, Cháoyáng; ⏲8am-8pm; Ⓢ Line 10 to Liangmaqiao, exit D) Offering 24-hour emergency medical care, with a high-quality clinic with English-speaking staff. Dental check-up ¥620; medical consultation ¥1320.

Peking Union Medical College Hospital (PUMCH; 协和医院; Xiéhé Yīyuàn; Map p302; ☎010 6915 6699, emergency 010 6915 9180; www.pumch.cn; 1 Shuaifuyuan; 东城区 王府井帅府园1号; ⏲24hr; Ⓢ Lines 1, 5 to Dongdan, exit A) Open 24 hours and with a full range of facilities for inpatient and outpatient care, plus a pharmacy. Head for International Medical Services, a wing reserved for foreigners which has English-speaking staff and telephone receptionists.

MONEY

Most ATMs accept foreign cards. Most large banks change money. Credit and debit cards are now used more widely than before, especially in hotels, shopping malls and upmarket restaurants, but cash remains king in Běijīng, so carry money with you at all times.

Bank of China (中国银行; Zhōngguó Yínháng; Map p302; ☎010 6513 2214; 19 Dong'anmen Dajie; 东安门大街19号; ⏲8.30am-5.30pm) One of dozens of branches around Běijīng with money-changing facilities.

HSBC (汇丰银行; Huìfēng Yínháng; Map p302; www.hsbc.com.cn; 1st fl, Block A, COFCO Plaza, 8 Jianguomennei Dajie; ⏲9am-5pm Mon-Fri, 10am-6pm Sat) One of around 15 branches in the capital, not including several standalone ATMs.

POST

Large post offices are generally open daily between 9am and 6pm. You can post letters via your hotel reception desk, or at green post boxes around town.

Letters and parcels marked 'Poste Restante, Běijīng Main Post Office' will arrive at the **International Post Office** (中国邮政; Zhōngguó Yóuzhèng; ☎010 6512 8114; Jianguomen Beidajie; 建国门北大街; ⏲8.30am-6pm; Ⓢ Lines 1, 2 to Jianguomen, exit B), 200m north of Jianguomen station. Outsized parcels going overseas should be sent from here (packaging can be bought at the post office); smaller parcels (up to around 20kg) can go from smaller post offices. Both outgoing and incoming packages will be opened and inspected. If you're sending a parcel, don't seal the package until you've had it inspected.

Letters take around a week to reach most overseas destinations. China charges extra for registered mail, but offers cheaper postal rates for printed matter, small packets, parcels, bulk mailings and so on.

Express Mail Service (EMS; 快递; *kuàidì*) is available for registered deliveries to domestic and international destinations from most post offices around town. Prices are very reasonable.

TOURIST INFORMATION

Tourist information offices are aimed at domestic tourists. Foreigners are better off using hotels or, better still, hostels.

Běijīng Tourist Information Centres have branches around the city, including at **Běijīng Railway Station** (Map p302; ☎010 6528 4848; 16 Laoqianju Hutong; tours ¥260-400; ⏲8.30am-6pm; Ⓢ Line 2 to Beijing Railway Station, exit B) and the **Hòuhǎi Lakes** (Map p302; 49 Di'anmenxi Dajie; 地安门西大街49号, Hòuhǎi Lakes; ⏲9am-6pm; Ⓢ Line 6 to Beihai North, exit B, or Lines 6, 8 to Nanluguxiang, exit E); this last branch can also arrange rickshaw tours of the *hùtòng* with English-speaking riders.

English skills at the information centres are limited and information is basic, but you can grab a free tourist map of the city and handfuls of free literature.

VISA EXTENSIONS

The Foreign Affairs Branch of the local PSB – the police force – handles visa extensions. The visa office at the **PSB main office** (北京公安局出入境管理处; Běijīngshì Gōng'ānjú Chūrùjìng

Guǎnlǐchù; Map p310; ☎010 8400 2101, 010 8402 0101; www.bjgaj.gov.cn; 2 Andingmen Dongdajie; 东城区安定门东大街2号; ⏲9am-5pm Mon-Sat; Ⓢ Line 2, 5 to Yonghegong-Lama Temple, exit B) is on the 2nd floor, accessed from the North 2nd Ring Rd. You can also apply for a residence permit here. You should apply for your visa extension at least seven days before your current visa expires, but this rule is not always enforced. Expect to wait up to five days for your visa extension to be processed.

Getting There & Away

TRAIN

International Tickets

Moscow, Ulaanbaatar and Harbin (Hā'ěrbīn) trains depart from, and arrive at **Běijīng Railway Station** (北京火车站; Běijīng Huǒchēzhàn; ☎010 5101 9999; Ⓢ Beijing train station), 2km east of Tiān'ānmén Sq. **Běijīng West Train Station** (北京西站; Běijīng Xī Zhàn; ☎010 5182 6253; Ⓢ Beijing West Railway Station) has trains for Hong Kong and Vietnam. Both these train stations are connected to the subway system.

For Mongolia, Russia and North Korea, buy tickets at the helpful office of the state-owned **CITS** (China International Travel Service; 中国国际旅行社; Zhōngguó Guójì Lǚxíngshè; Map p302; ☎010 6512 0507; Běijīng International Hotel, 9 Jianguomennei Dajie, Dōngchéng; ⏲9am-noon & 1.30-5pm Mon-Fri, to noon Sat; Ⓢ Lines 1, 2 to Jianguomen, exit A).

If you want to stop in Dàtóng on the way to Ulaanbaatar, it is possible to buy a Dàtóng–Ulaanbaatar ticket from CITS, then go to the Běijīng Railway Station and buy a separate ticket for Běijīng to Dàtóng. It can be difficult to snag sleeper tickets, but hard-seat tickets can usually be bought. Alternatively, there are frequent bus services to Dàtóng from Liùlǐqiáo Long-distance Bus Station.

For Vietnam, buy tickets at the office of **CRTS** (China Railway Travel Service; 中国铁道旅行社; Zhōngguó Tiědào Lǚxíngshè; ☎010 5182 6541, 010 5184 0985; 20 Beifengwo Lu; 北蜂窝路20号; ⏲8.30am-5.30pm; Ⓢ Military Museum). There's no English sign, but it's opposite the easy-to-spot Tiānyòu Hotel (天佑大厦; Tiānyòu Dàxià). Walk straight out of exit C1 of Military Museum subway station, take the first right and CRTS will be on your left (10 minutes).

For help with booking a tour to North Korea, Běijīng's leading tour company to the area is **Koryo Tours** (☎Běijīng 010 6416 7544; www.koryogroup.com; 27 Beisanlitun Nan; Ⓢ Line 2 to Dongsi Shitiao, exit C, or Line 10 to Tuanjiehu, exit A).

Premium Services

You can travel Běijīng to Moscow (莫斯科; Mòsīkē) via two routes:

Trans-Mongolian Railway train (K3; hard sleeper/deluxe ¥3500/5600, six days) Via Ulaanbaatar (hard sleeper/deluxe ¥1259/1849, 27 hours) leaves every Wednesday at 11.22am.

Trans-Manchurian Railway train (K19; hard sleeper/deluxe ¥3900/6000) leaves every Saturday at 11pm.

Also serving Ulaanbaatar is train K23 (¥1222/1888, 27 hours), which leaves on Tuesdays at 8.05am.

Domestic Tickets

Běijīng has three major train stations, but most trains for destinations along the Trans-Mongolian/Manchurian routes leave from Běijīng Railway Station (one bullet train to Harbin leaves from Běijīng South Train Station, and a few night-time trains to Dàtóng leave from Běijīng West Train Station).

There are no longer special ticket counters for foreigners, so you'll have to join the masses in the ticket queues at the station; arm yourself with some key Chinese phrases, and plenty of patience.

Now that tickets can be bought online (www.12306.cn; in Chinese), it's almost impossible to buy sleeper tickets on the day of departure, so try to buy your tickets in advance (they can be bought up to 30 days in advance). Hard-seat tickets, and seats on bullet trains, are easier to get, but it's still advisable to buy them in advance.

Youth hostels and hotels usually offer a ticket buying service, for a commission of around ¥50 per ticket. Alternatively, try the reliable China DIY Travel (www.china-diy-travel.com), which, for a US$10 commission, will prebook tickets for you to pick up at the train station in person.

AIR

Běijīng Capital International Airport (北京首都国际机场; Běijīng Shǒudū Guójì Jīchǎng; PEK; ☎010-6454 1100; http://en.bcia.com.cn) has three terminals. Terminal 3 (三号航站楼; *sān hào hángzhànlóu*) deals with most long-haul flights, although international flights also use Terminal 2 (二号航站楼; *èr hào hángzhànlóu*). Both are connected to the slick Airport Express, which links to Běijīng's subway system. The smaller Terminal 1 (一号航站楼; *yī hào hángzhànlóu*) is a 10-minute walk from Terminal 2. Free 24-hour shuttle buses connect all three terminals.

For good deals on flights to and from Běijīng, try Ctrip (www.ctrip.com) or eLong (www.elong.net).

BUS

No international buses leave from Běijīng.

Getting Around

TO/FROM THE AIRPORT

The **Airport Express** (机场快轨; Jīchǎng Kuàiguǐ; one-way ¥25; S Lines 2, 13 to Dongzhimen, exit B), also written as ABC (Airport Běijīng City), is quick and convenient and links terminals 2 and 3 to Běijīng's subway system at Sanyuanqiao station (Line 10) and Dongzhimen station (Lines 2 and 13). Avoid catching one of the waiting taxis on the road beside the Airport Express at Dongzhimen (not an official taxi rank). They invariably seek to overcharge tourists by not using the meter. Train times are as follows: Terminal 3 (6.21am to 10.51pm); Terminal 2 (6.35am to 11.10pm); Dongzhimen (6am to 10.30pm).

There are 17 different routes for the airport **shuttle bus** (机场巴士; Jīchǎng Bāshì; one way ¥15.50-30), including those listed here. They all leave from all three terminals and run from around 5am to midnight.

Line 3 To Běijīng train station (北京站; Běijīng Zhàn), via Dōngzhímén (东直门), Dōngsì Shítiáo (东四十条) and Cháoyángmén (朝阳门)

Line 7 To Běijīng west train station (西站; xī zhàn)

Line 10 To Běijīng south train station (南站; nán zhàn)

A taxi should cost ¥90 to ¥120 from the airport to the city centre; bank on it taking 40 minutes to one hour to get into town. Ignore unofficial drivers who may approach you as you exit customs and join the line for an official cab. When you get into the taxi, make sure the driver uses the meter (打表; *dǎ biǎo*). Have the name of your hotel written down in Chinese to show the driver. Very few drivers speak any English.

BICYCLE

Though it has largely been superseded by China's tidal wave of bike-sharing apps such as **Ofo** and **Mobike** (for which you will you need a Chinese bank account tied to a Chinese online payment solution, such as Alipay), Běijīng has an older bike-sharing scheme that can more readily be used by visitors. To use the red and white bikes, which, unlike the new apps, have to be docked and undocked from parking hubs outside central subway stations and on busy main streets, you must have an ordinary Běijīng travel card (refundable deposit ¥20) that is activated for bike-rental use.

To do that, head to either exit A2 of Tiantan Dongmen subway station or the kiosk just outside exit A of Dongzhimen subway station (marked with a bicycle logo). Both are only open Monday to Friday from 9.30am to 11.30am and from 2pm to 4pm. You will need your passport and a ¥400 deposit to activate the card for bike use, and the Běijīng travel card must also have at least ¥30 of credit.

Swipe your card at one of the bike sharing hubs to get a bike; then swipe it again when you put it back. Note that when swiping your card, don't remove it until you hear a click. Bike use is free for the first hour, so if you use them cleverly, swapping bikes at another kiosk before your hour is up, it means free bikes. After the first hour, it's ¥1 per hour to begin with, before it starts rising in price to ¥2, ¥3 or ¥4 per hour, depending on how long you keep the bike for.

PUBLIC TRANSPORT

The **Běijīng subway system** (地铁; Dìtiě; www.bjsubway.com; per trip ¥3-8; ⏲ 6am-11pm) is modern, safe, cheap and easy to use. It does get crowded, though. Fares are ¥3 to ¥8, depending on how far you are travelling. Get hold of a travel card (refundable deposit ¥20) if you don't want to queue for tickets each time you travel. The travel card also gets you a 50% discount on all bus journeys within the municipality of Běijīng.

The Metroman smartphone app reveals the Běijīng subway map in all its ever-expanding glory, with stations listed in both English and Chinese.

TAXI

Taxis (出租车; *chūzūchē*) are everywhere, although finding one can be a problem during rush hour, rainstorms and between 8pm and 10pm – prime time for people heading home after eating out.

Flag fall is ¥13, and lasts for 3km. After that it's ¥2.3 per kilometre. Rates increase slightly after 11pm.

It's rare for drivers to speak any English, so it's important to have the name and address of where you want to go written down in Chinese characters. Remember to keep your hotel's business card on you so you can get home at the end of the night.

Most Běijīng taxi drivers are honest and use the meter (打表; *dǎ biǎo*). If they refuse, get out and find another cab. The exception is for long, out-of-town trips to, say, the Great Wall, where prices are agreed (but not paid for) beforehand.

China's official taxi hailing app, Didi Dache (滴滴打车), which acquired Uber's China operations in 2016, now has an English-language version with features that include 'canned' messages you can send to drivers that are translated automatically. Using it requires a Chinese phone number and a WeChat payment account, although the company was in the process of adapting its service to accept foreign phone numbers and credit cards at time of research.

AROUND BĚIJĪNG

Great Wall of China 长城

China's most famous landmark, and one of the world's superlative human-made sights, the Great Wall snakes its way across northern China for almost 9000km, but nowhere beats Běijīng as a base for mounting your assault. Scattered throughout the municipality are more than a dozen fragmented stretches, from the perfectly chiselled to the charmingly dilapidated. You can get to them by bus, by train, by taxi...even by bicycle. And the adventurous can hike along it for days. The question isn't whether to see the Great Wall; it's how.

History

China's first sovereign emperor, Emperor Qin Shihuang, is credited with the 'original' construction of the Great Wall between 221 and 207 BC. He accomplished this feat by reconstructing and linking the ruins of older walls, which had been built by the vassal states under the Zhou dynasty in the 7th century BC. The result was a magnificent 4800km stretch of wall, which was meant to keep out the marauding nomads in the north (Huns, Turks and Mongols). The effort required hundreds of thousands of workers, many of them political prisoners.

By the collapse of the Qin, the Great Wall had already started to crumble due to years of neglect. Emperor Han Wu-Di once again undertook the task of rebuilding the existing wall, and extending it 480km further west into the Gobi Desert. During this period, the wall served mainly as an elevated highway, along which men and equipment could be transported across mountainous terrain. The stronger, bricked wall that you see today is largely a product of the Ming dynasty (1368–1644).

Mùtiányù 慕田峪

Famed for its Ming-era guard towers and excellent views, the 3km-long section of wall at **Mùtiányù** (慕田峪长城; Mùtiányù Chángchéng; adult ¥45; ⏲7am-7pm Apr-Oct, 7.30am-6.30pm Nov-Mar), northeast of Běijīng in Huáiróu County, is largely a recently restored Ming-dynasty structure that was built upon an earlier Northern Qi-dynasty edifice.

With 26 watchtowers, the wall is impressive and manageable, with most hawking reserved to the lower levels (the further you get away from Mùtiányù central the better). It's actually possible to hike from Mùtiányù all the way west to **Huánghuā** and the front section of **Jiànkòu**.

From the gargantuan ticket office at Mùtiányù, shuttle buses (¥15) run the 3km to the main entrance, from where three or four stepped pathways lead up to the wall itself. There's also a **cable car** (缆车; Lǎn Chē; one-way/return ¥100/120, kids half-price), a **chairlift** (索道; Suǒdào; one-way ¥100, with toboggan ¥120), called a 'ropeway' on the signs here, and a **toboggan ride** (滑道; Huá Dào; one-way ¥100, with chairlift ¥120), making this ideal for those who can't manage too many steps, or who have kids in tow.

Sleeping & Eating

There's a cluster of village guesthouses, with English signs, about 1km downhill from the Mùtiányù entrance. Expect to pay anything from ¥100 to ¥300 for an en suite room. For something more comfortable, reserve a room at the lovely **Brickyard Eco Retreat** (瓦厂; Wǎ Chǎng; ☎010 6162 6506; www.brickyardatmutianyu.com; Běigōu Village, Huáiróu District; 怀柔区渤海镇北沟村; r incl breakfast ¥1040-4745; ❄📶) 🍃 about 2km away.

Getting There & Away

From Běijīng's Dōngzhímén Wai bus stand, bus 867 makes a special detour to Mùtiányù twice every morning (¥16, 2½ hours, 7am and 8.30am, 15 March to 15 November only) and returns from Mùtiányù twice each afternoon (2pm and 4pm). Otherwise, go via Huáiróu: from Dōngzhímén Transport Hub (Dōngzhímén Shūniǔzhàn) take bus 916快 (the character is *'kuài'*, and means 'fast') to Huáiróu (¥11, one hour, 6.30am to 7.30pm). Get off at Míngzhū Guǎngchǎng (明珠广场) bus stop, where private taxis and minivans wait to take passengers to Mùtiányù (per person ¥20, 30 minutes). Note that after around 1pm, you'll probably have to charter your own car or van (¥60 one way). Return minivans start drying up at around 6pm. The last 916快 back to Běijīng leaves Huáiróu at around 7pm. If you miss that, catch a taxi from Huáiróu to Shunyi subway station (顺义地铁站; Shùnyì Dìtiě Zhàn; about ¥100) on Line 15, or all the way back to Dōngzhímén (¥220).

A taxi costs around ¥600 to ¥700 for a return day trip from Běijīng, the price being agreed in advance.

Gŭběikǒu 古北口

Although it an ever-expanding village these days, once upon a time Gŭběikǒu (¥45 through ticket, ¥20 town only) was an important, heavily guarded gateway into Běijīng from northeast China. The village, split into two sections by a ridge, with the Great Wall running along it and a small tunnel running through it, contains plenty of old courtyard homes (plus lots of rebuilt ones) and half a dozen small temples. Various stretches of the Wall meet in and around the village, in a kind of Great Wall crossroads with lots of hiking options. One short stony stretch of wall dates from the far-off Northern Qi dynasty (AD 550–577). The other stretches are Ming. There are well-worn dirt pathways on or beside them, so hiking here isn't as dangerous as it can be at other unrestored sections of the Wall. You should still take great care, though.

There are two main sections of Wall here: the **Coiled Dragon** (蟠龙; Pán Lóng), which runs along the ridge that cuts Gŭběikǒu village in two and which eventually leads to Jīnshānlǐng Great Wall, and **Crouching Tiger Mountain** (卧虎山; Wò Hǔ Shān), on the other side of the Cháo Hé River (walk through the tunnel, cross the river bridge, and follow the steps you'll soon see on your right). Both make for fabulous hiking, although Crouching Tiger is extraordinarily steep.

Sleeping & Eating

There's tourist accommodation in the redeveloped southern half of the village (before the Gŭběikǒu Tunnel), now called the **Folk Customs Village**. Get off the bus immediately before the tunnel (if you miss the stop, walk back through the tunnel from the next stop), and walk through the archway on the right, where the ticket office is. There are dozens of *nóngjiāyuàn* (农家院; village guesthouses), so there's no need to book. Although there is English signage, little if any English is spoken. Expect to pay ¥150 to ¥280 for a room with bathroom.

★ **Great Wall Box House** GUESTHOUSE $
(团园客栈; Tuán Yuán Kèzhàn; ☎010 8105 1123; http://en.greatwallbox.com; 18 Dongguan, Gŭběikǒu Village; 古北口镇东关甲18号; weekday/weekend incl dinner 6-bed dm ¥180/200, 4-bed ¥180/200, deluxe d ¥1200/1350; ⊙mid-Mar–mid-Nov; 🚭📶) Run by the friendly, English-speaking Joe, this wonderful place is housed in a 100-year-old courtyard building that was an abandoned chessboard factory before being lovingly renovated. Rooms surround a long, well-tended garden-courtyard, and are large (the dorm is enormous), bright, comfortable and spotlessly clean. Incredibly, a small, overgrown section of the Great Wall runs along one side of the property.

The shared bathroom is modern (with sit-down toilets), there's a small kitchen-dining area and a number of cats. Joe dishes out reliable hiking advice and offers free mountain-bike hire and tasty vegetarian meals. Get off the bus just before the Gŭběikǒu Tunnel and, instead of walking through the archway, walk along the lane to the south of the village stream. You'll see the Box House sign after about 500m.

ℹ Getting There & Away

Take bus 980快 from Dōngzhímén Transport Hub (Dōngzhímén Shūniŭzhàn) to its terminus at Mìyún bus station (密云汽车站; Mìyún *qìchēzhàn*; ¥17, 100 minutes, 6am to 8pm). The 快 *(kuài)* means 'fast'. Then, turn right out of the bus station, cross the main road and turn right and walk for 200m to find the stop for bus 25, which runs to Gŭběikǒu (¥10, 70 minutes). To catch the bus back to Mìyún from Gŭběikǒu, walk through the tunnel by the entrance to the village, cross the road and the bus stop is 400m ahead of you. The last bus 25 back to Mìyún leaves at 4.35pm. The last bus 980 back to Dōngzhímén is at 6.30pm.

Taxis cost ¥1000 to ¥1200 return for a day trip from Běijīng.

History

The Trans-Siberian Railway was spurred initially by the political whims and expansionist policies of Imperial Russia. The story of how it became a reality is but the prelude to an epic history that spans not only the great expanses of Siberia and the Russian Far East, but also monumental events of the 20th century, including revolution, civil and world wars, the Gulag and the highs and lows of the Soviet Union and modern-day Russia.

Birth of Russia's Railways

A latecomer to the Industrial Revolution, Russia had long been dominated by a bloated autocratic state tied to an obsolete, landowning aristocracy. By the mid-19th century, Russia was slipping from the ranks of Europe's great powers. In 1857, Tsar Alexander II issued a railway decree, through which the state determined to reinvigorate the economy's preindustrial infrastructure with modern railway routes.

The new railroads connected the central industrial region to the raw materials of the Ural Mountains and the agricultural products of the Black Earth region. Moscow became the hub of the national rail system, serving as the terminus of nine different lines. Initially this spurt of construction was mostly confined to European Russia, but fear of British encroachment from the Indian subcontinent prompted the construction of a trans-Caspian line, which penetrated deep into Central Asia in the 1880s. Much to the chagrin of Siberian nationalists, some of whom believed that forces in the capital were even deliberately trying to hinder their region's development, Siberia remained a distant, exotic land whose potential was not fully realised.

The Lure of the East

In the 1840s, a geological expedition discovered that the Chinese had left the Amur River region unsettled and unfortified. Shortly thereafter, Tsar Nicholas I appointed the ambitious and able Nikolai Muravyov as the governor-general of Eastern Siberia. Unlike his predecessors, Muravyov was not another corrupt official, but a strong advocate of developing the Siberian Far East. With the tsar's approval, he collected some Cossacks

TIMELINE

Early 1580s

Yermak Timofeyevich and his Cossack brigands capture Isker, the capital of the Turkic khanate Sibir, beginning Russia's expansion into Siberia.

1649–51

Siberian explorer Yerofei Khabarov leads 150 men from Yakutsk towards the Amur River, which he reaches in the winter of 1650, ruthlessly subduing Daur tribes and encroaching on Chinese territory.

1689

Russia and China sign the Treaty of Nerchinsk, defining the Sino-Siberian frontier and halting Russia's expansion east of the Amur. Russia gains right of passage to Běijīng for its traders.

and cruised the Amur, establishing towns for Russia and provoking fights with China. Preoccupied with foreign encroachment along the eastern seaboard, China was in no mood for hassles over Siberian forests. Without bloodshed, Muravyov was thus able to redraw the border with China along the Amur River in the north and the Ussuri River in the east in exchange for some cash and a promise of mutual security. At the tsar's request, Muravyov henceforth attached the sobriquet 'Amursky' to his name.

Muravyov-Amursky continued to pursue his vision of Siberian colonisation, becoming a leading advocate of a railway that would connect European Russia to the Far East. He attracted a long line of suitors from Russia, England and the USA, who offered their own proposals for a railroad to the Pacific. Nothing came of the proposals, however, until the late 19th century when centralism, the prestige of territorial possessions and a nationalist spirit that infused the Age of the Industrial Empire became cornerstones of the new tsar Alexander III's policies.

In March 1891 the tsar officially proclaimed the building of a Trans-Siberian Railway, from the Ural Mountains to the Pacific, and dispatched his son and heir apparent, Nicholas, to lay the first stone at Vladivostok.

Witte's State Within a State

The task of building the Trans-Siberian Railway fell to one of imperial Russia's most industrious and talented statesmen, Sergei Witte (1849–1915). Son of a colonial bureaucrat in the Caucasus and a graduate in mathematics, Witte had risen from lowly ticket seller in Odesa's Southwest Railway Company to stationmaster and then company director.

Even though Witte occupied a powerful position it was still a problem for him to find the enormous amount of cash needed for such a grand enterprise. He implemented a host of financial policies and did some sharp manoeuvring, including issuing bonds, raising taxes and taking out foreign loans. Finally, he triggered a wave of inflation by resorting to the printing presses to produce extra roubles to cover the soaring costs.

The Trans-Siberian Railway also provided Witte with the opportunity to play diplomat, when he proposed to build a 560km shortcut across Manchuria, rather than follow the northern bend in the Amur to Vladivostok. Already besieged with foreigners, the Chinese emperor rejected the proposal.

A determined Witte changed tactics. He bought the influence of senior Chinese statesmen, offered a generous loan to the close-to-bankrupt Chinese government and repackaged his proposal to look like a Chinese-Russian joint venture. The result was an 80-year lease agreement over a corridor of territory for the railway. The Manchurian diversion led to the formation of the East Chinese Railway Company and the Russo-Chinese Bank, which were both in fact fronts for the Russian Ministry of Finance.

History Books

A History of Russia (Nicholas Riasanovsky)

A Traveller's History of China (Stephen Haw)

The Modern History of Mongolia (Charles Bawden)

Rail historian Christian Wolmar's *To the Edge of the World* (2013) focuses on the development of the Trans-Siberian and BAM lines and is a pacy, fact-packed read summing up the route's construction and impact.

1730

Work begins on a full-scale Siberian Post Road, the only means of travel across Siberia to the Mongolian border. Over the centuries the route is gradually redirected south to Yekaterinburg.

1837

On 30 October, Russia's first passenger railway, the 24km Tsarskoe Selo line connecting St Petersburg with Pavlovsk, is opened in order to illustrate the value of railways to the country.

1851

On 1 November the first passenger train on the 649.7km St Petersburg–Moscow railway, Russia's second such transport line, departs on a journey of 21 hours and 45 minutes to Moscow.

1857

Tsar Alexander II issues a railway decree to build a Russian rail network, the same year in which American Perry McDonough Collins proposes an Amur Railroad between Chita and Irkutsk.

In 1898 Witte negotiated further territorial concessions, allowing Russia to build a Southern Manchurian line to a warm-water outlet at Port Arthur (Dàlián), located on the southern tip of the Liaodong Peninsula, west of the Korean Peninsula. The minister of finance, in effect, became the tsar's chief envoy to the Far East.

It's believed that Russia adopted the wider 5ft gauge track for its railways, as opposed to the 4ft 8.5in track favoured by the rest of Europe and American railways, to stop foreign invaders being able to use standard-width rolling stock.

Building the Trans-Siberian Railway

Construction on the railway began almost immediately after the tsar's decree was issued in 1891. Beginning at Chelyabinsk, in the southern Urals, the line would run parallel to the old post road as far as Irkutsk, from where an iron trail would blaze onwards through the untamed Baikal, Amur and Ussuri regions to Vladivostok, the eastern terminus on the Pacific.

This route was selected for the south's warmer weather conditions and more arable lands, which would hopefully encourage new agricultural settlements. But it didn't please local industrialists and merchants, since it bypassed many larger mining colonies and river towns in the north. The line was later altered to accommodate these influential economic lobbies by including Perm, Yekaterinburg and Tyumen.

Building the railroad across a formidable landscape posed ongoing challenges of engineering, supply and labour. The route cut through thick forests, crossed countless rivers, scaled rocky mountains and traversed soggy quagmires. Work brigades were poorly outfitted, using shovels and picks, and horses (and humans) for the hauling.

The Russian railway system, covering 85,500km of track, is the second-largest in the world after the USA's 228,464km of track.

Workers were recruited, or conscripted, from all over the empire as well as from abroad. Some of these were Siberian prisoners, others labour recruits from China or stonemasons from Italy, who worked on the tunnels. They toiled from dawn to dusk in the sweltering heat and freezing cold, and were preyed on by deadly diseases, forest bandits and hungry tigers. The construction work was divided into territorial segments, starting simultaneously from the eastern and western terminus points.

Western Siberian: 1892–96

From Chelyabinsk in the west (which is no longer part of the official Trans-Siberian route), the railway ran through Omsk and on to the Ob River, the site of present-day Novosibirsk. The Western Siberian section was 1440km long and the easiest to build. For the engineers, the main challenge was spanning the many rivers that fed the Ob Basin. The crossings for the Irtysh and Ob Rivers both required the building of bridges that were almost 1km long.

Ussuri: 1891–97

Meanwhile, construction was under way in the east on the Ussuri section of the railway. Beginning in Vladivostok, the line ran northward through the Ussuri River valley to Khabarovsk, a distance of about 800km. The

1860

The Treaty of Peking sees China cede to Russia all territory east of the Ussuri and south to the Korean border, including Vladivostok, the newly founded port.

1886–89

Following Tsar Alexander III's approval of the idea of a Trans-Siberian Railway, topographical surveys are taken along part of the proposed route between Tomsk and Sretensk, and around Vladivostok.

1891

Following a grand tour of Greece, Egypt, India, Indo-China and Japan (where he escaped assassination), Nicholas II lays the first stone in Vladivostok for the Ussuri line to Khabarovsk.

1892–96

Almost at the same time, construction of the Western Siberian segment from the tea-trading city of Chelyabinsk in the southern Urals to the Ob River (present-day Novosibirsk) begins.

forest terrain was more difficult for the engineers. Moreover, after the first tracks had been laid, it was discovered that the Amur rose as much as 10m during the spring, which meant redrawing the route and starting again.

The builders faced severe labour shortages in this remote corner of the Far East. Despite initial misgivings, the construction brigades recruited over 8000 workers from the local Korean population and migrant Chinese labourers, over one-half of the total workforce for this section. They received lower wages than the Russian workers because, the foremen said, their work was inferior (though it may have been because they did not run tabs in the company canteen).

The builders of the Ussuri line introduced convict labour to the railroad, when 600 prisoners destined for incarceration on Sakhalin Island were instead ordered to start digging. Some prisoners escaped from their inexperienced handlers and went on a local crime spree. The project as a whole eventually employed nearly 15,000 convicts and exiles, with far better results. Convicts could work time off their sentences, and the living conditions were a small improvement on the tsar's prisons.

Central Siberian: 1893–98

The Central Siberian section covered a distance of 1920km from the Ob through Krasnoyarsk and on to Irkutsk, west of Lake Baikal. The work of the engineers became more complicated on this leg, because of the

RUSSIA'S EARLY RAILS

In 1833, inspired by newfangled steam technology from overseas, EA Cherepanov and his son ME Cherepanov invented Russia's first steam railway locomotive at Nizhny Tagil in the Ural Mountains (there's a model of it in Yekaterinburg, opposite the railway station). The locomotive and first Russian rail line, just 2km long, were built to support the Urals' mining industry, although the Cherepanovs also sent one of their engines to Tsar Nicholas I in St Petersburg.

It was here in St Petersburg that Russia's first public railway opened, in 1836. Built by Austrian engineer Franz Anton von Gerstner and operating with British-built locomotives, it was a 24km line connecting the imperial capital to the tsar's summer residence, Tsarskoe Selo. Nicholas I was so impressed with this new form of transport that plans were quickly made to roll out a rail network across European Russia.

Legend has it that in 1850, when the tsar commanded that a 650km rail line be built between Moscow and St Petersburg, he accidentally drew around his own finger on the ruler as he traced out a straight line between the cities. Engineers, too afraid to point out the error, duly incorporated the kink into the plans, which became a 17km bend near the town of Novgorod.

The truth is somewhat more prosaic. The curve was actually built to circumvent a steep gradient that Russian steam locomotives of the time were not powerful enough to climb. In 2001, the line was closed for 24 hours so that workers could finally straighten it out.

1893–99

Mountainous terrain and the steep river valleys of central Siberia prove the chief challenges for the construction of the segment from the Ob River to Lake Baikal, via Krasnoyarsk.

1895

Construction starts on the Trans-Baikal line from Lake Baikal to Sretensk. Two years later torrential flooding washes away over 300km of the track and 15 bridges, wrecking another two irreparably.

1896

China grants Russia a concession to build the Chinese Eastern Railway (the Manchurian line) from Chita to Vladivostok via Harbin (Hā'ěrbīn) in Manchuria, avoiding the difficult terrain of Russia's Amur region.

1898

Work begins on the South Manchurian Railway 550km from Harbin to the ice-free, deep-water port at Port Arthur (Lüshun Port, present-day Dàlián) near the tip of the Liaodong Peninsula.

mountainous terrain and the steep river valleys. The Yenisey River required a steel bridge nearly 1km in length. The earth – frozen until July and then swampy after the thaw – was less than ideal for digging. Water from the drained bogs collected in stagnant pools, which bred swarms of bloodthirsty mosquitoes around work sites.

Worth tracking down is the out-of-print *To the Great Ocean* by Harmon Tupper, a well-researched, lively and interesting take on the construction of the Trans-Siberian Railway.

Supply and labour became chronic. Unlike on the plains, there were few settlements to tap for workers (particularly those skilled with stone) or provisions. The builders advertised throughout the empire, offering higher wages and bonuses to entice fresh forces. In August 1898, the first train rolled into the station at Irkutsk.

Trans-Baikal: 1895–1900

The Trans-Baikal section ran from the eastern shore of Lake Baikal past Ulan-Ude and Chita, then on to Sretensk on the Shilka River. For the engineers, this section of 1072km of dense forest was nearly as daunting as the Circumbaikal section was a few years later, and would prove more frustrating. The railroad had to scale the Yablonovy Mountains, rising 5630m above sea level. The rivers were not so wide, but they ran in torrents and cut steep valley walls. The tracks were laid on narrow beds along high mountain ledges. Harsh weather, including summer droughts and heavy rains, exacerbated the difficulties. The great flood of 1897 washed away over 300km of laid track and 15 completed bridges.

East Chinese: 1897–1901

In 1894 Russia secured an agreement from the weakened Chinese that allowed for a Manchurian section of the Trans-Siberian Railway. From Chita, the 1440km-long East Chinese Railway turned southeast, crossing the Argun River and rolling through Harbin (Hā'ěrbīn) to Vladivostok. It sliced over 600km off the journey and, after a one-sided negotiation, the Russian wide gauge was laid across the terrain of flat steppe lands, broad mountain passes and fertile river valleys.

From 1898 to 1901 the East Chinese Railway was extended in a branch line south from Harbin to the ice-free harbour of Port Arthur, which Russia was leasing from China. Sergei Witte vehemently opposed building this branch, saying it would inflame Chinese nationalism. He was right. In 1899 Chinese nationalism mobilised into a rancorous antiforeigner movement, which called itself 'Fists of Higher Justice'. Better known as the Boxer Rebellion, the movement quickly spread to Manchuria and the Russian-controlled railway. Stations and depots were set ablaze, 480km of track were torn up and besieged railroad workers took flight. The main East Chinese line was only able to return to service after the Russian military intervened, and in 1901 the entire main line and branch to Port Arthur came into service. Both were later integrated into the fully fledged Trans-Manchurian Railway used today.

1900

The first Trans-Siberian services go into operation, using the train-ferry Baikal to transport passengers across Lake Baikal. It's later supplemented by the Angara ferry, transporting passengers and freight only.

1901

With ferries proving a less-than-successful solution to crossing Baikal, the decision is taken to construct the Circumbaikal line along the southwestern shore of the lake.

1904

Port Arthur comes under attack from the Japanese, provoking the Russo-Japanese War. The Trans-Siberian Railway buckles under the strain of transporting troop reinforcements to the Far East.

1905

The Russian fleet is annihilated in the Tsushima Straits in May and Russia signs the Treaty of Portsmouth, turning Southern Manchuria over to Japan; Russia keeps the East Chinese Railway.

Circumbaikal: 1901–04

Heading east from Irkutsk, the builders encountered their most formidable obstacle: Lake Baikal. No previous experience prepared the engineers for the frigid lake's steep and rocky cliffs, which dominated the shoreline.

Engineers initially decided that construction of a railroad line around the lake would be impossibly expensive. Instead, the steamship *Baikal,* strong enough to smash through ice and big enough to carry train carriages, was commissioned from Britain. From April 1900, it transported trains and passengers between Port Baikal and Mysovaya (now Babushkin), while more passengers followed on the *Angara* – now moored in Irkutsk. However, the ships proved less than efficient against severe storms and sometimes impassable ice. This hindrance became a national security threat in 1904 – when Russia needed to transport troops and supplies to the front during the Russo-Japanese War, temporary tracks were actually laid across the ice in an attempt to expedite the military movement. Tragically, the first train to attempt this crossing sank through the cracked ice into Baikal's depths.

The decision was made in 1901 to construct a railway line that would skirt the southern edge of the lake, connecting Port Baikal and Mysovaya. The cliffs around the lake made this the most challenging section of all to build. Tsar Alexander III brought in Armenian and Italian masons to design the portals and arched bridges. The pride of Mother Russia at the time, this section was nicknamed 'the Tsar's Jewelled Buckle'.

In the 1950s the Angara River was dammed, raising the level of Lake Baikal by about 1.5m and submerging the railway line between Irkutsk and Port Baikal. A shortcut bypassing this flooded section was built between Irkutsk and Slyudyanka – today's Trans-Siberian main line. The remaining 94km of the Circumbaikal became a neglected branch line, along which a few weekly minitrains still chug, much to the delight of train buffs.

The Circumbaikal consumed four times as much stone as the entire Trans-Baikal section. Workers chiselled 39 tunnels into the lake's craggy capes and erected over 100 bridges and viaducts.

Amur: 1907–16

The 2080km-long Amur section presented similar engineering, supply and labour challenges. The section required some of the longest and most complicated bridges, including a span of almost 2km across the Amur. The builders relied heavily on convict labour, supplemented by army units and Chinese migrants. Building materials, including iron rails, had to be imported from British and North American suppliers.

The Amur was the last section of the Trans-Siberian Railway built, going into operation in 1916. The railway's first travellers transferred into boats at Sretensk for a long river voyage down the Amur to Khabarovsk, where they reboarded. The completion of the East Chinese Railway in 1898 bypassed the Amur, diverting passengers through northern China.

In 1999 a 2612m combined road and rail bridge over the Amur River replaced the original 18-span 2568m-long construction – the longest such bridge on the Trans-Siberian Railway.

1906

Japan founds the South Manchurian Railway Company within Japanese-controlled southern Manchuria. The railway runs to Harbin where it connects to the Chinese Eastern Railway.

1907

To protect Russia's Pacific access and territory in the Far East, Russia decides to construct the Amur line from Sretensk to Khabarovsk, the final portion of the Trans-Siberian Railway.

1914–21

About 60% of Russia's railway network, 90% of its locomotives and 80% of the country's railway carriages are destroyed during WWI and the civil war.

1915

Having declared its independence from the dying Manchu empire in 1911, Mongolia signs the Treaty of Kyakhta with China and Russia, and is granted limited autonomy.

The Promise of Luxury

At the dawn of the 20th century, Russia was ready to launch its engineering achievement to the world. Prince Mikhail Khilkov, the communication minister, made arrangements with a Belgian company to create what was later described by the explorer and travel writer Harry de Windt as 'an ambulant palace of luxury'. Promotional brochures were printed in four languages proclaiming how it would now only take 10 days to cover the 5500 miles between Moscow and Vladivostok, or Port Arthur.

An exquisite miniature version of a Trans-Siberian train, with luxury carriages and church car, was created in 1900 to go inside one of the jewelled eggs made by Fabergé for the tsar; today it's at the Armoury of Moscow's Kremlin.

To further press home the Trans-Siberian Railway's advantages, a 'Palace of Russian Asia' pavilion was constructed at the Exposition Universelle in Paris in 1900. Inside the pavilion, visitors were treated to images of Siberia's pristine rugged landscape and exotic native cultures – including, incongruously, stuffed polar bears clinging to papier mâché icebergs. Luxurious, mock 1st-class sleepers offered comfortable and commodious compartments decorated with French Empire and Chinese-style furnishings.

The imitation dining car served caviar, sturgeon and other Russian delicacies, while allowing visitors to admire moving Siberian scenery through the window, as recreated by a complex, multilayered painted panorama. The exhibit also featured a handsome smoking car, a music salon with piano, a well-stocked library, a fully equipped gymnasium and a marble-and-brass bath.

Trans-Siberian Reality

Travel along the early Trans-Siberian Railway, however, did not live up to its luxurious billing. East of Baikal, the train routinely ran out of food. 'Today we did not eat until 3pm, and then it was vile', wrote the cranky American traveller Michael Myers Shoemaker in 1902. 'There was one wretched little eating room filled with Russians. You may stand around and starve for all they care.'

Before the Trans-Siberian Railway was built, it was quicker to travel from St Petersburg to Vladivostok by crossing the Atlantic, North America and the Pacific than by going overland.

Nor did the hastily constructed Trans-Siberian succeed in providing a more expeditious route to the Far East. Travellers experienced frequent delays, sometimes lasting days. The Trans-Siberian had the highest accident rate of any line in the empire. Ties splintered, bridges buckled and rails warped. The locomotives chugged along at no more than 25km/h because of the risk of derailment.

Bound for Běijīng, Myers Shoemaker scribbled in resignation: 'A traveller in these far eastern lands gradually loses his impatience and finally ceases to care whether his train goes fast or slowly, or does not go at all. Certainly we have been two hours at this station for no apparent reason' – an observation that may still ring true for many contemporary Trans-Siberian travellers.

1916

The completion of the 2.6km Khabarovsk Bridge (the longest Trans-Siberian bridge) over the Amur River allows the opening of the 1920km Amur line, establishing the modern-day Trans-Siberian route.

1918

Following the October Revolution, Lenin pulls Russia out of WWI and moves the capital to Moscow. Civil war ensues. Nicholas II and family are executed in Yekaterinburg.

1918–20

The Czechoslovak Legion, a volunteer army who fought with Britain, France and Russia in WWI, seizes control of large parts of the Trans-Siberian Railway.

1920

Admiral Kolchak, leading the counter-revolutionary White Army, is defeated by the Red Army at Omsk. He retreats to Irkutsk where he's executed. The civil war ends two years later.

The 'Track of the Camel'

The completion of the Trans-Siberian Railway and its glamorous unveiling at the Paris Exhibition lured many a curious traveller onto the rails to Siberia. Among Russians it became known as the 'track of the camel', because it wound around and bypassed so many towns and ran through the middle of nowhere. A principal goal of the railway, however, was not to satisfy a craving for luxury among a travelling elite intent on sipping champagne in a spectacular wilderness. It was to facilitate the resettlement of Russian peasants to Siberia.

Restrictions on internal migration had been lifted in the 1800s, but a modest 500,000 people resettled in Siberia between 1860 and 1890. Once the train came on line, this turned into a raging torrent. Between 1891 and 1914, over five million new immigrants sought a better future there. Station halls were packed with hundreds of waiting peasants sleeping on the floor. One could travel for more than 3200km on the Trans-Siberian for less than R20 in 3rd class. These wagons dispensed with any pretension of style or comfort, packing passengers like proverbial sardines into carriages crammed with wooden bunks of up to six tiers.

- *Russia's Frozen Frontier* (Alan Wood)
- *A History of the Peoples of Siberia* (James Forsyth)
- *East of the Sun* (Benson Bobrick)

War & Revolution

Alexander III saw the Trans-Siberian Railway as the means for Russia to become a Far East power. Under his less able successor, Nicholas II, the construction of the railway instead provoked confrontations that exposed the many weaknesses of imperial Russia.

The Russo-Japanese War

The East Chinese Railway involved Russia in the multilateral dismemberment of the Chinese empire. In the subsequent grab for territorial and commercial concessions in Manchuria, Russia came into direct conflict with imperial Japan. Witte was always inclined towards diplomacy in Russia's Far Eastern policy, but Nicholas was poorly advised by his minister of interior who sketched out a quick victory over the Japanese to the tsar.

Russia's aggressive stance in the Far East provoked Japan to attack Port Arthur in February 1904. The overconfident Nicholas was dazed by the rapid string of defeats. Japanese forces quickly seized the advantage over Russia's outnumbered troops, while the reinforcements remained stalled at Lake Baikal. The single-track, light-rail Trans-Siberian was simply inadequate. The tsar dispatched his prized Baltic fleet. In May 1905 the war concluded when – upon reaching the Tsushima Straits – the fleet was annihilated in just one afternoon.

Nicholas summoned Witte to salvage Russia's dignity in the peace negotiations. Under the Treaty of Portsmouth, Russia vacated southern Manchuria, but managed to hold on to the main East Chinese Railway

1926
US correspondent Junius B Wood reports that the railway is falling apart and rarely punctual.

1929
Electrification of the Trans-Siberian line begins as part of the first of Stalin's five-year plans, designed to centralise the economy, boost heavy industry and make the USSR a superpower.

1930s
Slave labour from Siberia's Gulag system is used to start constructing the Baikal-Amur Mainline (BAM), an ambitious project to provide a backup Trans-Siberian Railway.

1931
A turn-of-the-century proposal to connect the Trans-Siberian Railway with the tsarist-built Trans-Caspian Railway is realised with the opening of the Turkestan–Siberian line from Novosibirsk to Lugovoi, in Kazakhstan.

line. Almost all of the branch line south to Port Arthur fell to the Japanese and was upgraded into the so-called South Manchurian Railway.

The 1905 Revolution

Russia's woeful performance in war unleashed a wave of anti-tsarist protest at home that culminated in the 1905 revolution. Railroad workers were quick to join the protest movement, with 27 different lines experiencing strikes in the first two months of 1905. In April, they coordinated their efforts by forming an All-Russia Union of Railroad Workers. At first they demanded economic concessions, such as higher wages and shorter hours, but soon their demands became more political, such as the rights to organise and strike.

It's estimated that by the time the Trans-Siberian Railway was completed in 1916 it had cost around R1400 million, over four times its original estimated cost of R300 million.

The government attempted to impose martial law over the railway system, and striking rail workers sparked a nationwide general strike.

The Bolshevik Revolution

Radical railroad workers also played a crucial role in the Bolshevik Revolution of 1917. Exhausted by its involvement in WWI, the tsarist regime fell to street demonstrators in February 1917. Nicholas' abdication created a power vacuum in the capital. The liberal provisional government was hesitant in dealing with the war issue, which swung public sentiment towards the more radical political parties.

In an attempt to restore order, General Kornilov ordered his troops at the front to march on St Petersburg, with the intention of declaring martial law. Radicals and liberals alike took cover. But Kornilov's men never made it. Railroad workers went on strike, refusing to transport them, and the putsch petered out. Within weeks, Vladimir Ilych Lenin and the Bolsheviks staged a palace coup, deposed the provisional government and declared themselves rulers of Russia.

The Russian Civil War

The Bolsheviks' claim on power was soon challenged. In the spring of 1918, as the war in Europe continued without Russia, a legion of Czech POWs tried to return home to rejoin the fighting. Unable to cross the front line in the west, they headed east. Along the way, they provoked a confrontation with the Bolsheviks. When the White Army, hostile to the Bolsheviks, came to support the Czechs, the Russian Civil War began.

The Czech legion seized control of the western half of the Trans-Siberian Railway; in the meantime, the Japanese, who had landed in Vladivostok, took control of the railway east of Baikal. A separatist Siberian Republic was formed in Omsk, until tsarist naval officer Admiral Kolchak overthrew the Omsk government and was declared supreme ruler of Siberia. Another former tsarist general reigned over the East Chinese

1935

Russia sells the East Chinese Railway in Manchuria to Japan for ¥170 million. Mao Zedong is recognised as the head of the Chinese Communist Party.

1937

Russia's railways, including the Trans-Siberian, are revived. The largest plant east of the Urals for building and repairing locomotives and rolling stock goes into operation in Ulan-Ude.

1939

Japan invades Mongolia from Manchuria in May. With help from the Soviet Union, and after heavy fighting, the Mongols defeat Japan in September – just as WWII starts in Europe.

1941

In June, Hitler invades the Soviet Union in Operation Barbarossa, beginning the 'Great Patriotic War'. During WWII, much Russian industry is transferred to Siberia.

Railway in Manchuria. Cossacks menaced the Trans-Baikal and Amur regions. Siberia had returned to the era of warlords.

It took the Bolsheviks more than three years to secure complete control over the Trans-Siberian Railway and to establish Soviet power across Siberia. Kolchak was arrested, tried and shot in Irkutsk.

World War II

In WWII, Nazi Germany's blitzkrieg invasion was an unintended impetus for Siberia's industrial development, when the industrial stock of European Russia was hastily evacuated to safer interior locations. Cities like Yekaterinburg, Tyumen, Novosibirsk, Barnaul (south of the Trans-Siberian) and Krasnoyarsk received an industrial boost, and Lenin's body was removed from its mausoleum in Moscow and freighted to Tyumen for safe-keeping. During the German occupation, the Trans-Siberian Railway served as a lifeline, furnishing the front with reinforcements and equipment.

Anne Applebaum's Pulitzer Prize–winning *Gulag: A History* is the definitive account of the forced-labour camps of Russia's most desolate regions.

Development of Siberia

While the Trans-Siberian Railway had brought Russia's peasants flocking to Siberia to share in a better life, it also meant increased demand for materials to feed the railway and helped spur a period of tremendous optimism on the subcontinent. A second track was built alongside the original single line and the light rails were replaced with heavier, more durable rails. Wooden bridges and supports were replaced with iron and steel.

From the late 1920s, the Soviet leader Josef Stalin (1878–1953) abandoned the New Economic Policy (NEP) begun by Lenin – who before his death in 1924 had set about liberalising sectors to bolster a stagnating economy – and put economic control firmly back into state hands with his First Five Year Plan. This was aimed at industrialising Russia's regions, especially Siberia, but it also foresaw collectivisation of agriculture, the breaking down of what it saw as 'backward' indigenous lifestyles by shifting children of the small nationalities of the north into boarding schools, and resulted in political paranoia and purges.

Bernardo Bertolucci's *The Last Emperor* (1988) is a lavish epic about Puyi, China's last imperial ruler. The film tells the story through the eyes of Puyi, using flashbacks to his childhood and days heading a Japanese puppet regime.

Stalin's drive for industrialisation was enormously successful, but it was also to a large extent achieved on the backs of prisoners of the Gulag camps, who were worked to death in slave labour camps.

In the 1950s and 1960s, oil and gas discoveries energised Siberia. These deposits were only in the north,but they promoted development in the cities along the railway.

Stalin's reform-minded successor, Nikita Khrushchev, denounced his former boss and liberated millions of labour-camp inmates. Meanwhile, incentive-laden offers lured new workers to the region and the Siberian population became highly skilled. A uniquely planned academic community was created near Novosibirsk. Military industry flourished in secret

1945

The USSR declares war against Japan. Soviet troops occupy Manchuria. When Japan surrenders, the Manchurian railway is placed under Sino-Russian administration.

1947–49

Construction of the Trans-Mongolian line begins in 1947, with an extension from Ulan-Ude south towards the border town of Naushki. In 1949 the line reaches Mongolia's capital of Ulaanbaatar.

1950–52

In 1950 the USSR signs a treaty with the People's Republic of China, shifting its support from the Nationalists to Mao's Communists. In 1952 China receives Manchuria's East Chinese Railway.

1956

The Gobi Desert is spanned; the Trans-Mongolian Railway connecting Moscow with Běijīng via Ulaanbaatar is completed. Due to different gauges, bogies have to be changed at the China–Mongolia border.

cities, sheltering well-tended scientists and technicians. By 1970, 13 Siberian cities had populations of 250,000 or more.

During this time, Siberia's native populations were increasingly assimilated into the lifestyle and culture of Soviet Russian society. In 1900 native peoples accounted for more than 15% of Siberia's total population; by 1970, this number was less than 4%. Simultaneously, Siberia's development was having detrimental effects on the environment.

For a very personal history of China through the 20th century read *Wild Swans* by Jung Chang. She followed this epic tale in 2005 with her collaborative warts-and-all portrait of Mao Zedong, *Mao: The Unknown Story*, cowritten with Jon Halliday.

Branching Out

The Soviet regime continued to develop overland rail access to the Eurasian continent so that travellers could reach ever more remote corners of the Far East. The construction and operation of branch lines throughout the Far East were entangled in the politics of the region for most of the 20th century.

The Trans-Manchurian

The Trans-Manchurian line connects Běijīng to the Trans-Siberian at Chita, via the Russian-built East Chinese Railway and also the section leading down to Port Arthur. The latter section was later known as the South Manchurian Railway, and had fallen to Japan as spoils of war in 1905. At this time, US railroad baron EH Harriman made several generous bids to buy these routes from their respective operators. He saw a rare opportunity to realise his ambition of building a railroad line that circumnavigated the globe. Harriman's offers, however, were rebuffed.

From 1917 until the early 1920s, revolution and civil war had thrown the Soviet Union into chaos. Gradually, however, the country recovered. Although Russia was good to its promises to renounce its privileges in Manchuria, it baulked at handing over its main-line segment of the East Chinese Railway across northern Manchuria. Instead it negotiated a temporary joint custody of the line, stacked positions with its own people and stalled all attempts by China to get it back.

Russian Railways have crafted a virtual Trans-Sib from Moscow to Vladivostok with a choice of views from different carriages and an audio soundtrack – view it at http://eng.rzd.ru/vtour/index.html.

The Russians had to continuously defend their (partial) claim to the railway line. During the 1920s the Russian managers were arrested by a Manchurian warlord and again by Chiang Kaishek (leader of the Kuomintang, the Chinese Nationalist Party), both of whom seized control of the railroad. In each case the aggressors were forced to relinquish their prizes and prisoners. In 1932 the Japanese took control of Manchuria, renaming it Manchukuo and installing the last Manchu emperor, Puyi, as a puppet ruler. Under pressure, Russia sold her interest in the main-line segment of the East Chinese Railway to the new rulers in 1935.

This was not the proverbial end of the line, however. According to the secret protocols negotiated at Yalta, Winston Churchill and Franklin D Roosevelt conceded back to Stalin the East Chinese and South Manchu-

1961

Mongolia is admitted to the UN as an independent country, but the Soviet Union continues to occupy Mongolia with troops and run it as a satellite state.

1961–63

The Trans-Siberian Railway is used to transport cosmonaut hardware to Baikonur (in present-day Kazakhstan). The first man in space, Yury Gagarin, blasts off in 1961.

1965

Oil begins to flow in Siberia as Prime Minister Alexey Kosygin tries to shift the Soviet economy over to light industry and consumer goods. Brezhnev's opposition brings economic stagnation.

1969

Political relations between China and Russia deteriorate and armed clashes erupt along the Ussuri River. The Trans-Mongolian and Trans-Manchurian routes into China are suspended.

rian rail lines as part of the price of Soviet entry into the Pacific War. The lines were given back to China in 1952 as a Soviet goodwill gesture to the new Chinese communist regime.

By the mid-1960s relations between China and Russia had soured and the border was closed, thus stopping the Trans-Manchurian service. The low point was reached in 1969 when armed clashes occurred over Damansky Island in the Ussuri River, part of the border between the two communist neighbours. The so-called Sino-Soviet Split lasted until the early 1980s, and since this time Russian-Chinese relations have warmed considerably, allowing the Trans-Siberian to be reconnected to the Trans-Manchurian, giving us the route you follow today.

Train buffs can flick through evocative historical and more contemporary images of past Trans-Siberian locos and carriages at Trains-World Expresses (http://trains-worldexpresses.com).

The Trans-Mongolian

Tracing the route travelled by the ancient tea caravans, from Běijīng through Mongolia to Ulan-Ude, the 2080km Trans-Mongolian line was built piecemeal, a direct result of fluctuations in the relationship between Russia and China.

During the late 19th century, Mongolia was formally part of the Chinese Manchu empire. China's officials became more interested in the region after centuries of neglect, much to the irritation of the Mongolians. Plans were made to construct a railroad from Běijīng to Örgöö (Ulaanbaatar). Instead, the Chinese empire collapsed in 1911.

Mongolia was very eager to be rid of its Chinese overlord but was too weak to fend for itself. Russia emerged conveniently as a protective patron of Mongolian independence. The Soviet Union consolidated its influence in 'independent' Mongolia and in 1936 a short rail route was announced, linking Mongolia and Soviet Buryatiya, whose peoples shared close ethnic ties. This new line between Ulan-Ude and Naushki was completed in 1940; in 1949, it was extended to the capital, Ulaanbaatar.

In the early 1950s, relations between the Soviet Union and communist China relaxed somewhat, allowing the Chinese to finally begin work on the long-planned railroad connecting Běijīng with Ulaanbaatar. Although train service began on this line in 1956, the Sino-Soviet Split of the 1960s closed the border. Like the Trans-Manchurian, the Trans-Mongolian line was reopened in the 1980s.

One of the most interesting and readable accounts of the BAM railway is *Brezhnev's Folly* by Christopher Ward. The author goes against the grain of most researchers and believes that, despite political stagnation, the Brezhnev era can also be seen as a dynamic period.

The Baikal-Amur Mainline

The 4234km Baikalo-Amurskaya Magistral (Baikal-Amur Mainline, or BAM) begins west of Irkutsk and passes north of Lake Baikal on its way east to the Pacific coast. The route was first considered as an option for the Trans-Siberian line in the 1880s, but it would not be until the 1930s that work actually started on its construction, beginning at Tayshet.

1974

As work resumes on the long-abandoned BAM, the railroad is styled by party general secretary Leonid Brezhnev as a huge Komsomol (Communist youth league) project, with completion scheduled for 1982.

1980s

Following a thaw in international relations between Russia and China, the Trans-Mongolian and Trans-Manchurian lines reopen for business and travellers begin writing about the routes again.

1990

Democracy demonstrations occur in Ulaanbaatar. Soviet troops begin withdrawing, and in the first free, multiparty elections the Mongolian People's Revolutionary Party wins 85% of the vote.

1991

The BAM's second official opening is overshadowed by an attempted coup against USSR president Mikhail Gorbachev and the demise of the Soviet Union. Boris Yeltsin becomes Russia's president.

FUTURE INTERNATIONAL CONNECTIONS

London to New York by train via a tunnel beneath the Bering Strait is an idea almost as old as the Trans-Siberian Railway itself, but now engineers believe it's possible. The cost is reckoned (conservatively) to be US$65 billion for the Russian side and tunnel alone, which would be about 103km, twice the length of the Channel Tunnel linking Britain with continental Europe. Legislators in Russia have given a green light to the project and it has been reported that the Chinese are also keen to join the railway building party, envisioning a grand China–Russia–Canada–USA line.

In the meantime Russia continues to expand its high-speed services, which already reach Nizhny Novgorod and are set to connect with Kazan by 2020. A long way in the future this high-speed line may even stretch as far as Běijīng. The Russian government has also said it plans to upgrade the BAM. There are even discussions about a tunnel to extend this line to Sakhalin Island (a project first started during Stalin's rule and abandoned after his death) *and* for a 45km bridge to link from Sakhalin to Japan.

Although parts of the far-eastern end of the line were built from 1944 (partly using Japanese and German POWs as labour), the project was put on indefinite hold in 1953 after the death of Stalin. Its resumption, amid much fanfare, came in 1974, when Leonid Brezhnev hailed it the 'Hero Project of the Century'. The call went out to the youth of the Soviet Union to rally to the challenge of constructing the BAM.

Even though the project employed 100,000 workers, including 20,000 communist youth league 'volunteers', it was poorly coordinated and badly mismanaged. It had to overcome Siberia's swamps, its seven mountain ranges, its seemingly infinite number of rivers and, in particular, its vast swath of permafrost. Lacking adequate housing and electricity, few workers reenlisted and others simply deserted.

In 2005 China and Russia settled a post-WWII dispute over 2% of their 4300km common border. For the first time, the whole border was legally defined.

The line was officially opened in 1991, when it became possible to travel the whole length from Tayshet to Sovetskaya Gavan on the Pacific coast. However, the BAM's 15.3km Severomuysky tunnel, the longest in Russia, was only completed in 2003. The official cost of the project (US$11 billion) hardly covers the true bill – an enormous amount that will never be fully known.

The AYaM (Amuro-Yakutskaya Mainline or Amuro-Yakutskaya Magistral) is a branch line that already extends south from Tynda on the BAM to Bamovskaya on the Trans-Siberian line, and will eventually terminate in the north at Yakutsk, capital of the Republic of Sakha. At the time of research, passenger trains went as far as the coal-mining town of Neryungri on the AYaM.

1992

A third route from Russia to China is established via a railway from Ürümqi to Kazakhstan, connecting with a line completed in 1960 to Aktogay, between Almaty and Semey.

2002

The electrification of the Trans-Siberian line, started in 1929, is finally completed. Train weights can be doubled to 6000 tonnes on this route covering one-sixth of the globe.

2005

The private Golden Eagle luxury train service commences between Vladivostok and Moscow, making a detour on some services to Ulaanbaatar in Mongolia, complementing the private Tsar's Gold service.

2014

The first cargo trains run along the Amur-Yakutsk (AYaM) spur from the BAM as far as Nizhny Bestyakh on the opposite bank of the Lena River.

Siberian & Far East Travellers

The magnetic lure of Siberia, the Russian Far East, Mongolia and China tempted many an adventurer and hardy traveller to battle their way through the taiga long before the railway made the going a hell of a lot easier. Vivid accounts of these journeys, provided by writers as great as Dostoevsky and Chekov, make for fascinating reading before or during a contemporary Trans-Siberian trip.

Zhang Qian & the Silk Road

Although he travelled only to Siberia's fringes, Chinese explorer Zhang Qian (195–114 BC) was the most influential of the early explorers of Northern and Central Asia. He brought back to China the first descriptions of Central Asia, leading to the development of the ancient trading routes that became the Silk Road.

The northern Silk Road through Samarkand would have a considerable impact on Siberia; even prior to Russian colonisation, traders from Bukhara (in modern-day Uzbekistan) provided a trade lifeline between the towns of the khanate of Sibir and the Silk Road. The Bukharans also conducted the religious education of the Tartar khans of Sibir. Once the Russians arrived, the Bukharan trade caravans and their wares were a common sight at Siberian markets and in the Tartar quarters of towns such as Tobolsk.

The Real Siberia, Together With an Account of a Dash Through Manchuria (1902) by John Foster Fraser describes Siberia during its boom years and avoids many of the prejudices of the period.

Yermak's Conquest of Siberia

At the forefront of Russia's concerted expansion into Siberia was the Volga brigand and Cossack Yermak Timofeevich, who was later glorified in a series of religious stories known as the *Siberian Chronicles,* compiled over later centuries. Some historians liked to colour him as a Russian Hernán Cortés, the conquistador of South America.

From 1563 Sibir began raiding what were then Russia's easternmost flanks on the cusp of the Ural Mountains. Funded and given firearms by the Stroganov industrial family, Yermak led his group of 840 Cossacks into the khanate of Sibir. He marched and sailed the rivers into Siberia, probably armed only with the tacit agreement of Ivan the Terrible, taking Tyumen (on the Trans-Siberian line today) as his first major possession. In late 1582 or 1583 (dates are conflicting) Yermak reached an abandoned Isker (the capital of Sibir, buried in the river meadows near today's Tobolsk), triggering what would later become Russia's extraordinary drive across Siberia to the Pacific, culminating in Russians reaching Alaska by the 1730s.

In Xanadu (1989) by William Dalrymple is the best of a bunch of books following in the footsteps of Marco Polo, who travelled from Jerusalem to Shàngdū (about 280km north of Běijīng; better known in the West as Xanadu), the summer residence of Kublai Khaan.

China's First Embassy to Russia

The first full-scale embassy from Manchu China through Mongolia to Russia took place in 1712, when the ambassador of the Qing dynasty, Túlǐshēn (1667–1741), travelled on a roundabout route through Russia to negotiate with the Kalmyks on the Volga. Túlǐshēn records the journey in his *Yìyùlù*, first published in English translation by George Thomas Staunton as *Narrative of the Chinese Embassy to the Khan of the Tourgouth Tartars, in the years 1712, 13, 14, and 15, by the Chinese Ambassador, and published by the Emperor's Authority, at Peking* (1821).

After crossing the Russia–Mongolia border, Túlǐshēn and his attendants met a messenger sent by the governor of the Selenga district, who was taking an active interest in the (self-proclaimed) 'imperial ambassadors and heavenly messengers of his most excellent majesty, emperor of China'. The governor arranged accompaniment and the embassy was taken in boats on the Selenga River to Lake Baikal, where Túlǐshēn wrote: 'The Baykale Lake is surrounded by mountains; its banks are overgrown with reeds, and upon its surface thick fogs and noxious vapours collect from the vast forests and deserts in the vicinity. It is a great expanse of waters, extending further than the eye can reach, and its waves are like those in the ocean.'

In *A Ribbon of Iron* (1901), Annette Meakin, the first Englishwoman to circumnavigate the globe by rail, recounts her generally favourable impression of the early Trans-Siberian services.

18th- & 19th-Century Travellers

Some of the best travel writing is from the early 18th century, a time when travellers were less susceptible to nationalist prejudices. Standing out among the early crop is the Scottish-born physician John Bell (1691–1780), who travelled with an embassy to Běijīng in 1719. Bell's embassy was typically large, consisting of guards, valets, footmen, interpreters, clerks and even musicians – anything between 60 and 100 people. His recollections, published in 1763 as *Travels from St. Petersburg in Russia to Diverse Parts of Asia,* are refreshing and interesting.

The retinue received camels on the Mongolian border to complement their horses. Later, once in China itself, Bell described the turreted post houses he saw, set about 2.5 miles apart and within sight of each other. Each post house was guarded by several soldiers, part of a network of stations for running messages across Qing China and which also served

TRAVELLING THE TRAKT

The Sibirsky Trakt, the post road leading across Siberia (really nothing more than a rough track), was the main route across the subcontinent before the advent of today's Trans-Siberian Railway. Siberia had been colonised by its rivers, with short portages between them, but once construction of a post road was stepped up in the 1730s, travellers, explorers and settlers often followed routes between isolated post stations set about 30km to 40km apart. The stations housed a postmaster, his family, and the *yamshchiki*, the drivers that were hired along with horses and a *telega* (a rudimentary one-horse cart without suspension).

During the travels of George Kennan, the American who surveyed a proposed telegraph route across Siberia in the 1860s and later wrote *Tent Life in Siberia* (1877), the post road connected Yekaterinburg with the Amur River, petering out on the border to Mongolia almost 5000km later.

Kennan said he used to feel ashamed waking up a driver in the dead of night to be driven across dangerous country for a pittance. Sometimes the drivers were so drunk or tired that they toppled off the carts, and travelling in a *telega* often meant holding on tight, with your legs dangling over the sides. Even so he wrote that transport along the *trakt* was the world's best-organised horse express service.

Travellers could also use the hired horses – usually a *troika* (group of three) and driver for their own vehicles. Anton Chekhov travelled to Sakhalin Island in his own *tarantass* – the most comfortable vehicle because it was fully enclosed and had suspension – and another option was the *kibitka,* which resembled a baby's rocking cradle on wheels and had struts jutting out on each side to prevent a complete capsize. In winter, the *kibitka* and *tarantass* were adapted into sleds.

to keep highway robbers at bay. After passing the Great Wall, Bell was met by the former Chinese ambassador, Túlīshēn. Once in Běijīng, the Russian ambassador and Bell were granted an audience with the ageing Emperor Kangxi (1654–1722), who received gifts in the name of Peter the Great – furs, clocks, watches set in diamonds and mirrors.

In 1890, even though he was ill with tuberculosis, the 30-year-old Russian playwright Anton Chekhov embarked on an 11-week journey across Siberia to Sakhalin Island to witness and later describe prison conditions there, in *Sakhalin Island*. Some modern-day editions of this title are published along with an account of his Siberian journey and letters penned on the way, including the ones in which he described Tomsk as 'dull' and his visit to a brothel in Blagoveshchensk.

Frostbitten and broken by a mock execution in St Petersburg, Fyodor Dostoevsky (1821–81) shuffled across Siberia in shackles in the mid-19th century, pausing in Tobolsk and Omsk, and reworked his hardships into the novel *The House of the Dead* (1862).

Early Trans-Siberian Railway Travellers

The advent of the Trans-Siberian Railway generated enormous interest in Siberia and produced a flood of books about rail travel. The best are insightful, the worst are culturally jaundiced or xenophobic. Mrs John Clarence Lee's *Across Siberia Alone: An American Woman's Adventures* (1913) is both, but interesting for a take on the Trans-Manchurian.

The New York politician and engineer Lindon Bates Jr (1883–1915) had the misfortune to perish in 1915 on the *Lusitania,* a British passenger ship, but his *The Russian Road to China* (1910) remains a nice blend of history, railway description and travel with occasional literary glimpses of life on the train.

In the 1896 title *The New Siberia* (partly about the penal colonies), Harry de Windt (1856–1933), a rail and road traveller, journeyed much of the way on a *telega*. De Windt reckoned he could hardly keep a cigarette between his teeth because of the jolting, adding that he had blisters from trying to hold on.

Journey Into the Mind's Eye (1968) by Lesley Blanch is a semi-autobiographical tale about a romantic obsession with Russia and the Trans-Siberian Railway, which the author eventually travels along in the 1960s.

20th- & 21st-Century Travellers

In late 1973 Paul Theroux boarded the Trans-Siberian for the first time on the final leg of his global train odyssey for *The Great Railway Bazaar* (1975). The train was delayed and, depressed and homesick, Theroux ended up spending Christmas on it. He would tackle the route again in the late 1980s as a prelude to covering China's rail network in *Riding the Iron Rooster* (1988) and, once again, found the experience monotonous. It clearly didn't put him off as a third Trans-Siberian trip appears in *Ghost Train to the Eastern Star* (2008), by which time Theroux had graduated to travelling in soft class.

Enjoying himself much more was Eric Newby, whose classic *The Big Red Train Ride* (1978) stands out as a hilarious and vivid snapshot of the Soviet era. Minders dogged a traveller's every step and disembarking at many Siberian locations was banned (the train during this era started and terminated its journey in Nakhodka rather than Vladivostok, which was closed to non-residents).

Opting instead for the BAM, Irish octogenarian Dervla Murphy penned two books on her travels around Siberia in the early 21st century (*Through Siberia by Accident* and *Silverland*). *Platskart* was the only way to roll for the famously frugal 'Irish babushka', as she dubbed herself. Travelling alone and speaking not a word of Russian, Murphy brought out the best in Siberian people, whose hospitality she describes as nothing short of legendary.

Dedicated to a carbon-friendly, organic lifestyle, ferociously anti-war and an avowed technophobe and critic of today's gadget-obsessed world, Murphy mixes colourful vignettes about her travels with evocative landscape descriptions and riveting historical asides about the

Colin Thurbon's *In Siberia* (1999) details the 24,000km journey from the Ural Mountains to Magadan; it captures the bleak majesty of the landscape and the pain of Siberian existence with poetic force.

BOWIE ON THE TRANS-SIBERIAN

Could there have been a more vivid culture shock experience – for both Russians and the Brixton-born musician at its centre – than David Bowie's trip on the Trans-Siberian in 1973? For years rumours of this near-mythical event circulated across Russia, including ones that had Bowie and Iggy Pop tearing up the streets of Vladivostok. The truth, as documented in Geoffrey MacCormack's *From Station to Station,* a memoir and photo book published in 2007 about life on tour with Bowie, is both less fanciful and way more bizarre.

Apparently, Bowie took the train following the end of his Ziggy Stardust tour in Japan because he was afraid of flying. To get to Russia, Bowie and MacCormack sailed on the Soviet cruise ship the *Felix Dzerzhinsky* to the port of Nakhodka. During the voyage, Bowie thrilled passengers and crew with an impromptu concert including his hit 'Space Oddity'. The henna-haired pop star later charmed the Trans-Siberian *provodnitsas* (carriage attendants) Danya and Nadya by singing songs for them.

In Khabarovsk the singer was joined on the train by veteran UPI correspondent Robert Muesel (read his fascinating account of the trip on www.5years.com/jtswdb.htm). A week later, by the time Bowie & Co reached Moscow, they were greeted like the Spiders from Mars. Muscovites stopped in their tracks, never having seen anything like the red-haired pop star – who was dressed in 3in-high yellow platform boots, matching yellow trousers and silk jacket trimmed with sequins – in their lives.

BAM and Siberia in general. She also excels at bringing to life the Cossack 'heroes' who conquered and ruled these unforgiving lands centuries ago.

One of the best travel books on the region is Ian Frazer's *Travels in Siberia* (2010), which vividly recounts the American author's experiences there during several visits to Russia. Frazer's great-great-great grandfather was the editor of a newspaper that had published letters sent by George Kennan in the mid-19th century about his Siberian journey. Retracing Kennan's steps across the country, Frazer travels mainly by road, at one point having to load his vehicle onto a Trans-Siberian carriage with no windows to cover part of the route.

In her 2015 TV documentary *Joanna Lumley's Trans-Siberian Adventure,* the actress and former model travelled in a fair bit more comfort (and with an ab fab wardrobe of fur coats) from Hong Kong to Moscow by rail. The three-part series is available on DVD and includes some wry comments from Lumley on the journey and sights along the way.

Midnight in Siberia (2014) by David Greene is an entertaining and insightful travelogue from the former Moscow bureau chief for the USA's National Public Radio (NPR), as he hops on and off the Trans-Siberian and meets a cross-section of Russians.

Russia Today

From its relations with the US, to its key involvement in conflicts in Syria and Ukraine, Russia is resurgent on the international stage. Front and centre is President Vladimir Putin, who, should he choose to run for re-election in 2018, appears unassailable despite opposition politician Alexey Navalny nipping at his heels. Whatever happens, you can be sure that little will be allowed to spoil the success of Russia's hosting of the 2018 FIFA World Cup.

Best on Film

Loveless (2017) Winner of the Jury Prize at the Cannes Film Festival in 2017, Andrei Zvyagintsev's follow-up to *Leviathan* is another subtle critique of contemporary Russian society.

My Perestroika (2010) Robin Hessman's film focuses on five Russians and the effect of the past 20 turbulent years on their lives.

Bolshoi Babylon (2015) Behind-the-scenes documentary exposing the violent rivalries in Russia's most famous ballet troupe.

Best in Print

Nothing Is True and Everything Is Possible: Adventures in Modern Russia (Peter Pomerantsev; 2014) Darkly entertaining tales of contemporary Russian life by TV producer Peter Pomerantsev.

The Last Man in Russia (Oliver Bullough; 2013) A spot-on portrait of modern Russia, told through the tumultuous and tragic life of an Orthodox priest.

Lost Cosmonaut and **Strange Telescopes** (Daniel Kalder; 2006 and 2009) Kalder's books explore some of Russia's quirkiest and least-visited locations.

Complex International Relations

With his approval rating running around 84% at home, Russia's President Putin has been emboldened to follow a more aggressive international political agenda. There's the possibility that the Russians had a hand in the election of Donald Trump to the US presidency in 2016. There's its controversial military support for Syria's President Bashar al-Assad under the guise of keeping Islamic militants in check. And there's its military backing for separatists in eastern Ukraine where, three years on from Russia's annexation of Crimea, heavy fighting continues. In response to EU sanctions imposed on Russia because of that annexation, the Kremlin imposed its own embargo on certain EU agricultural products.

Putin Can Fix It

At the time of research Putin had yet to confirm his candidacy for the 2018 presidential election. The Kremlin is known for pulling surprises, but few believe Putin is ready to relinquish control of the nation he has effectively ruled since 2000. The 64-year-old ex-KGB agent certainly appeared in command during an annual live national TV program in June 2017, during which he answered a selection from some 2.6 million questions raised by the public. The show – which could easily be called 'Putin Can Fix It' – saw the president promise to solve problems ranging from pot-holed streets and low wages to what to do with fired FBI director James Comey (offer him asylum in Russia, like Edward Snowden).

However, one problem that Putin is somewhat at a loss of how to fix is that of a growing opposition to his rule. Days prior to the TV Q&A, tens of thousands of demonstrators had gathered in over 100 cities across Russia to march against corruption and Putin's regime. Along with a thousand other people, the protest's architect and Russia's leading opposition figure

Alexey Navalny was arrested and sentenced to 25 days in jail.

The Problem with Navalny

Lawyer turned anticorruption crusader Navalny has been a thorn in Putin's side since 2008, when he started blogging about state graft. The 41-year-old emerged as an effective opposition leader during the parliamentary elections of 2011, when he urged his supporters not to vote for United Russia, which he dubbed the 'party of crooks and thieves'. Standing as a candidate in the Moscow mayoral elections of 2013, Navalny captured 27% of the vote despite a concerted attempt by the establishment to sideline him.

In the latest of several criminal prosecutions against him, Navalny was convicted of embezzlement in 2014. He claims this verdict, like those before it, is politically motivated; candidates with a criminal record are barred from standing for the presidency. Nevertheless, Navalny is determined to run, and has began campaigning across the country, taking his message as far afield as Siberia. Barred from national TV, Navalny – for all his team's internet and social media savvy – has a mountain to climb. Less than 50% of Russians know who he is, according to independent pollsters the Levada Center. Those that do know him are also likely to be aware of his strong nationalist views, which come with an unrepentant tinge of antimigrant rhetoric. This makes him a controversial figure that not all Russian liberals are in a hurry to support.

Patriot Games

Since the demise of the Soviet Union, Russian politicians have been in search of a national ideology to replace communism. In 2016, the president named patriotism as that ideology, confirming many academics' and commentators' suspicions that the state had, in effect, hijacked the concept to serve its own agenda (ie keeping Putin in power). Patriotism is encouraged through celebrations of the country's sacrifices and victories in WWII (known in Russia as the Great Patriotic War) and glorification of historical figures such as Ivan the Terrible and Vladimir the Great, both of whom have had recent public statues unveiled in their honour.

National pride will also be riding on Russia's successful hosting of 2018's FIFA World Cup. Improved and new airports, better roads and speedier rail links are all making it easier for travellers and football fans to get around Russia. However, Human Rights Watch have also documented abuses at six stadium construction sites, including unpaid wages and hazardous working conditions that have led to deaths. This includes the decade-overdue Krestovsky Stadium in St Petersburg where the budget has ballooned to as much as US$1.5 billion (the government claims US$700 million).

POPULATION: **144.5 MILLION**

AREA: **17,098,242 SQ KM**

GDP: **US$1.326 TRILLION**

INFLATION: **4.1%**

UNEMPLOYMENT: **5.5%**

if Russia were 100 people

80 would be Russian
4 would be Tatar
2 would be Ukrainian
1 would be Bashkir
1 would be Chuvash
12 would be other

belief systems
(% of population)

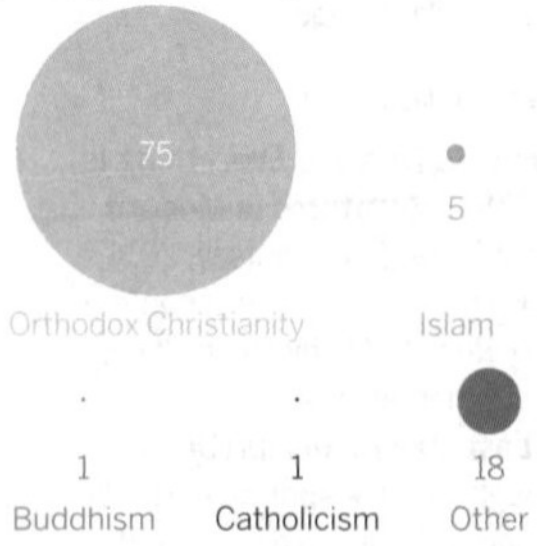

population per sq km

≈ 8 people

Russian Culture & Cuisine

Russia's multiethnic society is the result of imperial expansion, forced movements, migration and the mingling of ethnic groups over many thousands of years. Within the Russian Federation, one's 'nationality' refers to one's ethnicity rather than one's passport – and Russia has over 160 nationalities. Despite such enormous ethnic and cultural variation, there is much that Russian citizens have in common.

The Russian People

The overwhelming majority of Russia's population – about 80% – have Slavic European-Russian roots. Almost 4% are Tartars who descend from the Mongol armies of Chinggis (Genghis) Khaan, his successors and from earlier Hunnic, Turkic and mostly Finno-Ugric settlers.

The remainder of Russia's population consists of smaller ethnic groups such as Ukrainians (2%), Muslim Bashkirs (1.2%) and Orthodox Christian Chuvash (about 1.15%). In Siberia, the largest ethnic groups are the ethnic Mongol Buryats (500,000), who speak a language closely related to Mongolian, and the peoples who speak languages with Turkic roots or Turkic influences: Yakuts or Sakha (around 480,000), Tuvans (300,000), Altai (70,000) and Khakass (63,500). In addition there are the so-called 'small-numbered peoples of the North' – indigenous groups mostly spread across Siberia's northern regions.

Russian Lifestyle

There is a vast difference in the quality of life of urban and rural Russians. The glittering skyscrapers of Moscow are far from the norm, with many areas of Russia seemingly unchanged from the days of the USSR – as witnessed in any of the preserved-in-Soviet-formaldehyde towns along the Baikal-Amur Mainline (BAM).

This said, some common features of contemporary life across Russia stand out, such as the Soviet-era flats, the dacha (summer country house), education and weekly visits to the *banya* (bathhouse). Cohabitation remains less common than in the West, so when young couples get together, often marry.

As the economy has improved so too has the average Russian's lifestyle, with more people than ever before owning a

RUSSIAN HISTORY

862

The legendary Varangian (Scandinavian) Rurik of Jutland gains control of the village Staraya Ladoga near Novgorod and Rus, the infant version of Russia, is born.

10th–11th Centuries

Oleg of Novgorod shifts the centre of Rus to Kyiv (Kiev) in the early 10th century, where the powerful Kyivan Rus reach their zenith, eventually uniting Kyiv with the Novgorod principality.

1223

Chinggis (Ghengis) Khaan's defeat of the Russian princes at the Battle of Kalka River sparks Mongol incursions into Rus territory, followed by Batu Khaan's massive invasion from 1236 to 1240.

1552–56

Ivan IV (aka 'the Terrible' for his fearsome temper) defeats the splinter khanates of Kazan (once Batu's headquarters) and Astrakhan. The Volga region also falls to Russia; Siberia beckons.

Early 1580s–1613

Yermak Timofeevich and his Cossacks cross the Ural Mountains and capture Tyumen and Isker, the capital of the surviving khanate of Sibir based in Western Siberia. The Romanov dynasty begins in 1613.

1660

Nikon, Patriarch of the Orthodox Church, enacts reforms and creates a schism, leading to his being deposed. Many 'Old Believers', who reject the reforms, flee to Siberia and form communities.

car, a computer and a mobile phone, and taking holidays abroad. The lives of Russian teenagers today couldn't be more different from those of their parents, who just a generation ago had to endure shortages of all kinds of goods on top of the ideology of Soviet communism. It's not uncommon to come across young adults who have only the vaguest, if any, idea of who Lenin or Stalin are.

Indigenous Peoples of Siberia

James Forsyth's *A History of the Peoples of Siberia* (2008) traces the history of Siberia's native peoples from the Russian conquest onwards.

Russians who ventured across the Ural Mountains before the 16th century returned with excited reports of an endless forest rich in fur-bearing sable. They also told of bizarre people who didn't stop short of hacking up their own children to feed a guest (an unlikely form of hospitality) or who died each winter because water trickled out of their noses and caused their feet to freeze to the ground.

The rumours were fanciful; the reality, however, was that Orthodox Russians had begun to weave themselves into a complex cultural region and dominate it. This region included the Turkic-speaking Tartars (but also other Turkic-speaking groups, such as the peoples of Altai), Mongol-speaking Buryats, as well as Khanty and Mansi peoples who inhabited the plains and taiga of Western Siberia, spoke a Finno-Ugric language and lived off hunting, fishing and sometimes reindeer herding.

In the north of Siberia, Orthodox Russians encountered clans of Samoyeds along a vast stretch of tundra and taiga from the Urals region to the Lena River in Eastern Siberia. So-called Samoyeds included Nenets (today centred on the capital, Salekhard, in Western Siberia), Enets, Nganasans and other tundra peoples whose lifestyle was often based around reindeer herding, hunting and fishing. Small related groups of Selkups (earlier known as Yenisey Ostyaks or Ostyak Samoyeds) lived south in forests around the Yenisey River, and even further south Russians met upon descendants of the Kets, some of whom even lived on houseboats similar to the sampans of China.

Anna Reid's *The Shaman's Coat* is both a fascinating history of the major native peoples of Siberia and the Russian Far East and a lively travelogue.

Further east across the north of Siberia were peoples such as the reindeer-herding Chukchi, seafaring Aleuts, reindeer-herding Koryaks, and Koryaks and Itelmeni of Kamchatka who mostly hunted and fished. In the southern regions of the Far East lived over half a dozen ethnic groups of fishing or hunting peoples such as the Nivkhi of Sakhalin Island.

In terms of land area, the most widespread ethnic group in Siberia comprised the Evenki (and Evens, together often called Tungusi), who populated pockets of Western Siberia, a vast heartland of Central Siberia and the north

THE TRADITIONS OF THE BANYA

For centuries, travellers to Russia have commented on the particular (in many people's eyes, peculiar) traditions of the *banya* (bathhouse). To this day, Russians make it an important part of their week and you can't say you've really been to Russia unless you've visited a *banya*.

The main element of the *banya* is the *parilka* (steam room). Here, rocks are heated by a furnace, with water poured onto them using a long-handled ladle. A few drops of eucalyptus or pine oils (sometimes even beer) are often added to the water, creating an aroma-filled burst of steam that's released into the room. You'll note that even though people are naked in the *banya*, some wear a *chapka* (felt cap) to protect their hair from the effects of the heat.

As they sweat it out, some bathers grab hold of a *venik* (a tied bundle of birch branches) and beat themselves or each other with it. Though it can be painful, the effect can also be pleasant and cleansing: the birch leaves (sometimes oak or, agonisingly, juniper branches) and their secretions are supposed to help rid the skin of toxins. After the birch-branch thrashing, bathers run outside and, depending on their nerve, plunge into the *basseyn* (ice-cold pool) or take a cooling shower. The whole process is then repeated several times for up to two hours.

Russia's big cities all offer *banya* complexes with Moscow's Sanduny Baths being the most luxurious (and expensive). Grab any chance to try a traditional countryside *banya*: nearly all the guesthouses on Olkhon Island in Lake Baikal have them.

that took in Central Siberia, a large swath of Yakutia and even parts of the Pacific seaboard. In the south, Tungusi populated large portions of the Lake Baikal and Amur River regions, and even the northern fringes of Mongolia and China, where they adopted Mongolian equestrian culture. Most Tungusi, however, were forest people who hunted and fished. Many were reindeer people; they revered bears and practised shamanism like almost all of the Siberian peoples, and they lived in groups of a couple of families, or up to a dozen in summer.

Today there are about 38,000 Evenki living in Russia and they are one of the 40 indigenous groups who number less than 50,000 and make up the 'small-numbered peoples of the North'.

Peoples of the Borderlands

For the Trans-Siberian traveller, the Lake Baikal and Amur regions are especially interesting as it's here that one enters a historical and contemporary conflux of Russian, Mongolian and Chinese cultures. While Russia was expanding eastwards, China, ruled by the Manchus of the Qing dynasty, was gradually expanding into present-day Mongolia. With the Treaty of Kyakhta in 1727 between Russia and China, many Khalkh Mongolians – a tribe that makes up about 86% of all Mongolians today – were stranded on the Russian side. They became integrated into Buryat culture and had an enormous influence on Buryatiya.

The Amur region was traditionally inhabited by Mongol-speaking Daurs, and further east of the Daurs were the Jurchen, a group related to the Tungusi and the Manchus. Beyond these were various other Manchu-Tungusi peoples, including the predecessors of today's 12,000-strong community of Nanai (also known as Goldi) who live around both the Amur and the Ussuri rivers and across the Amur in Hēilóngjiāng province in China. In China, the Amur is known as the Black Dragon River.

Religion

Since 1997 the Russian Orthodox Church has been legally recognised as the country's leading faith. Russia also has a major Muslim population (anything between 6.5% and 15% of the population depending on different surveys), between 158,000 and 194,000 practising Jews and between 700,000 and 1.5 million Buddhists, as well as smaller groups that adhere to shamanism.

Russian Orthodox Church

The Orthodox Church flourished until 1653, when it was split by reforms of Patriarch Nikon (1605–81), who insisted on a new translation of the Bible to bring it closer to the Greek original and that the sign of the cross be made with three fingers. This led to a schism, with many of the persecuted Starovery (Old Believers) fleeing. A large number settled in remote pockets of Siberia and Central Asia.

For the most part, Soviet leaders dealt blow after blow to the Church, but today about 75% of Russians identify with the Orthodox Church, even if only a much smaller percentage practise the religion on a daily basis.

1689

Russia and China sign the Treaty of Nerchinsk. Russia withdraws from the Amur basin; it retains the Transbaikal and trade caravans receive rights of passage to travel to Běijīng.

1696–1725

Peter I ('the Great') becomes sole tsar after a period co-ruling with his half-brother. Under Peter the Great, St Petersburg is founded and Russia modernises and becomes more European.

1812–14

Napoleon's invasion of Russia (1812) culminates in his ill-fated march on Moscow, when Muscovites burn two-thirds of the capital rather than see it occupied. Russians briefly occupy Paris in 1814.

1904–05

The Russo-Japanese War results in Russia's defeat. Abysmal social and political conditions lead to the revolution of 1905, when Russia nominally becomes a constitutional monarchy, but reform remains patchy.

1914–18

WWI rages. In February 1917 Nicholas II abdicates; in October Bolsheviks seize power. In 1918 Lenin pulls Russia out of WWI and Nicholas II is murdered during Russia's civil war.

1922–53

Stalin rules over an era that brings brutal collectivisation, purges and Gulag camps. Russia industrialises and liberates parts of Europe in WWII, but it establishes a stifling hegemony over Eastern Europe.

THE SOVIET SUN GOD

Soviet authorities liked to depict shamans in propaganda as forces of evil. In practice, shamans were simply a threat to the Soviet ideologists' own influence over the native peoples. But in an interesting turn of events, the ideologists even tried to win hearts and minds by depicting Lenin and Stalin as uber-shamans who battled evil spirits.

In his book *The Peoples of the Soviet Far East*, Walter Kolarz mentions a 'Nanai' tale in which Lenin is depicted as a kind of sun god who resides far away and spreads light into the darkness and upon the oppressed of the land. With the death of Lenin, evil seems to triumph, but no, along comes an omniscient Stalin, Lenin's great friend, who sees and hears everything (the propagandists were almost right about that): 'Nobody can equal the strength of that hero. He sees everything that goes on on Earth. His ears hear everything people say. His brain knows all that people think.'

Top Sacred Visits

- *Church upon the Blood, Yekaterinburg*
- *Trinity Monastery, Tyumen*
- *St Sofia & Intercession Cathedrals, Toblosk*
- *Znamensky Monastery, Irkutsk*

Buddhism

The Kalmyks (from the Republic of Kalmykia north of the Caspian Sea) form the largest group of Russian Buddhists. These are Gelugpa or 'Yellow Hat' Buddhists, as in Tibet. The Gelugpa sect reached eastern Buryatiya via Mongolia in the 18th century, but only in the 19th century did it really take root. Stalin's ideologues and henchmen destroyed hundreds of *datsany* (Buddhist temples) in the 1930s, and executed or exiled thousands of peaceable lamas. At the end of WWII two *datsany* were opened – a new one at Ivolginsk near Ulan-Ude, which houses Russia's largest collection of Buddhist texts, and another at Aginskoe (southeast of Chita). The glorious 1820 Tsugol Datsan is the only other Siberian *datsan* to survive virtually intact.

Islam

Muslim history dates back about 1000 years in Russia. The majority of Muslims live in the Caucasus region. Kazan, situated on the Volga River, is the capital of the Tatarstan Republic, where about 48% of the population is Tatar and 43% Russian. Other cities on the middle Volga with large Muslim populations are Ulyanovsk, Samara and Nizhny Novgorod, while significant communities also live in Moscow and St Petersburg. Tyumen, Tobolsk, the Baraba Steppe and Tomsk in Siberia have significant Muslim Tartar populations.

Shamanism & Animism

Many cultures, from the Finno-Ugric Mari and Udmurts to the nominally Buddhist Mongol Buryats, retain varying degrees of animism. This is often submerged beneath, or accepted in parallel with, other religions. Animism is a primal belief in the presence of spirits or spiritual qualities in objects of the natural world. Peaks and springs are especially revered and their spirits are thanked with token offerings. This explains (especially in Tuva and Altai) the coins, stone cairns, vodka bottles and abundant prayer ribbons that you'll commonly find around holy trees and mountain passes.

Spiritual guidance is through a shaman – a high priest, prophet and doctor in one. Animal skins, trance dances and a special drum are typical shamanic tools, though different shamans have different spiritual and medical gifts.

Russkiy Mir (www.russkiymir.ru) is a Russian government-sponsored organisation to preserve and promote the Russian language and culture throughout the world.

The Arts

With 19th-century composers such as Modest Mussorgsky (1839–81) and Pyotr Tchaikovsky (1840–93), later greats like Sergei Rachmaninov (1873–1943) and Dmitry Shostakovich (1906–75), and the contemporary soprano star Anna Netrebko (b 1971), Russia has a lot to offer the classical-music buff. Understandably, Moscow and St Petersburg take the lead role in stage, music and theatre in Russia, and galleries like the Tretyakov Gallery or the Pushkin Museum of Fine Arts in Moscow and the Hermitage in St Petersburg are highlights.

The Tretyakov has a large collection of paintings by the Krasnoyarsk-born painter Vasily Surikov (1848–1916), including details of *The Conquest of Siberia by Yermak*. The full-scale painting is in the Russian Museum in St Petersburg.

In Siberia itself, Surikov's house in Krasnoyarsk is a splendid inner-city retreat, and there are works by the artist and spiritualist Nikolai Rerikh (1874–1947; known internationally as Nicholas Roerich) in the State Art Museum in Novosibirsk. In Irkutsk's Art Gallery are a couple of works by Ilya Repin (1844–1930) and Ivan Shishkin (1832–98). Both are closely tied to the Peredvizhniki (Wanderers) movement, a 19th-century breakaway group that began staging exhibitions at temporary locations and focused on national and Slavic themes in its paintings. The regional museums across Siberia are excellent places to learn about indigenous arts and crafts.

Near Irkutsk, the Taltsy Museum of Wooden Architecture is excellent, including original 17th-century structures from the Ilimsk fort. Further east, just outside Ulan-Ude, the Ethnographic Museum has Old Believer houses and Buryat artefacts. In Listvyanka, check out the small artists colony with a picture gallery *(kartinaya galeriya)* in the side valley at Chapaeva 76 (a sign points to it).

In literature, Valentin Rasputin (1937–2015) wrote some evocative and thought-provoking works about Siberia and was associated with the Village Prose movement, which focused on traditional Russian values. Another acclaimed Siberian is Vasily Shukshin (1929–74), a famous Soviet-era director, screenwriter and writer who hailed from the Altai region and wrote *Stories from a Siberian Village*.

1953–82

Nikita Khrushchev becomes first secretary and condemns Stalin's brutal policies. The years from 1964 under successor Leonid Brezhnev are marked by stagnation. Siberian oil discoveries hide Soviet economic flaws.

1985–91

Mikhail Gorbachev is elected first secretary and initiates *perestroika* and *glasnost* reforms. A failed coup in August 1991 causes the collapse of the USSR and the rise of Boris Yeltsin.

1990s

Yeltsin uses force in 1993 to crush dissenters in parliament; the decade brings civil freedoms but also powerful oligarchs, crime, poverty, and war in breakaway Chechnya. Yeltsin resigns in 1999.

2000–present

A 'tandem' of Vladimir Putin and Dmitry Medvedev ruling variously as president and prime minister oversees relative re-stabilisation of Russia. Power is re-centralised, but many Russians seek greater civil freedoms.

Russian Cuisine

Russia's food heritage is enriched by influences from the Baltic to the Far East as well as pan-European trends. A culinary highlight of a rail journey through Russia will be the freshwater fish of Lake Baikal, and in Moscow or St Petersburg don't forgo a meal in a good Georgian restaurant.

Russians like to eat till late, and they also like to enjoy a crossover of eating, drinking, dancing and entertainment (often karaoke these days) in one session. So while the traditional Slavic kitchen might lack the culinary peaks of, say, French or Italian cooking, a night out in a restaurant in Russia can be a splendid 'universal' experience.

Staples

A typical *zavtrak* (breakfast) will include bliny (pancakes) with savoury or sweet fillings, various types of *kasha* (porridge), and *syrniki* (cottage-cheese fritters), delicious with jam, sugar and the universal Russian condiment, *smetana* (sour cream). Russians excel in dairy products such as *tvorog* (soft curd) and dairy drinks, so make sure you sample these.

Lunch or dinner usually starts with *zakuski* (appetisers) then progresses to soup – often served with piles of bread and a thick dollop of sour cream – such as borsch, made with beetroot and mostly beef; *lapsha* (chicken noodle); *solyanka* (a thick broth with meat, fish and a host of vegetables); *ukho* (fish soup); and *shchi* (cabbage soup).

Main dishes often come with a small salad garnish, and side dishes are almost always ordered separately on the menu as *garniry*. Lamb from the steppes of Kalmykia and beef from Altai are excellent. *Pelmeni* (ravioli) has been elevated to an art form in Siberia.

Siberia Movies

How I Ended This Summer (Kak ya provyol etim letom; 2010)

Sibir. Monamur (2011)

The Edge (Krai; 2010)

During summer, outdoor pizza and shashlyk (kebab) stalls pop up all over the place – in Krasnoyarsk you will find an enormous row of shashlyk stands and beer tents along the Yenisey River. Not to be missed are *pirozhki* (savoury pies). In most Russian cities it's common to find restaurants serving set three-course *biznes* lunches from noon to 4pm Monday to Friday; these cost as little as R300 (R500 in Moscow and St Petersburg).

Sweet-toothed Russians adore *morozhenoye* (ice cream) and gooey *torty* (cream cakes), often decorated in lurid colours. *Pecheniye* (sweet pastries) are eaten at tea time in the traditional English style and are available at any *bulochnaya* (bakery). Locally made chocolate and *konfetki* (sweets) are also excellent and, with their colourful wrappings, make great presents.

Specialities

You'll find the following regional food specialities along the rail routes.

kasylyk (dried horsemeat sausages) – along with *zur balish* (meat pies), this is from Tatarstan, where *chek chek* (honey-drenched, macaroni-shaped pieces of fried dough) are also an essential part of celebrations

manti (steamed, palm-sized dumplings) – known as *buuz* or *buuzy* in Buryatiya and *pyan-se* (a peppery version) in the Russian Far East

oblyoma (dried, salty fish found in the Volga) – often eaten as a snack food with beer

omul (a cousin of salmon and trout) – endemic to Lake Baikal and considered a great delicacy; *kharius* (grayling) is also delicious

Vegetarians & Vegans

Russia restaurants are tough on vegetarians, Georgian ones less so. Salmon is widespread for those who eat fish. *Zakuski* include quite a lot of meatless ingredients, such as eggs and mushrooms. Failing that, a Greek salad with feta cheese is fairly widespread in cities. If you're travelling during Lent, you'll find that many restaurants have special nonmeat menus.

Drinks

Russia produces hundreds of different brands of vodka, including ones that you'll certainly have heard of such as Stolichnaya and Smirnoff. Also look out for Moskovskaya, Flagman and Gzhelka. As well as 'plain' vodka you'll find *klyukovka* (cranberry vodka), *pertsovka* (pepper vodka), *starka* (vodka flavoured with apple and pear leaves), *limonnaya* (vodka with lemon) and *okhotnichya* (meaning 'hunter's vodka', with about a dozen ingredients, including peppers, juniper berries, ginger and cloves).

In *A Year of Russian Feasts*, Catherine Cheremeteff Jones recounts how Russia's finest dishes have been preserved and passed down through the feast days of the Russian Orthodox Church.

Far more popular as a drink than vodka is beer. The local market leader is Baltika, but there are scores of other palatable local brands and a fast-growing sector of microbreweries producing craft beers.

Most wines in Russia are foreign, and although you will find some decent ones, there will be little unique about them. The word for 'dry' is *sukhoe*. Russian *konyak* (brandy) from the Caucasus is often a pleasant surprise.

Kvas is fermented rye-bread water, and in summer is dispensed on the street from big wheeled tanks. It tastes not unlike ginger beer, and is a wonderfully cool and refreshing drink. *Mors*, a fruit drink made from cranberries and other fruits, is popular in summer.

Russians are world-class tea drinkers, and this partly explains the samovars at the end of every railway carriage. In Russian homes, the traditional brewing method is to make an extremely strong pot, pour small shots of it into glasses and fill the glasses with hot water from the kettle. Putting jam, instead of sugar, in tea is quite common.

Coffee comes in small cups, and unless you buy it at kiosks or stand-up eateries, it's usually quite good. There's been an explosion of Starbucks-style cafes all across Russia's bigger cities – cappuccino, espresso, latte and mocha are now as much a part of the average Russian lexicon as elsewhere.

Other drinks include *sok* (juice) and *kefir* (yoghurt-like sour milk).

Mongolia Today

Mongolia's importance on the world stage is growing. 'Mine-golia', as it's sometimes called, has enormous mineral wealth, including vast reserves of coal and copper. Despite this golden economic potential, there have been downturns, as various governments overspent mining revenues. Hard lessons learned, Mongolia now seems more committed to fiscal stability, cautious spending and diversification away from mining to focus on other sectors, including agriculture and tourism.

Best on Film

The Weeping Camel (2005) Docu-drama that follows a camel herder family in the Gobi.

Mongol (2007) Dramatic depiction of the rise of Chinggis Khaan.

The Eagle Huntress (2016) Docu-drama about a 13-year-girl and her quest to become the first female champion in Bayan-Ölgii's eagle-hunting competition.

Best in Print

Ghengis Khan and the Making of the Modern World (Jack Weatherford; 2005) Groundbreaking book and a bestseller on the Mongol empire.

Mörön to Mörön (Tom Doig; 2013) Wacky adventures of two Aussies making their way across Mongolia on pushbikes.

Dateline Mongolia (Michael Kohn; 2017) An American journalist crosses the country, recounting misadventures and bizarre news events.

Sky Shamans of Mongolia (Kevin Turner; 2016) Eye-opening and well-researched account by a practising shaman describing his encounters with a Mongolian shaman.

The Great Leap Forward

Mongolia's biggest driver of growth is the US$10-billion Oyu Tolgoi copper and gold underground mine, developed by the Anglo-Australian company Rio Tinto, but 34% owned by the Mongolian government. When complete in around 2021, the mine could account for one-third of the country's total GDP. The hope is that this single world-class deposit will lift the whole country up by the bootstraps. The nearby Tavan Tolgoi mine, another big revenue earner, exports coking coal to China where it's used in the production of steel.

China is a ready market for Mongolia's raw materials and the government is rapidly trying to build up its infrastructure to deliver the goods. New rail and road links to China are being built, and in a bid to diversify its markets, Mongolia is also planning a 1000km railway from the southernmost Gobi all the way to Russia (via Choibalsan).

Mongolia's political leaders seem keenly aware of the need to invest the newfound wealth back into the country. A copper smelter, an oil refinery and coal washing plants are a few of the planned factories. A new international airport is expected to open in 2018. The government is also planning to construct enormous power plants to export energy to China, Korea and Japan. While most of these plans include dirty coal-fired plants, Mongolia insists that by 2030, more than 20 percent of its energy will come from renewable sources including solar and wind farms.

Bankrupt Nation

Mongolians went to the polls in June 2016 and gave the Mongolian People's Party (MPP) a decisive victory over the ruling Democrats. The MPP took over a country nearly bankrupt after the Democrats spent the country's mineral wealth on populist projects, including subsidised mortgages, cash handouts and highways.

In 2017 the International Monetary Fund (IMF) and other partners bailed Mongolia out of debt with a long-term loan worth US$5.5 billion, an amount nearly half the country's GDP.

To receive the massive loan, Mongolia agreed to cut spending and raise taxes, particularly on vehicles, petrol, cigarettes and alcohol. Income taxes shot up for higher earners and state executives saw salaries cut by up to 50%. While the loan was under negotiation, protestors on Sükhbaatar Sq demanded officials get out of debt by repatriating monies hidden in offshore bank accounts. The organisers claimed some US$16 billion had been embezzled overseas.

The MPP also faces numerous social challenges, especially in Ulaanbaatar, where public anger over air pollution and lack of modern housing has boiled over to street protests. In response, the government has promised to redevelop the ger districts and ban the use of raw coal for heating. In the countryside, officials are promising more jobs by developing meat and dairy farms that will export products to China.

In mid-2017 Battulga Khaltmaa became Mongolia's fifth president after an unprecedented two rounds of voting.

The Future

Mongolia's journey over the past three decades since the fall of the Iron Curtain has been a two-step-forward, one-step-back process. One of its greatest successes is the establishment of an open society. Its people are now increasingly online, obsessed with social media and using new technologies to better society. Young Mongolians are forging unique identities, often driven by nationalist ideas.

Mongolia is looking to expand its network of railways and highways. Mineral processing factories, coal-fired power plants and farms are also planned. The challenge lies in growing the industrial sector without causing harm to the environment. Mongolia is already suffering from wildlife habitat loss and desertification due to poorly enforced mining and agriculture regulations.

While increased industrialisation will bring jobs, revenue and prosperity, it will be some time before the benefits reach low income households. In poor areas, schools are overcrowded, public hospitals are crumbling and basic infrastructure is generally nonexistent. While the government has been slow to address infrastructure needs in poor areas, the private sector has turned pockets of Ulaanbaatar into self-sustaining gated communities.

Despite the challenges ahead, public surveys show widespread support for the economic reforms. There is strong optimism among most of the population, but the country still has a long way to go before it can claim success.to as much as US$1.5 billion (the government claims US$700 million).

POPULATION: **3,140,000**

GDP: **US$3870 PER CAPITA (2015)**

GDP GROWTH: **1% (2016)**

INFLATION: **2.5%**

LITERACY RATE: **98%**

if Mongolia were 100 people

66 would be settled
34 would be nomadic

belief systems

(% of population)

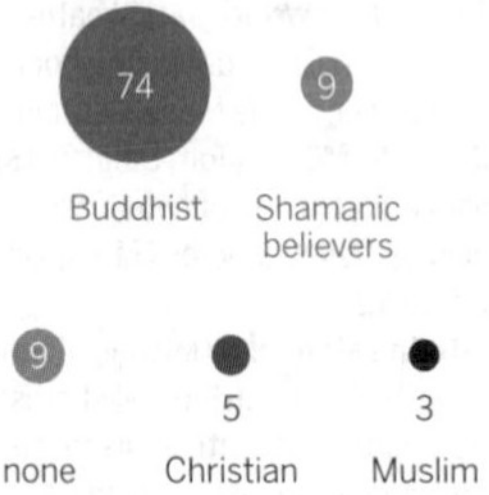

population per sq km

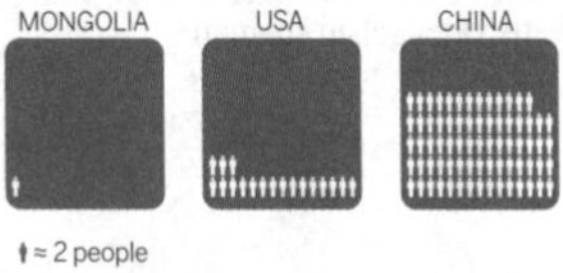

Mongolian Culture & Cuisine

Nomadic herders speed over the steppes on motorcycles to herd their flocks while Buddhist monks tap away at iPhones between prayer sessions – these are some of the paradoxes that visitors come across in Mongolia. It's a constant battle here to keep the traditional lifestyle alive amid the advances of modern society. Yet Mongolia is pulling it off, even fusing traditional and modern music, food and spiritual beliefs. This uncanny ability to adapt to changing times has helped usher in the new era of democracy.

The Mongolian People

Mongolians have traditionally been a nomadic people. This way of life was born out of necessity, as herders were forced to move their animals over the harsh landscape in search of fresh pasture. This lifestyle has shaped Mongolians' psyche, worldview, philosophy, ethics and relationship with their neighbours.

Livestock, especially horses, play a crucial role in Mongolian culture. It was the horse that allowed ancient tribespeople to spread across the steppes and cover great distances as they tended their animals. Later it was the horse that carried Mongol warriors across Asia as they built their empire. An old Mongolian proverb says: 'A man without a horse is like a bird without wings'.

Nomadic peoples are greatly affected by the climate and other natural forces. Because good pastures are a requirement for the survival of the herds (and therefore the people), traditional beliefs eschew mining, construction or other development of the land. Throughout the ages, Mongolians have believed that nature is not something to be tamed or dominated but something that's better left untouched. These traditional beliefs are now giving way to other considerations as politicians and businesspeople seek to develop mines and other infrastructure.

Seasons also shape Mongolian life. Spring in particular is a crucial time. Because the country's rainy season comes towards the end of summer, spring is dry, dusty, windy and unforgiving. This is the time when the weaker animals die and, it is said, when people die. Despite

MONGOLIAN HISTORY

209–174 BC

Reign of Modun, as *shanyu* of the Huns; the first great steppe empire of Mongolia stretches from Korea to Lake Baikal and south into northern China.

AD 552–744

Succession of two Turkic empires; the greatest ruler is Bilge Khan. Following his death in 734 a monument is erected near Lake Ögii.

744–840

The Uyghur empire occupies central Mongolia until expelled by the Kyrgyz tribe; the Uyghur move south into western China and control the Silk Road for nearly 1000 years.

1162

Birth of Temujin, the child destined to become Chinggis Khaan, near the Onon River. According to legend, Temujin emerges with a blood clot clutched in his fist.

1206

Chinggis Khaan calls a massive conclave at Kherlen Gol and creates his empire, which he names the Great Mongol Nation.

1368

Yuan dynasty collapses in China. The Mongol government returns to Mongolia, refusing to submit to the newly created Ming dynasty. They continue ruling 'Northern Yuan'.

1585

Founding of Erdene Zuu, first Buddhist monastery in Mongolia, at the site of the Mongol capital, Karakorum (modern Kharkhorin).

CHINGGIS KHAAN

Known to the world as a bloodthirsty conqueror, Chinggis (Genghis) Khaan is remembered by Mongolians as the great lawgiver, whose laws derived from practical considerations more than from ideology or religion, and they proudly refer to him as the Man of the Millennium (a title bestowed on him by the *Washington Post* in 1995).

After the abduction of his wife Borte, Chinggis Khaan recognised the role of kidnapping in perpetuating feuds among clans and outlawed it. Similarly, he perceived religious intolerance as being a source of violence in sedentary society and so decreed religious freedom for everyone and exempted religious scholars and priests from taxes.

To promote trade and communications, Chinggis Khaan built an international network of postal stations that also served as hostels for merchants. He decreased and standardised taxes on goods so that they would not be repeatedly taxed. Under these laws the Mongol empire formed the first intercontinental free-trade zone.

In an era when ambassadors served as hostages to be publicly tortured or killed during times of hostilities, Chinggis Khaan ordered that every ambassador be considered an envoy of peace. This law marked the beginning of diplomatic immunity and international law. Today nearly every country accepts and promotes, at least in theory, the ideas and policies behind the 'Great Law of Chinggis Khaan'.

the severe temperatures, it's during winter that Mongolians feel most comfortable. After a difficult summer filled with chores and moving around the herds, winter is a time to relax inside a ger (yurt) and fatten up against the cold.

Nearly all nomadic families have a short-wave radio to get national and world news. Many receive satellite TV and certainly everyone reads newspapers when they're available (98% of Mongolians are literate).

Mongolia's vast, open steppes and great distances have made hospitality a matter of sheer necessity rather than simply a social obligation. It would be difficult for anyone to travel across this vast, sparsely populated country without the hospitality that has developed, as each ger is able to serve travellers as a hotel, restaurant, pub and repair shop. As a result, Mongolians are able to travel rapidly over long distances without the weight of provisions.

Life on the steppes is by no means easy or idyllic. Constant work is required to care for the animals, cook food and collect dung and water. It's also a precarious life: a harsh winter can kill millions of head of livestock, as happened in 2009. The government can resupply some herders who lose animals in a severe storm, but many have ended up jobless in the sprawling suburbs around Ulaanbaatar.

In the capital, urban Mongolians have developed their own unique blend of Mongolian and Western lifestyles. You'll see young people wearing the latest European or American fashions, sporting mohawks, hoop earrings, gangsta garb and iPhones. Materialism is apparent in all the flashy SUVs bounding around the city. But talk to some young locals and you'll soon realise that their hopes and dreams lie not only in the West but also in the future of Mongolia, its success and prosperity and the continuation of its unique culture.

Ovoos, the large piles of rocks found on mountain passes, are repositories of offerings for local spirits. Upon arriving at an *ovoo*, walk around it clockwise three times, toss an offering onto the pile (another rock should suffice) and make a wish.

Religion

Spirituality in Mongolia comes in many forms, with many day-to-day rituals rooted in Mongolia's shamanic past. The ancient animist beliefs of the Siberian and steppe tribes who worshipped the sun, earth and sky are still very much alive, woven intimately into the fabric of modern Mongolia.

Shamanism

Mongolians have long believed in the spirit world as their shamans described it to them. Their cosmic view of the universe did not differentiate between the worlds of the living and the dead, nor did they consider themselves any greater than other creatures in this or other worlds. Any imbalance between the human and natural worlds could cause calamity.

Shamanism centres on the shaman – called a *bo* if a man or *udgan* if a woman – who has special medical and religious powers. A shaman's main functions are to cure any sickness caused by the soul straying and to accompany the soul of a dead person into the afterlife. Shamans act as intermediaries between the human and spirit worlds, and communicate with spirits during trances, which can last up to six hours.

Sky worship is another integral part of shamanism and you'll see Mongolians leaving blue scarves (representing the sky) on *ovoos* (piles of stones built to honour earth spirits). Sky gods are likewise honoured by flicking droplets of vodka into the air before drinking.

Buddhism

The Mongols had limited contact with organised religion before their great empire of the 13th century. It was Kublai Khaan who first found himself with a court in which all philosophies of his empire were represented, but it was a Tibetan Buddhist, Phagpa, who wielded the greatest influence on the khaan.

In 1578 Altan Khaan, a descendant of Chinggis Khaan, met the Tibetan leader Sonam Gyatso, was converted, and subsequently bestowed on Sonam Gyatso the title Dalai Lama (*dalai* means 'ocean' in Mongolian). Sonam Gyatso was named as the third Dalai Lama and his two predecessors were named posthumously.

Mass conversions occurred under Altan Khaan. As Mongolian males were conscripted to monasteries, rather than the army, the centuries of constant fighting seemed to wane (much to the relief of China, which subsequently funded more monasteries in Mongolia).

Buddhist opposition to needless killing reinforced strict hunting laws already set in place by shamanism. Today, Buddhist monks are still influential in convincing local populations to protect their environment and wildlife.

Buddhism in Mongolia was nearly destroyed in 1937 when the young communist government, fearing competition, launched a purge that wiped out nearly all of the country's 700 monasteries. Up to 30,000 monks were massacred and thousands more sent to Siberian labour camps. Freedom of religion was only restored in 1990 following Mongolia's peaceful democratic revolution.

Restoring Buddhism has been no easy task, as two generations were essentially raised atheist. While many Mongolians will make the occasional visit to their local temple, Buddhist rituals and meanings are not well understood. Despite this, numbers swell at Ulaanbaatar's Gandan monastery when well-known Buddhist monks from Tibet or India (or even Western countries) visit Mongolia.

Islam

The country has a significant minority of Sunni Muslims, most of them ethnic Kazakhs who live primarily in

1639

Zanabazar, a direct descendent of Chinggis Khaan and the greatest artist in Mongolian history, is recognised as the first Jebtzun Damba, the supreme religious leader of Mongolia.

1696

The Manchus defeat Galdan Khaan of Dzungaria and claim western Mongolia for the Qing dynasty, but some western Mongolians continue to resist for several generations.

1911

Mongolia declares independence from China and sets up religious leader Bogd Khan as the head of state.

1915

Treaty of Khyakhta is signed by Mongolia, China and Russia, granting Mongolia limited autonomy.

1921

The Mad Baron, von Ungern-Sternberg, briefly conquers Mongolia, but the Red Army and Mongolian forces under D Sükhbaatar defeat him.

1924

The Bogd Khan, the eighth reincarnation of the Jebtzun Damba, dies; the People's Republic of Mongolia is created on 26 November.

1937

Choibalsan's Buddhist purge leaves 700 monasteries destroyed and 27,000 monks and civilians dead. Purge victims include former prime minister P Genden.

1939

Japan invades Mongolia from Manchuria in May. With help from the Soviet Union, and after heavy fighting along the Khalkh

Bayan-Ölgii. Because of Mongolia's great isolation and distance from the major Islamic centres of the Middle East, Islam has never been a major force in Bayan-Ölgii. However, most villages have a mosque and contacts have been established with Islamic groups in Turkey. Several prominent figures in the community have been on a hajj to Mecca. A small population of Kazakhs live in the city of Nalaikh, 35km southeast of Ulaanbaatar.

Christianity

The fastest-growing religion in Mongolia is Christianity. A whole spectrum of mainstream and fundamentalist sects have set up shop in Ulaanbaatar, each of them competing to convert a nation whose native faith is not well supported. In 1990 the number of Christians was negligible. Today there are an estimated 65,000 Christians and more than 150 churches.

Nestorian Christianity was part of the Mongol empire long before Western missionaries arrived. The Nestorians followed the doctrine of Nestorius (358–451), patriarch of Constantinople (428–31), who proclaimed that Jesus exists as two separate persons: the man Jesus and the divine son of God.

The 2010 documentary *Babies* featured four newborns from different corners of the globe: Namibia, San Francisco, Tokyo and Mongolia. Watching the film gives unique insight into the life of a typical Mongolian rural family.

The Arts

From prehistoric oral epics to the latest movie from MongolKino film studios in Ulaanbaatar, the many arts of Mongolia convey the flavour of nomadic life and the spirit of the land.

Music

Traditional Mongolian music, which can be heard at concerts in Ulaanbaatar, is usually played on a *morin khuur* (horsehead fiddle), a two-stringed vertical violin and a lute. These instruments are also used by some of Mongolia's popular rock bands, including Altan Urag and Boerte Ensemble.

There are also several unique traditional singing styles. The enigmatic *khöömii* – throat singing – has the remarkable effect of producing two notes simultaneously – one a low growl and the other an ethereal whistling. Translated as 'long songs', *urtyn-duu* use long trills to relate traditional stories about love and the countryside.

There is a thriving contemporary music scene in Ulaanbaatar and you can hear live music at many downtown bars like Gandan Live House or Grand Khaan Irish Pub. Popular music genres include pop, rap and hip-hop, as well as a totally Mongolian brand of folklore-rock fusion music

THE MAD BARON

Throughout their history the disparate countries of Mongolia, Russia and China have had few agreements. It was only in 1920 that the three found themselves facing a common enemy – one Baron Roman Nikolaus Fyodorovich von Ungern-Sternberg, aka the Mad Baron.

A renegade White Russian officer who believed he was the reincarnation of Chinggis (Genghis) Khaan, the Baron was described by his contemporaries as a psychotic killer whose army consisted of escaped convicts and bandits.

In the summer of 1920 the Baron led his 6000-strong army on an assault of Ulaanbaatar, chasing out the Chinese army that occupied the city. The Baron declared himself emperor of Mongolia and Russia, and then sent his men on a three-day orgy of looting, burning and killing.

After only a few months, the Bolshevik advance across Siberia forced the Baron to abandon Urga. Out on the steppes, his own followers tried to kill him by shooting him in his tent, but he managed to escape. He was eventually captured by the Bolsheviks, deported to Novosibirsk and shot on 15 September 1921.

The Bloody White Baron (2010) by Stephen Palmer is a vivid account of the rise and fall of this legendary character.

that includes drums and guitars along with traditional instruments.

For folklore-rock, Altan Urag is regarded as one of the best. Their mash-ups of Western percussion and Mongolian string instruments will have you entranced. We are also fans of the Boerte Ensemble, which fuses all sorts of instruments into a mellow sound good for long road trips. Their videos are available on YouTube. Another band enjoying some success is Khusugtun (www.khusugtun-group.com).

If you're into hip-hop, look out for upcoming artists Opozit, Quiza, Tatar and Tsetse. Their lyrics combine inner-city struggles as well as traditional themes of lost love and wild nature. Rock groups include the Lemons, Pips and Nisvanis.

The recent breakout in Mongolian rap has not gone unnoticed. Australian filmmaker Benj Binks has documented the phenomenon in *Mongolian Bling* (http://mongolianbling.com) as has American Lauren Knapp in *Live From UB* (www.livefromub.com), a documentary exploring Mongolian rock music.

Theatre & Film

Mongolia's best-known modern poet and playwright is Dashdorjiin Natsagdorj (1906–37), regarded as the founder of Mongolian literature. His dramatic nationalist poems and plays are still performed in Mongolian theatres today. There's also been a revival in Mongolian cinema, its brightest star being director Byambasuren Davaa. Her best-known films, *The Story of the Weeping Camel* (2003) and *The Cave of the Yellow Dog* (2005), depict nomadic life, the simplicity of the steppes and Mongolia's transition into the 21st century.

Visual Arts

Many of Mongolia's visual arts are religious in nature. Religious scroll paintings, depicting deities and their enlightened qualities, can be found on family altars in many homes. Another traditional style of painting is *zurag* – landscape storytelling. These landscapes include intricate sketches depicting every aspect of Mongolian life. Balduugiyn Sharav (1869–1939) is Mongolia's best-known painter in this style. The sculptor Zanabazar (1635–1723) is one of Mongolia's most revered artists, as well as a religious and political leader. He is known primarily for his cast-bronze statues, which are now on display in monasteries and museums around Ulaanbaatar.

Ulaanbaatar has a vibrant modern-art scene, with several commercial galleries across the capital holding regularly changing exhibitions.

Mongolian Cuisine

Mongolian cuisine evolved from nomadic traditions and the types of food available on Mongolia's barren steppes. Livestock (which offer meat and milk) have long been in plentiful supply. Fruit, vegetables, nuts, herbs and spices are mostly absent, due to the fact that nomadic people move frequently and crops do not.

Gol, the Mongols defeat Japan by September.

1956

The Trans-Siberian railroad through Mongolia is completed, connecting Běijīng with Moscow.

1961

Mongolia is admitted to the UN as an independent country, but the USSR continues to occupy Mongolia with troops and run the country as a satellite state.

1990

Democracy demonstrations in Ulaanbaatar. In June the first free, multiparty elections are held, with the Mongolian People's Revolutionary Party (MPRP) winning 85% of the vote.

1996

The Democratic Coalition becomes the first noncommunist government to win an election (although a series of scandals causes the fall of four successive governments).

1998

S Zorig, the leader of the 1990 democratic revolution, is assassinated in his apartment on 2 October. The killers are never found.

2008

In hotly contested parliamentary elections the MPRP narrowly defeats the Democratic Coalition. Protestors allege vote rigging, and subsequent riots end with four people shot dead and hundreds arrested.

2017

After an election victory the Mongolian People's Party acknowledges severe debts and accepts a US$5.5 billion bailout from the IMF to stabilise the economy over the next decade.

Mongolians have long traded for goods such as rice and flour, but more perishable products rarely made it north of the Gobi.

Mongolian food tends to be seasonal. In the summer months, when animals provide milk, dairy products become the staple. Meat (and fat) takes over in winter, supplemented with flour (in some form) and potatoes or rice if these are available.

The well-researched www.mongolfood.info includes notes on Mongolian cuisine, plus cooking techniques and recipes, dispelling the myth that Mongolian menus stop at boiled mutton.

Almost any Mongolian dish can be created with meat, rice, flour and potatoes. Most meals consist of *talkh* (bread) in the towns and cities and *bortzig* (fried unleavened bread) in the gers, and the uncomplicated *shölte khool* (literally, soup with food) – a meal involving hot broth, pasta slivers, boiled mutton and a few potato chunks. Nowadays, you can find plenty of international cuisine in the capital.

Buuz (steamed meat dumplings) and *khuushuur* (deep-fried meat pancakes) are two of the most popular menu options you'll find in restaurants. Miniature *buuz,* known as *bansh,* are usually dunked in milk tea. If you are travelling north from Běijīng, *buuz* may seem familiar – they are distant cousins of Chinese *bāozi.*

The classic Mongolian dinner staple is referred to simply as *makh* (meat) and consists of boiled sheep bits (bones, fat, various organs and the head) with some sliced potato, served in a plastic bucket. This meal does not require silverware; just trawl around the bucket of bones until a slab catches your fancy. There'll be a knife to slice off larger chunks.

The other main highlight of Mongolian cuisine is *khorkhog,* made by placing hot stones from an open fire into a pot or urn with chopped mutton, some water and sometimes vodka. The container is then sealed and left on the fire. When eating this meal, it's customary to pass the hot, greasy rocks from hand to hand, as this is thought to be good for your health.

In summer you can subsist as Mongolians do on *tsagaan idee* (dairy products; literally 'white foods'): yoghurt, milk, delicious fresh cream, cheese and fermented milk drinks. When you visit a ger you will be offered dairy snacks such as *aaruul* (dried milk curds), which are as hard as a rock and often about as tasty.

Finally, if you get a chance, don't miss the opportunity to try blowtorched marmot (prairie dog), a delicacy of the steppes.

Meals are occasionally interrupted for a round of vodka. Before taking a swig, a short ritual is employed to honour the sky gods and the four cardinal directions. There is no one way of doing this, but it usually involves dipping the left ring finger into the vodka and flicking droplets into the air four times before wiping your finger across your forehead.

Drinks

Mongolians are big tea drinkers and will almost never start a meal until they've had a cup of tea, as it's thought to aid digestion.

Süütei tsai, a classic Mongolian drink, is milk tea with salt. If you can't get used to the salty brew, try asking for *khar tsai* (black tea), which is like European tea, with sugar and no milk.

Alcoholic drinks are readily available and Mongolians can drink you under the table if you challenge them. There is much social pressure to drink, especially on males – those who refuse to drink *arkhi* (homemade vodka) are considered wimps.

Locally produced beer labels include Mongol, Chinggis, Borigo and Khan Brau. Popular vodkas include the very smooth Chinggis black label, which costs just US$8 a bottle.

While it may not seem obvious at first, every countryside ger doubles as a tiny distillery. One corner of the ger usually contains a tall, thin jug with a plunger that is used for fermenting mares' milk. The drink, known as *airag* or *koumiss,* has an alcohol content of about 3%. Go easy on the *airag* from the start or your guts will pay for it later.

China Today

A highly idiosyncratic mix of can-do entrepreneurs, inward-looking Buddhists, textbook Marxists, overnight millionaires, out-of-pocket, leather-faced farmers, unflagging migrant workers and round-the-clock McJobbers, China today is as multifaceted as its challenges are diverse. From the outside, China's autocratic decision-making may suggest national uniformity, but things are actually more in a state of controlled, and not so controlled, chaos.

Best in Print

Country Driving: A Chinese Road Trip (Peter Hessler; 2009) Hessler's amusing and insightful journey at the wheel around the highways and byways of China.

Tiger Head, Snake Tails (Jonathan Fenby; 2012) Compelling account of contemporary China's myriad challenges and contradictions.

Diary of a Madman & Other Stories (Lu Xun; 1918) Astonishing tales from the father of modern Chinese fiction.

Best on Film

Still Life (Jia Zhangke; 2005) Bleak and hauntingly beautiful portrayal of a family devastated by the construction of the Three Gorges Dam.

Raise the Red Lantern (Zhang Yimou; 1991) Exquisitely fashioned tragedy from the sumptuous palette of the Fifth Generation.

In the Mood for Love (Wong Kar-Wai; 2000) Seductive, stylishly costumed and slow-burning Hong Kong romance.

China Goes Travelling

China's crashing stock market seems to have done little to stop the Chinese from joining the top league of travelling nations for the first time in their tumultuous and predominantly inward-looking recent history. So while the world goes to China, China is increasingly going to the world. In 2015 a record 120 million (a bit less than the population of Mexico) outbound visitors left China. In the same year, Chinese arrivals to the UK were up by 40% in the first nine months of 2015. Chinese travellers spent a staggering US$215 billion abroad in 2015 (more than the GDP of Portugal), up 53% on the previous 12 months, while Chinese tourism is predicted to account for 14% of worldwide tourism revenue by 2020. Relaxed visa rulings from several nations, including the US and UK, have helped get Chinese feet into their outbound travelling shoes. It doesn't quite mean you'll find China deserted when you get there – the Chinese are more actively travelling around their home nation too: Běijing is hoping that domestic travellers will outlay ¥5.5 trillion on travel around China by 2020.

The Economy: Speed Bump or Cul-de-Sac?

China's eye-watering growth appears to be nearing the end of its blinding three-decade run, although experts remain divided over long-term implications for its US$11 trillion economy. Confrontingly high levels of debt, chronic overcapacity in manufacturing, a constellation of real-estate bubbles dotted around the land and a stock market prone to sudden dives, mean the days of easy, double-digit growth have given way to more sober forecasts. The economy may not be coming off the rails, but China's ambitious proposals in its current five-year plan could take a bruising, including its commitment to hugely expand social security and feed the country's large and demanding military budget. The latter expenditure is perhaps most crucial, to satisfy a growing domestic appetite for a strong nation when rivalries within the region and with the US are at their keenest. While a bust is perhaps unlikely, China may need to prepare for a period of middle-income blues with fewer jobs, reduced expectations and the days of double-digit growth a thing of the past.

Troubled Waters and Restive Borderlands

China's dazzling economic trajectory over the last three decades has been watched with awe by the West and increasing consternation by the Middle Kingdom's neighbours. By virtue of its sheer size and population, a dominant China will ruffle some East Asian feathers. The long-festering dispute between China and Vietnam, the Philippines and other nations over the control of waters, islands, reefs, atolls and rocky outcrops of the Paracel (Xīshā) and Spratly (Nánshā) Islands in the South China Sea worsened in recent years when China unilaterally began reclaiming land around, and building on, contested reefs. China has attempted to enforce a 12-nautical-mile exclusion zone around these reefs, which has been tested by the US Navy conducting 'freedom of navigation' exercises. The possibility of miscalculation, which could lead to conflict, has never been greater.

Meanwhile, the seemingly intractable spat over the contested and uninhabited Diàoyú Islands (Senkaku Islands to the Japanese) continues to sour relations between China and Japan. While keeping an eye on maritime issues, at home President Xi Jinping has had to deal with unrest in Xīnjiāng province, where Uyghur disquiet has prompted an increasingly harsh security clampdown from Běijīng, which may threaten to inflame sentiments further.

POPULATION: **1.41 BILLION**

GDP (PER CAPITA; PPP): **$16,676**

LABOUR FORCE: **807 MILLION**

UNEMPLOYMENT: **3.9%**

HIGHEST POINT: **MT EVEREST (8848M ABOVE SEA LEVEL)**

if China were 100 people

92 would be Han Chinese
8 would be ethnic minorities, eg Zhuang, Manchu, Uyghur etc

belief systems

(% of population)

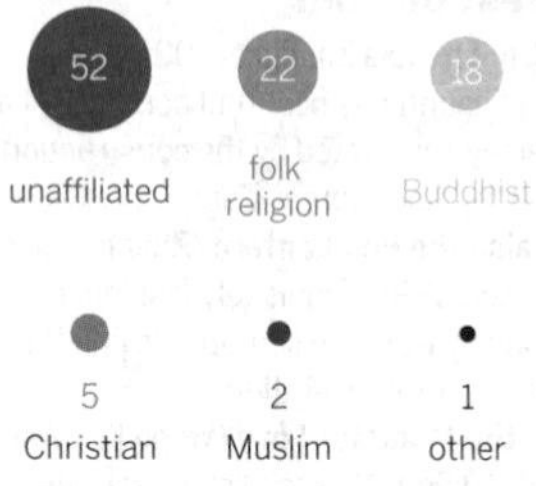

population per sq km

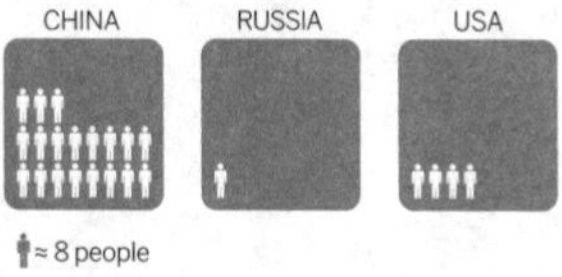

Chinese Culture & Cuisine

Powerful links connect the Chinese of today with their ancestors 5000 or 6000 years ago, making this the longest-lasting complex civilisation on earth. No wonder then that China, home to roughly one-fifth of humanity, is custodian of one of the world's richest cultural and artistic legacies.

The Chinese People

The Chinese Character

Shaped by Confucian principles, the Chinese are thoughtful and discreet, subtle but also pragmatic and practically minded. Conservative and somewhat introverted, they favour dark clothing over bright or loud colours while their body language is usually reserved and undemonstrative, yet attentive.

The Chinese (apart from the Shanghainese, some Chinese insist) are particularly generous. Don't be surprised if a person you have just met on a train invites you for a meal in the dining carriage; they will insist on paying, in which case do not try to thwart their efforts. The Chinese also adore children and delight in showing them affection.

Particularly diligent, the Chinese are inured to the kind of hours that may prompt a workers' insurrection elsewhere. This is partly due to a traditional culture of hard work but is also a response to inadequate social-security safety nets and an expression of anxiety regarding economic and political uncertainties. The Chinese impressively save much of what they earn, emphasising the virtue of prudence. Despite this restraint, however, wastefulness can be astounding when 'face' is involved: mountains of food are often left on restaurant dining tables, particularly if important guests are present.

The Chinese are also an exceptionally dignified people. They are proud of their civilisation and history, their written language and of their inventions and achievements. This pride rarely comes across as arrogance or self-assurance, however, and may be tinged with a lack of confidence. The Chinese may, for example, be very gratified by China's newfound world status, but may squirm at the mention of food safety and hygiene.

c 4000 BC

Archaeological evidence for the first settlements along the Yellow River (Huáng Hé). Even today the river remains a central cultural reference point for the Chinese.

551 BC

Birth of Confucius. Collected in the *Analects*, his ideas of an ethical, ordered society that operated through hierarchy and self-development would dominate Chinese culture until the early 20th century.

214 BC

Emperor Qin indentures thousands of labourers to link existing city walls into one Great Wall, in hope of reducing attacks on his country by nomadic warriors from Mongolia.

c 100 BC

Buddhism arrives in China from India. This religious system ends up thoroughly assimilated into the culture and becomes more powerful in China than in its country of origin.

1215

Chinggis (Genghis) Khaan conquers Běijīng as part of his creation of a massive Eurasian empire under Mongol rule.

1368

Zhu Yuanzhang founds the Ming dynasty and tries to impose a rigid Confucian social order on the population. However, China is too commercialised for the policy to work.

1644

Běijīng falls to peasant rebel Li Zicheng and the last Ming emperor, Chongzhen, hangs himself in Jǐngshān Park; the Qing dynasty is established.

CHINA'S ONE-CHILD POLICY

The 'one-child policy' (actually a misnomer, as the policy allows many exceptions and ethnic minorities are exempt) came into effect in 1979 in a bid to keep China's population to one billion by the year 2000; the latest government estimate is that the population will peak at 1.5 billion in 2033. The policy was originally harshly implemented, but rural revolt led to a softer stance; nonetheless, it has generated much bad feeling between local officials and the rural population.

Rural families were later allowed two children if the first child was a girl, but some couples have upwards of three or four kids. Additional offspring can result in fines and families having to shoulder the cost of education themselves, without government assistance. Official stated policy opposes forced abortion or sterilisation, but allegations of coercion continue as local officials strive to meet population quotas. Families who do abide by the one-child policy often go to great lengths to make sure their child is male, which has resulted in a lopsided male-to-female ratio of 111 boys to 100 girls.

In October 2015 China announced an end to the one-child policy, allowing couples to have two children.

The modern Chinese character has been shaped by recent political realities, and while Chinese people have always been reserved and circumspect, in today's China they can appear even more prudent. Impressive mental gymnastics are performed to detour contentious domestic political issues, which can make the mainland Chinese appear complicated, despite their reputation for being straightforward and down-to-earth.

Far West China (www.farwest-china.com) is a useful website and blog covering the people, culture and landscapes of Xīnjiāng, in China's northwest.

Ethnic Groups

When we think of China, we think of the world's most populous nation, dominated by the Han Chinese. While 92% of the population is Han, China is also home to 55 other ethnic minorities, including Tibetans, Uyghurs and Mongols. Most of the minorities live on China's borderlands. In the northeast, near Hǎilāěr, there are small pockets of Evenki (reindeer herders) and even ethnic Russians who speak Mandarin as their native tongue.

But it is indeed the Han Chinese who dominate, not only in the population figures but in every aspect of life in China – including writing, the arts, literature, sport and politics. For the minorities, the ability to operate comfortably in Han culture and language is essential for moving ahead in society.

The Han are distributed throughout the country but predominantly concentrated along the Yellow River, Yangzi River and Pearl River basins. These core areas are but a small fraction of the total area of China – the colossal areas of Tibet, Qīnghǎi, Xīnjiāng, Inner Mongolia and the northeast (Manchuria) are historically non-Han areas but were slowly brought into the motherland following centuries of warfare and occupation.

Falun Gong is a quasi-religious lifestyle philosophy that gained so much traction in the 1990s that it was labelled a cult by Chinese authorities, and subsequently outlawed. Its followers at the time numbered between 60 and 70 million.

Religion

Religion in China has been influenced by three streams of thought: Taoism, Confucianism and Buddhism. All three have been inextricably entwined in popular Chinese religion along with ancient animist beliefs. The founders of these traditions have been deified; the Chinese worship them and their disciples as fervently as they worship their own ancestors and a pantheon of gods and spirits.

The Chinese Communist government professes atheism. It considers religion to be base superstition, a remnant of old China used by the ruling classes to maintain power. Nevertheless, in an effort to improve relations with the Muslim, Buddhist and Lamaist minorities, in 1982 the

Chinese government amended its constitution to allow freedom of religion. However, only atheists are permitted to be members of the Chinese Communist Party (CCP). Since almost all of China's 55 minority groups adhere to one religion or another, this rule precludes most of them from party membership.

Muslims and Christians are believed to be the largest identifiable religious groups still active in China today, each numbering perhaps 3% to 5% of the nation's population. The government has not published official figures of the number of Buddhists – hardly surprising given the ideological battle it has been waging with Tibetan Buddhists, who have been fighting for decades to preserve their culture and their nation. It's impossible to determine the number of Taoists, but the number of Taoist priests is very small.

Traditional Chinese religious beliefs took a battering during the Cultural Revolution when monasteries were disbanded, temples were destroyed and the monks were sometimes killed or sent to the fields to labour. Since Mao's death, the Chinese government has allowed many temples (sometimes with their own contingent of monks and novices) to reopen as active places of worship. All religious activity is firmly under state control and many of the monks are caretakers within renovated shells of monasteries, which serve principally as tourist attractions and are pale shadows of their former selves.

The Arts

China is the custodian of one of the world's richest cultural and artistic legacies. Until the 20th century, China's arts were deeply conservative and resistant to change; over the last century, revolutions in technique and content have fashioned a dramatic transformation. Despite this evolution, China's arts – whatever the period – remain united by a common aesthetic that taps into the very soul of the nation.

In reflection of the Chinese character, Chinese aesthetics have traditionally been marked by restraint and understatement, a preference for oblique references over direct explanation, vagueness in place of specificity. These guiding principles compellingly find their way into virtually every Chinese art form.

Calligraphy

Perhaps the most iconic of China's arts is calligraphy. However, it can be tricky for Westerners to comprehend calligraphy as an art form, unless they have a sound understanding of written Chinese. This is because the characters represent both an image of beauty as well as a description or concept. Less 'insider' knowledge is needed, however, to appreciate Chinese traditional painting. There may be subtle meanings behind the work, but in general Chinese landscapes are accessible to any eye and have long been treasured in the West for their beauty.

1842

The treaty of Nánjīng concludes the first Opium War. China is forced to hand over Hong Kong island to the British and open up Chinese ports to foreign trade.

1898

The New Territories adjoining Kowloon in Hong Kong are leased to the British for 99 years, eventually being returned, along with all of Hong Kong, in 1997.

1904–05

The Russo-Japanese War is fought entirely on Chinese territory. Japan's victory is the first triumph by an Asian power over a European one.

1911

Revolution spreads across China as local governments withdraw support for the Qing dynasty, and instead support a republic under Sun Yatsen.

1931

Japan invades Manchuria (northeast China), provoking an international crisis and forcing Kuomintang leader Chiang Kaishek to consider anti-Japanese as well as anti-communist strategies.

1949

Mao Zedong stands on top of the Gate of Heavenly Peace in Běijīng on 1 October and announces the formation of the People's Republic of China, saying 'The Chinese people have stood up'.

1962

Mao initiates the Great Leap Forward; at least 20 million people starve when his plan to industrialise the country causes agricultural collapse.

1966

The Cultural Revolution breaks out, and Red Guards demon-

Visual Arts

China turned an artistic corner of sorts after 1949, when artists eschewed washes on silk in favour of oil on canvas. The Chinese obsession with the mysterious and the ineffable made way for attention to detail and realism. By the 1970s Chinese artists aspired to master the art of socialist realism. Saturated with political symbolism and propaganda, the blunt artistic style was produced on an industrial scale. Traditional Taoist and Buddhist philosophy was overturned; humans were now the masters of nature, which would bend to their will.

The five fundamental brushstrokes necessary to master calligraphy can be found in the character 永 *(yǒng)*, which means eternal or forever.

Mao's death ended the era of 'art for the masses' and a new school of artists began exploring a variety of themes, largely influenced by the Western art world. After the Tiān'ānmén Square protests in 1989 the Chinese art world turned cynical, with many works mocking Chinese consumerism and political ideology. Today there is a vast array of subjects as Chinese artists have moved away from overtly political work towards more universal concerns.

Ceramics

One of China's biggest art exports is ceramics, for which it has been developing techniques for thousands of years. Some of the best pieces date from the Yuan dynasty, when the 'blue-and-white' *(qīnghuā)* porcelain, made with cobalt-blue paint from Persia, was developed. The porcelain became famous the world over, eventually acquiring the name 'China' whether the pieces were produced in China or not.

Sculpture

Ai Weiwei: Never Sorry (2012) is an acclaimed documentary that chronicles three years in the life of the outspoken Chinese artist and activist Ai Weiwei.

Sculpture in China reached its zenith after the arrival of Buddhism, when artists across the land were commissioned to carve enormous statues of the Buddha. Early concepts for Buddhist sculpture came from India, so it's not surprising that some of China's most spectacular Buddhist statues are found along the Silk Road west of Xī'ān.

Dàtóng, on the train line from Běijīng to Ulaanbaatar, is home to one of China's four most celebrated sites of Buddhist sculptures, the magnificent Yungang Caves.

ANCESTORS, GHOSTS & KITCHEN GODS

Beliefs about ancestor worship permeate almost every aspect of Chinese philosophy. Many homes have their own altar, where family members pay their respects to deceased relatives by burning spirit money and providing offerings. It's believed that a person possesses two 'souls' – a *guǐ* (literally 'ghost'), which is yin and represents everything dark, damp and earthly, and a *shén* (literally 'spirit'), which is yang, and represents light, goodness and strength. When a person dies the two souls go in separate directions – the *shén* to heaven and the *guǐ* to the underworld. If a person has suffered a tragic death or if the body is neglected the *guǐ* lingers on earth, often seeking revenge.

Closely tied to ancestor worship is popular religion, which consists of an immense celestial bureaucracy of gods and spirits, from the lowly but all-important kitchen god *(zào jun)* to the celestial emperor himself *(tiāndì)*. Each god has a particular role to fulfil and can be either promoted or demoted depending on his or her performance. Lower-ranking gods who protect homes, doors and neighbourhoods from evil spirits *(guǐ)* are of particular interest, and in pre-Communist China tiny altars and shrines were a ubiquitous sight. Offerings to the gods consisted not only of food and incense but also opera performances, birthday parties (to which the other local gods were invited) and the occasional procession around town.

Architecture

Balance and symmetry are important features of traditional Chinese architecture and can be found in all types of buildings, from humble farmhouses to great imperial palaces. Another common feature is the idea of enclosure. Whereas contemporary Western architectural practices typically involve surrounding a building by an open yard or garden, traditional Chinese architecture involves constructing buildings that take up an entire property but enclose open spaces within themselves. These enclosed spaces come in two forms: the courtyard (more common in north China, including Běijīng) and the 'sky well' (more common in the south).

Classical Chinese buildings, especially those of the wealthy, are built with an emphasis on breadth rather than height, featuring an enclosed heavy platform and a large roof that floats over this base, with the vertical walls not well emphasised. This contrasts Western architecture, which tends to grow in height and depth.

The halls and palaces in Běijīng's Forbidden City, for example, have relatively low ceilings when compared to equivalent stately buildings in the West, but their external appearances suggest the all-embracing, sweeping nature of imperial China; a concept you can visualise yourself when you stand on top of Coal Hill in Jǐngshān Park and look out over the vast Forbidden City below you.

Along the Trans-Manchurian route the architecture is distinct from much of the rest of China, primarily as a result of foreign influences in the region. At the turn of the 20th century, much of Manchuria was occupied – either economically or militarily – by Russia, Japan and various European powers, all of whom left their mark on the cities in this region. The best example is Tiānjīn, which contains quarters once dominated by Austro-Hungarians, Belgians, Germans, Italians and Japanese. In Dàolǐqū, the oldest part of Harbin (Hā'ěrbīn), onion domes and ornamental facades reveal the city's Russian roots.

If modern architecture in China is defined as anything post-1949, then China has ridden a roller-coaster ride of styles and fashions. In Běijīng, stand between the Great Hall of the People and the National Centre for the Performing Arts and weigh up how far China has travelled in 50 years. Interestingly, neither building has clear Chinese motifs. The same applies to the complex form of Běijīng's CCTV Building, where a continuous loop through horizontal and vertical planes required some audacious engineering.

Many of the top names in world architecture – IM Pei, Rem Koolhaas, Norman Foster, Herzog & de Meuron – have designed at least one building in China in the 21st century. Other impressive examples in Běijīng include the National Stadium (aka the 'Bird's Nest'), the National Aquatics Centre (aka the 'Water Cube') and Běijīng South Train Station.

strate in cities across China. The movement is marked by a fetish for violence as a catalyst for transforming society.

1976

Mao Zedong dies, aged 83. The Gang of Four (led by Mao's wife Jiang Qing) are arrested by his successor and put on trial, where they are blamed for all the disasters of the Cultural Revolution.

1979

The one-child policy is adopted by the state to reduce the population. At the same time it imposes unprecedented control over women's personal liberty.

1989

Hundreds of civilians are killed by Chinese troops in the streets around Tiān'ānmén Sq. No official reassessment has been made, but rumours persist of deep conflict within the party.

2008

Běijīng hosts the Summer Olympic Games and Paralympics. The Games go smoothly and are widely considered to be a great success in burnishing China's image overseas.

August 2008

The Běijīng–Tiānjīn 'bullet train' opens, reaching a top speed of 330km/h and setting the record for the fastest conventional train service in the world.

2015

China's economic growth falls to its lowest level since 1990. The Communist Party announces the end of the one-child policy.

2017

Economic growth continues to slow. A new cyber-security law is passed giving the government more control over foreign and domestic firms' data.

Chinese Cuisine

China is a gastronome's paradise. Cooking is a way of life here and first-time visitors will find a world of culinary delights far greater than what is on offer in Chinatowns the world over. Food plays a prominent role in the national psyche – work, play, romance, business and family life all revolve around it. When people meet, a common greeting is *'nǐ chīfàn le ma?'* ('have you eaten yet?').

The food in China varies greatly by region and is influenced by the topographical and climatic disparities that exist across this vast nation. Naturally, seafood is plentiful near the coast and meat dominates in interior regions like Inner Mongolia. Likewise, grains are more prevalent in the north, while rice is the staple in the south.

China Demographics

Population: 1.38 billion

Birth rate: 13.3 births per 1000 people

Percentage of people aged over 65 years: 9%

Urbanisation rate: 3.05%

Life expectancy: 76 years

The Northern School

The northern school of cooking is what you'll experience when travelling along the Trans-Mongolian and Trans-Manchurian railway lines, although big cities like Běijīng and Harbin will also have restaurants that represent the southern, eastern and western schools.

The northern school has a reputation for being bland and unsophisticated, but it's filling, appetising and well suited to the harsh winter climate. There's a particular accent on millet, sorghum, maize, barley and wheat rather than rice (which requires a lot of water). The spectrum of flavours is somewhat muted compared to southern cooking, as salt is preferred to spice.

Roasting meat is also more common in the north than in other parts of China. Meats in northern China are braised until they're falling off the bone, or brushed with spices and barbecued until smoky. Pungent garlic, chives and spring onions are used with abandon and are also used raw.

Culinary Influences

The influence of Manchurian cooking and the cold climate of the north-eastern provinces have left a legacy of rich and hearty stews, dense breads and dumplings. The cooking of the nomadic Mongolians has also left a pronounced mark on northern meat cooking, especially in the development of northern hotpot. Milk from nomadic herds of cattle, goats and horses has also made its way into northern cuisine, as yoghurts, for example. In Běijīng it's common to spot small clay jars of yoghurt being sold at streetside stalls.

HALLMARK NORTHERN DISHES

PINYIN	SCRIPT	ENGLISH
Běijīng kǎoyā	北京烤鸭	Peking duck
jiāo zhá yángròu	焦炸羊肉	deep-fried mutton
qīng xiāng shāo jī	清香烧鸡	chicken wrapped in lotus leaf
shuàn yángròu	涮羊肉	lamb hotpot
mántou	馒头	steamed buns
jiǎozi	饺子	dumplings
ròu bāozi	肉包子	steamed meat buns
sān měi dòufu	三美豆腐	sliced bean curd with Chinese cabbage
yuán bào lǐ jí	芫爆里脊	stir-fried pork tenderloin with coriander
zào liū sān bái	糟溜三白	stir-fried chicken, fish and bamboo shoots

Landscapes & Wildlife

One of the attractions of the Trans-Siberian routes is the opportunity to experience the vast changes in landscape across Russia, Mongolia and China. Much of the wildlife is naturally shy, hidden from view or too distant to be observed well from the train itself, so the best way to appreciate the nature is to alight and spend a few days exploring the countryside.

Taiga

The most prevalent of the vegetation zones traversed by the railway is the iconic Russian taiga, a dense forest belt running from Scandinavia across Siberia to the Pacific coast. Hints of the vast taiga lying ahead can be found even as Trans-Siberian trains crawl across European Russia, but train travellers get a sense of what writer Anton Chekhov called the true Siberian taiga once they have crossed the Yenisey River at Krasnoyarsk. The BAM route (from Tayshet) is wall-to-wall taiga for days on end.

True taiga is coniferous forest, particularly Siberian pine *(Pinus sibirica),* but you will often find mixed conifer and deciduous forest, and in some places completely deciduous forest. Silver firs, spruce, larch and birch often mingle with maple and aspen, while willows and poplars dominate the innumerable rivers, lakes and ponds. Typically, as you cross Siberia, the mixed and coniferous forest is broken by clearings or farmland, which in turn are punctuated by towns, villages and settlements. In Eastern Siberia and the Far East the landscape folds and rises in parts into forested mountains, such as the Barguzin Mountains that flank the eastern shore of Lake Baikal.

The Gobi Desert is encroaching on Běijīng at a rate of 2km per year. To stop it, the Chinese government is trying to create a 5700km long 'green wall' by paying farmers to plant trees.

Ussuriland

Towards the far eastern end of the main Trans-Siberian route you will encounter Ussuriland. This unique environment is largely covered by a monsoon forest filled with an exotic array of flora and fauna, many species of which are found nowhere else in Russia. The topography is dominated by the Sikhote-Alin Range, which runs for more than 1000km in a spine parallel to the coast. Unlike the sparsely vegetated woodland floor of the taiga, the forests of Ussuriland have a lush undergrowth, with lianas and vines twined around trunks and draped from branches.

Russian Railways collaborated with photographer Anton Lange on *Russia Through a Train Window* (http://fotorussia.su), an exhibition of images shot across the country and featuring Russia's most magnificent scenery.

Steppe

As the Trans-Mongolian Railway crosses Mongolia, it passes through the pastures of the Selenga Gol (Selenga River) Valley. Gradually, however, the landscape changes to steppe. The steppe (some of it mountain forest steppe) spans the continent from the plains north of the Black Sea across Central Asia through Mongolia to the western edge of China. This gently rolling and – in its driest form – semiarid grassland is often unsuitable for cultivation, but it provides sufficient vegetation to support large herds of grazing animals.

SIBERIAN LANDSCAPES & BELIEFS

Landscapes, perhaps more than anything else, shape the lives and beliefs of a people.

In Russia, the countryside is imbued with aspects of both Christian and traditional lifestyles. After the Cossack Yermak drowned in the Irtysh River near Tobolsk during a Tatar ambush, his corpse was described in the early semireligious *Siberian Chronicles* as being too miraculous to be touched even by birds. Almost a century later, the exiled Old Believer Archpriest Avvakum (1621–82) was flogged and tormented across Siberia and on reaching Lake Baikal he described it as a paradise on earth, where everything was larger than life. Later still, in 17th-century Russia, the Daur region in the Amur Basin was widely seen by Cossacks as a land of milk and honey to which they could flee and where they might find refuge from brutal masters. For Russian peasants as a whole, Siberia stood for freedom from serfdom.

In the 18th century, a bizarre castrati sect (called Skoptsy in Russian) established itself in Siberia and several other regions. As the name suggests, the sect practised castration of its male followers. If there were one religious movement you'd think would have no future, it would be the castrati; however, bizarrely enough, it later spawned an offshoot 'neo-castrati' sect in the Balkans. Even today, sects and gurus are attracted to Siberia, the most famous being the neo-Jesus Vissarion (aka Sergei Torop), whose Abode of Dawn community is tucked away in forest near the town of Abakan, south of Krasnoyarsk.

South of the Trans-Siberian at Novosibirsk, in the Altai Republic, the Russian painter and mystic Nikolai Rerikh (known internationally as Nicholas Roerich) sought the mythical, heavenly kingdom of Shambhala, and today ordinary Russians popularly perceive the picturesque Altai as a 'sacred' place imbued with spiritual energy.

The tie between landscape and shamanism among Buryats of the regions around Lake Baikal is very similar to those of Mongolians across the border. The sky is an integral aspect of shamanist belief, and in Mongolia blue scarves are placed on *ovoos* (stone cairns) to represent it. Mongolians also flick droplets of vodka into the air before they drink, in order to honour the sky gods.

In China a special role is played by its sacred mountains. Beyond Tibet, there are four sacred Buddhist mountains, each one the home of a specific bodhisattva, an enlightened being or source of enlightenment. The two most famous are Wŭtái Shān and Éméi Shān, respectively ruled over by Wenshu and Puxiang.

To the south, the steppe becomes arid and gives way to the deserts of Central Asia. The Gobi Desert in Mongolia and China retains a thin grass cover that sustains some of the hardier herbivores. The section traversed by the Trans-Mongolian south of Choir gets grass in a good year.

Rivers & Lakes on the Routes

Russia has six of the world's 20 longest rivers. Forming the China–Russia border, the east-flowing Amur (4416km) is the longest, along with the Lena (4400km), Yenisey (4090km), Irtysh (4245km) and Ob (3680km), all of which flow north across Siberia and end up in the Arctic Ocean.

Beautiful Lake Baikal itself is the world's deepest lake, holding nearly one-fifth of all the globe's unfrozen fresh water. Formed by rifting tectonic plates, Baikal is also the world's oldest lake, dating back 25 million years. The rift, which widens by about 2cm per year, is thought to be 9km deep, of which 7km of depth is covered by sediment.

Europe's longest river, the Volga (3690km), rises northwest of Moscow and flows via Nizhny Novgorod and Kazan into the Caspian Sea.

National Parks & Reserves

Along or close by the Trans-Siberian routes you'll find easily reached national parks and reserves.

- Perm, Kungur and Yekaterinburg are good springboards into the Ural Mountains' landscapes and parks.
- Irkutsk (Listvyanka) provides access to spectacular walking trails, whereas Ulan-Ude is best for the Barguzin National Reserve within Zabaikalsky National Park.
- Krasnoyarsk has the unusual Stolby Nature Reserve.
- Close to Ulaanbaatar, you'll find Gorkhi-Terelj National Park and Khustain National Park.

One of the best places to spot waterfowl is on the Baraba Steppe between Omsk and Novosibirsk. Part of this is an outlier of the Vasyugian Swamp, the largest swamp in the northern hemisphere.

Wildlife

Wildlife flourishes in the taiga; the indigenous cast includes squirrels, chipmunks (which dine on pine-cone seeds), voles and lemmings, as well as small carnivores such as polecats, foxes, wolverines and, less commonly, the sable – a weasel-like creature whose luxuriant pelt played an important role in the early exploration of Siberia.

The most common species of large mammal in the taiga is the elk, a large deer that can measure over 2m at the shoulder and weighs almost as much as a bear. The brown bear itself is also a Siberian inhabitant that you may come across, despite the Russian penchant for hunting it. Other taiga-dwelling animals include deer, wolves and lynx.

Ussuriland's animal life includes wolves, sables, Asian black bears (tree-climbing, herbivorous cousins to the more common brown bears, also found here), as well as the rare Siberian or Amur tiger. The largest of all wild cats, the Siberian tiger can measure up to 3.5m in length. They prey on boar, though they've been known to hunt and kill bears, livestock and even humans.

Ussuriland is also home to the Amur leopard, a big cat significantly rarer than the tiger, though less impressive and consequently less well known. Around 70 of these leopards roam the lands bordering China and North Korea. Sadly, both the leopard and tiger are under threat from constant poaching by Chinese and Russian hunters. For more about this beautiful animal see the website of the Amur Leopard & Tiger Alliance (ALTA; www.altaconservation.org).

SPECIES UNDER THREAT

The largest of all wild cats, the Siberian tiger can measure up to 3.5m in length. A 2015 census showed there to be only 480 to 540 tigers in Russia's Far East, out of a total population of 562 in the whole country. Across the border in China the situation is even less rosy – perhaps 60 are divided between Hēilóngjiāng and Jílín provinces in China, and none are left in South Korea.

Though protected by Chinese law and recognised as one of the world's most endangered species, the animals' survival hangs by a thread due to urban encroachment on its territory and a lucrative poaching industry. Tiger bones are prized in traditional Chinese medicine, while tiger skins also fetch a hefty price on the black market.

In 1986 the Chinese government set about boosting numbers by establishing the world's largest tiger-breeding centre in Harbin. The majority of these tigers are in captivity, with 28 born in the first half of 2016, but the centre's conditions are dubious. This makes any wild sighting a cause for celebration. In December 2015 the figurative champagne flowed when Amur tigers were captured on film in Jílín province in the Tiānqiáolǐng area, a zone they had been absent from since the 1980s. This was evidence that the cats are expanding their range south – back into traditional Chinese territory.

Lake Baikal

Lake Baikal's wildlife is unique. Thanks to warm water entering from vents in the bottom of the lake, and the filtering action of countless millions of minute crustaceans called *epischura,* the water is exceptionally clear and pure. More than 1700 species of plants and animals live in the lake (nearly all endemic), including more than 200 types of shrimp and 80 types of flatworm; one species of flatworm is the world's largest and eats fish.

The many kinds of fish include the endemic *omul,* Baikal's main commercial fish. A remarkable species, the *omul* (a white fish of the salmon family) is reputed to emit a shrill cry when caught. It spawns in the Selenga River, but its main food source is the endemic Baikal alga, *melosira,* which has declined drastically because of pollution.

The *golomyanka* – a pink, translucent oilfish with large pectoral fins – is endemic to Baikal. It's unusual in having no scales and being viviparous – giving birth to live young, about 2000 at a time. It is the lake's most common fish, although its numbers have been depleted by pollution. By day it lives in the deep, dark depths; at night it rises close to the surface.

Golomyanka is the preferred food of the *nerpa* (Baikal seal, *Phoca siberica*), the world's only freshwater seal, with no relatives nearer than the ringed seal of the Arctic. The *nerpa* is an attractive, gentle creature with unusually large eyes set in a round, flat face, enabling it to hunt down to at least 1500m below the surface – even at night. Despite their size (less than 1.5m, making them the world's smallest seal), they have particularly strong claws for forcing their way through winter ice and keeping their breathing holes open. Pups are born in late winter and there's estimated to be a sustainable population of between 80,000 and 100,000 currently living in Baikal.

There is plenty of other wildlife around the lake. The huge delta, nearly 40km wide, formed by the sediment brought down to the lake by the Selenga River, is a great attraction to wild fowl and wading birds. In summer such beautiful and rare species as the Asiatic dowitcher and white-winged black tern nest in the delta, while in autumn vast numbers of waterfowl from the north use the mudflats and marshes to rest and feed on their migration south. It's a sort of international bird airport, with many birds overwintering there, too.

Vast numbers of caddis flies and other insects hatch and swarm on the lake in summer, providing a rich and vital food source for all kinds of wildlife from fish to birds. Despite their lack of visual impact for the Trans-Siberian traveller, these tiny insects, along with the microscopic plant and animal organisms, form the base of the pyramid of wildlife that graces this unique area.

Directory A–Z

Accommodation

For much of your Trans-Siberian journey your bed will be on the train, but at either end of your trip and most likely at points along it you'll be looking for more traditional accommodation.

➡ Listed prices are generally for a standard twin or double room in the high season (summer), including breakfast, and with a private bathroom.

➡ Big discounts on rack rates can be had for online bookings on sites such as www.booking.com.

➡ It's a good idea to book a few nights in advance for big cities in each country, but elsewhere it's usually not necessary

Russia

➡ Make bookings by email or fax rather than telephone so you get a written copy of your reservation.

➡ For cheaper places to stay, head for the smaller towns or consider a homestay or serviced apartment; many travel agencies can arrange these.

➡ Occasionally, twin rooms are cheaper than singles, but you may end up sharing with a stranger unless you make it clear that you'd prefer single occupancy.

➡ Types of accommodation include hotels, hostels, B&Bs, homestays and apartments.

➡ Resting rooms *(komnaty otdykha)* are found at all major train stations and several of the smaller ones, as well as at a few larger bus stations. Generally they have basic (but often quite clean) shared accommodation with communal sinks and toilets. Some have showers but you'll often pay an extra fee to use them. Sometimes there are single and double rooms and, rarely, more luxurious ones with private bathrooms. The beds generally can be rented by the half-day (₽50 to ₽1000) or 24-hour (₽800 to ₽1700) period. Some places will ask to see your train ticket before allowing you to stay.

➡ *Kempingi* (organised camping grounds) are rare and usually only open from June to September. Camping is generally not allowed in the wild – check with locals if you're in doubt. *Turbazy*, tourist bases with shared bungalows or sometimes spaces for tents, are good alternatives.

China

➡ Options include rustic homesteads, homestays, youth hostels, student dormitories, guesthouses,

ACCOMMODATION PRICES

The following price ranges are generally for a standard twin or double room in the high season (summer), including breakfast, and with a private bathroom.

Symbol	Moscow & St Petersburg	Rest of Russia	Mongolia/ Ulaanbaatar	China
€ or $	less than ₽3000	less than ₽1500	less than T50,000/168,000	less than ¥400
€€ or $$	₽3000–15,000	₽1500–₽4000	T50,000–80,000/ T168,000–288,000	¥400–1000
€€€ or $$$	more than ₽15,000	more than ₽4000	more than T80,000/288,000	more than ¥1000

courtyard lodgings, boutique hotels and five-star towers.

- Dorms in hostels usually cost between ¥40 and ¥100 around the centre of Běijīng. Doubles or twin rooms in Beǐjīng hostels start at around ¥200 with a shared bathroom.
- Useful accommodation websites include **Ctrip** (http://english.ctrip.com) and **Agoda** (www.agoda.com).

Mongolia

- Mongolia has excellent campsites everywhere, even near Ulaanbaatar in places such as Terelj. Camping is the better option if you are travelling in the countryside, considering the lack of hotels and the expense of ger (yurt) camps.
- A tourist ger camp is a 'camping ground' with traditional ger, a separate building for toilets and showers, and a restaurant-bar. The gers are furnished with two to four beds. Toilets and bathrooms, which are shared, are usually clean. Most ger camps in Terelj are open from June to September. In the Gobi Desert they are open from May to October.
- Ulaanbaatar (UB) has an abundant range of guesthouses targeting foreign backpackers. Most guesthouses are in apartment blocks and have dorm beds as well as private rooms.
- At US$20 to US$60 per day, apartments are much better value than Ulaanbaatar's hotels, which are decent but overpriced.
- Dorm beds at UB guesthouses cost US$6 to US$8, private rooms around US$10.
- Ger camps charge US$20 to US$50 per person per night, including three hearty meals, but prices are negotiable, and they may drop considerably if you bring your own food. Tour agencies and travel agencies in Ulaanbaatar can arrange visits.

HOMESTAYS

As well as the agencies that can arrange homestays in Russia and China, there are growing Couchsurfing, Airbnb and Homestay (www.homestay.com) participants in both countries providing rooms or even whole homes for short-term rent. Rates start from as little as US$15 a day, but more commonly US$40 to $100, depending on location and quality of accommodation.

Russia

Host Families Association (www.hofa.ru)

International Homestay Agency (https://homestayagency.com)

Worldwide Homestay (www.worldwidehomestay.com/Russia.htm)

China

Homestay China (http://homestaychina.org)

China Study Abroad (www.chinastudyabroad.org)

Activities

Below is a brief overview of when a permit is required.

Parks, Reserves & Protected Areas

Most tourist destinations can be entered without special permits, but you will usually have to pay an admission/permit fee at the entrance.

Fishing

Russia and Mongolia are the two places you are likely to go fishing.

RUSSIA

Fishermen will take you out onto the waters (or the winter ice) of Lake Baikal. Rules on when you can fish, how and for what species vary from region to region and the time of year; your local boat operator or tour company can take care of permits where required.

MONGOLIA

For national parks, you can get a fishing permit from park offices. Permits are valid for two days or 10 fish, whichever comes first. While it's relatively easy to get a fishing permit in a national park, buying one for other areas is much more difficult. Anglers must have a special permit authorised by the **Ministry of Nature & Green Development** (☎51-261 966, 51-266 171; www.mne.mn; United Nations St 5/2, Government Bldg II, Ulaanbaatar, What3words: dampen.carbonate.doped), which costs US$330 a week. As a tourist you cannot get one on your own, but instead through a tour operator (and only a few

BOOK YOUR STAY ONLINE

For more accommodation reviews by Lonely Planet authors, check out http://lonelyplanet.com/hotels. You'll find independent reviews, as well as recommendations on the best places to stay. Best of all, you can book online.

operators qualify to receive them). Before signing up, make sure your outfitter has the necessary permits; some take the risk of fishing illegally, which can get you in big trouble if you're caught.

Activities in Border Regions

RUSSIA

Designated border zones throughout Russia can only be entered with a permit from the local Federalnaya Sluzhba Bezopasnosti (FSB), the Russian Federal Security Service (formerly known as the KGB). No special permits are required for most tourist rail routes and the border crossings. Nor do you usually need one if you are transiting on a main road, but for side trips or deeper exploration inside border regions, such as the Mongolia–Russia border zone in the Altai Republic or Tuva, you certainly will require one. Permits can take up to two months to arrange.

CHINA

Much of the northeastern border between China and Siberia follows the Black Dragon River (Hēilóng Jiāng), known to the Russians as the Amur River. At the time of research, you didn't need permits to visit any areas along the border.

MONGOLIA

If you are travelling to border areas such as Altai Tavan Bogd National Park in Bayan-Ölgii, the **General Office of Border Protection** (☎51-266 638; Border Defence Bldg, What3words: extensive.bunkers.gadgets; ⏲10am-12.30pm & 2-5pm Mon-Fri), in the east of Ulaanbaatar, is the place to go for permits. You must send a Mongolian on your behalf to apply with a passport photocopy and a map showing your route.

Children

Travelling in Russia, China or Mongolia with children can be a breeze as long as you come well prepared with the right attitudes, equipment and patience.

- Baby-changing rooms are uncommon.
- Public toilets are often in poor condition.
- Nappies (diapers), powdered milk and baby food are widely available except in rural areas.
- Finding English-language kids' publications is difficult; toy shops are plentiful.
- On Russian trains infants and babies travelling for free (up to four years old) must have a (free of charge) ticket with their name on it.
- If you are travelling alone with a child on a train, carriage attendants will briefly watch over children while you use the toilet.
- Lonely Planet's *Travel with Children* contains useful advice on how to cope with kids on the road and what to bring to make things go more smoothly.

Customs Regulations

Russia

- Searches beyond the perfunctory are quite rare, but clearing customs when you leave Russia by a land border can be lengthy.
- If you declared foreign currency when you entered Russia, make sure you are carrying less when leaving, otherwise you may have to change the excess into roubles.
- Visitors are allowed to bring in and take out up to US$10,000 (or its equivalent) in currency, and goods up to the value of €10,000 and weighing less than 50kg, without making a customs declaration.
- Fill in a customs declaration form if you're bringing into Russia major equipment, antiques, artworks or musical instruments (including a guitar) that you plan to take out with you – get it stamped in the red channel of customs to avoid any problems leaving with the same goods.

PRACTICALITIES

Russia

- **Newspapers** The main newspapers are government-owned *Rossiyskaya Gazeta*, the popular dailies *Izvestia* and *Komsomolskaya Pravda*, and the left-leaning daily *Trud*. *Novaya Gazeta* is known for its investigative journalism, as is the online news site *Meduza* (https://meduza.io), which has an English version. The *Moscow Times* (https://themoscowtimes.com) is also in English, as is the *Siberian Times* (http://siberiantimes.com).

Mongolia

- **Newspapers** The English-language *UB Post* (http://theubpost.mn) has good articles, events listings and a classified section.

China

- **Newspapers** The standard English-language newspaper is the (censored) *China Daily* (www.chinadaily.com.cn). China's largest-circulation Chinese-language daily is the *People's Daily (Rénmín Rìbào)*; it has an English-language edition on http://english.peopledaily.com.cn.

➡ If you plan to export anything vaguely 'arty' – instruments, coins, jewellery, antiques, antiquarian manuscripts and books (older than 50 years) or art (also older than 50 years) – it should first be assessed by the **Expert Collegium** (Коллегия экспертизы; ☎499-391 4212; ul Akademika Korolyova 21, bldg 1, office 505, 5th fl; ⏲11am-5pm Mon-Fri; Ⓜ VDNKh) in Moscow; it is very difficult to export anything over 100 years old. Bring your item (or a photograph, if the item is large) and your receipt. If export is allowed, you'll be issued a receipt for tax paid, which you show to customs officers on your way out of the country.

China

➡ Chinese customs officers generally pay tourists little attention.

➡ There are no restrictions on foreign currency, but you should declare any cash exceeding US$5000 (or its equivalent in another currency).

➡ Objects considered antiques require a certificate and a red seal to clear customs when leaving China. Anything made before 1949 is considered an antique, and if it was made before 1795 it cannot legally be taken out of the country. To get the proper certificate and red seal, your antiques must be inspected by the **State Administration of Cultural Heritage** (Guójiā Wénwù Jú; ☎010 5679 2211; www.sach.gov.cn; 83 Beiheyan Dajie; ⏲8.30am-5pm; Ⓢ Lines 6, 8 to Nanluoguxiang, exit B or Line 5 to Zhangzizhonglu, exit D) in Běijīng.

Mongolia

➡ To export antiques you must have a receipt and customs certificate from the place you bought them; most reliable shops in Ulaanbaatar provide this. You'll need to fill in a form giving your passport number, details of where the antique was purchased and two photos of the antique itself.

➡ If you have anything that even *looks* old, it is a good idea to get a document to indicate that it is not an antique. That goes for Buddha images and statues as well.

Discount Cards

Full-time students and people aged under 26 can sometimes (but not always) get a discount on admissions – flash your student card or International Student Identity Card (ISIC) before paying. If you're not a student but are under 26, ask a student agency at home for an ISIC Youth Card (www.isic.org).

Senior citizens also *might* get a discount, but no promises: carry your pension card or passport anyway.

Electricity

➡ Electrical power in Russia, China and Mongolia is 220V, 50Hz.

➡ Sockets in Russia and Mongolia are designed to accommodate two round prongs in the European style. Chinese plugs come in at least four designs: three-pronged angled pins as used in Australia; three-pronged round pins as in Hong Kong; two-pronged flat pins as in the USA; or two narrow round pins as in Europe.

Embassies & Consulates

Russia

IRKUTSK

Mongolian Consulate (☎395-234 2295; www.irkutsk.mfa.gov.mn; ul Lapina 11; ⏲9am-1pm)

KHABAROVSK

Chinese Consulate (☎4212-302 590; www.chinaconsulate.khb.ru/rus; Southern Bldg, Lenin Stadium 1; ⏲11am-1pm Mon, Wed & Fri)

Japanese Consulate (☎4212-413 048; www.khabarovsk.ru.emb-japan.go.jp; ul Turgeneva 46; ⏲10am-noon & 3-5pm Mon-Fri)

MOSCOW

Australian Embassy (Посольство Австралии; ☎495-956 6070; www.russia.embassy.gov.au; Podkolokolny per 10a/2; Ⓜ Kitay-Gorod)

Belarusian Embassy (Посольство Белорусии; ☎495-777 6644; www.embassybel.ru; ul Maroseyka 17/6; Ⓜ Kitay-Gorod)

Canadian Embassy (Посольство Канады; ☎495-925 6000; http://russia.gc.ca; Starokonyushenny per 23; ⏲8.30am-5pm; Ⓜ Kropotkinskaya)

Chinese Embassy (Посольство Китая; ☎consular 499-951 8436; http://ru.chineseembassy.org/rus; ul Druzhby 6; ⏲9am-noon Mon-Fri; Ⓜ Universitet)

Finnish Embassy (Посольство Финляндии; ☎495-787 4174; www.finland.org.ru; Kropotkinsky per 15/17; ⏲9am-5pm; Ⓜ Park Kultury)

French Embassy (Посольство Франции; ☎495-937 1500; www.ambafrance-ru.org; ul Bolshaya Yakimanka 45; Ⓜ Oktyabrskaya)

German Embassy (Посольство Германии; ☎495-937 9500; www.germania.diplo.de; Mosfilmovskaya ul 56; ⏲9am-3pm; 🚌119, Ⓜ Universitet)

Irish Embassy (Посольство Ирландии; ☎495-937 5911; www.embassyofireland.ru; Grokholsky per 5; Ⓜ Prospekt Mira)

Japanese Embassy (Посольство Японии; ☎495-229 2550; www.ru.emb-japan.go.jp; Grokholsky per 27; Ⓜ Arbatskaya)

Mongolian Embassy (Посольство Монголии; ☎495-690 4636; http://embassymongolia.ru; Borisoglebsky per 11;

Ⓜ Arbartskaya) The Visa section (Посольство Монголии (Визовый отдел); ☎499-241 1557; http://embassymongolia.ru; Spasopeskovsky per 7/1; Ⓜ Smolenskaya) is in a different location.

Netherlands Embassy (Посольство Королевства Нидерландов; ☎495-797 2900; www.netherlands-embassy.ru; Kalashny per 6; Ⓜ Arbatskaya)

New Zealand Embassy (☎495-956 3579; www.nzembassy.com; Povarskaya ul 44; Ⓜ Arbatskaya)

UK Embassy (Посольство Великобритании; ☎495-956 7200; www.gov.uk/government/world/russia; Smolenskaya nab 10; ⏲9am-5pm; Ⓜ Smolenskaya)

Ukrainian Embassy (Посольство Украины; ☎495-629 3542, consular questions 495-629 9742; http://russia.mfa.gov.ua; Leontevsky per 18; Ⓜ Pushkinskaya)

US Embassy (Посольство США; ☎495-728 5000; http://moscow.usembassy.gov; Bolshoy Devyatinsky per 8; Ⓜ Barrikadnaya)

ST PETERSBURG

Belarusian Embassy (☎812-274 7212; www.embassybel.ru; ul Bonch-Bruevicha 3a; Ⓜ Chernyshevskaya)

Chinese Consulate (Посольство Китая; ☎812-714 7670; http://saint-petersburg.chineseconsulate.org/rus/; nab kanala Griboyedova 134; Ⓜ Sadovaya, Sennaya Ploshchad)

Finnish Consulate (☎812-331 7600; www.finland.org.ru; Preobrazhenskaya pl 4; Ⓜ Chernyshevskaya)

French Consulate (☎812-332 2270; https://ru.ambafrance.org; 5th fl, Nevsky pr 12; Ⓜ Admiralteyskaya)

German Consulate (☎812-320 2400; www.germania.diplo.de; Furshtatskaya ul 39; Ⓜ Chernyshevskaya)

Japanese Embassy (Посольство Японии; ☎812-314 1434; www.st-petersburg.ru.emb-japan.go.jp; nab reki Moyki 29; Ⓜ Admiralteskaya)

UK Consulate (☎812-320 3200; pl Proletarskoy Diktatury 5; Ⓜ Chernyshevskaya)

US Consulate (☎812-331 2600; www.stpetersburg.usconsulate.gov; Furshtatskaya ul 15; Ⓜ Chernyshevskaya)

ULAN-UDE

Mongolian Consulate (Консульство Монголии; ☎3012-215 275; ul Profsoyuznaya 6; ⏲9am-6pm Mon-Fri)

YEKATERINBURG

UK Consulate (☎343-253 5600; ul Gogolya 15a; ⏲9am-5pm Mon-Fri)

China

BĚIJĪNG

Embassies (大使馆; *dàshǐguǎn*) in Běijīng are open from 9am to noon and from 1.30pm to 4pm Monday to Friday. Visa departments, which are often in separate, usually adjoining, buildings (check the embassy website), are sometimes only open in the morning. There are three main embassy areas: Jiànguóménwài, Sānlǐtún and Liàngmǎqiáo.

It has become increasingly common in recent years for embassies to turn down visa applications from foreigners who do not live in China. It's always best to arrange visas in your home country.

Australian Embassy (澳大利亚大使馆; Àodàlìyà Dàshǐguǎn; ☎010 5140 4111; www.china.embassy.gov.au; 21 Dongzhimenwai Dajie; 东直门外大街21号; ⏲9am-noon & 2-3.30pm Mon-Fri; Ⓢ Line 2 to Dongzhimen, exit B)

Canadian Embassy (加拿大大使馆; Jiānádà Dàshǐguǎn; ☎010 5139 4000; www.china.gc.ca; 19 Dongzhimenwai Dajie; 东直门外大街19号; ⏲8.30-11am Mon-Fri & 1.30-3pm Tue & Thu; Ⓢ Line 2 to Dongzhimen, exit B)

French Embassy (法国驻华大使馆; Fàguó Zhùhuá Dàshǐguǎn; ☎010 8531 2000; www.ambafrance-cn.org; 60 Tianze Lu; 天泽路60号; ⏲8.30am-noon Mon-Fri; 9am-noon last Sat of month; Ⓢ Line 10 to Liangmaqiao, exit B)

German Embassy (德国大使馆; Déguó Dàshǐguǎn; ☎010 8532 9000; www.china.diplo.de; 17 Dongzhimenwai Dajie; 东直门外大街17号; ⏲8am-noon & 1-5pm Mon, to 5.30pm Tue-Thu, 8am-noon & 12.30-3pm Fri; Ⓢ Line 2 to Dongzhimen, exit B)

Indian Embassy (印度大使馆; Yìndù Dàshǐguǎn; ☎010 8531 2500; www.indianembassy.org.cn; 5 Liangmaqiao Beijie; 亮马桥北街5号; ⏲8.30am-5.30pm Mon-Fri; Ⓢ Line 10 to Liangmaqiao, exit B) Visa applications are handled are handled nearby at the India Visa Application Centre (印度签证申请中心; Yìndù Qiānzhèng Shēnqǐng Zhōngxīn; ☎010 8446 3955; www.blsindia-china.com; B-505, Xiaoyun Centre, 15 Xiaguangli; 霄云中心霞光里15号; ⏲8.30am-5.30pm Mon-Fri; Ⓢ Line 10 to Sanyuanqiao Station, exit C2).

Irish Embassy (爱尔兰大使馆; Ài'ěrlán Dàshǐguǎn; ☎010 8531 6200; www.irishembassy.cn; 3 Ritan Donglu; 日坛东路3号; ⏲9am-12.30pm & 2-5pm Mon-Fri; Ⓢ Line 1 to Yonganli, exit A1)

Kazakhstan Embassy (哈萨克斯坦使馆; Hāsàkè Sītǎn Shǐguǎn; ☎010 6532 4189, 010 6532 6182; www.mfa.gov.kz/en/beijing; 9 Sanlitun Dongliu Jie; 三里屯东六街9号; ⏲visa applications 9am-1pm Mon & Wed-Fri; Ⓢ Liangmaqiao) Come here for visas to Kazakhstan.

Mongolian Embassy (蒙古大使馆; Ménggǔ Dàshǐguǎn; ☎010 6532 1203; www.beijing.mfa.gov.mn; 2 Xiushui Beijie; 秀水北街2号; Ⓢ Line 1 to Yonganli, exit A1) There is a separate visa section (☎010 6532 1203, 010 6532 6512; www.beijing.mfa.gov.mn; 2 Xiushui Beijie; 秀水北街2号; ⏲visa application 9am-noon Mon-Fri, passport collection 4-5pm Mon-Fri; Ⓢ Line 1 to Yonganli, exit A1).

Netherlands Embassy (荷兰大使馆; Hélán Dàshǐguǎn; ☎010 8532 0200; http://china.nlembassy.org; 4 Liangmahe Nanlu; 亮马河南路4号; ⏲9am-12.30pm & 2-5.30pm Mon-Fri;

Ⓢ Line 10 to Liangmaqiao, exit B)

New Zealand Embassy (新西兰大使馆, Xīnxīlán Dàshǐguǎn; ☎010 8531 2700; www.mfat.govt.nz; 3 Sanlitun Dongsanjie, 三里屯东三街3号; ⏲8.30am-5pm Mon-Fri; Ⓢ Line 10 to Agricultural Exhibition Center, exit D2)

North Korean Embassy (北朝鲜驻华使馆; Běi Cháoxiǎn Zhùhuá Shǐguǎn; ☎010 6532 1186; 11 Ritan Beilu; 日坛北路11号; Ⓢ Line 6 to Dongdaqiao, exit D)

Pakistan Embassy (巴基斯坦大使馆; Bājīsītǎn Dàshǐguǎn; ☎010 6532 2504; www.pakbj.org.pk; 1 Dongzhimenwai Dajie; 东直门外大街1号; ⏲9-11.30am Mon-Fri; Ⓢ Line 10 to Agricultural Exhibition Center, exit A)

Russian Embassy (俄罗斯大使馆; Èluósī Dàshǐguǎn; Map p310; ☎010 6532 1381, visa section 2-6pm Mon-Fri 010 6532 1267; www.russia.org.cn; 4 Dongzhimen Beizhongjie, off Dongzhimennei Dajie; 东直门内大街东直门北中街4号, off Dongzhimennei Dajie; ⏲9am-noon Mon-Fri; Ⓢ Lines 2, 13 to Dongzhimen, exit A)

UK Embassy (联合王国大使馆; Liánhé Wángguó Dàshǐguǎn; ☎010 5192 4000; www.gov.uk; 11 Guanghua Lu; 光华路11号; ⏲9am-noon Mon, Tue, Thu & Fri; Ⓢ Line 1 to Yonganli, exit A1) Consular Section (英国大使馆; ☎010 8529 6600; www.gov.uk; 21st fl, Kerry Center, 1 Guanghua Lu; 光华路1号家里中心21层; ⏲8.30am-noon & 1.30-4pm Mon-Fri; Ⓢ Line 10 to Jintaixizhao, exit D)

US Embassy (美国大使馆; Měiguó Dàshǐguǎn; ☎010 8531 3300; https://china.usembassy-china.org.cn/; 55 Anjialou Lu, off Liangmaqiao Lu; 亮马桥安家楼路55号; ⏲8.30am-noon & 2-4pm Mon, Tue & Fri; 8:30am-noon Wed & Fri; Ⓢ Line 10 to Liangmaqiao, exit B)

Vietnamese Embassy (越南大使馆; Yuènán Dàshǐguǎn; ☎010 6532 1155; https://vnembassy-beijing.mofa.gov.vn; 32 Guanghua Lu; 光华路32号; ⏲9am-5pm Mon-Fri; Ⓢ Line 1 to Yonganli, exit A1)

HOHHOT

Mongolian Consulate (蒙古领事馆; Měnggǔ Lǐngshìguǎn; ☎0471 468 5161, 0471 492 3819; Unit 1, Bldg 5, Wulan Residential Area, Sai Han District; 赛罕区乌兰小区五号楼一单元; ⏲9am-noon Mon, Tue & Thu)

Mongolia

The German embassy also looks after the interests of Dutch, Belgian, Greek and Portuguese citizens. The British embassy can handle normal consular duties for Commonwealth countries that do not already have an embassy or consulate.

ULAANBAATAR

Canadian Embassy (☎11-332 500; www.canadainternational.gc.ca/mongolia-mongolie; Peace Ave, Central Tower, 6th fl, What3words: devoured.village.trooper; ⏲9am-noon Mon-Fri)

Chinese Embassy (☎11-323 940; http://mn.china-embassy.org; Zaluuchuudyn Örgön Chölöö 5, What3words: adults.reputable.breathy; ⏲visas 9.30am-noon Mon, Wed & Fri) The consular section is actually on Baga Toiruu.

French Embassy (☎11-324 519; www.ambafrance-mn.org; Peace Ave 3, What3words: broker.overdrive.glimmers; ⏲8.30am-12.30pm & 1.30-5pm Mon-Fri)

German Embassy (☎011-323 915, 11-323 325; www.ulan-bator.diplo.de; United Nations St 16, What3words: scan.redeeming.regaining; ⏲8.30am-12.30pm & 1-5pm Mon-Thu, 8.30am-12.30pm Fri)

Japanese Embassy (☎11-320 777; www.mn.emb-japan.go.jp; Embassy Rd 10, What3words.carriage.parsnips.shut; ⏲9am-1pm & 2-4.45pm Mon-Fri)

Kazakhstan Embassy (☎11-345 408; ulaanbaatar@mfa.kz; Zaisan St 31/6, Khan Uul District, What3words: forgets.indicated.fantastic) The embassy is located on the way to Zaisan; take the last right turn before the bridge, into an alley with hideous-looking villas. Look for the Kazakh flag on the right.

Russian Embassy (☎11-326 037; www.mongolia.mid.ru/en; Peace Ave 6A, What3words: prime.slant.beaker; ⏲visas 9am-noon Mon-Fri)

UK Embassy (☎11-458 133; www.gov.uk/world/mongolia; Peace Ave 30, What3words: nets.cases.dummy; ⏲8.30am-1pm & 2-5pm Mon-Thu, to 1.30pm Fri)

US Embassy (☎7007 6001; https://mn.usembassy.gov; Denver St 3, What3words: craftsman.memo.rags; ⏲8.30am-5pm Mon-Fri)

Food

For more on Chinese food, see p364.

For more on Mongolian food, see p355.

For more on Russian food, see p347.

Gay & Lesbian Travellers

Russia

- Russia is a conservative country and being gay is generally frowned upon. LGBT people face stigma, harassment and violence in their everyday lives.
- Homosexuality isn't illegal, but promoting it (and other LGBT lifestyles) is. What constitutes promotion is at the discretion of the authorities.
- There are active and relatively open gay and lesbian scenes in both Moscow and St Petersburg. Elsewhere the gay scene tends to be underground.
- For a good overview visit http://english.gay.ru, which has up-to-date information, good links and a resource for putting you in touch with personal guides for Moscow and St Petersburg.

MEAL PRICES

The following price ranges are for a standard main course.

Symbol	Russia/ Moscow & St Petersburg	Mongolia	China
€ or $	less than ₽300/500	less than T9000	less than ¥40
€€ or $$	₽300–800/ ₽500–1000	T9000–16,000	¥40–100
€€€ or $$$	more than ₽800/1000	more than T16,000	more than ¥100

China

Despite China's florid homosexual traditions, the puritanical overseers of the Chinese Communist Party (CCP) have worked tirelessly to suppress the LGBT community. Even in urban areas, gay and lesbian visitors should not be too open about their sexual orientation in public. **Utopia** (www.utopia-asia.com/tipschin.htm) has tips on travelling in China and a complete listing of gay bars nationwide.

Mongolia

Mongolia is not an LGBT-friendly place, nor one to test local attitudes towards homosexuality. Ulaanbaatar has a small gay community that will occasionally convene at a tolerant restaurant or bar, but it moves around every few months, so you'll need to quietly tap into the scene and ask. Insight can be found at www.utopia-asia.com/tipsmong.htm.

Insurance

We strongly recommend taking out travel insurance. Check the small print to see if the policy covers potentially dangerous sporting activities, such as diving or trekking. For medical treatment, some policies pay doctors or hospitals directly but most require you to pay on the spot and claim later (keep all receipts and documentation). Check that the policy covers ambulances or an emergency flight home.

Worldwide travel insurance is available at www.lonelyplanet.com/travel-insurance. You can buy, extend and claim online anytime – even if you're already on the road.

Internet Access

Wi-fi accessibility in hotels, cafes, restaurants and bars along the Tran-Sib routes is generally good. The best option is to bring a wi-fi-equipped smartphone, tablet or laptop or use your hotel computer or broadband internet connection.

Russia

Wi-fi is common across Russia and usually access is free (or available for the cost of a cup of coffee). You may have to ask for a password, or *parol*, to get online, and also input your mobile phone number. Sometimes this will need to be a Russian number (ie one starting with +7); if you don't have one, ask a local if you can use their number.

China

The Chinese authorities remain mistrustful of the internet, and censorship is heavy-handed. Around 10% of websites are blocked; the list is constantly changing but includes sites and apps such as Facebook, Twitter, Instagram, Google-owned sites (YouTube, Google Maps, Gmail, Google Drive), Dropbox and Telegram, so plan ahead. Google's search function is blocked, but a limited Chinese version of Yahoo and Bing are accessible. Newspaper sites such as the *New York Times* are also blocked, as is Bloomberg, though the *Guardian* is allowed.

Users can gain access to blocked websites by using a VPN (virtual private network) service such as VyprVPN (www.goldenfrog.com). Be aware that using VPNs can be slow, and often they are blocked sites themselves so must be installed before arriving in China – and not all even work in China.

Many internet cafes only accept customers with Chinese ID, thus barring foreigners. In large cities and towns, the area around the train station generally has internet cafes.

Mongolia

A handful of internet cafes can be found in Ulaanbaatar and other cities. Signs are often in English or Mongolian (Интэрнэт Кафэ). Wi-fi hot spots are just about everywhere in bigger cities. In villages you'll need to ask around.

The capitals of each *aimag* (province) will have internet access at the central Telecom office. Some *sum* (district) centres also have internet access. Expect to pay around T800 per hour at internet cafes, double or triple that for hotel business centres.

Internet service providers (ISPs) such as Skytel charge T10,000 for 1GB of data for a month.

Mobile broadband 4G is available in Ulaanbaatar and *aimag* capitals; elsewhere, coverage is patchy. Use it sparingly as it tends to drain your phone battery.

Legal Matters

In Russia, and to a lesser extent in Mongolia, it's generally best to avoid contact with the police. It's not uncommon for Russian police to bolster their puny incomes by extracting sham 'fines' from the unaware; you always have the right to insist to be taken to a police station (we don't recommend this) or that the 'fine' be paid the legal way through Sberbank. If you do need police assistance (ie you've been the victim of a robbery or an assault) go to a station with a Russian for both language and moral support.

Note anyone caught smoking in a public place in Russia can be subjected to fines of up to ₽1500, according to a law that came into force in 2014. This includes bars, restaurants, children's playgrounds, station platforms or at the end of carriages on long-distance trains.

If you are arrested, the police in Russia, China and Mongolia are obliged to inform your embassy or consulate immediately and allow you to communicate with it without delay. Although you can insist on seeing an embassy or consular official straight away, you can't count on the rules being followed, so be polite and respectful towards officials and hopefully things will go far more smoothly for you.

Maps

Maps of all the major cities along the Trans-Siberian routes are on sale in each city.

Russia

City and regional maps for Russia are available from bookshops and map shops in Moscow and St Petersburg. Magazine kiosks at larger Russian train stations usually sell city maps.

China

In Běijīng, English-language maps of the city are available for free at most big hotels and branches of the Běijīng Tourist Information Center.

Mongolia

Conservation Ink (www.conservationink.org) produces maps (US$8) using satellite images combined with useful information on culture, wildlife and tourist facilities. The national park series includes Gorkhi-Terelj and Khustain Nuruu.

Money

ATMs

RUSSIA

Use your credit or debit card as you would in ATMs at home and you can obtain cash as you need it – usually in roubles, but sometimes in US dollars or euros, too. You're rarely a block or so from an ATM: look for signs that say *bankomat* (БАНКОМАТ).

CHINA

Bank of China and the Industrial & Commercial Bank of China (ICBC) 24-hour ATMs are plentiful, and you can use Visa, MasterCard, Cirrus, Maestro Plus and American Express to withdraw cash. All ATMs accepting international cards have dual-language ability.

MONGOLIA

Golomt, Trade & Development Bank, Khan Bank and Khas Bank all have ATMs in their Ulaanbaatar and countryside branches. These ATMs accept Visa and MasterCard and work most of the time, allowing you to withdraw up to T800,000 per day.

Cash

Any currency you bring should be in pristine condition: banks and exchange bureaus do not accept old, tatty bills with rips or tears. Wrap notes in plastic if you're carrying them anywhere sweaty.

There are no official facilities for exchanging money on the train but some *provodnitsas* (train carriage attendants) or the restaurant staff will accept foreign cash at very poor exchange rates – don't count on this. Stock up at major stops, where you should find ATMs. There are usually exchange places at border-town train stations.

Get rid of your *tögrög* before you leave Mongolia, as almost no one will want to touch them once you are outside the country.

Credit Cards

Credit cards are accepted in Russian cities and towns, but don't rely on them in more rural areas. When using a credit card at Russian stations to buy tickets, say so early on by showing it. Cash is usually required for train tickets in China and Mongolia.

Most sizeable cities in Russia have banks or exchange bureaus that will

RUSSIAN STREET NAMES

We use the Russian names of all streets and squares to help you when deciphering Cyrillic signs and asking locals the way. To save space, we use the following abbreviations.

bul	bulvar	бульвар	boulevard
nab	naberezhnaya	набережная	embankment
per	pereulok	переулок	side street
pl	ploshchad	площадь	square
pr	prospekt	проспект	avenue
sh	shosse	шоссе	road
ul	ulitsa	улица	street

give you a cash advance on your credit card, but be prepared for paperwork in the local language. Always carry enough cash for a night in a hotel – hand-held card machines in Russian hotels may suffer communication breakdowns.

In Mongolia, credit cards are often accepted at top-end hotels, the expensive souvenir shops, airline offices and travel agencies, but usually with an additional 3% charge. Banks can give cash advances from credit cards, often for no charge if you have Visa, but as much as 4% with MasterCard.

In China, credit cards are useful for withdrawing money at ATMs, but are much less useful for buying goods and services.

Tipping

RUSSIA

Common in restaurants – about 10% is good. Tip your guide, if you have one, a similar amount of their daily rate; a small gift is appropriate if service is especially good.

CHINA

Neither required nor expected, except in the case of porters in upmarket hotels.

MONGOLIA

Optional; if you round up the bill, then your server will be satisfied.

Travellers Cheques

Travellers cheques are no longer a preferred method of carrying funds and will prove difficult to exchange in Russia, China and Mongolia.

Opening Hours

Russia

Banks 9am–6pm Monday to Friday, some open 9am–5pm Saturday

Museums Hours are not uniform; they close one day a week and there will be one extra 'sanitary' day per month when the facility is closed for cleaning.

Restaurants and bars Noon–midnight, bars usually until 6am Friday and Saturday

Shops 10am–8pm Monday to Friday, supermarkets 24 hours

China

Banks 9am–noon and 2–5pm Monday to Friday

Restaurants 10.30am–11pm

Shops 10am–10pm

Mongolia

Banks 9am–6pm Monday to Friday, 10am–3pm Saturday

Restaurants 10am–10pm

Shops 9am–6pm (to 10pm in Ulaanbaatar)

Photography

For more professional tips on taking some decent photos, read Lonely Planet's *Travel Photography* by Richard I'Anson.

Equipment & Back-Up

All major towns have photographic shops for digital burning to CD, printing and film purchases. Slide film is rare.

Photographing People

Always ask before photographing someone, especially on the train (including the *provodnitsa*). In Russian, 'May I take a photograph of you?' is *'Mozhno vas sfotografirovat?'*; in Mongolian it is *'Bi tany zurgiig avch bolokh uu?'*. Remember that many people will be touchy if you photograph 'embarrassments' such as drunks, run-down housing and other signs of social decay.

Restrictions

SENSITIVE INFRASTRUCTURE

In Russia, China and Mongolia (but especially in Russia) be particularly careful about taking photographs of stations, official-looking buildings and any type of military/security structure. Sometimes over-eager police in Russia will stop you taking a platform photo.

MUSEUMS & GALLERIES

Many forbid flash pictures, some ban all photos and most will charge you extra to snap away. Some caretakers in historical buildings and churches charge mercilessly for the privilege of using a still or video camera.

RELIGIOUS BUILDINGS

Taking photos inside churches, monasteries and temples is discourteous and, in the case of temples in Mongolia, forbidden; you may photograph building exteriors and monastery grounds.

Post

The postal service in Russia, China and Mongolia is generally reliable, although in Russia it can be slow. Allow at least a couple of weeks for letters and postcards to arrive home from Mongolia, more like four or five from Russia (although it can be quicker), and about five to 10 days from China. The major Russian cities, plus Běijīng and Ulaanbaatar, have international private courier firms such as **FedEx** (www.fedex.com), **UPS** (www.ups.com), **DHL** (www.dhl.com) and **TNT Express** (www.tnt.com).

For receiving post along the Trans-Mongolian, Běijīng's **International Post Office** (中国邮政; Zhōngguó Yóuzhèng; Map p302; ☎010 6512 8114; Jianguomen Beidajie; 建国门北大街; ⏰8.30am-6pm; Ⓢ Lines 1, 2 to Jianguomen, exit B) and Ulaanbaatar's **Central Post Office** (CPO, Töv Shuudangiin Salbar; ☎11-313 421; cnr Peace Ave & Sükhbaataryn Gudamj, What3words: wicked.greet.conjured; ⏰7.30am-9pm Mon-Fri, 9am-8pm Sat & Sun) are useful for poste restante (in Russia there's no poste restante, and embassies and consulates won't hold mail for transient visitors). Bring along your passport as proof of identification.

Public Holidays

Russia

In addition to the following official days, many businesses (but not restaurants, shops and museums) close for a week of bank holidays between 1 January and at least 8 January. Bank holidays are typically declared to merge national holidays with the nearest weekend.

New Year's Day 1 January

Russian Orthodox Christmas Day 7 January

Defender of the Fatherland Day 23 February

International Women's Day 8 March

International Labour Day/ Spring Festival 1 May

Victory Day 9 May

Russian Independence Day 12 June

Unity Day 4 November

China

The People's Republic of China has a number of national holidays. Some of the following are nominal holidays that do not result in leave. It's not a great idea to arrive in China or go travelling during the big holiday periods as hotel prices reach their maximum and transport can become very tricky. It is also possible to contact a hotel and ask when large conferences occur in the area.

New Year's Day 1 January

Chinese New Year 16 February 2018, 5 February 2019; a week-long holiday for most.

International Women's Day 8 March

Tomb Sweeping Festival First weekend in April; a popular three-day holiday period.

International Labour Day 1 May; for many it's a three-day holiday.

Youth Day 4 May

International Children's Day 1 June

Dragon Boat Festival 30 May 2017, 18 June 2018, 7 June 2019

Birthday of the Chinese Communist Party 1 July (not a public holiday)

Anniversary of the Founding of the People's Liberation Army 1 August

Mid-Autumn Festival 24 September 2018, 13 September 2019

National Day 1 October; the big one – a week-long holiday.

Mongolia

The Naadam Festival and Tsagaan Sar each warrant three days off, plus there's a day off for Children's Day, New Years and Chinggis Khaan's birthday. Most tourist facilities remain open during holidays, but shops and offices will close down. The following holidays are observed:

Shin Jil (New Year's Day) 1 January

Constitution Day 13 January; to celebrate the adoption of the 1992 constitution (generally a normal working day).

Tsagaan Sar (Lunar New Year) January/February; a three-day holiday celebrating the Mongolian New Year.

Women's Day 8 March (generally a normal working day).

Mothers' & Children's Day 1 June; a great time to visit parks.

Naadam Festival 11 and 12 July; also known as National Day celebrations.

Chinggis Khaan's Birthday Early November; the date is the first day of the first winter month, based on the lunar calendar. Most government offices and banks are closed.

Safe Travel

Russia, China and Mongolia are generally safe countries and crime against foreigners is rare.

➡ Traffic will be the biggest danger in all three countries – always keep your wits about you.

➡ On the whole, the trains are reasonably safe, but it always pays to take simple precautions with your luggage. If you've got the compartment to yourself, ask the carriage attendant to lock it when you leave for the restaurant car or get out at the station platforms.

Scams

RUSSIAN POLICE

They may want to see your documents, find fault (such as not being registered, even when it's not necessary) then demand you to pay a 'fine' to get the documents back. It's ransom, and fortunately it's happening less often these days. The only course of action is to remain calm, polite and stand your ground. Show copies, not originals, whenever possible. Try to enlist the help of a passer-by to translate for you (or at least witness what is going on).

GOVERNMENT TRAVEL ADVICE

The following government websites offer travel advisories and information on current hot spots.

Australian Department of Foreign Affairs (www.smartraveller.gov.au)

British Foreign Office (www.gov.uk/foreign-travel-advice)

Canadian Department of Foreign Affairs (www.dfait-maeci.gc.ca)

US State Department (http://travel.state.gov)

BĚIJĪNG AIRPORT TAXIS

Taxi scams at the airport are legendary; always join the queue at the taxi rank and insist that the taxi driver uses his or her meter. If anyone approaches you offering a taxi ride, ignore them.

PRETTY-WOMAN SCAM

On Běijīng's Wangfujing Dajie, well-dressed girls flock to drag single men to expensive cafes or Chinese teahouses, leaving them to foot monstrous bills.

Racism & Discrimination

Sadly, racism is a problem in Russia. Frightening reports of racial violence appear from time to time in the media, and it's a sure thing that if you are non-Caucasian you'll be targeted with suspicion by many (the police, in particular).

Telephone & Fax

In Russia, China and Mongolia faxes can be sent from most post offices and upmarket hotels.

Russia

- The country code for Russia is ☎7.
- Local calls from homes and most hotels are free.
- To make a long-distance call from most phones first dial ☎8, wait for a second dial tone, then dial the city code and number.
- To make an international call dial ☎8, wait for a second dial tone, then dial ☎10, then the country code etc. Some phones are for local calls only and won't give you that second dial tone. From mobile phones, just dial + followed by the country code to place an international call.

MOBILE PHONES

Prepaid SIM cards are readily available. International roaming possible.

China

- The country code for China is ☎86.
- To call internationally from China, drop the first zero of the area or city code after dialling the international access code, and then dial the number you wish to call.
- Local calls from hotel-room phones are generally cheap (and sometimes free), although international phone calls are expensive; it's best to use a phonecard.

MOBILE PHONES

A mobile phone should be the first choice for calls, but ensure your mobile is unlocked for use in China if taking your own. SIM cards can be bought at the arrivals area at major airports.

PAY PHONES

If making a domestic call, look out for very cheap public phones at newspaper stands (报刊亭; *bàokāntíng*) and hole-in-the-wall shops (小卖部; *xiǎomàibù*); you make your call and then pay the owner. Domestic and international long-distance phone calls can also be made from main telecommunications offices and 'phone bars' (话吧; *huàbā*).

Cardless international calls are expensive and it's far cheaper to use an IP card. You dial a local number, then punch in your account number, followed by a pin number and finally the number you wish to call. English-language service is usually available. IP cards can be found at newspaper kiosks, hole-in-the-wall shops, internet cafes and from any China Telecom office, although in some cities they can be hard to find. Some IP cards can only be used locally, while others can be used nationwide, so it is important to buy the right card (and check the expiry date).

Public telephone booths are rarely used now in China but may serve as wi-fi hot spots (as in Shànghǎi).

Mongolia

- The country code for Mongolia is ☎976.
- Ulaanbaatar has several area codes: 11 is the most widely used. If a phone number begins with a 23, 24 or 25, then the area code is ☎21. If the phone number begins with a 26, the code is ☎51.
- If you are calling out of Mongolia and are using an international direct dial (IDD) phone, just dial 00 and then your international country code. On non-IDD phones you can make direct long-distance calls by dialling the international operator (☎106), who may know enough English to make the right connection (but don't count on it).
- It's easy to make international or domestic calls in Ulaanbaatar and the *aimag* capitals. Technology is still lagging in many *sum* centres; however, it's now possible to use mobile (cell) phones in most of the country.

MOBILE PHONES

Local SIM cards can be used in whatever phone you bring. You can also keep your own SIM card if you have a plan that allows roaming, but be wary of roaming charges.

Time

One of the most disorienting aspects of a Trans-Siberian trip is working out what time it is. The important thing to remember is that all long-distance trains run on Moscow time – so check carefully when you buy a ticket exactly what time *locally* you should be at the station. Once inside the station and on the train all clocks are set to Moscow time.

Mongolia is divided into two time zones: the three western *aimags* of Bayan-Ölgii, Uvs and Khovd are one hour behind Ulaanbaatar and the rest of the country. China has only one time zone, which is the same as the time in Ulaanbaatar. Russia has 11 time zones.

Russia, China and Mongolia do not change clocks to daylight-saving time.

Toilets

It's rare that paper will actually be available in the stalls of public toilets, so always bring a supply of toilet paper or tissue with you. Plumbing systems in Russia, China and Mongolia often have problems digesting toilet paper. If there is a rubbish basket next to the toilet, this is where the paper should go.

Russia

Pay toilets are identified by the words платный туалет *(platny tualet)*. In any toilet Ж *(zhensky)* stands for women's, while М *(muzhskoy)* stands for men's.

In cities, you'll now find clusters of temporary plastic toilet cubicles in popular public places, although other public toilets are rare and often dingy and uninviting. A much better option are the loos in major hotels or in modern food outlets. In all public toilets, the attendant who you pay your ₽10 to can provide miserly rations of toilet paper.

China & Mongolia

Public toilets in hotels, ger camps and restaurants are usually European-style, with moderately clean facilities. In contrast, public facilities in parks, stores and train stations usually require that you squat over a smelly hole. In China you'll also come across toilets without doors and separated only by a low partition, making it easy to strike up a conversation with the person squatting next to you.

Toilets along the Route

- On Russian and Mongolian trains the toilets are of the Western variety. The bowl on older toilets is designed to allow you to squat. The carriage attendants generally do a good job of keeping them clean, particularly on the more prestigious class of trains.
- Before and after any major stops, and along any densely populated stretches of the line, the toilets will be locked; a timetable for this is usually posted on the toilet door.
- On Chinese trains (but not train 3/4) toilets are often of the squat variety.

Tourist Information

Russia

Official tourist offices are rare in Russia. Along the main trans-Siberian route, Western-style hostels are good sources of local information.

You're mainly dependent on hotel receptionists and administrators, service bureaus and travel firms for information. The latter two exist primarily to sell accommodation, excursions and transport – if you don't look like you want to book something, staff may or may not answer questions.

China

Tourist information continues to improve, with modern booths with pamphlets springing up even in smaller cities. The quality of spoken English can be hit-and-miss, though.

- **China National Tourist Office** www.cnto.org

Mongolia

- There are two tourist information desks in Ulaanbaatar: at the **Ulaanbaatar Bank building** (☎7010 8687; www.tourism.ub.gov.mn; Baga Toiruu W 15, What3words: float.unscathed.snippets; ⏰8am-5pm Mon-Fri) and the **Guide Tourist Information Centre** (☎7010 1011; www.touristinfocenter.mn; Peace Ave, State Department Store, 1st fl, What3words: bravo.hexes.steamed; ⏰9am-9pm Mon-Fri, 10am-9pm Sat & Sun May-Sep, to 6pm Oct-Apr)

TIME ZONES

Moscow	Noon	(GMT/UTC +3 hours)
San Francisco	1am	(GMT/UTC -8 hours)
New York	4am	(GMT/UTC -5 hours)
London	9am	(GMT/UTC +0 hours)
Paris, Berlin	10am	(GMT/UTC +1 hour)
Helsinki	11am	(GMT/UTC +2 hours)
Krasnoyarsk, Tuva	4pm	(GMT/UTC +7 hours)
Irkutsk, Ulan-Ude	5pm	(GMT/UTC +8 hours)
Běijīng, Ulaanbaatar, Perth	5pm	(GMT/UTC +8 hours)
Vladivostok, Sydney	7pm	(GMT/UTC +10 hours)

inside the State Department Store. Each is run by a separate entity.

➡ Outside UB, there is a **tourist information centre** (☎9938 2050; www.huvsgul.wix.com/info; What3words: submits.loved.sometimes; ⌚9am-6pm) in Mörön.

Travellers with Disabilities

Russia, China and Mongolia can be difficult places for disabled travellers. Most buildings, buses and trains are not wheelchair accessible. In China and Russia, crossing busy streets often requires using underground walkways with many steps. Uneven pavements in the cities and rough roads in the countryside make for uncomfortable and potentially dangerous travel.

Across its system, Russian Railways offers 615 carriages with compartments for people with disabilities and 609 carriages equipped with lifting devices for them. Failing these, travellers in wheelchairs will have to be carried on and off the train and into their compartments and will have difficulty with the toilets, which are utterly unfriendly for wheelchairs. If you need assistance, call the Mobility Assistance Centre at Russian Railways on ☎8-800-510 1111.

Download Lonely Planet's free Accessible Travel guides from http://lptravel.to/AccessibleTravel.

Visas

For information about obtaining, registering and extending visas for Russia, China and Mongolia, see p40.

Women Travellers

Russian women are very independent and, in general, you won't attract attention by travelling alone.

That said, a woman alone should certainly avoid private taxis at night. Never get in any taxi with more than one person – the driver – already in it. You're unlikely to experience sexual harassment on the streets in most parts of Russia, though sexual stereotyping remains strong. In rural areas, revealing clothing will probably attract unwanted attention (whereas on hot days in Moscow women wear as little as possible).

On the train consider buying a *platskart* ticket (*platskartny;* open carriage) rather than one in a *kupe* (*kupeyny;* compartmentalised carriage), to avoid the risk of getting stuck in a closed compartment with three shady male characters. Some Russian trains offer a female *(zhensky)* compartment. If you travel *kupe* and don't like your cabin mates, tell the conductor, who will more than likely find you a new place. If a drunk starts accosting you, especially on trains or in minibus taxis, simply do what Russian women do: ignore him and avoid eye contact.

China is probably among the safest places in the world for foreign women to travel alone. Women are generally treated respectfully, because principles of decorum are ingrained deeply in the culture.

Mongolia doesn't present too many problems for foreign women travelling independently. The majority of Mongolian men behave in a friendly and respectful manner. However, you may come across an annoying drunk or the occasional macho idiot. The phrase for 'Go away!' is '*Sasha be!*'.

There are occasional incidents of solo female travellers reporting being harassed by their male guide. If your guide is male, it is best to keep in touch with your tour agency in Ulaanbaatar, perhaps making contingency plans with them if things go awry. Better yet, take a female guide whenever possible.

Transport

GETTING THERE & AWAY

Most travellers will start their Trans-Siberian or Trans-Mongolian trip in either Moscow or Běijīng. It's also possible to fly into or out of other major gateways, such as St Petersburg, Irkutsk, Vladivostok or Ulaanbaatar.

Flights, tours and rail tickets can be booked online at lonelyplanet.com/bookings.

Air

Airports & Airlines

Moscow's **Sheremetyevo** (Шереметьево; ☎495-578 6565; www.svo.aero) and **Domodedovo** (Домодедово; ☎495-933 6666; www.domodedovo.ru) airports host the bulk of Russia's international flights. There are also many daily international services to St Petersburg's **Pulkovo International Airport** (LED; ☎812-337 3822; www.pulkovoairport.ru; Pulkovskoye sh).

Plenty of other trans-Siberian cities have direct international connections, including Irkutsk, Kazan, Khabarovsk, Nizhny Novgorod, Novosibirsk, Perm, Ulan-Ude, Vladivostok and Yekaterinburg.

Běijīng Capital International Airport (北京首都国际机场; Běijīng Shǒudū Guójì Jīchǎng; PEK; ☎010-6454 1100; http://en.bcia.com.cn) is served by both international and domestic connections, as is Ulaanbaatar's **Chinggis Khaan Airport** (☎1900 1980; http://en.airport.gov.mn; What3words: inspects.roaring.nags; 📶).

Flights to/from Ulaanbaatar can be pricey, as there is a limited number of carriers. The main carriers are MIAT, Air China, Korean Air, Turkish Airlines and Aeroflot. Apart from flights to major cities such as Běijīng, Seoul and Moscow, there are some to smaller destinations in China and Russia. These include an Aero Mongolia flight to/from Hohhot four times a week for US$125 one way. Other regional flights to places like Mǎnzhōulǐ, Ulan-Ude and Èrlián, however, change with the seasons.

The choice of airlines for Russia and China is much greater, and tickets are usually cheaper.

Tickets

Some agencies specialise in tours and may offer discount fares.

The peculiarity about flying to and from the railheads for travel on the Trans-Siberian routes is that you will probably be flying in and out of two different cities on one-way tickets, and perhaps using two different airlines.

The cheapest tickets to Hong Kong and China can often be found in discount agencies in Chinatowns around the world.

Land

Train fares stated by Lonely Planet for trips to/from Russia are usually for a 2nd-class *kupe* ticket in a four-berth compartment. Most routes also offer cheaper *platskart* (3rd-class open carriage) fares. See **Russian Railways** (http://pass.rzd.ru/main-pass/public/en) for a complete list of international services.

AIR TICKETS VIA THE WEB

Online gencies with English-language websites specialising in Russian air tickets include **Anywayanyday** (www.anywayanyday.com) and **Pososhok.ru** (www.pososhok.ru).

Major Russian airlines, including **Aeroflot** (☎495-223 5555, toll free in Russia 8-800 444 5555; www.aeroflot.com), **Rossiya** (☎8-495 139 7777, 8-800 444 5555; www.rossiya-airlines.com), **S7 Airlines** (☎495-783-0707, 8-800 700-0707; www.s7.ru) and **UTAir** (www.utair.ru/en) have online bookings, with the usual discounts for advance purchases.

Border Crossings

RUSSIA–MONGOLIA

The border crossed by the Trans-Mongolian trains is at Naushki (Russia) and Sükhbaatar (Mongolia). It's also possible to cross borders by minivan or local train. In addition, there are two road crossings: Tashanta–Tsagaannuur in Bayan-Ölgii *aimag* and Kyakhta–Altanbulag (near Sükhbaatar) in Selenge. The crossings are open from 9am to noon and 2pm to 6pm daily except holidays. The Mondy–Khankh border in northern Khövsgöl and the Solovyevsk–Ereentsav crossing in Dornod are not open to third-country nationals.

MONGOLIA–CHINA

The border crossing is at Zamyn-Üüd and Ereen (Érliàn or Erenhot in Chinese). Don't be concerned if you get off at Ereen (on the Chinese side of the border) and the train disappears from the platform. About an hour is spent changing the bogies (wheel assemblies) because the Russians (and, therefore, the Mongolians) and the Chinese use different railway gauges.

RUSSIA–CHINA

The Trans-Manchurian train crosses the border at Zabaikalsk (Russia) and Mǎnzhōulǐ (China). The bogies are changed here to account for the different rail gauges.

Buses to Zabaikalsk (后贝加尔; Hòubèijiā'ěr; ¥92, five hours), over the Russian border, depart eight times daily between 7.40am and 1.30pm from Mǎnzhōulǐ's **International Bus Passenger Terminal** (际客运站; Guójì Kèyùn Zhàn; ☎0470 622 0358; Huabu Dajie; 华埠大街), but they tend to be much slower than a private car (the Chinese traders on your bus will take ages to get through customs). In Mǎnzhōulǐ you could ask around for a ride from a Russian trader (Russians get through faster). Otherwise, take a taxi to the border (¥40), 9km from town, and get a ride across from there with a Russian driver.

Belarus

Russia and Belarus are members of a Customs Union, so there is no border control. That doesn't mean you can legally cross if you don't have both visas. Crossing without a visa is a criminal offence in both countries.

TRAIN

There are services to/from Kaliningrad, Moscow, Smolensk and St Petersburg, but be aware of the potential problems with using the Russian–Belarus border.

BUS

There are several daily buses between Minsk and Moscow (12 hours), but be aware of the potential problems with using the Russian–Belarus border.

CAR & MOTORCYCLE

Highway crossings between Russia and Belarus can't be used by the citizens of third countries. Non-Russian and Belarus passport holders travelling from the EU by road should use border crossings with Latvia or Estonia.

> **RUSSIA–BELARUS BORDER PROBLEM**
>
> There are potentially serious implications for those transiting into Russia via Belarus on an international bus or train as you will not receive a Russian border stamp or an immigration form on entering the country. If you plan to exit Russia via a different route, this will be a problem and you could be fined.
>
> We've not heard of any travellers running into serious difficulties but it would still be wise to make careful enquiries with visa authorities in both Belarus and Russia before you've confirmed your travel arrangements.

Estonia

There are three border crossings, of which Narva is nearest to Tallinn. Conveniently for motorists, you can avoid queues by booking a time slot for your crossing from (but not into) Estonia for a small fee at www.estonianborder.eu.

There are daily trains between Tallinn and Moscow (*kupe* R5585, 15 hours, 30 minutes) and St Petersburg (R2855, seven hours and 20 minutes). By bus you can connect to/from Tallinn with St Petersburg (from €15, seven hours, seven daily) and Pskov (R1000, six hours, daily).

Finland

TRAIN

High-speed Allegro trains (from R3830, 3½ hours, four daily) connect St Petersburg and Helsinki. The daily 31/34 Leo Tolstoy service between Moscow and Helsinki (R6035, 14 hours and 20 minutes) also passes through St Petersburg (R4100, seven hours, 30 minutes).

BUS

There are many daily buses between Helsinki and St Petersburg.

CAR & MOTORCYCLE

Highways cross at the Finnish border posts of Nuijamaa and Vaalimaa (Brusnichnoe and Torfyanovka, respectively, on the Russian side).

Kazakhstan

Roads into Kazakhstan head east from Astrakhan and south from Samara, Chelyabinsk, Orenburg and Omsk. There are buses (R1000, two daily, 11 hours) between Omsk and Astana, Kazakhstan's capital.

There are direct trains on even days between Moscow and Astana (*platzkart/kupe* R10,050/14,050, two days and six hours) in addition to

CLIMATE CHANGE & TRAVEL

Every form of transport that relies on carbon-based fuel generates CO_2, the main cause of human-induced climate change. Modern travel is dependent on aeroplanes, which might use less fuel per kilometre per person than most cars but travel much greater distances. The altitude at which aircraft emit gases (including CO_2) and particles also contributes to their climate change impact. Many websites offer 'carbon calculators' that allow people to estimate the carbon emissions generated by their journey and, for those who wish to do so, to offset the impact of the greenhouse gases emitted with contributions to portfolios of climate-friendly initiatives throughout the world. Lonely Planet offsets the carbon footprint of all staff and author travel.

services connecting Samara and Novosibirsk with Almaty.

Latvia

BUS

Rīga is connected by bus to Moscow (from €50, 15 hours, daily) and St Petersburg (from €20, 11 hours, four daily).

CAR & MOTORCYCLE

The M9 Rīga–Moscow road crosses the border east of Zilupe (Latvia). Be prepared to lose a few hours at the border as checks are slow, especially on the Latvian side. The A212 road from Rīga leads to Pskov, crossing a corner of Estonia en route.

TRAIN

Overnight trains run between Rīga and Moscow (*platzkartny/kupe* R5400/9070, 16 hours, daily) and St Petersburg (*platzkart/kupe* R3365/5985, 16 hours, daily).

Lithuania

Trains link Vilnius with Moscow (*platzkart/kupe* R5470/10,170, 14 hours, two daily) and St Petersburg (*platzkart/kupe* R5580/10,580, 17 hours, daily). The St Petersburg trains cross Latvia and the Moscow ones cross Belarus, for which you'll need a Belarus visa or transit visa.

Poland

Warsaw is connected with Moscow (from R8730, 18 hours, daily) by train. The Moscow trains enter Belarus near Brest, so you'll need a Belarus visa or transit visa.

UK & Western Europe

Travelling overland by train from the UK or Western Europe takes a minimum of two days and nights.

There are no direct trains from the UK to Russia. The cheapest route you can take is on the Eurostar (www.eurostar.com) to Brussels, and then via Cologne and Warsaw to Moscow. This journey passes through Minsk (Belarus), which may be problematic. All foreigners visiting Belarus need a visa, including those transiting by train – sort this out before arriving in Belarus. There may also be an issue crossing into Russia as you're unlikely to receive a visa stamp into the country or an immigration card.

To avoid such hassles consider taking the train to St Petersburg from Vilnius in Lithuania, which runs several times a week via Latvia. There are daily connections between Vilnius and Warsaw.

From Moscow and St Petersburg there are also regular direct international services to Berlin, Nice, Paris, Prague and Vienna (note all these services go via Belarus).

For European rail timetables check www.railfaneurope.net, which has links to all of Europe's national railways.

Ukraine

The two countries were essentially at war with each other at the time of writing, but it was still possible to cross in both directions by vehicle or train, with the exception of rebel-held zones in southeastern Ukraine and Crimea. Note that crossing into the rebel-held zones or Crimea from the Russian side is a criminal offence under Ukrainian law. To enter Crimea from Ukraine, you need special permission from the Ukrainian authorities and you must return by the same route.

TRAIN

Trains from Kyiv to Moscow cross at the Ukrainian border town of Seredyna-Buda. Trains on this route include the following:

Moscow–Kyiv *platzkart/kupe* R3735/6570, 12 to 13 hours, 30 minutes, six daily

Moscow–Lviv *platzkart/kupe* R4980/8620, 23 hours, 45 minutes, daily via Kyiv

Moscow–Odesa *kupe* R8660, 23 hours, daily via Kyiv

St Petersburg–Kyiv *platzkart/kupe* R4985/9020, 22 hours, 30 minutes, daily

BUS

Several daily buses run between Moscow and Kyiv (from R1400, 15 to 17 hours) as well as Kharkiv (from R1100, 14 hours) and other major Ukrainian cities.

CAR & MOTORCYCLE

The main auto route between Kyiv and Moscow starts as the E93 (M20) north of Kyiv, but becomes the M3 when it branches off to the east some 50km south of Chernihiv. Kharkiv is connected to Moscow by the M2 road.

River & Sea

St Petersburg Between early April and late September international passenger ferries connect with Stockholm, Helsinki and Tallinn.

Vladivostok Year-round DBS Cruise Ferry (www.dbsferry.com) has connections with Donghae in South Korea, continuing onto Sakaiminato in Japan.

Khabarovsk There are daily ferries across the Amur River to Fuyuan in China.

Travel Agencies & Organised Tours

A number of travel agencies, such as **Imaginative Traveller** (www.imaginative-traveller.com) and **Travman Tours** (www.travman.com.au), offer organised tours on the Trans-Siberian routes. They can also arrange individual tickets and itineraries.

GETTING AROUND

For most, if not all, of your Trans-Siberian journey you're going to be getting around on the train, but sometimes you might need or want to take an internal flight, a boat or a bus.

Air

Unless you plan to explore destinations off the main Trans-Mongolian and Trans-Manchurian railways in China and Mongolia, it is unlikely you will need to fly within those countries. Russia is a different matter, as flights can shorten a route or may be necessary to return from, say, Vladivostok to Moscow.

Russia

- Major Russian airlines allow you to book over the internet. Otherwise it's no problem buying a ticket at ubiquitous *aviakassa* (ticket offices).
- Most internal flights in Moscow use either **Domodedovo** (Домодедово; ☎495-933 6666; www.domodedovo.ru) or **Vnukovo** (Внуково; ☎495-937 5555; www.vnukovo.ru) airports; if you're connecting to **Sheremetyevo** (Шереметьево; ☎495-578 6565; www.svo.aero) for an international flight, allow a few hours to cross town (at least three hours if you need to go by taxi, rather than train and metro).

China & Mongolia

- **China** The Civil Aviation Administration of China (CAAC; Zhōngguó Mínháng) is the authority for numerous airlines, including **Air China** (www.airchina.com.cn), **China Eastern Airlines** (www.flychinaeastern.com) and **China Southern Airlines** (www.csair.com). Check timetables at www.elong.net.
- **Mongolia** Dirt airstrips are the norm, and almost all destinations are served from Ulaanbaatar. If you plan to fly in one direction and travel overland in another, try to book and fly from Ulaanbaatar, as flying from rural towns can mean waiting several days for a seat, especially in summer. See www.aeromongolia.mn for inland routes and ticket purchases.

Train

Russia

Russian Railways (РЖД, RZD; ☎8-800 775 0000; www.rzd.ru) trains are generally comfortable and, depending on the class

AIRLINE SAFETY IN RUSSIA

Deadly lapses in Russian airline safety are frighteningly common. Hardly a year passes without a massive civil-aviation disaster. If you're worried about airline safety, the good news is that for many destinations in Russia, getting there by train or bus is practical and often preferable (if you have the time). But in some cases – where you're short of time or where your intended destination doesn't have reliable rail or road connections – you will have no choice but to take a flight.

Industry experts recommend taking the following factors into account when deciding whether an airline is safe to fly with in Russia:

- If there's a choice, stick to major airlines that are members of the International Air Transport Association (IATA) – these include Aeroflot, S7 and UTAir.
- A Class 1 Russian airport, which hosts more than seven million passengers per year, is much more likely to be safe to fly in and out of than a Class 5 airport, which serves less than 100,000 passengers a year.
- Fly with an airline that has regularly scheduled flights, not a charter. The accident rate for charter flights is about three times higher than for regular flights.
- Check https://aviation-safety.net or www.airlines-inform.com to see the number of accidents and incidents at an airport and to read traveller reviews.

of travel, relatively inexpensive for the distances covered. For more information on Russian train travel see Choosing Your Route (p24) and Booking Tickets (p33).

LEFT LUGGAGE

Many train stations have a left-luggage room (камера хранения, *kamera khranenia*) or left-luggage lockers (автоматические камеры хранения, *avtomaticheskiye kamery khranenia*). These are generally secure, but make sure you note down the room's opening and closing hours and, if in doubt, establish how long you can leave your stuff. Typical costs are around R200 per bag per day (according to size) or R200 per locker.

Here is how to work the left-luggage lockers (they're generally the same everywhere). Be suspicious of people who offer to help you work them, above all when it comes to selecting your combination.

- Put your stuff in an empty locker.
- Decide on a combination of one Russian letter and three numbers and write it down or remember it.
- Set the combination on the inside of the locker door.
- Close the locker.
- Pay the attendant the fee.

To open the locker, set your combination on the outside of your locker door. Note that even though it seems as if the knobs on the outside of the door should correspond directly with those on the inside, the letter is always the left-most knob, followed by three numbers, on both the inside and the outside. After you've set your combination, wait a second or two for the electrical humming sound and then pull open the locker.

China

Although carriages can be crowded, trains are the best way to get around the country in reasonable speed and comfort.

The following classes are available on Chinese trains:

Hard seat (硬座; *yìngzuò*) Generally padded, but this class can still be hard on one's sanity – it can be dirty, noisy and crowded. You may or may not have a seat reservation.

Soft seat (软座; *ruǎnzuò*) Less crowded, on some shorter routes.

Hard sleeper (硬卧; *yìngwò*) Doorless compartments with half a dozen bunks in three tiers; sheets, pillows and blankets are provided.

Soft sleeper (软卧; *ruǎnwò*) Four comfortable bunks in a closed compartment; on Z-class trains (the best) you'll also have your own TV. Z-class trains also have luxury two-berth compartments with their own shower and toilet facilities. It does very nicely as an overnight hotel.

Once you are on the train, the conductor may be able to upgrade your ticket if space is available in other carriages. The cost of the upgraded ticket is pro rata to the distance travelled in the higher class.

For tips on reading tickets, see http://cnvol.com/read-china-train-ticket.htm. For more info on China's railways and trains, consult the following sites:

Duncan Peattie's Chinese Railways Home Page (www.chinatt.org) English-language timetable information for trains in China.

Man in Seat 61 (www.seat61.com/china.htm)

Railways of China (www.railwaysofchina.com)

Mongolia

Note that you can't use the Trans-Mongolian Railway for domestic transport. If you're travelling from Ulaanbaatar, it is important to book a soft seat well in advance – this can be done up to 10 days before departure. There may be a small booking fee. In general, booking ahead is a good idea for any class, though there will always be hard-seat tickets available.

There are usually three classes on domestic passenger trains:

Hard seat Padded bunks, but none are assigned, nor is there any limit to the amount of tickets sold; carriages are always crowded and dirty.

Hard sleeper (platzkartnuu) Looks just like the hard seat but everyone gets their own bunk and optional sheets and a blanket (T1000). Upgrades available to soft seat.

Soft seat Compartments with four assigned beds. If you travel at night, clean sheets are provided for about T1500; a wise investment since some of the quilts smell of mutton.

Boat

Russia

In summer it's possible to travel long distances across Russia on passenger boats. You can do this either by taking a cruise, which you can book through agencies at home or in Russia, or by using scheduled river passenger services. The season runs from late May through to mid-October, but is shorter on some routes.

Numerous boats ply routes between Moscow and St Petersburg, many stopping at some of the Golden Ring cities on the way, and along the Volga River from Moscow to other Trans-Siberian cities such as Nizhny Novgorod and Kazan. In Siberia and the Russian Far East there are services along the Ob and Irtysh Rivers (between Omsk and Tobolsk), the Yenisey from Krasnoyarsk, the Lena from Ust-Kut via Lensk to Yakutsk, as well as across Lake Baikal from Irkutsk to Nizhneangarsk.

Beware that boat schedules can change radically from year to year (especially on Lake Baikal) and are only published infuriatingly close to the first sailing of each season.

Bus

Long-distance buses generally serve areas with no railway or routes on which trains are slow, infrequent or overloaded.

Russia

Most cities have a main intercity *avtovokzal* (автовокзал; bus station). Tickets are sold at the station or on the bus. Fares are normally listed on the timetable and posted on a wall. As often as not you'll get a ticket with a seat assignment, scribbled almost illegibly on a till receipt. Buses are cheaper than trains and often faster. You need to pay a baggage fee for items that are too large for racks.

Marshrutky (just a diminutive form of *marshrutnoye taksi*, meaning a fixed-route taxi) are minibuses that are quicker than the rusty old buses and rarely cost much more. Where roads are good and villages frequent, *marshrutky* can be twice as fast as buses, and well worth the double fare.

China

Chángtú gōnggōngqìchē (long-distance buses) are one of the best means of getting around China. On popular long-haul routes, *wòpù qìchē* (sleeper buses) may cost around double the price of a normal bus service. Some have comfortable reclining seats, while others have two-tier bunks. Watch out for your belongings on them, however.

In many cities, the train station forecourt doubles as a bus station. Tickets are easy to purchase and often you can just turn up at the bus station and buy them. Booking in advance, however, can secure you a better seat, as many buses have numbered seats; the earlier you buy your ticket, the closer to the front of the bus you will sit.

Car & Motorcycle

A useful general site for motorcyclists, with some information on Russian road conditions, is www.horizonsunlimited.com.

In Russia, China and Mongolia vehicles are driven on the right-hand side of the road.

READING A TRAIN TIMETABLE

Russian train timetables vary from place to place but generally list a destination; number and category of train; frequency of service; and time of departure and arrival, in Moscow time unless otherwise noted. For services that originate somewhere else, you'll see a starting point and the final destination on the timetable. For example, when catching a train from Yekaterinburg to Irkutsk, the timetable may list Moscow as the origin and Irkutsk as the destination.

Number

Generally, the higher the Номер (*nomer*, number) of a train, the slower it is; anything over 900 is likely to be a mail train. High-speed trains, however, go under the numbers 151 through 198.

Category

- Скоростной (*Skorostnoy*, high-speed trains)
- Скорый (*Skory*, fast trains)
- Пассажирский (*Passazhirsky*, passenger trains)
- Почтово – багажный (*Pochtovo-bagazhny*, post-cargo trains)
- Пригородный (*Prigorodny*, suburban trains)

There may also be the name of the train, usually in quotation marks, eg 'Россия' ('Rossiya').

Frequency

- ежедневно (*yezhednevno*, daily; abbreviated еж)
- чётные (*chyotnye*, even-numbered dates; abbreviated ч)
- нечётные (*nechyotnye*, odd-numbered dates; abbreviated не)
- отменён (*otmenyon*, cancelled; abbreviated отмен)

Days of the week are listed usually as numbers (where 1 is Monday and 7 Sunday) or as abbreviations of the name of the day (Пон, Вт, Ср, Чт, Пт, Суб and Вск are, respectively, Monday to Sunday). Remember that time-zone differences can affect these days. So in Chita (Moscow +6hr) a train timetabled at 23.20 on Tuesday actually leaves at 5.20am on Wednesday. In

Russia

Siberian roads are atrocious, with potholes large enough to consume an entire vehicle – which is why vehicle workshops with puncture-repair services (шиномонтаж; *shinomontazh*) are everywhere in cities. If you are driving, this will be the most useful word to learn.

You'll need to be 18 years old and have an International Driving Permit with a Russian translation of your licence, or a certified Russian translation of your full licence (you can certify translations at a Russian embassy or consulate).

Don't forget your vehicle's registration papers, proof of insurance (be sure it covers you in Russia) and a customs declaration promising that you will take your vehicle with you when you leave. To get the exact details on all this it's best to contact your automobile association (eg the AA or RAC in the UK) at least three months before your trip.

China

Road conditions in China should abolish any remaining desire to drive. Bilingual road signs are making a slow appearance along some highways, but much remains to confuse would-be drivers from abroad.

Both Běijīng's Capital International Airport and Shànghǎi's Pǔdōng International Airport have a Vehicle Administration Office (车管所; *chēguǎnsuǒ*) where you can have a temporary three-month driving licence issued. This involves checking your driving licence and a simple medical exam (including an eyesight test). You will need this licence before you can hire a car from reputable companies.

Wikitravel (http://wikitravel.org/en/Driving_in_China) has useful information.

Mongolia

Travellers can use an International Driving Permit to drive any vehicle in Mongolia. The roads are worse than atrocious. Accidents occur frequently. Try to avoid travelling at night, when unseen potholes, drunk drivers and wildlife can wreak havoc. Driving in the dark is also a great way to get completely and utterly lost in Mongolia.

What look like main roads on the map are often little more than tyre tracks in

months with an odd number of days, two odd days follow one another (eg 31 May, 1 June). This throws out trains working on an alternate-day cycle so if travelling near the end of the month pay special attention to the hard-to-decipher footnotes on a timetable. For example, '27/V – 3/VI Ч' means that from 27 May to 3 June the train runs on even dates. On some trains, frequency depends on the time of year, in which case details are usually given in similar abbreviated small print: eg '27/VI – 31/VIII Ч; 1/IX – 25/VI 2, 5' means that from 27 June to 31 August the train runs on even dates, while from 1 September to 25 June it runs on Tuesday and Friday.

Arrival & Departure Times

Corresponding trains running in opposite directions on the same route may appear on the same line of the timetable. In this case you may find route entries such as время отправления с конечного пункта *(vremya otpravlenia s konechnogo punkta)*, or the time the return train leaves its station of origin. Train times are given in a 24-hour time format, and almost always in Moscow time (Московское время, *Moskovskoye vremya*). But suburban trains are usually marked in local time (местное время, *mestnoe vremya*). From here on it gets tricky (as though the rest wasn't), so don't confuse the following:

- время отправления *(vremya otpravleniya)* Time of departure
- время отправления с начального пункта*(vremya otpravleniya s nachalnogo punkta)* Time of departure from the train's starting point
- время прибытия *(vremya pribytiya)* Time of arrival at the station you're in
- время прибытия на конечный пункт *(vremya pribytiya v konechny punkt)* Time of arrival at the destination
- время в пути *(vremya v puti)* Duration of the journey

Distance

You may sometimes see the расстояние *(rasstoyaniye)* – distance in kilometres from the point of departure – on the timetable as well. These are rarely accurate and usually refer to the kilometre distance used to calculate the fare.

the dirt, sand or mud, and there is hardly a signpost in the whole country. Remote tracks quickly turn into eight-lane dirt highways devoid of any traffic, making navigation tricky – some drivers follow the telephone lines when there are any, or else ask for directions at gers along the way. Towns with food and water are few and far between, and very few people in the countryside will speak anything but Mongolian or, if you are lucky, Russian.

Hitching

Hitching is never entirely safe, and we don't recommend it. Travellers who hitch should understand that they are taking a small but potentially serious risk.

Russia

Hitching in Russia is a very common method of getting around. Hitching in cities in private vehicles is less common these days but in the countryside, especially in remote areas not well served by public transport, it's a major mode of transport. You are expected to pitch in for petrol; paying what would be the normal bus fare for a long-haul ride is appropriate.

China

Hitching in China is more difficult than in Russia. Sometimes even a moderate, agreed-upon price can be inflated by the driver on arrival. Unless you travel into extremely remote regions, there is little reason to hitch, as it's neither cost-saving nor necessary.

Mongolia

Because the country is so vast, public transport so limited and the people so poor, hitching (usually on trucks) is a recognised – and, often, the only – form of transport in the countryside. Hitching is seldom free and often no different from just waiting for public transport to turn up. It is *always* slow – with stops, a truck can take 48 hours to cover 200km.

Hitching here is not generally dangerous personally, but it is still hazardous and often extremely uncomfortable. Don't expect much traffic in remote rural areas; you might see one or two vehicles a day on many roads, and sometimes nobody at all for several days. The best place to wait is a petrol station on the outskirts of town, where most vehicles stop before any journey. Pay truck drivers about T5000 per hour travelled.

Local Transport

Russia & Mongolia

In Russia and Mongolia, using buses and minibuses is easier than in China.

For a taxi in Ulaanbaatar, just flag down any driver. All charge a standard T800 per kilometre (check the latest rate, as it increases regularly). Don't agree to a set daily price because it will always be more than the standard rate per kilometre.

Across Russia, phone apps such as Gett and Yandex Taxi have made cabs much more affordable and easy to use. Elsewhere, taxis are ordered by phone. If you need one, watch out for a taxi that has its phone number written on it. English-speaking operators are rare. It's less common these days, but it's still possible to flag down a taxi, or just a random driver whose owner needs some extra cash, on the street. Check with locals to determine the average taxi fare in that city at the time of your visit; taxi prices around the country vary widely. Practise saying your destination and the amount you want to pay so that it comes out properly. Generally, the better your Russian, the lower the fare. If possible, let a Russian friend negotiate for you: they'll do better than you will.

China

Navigation on buses can be tricky for non-Chinese speakers as Chinese without pinyin appears on stops. Taxis (出租汽车; *chūzū qìchē*) are cheap, plentiful and easy to find. Taxi drivers rarely speak any English so have your destination written down in characters. To use the same driver again, ask for his card (名片; *míngpiàn*). Taxi rates per kilometre are clearly marked on a sticker on the rear side window of the taxi, and there's a flagfall. China also has motorcycles, motor tricycles and pedal-powered tricycles, all mustering outside train and bus stations. Agree on prices first for these.

Health

Russia, China and Mongolia present few serious health problems. If you are dependent upon strong or finely dosed medication, you should consult your doctor about dosages due to the changes in time zones. Apart from injury due to bad drivers or a traffic accident on the busy streets, the main dangers are ticks in some regions, bacteria in drinking water and coping with heat or cold. HIV infection is a serious problem, especially in Siberia – *always* take precautions.

BEFORE YOU GO

Insurance

Make sure you are covered for all regions and activities and find out in advance what is excluded and how payment is arranged. If your health insurance does not cover you for medical expenses abroad, consider supplemental insurance. Check the Lonely Planet website at www.lonelyplanet.com/travel-insurance for more information. Make copies of your policy (a digital photograph uploaded to an email account is useful for all documentation). Declare any pre-existing conditions.

Medical Checklist

Following is a list of items you should consider including in your medical kit – consult your pharmacist for brands available in your country.

- Antibacterial cream (eg Muciprocin)
- Antibiotics (prescription only) – for travel well off the beaten track; carry the prescription with you in case you need it refilled
- Antifungal cream or powder (eg Clotrimazole) – for fungal skin infections and thrush
- Anti-nausea medication (eg Prochlorperazine)
- Antiseptic (such as povidone-iodine) – for cuts and grazes
- Aspirin or paracetamol (acetaminophen in the USA) – for pain or fever
- Bandages, Band-Aids (plasters) and other wound dressings
- Calamine lotion, sting-relief spray or aloe vera – to ease irritation from sunburn and insect bites or stings
- Cold and flu tablets, throat lozenges and nasal decongestant
- Insect repellent (DEET-based)
- Loperamide or diphenoxylate – 'blockers' for diarrhoea
- Multivitamins – consider them for long trips, when dietary vitamin intake may be inadequate
- Rehydration mixture (eg Gastrolyte) – to prevent dehydration, which may occur during bouts of diarrhoea (particularly important when travelling with children)
- Scissors, tweezers and a thermometer – note that mercury thermometers are prohibited by airlines
- Sunscreen, lip balm, face cream against cold and eye drops
- Water-purification tablets or iodine (iodine is not to be used by pregnant women or people with thyroid problems)

Further Reading

Lonely Planet Healthy Travel – Asia & India is a handy pocket size and is packed with useful information. Also recommended is *Traveller's Health* by Dr Richard Dawood and *Travelling Well* (www.travellingwell.com.au) by Dr Deborah Mills.

IN RUSSIA, CHINA & MONGOLIA

Availability & Cost of Health Care

Medical care is readily available across Russia but the quality can vary enormously. The biggest cities and towns have the widest choice of places, with both

Moscow and St Petersburg well served by international-style clinics. In remote areas, the standard of care is lower.

Good clinics catering to travellers can be found in major cities of China. They are more expensive than local facilities. These clinics usually have a good understanding of the best local hospital facilities and close contacts with insurance companies.

Mongolia suffers from a serious lack of medical facilities. Health care is readily available in Ulaanbaatar, but choose your hospital and doctor carefully. Ordinary Mongolians won't know the best place to go, but a reputable travel agency or top-end hotel might. The best advice will come from your embassy. In the countryside the availability of health services is generally poor. You may be better off travelling on to Běijīng.

Apart from the chief *provodnitsa* (carriage attendant) probably having a first-aid box, there is no medical assistance available on the Trans-Siberian train itself.

Infectious Diseases

Rabies

This is a problem in Russia, China and Mongolia. It is spread through bites or licks on broken skin from an infected animal. It's always fatal unless treated promptly. Vaccination is advisable for those travelling to remote areas where a reliable source of postbite vaccine is not available within 24 hours. A simple precaution against dog attack is to carry a high-pitched whistle.

Tick-borne Encephalitis & Japanese B Encephalitis

Tick-borne encephalitis is spread by tick bites and is a serious infection of the brain; vaccination is advised for those in risk areas who are unable to avoid tick bites (such as campers, forestry workers and walkers). The risk is highest in spring and summer, when ticks are active. The Ural Mountains, Siberia, the Far East and China's north are particular problem zones.

Two doses of vaccine will give a year's protection; three doses will last up to three years.

Typhoid & Hepatitis A

Spread through contaminated food (particularly shellfish) and water, typhoid can cause septicaemia (blood poisoning). Hepatitis A causes liver inflammation and jaundice. Neither is usually fatal but recovery can be delayed if you don't see your doctor immediately.

Traveller's Diarrhoea

Diarrhoea on a train is not much fun, and off the train it leaves much to be desired as well. Treatment consists of staying well hydrated; rehydration solutions such as Gastrolyte are best. Antibiotics such as norfloxacin, ciprofloxacin or azithromycin will kill the bacteria quickly. Loperamide is just a 'stopper' and doesn't cure the problem; it can be helpful, however, for long rides. Don't take loperamide if you have a fever, or blood in your stool. Seek medical attention quickly if you do not respond to an appropriate antibiotic.

- Don't drink tap water on the trains or anywhere in Russia, China or Mongolia unless it's been boiled (eg in the samovar).
- Brush your teeth using bottled water.
- In all three countries avoid ice and unpeeled fruit and vegetables that have been washed in tap water.
- Check use-by dates of food sold on train platforms.
- If a restaurant is full of locals, the food is probably safe.

DRINKING WATER

The quality of drinking water varies greatly from region to region, so it's best to play it safe.

- Never drink tap water.
- Check that the seal on bottled water is intact at the time of purchase.
- Avoid ice and fresh juices if you suspect they have been watered down.
- Boiling water is the most efficient method of purifying it. Trains have a samovar (hot-water heater) in every carriage.
- Never use the tap in the train toilet for drinking water or washing vegetables.
- The best chemical purifier is iodine. It should not be used by pregnant women or those with thyroid problems.
- Water filters should also filter out viruses. Ensure your filter has a chemical barrier such as iodine and a small pore size, eg less than four microns.

Environmental Hazards

The temperatures on the trains are generally kept at a comfortable level, but once out in the wide open spaces of Russia, Mongolia and China, the main environmental hazards to be careful of are heat exhaustion in summer and frostbite in winter.

Heat Exhaustion & Heat Stroke

Heat exhaustion is best avoided by drinking water on a constant basis. Train carriages can get hot in summer and be overheated in winter, so make sure you have sufficient bottled water with you.

Heat stroke is much more serious, resulting in irrational and hyperactive behaviour and eventually loss of consciousness and death. Rapid cooling by spraying the body with water and fanning is ideal. Emergency fluid and electrolyte replacement by intravenous drip is recommended.

Hypothermia & Frostbite

Winters are cold on the Trans-Siberian routes and proper clothing will reduce the risks of getting hypothermia. Make sure you have a heavy coat ready for station stops. Don't overdo outdoor sightseeing if you are not well prepared against the cold.

Frostbite is caused by freezing and subsequent damage to bodily extremities. As it develops, the skin blisters and then becomes black. Adequate clothing, staying dry, keeping well hydrated and ensuring adequate calorie intake will help prevent frostbite. Treatment involves rapid rewarming. Avoid refreezing and rubbing the affected areas.

Ticks & Mosquitoes

Ticks can transmit Lyme disease, an infection that may be acquired throughout the region. The illness usually begins with a spreading rash at the site of the tick bite, accompanied by fever, headache, extreme fatigue, aching joints and muscles, and mild neck stiffness. It is essential that you receive medical treatment as serious long-term complications can arise.

Always check all over your body after hiking or outdoor activities. The best way to remove a tick is to use dedicated plastic or metal tweezers designed to grip the head of the tick. Rotate it out of the skin. Ordinary tweezers can also be used.

Mosquitoes are a problem in summer all across Russia. From May to September in the rural areas bordering Mongolia, China and North Korea, take extra-special care as mosquito bites can cause Japanese encephalitis. If visiting rural areas you should consider being immunised.

Travelling with Children

Children should be encouraged to avoid and mistrust any dogs or other mammals because of the risk of rabies and other diseases. Any bite, scratch or lick from a warm-blooded, furry animal should immediately be thoroughly cleaned. If there is any possibility that the animal is infected with rabies, immediate medical assistance should be sought.

Vaccinations

Ask your doctor for an International Certificate of Vaccination (otherwise known as the yellow booklet), which will list all of the vaccinations you have received, and take it with you. If travelling from a yellow fever zone within six days of entering China, proof of vaccination is required.

The following vaccinations are recommended.

Adult Diphtheria & Tetanus

Hepatitis A

Hepatitis B Routine for most travellers today.

Measles, Mumps & Rubella (MMR) Two doses are recommended unless you have had the diseases.

Typhoid

Varicella If you haven't had chickenpox, discuss this vaccination with your doctor.

Depending on circumstances and age, the following are worth keeping in mind.

Influenza A Especially for those over 65 years of age or with underlying medical conditions.

Pneumonia A single injection with a booster after five years is recommended for all travellers over 65 years of age or with underlying medical conditions that compromise immunity.

Rabies Three injections are required. A booster after one year will then provide 10 years' protection.

Tuberculosis (TB) It's usually recommended that high-risk adult long-term travellers have a TB skin test before and after travel, rather than a vaccination. Only one vaccine is given in a lifetime.

Japanese B Encephalitis Consider vaccination if spending a month or longer in parts of the Russian Far East and Siberia, in China, or if making repeated trips to at-risk areas.

Women's Health

Emotional stress, exhaustion and travelling through time zones can all contribute to an upset in the menstrual cycle.

Travelling along the Trans-Siberia routes while pregnant is not really advisable because emergency treatment can be patchy in remote segments. Always consult your doctor before planning your trip. The most risky times for travel are during the first 12 weeks of pregnancy and after 30 weeks.

Language

In this chapter, we're providing some basic travel words and phrases in Mandarin, Mongolian and Russian that might come in handy during your travels.

MANDARIN

Pinyin & Pronunciation

In 1958 the Chinese adopted a system of writing their language using the Roman alphabet. It's known as Pinyin. The original idea was to eventually do away with Chinese characters. However, tradition dies hard, and the idea has been abandoned. Pinyin, which we've provided alongside the Mandarin script in this chapter, is often used on shop fronts, street signs and advertising billboards. Don't expect all Chinese people to be able to use Pinyin, however. In the countryside and the smaller towns you may not see a single Pinyin sign anywhere, just Chinese characters. Below are some basic guidelines as to how to pronounce Pinyin sounds (in blue in this chapter):

a	as in 'father'
ai	as in 'aisle'
ao	as the 'ow' in 'cow'
e	as in 'her', without audible 'r' sound
ei	as in 'weigh'
i	as the 'ee' in 'meet' (or like a light 'r' as in 'Grrr!' after c, ch, r, s, sh, z, zh)
ian	as the word 'yen'
ie	as the English word 'yeah'
o	as in 'or', without audible 'r' sound
ou	as the 'oa' in 'boat'
u	as in 'flute'
ui	as the word 'way'
uo	like a 'w' followed by 'o'
yu/ü	like 'ee' with lips pursed

c	as the 'ts' in 'bits'
ch	as in 'chop' *
h	as in 'hay', but articulated from further back in the throat
q	as the 'ch' in 'cheese'
sh	as in 'ship' *
x	as in 'ship'
z	as the 'ds' in 'suds'
zh	as the 'j' in 'judge'*

* but with the tongue curled up and back

In Pinyin, the only consonant sounds that occur at the end of a syllable are n, ng and r. Also, apostrophes are occasionally used to separate syllables in order to prevent ambiguity, eg the word píng'ān can be written with an apostrophe after the 'g' to prevent it being pronounced as pín'gān.

Finally, Mandarin is a language with a large number of words with the same pronunciation but a different meaning. The only thing that distinguishes these words are tones – the raising and the lowering of pitch on certain syllables. Mandarin has four tones (high, rising, falling-rising and falling), indicated by accent marks over the vowels. The word ma, for example, has four different meanings according to tone:

high tone	mā (mother)
rising tone	má (hemp, numb)
falling-rising tone	mǎ (horse)
falling tone	mà (scold, swear)

There's a fifth 'neutral' tone (without accent mark) that you can all but ignore.

Basics

When asking a question it is polite to start with qǐng wèn – literally, 'may I ask?'.

Hello	你好。	Nǐhǎo.
Goodbye	再见。	Zàijiàn.
Excuse me (to get attention)	劳驾。	Láojià.
(to get past)	借光。	Jièguāng.
Sorry	对不起。	Duìbùqǐ.
Yes./No	是。/不是。	Shì./Bùshì.
Please ...	请……	Qǐng ...
Thank you	谢谢你。	Xièxie nǐ.
You're welcome	不客气。	Bù kèqi.

What's your name?
你叫什么名字？ Nǐ jiào shénme míngzi?

My name is ...
我叫…… Wǒ jiào ...

Do you speak English?
你会说英文吗？ Nǐ huìshuō Yīngwén ma?

I don't understand
我不明白。 Wǒ bù míngbái.

Accommodation

Do you have a single/double room?
有没有(单人/套)房？ Yǒuméiyǒu (dānrén/tào) fáng?

How much is it per night/person?
每天/人多少钱？ Měi tiān/rén duōshǎo qián?

air-con	空调	kōngtiáo
bathroom	浴室	yùshì
bed	床	chuáng
campsite	露营地	lùyíngdì
guesthouse	宾馆	bīnguǎn
hostel	招待所	zhāodàisuǒ
hotel	酒店	jiǔdiàn
window	窗	chuāng

Directions

Where's (a bank)?
(银行)在哪儿？ (Yínháng) zài nǎr?

What's the address?
地址在哪儿？ Dìzhǐ zài nǎr?

Could you write the address, please?
能不能请你把地址写下来？ Néngbunéng qǐng nǐ bǎ dìzhǐ xiě xiàlái?

Please show me on the map where it is.
请帮我找它在地图上的位置。 Qǐng bāngwǒ zhǎo tā zài dìtú shàng de wèizhi.

behind	背面	bèimiàn
far	远	yuǎn
in front of ...	……的前面	... de qiánmian
near	近	jìn
next to	旁边	pángbiān
opposite	对面	duìmiàn
turn left	左转。	Zuǒ zhuǎn.
turn right	右转。	Yòu zhuǎn.

Eating & Drinking

What would you recommend?
有什么菜可以推荐的？ Yǒu shénme cài kěyǐ tuījiàn de?

What's in that dish?
这道菜用什么东西做的？ Zhèdào cài yòng shénme dōngxi zuòde?

I don't eat (red meat)
我不吃(牛羊肉)。 Wǒ bùchī (niúyángròu)

Cheers!
干杯！ Gānbēi!

That was delicious!
真好吃！ Zhēn hǎochī!

The bill, please
买单！ Mǎidān!

Key Words

appetisers	凉菜	liángcài
bar	酒吧	jiǔbā
bottle	瓶子	píngzi
bowl	碗	wǎn
bread	面包	miànbāo
breakfast	早饭	zǎofàn
butter	黄油	huángyóu
cafe	咖啡屋	kāfēiwū
children's menu	儿童菜单	értóng càidān
(too) cold	(太)凉	(tài) liáng
dinner	晚饭	wǎnfàn
dish (food)	盘	pán
egg	蛋	dàn
food	食品	shípǐn
fork	叉子	chāzi
glass	杯子	bēizi
halal	清真	qīngzhēn
herbs/spices	香料	xiāngliào
highchair	高凳	gāodèng
hot (warm)	热	rè
knife	刀	dāo
kosher	犹太	yóutài
local specialities	地方小吃	dìfāng xiǎochī

lunch	午饭	wǔfàn
main courses	主菜	zhǔ cài
market	菜市	càishì
menu (in English)	(英文)菜单	(Yīngwén) càidān
noodles	面条	miàntiáo
nuts	果仁	guǒrén
pepper	胡椒粉	hújiāo fěn
plate	碟子	diézi
restaurant	餐馆	cānguǎn
rice (raw/cooked)	大米/米饭	dàmǐ/mǐfàn
salt	盐	yán
soy sauce	酱油	jiàngyóu
(too) spicy	(太)辣	(tài) là
spoon	勺	sháo
sugar	砂糖	shātáng
tofu	豆腐	dòufu
vegetable oil	菜油	càiyóu
vegetarian food	素食食品	sùshí shípín
vinegar	醋	cù
yoghurt	酸奶	suānnǎi

Meat & Fish

beef	牛肉	niúròu
chicken	鸡肉	jīròu
duck	鸭	yā
fish	鱼	yú
lamb	羊肉	yángròu
pork	猪肉	zhūròu
poultry	家禽	jiāqín
seafood	海鲜	hǎixiān

Fruit & Vegetables

apple	苹果	píngguǒ
banana	香蕉	xiāngjiāo
bok choy	小白菜	xiǎo báicài
carrot	胡萝卜	húluóbo
cucumber	黄瓜	huángguā
'dragon eyes' fruit	龙眼水果	lóngyǎn shuǐguǒ
grape	葡萄	pútáo
green beans	扁豆	biǎndòu
guava	石榴	shíliu
lychee	荔枝	lìzhī
mango	芒果	mángguǒ
mushroom	蘑菇	mógū
onion	洋葱	yáng cōng
orange	橙子	chéngzi
pear	梨	lí
pineapple	凤梨	fènglí
plum	梅子	méizi
potato	土豆	tǔdòu
radish	萝卜	luóbo
spring onion	小葱	xiǎo cōng
sweet potato	地瓜	dìguā
vegetable	蔬菜	shūcài

Drinks

beer	啤酒	píjiǔ
Chinese spirits	白酒	báijiǔ
coffee	咖啡	kāfēi
(orange) juice	(橙)汁	(chéng) zhī
milk	牛奶	niúnǎi
mineral water	矿泉水	kuàngquán shuǐ
red wine	红葡萄酒	hóng pútáo jiǔ
rice wine	米酒	mǐjiǔ
soft drink	汽水	qìshuǐ
tea	茶	chá
(boiled) water	(开)水	(kāi) shuǐ
white wine	白葡萄酒	bái pútáo jiǔ

SIGNS – MANDARIN

入口	Rùkǒu	**Entrance**
出口	Chūkǒu	**Exit**
问讯处	Wènxùnchù	**Information**
开	Kāi	**Open**
关	Guān	**Closed**
禁止	Jìnzhǐ	**Prohibited**
厕所	Cèsuǒ	**Toilets**
男	Nán	**Men**
女	Nǚ	**Women**

Emergencies

Help!	救命！	Jiùmìng!
Go away!	走开！	Zǒukāi!
I'm lost	我迷路了。	Wǒ mílù le.

There's been an accident!
出事了！ Chūshì le!

Call a doctor!
请叫医生来！ Qǐng jiào yīshēng lái!

Call the police!
请叫警察！ Qǐng jiào jǐngchá!

I'm ill
我生病了。 Wǒ shēngbìng le.

It hurts here
这里痛。 Zhèlǐ tòng.

Where are the toilets?
厕所在哪儿？ Cèsuǒ zài nǎr?

Shopping & Services

I'd like to buy ...
我想买…… Wǒ xiǎng mǎi ...

How much is it?
多少钱? Duōshǎo qián?

Can you lower the price?
能便宜一点吗? Néng piányi yīdiǎn ma?

There's a mistake in the bill
帐单上有问题。 Zhàngdān shàng yǒu wèntí.

ATM	自动取款机	zìdòng qǔkuǎn jī
credit card	信用卡	xìnyòng kǎ
internet cafe	网吧	wǎngbā
market	市场	shìchǎng
post office	邮局	yóujú
supermarket	超市	chāoshì
tourist office	旅行店	lǚxíng diàn

Time, Dates & Numbers

What time is it?
现在几点钟? Xiànzài jǐdiǎn zhōng?

morning	早上	zǎoshang
afternoon	下午	xiàwǔ
evening	晚上	wǎnshàng
yesterday	昨天	zuótiān
today	今天	jīntiān
tomorrow	明天	míngtiān

Monday	星期一	xīngqī yī
Tuesday	星期二	xīngqī èr
Wednesday	星期三	xīngqī sān
Thursday	星期四	xīngqī sì
Friday	星期五	xīngqī wǔ
Saturday	星期六	xīngqī liù
Sunday	星期天	xīngqī tiān

January	一月	yīyuè
February	二月	èryuè
March	三月	sānyuè
April	四月	sìyuè
May	五月	wǔyuè
June	六月	liùyuè
July	七月	qīyuè
August	八月	bāyuè
September	九月	jiǔyuè
October	十月	shíyuè
November	十一月	shíyīyuè
December	十二月	shí'èryuè

1	一	yī
2	二/两	èr/liǎng
3	三	sān
4	四	sì
5	五	wǔ
6	六	liù
7	七	qī
8	八	bā
9	九	jiǔ
10	十	shí
100	一百	yībǎi
1000	一千	yīqiān

Transport

boat	船	chuán
bus (city)	大巴	dàbā
bus (intercity)	长途车	chángtú chē
plane	飞机	fēijī
taxi	出租车	chūzū chē
train	火车	huǒchē
tram	电车	diànchē

I want to go to ...
我要去…… Wǒ yào qù ...

Does it stop at (Hāērbīn)?
在(哈尔滨)能下车吗? Zài (Hā'ěrbīn) néng xià chē ma?

What time does it leave?
几点钟出发? Jǐdiǎnzhōng chūfā?

What time does it get to (Hángzhōu)?
几点钟到(杭州)? Jǐdiǎnzhōng dào (Hángzhōu)?

Can you tell me when we get to (Hángzhōu)?
到了(杭州)请叫我,好吗? Dàole (Hángzhōu) qǐng jiào wǒ, hǎoma?

I want to get off here
我想这儿下车。 Wǒ xiǎng zhèr xiàchē.

When's the ... (bus)?	……(车)几点走?	... (chē) jǐdiǎn zǒu?
first	首趟	Shǒutàng
last	末趟	Mòtàng
next	下一趟	Xià yītàng

A ... ticket to (Dàlián).	一张到(大连)的……票。	Yīzhāng dào (Dàlián) de ... piào.
1st-class	头等	tóuděng
2nd-class	二等	èrděng
one-way	单程	dānchéng
return	双程	shuāngchéng

aisle seat	走廊的座位	zǒuláng de zuòwèi
buy a ticket	买票	mǎi piào
cancelled	取消	qǔxiāo
delayed	晚点	wǎndiǎn
hard-seat	硬席/硬座	yìngxí/yìngzuò
hard-sleeper	硬卧	yìngwò
one ticket	一张票	yìzhāng piào
platform	站台	zhàntái
soft-seat	软席/软座	ruǎnxí/ruǎnzuò
soft-sleeper	软卧	ruǎnwò
ticket office	售票处	shòupiàochù
timetable	时刻表	shíkè biǎo
train station	火车站	huǒchēzhàn
two tickets	两张票	liǎngzhāng piào
window seat	窗户的座位	chuānghu de zuòwèi

MONGOLIAN

Mongolian is a member of the Ural-Altaic family of languages, and as such it is distantly related to Turkish, Kazakh, Uzbek and Korean. It has around 10 million speakers worldwide. The traditional Mongolian script (cursive, vertical and read from left to right) is still used by the Mongolians living in the Inner Mongolia Autonomous Region of China. In 1944 the Cyrillic alphabet was adopted and is in use in Mongolia and two autonomous regions of Russia (Buryatiya and Kalmykia). We've used the Cyrillic script in this chapter. The only difference between Mongolian and Russian Cyrillic is that the Mongolian version has two added characters (**ө** and **ү**).

It's well worth the effort to familiarise yourself with the Cyrillic alphabet so that you can read maps and street signs. Mongolian pronunciation is also explained in the Cyrillic alphabet table, but if you just read the coloured pronunciation guides given next to each word below as if they were English, you'll be understood.

Just remember to pronounce double vowel letters as long sounds, because vowel length can affect meaning. In our pronunciation guides the stressed syllables are in italics.

CYRILLIC ALPHABET

Cyrillic	Sound (Mongolian)	
А а	a	as the 'u' in 'but'
Г г	g	as in 'get'
Ё ё	yo	as in 'yonder'
И и	i	as in 'tin'
Л л	l	as in 'lamp'
О о	o	as in 'hot'
Р р	r	as in 'rub'
У у	u	as in 'rude'
Х х	kh	as the 'ch' in the Scottish *loch*
Ш ш	sh	as in 'shoe'
Ы ы	y	as the 'i' in 'ill'
Ю ю	yu	as the 'yo' in 'yoyo'
	yü	long, as the word 'you'
Б б	b	as in 'but'
Д д	d	as in 'dog'
Ж ж	j	as in 'jewel'
Й й	i	as in 'tin'
М м	m	as in 'mat'
Ө ө	ö	long, as the 'u' in 'fur'
С с	s	as in 'sun'
Ү ү	ü	long, as the 'o' in 'who'
Ц ц	ts	as in 'cats'
Щ щ	shch	as in 'fresh chips'
Ь ь		'soft sign' meaning the preceding consonant is pronounced with a faint y after it.
Я я	ya	as in 'yard'
В в	v	as in 'van'
Е е	ye	as in 'yet'
	yö	as the 'yea' in 'yearn'
З з	z	as the 'ds' in 'suds'
К к	k	as in 'kit'
Н н	n	as in 'neat'
П п	p	as in 'pat'
Т т	t	as in 'tin'
Ф ф	f	as in 'five'
Ч ч	ch	as in 'chat'
Ъ ъ		'hard sign' meaning the preceding consonant is pronounced without a faint y after it.
Э э	e	as in 'den'

Basics

Hello	Сайн байна уу?	sain *bai*·na uu
Goodbye	Баяртай.	ba·yar·*tai*
Excuse me	Уучлаарай.	uuch·*laa*·rai
Sorry	Уучлаарай.	uuch·*laa*·rai
Yes	Тийм.	tiim
No	Үгүй.	ü·*güi*
Thank you	Баярлалаа.	ba·yar·la·*laa*
You're welcome	Зүгээр.	zü·*geer*

What's your name?
Таны нэрийг хэн гэдэг вэ? — ta·*ny* ne·*riig* khen *ge*·deg ve

My name is ...
Миний нэрийг ... гэдэг. — mi·*nii* ne·*riig* ... *ge*·deg

Do you speak English?
Та англиар ярьдаг уу? — ta an·*gliar yair*·dag uu

I don't understand
Би ойлгохгүй байна. — bi *oil*·gokh·güi *bai*·na

Accommodation

I'd like a single/double room

Би нэг/хоёр хүний өрөө авмаар байна.	bi neg/*kho*·yor khü·*nii* ö·*röö* av·*maar* *bai*·na

How much is it per night/week?

Энэ өрөө хоногт/ долоо хоногт ямар үнэтэй вэ?	e·ne ö·*röö* *kho*·nogt/ do·*loo* *kho*·nogt *ya*·mar ün·*tei* ve

air-con	агааржуулалт	a·gaar·*juul*·alt
bathroom	угаалгын өрөө	u·*gaal*·gyn ö·*röö*
cot	хүүхдийн ор	khüükh·*diin* or
dormitory	нийтийн байр	*nii*·tiin bair
hotel	зочид буудал	*zo*·chid *buu*·dal
window	цонх	tsonkh
youth hostel	залуучуудын байр	za·*luu*·chuu·dyn bair

Directions

Where's ...?

… хаана байна вэ?	... khaan *bai*·na ve

How can I get to ...?

... руу би яаж очих вэ?	... ruu bi yaj *o*·chikh ve

Can you show me on the map?

Та газрын зураг дээр зааж өгнө үү?	ta gaz·*ryn* *zu*·rag deer zaaj *ög*·nö *üü*

address	хаяг	*kha*·yag
after	ард	ard
before	урд	urd
behind	хойно	*khoi*·no
in front of	өмнө	*öm*·nö
straight ahead	чигээрээ урагшаа	chi·*gee*·ree u·rag·*shaa*
to the left	зүүн тийш	züün tiish
to the right	баруун тийш	ba·*ruun* tiish

Eating & Drinking

Can I have a menu, please?

Би хоолны цэс авч болох уу?	bi *khool*·nii tses avch *bo*·lokh uu

What food do you have today?

Өнөөдөр ямар хоол байна вэ?	ö·*nöö*·dör *ya*·mar khool *bai*·na ve

I'd like to have this

Би энэ хоолыг авья.	bi en *khoo*·lyg a·*vi*

I don't eat (meat)

Би (мах) иддэггүй.	bi (makh) *id*·deg·gui

We'd like to drink some koumiss

Бид айраг уух гэсэн юм.	bid *ai*·rag uukh *ge*·sen yum

Cheers!

Эрүүл мэндийн төлөө!	e·*rüül* men·*diin* tö·*löö*

The bill, please

Тооцоогоо бодуулъя.	too·*tsoo*·goo bo·*duu*·li

Key Words

appetisers	хүйтэн зууш	*khüi*·ten zuush
bottle	шил	shil
bread	талх	talkh
breakfast	өглөөний хоол	ög·*löö*·nii khool
butter	цөцгийн тос	tsöts·*giin* tos
cake	бялуу	bya·*luu*
camel yogurt	хоормог	*khoor*·mog
canteen	гуанз	guanz
cold	хүйтэн	*khüi*·ten
cheese	бяслаг	*byas*·lag
cream	өрөм	ö·röm
cup	аяга	*a*·yag
(dried) curds	ааруул	*aa*·ruul
dairy	цагаан-идээ	tsa·*gaan* i·*dee*
dessert	амтат зууш	*am*·tat zuush
dinner	оройн хоол	o·*roin* khool
dining room	зоогийн газар	*zoo*·giin *ga*·zar
dumplings	банштай	*ban*·shtai
egg	өндөг	*ön*·dög
food	хоол	khool
fork	сэрээ	se·*ree*
fried	шарсан	*shar*·san
fried food	хуураг	*khuu*·rag
glass	шилэн аяга	*shi*·len *a*·yag
honey	зөгийн бал	zö·*giin* bal
hot	халуун	kha·*luun*
ice cream	зайрмаг	*zair*·mag
jam	жимсний чанамал	jims·*nii* *cha*·na·mal
knife	хутга	*khu*·tag
lunch	үдийн хоол	ü·*diin* khool
market	зах	zakh
menu	хоолны цэс	khool·*ny* tses
noodle soup	гоймонтой шөл	*goi*·mon·toi shöl
pasta	хөндий гоймон	khön·*diin* *goi*·mon
pepper	поваарь	po·*vaair*
plate	таваг	*ta*·vag
restaurant	ресторан	res·to·*ran*

SIGNS – MONGOLIAN

ГАРЦ	Exit
ЛАВЛАГАА	Information
ОРЦ	Entrance
ХААСАН	Closed
ХАДГАЛСАН	Reserved/Engaged
ЭРЭГТЭЙН	Men
ЭМЭГТЭЙН	Women

rice	цагаан будаа	tsa·*gaan* bu·*daa*
salad	ногоон зууш	no·*goon* zuush
salt	давс	davs
set dish	бэлэн хоол	*be*·len khool
soup	шөл	shöl
sour cream	тараг/цөцгий	*ta*·rag/tsöts·*gii*
spoon	халбага	*khal*·bag
tea shop	цайны газар	*tsai*·ny *ga*·zar
sugar	чихэр	*chi*·kher
vegetarian	ногоон хоолтон	no·*goon* *khool*·ton
with rice	будаатай	bu·*daa*·tai

Meat & Fish

antelope	цагаан зээр	tsa·*gaan* zeer
beef	үхрийн мах	ü·*khriin* makh
carp	булуу цагаан	bu·*luu* tsa·*gaan*
chicken	тахианы мах	ta·khia·*ny* makh
duck	нугас	*nu*·gas
fillet	гол мах	*gol* makh
fish	загас	*za*·gas
goat	ямаа	*ya*·*maa*
kebab	шорлог	*shor*·log
marmot	тарвага	*tar*·vag
meat	мах	makh
(fried) meat pancake	хуушуур	*khuu*·shuur
meat with rice	будаатай хуураг	bu·*daa*·tai *khuu*·rag
mutton	хонины мах	kho·ni·*ny* makh
mutton dumplings	бууз	buuz
patty	бифштекс	*bif*·shteks
perch	алгана	*al*·gan
pike	цурхай	tsurh·*kai*
pork	гахайн мах	ga·*khain* makh
salmon	омуль	o·*mul*
sausage	хиам/зайдас/сосик	khiam/*zai*·das/*so*·sisk
sturgeon	хилэм	*khi*·lem
antevenison	бугын мах	bu·*gyn* makh
wild boar	бодон гахай	*bo*·don ga·*khai*

Fruit & Vegetables

apple	алим	*a*·lim
cabbage	байцаа	*bai*·tsaa
carrot	шар лууван	shar *luu*·van
cucumber	өргөст хэмэх	ör·göst *khe*·mekh
fruit	жимс	jims
onion	сонгино	*son*·gin
potato	төмс	töms
radish	улаан лууван	u·*laan* *luu*·van
salad	салат	*sa*·lad
tomato	улаан лооль	u·*laan* *loo*·il
turnip	манжин	*man*·jin
vegetable	ногоо	no·*goo*

Drinks

beer	пиво	piv
coffee	кофе	*ko*·fi
(buckthorn) juice	(чацарганы) шүүс	(cha·tsar·ga·*ny*) shüüs
koumiss	айраг	*ai*·rag
lemonade	нимбэгний ундаа	nim·beg·*nii* un·*daa*
milk	сүү	süü
milk tea	сүүтэй цай	*süü*·tei tsai
milk with rice	сүүтэй будаа	*süü*·tei bu·*daa*
mineral water	рашаан ус	ra·*shaan* us
tea	цай	tsai
vodka	архи	*a*·rikh
wine	дарс	dars

Emergencies

Help!	Туслаарай!	tus·*laa*·rai
Go away!	Зайл!	zail
I'm lost	Би төөрчихлөө.	bi töör·chikh·*löö*

There's been an accident
Осол гарчээ. — o·sol gar·*chee*

Call a doctor/the police!
Эмч/Цагдаа дуудаарай! — emch/tsag·*daa* duu·*daa*·rai

I'm ill
Би өвчтэй байна. — bi övch·*tei* *bai*·na

It hurts here
Энд өвдөж байна. — end *öv*·döj *bai*·na

Where is the toilet?
Хорлон хаана байна вэ? — jor·long khaan *bai*·na ve

Shopping & Services

I'd like to buy ...
Би ... авмаар байна. — bi ... av·*maar* *bai*·na

How much is it?
Энэ ямар үнэтэй вэ? — en *ya*·mar ün·*tei* ve

Can you reduce the price?
Та үнэ буулгах уу? — ta ün *buul*·gakh uu

exchange rate	мөнгөний ханш	möng·*nii* khansh
post office	шуудан	*shuu*·dan
public phone	нийтийн утас	*nii*·tiin *u*·tas
signature	гарын үсэг	ga·*ryn* *ü*·seg
travellers check	жуулчны чек	*juulch*·ny chek

Time, Dates & Numbers

What time is it?
Хэдэн цаг болж байна? *khe*·den tsag bolj *bai*·na

morning	өглөө	ög·*löö*
afternoon	өдөр	*ö*·dör
evening	орой	o·*roi*
yesterday	өчигдөр	ö·*chig*·dör
today	өнөөдөр	ö·*nöö*·dör
tomorrow	маргааш	mar·*gaash*

Monday	даваа	da·*vaa*
Tuesday	мягмар	*myag*·mar
Wednesday	лхагва	*lkha*·vag
Thursday	пүрэв	*pü*·rev
Friday	баасан	*baa*·sang
Saturday	бямба	byamb
Sunday	ням	nyam

Remember to add the word сар sar (literally 'month', 'moon') after the following words:

January	нэгдүгээр	neg·dü·*geer*
February	хоёрдугаар	kho·yor·du·*gaar*
March	гуравдугаар	gu·rav·du·*gaar*
April	дөрөвдүгээр	dö·röv·dü·*geer*
May	тавдугаар	tav·du·*gaar*
June	зургадугаар	zur·ga·du·*gaar*
July	долдугаар	dol·du·*gaar*
August	наймдугаар	naim·du·*gaar*
September	есдүгээр	yes·dü·*geer*
October	аравдугаар	a·rav·du·*gaar*
November	арваннэгдүгээр	ar·van·neg·dü·*geer*
December	арванхоёрдугаар	ar·van·kho·yor·du·*gaar*

1	нэг	neg
2	хоёр	*kho*·yor
3	гурав	*gu*·rav
4	дөрөв	*dö*·röv
5	тав	tav
6	зургаа	zur·*gaa*
7	долоо	do·*loo*
8	найм	naim
9	ес	yös
10	арав	*ar*·av
100	зуу	zuu
1000	мянга	*myang*·ga

Transport

What times does the ... leave/arrive?
... хэдэн цагт явдаг/ирдэг вэ? ... *khe*·den tsagt *yav*·dag/*ir*·deg ve

bus	Автобус	av·*to*·bus
plane	Нисэх онгоц	*ni*·seh *on*·gots
train	Галт тэрэг	galt *te*·reg
trolleybus	Троллейбус	trol·*lei*·bus

I want to go to ...
Би ... руу явмаар байна. bi ... ruu yav·*maar bai*·na

Can you tell me when we get to ...?
Бид хэзээ ... хүрэхийг хэлж өгнө үү? bid khe·*zee* ... khu·re·*hiig* helj *ög*·nö uu

I want to get off!
Би буумаар байна! bi *buu*·maar *bai*·na

1st class	нэгдүгээр зэрэг	neg·dü·*geer* *ze*·reg
2nd class	хоёрдугаар зэрэг	kho·yor·du·*gaar* *ze*·reg
one-way ticket	нэг талын билет	neg ta·*lyn* bi·*let*
return ticket	хоёр талын билет	*kho*·yor ta·*lyn* bi·*let*

first	анхны	ankh·*ny*
next	дараа	da·*raa*
last	сүүлийн	*süü*·liin

airport	нисэх онгоцны буудал	*ni*·sekh on·gots·*ny* *buu*·dal
bus stop	автобусны зогсоол	av·*to*·bus·ny zog·*sool*
platform	давцан	*dav*·tsan
ticket office	билетийн касс	bi·le·*tiin* kass
timetable	цагийн хуваарь	tsa·*giin* khu·*vaair*
train station	галт тэрэгний буудал	galt te·re·ge·*nii* *buu*·dal

RUSSIAN

Russian belongs to the Slavonic language family and is closely related to Belarusian and Ukrainian. It has more than 150 million speakers within the Russian Federation and is used as a second language in the former republics of the USSR, with a total number of speakers of more than 270 million.

Russian is written in the Cyrillic alphabet (see p403), and it's well worth the effort familiarising yourself with it so that you can read maps, timetables, menus and street signs. Otherwise, just read the coloured pronunciation guides given next to each Russian phrase in this chapter as if they were English, and you'll be understood. Most sounds are the same as in English, and the few differences in pronunciation are explained in the alphabet table. The stressed syllables are indicated with italics.

Basics

Hello	Здравствуйте.	*zdrast*·vuy·tye
Goodbye	До свидания.	da svi·*da*·nya
Excuse me	Простите.	pras·*ti*·tye
Sorry	Извините.	iz·vi·*ni*·tye
Yes/No	Да./Нет.	da/nyet
Please	Пожалуйста.	pa·*zhal*·sta
Thank you	Спасибо.	spa·*si*·ba
You're welcome	Пожалуйста.	pa·*zhal*·sta

What's your name?
Как вас зовут? kak vas za·*vut*

My name is ...
Меня зовут ... mi·*nya za*·vut ...

Do you speak English?
Вы говорите по-английски? vi ga·va·*ri*·tye pa·an·*gli*·ski

I don't understand
Я не понимаю. ya nye pa·ni·*ma*·yu

Accommodation

Do you have a ... room?	У вас есть ...?	u vas yest' ...
single	одноместный номер	ad·na·*myest*·nih *no*·mir
double	номер с двуспальной кроватью	*no*·mir z dvu·*spal'*·noy kra·*va*·tyu
How much is it for ...?	Сколько стоит за ...?	*skol'*·ka *sto*·it za ...
a night	ночь	noch'
two people	двоих	dva·*ikh*

boarding house	пансионат	pan·si·a·*nat*
campsite	кемпинг	*kyem*·ping
heating	отопление	a·ta·*plye*·ni·ye
hot water	горячий вода	go·*rya*·chiy va·*da*
hotel	отель	o.*tel*
youth hostel	хостел	*ho*.stel
light	свет	svyet

Directions

Where is ...?
Где ...? gdye ...

What's the address?
Какой адрес? ka·*koy a*·dris

Could you write it down, please?
Запишите, пожалуйста. za·pi·*shih*·tye pa·*zhal*·sta

Can you show me (on the map)?
Покажите мне, пожалуйста (на карте). pa·ka·*zhih*·tye mnye pa·*zhal*·sta (na *kar*·tye)

behind ...	за ...	za ...
far	далеко	da·li·*ko*
in front of ...	перед ...	*pye*·rit ...
near	близко	*blis*·ka
next to ...	рядом с ...	*rya*·dam s ...
opposite ...	напротив ...	na·*pro*·tif ...
straight ahead	прямо	*prya*·ma

Eating & Drinking

What would you recommend?
Что вы рекомендуете? shto vih ri·ka·min·*du*·it·ye

What's in that dish?
Что входит в это блюдо? shto *fkho*·dit v e·ta *blyu*·da

I don't eat (meat)
Я не ем (мясо). ya nye yem (*mya*·so)

To your health!
За ваше здоровье! za *va*·shih zda·*rov*·ye

That was delicious!
Было очень вкусно! *bih*·la o·chin' *fkus*·na

Please bring the bill
Принесите, пожалуйста счёт. pri·ni·*sit*·ye pa·*zhal*·sta shot

Key Words

bottle	бутылка	bu·*tihl*·ka
bowl	миска	*mis*·ka
bread	хлеб	khlyep
breakfast	завтрак	*zaf*·trak
cheese	сыр	sihr
cold	холодный	kha·*lod*·nih
dinner	ужин	*u*·zhihn
dish	блюдо	*blyu*·da
egg	яйцо	yeyt·*so*
fork	вилка	*vil*·ka
glass	стакан	sta·*kan*
honey	мёд	myot

hot (warm)	жаркий	*zhar*·ki
knife	нож	nosh
lunch	обед	ab·*yet*
menu	меню	min·*yu*
nut	орех	ar·*yekh*
oil	масло	*mas*·la
pasta	паста	*pa*·sta
pepper	перец	*pye*·rits
plate	тарелка	tar·*yel*·ka
restaurant	ресторан	ris·ta·*ran*
rice	рис	ris
salt	соль	sol'
spoon	ложка	*losh*·ka
sugar	сахар	*sa*·khar
vinegar	уксус	*uk*·sus
with	с	s
without	без	byez

Meat & Fish

beef	говядина	gav·*ya*·di·na
caviar	икра	i·*kra*
chicken	курица	*ku*·rit·sa
duck	утка	*ut*·ka
fish	рыба	*rih*·ba
herring	сельдь	syelt'
lamb	баранина	ba·*ra*·ni·na
meat	мяса	*mya*·sa
oyster	устрица	*ust*·rit·sa
pork	свинина	svi·*ni*·na
prawn	креветка	kriv·*yet*·ka
salmon	лосось	la·*sauce*
veal	телятина	til·*ya*·ti·na
turkey	индейка	ind·*yey*·ka

Fruit & Vegetables

apple	яблоко	*yab*·la·ka
bean	фасоль	fa·*sol'*
cabbage	капуста	ka·*pu*·sta
capsicum	перец	*pye*·rits
carrot	морковь	mar·*kof'*
cauliflower	цветная капуста	tsvit·*na*·ya ka·*pu*·sta
cucumber	огурец	a·gur·*yets*
fruit	фрукты	*fruk*·tih
mushroom	гриб	grip
onion	лук	luk
orange	апельсин	a·pil'·*sin*
peach	персик	*pyer*·sik
pear	груша	*gru*·sha
plum	слива	*sli*·va
potato	картошка	kar·*tosh*·ka
spinach	шпинат	shpi·*nat*
tomato	помидор	pa·mi·*dor*
vegetable	овощ	*o*·vash

CYRILLIC ALPHABET

Cyrillic	Sound (Russian)	
А а	a	as in 'father' (in a stressed syllable);
		as in 'ago' (in an unstressed syllable)
Б б	b	as in 'but'
В в	v	as in 'van'
Г г	g	as in 'get'
Д д	d	as in 'dog'
Е е	ye	as in 'yet' (in a stressed syllable and at the end of a word);
	i	as in 'tin' (in an unstressed syllable)
Ё ё	yo	as in 'yore' (often printed without dots)
Ж ж	zh	as the 's' in 'measure'
З з	z	as in 'zoo'
И и	i	as the 'ee' in 'meet'
Й й	y	as in 'boy' (not transliterated after **ы** or **и**)
К к	k	as in 'kind'
Л л	l	as in 'lamp'
М м	m	as in 'mad'
Н н	n	as in 'not'
О о	o	as in 'more' (in a stressed syllable);
	a	as in 'hard' (in an unstressed syllable)
П п	p	as in 'pig'
Р р	r	as in 'rub' (rolled)
С с	s	as in 'sing'
Т т	t	as in 'ten'
У у	u	as the 'oo' in 'fool'
Ф ф	f	as in 'fan'
Х х	kh	as the 'ch' in 'Bach'
Ц ц	ts	as in 'bits'
Ч ч	ch	as in 'chin'
Ш ш	sh	as in 'shop'
Щ щ	shch	as 'sh-ch' in 'fresh chips'
Ъ ъ	–	'hard sign' meaning the preceding consonant is pronounced as it's written
Ы ы	ih	as the 'y' in 'any'
Ь ь	'	'soft sign' meaning the preceding consonant is pronounced like a faint y
Э э	e	as in 'end'
Ю ю	yu	as the 'u' in 'use'
Я я	ya	as in 'yard' (in a stressed syllable);
	ye	as in 'yearn' (in an unstressed syllable)

SIGNS – RUSSIAN

Вход	Entrance
Выход	Exit
Открыто	Open
Закрыто	Closed
Информация	Information
Запрещено	Prohibited
Туалет	Toilets
Мужской (М)	Men
Женский (Ж)	Women

Drinks

beer	пиво	*pi*·va
'soviet-brand' champagne	советское шампанское	sav·*yet*·ska·ye sham·*pan*·ska·ye
coffee	кофе	*kof*·ye
(orange) juice	(апельсин-овый) сок	(a·pil'·*si*·na·vih) sok
milk	молоко	ma·la·*ko*
tea	чай	chey
(mineral) water	(минеральная) вода	(mi·ni·*ral'*·na·ya) va·*da*
vodka	водка	*vot*·ka
(home-made) vodka	самогон	sa·ma·*gon*
wine	вино	vi·*no*

Emergencies

Help!
Помогите! pa·ma·*gi*·tye

Leave me alone!
отвали! ot·va·*li*

I'm lost
Я заблудился/заблудилась. (m/f) ya za·blu·*dil*·sa/za·blu·*di*·las'

There's been an accident
Произошёл несчастный случай. pra·i·za·*shol* ne·*shas*·nih *slu*·chai

Call a doctor!
Вызовите врача! *vih*·za·vi·tye vra·*cha*

Call the police!
Вызовите полицию! *vih*·za·vi·tye pol·*li*·tsih·yu

I'm ill
Я болен/больна. (m/f) ya *bo*·lin/bal'·*na*

It hurts here
Здесь болит. zdyes' ba·*lit*

Where are the toilets?
Где здесь туалет? gdye zdyes' tu·al·*yet*

Shopping & Services

I need ...
Мне нужно ... mnye *nuzh*·na ...

How much is it?
Сколько стоит? *skol'*·ka *sto*·it

That's too expensive
Это очень дорого. *e*·ta *o*·chen' *do*·ra·ga

There's a mistake in the bill
Меня обсчитали. min·*ya* ap·shi·*ta*·li

bank	банк	bank
market	рынок	*rih*·nak
post office	почта	*poch*·ta
telephone office	телефонный пункт	ti·li·*fo*·nih punkt

Time, Dates & Numbers

What time is it?
Который час? ka·*to*·rih chas

Is this Moscow time?
Это московское время? *e*·ta ma·*skof*·ska·ye *vryem*·ya

Is this local time?
Это местное время? *e*·ta *myes*·na·ye *vryem*·ya

morning	утро	*ut*·ra
afternoon	день	den
evening	вечер	*vye*·chir
yesterday	вчера	vchi·*ra*
today	сегодня	si·*vod*·nya
tomorrow	завтра	*zaft*·ra
Monday	понедельник	pa·ni·*dyel'*·nik
Tuesday	вторник	*ftor*·nik
Wednesday	среда	sri·*da*
Thursday	четверг	chit·*vyerk*
Friday	пятница	*pyat*·ni·tsa
Saturday	суббота	su·*bo*·ta
Sunday	воскресенье	vas·kri·*syen*·ye
January	январь	yan·*var'*
February	февраль	fiv·*ral'*
March	март	mart
April	апрель	ap·*ryel'*
May	май	mai
June	июнь	i·*yun'*
July	июль	i·*yul'*
August	август	*av*·gust
September	сентябрь	sin·*tyabr'*

October	октябрь	ak·*tyabr'*
November	ноябрь	na·*yabr'*
December	декабрь	di·*kabr'*

1	один	a·*din*
2	два	dva
3	три	tri
4	четыре	chi·*tih*·ri
5	пять	pyat'
6	шесть	shest'
7	семь	syem'
8	восемь	*vo*·sim'
9	девять	*dye*·vyat'
10	десять	*dye*·syat'
100	сто	sto
1000	тысяча	*tih*·si·cha

Transport

A ... ticket (to Novgorod).	Билет ... (на Новгород).	bil·*yet* ... (na *nov*·ga·rat)
one-way	в один конец	v a·*din* kan·*yets*
return	туда-обратно	tu·*da*·ob·*rat*·no
arrival	прибытие	pri·*bih*·ti·ye
baggage	багаж	ba·*gash*
bus	автобус	af·*to*·bus
conductor/ carriage attendant	проводник	pra·*vad*·nik
departure	отправление	at·prav·*lye*·ni·ye
first	первый	*pyer*·vih
last	последний	pas·*lyed*·ni
map	карта	*kar*·ta
metro token	жетон	zhi·*ton*
platform	платформа	plat·*for*·ma
(bus) stop	остановка	a·sta·*nof*·ka
ticket	билет	bil·*yet*
ticket office	билетная касса	bil·*yet*·na·ya *ka*·sa
timetable	расписание	ras·pi·*sa*·ni·ye
train	поезд	*po*·ist
tram	трамвай	tram·*vai*
trolleybus	троллейбус	tra·*lyey*·bus

I want to go to ...
Я хочу ехать в ... — ya kha·*chu ye*·khat' v ...

Does it stop at ...?
Поезд останавливается в ...? — *po*·yist a·sta·*nav*·li·va·yit·sa v ...

When does it leave?
Когда отправляется? — kag·*da* at·prav·*lya*·it·sa

When is the next train?
Когда следующий поезд? — kag·*da slye*·du·yu·shi *po*·ist

Which platform does the train leave from?
С какой платформы отходит поезд? — s ka·*koy* plat·*for*·mih at·*kho*·dit *po*·ist

How long does it take to get to ...?
Сколько времени нужно ехать до ...? — *skol'*·ka *vrye*·mi·ni *nuzh*·na *ye*·khat' da ...

What station is this?
Какая эта станция? — ka·*ka*·ya e·ta *stant*·sih·ya

What's the next station?
Какая следующая станция? — ka·*ka*·ya *slye*·du·yu·sha·ya *stant*·sih·ya

Please stop here
Остановитесь здесь, пожалуйста! — a·sta·na·*vit*·yes' zdyes' pa·*zhal*·sta

I need (assistance)
Мне нужна (помощь). — mnye nuzh·*na* (*po*·mash)

I'd like to buy an SV/kupe/platstkartny ticket for train number ... to ...
Я хотел/хотела бы купить билет для СВ/для купе/ в плацкарте на поезд номер ... до ... (m/f) — ya kha·*tyel*/kha·*tye*·la bih ku·*pit'* bil·*yet* dlya es ve/dlya ku·*pe*/ f plats·*kar*·tye na *po*·ist *no*·mir ... na ...

RUSSIAN TRAIN TALK

Passports, please!
Предъявите паспорт! — prid·yi·*vit*·ye *pas*·part

There's no train today
Сегодня не будет поезда. — si·*vod*·nya nye *bu*·dit pa·iz·*da*

The train is full
Все билеты на этот поезд проданы. — fsye bil·*ye*·tih na *et*·at *po*·ist *pro*·da·nih

There are no SV/kupe/platskart tickets left for the train
Билеты для СВ/ для купе/ в плацкарте уже все распродались. — bil·*lye*·tih dlya es ve/ dlya ku·*pe*/ f plats·*kar*·tye u·*zhye* vsye ras·pra·*da*·lis'

Tickets for that service aren't on sale until ...
Билеты на этот город будут на продаже с ... — bil·*ye*·tih na *e*·tat *go*·rat *bu*·dut na pra·*da*·zhye s ...

You're at the wrong ticket window
Вы стоите не в том месте. — vi sta·*i*·tye nye f tom *myes*·tye

Please go to window ...
Обращайтесь к окошку ... — a·bra·*shai*·tyes k a·*kosh*·ku ...

GLOSSARY

This glossary is a list of Russian (R), Chinese (C) and Mongolian (M) terms you may come across during your journey. See p347, p355, and p364 for words that will help you while dining.

aimag (M) – Mongolian province

airag (M) – fermented mare's milk

apteka (R) – pharmacy

arkhi (M) – homemade vodka

aviakassa (R) – air-ticket office

avtovokzal (R) – bus terminal

AYaM (R) – Amur-Yakutsk Mainline, in Russian Amuro-Yakutskaya Magistral

BAM (R) – Baikal-Amur Mainline, in Russian Baikalo-Amurskaya Magistral

bankomat (R) – ATM

banya (R) – bathhouse

bei (C) – north

bilet (R) – ticket

bīnguǎn (C) – tourist hotel

bolnitsa (R) – hospital

CAAC (C) – Civil Aviation Administration of China, which controls most of China's airlines

CITS (C) – China International Travel Service

CTS (C) – China Travel Service

dacha (R) – country cottage

dajie (C) – avenue

datsan (R) – Buddhist monastery

detsky (R) – child's, children's

dong (C) – east

duma (R) – parliament

elektrichka (R) – also *prigorodny poezd*; suburban train

firmeny poezda (R) – trains with names (eg *Rossiya*); these are usually of a higher standard

gol (M) – river

gudamj (M) – street

Gulag (R) – Glavnoe Upravlenie Lagerey (Main Administration for Camps); the Soviet network of concentration camps

hútòng (C) – narrow alleyway

Inner Mongolia (M) – a separate province within China

Intourist (R) – the old Soviet State Committee for Tourism, now split up and in competition with hundreds of other travel agencies

izba (R & M) – wooden cottage

jie (C) – street

kassa (R) – ticket office

Kazakh (M) – Turkic ethnic group from Central Asia

khaan (M) – a king or chief

Khalkh (M) – the major ethnic group living in Mongolia

khiid (M) – Buddhist monastery

khram (R) – church

komnaty otdykha (R) – literally 'resting rooms'; cheap lodgings in Siberian train stations

kupeyny (R) – *kupe*; compartmentalised carriage; 4-berth compartment

lu (C) – road

lyuk (R) – 2-berth compartment

lyux (R) – hotel suite with a sitting room, bedroom and bathroom

Mafia (R) – any kind of criminal

magazin (R) – shop

marshrutky (R) – minibus that runs along a fixed route

most (R) – bridge

muzhskoy (R) – men's (toilet)

nan (C) – south

oblast (R) – region

obshchiy (R) – 4th-class train compartment

okrug (R) – district

örgön chölöö (M) – avenue

pereryv (R) – break (when shops close for an hour or two)

Pinyin (C) – Chinese written in the Roman alphabet

platskartny (R) – *platskart*, also *zhyosky*; 3rd class (or hard seat) in an open carriage of a train

poezd (R) – train

posolstvo (R) – embassy

prigorodny poezd (R) – also *elektrichka*; suburban train

provodnik/provodnitsa (R) – male/female carriage attendant on a train

PSB (C) – Public Security Bureau; the arm of the police force that deals with foreigners

rayon (R) – district

rechnoy vokzal (R) – river terminal

Renminbi (C) – literally 'people's money', the currency of China; shortened to RMB

samovar (R) – hot water urn containing hot charcoal

sever (R) – north

skory (R) – fast

spalny vagon (R) – also SV; sleeping wagon

stupa (M) – Buddhist religious monument with a solid hemisphere topped by a spire

taiga (R) – northern pine, fir, spruce and larch forest

tögrög (M) – unit of currency in Mongolia

UFMS (R) – Upravleniye Federalnoy Migratsionnoy Slyzhby (Federal Migration Service), often shortened to UFMS or FMS.

vokzal (R) – station

vostok (R) – east

xi (C) – west

yezhednevno (R) – daily

yuán (C) – the Chinese unit of currency, also referred to as RMB

yurt (R) – nomad's portable, round tent-house; also called *ger*

zheton (R) – token

Behind the Scenes

SEND US YOUR FEEDBACK

We love to hear from travellers – your comments keep us on our toes and help make our books better. Our well-travelled team reads every word on what you loved or loathed about this book. Although we cannot reply individually to your submissions, we always guarantee that your feedback goes straight to the appropriate authors, in time for the next edition. Each person who sends us information is thanked in the next edition – the most useful submissions are rewarded with a selection of digital PDF chapters.

Visit **lonelyplanet.com/contact** to submit your updates and suggestions or to ask for help. Our award-winning website also features inspirational travel stories, news and discussions.

Note: We may edit, reproduce and incorporate your comments in Lonely Planet products such as guidebooks, websites and digital products, so let us know if you don't want your comments reproduced or your name acknowledged. For a copy of our privacy policy visit lonelyplanet.com/privacy.

OUR READERS

Many thanks to the travellers who used the last edition and wrote to us with helpful hints, useful advice and interesting anecdotes:

Amanda Chilcott, Antoine Atallah, Benoit Cambron, Bruce Ellingsen, Danielle Edwards, Donald Fisher, Sophie Hunter

WRITER THANKS

Simon Richmond

Many thanks to my fellow author Regis and to Peter Kozyrev, Andrey and Sasha, Yegor Churakov, Vladimir Stolyarov, Dima Alimov, Konstantin Yurganov and Darina Gribova.

Mark Baker

I would like to thank all the friendly people who helped me along the way down the Volga and around Kaliningrad. Special thanks to friends Alsu Kurmash, Andrey Grigoriev and his wife, Alina, Julia Ziyatdinova and Ildar Gabidullin. Lubomir Hyska in Prague was especially helpful in sorting out my visas.

Stuart Butler

First and foremost – thank you to my ever-patient wife, Heather, and children, Jake and Grace, for putting up with everything while I worked on this project. Thank you also to Olga and Alexander of Altair Tur for visa papers and helping with the fab trek in Chuya Mountains. Also, thank you to (a different) Alexander for the driving and company along the Chuysky Trakt. Finally, thanks to Simon and Brana for encouragement.

Ali Lemer

Thanks to Jon Earle; Tara Kennaway; Dmitry Doronin, Ilaria Doronina & Babuskha Tamara; Gennady Gavrikov & Ilya Zlotnikov; Nikita and everyone in Pereslavl-Zalessky's English Club; to fellow authors Leonid Ragozin, Regis St Louis, Trent Holden, Simon Richmond and Mara Voorhees; and Kira Tverskaya. Big thanks also to Brana Vladisavljevic, Tasmin Waby and Jane Atkin, and especially to all of the Lonely Planet eds and cartos who worked on this book.

Tom Masters

A huge thanks to all those who helped me in the Far East, but particularly to Anna Konevskaya at Kamchatintour, Martha Madson at Explore Kamchatka, Alexei Podprugin at Nata Tour, Aleksei Shein in Vladivostok, Masha Gessen, Sarah Weinknecht, Sergei Kromykh in Khabarovsk, Tolya Buzinsky, Bolot Bochkarev, Bogdan Chernov and Simon Patterson, as ever.

Leonid Ragozin

I would like to thank Anatoly Bryukhanov and Aleksey Makeyev for their invaluable help in Krasnoyarsk; Jack Sheremetoff and Denis Sobnakov for explaining Baikal and fun conversations; Igor Ozerov in Ulan-Ude for all his stories and a wonderful trip to the eastern coast; the charming Ilona Baikara for driving me around Tuva and to the Saryglar family for making it happen; Igor Shalygin in Taishet for a superb and much-needed banya; Aleksandr Maryasov for helping out in Severobaikalsk. Finally, many huge thanks to my wife, Maria Makeeva, for helping out with the research, keeping me company on Olkhon and enduring my absence for the rest of the trip.

Regis St Louis

Many thanks to Tatiana and Vlad for the warm welcome in Petersburg; Peter Kozyrev for Chkalovsky knowledge and the late-night strolling seminar; Darina Gribova for the street art tour; Vladimir, Yegor and Natasha of Wild Russia for many local recommendations; and friend and fellow author Simon Richmond for his many helpful tips. Warm thanks to Cassandra and daughters, Magdalena and Genevieve, for all their support.

Mara Vorhees

Many thanks to my coauthors and resident Moscow experts Marc Bennetts and Leonid Ragozin. Always a pleasure to work with colleagues so insightful and well informed. I also received useful information from Andrei Musiano and Sasha Serbina at Garage Museum of Contemporary Art and Dmitry Elovsky at Zaryadye Project, as well as Andrey Muchnik and Marina Dedozhdy. Unlimited thanks and love to мои самые любимые – Van, Shay and Jerry - for coming along for the adventure.

ACKNOWLEDGEMENTS

Climate map data adapted from Peel MC, Finlayson BL & McMahon TA (2007) 'Updated World Map of the Köppen-Geiger Climate Classification', Hydrology and Earth System Sciences, 11, 163344.

Illustrations pp58-9 and pp90-91 by Javier Zarracina

Cover photograph: Train skirting Lake Baikal, Tuul & Bruno Morandi/Getty Images ©

THIS BOOK

This 6th edition of Lonely Planet's *Trans-Siberian Railway* guidebook was researched and written by Simon Richmond, Mark Baker, Stuart Butler, Trent Holden, Adam Karlin, Michael Kohn, Ali Lemer, Tatyana Leonov, Tom Masters, Thomas O'Malley, Leonid Ragozin, Regis St Louis and Mara Vorhees.

This guidebook was produced by the following:

Destination Editors Megan Eaves, Brana Vladislavljevic

Product Editors Heather Champion, Anne Mason

Senior Cartographers David Kemp, Valentina Kremenchutskaya

Book Designer Gwen Cotter

Assisting Editors Imogen Bannister, Nigel Chin, Bruce Evans, Kate Mathews, Anne Mulvaney, Susan Paterson, Tamara Sheward, Sarah Stewart, Ross Taylor, Saralinda Turner, Maja Vatric

Cover Researcher Naomi Parker

Thanks to Baigalmaa Batsukh, Dan Corbett, Sandie Kestell, Seb Neylan, Trisha Ping, Jessica Ryan, Kate Sullivan, Angela Tinson, Kira Tverskaya

Index

Map Pages **000**
Photo Pages 000

Map Pages **000**
Photo Pages 000

Map Legend

Sights
- Beach
- Bird Sanctuary
- Buddhist
- Castle/Palace
- Christian
- Confucian
- Hindu
- Islamic
- Jain
- Jewish
- Monument
- Museum/Gallery/Historic Building
- Ruin
- Shinto
- Sikh
- Taoist
- Winery/Vineyard
- Zoo/Wildlife Sanctuary
- Other Sight

Activities, Courses & Tours
- Bodysurfing
- Diving
- Canoeing/Kayaking
- Course/Tour
- Sento Hot Baths/Onsen
- Skiing
- Snorkelling
- Surfing
- Swimming/Pool
- Walking
- Windsurfing
- Other Activity

Sleeping
- Sleeping
- Camping
- Hut/Shelter

Eating
- Eating

Drinking & Nightlife
- Drinking & Nightlife
- Cafe

Entertainment
- Entertainment

Shopping
- Shopping

Information
- Bank
- Embassy/Consulate
- Hospital/Medical
- Internet
- Police
- Post Office
- Telephone
- Toilet
- Tourist Information
- Other Information

Geographic
- Beach
- Gate
- Hut/Shelter
- Lighthouse
- Lookout
- Mountain/Volcano
- Oasis
- Park
- Pass
- Picnic Area
- Waterfall

Population
- Capital (National)
- Capital (State/Province)
- City/Large Town
- Town/Village

Transport
- Airport
- Border crossing
- Bus
- Cable car/Funicular
- Cycling
- Ferry
- Metro station
- Monorail
- Parking
- Petrol station
- S-Bahn/Subway station
- Taxi
- T-bane/Tunnelbana station
- Train station/Railway
- Tram
- Tube station
- U-Bahn/Underground station
- Other Transport

Routes
- Tollway
- Freeway
- Primary
- Secondary
- Tertiary
- Lane
- Unsealed road
- Road under construction
- Plaza/Mall
- Steps
- Tunnel
- Pedestrian overpass
- Walking Tour
- Walking Tour detour
- Path/Walking Trail

Boundaries
- International
- State/Province
- Disputed
- Regional/Suburb
- Marine Park
- Cliff
- Wall

Hydrography
- River, Creek
- Intermittent River
- Canal
- Water
- Dry/Salt/Intermittent Lake
- Reef

Areas
- Airport/Runway
- Beach/Desert
- Cemetery (Christian)
- Cemetery (Other)
- Glacier
- Mudflat
- Park/Forest
- Sight (Building)
- Sportsground
- Swamp/Mangrove

Note: Not all symbols displayed above appear on the maps in this book